Chinese Circulations

Chinese Circulations

CAPITAL, COMMODITIES, AND NETWORKS IN SOUTHEAST ASIA

Eric Tagliacozzo and Wen-Chin Chang, eds.

Foreword by Wang Gungwu

Duke University Press   Durham and London   2011

Printed in the United States of America on acid-free paper ∞

Designed by Heather Hensley

Typeset in Quadraat by Tseng Information Systems, Inc.

Library of Congress Cataloging-in-Publication Data appear
on the last printed page of this book.

Duke University Press gratefully acknowledges the support
of the Chiang Ching-Kuo Foundation for International
Scholarly Exchange, which provided funds toward the
production of this book. A portion of the royalties from the
sale of this book will be donated to the Central Asia Institute.

CONTENTS

LIST OF MAPS

Several books concerning the Chinese overseas and their commercial ventures are now available, some with special reference to the business acumen of sojourners turned settlers. New basic research examines the history of their wide-ranging activities and the methods and organizations they employed wherever they went. Some studies of their regional and global networks confirm that the Chinese did well in some countries and less so in others, and suggest the reasons why. While it is clear that these trading communities were remarkably adaptable in what they achieved in many parts of Southeast Asia, the studies covering the commodities in which they traded have been uneven, desultory, and even fragmentary. It has therefore been difficult to develop a clear picture of why the Chinese concentrated on certain trade items, and how they came to dominate certain regional and colonial markets. This collection, edited by Eric Tagliacozzo and Wen-Chin Chang, is a welcome addition to the body of literature on that subject, providing a comprehensive assessment of the range of trade items that made the Chinese so formidable and so necessary for the development of local economies.

The four essays in the first section offer valuable theoretical insights, some preliminary, that put the long history of Chinese trade in Southeast Asia in historical perspective. Each makes a distinctive contribution, and together they capture slices of the rich experience with commodities that different generations of Chinese were able to trade in. Building on earlier work, Anthony Reid and Carl Trocki both illuminate the broader dimensions of the mining and opium industries that engaged so many Chinese workers and merchants. Of particular interest is Adam McKeown's picture of human labor as a commodity; although this constituted a rather special trade, the so-called coolie trade, it is enlightening to have it set beside goods that are no less valuable, but usually inanimate. The fourth of the essays, by C. Patter-

son Giersch, examines less-well-known trading conditions in southwestern China, highlighting the fact that less research has been done on overland merchandise across the porous Chinese borders of mainland Southeast Asia. Indeed, at least five essays in this volume deal with this relatively neglected area of study, and all make useful suggestions about possible future research.

The remaining four parts are arranged more or less chronologically, from precolonial to early colonial, from high colonial to postcolonial. Scholars of commodity trade through the centuries, especially those working on the trade between China and Southeast Asia and on the economic role of the Chinese overseas, will benefit greatly from this volume. Social and economic historians of Asia in general will also find much to learn. For myself, I am gratified to see how far the field has come since I started writing, in 1953, about the early centuries of the ancient Nanhai trade in the South China Sea. At the time, I was disappointed to find that efforts to develop trade with the southern seas seemed always to come from Chinese officials who were responsible for foreign relations. The vast majority of the records dealt with tribute envoys coming by sea to bring merchandise as gifts and the Chinese emperors giving gifts in return. In between, the officials in charge profited greatly from the monopolistic conditions at the Chinese ports. Where private enterprise was concerned, it was foreign merchants from the south and the west who opened up trade routes. I was particularly surprised at the lack of early documentation about Chinese seagoing vessels competing with those coming from South and Southeast Asia. The Chinese seemed to have been content to travel on foreign bottoms when they sailed to and from the Indian Ocean. Nevertheless, I speculated that the proto-Chinese Yue peoples of what became the southern coastal provinces of Fujian, Guangdong, and Guangxi were engaged in the maritime trade, and that their Chinese descendants eventually led the way as late Tang (ninth century), Wudai (907–959), and Song (960–1279) China increasingly launched their own ships to compete against well-established Muslim fleets.

By the time of Zheng He's Indian Ocean naval expeditions in the 15th century, the Chinese were poised to dominate the southern seas. But continental power prevailed and that initiative did not go any further. For much of the next six centuries, Chinese private merchants operated in the interstices of European trading empires. Without state support, they had little choice but to adapt the best they could by utilizing the power of others while they wove their own networks wherever they were given operational space. The strategies for survival and prosperity depended a great deal on resilience,

transactional skills, and good fortune. It was astonishing how the many disparate groups of Chinese, compatriots as well as competitors, managed to devise ways to serve foreign rulers, powerful mercantile companies as well as themselves, even while European powers consolidated control over new colonial states. No port was too small, no corner of the region too remote, as they sought new commodities for the markets of China and the West.

When Chinese governments after the late 1890s finally came to appreciate their achievements, the overseas Chinese classes discovered that official attention was not always helpful for their manifold businesses. For the past century, these classes have been both sought after by a rejuvenated Chinese state and, after the colonial powers withdrew, constrained by new loyalties to their adopted countries. A new set of dynamics has been set in motion, and the Chinese merchants trading abroad must again reassess the parameters within which they hope to thrive—this is still very much work in progress. How they will emerge from the new mix of responsibilities depends on many factors, not least the fact of globalization, which has exposed them to conditions beyond their control. But, not least, they will be experimenting with new kinds of commodities, whether natural or manufactured, that they must learn to handle. Under these circumstances, Chinese merchants could benefit from reading this volume and learn about how their predecessors managed the trade goods of earlier times. Some might even draw lessons about how to meet changing conditions of trade, something that they face every day. But the studies in this volume have a larger purpose. The authors have used their great professional skills to paint a picture of extensive and precarious trading activity that illuminates the underpinnings of Southeast Asian economic development for the last millennium. It is their success in doing so that recommends this collection to all who wish to understand why the region is what it is today.

Wang Gungwu
East Asian Institute, National University of Singapore
24 February 2009

ACKNOWLEDGMENTS

The editors wish to thank Hsin-Huang Michael Hsiao, the former director of the Center for Asia-Pacific Area Studies, in the Research Center for Humanities and Social Science, Academia Sinica, Taiwan, for his great support of the two workshops in late 2005 and early 2007 that eventually led to this book. We are also grateful for a competitive publishing subvention that we received from the Chiang Ching-kuo Foundation. Finally, the editors wish to thank the Yenching Institute at Harvard University and the Center for Southeast Asian Studies at Kyoto University for sabbatical leaves spent by the editors at these two institutions. We also wish to thank Valerie Millholland, Miriam Angress, Danielle Szulczewski, and Neal McTighe, all at Duke University Press, for all of their persistent efforts and help with this book.

THE ARC OF HISTORICAL COMMERCIAL
RELATIONS BETWEEN CHINA AND SOUTHEAST ASIA

~~~~~ Wen-Chin Chang and Eric Tagliacozzo

Theoretical Review

Chinese merchants have been trading down to Southeast Asia for centuries, sojourning—and sometimes settling—during the course of their voyages. These ventures have taken place by land and by sea, linking the wider orbit of the Chinese homeland with vast stretches of Southeast Asia in a broad, mercantile embrace. The present volume aims to examine these contacts, transactions, and transmissions over what the great French historian Fernand Braudel called the *longue durée*. Despite the presence of several foundational volumes by Wang Gungwu and others, which have charted the directions of this field of study over the past several decades, the field of Chinese trade in Southeast Asia has become so large and so complex that a syncretic book on its parameters seems long overdue.[1] We hope to build on past achievements and outline the scope, diversity, and complexity of Chinese trade interactions over a vast geography and an equally broad temporal spectrum. Because the languages, archives, and sources needed to master a task such as this are beyond the grasp of any one person, we hope that this book will make a signal contribution to the field, in summarizing where our knowledge now stands and where future directions of research may wish to go.

The idea of networks as being crucial to the linking of human societies has received much attention in the past several decades. Philip Curtin was among the first to point this out in his broad and wide-ranging study *Cross-Cultural Trade in World History*.[2] In that book, he linked the Phoenicians of Mediterranean antiquity, the Hanseatic merchants of the early-modern Baltic, and Bugis traders of modern Indonesia in a single, coherent narrative, showing how merchant diasporas could be analyzed with theoretical rigor

over the centuries. Scholars brought this global vantage down to a regional scope, such as Christine Dobbin in her fascinating *Asian Entrepreneurial Minorities: Conjoint Communities in the Indian Ocean*.[3] Where Curtin saw "types" of ethnicized commercial ventures, Dobbin stressed communities, borrowing a page out of Tönnies and the Frankfurt school of sociology. To bring this line of thinking even closer to the subject of this volume, Aihwa Ong's recent work has also shown how ideas of traveling subjects—often involved in trade—can be seen as crucial transnational actors in the making of political economies.[4] Ong's focus on the Chinese in this respect brought a new theoretical sophistication to the idea of including Asians in Western social-science paradigms involving diaspora, a much-needed corrective that has subsequently received huge attention in the literature.

Merchants transport products, not just themselves, over vast distances of mountains, deserts, or seas, so an analysis of commodities—and not just the networks that carry them—is also a vital part of this volume. Here again, recent social-science research, particularly by scholars such as Arjun Appadurai and Igor Kopytoff, is crucial to our aims.[5] Appadurai and Kopytoff have spoken of the social histories and cultural biographies of "things." According to Appadurai, commodities are like persons; they have social lives and move in and out of different regimes of value in discrete space and time. The "total trajectory" of commodities—that is, from the course of their production, through their exchange and distribution, to their eventual consumption—involves different stages, and is enmeshed in complex intersections of economic, political, and cultural factors. We have endeavored in this book to foreground the commodities themselves that have linked China and Southeast Asia over the centuries, at least as much as the actors who have transported them. For the present study, these commodities include a bewildering array of objects, and many of them—including books and other forms of traveling print, human labor, fish (dried and fresh), and jade stones—have not been thoroughly explored in existing studies on this part of the world.

Chinese merchants have been involved in the transit of most "things," historically, between Southeast Asia and the Chinese mainland, and it is difficult to find any single line of trade where they have not played a part, in some form or another.[6] Yet linking a great variety of trades over a long period of time and even wider geographies is a very tall order. Nevertheless this is one of the primary aims of this volume. How similar were the dynamics of these ventures, and how different? Are there mechanics or dynamics of the trades that we can point to as being analogous? Does our vantage of analysis shift if we make the commodities themselves as important as the

people carrying them, or is this altering of locus irrelevant? We have asked each scholar in the volume to highlight one particular commodity or class of commodities, in addition to a period of time or a proscribed geography, so that we might see what comparative insights might be achieved by bringing these essays together in one coherent study.

This volume, by its very scope, also fits into a wider general debate over the nature of Chinese trade and capital over the past several centuries. Max Weber and Karl Marx were foundational in these debates more than a century ago, but since that time ideas on how to study Chinese economic structures and particularities—especially as part of regional or transregional units—have changed.[7] G. William Skinner made an impressive contribution in this respect in the 1960s and 1970s, and he was later joined by a coterie of scholars—including Mark Elvin, Philip Huang, Peter Purdue, R. Bin Wong, and Ken Pomeranz—in trying to decipher how Chinese market mechanisms have worked over time.[8] Much of this discussion has focused on rural macroregions, but with the more recent work of Sherman Cochran on Shanghai and William Rowe on Hankow, among others, an urban component has emerged in these discussions as well.[9]

One of the issues at stake, in fact, is whether there has been any such thing as "capitalism" or "Chinese capitalism" in the passage of Chinese history, and if so, when these processes started, and what forms they may have taken. Terence Gomez and Michael Hsiao, again among other scholars, have critiqued essentializations of the cultural aspects of Chinese business-networking, showing how these patterns have been both similar to and different from Western variants.[10] Other scholars, such as Timothy Brook and Gregory Blue in a particularly useful volume on the historical period, and Gary Hamilton in a more contemporary era, have questioned capitalism's place in a Chinese context, both as a historical reality in a proscribed time and place and as a useful concept altogether.[11] David Faure has even attempted to connect freewheeling notions of Chinese-style "capitalism" and family/business enterprise into a single, concerted whole in his treatment of the topic.[12] These analyses tend to be sociological or economic in nature, but scholars such as Philip Kuhn have shown that they can be human stories as well, with an emphasis on the lived experience of actual human beings.[13] All of these studies have brought an impressive edifice of data, interpretation, and methodology to bear in helping us think about how these Chinese merchant connections have stretched from China itself to a variety of landscapes (Southeast Asian and otherwise) into the wider world.

In bringing together twenty scholars, we have hoped, among other things, to achieve a blending of generations: scholars whose shoulders we all stand on now; mid-level professors who are now beginning to shape this field; and younger scholars who will follow new avenues of inquiry in the years to come. Anthony Reid opens the volume with an essay entitled "Chinese on the Mining Frontier in Southeast Asia," which is inclusive of the region as a whole. Reid argues that Chinese technologies of mining and metalworking have been influential in Southeast Asia at least since Dong-Son times, stretching far back into the region's antiquity. Since Sung times, and probably long before, iron and bronze artifacts were imported to Southeast Asia from China because larger-scale Chinese methods of extraction and manufacture could produce them more cheaply. Reid points out that Chinese miners and metalworkers no doubt interacted with Vietnam over a longer period, but began to travel southward by sea from the Mongol period. His essay examines what little we know about these early interactions, but necessarily focuses on the eighteenth and nineteenth centuries, when Chinese miners revolutionized the Southeast Asian tin industry.[14]

In a similarly encompassing essay, titled "Cotton, Copper, and Caravans: Trade and the Transformation of Southwest China," C. Patterson Giersch picks up the *longue durée* thread laid down by Reid. Giersch examines the overland trade of two commodities, copper and cotton, which dominated Yunnan Province's early modern trade with both Southeast Asia and eastern China. Giersch asserts that previous work on the caravan trade and mining has challenged accepted economic-geography paradigms that divide Southeast Asia from China, and has demonstrated how Southwest China's commercialization produced profound economic and political transformations in Southeast Asia as well. His essay builds on past scholarly accomplishments by explaining how Chinese merchants organized long-distance trade across rugged terrain, and how this contributed to profound, long-term transformations in Yunnan's society and economy. More specifically, Giersch argues that the changing nature of long-distance trade over the *longue durée* was linked to broad patterns of migration, urbanization, and economic development across much of what now constitutes Yunnan Province proper.[15]

Adam McKeown likewise takes a wide-angled approach with his essay, "The Social Life of Chinese Labor." McKeown suggests that labor can easily be understood as a commodity; a person may sell or lease his own labor, and

merchants may also profit from the organization and sale of other people and their labor. The conceptualization and historiography of labor as a commodity, however, presents several difficulties, especially with regard to Chinese migrant labor. The radical polarization between freedom and slavery that has shaped the understanding of labor and migration since the abolition of African slavery has made it difficult to understand the many forms of obligation, control, and private organization that fall between these poles. McKeown argues that much understanding of Chinese migration can still be traced to categories established in the extensive debates surrounding the "coolie trade" from the 1840s to 1880s. He therefore problematizes the debate in his own essay, arguing for a new and more syncretic understanding of the position of Chinese human beings in forging the links between places like China and Southeast Asia.[16]

Carl A. Trocki follows this approach in his essay, "Opium as a Commodity in the Chinese Nanyang Trade," offering a periodization of the rise and decline of opium as a key element in the Chinese economy of the Nanyang. He focuses primarily on the role of opium revenue farming, and looks at the changing importance of these institutions in the region. Trocki argues that opium as a commodity in the Chinese trade of Southeast Asia can be traced through three relatively distinct phases. The first lasted from about 1760 to 1820; during these years opium was traded much like any other commodity, throughout the region and to China itself. Between 1820 and 1880, the revenue farms grew in value and influence. An interdependence developed between opium, labor, commodity production, and Chinese capital, which agglomerated around the farming system. After 1880, the farms grew beyond their local economic bases and became large international syndicates. Groups of investors from the various capitals of the region sought to build syndicates controlling the flow of opium to many major settlements. By 1915, even though Chinese workers continued to be among the most important opium consumers, opium processing and retail distribution were both taken over by colonial states.[17]

The second section of the volume focuses on the precolonial interactions between China and Southeast Asia. Takeshi Hamashita opens this part by focusing attention on the *Lidai Baoan* (the precious documents of successive generations of the Ryukyu Kingdom). This is a compilation of several large volumes of documents, written in Chinese with some inflection of local Fujian dialect, relating to Ryukyuan contacts with China and eight Southeast Asian countries (or, more exactly, port towns), covering the period from 1424 to 1867. The eight Southeast Asian locations include Siam, Melaka,

Table 1 Commodities, Geographies, and Time Periods

Author/Time Period	Commodity	Geography
I. THEORETICAL/LONGUE DURÉE		
Anthony Reid	precious metals	Pan–Southeast Asia
C. Patterson Giersch	cotton and copper	China and mainland Southeast Asia
Adam McKeown	labor	China and Southeast Asia
Carl A. Trocki	opium	Pan–Southeast Asia
II. PRECOLONIAL		
Takeshi Hamashita	pepper and sappanwood	South China Sea
Li Tana	coins	Vietnam
Masuda Erika	luxury goods	Thailand
Heather Sutherland	tortoiseshell	Indonesia
III. EARLY COLONIAL		
Sun Laichen	gems	Burma
Leonard Blussé	junk cargoes	Java
Lucille Chia	books	Philippines
Kwee Hui Kian	textiles	Indonesia
IV. HIGH COLONIAL		
Man-houng Lin	capital	Taiwan, South China, and Southeast Asia
Wu Xiao An	rice	Malaysia
Nola Cooke	fish	Cambodia
Jean DeBernardi	Bibles	China and Southeast Asia
V. POSTCOLONIAL		
Bien Chiang	birds' nests	Sarawak
Eric Tagliacozzo	marine products	Coastal Southeast Asia
Wen-Chin Chang	jade stones	Burma and Thailand
Kevin Woods	timber	Burma

Palembang, "Jawa," "Samudera," Sunda, Patani, and Annam. Hamashita's essay examines the role of the Ryukyu tributary trade network with Fujian merchants' networks in East and Southeast Asia, concentrating particularly on the pepper and sappanwood trades.[18] In many ways, it is a specific commodity history of the South China Sea in miniature.

Li Tana then picks up the precolonial thread in her essay, "Cochinchinese Coin Casting and Circulating in Eighteenth-Century Southeast Asia." Li argues that while much has been said about Chinese business networks in modern Southeast Asia, little is known about the coins they used in these ports and about the origins of the coins. Locating the coin business in a regional trade system, Li's essay explores the links of the coin business between eighteenth-century China and Southeast Asia, and particularly between the different ports of Southeast Asia. The evidence she introduces suggests that there were much closer connections than previously supposed in this important branch of Chinese business, namely between mining in Tongkin, copper and zinc importing from Japan and China, and coin-casting in Cochinchina. These coins eventually circulated on to neighboring polities as well, such as Siam and even inland to landlocked Laos.[19]

Masuda Erika extends the vision of precolonial interactions between Southeast Asia and China in her essay, "Import of Prosperity: Luxurious Items Imported from China to Siam during the Thonburi and Early Rattanakosin Periods (1767–1854)." Masuda argues that previous studies on the rise and fall of the Sino-Siamese junk trade demonstrated that after the trade reached its peak in the early 1830s, it gradually declined, with Siam being keenly aware of this decay. These studies, Masuda asserts, give the misleading impression that Siam abruptly stopped paying attention to China, and that the latter disappeared entirely from the former's external perspective. However, she continues, Siamese documents indicate that the degradation of China's political prestige due to the opium war and the loss of trading privileges in Guangzhou under the tributary system did not change the prosperous image China held in Siam, nor did it affect the image of Guangzhou as a desirable outlet for commerce. Masuda emphasizes the Siamese ruling class's continuing appetite for luxurious or ornamental items imported from China to Siam during the early Rattanakosin period. She also emphasizes how these items were enjoyed by the Siamese ruling class, and often embellished and justified Siamese monarchs' claims to royal power.[20]

Adopting a commodity-chain approach, Heather Sutherland also makes a case for continuity in her stimulating essay, "A Sino-Indonesian Commodity Chain: The Trade in Tortoiseshell in the Late Seventeenth and Eighteenth

Centuries." Sutherland argues that during the seventeenth-century Chinese consumption of trepang (*bêche-de-mer*, or edible sea cucumbers) increased, so much so that early-eighteenth-century Makassar emerged as a transit port for this new commodity, enabling it to become again a center of regional commercial networks after a hiatus of many decades. At first trepang was sent through intermediate ports (especially Batavia), but during the second half of the eighteenth century Makassar was allowed a direct junk link to Xiamen in South China. In fact, in the 1770s Xiamen passed even the colonial Dutch capital of Batavia as Makassar's main trading partner. If in the 1720s Makassar's most valuable imports and exports were Indian textiles and rice, by the 1780s they were both trepang. China was always the principal market for this highly profitable cargo, Sutherland argues, and eagerly sought out a continuing, stable supply of the shells.[21]

COLONIAL AND POSTCOLONIAL VANTAGES

In the early colonial period, some of these patterns of interaction began to change. One of the best places to examine these echoes is in the upland frontier areas separating mainland Southeast Asia and Southwest China. Sun Laichen focuses on the gem trade between Ming and Qing China and Burma to the south. He explores the changes in and continuities of gem trade from the Ming into the Qing, looking in particular into the development of Chinese terminologies related to specific precious stones. He points out that rubies and sapphires (called *baoshi* 寶石 in Chinese) dominated the flow of gems into Ming China, whereas during the Qing, especially from the eighteenth century onward, Burmese jadeite (*feicui* 翡翠) overtook baoshi as the most popular gemstone. This shift of fashion resulted in the booming of jade mine excavation in the Kachin state of Burma. The history of jade commerce thus effectively demonstrates how China's demand helped drive economic and political changes in Southeast Asian history, particularly along this one landlocked frontier.[22]

Complementing Sun's work in the maritime corridors of Asia is Leonard Blussé's essay, "Junks to Java: Chinese Shipping to the Nanyang in the Second Half of the Eighteenth Century." Blussé points out that there is almost no quantitative research on the import and export cargoes of the junks that plied between the "primate city" of Batavia and Southeastern China, apart from the more qualitative studies on sea products such as *bêche-de-mer*, shark fins, and delicacies like edible birds' nests. Blussé has made a long-term project of collecting from archival sources any available quantitative ma-

terial about the cargoes of individual junks or series of junks. He argues for the vast importance of this subject given that the junk trade formed a metaphorical umbilical cord between Southeast China and overseas Chinese port towns. Taken together, Sun's and Blussé's essays provide a fascinating overview of early modern relationships as they were acted out between China and Southeast Asia over the course of the eighteenth century and beyond, both by land and by sea.[23]

Lucille Chia draws attention to the striking fact that very little Chinese culture was introduced through print to local societies before the nineteenth century, while many other cultural elements diffused into Southeast Asia following the arrival of both humans and goods from China. In spite of this centuries-long paucity in print was the anomalous appearance of Chinese books in the early Spanish Philippines. These books were largely religious in nature, reflecting the efforts of Spanish missionaries to proselytize the Chinese in the Philippines. The success of these campaigns, Chia argues, often turned both the Chinese and local Filipinos away from their native cultures. Later, when the printing of books in Chinese and Chinese works in translation gained a foothold in Southeast Asia, following large-scale arrivals of Chinese immigrants in the nineteenth century, the Philippines was the country in the region the least receptive to establishing a long-term Chinese publishing tradition.[24]

Following these paradigms even further south, to the nascent Dutch East Indies, Kwee Hui Kian examines the place of Chinese merchants in the trade of South Asian textiles. She argues that the consumption of Indian textiles in the Indonesian archipelago was dependent on the competitiveness of the price and quality of the commodity relative to those produced locally in the region. When the prices of Indian textiles were driven up by increasing European demand during the late seventeenth century, island Southeast Asians turned to regional sourcing to procure higher quality, cheaper textiles. The decrease in the demand for the Indian product within the Indonesian archipelago was therefore primarily a factor of the region's resourcefulness, rather than a sign of its economic decline. Kwee shows the vital place of Chinese merchants in these processes, especially in the warp and weft of the early colonial period, when it was by no means clear who would be controlling the future of this profitable line of commerce.[25]

As we move into the high-colonial period of the nineteenth and early twentieth centuries, the essays in this volume increasingly emphasize the role of capital in binding Chinese trade networks between China and South-

east Asia. Man-houng Lin examines these processes by exploring the role of cultural ties in the shaping of economic networks. Lin focuses specifically on Taiwanese merchants' overseas business relations with South China, Southeast Asia, and Manchuria during the period of Japanese colonial rule. She first explores the power of cultural ties that contributed to Taiwanese traders' high investment in South Fujian and north Guangdong provinces, where most Taiwanese immigrants' families had originally come from, several generations back. Southeast Asia was also very important to the interests of Taiwanese traders because they knew overseas Chinese there shared common cultural backgrounds and ties to the southeastern coasts of China proper. Manchuria, which did not share these cultural links, ranked last in Taiwanese traders' estimations. However, following Japan's growing political and economic influence in Manchuria after Manchukuo was established, in 1932, Taiwanese traders' investments there grew substantially. This shift was further stimulated by other factors, such as the benefit Taiwan derived from a regional division of labor with Manchuria. As this case study suggests, economic comparative advantage can trump cultural ties in economic engagement, which, Lin argues, disproves culture-based concepts, such as the "Greater China Economic Zone" and the idea of a "global Chinese network."[26]

Wu Xiao An agrees with Carl Trocki that, as was the case with the opium business, commercialization of the rice industry in Southeast Asia was tied through Chinese traders to the global capitalist economy. This was true both in terms of production and consumption, as all of these products were closely related to the larger colonial tin, rubber, and other cash-cropping economies. Wu shows that prior to the Second World War, British Malaya depended primarily on imports of rice, comprising over 60 percent of the colony's total consumption. The rice trade in British Malaya was largely monopolized by Chinese merchants (mostly Hokkien and Teochieu), who formed close-knit trading networks through credit, kinship, and guild associations. Another pattern of rice trading that concerns Wu is the local rice-milling economy in northern Malaya, a case study of Chinese trade in the region that Wu is able to explore in some detail.[27]

Nola Cooke focuses on a different industry: the Chinese contribution to fish farming in Cambodia in the high-colonial period. In certain respects, Chinese (and Sino-Khmer) commodity production in nineteenth-century Cambodia remained remarkably unchanged by the advent of French colonial protection, in 1863. Along the major rivers, Cooke argues, Chinese agri-

culturalists continued to rent the most fertile river banks and islands from the Cambodian king, and to plant them with a variety of cash crops which included indigo, tobacco, and cotton. Chinese (and Vietnamese) junk traders continued to transport these products downriver to the markets of Cochinchina. The most important change to occur in commodity production, however, involved the fishing industry, especially on Tonle Sap, the Great Lake. Where this activity had involved all resident ethnic groups in the first half of the century and produced relatively small catches, by the 1890s a major industry had emerged. This industry was overwhelmingly run by Chinese and Vietnamese, and its produce was exported to markets in coastal China and much of Southeast Asia. Cooke's paper examines how this fishing industry developed and, by the 1890s, assumed the form that would persist throughout the colonial era.[28]

The last essay in the high-colonial rubric focuses on Singapore and its connections with China. Jean DeBernardi uncovers a rather unexpected link between these two places: the commodity of a single book, the Bible. DeBernardi argues that evangelical Protestant Christians, excited and perhaps even compelled by the challenge posed by China's enormous population, aspired to distribute the Bible to every living person in the Middle Kingdom. With this in mind, in 1815 the London Missionary Society launched an important program of Chinese translation and printing in Southeast Asia under the umbrella of colonial rule. DeBernardi traces the history of Chinese and Southeast Asian Bible production and transmission since that time, with an emphasis on the high-colonial years, when records for this practice became particularly important. She also makes use of ethnographic research to bring this study into the present, linking history and anthropology in novel and interesting ways along the way.[29]

The last section of the volume deals with postcolonial developments and connections in the binding of China and Southeast Asia through the trade in various "commodities." Bien Chiang explores the trade of edible birds' nests in Sarawak to Chinese consumer markets back in China. He reviews the Chinese medicinal tradition, which contains a hierarchy of birds' nest categories and has triggered a huge demand for this commodity among Chinese consumers, resulting in the formation of a lucrative circum-South China Sea birds' nest market. Chiang discusses the interactions between Chinese traders and indigenous communities in Sarawak, pointing out that local people are not just passive workers exploited by these same Chinese merchants, but instead carve out a share, as well as a career, for themselves,

by working as collectors and guardsmen in the caves where birds' nests are found.[30]

Continuing the emphasis on natural, environmental produce, Eric Tagliacozzo investigates the marine-products trade between East and Southeast Asia. His essay draws on oral-history work completed among wholesalers, retailers, and fishing communities throughout coastal Southeast Asia, and is backed up with interviews conducted in the "Chinese core" areas of Hong Kong, China, and Taiwan as well. He argues that this trade, one of the oldest of the commercial linkages between China and Southeast Asia, is still vital and important, despite having gone through a number of changes over time. It has acquired regional variations in hierarchy and function that are readily apparent.[31]

Wen-Chin Chang then orients our vantage to the mountains of mainland Southeast Asia, where she has been tracing legal and illegal jade networks among migrant Yunnanese Chinese through ethnographic research. Her essay looks into Yunnanese migration and resettlement in Thailand and Burma, these peoples' interaction with state agents and other ethnic communities, and mining and trading regulations, as well as the operation of capital flows in the region. She argues that a state-centered slant must be avoided in order to obtain real insights into the traders' economic dynamism, beyond the restrictions imposed by area regimes. Employing a non-state perspective, she analyzes contemporary field data as well as relevant historical sources to illustrate the intertwining of historical contingency and continuity in this particular underground transnational business.[32]

Finally Kevin Woods, an NGO worker embedded in Chiang Mai, takes a global commodity chain approach by looking at another "liminal" product: the timber trade in Burma (Myanmar), much of it carried through ethnically Chinese hands. Northern Burma, Kevin Woods argues, has played an important role in Southeast Asian regional trading for the past millennium, which has relied on natural-resource wealth and the control of strategic border checkpoints passing from landlocked Yunnan into mainland Southeast Asia, even on to India. Using the case of the timber economy along the China-Burma border today, Woods traces the connections of the three successive nodes of this commodity trade. The first node is timber production in the Kachin state of Upper Burma; the second node is that of procession, controlled by Chinese merchants along the China-Burma border, to Shanghai, Guangdong, and Hong Kong; and the third node is consumption of this illegal timber in different parts of the world. This case study reveals the violence

of the insurgent economy in Burma, the role of Chinese merchants in this trade, and the erasure of the violence at the consumption end of this many-miles-long process.

Charting Directions

The field of Sino-Southeast Asian Studies is now so large and complex that a synthesis of information, ideas, and approaches seems highly desirable. Sources have become available that were previously inaccessible, and disciplinary boundaries have begun to be crossed, as interpreters of this academic field strive to stretch the bounds of what is knowable about Chinese movements in Southeast Asia, both historically and today. The languages in this volume alone include Chinese, Japanese, Vietnamese, Thai, Burmese, Malay, and Indonesian—and that covers only the Asian languages, leaving out Western scholarship (read here in English, French, Spanish, and Dutch). Because no single scholar can hope to know all of these languages, let alone the geographies, time periods, and most important, the varied contexts of Chinese trade in the Nanyang, bringing these essays together to see what they can tell us as a collective seems like a very good idea. As a group, they elucidate the hardship, toil, failure, and success of Chinese merchant ventures into Southeast Asia, both in the now darkening glow of past centuries and in our own ethnographic present, as several of the later contributions clearly show.

Chinese merchants have not been alone in the Nanyang; they were joined by Indians, Arabs, Parsees, Armenians, and Jews, all conducting their own commerce and often along their own commercial lines. Equally often these diasporas have found cause to work together. It is conceivable that companion volumes to this one might usefully appear on any one (or all) of these other merchant diasporas, and the products they transited between Southeast Asia and other lands. A start has been made toward that goal already. Ravi Shankar, for example, has written on the Tamil Muslim connections between South India and Southeast Asia (particularly Malaysia and Singapore), and David Rudner has concentrated on the merchant caste known as "Chettiars" specifically in this context.[33] Gene Ammarell has looked at Bugis networks in a similar vein, using an anthropological lens, while Christian Pelras has done the same from a historical vantage.[34] The connections, both actual and conceptual, between Jewish trading networks (mostly in Europe) and Chinese merchant diasporas (mostly in Southeast Asia) have been problematized by Daniel Chirot and Anthony Reid to very good effect,

for thinking about how these processes work both in cross-cultural and in comparative terms across large swaths of the earth.[35]

We hope that this volume will provide a broad and wide-ranging perspective on these mercantile processes, elucidating not only the dynamics and mechanics of the Chinese as a merchant diaspora far from home, but also the workings of one group among many engaged in the pursuit of commerce in lands not originally their own. Taking seriously the conjuncture of geography, temporality, and the commodities themselves, this book asks how merchant diasporas operate, both actually and conceptually over long periods of time. As such, we hope it contributes to the ever-deepening field of Chinese studies overseas, but also to the critique and analysis of globalization as this has happened in past centuries, and in our own lifetime. That lofty goal is one of the signal aims of this book.

Notes

1. Some frequently quoted works are: Wang Gungwu, *China and the Chinese Overseas* (Singapore: Times Academic Press, 1991); Wang Gungwu, *Don't Leave Home: Migration and the Chinese* (Singapore: Times Academic Press, 2001); Wang Gungwu and Ng Chin-keong, eds., *Maritime China in Transition 1790–1850* (Wiesbaden: Harrassowitz Verlag, 2004); Lynn Pan, *Sons of the Yellow Emperor* (New York: Kodansha, 1990); Roderich Ptak, *China's Seaborne Trade with South and Southeast Asia (1200–1750)* (Aldershot: Ashgate, 1999); Cao Yonghe, *Zhongguo haiyangshi lunji* [Anthology of Chinese maritime history] (Taibei: Lianjing, 2000); Anthony Reid, *Sojourners and Settlers: Histories of Southeast Asia and the Chinese* (Honolulu: University of Hawaii Press, 1996); Chen Guodong, *Dongya haiyu yi qiannian* [A thousand years of East Asian Seas] (Taibei: Yuanliu, 2005); Leo Suryadinata, ed., *Southeast Asia's Chinese Businesses in an Era of Globalization: Coping with the Rise of China* (Singapore: Institute of Southeast Asian Studies, 2006).
2. Philip D. Curtin, *Cross-Cultural Trade in World History* (Cambridge: Cambridge University Press, 1984).
3. Christine E. Dobbin, *Asian Entrepreneurial Minorities: Conjoint Communities in the Making of the World-economy, 1570–1940* (Richmond, Surrey: Curzon, 1996).
4. Aihwa Ong, *Flexible Citizenship* (Durham: Duke University Press, 1999); see also Aihwa Ong and Donald M. Nonini, eds., *Ungrounded Empires: The Cultural Politics of Modern Chinese Transnationalism* (New York: Routledge, 1997).
5. Arjun Appadurai, "Introduction: Commodities and the Politics of Value," *The Social Life of Things: Commodities in Cultural Perspective*, ed. Arjun Appadurai (Cambridge: Cambridge University Press, 1986), 3–63; Igor Kopytoff, "The Cultural Biography of Things: Commoditization as Process," *The Social Life of Things: Commodities in Cultural Perspective*, ed. Arjun Appadurai (Cambridge: Cambridge University Press, 1986), 64–91.
6. Ayurvedic medicines from India might be one of these lines; the transit of Korans from the Middle East to Southeast Asia might be another.

7. Max Weber, The Protestant Ethic and the Spirit of Capitalism (1904; Los Angeles: Roxbury, 2000); Karl Marx, Capital: A Critique of Political Economy (Chicago: C. H. Kerr, 1906–9).

8. G. William Skinner, "Regional Urbanization in Nineteenth Century China," Urban Development in Imperial China (Stanford: Stanford University Press, 1977), 211–17; Mark Elvin, The Pattern of the Chinese Past (Stanford: Stanford University Press, 1973); Roy Bin Wong, China Transformed: Historical Change and the Limits of European Experience (Ithaca: Cornell University Press, 1997); Peter C. Perdue, Exhausting the Earth: State and Peasant in Hunan, 1500–1850 (Cambridge: Council on East Asian Studies, Harvard University, 1987); Philip Huang, The Peasant Economy and Social Change in North China (Stanford: Stanford University Press, 1985); Kenneth Pomeranz, The Great Divergence: China, Europe, and the Making of the Modern World Economy (Princeton: Princeton University Press, 2000).

9. Sherman Cochran, Encountering Chinese Networks: Western, Japanese, and Chinese Corporations in China, 1880–1937 (Berkeley: University of California Press, 2000); William T. Rowe, Hankow: Conflict and Community in a Chinese City, 1796–1895 (Stanford: Stanford University Press, 1989).

10. Edmund Terence Gomez and Hsin-Huang Michael Hsiao, eds., Chinese Business in Southeast Asia: Contesting Cultural Explanations, Researching Entrepreneurship (Richmond, Surrey: Curzon, 2001).

11. Timothy Brook and Gregory Blue, eds., China and Historical Capitalism: Genealogies of Sinological Knowledge (Cambridge: Cambridge University Press, 1999); Gary Hamilton, Commerce and Capitalism in Chinese Societies (New York: Routledge, 2006).

12. David Faure, China and Capitalism: A History of Business Enterprise in Modern China (Hong Kong: Hong Kong University Press, 2006).

13. Philip Kuhn, Chinese among Others: Emigration in Modern Times (Lanham, Md.: Rowman and Littlefield, 2008).

14. See also Anthony Reid, "The Unthreatening Alternative: Chinese Shipping in Southeast Asia, 1567–1842," Review of Indonesian and Malaysian Affairs 27.1–2 (1993): 13–33.

15. See also C. Patterson Giersch, Asian Borderlands: The Transformation of Qing China's Yunnan Frontier (Cambridge: Harvard University Press, 2006).

16. Also see Adam McKeown, Chinese Migrant Networks and Cultural Change: Peru, Chicago, Hawaii, 1900–1936 (Chicago: University of Chicago Press, 2001).

17. Also see Carl Trocki, Opium, Empire and the Global Political Economy: A Study of the Asian Opium Trade, 1750–1950 (London: Routledge, 1999).

18. Takeshi Hamashita, Choko shisutemu to kindai ajia (朝貢システムと近代アジア) (Tokyo: Iwanami Shoten, 1997).

19. Li Tana, Nguyen Cochinchina: Southern Vietnam in the Seventeenth and Eighteenth Centuries (Ithaca: Southeast Asia Program, Cornell University, 1998).

20. See also Masuda Erika, "The Last Siamese Tributary Missions to China, 1851–1854, and the 'Rejected' Value of Chim Kong," Maritime China in Transition 1750–1850, ed. Wang Gungwu and Ng Chin-keong (Wiesbaden: Harrassowitz Verlag, 2004), 33–42.

21. See also Gerrit Knaap and Heather Sutherland, Monsoon Traders: Ships, Skippers and Commodities in Eighteenth-century Makassar (Leiden: KITLV Press, 2004).

22. Sun Laichen, "Shan Gems, Chinese Silver, and the Rise of Shan Principalities in

Northern Burma, c. 1450–1527," *Southeast Asia in the Fifteenth Century: The Ming Factor*, ed. Geoffrey Wade and Sun Laichen (Singapore: NUS Press, 2009).

23. Also see Leonard Blussé, *Strange Company: Chinese Settlers, Mestizo Women, and the Dutch in VOC Batavia* (Dordrecht, Holland: Foris, 1986).

24. See also Lucille Chia, *Printing for Profit: The Commercial Publishers of Jianyang, Fujian (Eleventh–Seventeenth Centuries)* (Cambridge: Center for Harvard-Yenching Institute, Harvard University Asia, 2002).

25. See also Kwee Hui Kian, *The Political Economy of Java's Northeast Coast, c. 1740–1800: Elite Synergy* (London: Brill, 2006).

26. See also Man-houng Lin, *China Upside Down: Currency, Society, and Ideologies, 1808–1856* (Cambridge: Asian Center, Harvard University, 2006).

27. See also Wu Xiao An, *Chinese Business in the Making of a Malay State, 1882–1941: Kedah and Penang* (London: Routledge, 2003).

28. See also Nola Cooke, "Water World: Chinese and Vietnamese on the Riverine, from Ca Mau to Tonle Sap (c. 1850–1884)," *Water Frontier: Commerce and the Chinese in the Lower Mekong Region, 1750–1880*, ed. Nola Cooke and Li Tana (Singapore: Rowman and Littlefield, 2004), 139–57.

29. See Jean DeBernardi, *Rites of Belonging: Memory, Modernity, and Identity in a Malaysian Chinese Community* (Stanford: Stanford University Press, 2004); DeBernardi, *The Way that Lives in the Heart: Chinese Popular Religion and Spirit Mediums in Penang, Malaysia* (Stanford: Stanford University Press, 2006).

30. See also Bien Chiang, "Zhang changwu: Yige salauyue yibanzu de changwu shequn, lishi yu maoyi chutan" [Rumah chang: Community, history and regional trading relationship of an Iban long-house of Sarawak], *Shequn yanjiu de shengsi*, ed. Chen Wende and Huang Yingkui (Taibei: Zhongyang yanjiuyuan minzuxue yanjiu suo, 2002), 199–255.

31. See also Eric Tagliacozzo, *Secret Trades, Porous Borders: Smuggling and States along a Southeast Asian Frontier, 1865–1915* (New Haven: Yale University Press, 2005); Tagliacozzo, "Onto the Coast and Into the Forest: Ramifications of the China Trade on the History of Northwest Borneo, 900–1900," *Histories of the Borneo Environment*, ed. Reed Wadley (Leiden: KITLV Press, 2005), 25–60; Tagliacozzo, "Border-Line Legal: Chinese Communities and 'Illicit' Activity in Insular Southeast Asia," *Maritime China and the Overseas Chinese in Transition, 1750–1850*, ed. Wang Gungwu and Ng Chin Keong (Wiesbaden: Harrassowitz Verlag, 2004), 61–76.

32. See also Wen-Chin Chang, "Guanxi and Regulation in Network: The Yunnanese Jade Trade between Burma and Thailand, 1962–88," *Journal of Southeast Asian Studies* 35.3 (2004): 479–501; Chang, "Home away from Home: The Migrant Yunnanese in Northern Thailand," *International Journal of Asian Studies*, 3.1 (2006): 49–76; Chang, "Venturing into Barbarous Regions: Trans-border Trade among Migrant Yunnanese between Thailand and Burma," *Asian Studies* 68.2 (2009): 543–72.

33. Ravi Shankar, *Tamil Muslims in Tamil Nadu, Malaysia, and Singapore: Historical Identity, Problems of Adjustment, and Change in the Twentieth Century* (Kuala Lumpur: Jayanath, 2001); David Rudner, *Caste and Capitalism in Colonial India: The Nattukottai Chettiars* (Berkeley: University of California Press, 1994).

34. Gene Ammarell, *Bugis Navigation* (New Haven: Yale University Southeast Asia Program, 1999); Christian Pelras, *The Bugis* (Oxford: Blackwell Publishers, 1996).

35. See Daniel Chirot and Anthony Reid, eds., *Essential Outsiders: Chinese and Jews in the Modern Transformation of Southeast Asia and Central Europe* (Seattle: University of Washington Press, 1997).

PART I ~~~~ Theoretical/Longue Durée

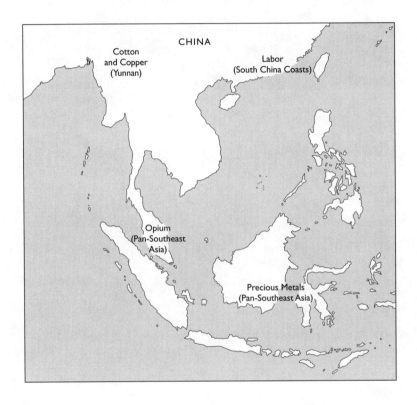

CHINA

Cotton
and Copper
(Yunnan)

Labor
(South China Coasts)

Opium
(Pan-Southeast
Asia)

Precious Metals
(Pan-Southeast Asia)

CHINESE ON THE MINING FRONTIER IN SOUTHEAST ASIA

——— Anthony Reid

The influx of Chinese into Malaysia in particular and "Central Southeast Asia" more generally is often popularly attributed to colonial rule, as if the pluralism they exemplified were not "natural" to the region. In reality, the Peninsula has always been highly plural, and the advance of the Chinese mining frontier within it preceded the British.[1] This essay documents some of the means by which Chinese mining advanced the economic frontiers in Southeast Asia ahead of European capital. Tin, being the most obvious example, takes center stage in this story.

Early Controversies

How metals technology spread in Southeast Asia in the earliest periods is a matter of considerable and long-standing debate, particularly since the Ban Chiang excavations in Thailand in the 1970s raised the possibility that bronze-working there may have been as old as that in China. The earliest Ban Chiang periodizations have now been largely discredited, however, and a consensus is emerging that the Southeast Asian bronze age began in the middle of the second century B.C.E., that it was distinct from any of the older "Chinese" traditions, yet somehow related to them, and that it long predated the rise of states in Southeast Asia. Gold, iron, copper, and tin were undoubtedly mined, smelted, and worked into ornaments, utensils, and weapons in Southeast Asia before the Common Era (C.E.), and Chinese records of contact with Lao peoples at the end of the sixth century C.E. declare that they made their own bronze drums in a manner different from the Chinese. We know little, however, about how the relevant technologies were disseminated or developed.[2]

Until the era of bulk imports in the sixteenth and seventeenth centuries, iron and copper remained relatively scarce in island Southeast Asia, and trav-

elers from Europe and China found that their everyday nails, knives, and needles were in great demand from the locals. The reasons appear to have been not so much the lack of minerals in the ground (although Java and Bali were particularly disadvantaged in that regard) as the sparse population (by Chinese standards) in the vicinity of most of these minerals, and consequently smaller scale, less efficient methods of both mining and smelting.

As trade developed in the second millennium of the Common Era, everyday metal items became cheaper to import from afar than to produce locally. In Sung times, iron and ironware were "among the commonest commodities" exported to Southeast Asia from China.[3] By 1500, the needs of Southeast Asian maritime centers like Melaka were provided principally from China, including "copper, iron . . . cast iron kettles, bowls, basins . . . plenty of needles of a hundred different kinds, some of them very fine and well made . . . and things of very poor quality like those that come to Portugal from Flanders."[4] These items could be produced far more cheaply in China than in any of the Southeast Asian cities because of more advanced mining and smelting methods, so that Southeast Asian mining and metalwork tended to retreat with time to less accessible areas in the interior.

Was There a Chinese Role in Borneo Ironworking?

Iron is found in the northerly areas of the mainland states, and in the hills between Siam and Burma, as well as in the islands in central Sumatra, Belitung, western Borneo, and central Sulawesi. Weapons, tools, and ploughtips manufactured in these places had to circulate to many other populous centers, such as Java and Bali, where iron was not found.

The ready availability of brown iron ores near the surface in many parts of western Borneo, and the islands of Belitung and Karimata off its shores, make this region particularly interesting. The ironworking site at the mouth of the Sarawak River was somewhat controversially investigated by Tom Harrison in the 1960s. He and Stanley O'Connor claimed as many as 40,000 tons of slag were left behind in three adjacent sites where iron was extracted from ores between around 900 and 1350. The technology for smelting the iron was not of Chinese type, with a fixed furnace, but rather by using open charcoal fires in bowl-like recessions in the ground. This relatively simple technology was still in use in the nineteenth century among peoples of interior Borneo such as the Kayan and Kenyah, whom imported iron was the last to reach.[5] Karl Hutterer also found large amounts of slag in Cebu that he dated to iron-smelting processes of the thirteenth to fifteenth centuries.[6]

Both sites were relatively accessible to the China trade. In particular, West

Borneo was on the standard sailing routes between south China and the Majapahit heartland of Java. While discounting Chinese technological influences on ironworking in Borneo, Harrison and O'Connor argue that Sarawak iron may have been carried to China by Arab and other ships, since too much was being produced for local consumption. Wheatley had already argued that wi-mung-i, which was listed in the Sung chronicle as being brought to China by Arab merchants, was probably "the hydrated iron oxide known as limonite."[7]

Around 1600, a time for which evidence of the internal Southeast Asia trade is more abundant, the most important archipelago center for exporting parangs and other iron tools was Karimata, about 60 kilometers off the coast of Southwest Borneo. Java and Makasar imported their axes and parangs from Karimata, while Malays of the Peninsula were said to carry krisses of Karimata steel. When the Dutch found a way to access this supply, in 1630, they purchased almost 10,000 axes and parangs in one lot.[8] Although Belitung was also a source for this kind of trade, with "more parangs but fewer axes," the reputation of tiny Karimata for superior workmanship was such that the label "Karimata" was applied more widely.[9]

So centrally were the Karimata islands located on the sailing routes between China and Java that the major strait on that route was named the Karimata Strait, between those islands and Belitung. Whatever the case in the Sarawak River area, there is firm evidence in Karimata of Chinese craftsmen settling as early as the thirteenth century. Wang Dayuan, describing the Nanyang a half-century after the Mongol fleet set off to conquer Java in 1293, had this to say of an island he called Goulan Shan.

> When the [Yuan] dynasty was founded, the forces to attack Java were driven by the wind to this island, and the ships wrecked. One ship fortunately escaped with stores of nails and mortar. Seeing that there was a great deal of timber on this island, they built some tens of ships, everything from ribs to sails and bamboo poles were supplied [from the island]. Over a hundred men who were ill from the long beating about in the storm and were unable to leave were left on the island, and today the Chinese live mixed up with the native families.[10]

Rockhill sought to identify this mysterious island with the tiny island of Gelam off the coast of Southwest Borneo, though the Karimata group seem more likely in view of their location on the sailing routes. Whether or not this group of Chinese transferred smelting technology to Karimata and Belitung, there were many other Chinese craftsmen who passed this way in

Ming times, some of whom may also have been shipwrecked or defected voluntarily. As Zhou Daguan put it of Angkor in the 1290s, since "women are easily had . . . a great many sailors desert to take up permanent residence."[11]

Whatever technology transfer there may have been to iron-production in this Karimata-Belitung area cannot have been continuous. The gap between economies of scale in production in China and in the archipelago grew wider with more frequent shipping in the seventeenth century. In the eighteenth century, cheaper imported Chinese iron- and metalwork drove out most of the production in accessible coastal areas of the archipelago. The dwindling community of ironworkers of Karimata left for the mainland in 1808.[12]

Chinese Expansion of the Mining Frontier in the Eighteenth Century

In the eighteenth century, China's population grew markedly, stimulating an increase in the demand for silver, gold, copper, and lead as currency to fuel the expanding economy. The quest for minerals was one factor propelling Chinese explorers, miners, traders, and officials south and west, eventually bringing the empire's extent to its historic maximum. Yunnan was the largest mining frontier for Chinese, with 300,000 Han miners reportedly working there in 1750 and 500,000 in 1800.[13] Sources of silver, lead, and zinc were particularly abundant around what is today the boundary between southern Yunnan and Burma's Shan state. The massive Munai and Maolong mines peaked in production in the mid-eighteenth century, and eventually came under permanent Qing control.[14] Chinese miners went beyond imperial control, into the hills in the north of Dai Viet and what is today Burmese and Lao territory.

The huge Bawdwin opencast mine in Shan territory was the most important Chinese-worked mine of the border area that never fell under Qing control. It may have been "protected" from this fate by malaria, which Herbert Hoover contracted when inspecting the mine for its modern rebirth in the British period. Ming records suggest that it was Chinese miners who first brought the mine into production in 1412, and they continued to extract silver from it in increasing amounts throughout the eighteenth century.

Copper, lead, and silver also occur in the border area of northern Vietnam, where geographical barriers to an influx of Chinese miners were less intimidating, but political ones were better established along one of Asia's oldest frontiers. Here, too, the eighteenth century was the peak period for the expansion of Chinese mining. The Trinh regime that governed northern Vietnam (Tonkin) profited greatly from the booming output of the mines

and in the 1760s was reportedly drawing half its revenue from levies on these northern mines. By midcentury, there were upward of 20,000 Cantonese at the Tong-tinh copper mines alone, despite a series of royal decrees seeking to limit their numbers. In the second half of the century, the copper-mining operation in the border areas was thought to have averaged over 500 tons output per annum, making it one of the largest in Asia. The tenuous control the court exercised over the Chinese mining kongsis caused increasing difficulties, however, and in 1767 the Trinh attempted to expel them from Vietnam. The economic stakes were too high, however, and the attempt failed.[15]

Gold-Working

Precious metals were the most ancient and valued of Southeast Asia's precious minerals, particularly the silver of the northern mainland close to Yunnan, and the gold of Sumatra, Borneo, and the Peninsula. Chinese miners were also attracted to these commodities, although they never became as dominant as they were on the nineteenth-century tin fields. Sumatran gold, which gave rise to the Sanskrit soubriquet Suvarna-bhumi (gold-land), was for the most part off limits to Chinese miners. It was considered so precious an item of royal monopoly that outsiders were discouraged. William Dampier related that in Aceh in the 1680s, when gold had become the principal export of the state, only Muslims were permitted to go to the rich mining areas of Kawaj XIII in the hills behind Pidië. Huge profits were reportedly made in these goldfields, discovered only about thirty years earlier, and the wealth they produced brought Chinese traders and craftsmen to the Aceh capital every year. However, to prevent them reaching the goldfields, armed guards were posted along the route.[16]

Central Southeast Asia—western Borneo, eastern Sumatra and its islands, and the Peninsula—with its sparse populations and states largely dependent on the economic activities of outsiders, was the major Southeast Asian theater of Chinese mining. Gold had been extracted from Borneo and the Peninsula for more than a millennium, by simple methods of panning. However, as with tin, the larger-scale labor organization of Cantonese and Hakka miners was introduced to archipelago gold-mining in the middle of the eighteenth century. In most cases, river-mouth chiefs and rajas engaged them to work more efficiently interior mineral resources hitherto dependent on the part-time attention of agriculturalists.

One such early settlement on the Peninsula was Pulai, in upper Kelantan, which Hakka gold-miners had opened by the second half of the eighteenth

century.[17] Graham, however, suggests it was considerably older, and that in earlier times "the mineral products of Kelantan considerably exceeded in value those of any other State" in the Peninsula.[18] During the reign of Sultan Mahmat in Kelantan (1807–1837), the ruler's son was killed by the previously self-governing Chinese miners when he tried to enforce his newly granted monopoly of rice distribution by cutting off the mining settlement from all supplies coming up the river to them. The dead prince's son then organized a massacre of the whole Chinese settlement, "and the gold mining industry of Kelantan came to a sudden end."[19]

But it was the goldfields north of the Kapuas River in West Borneo that drew the largest number of Chinese pioneers. As early as 1740, the ruler of Mempawah, or in some accounts the Sultan of Sambas, decided to bring Chinese miners in to work the gold-bearing rivers he sought to control. Production had previously depended on the part-time labor of Dayaks. The Malay rulers used terms that had been effective on a small scale with the Dayaks, providing salt, rice, opium, and cloth at inflated monopoly prices in return for a monopoly of the gold extracted. In addition, the Chinese as outsiders were forbidden to engage in agriculture (to increase their dependence on the ruler's supplies) and were charged a head tax on entering or leaving Borneo through the ruler's port.[20]

The Chinese miners set to work initially on mines abandoned by the Dayaks, but used more intense and mechanized methods to sluice away the topsoil above the gold-bearing lode. They were also much more centrally organized through their kongsi, a ritual brotherhood in which capital and labor were shared in acknowledged portions.[21] Gradually the kongsis became autonomous by forming their own relations with interior Dayaks (including marriage), farming the surrounding land, and smuggling their gold out through channels not controlled by the rulers. The capitalists who established the mine and funded the importation of workers of course had the largest share, and laborers still indebted for their passage had none, but older workers did share decision-making and often rotated the leadership among themselves.

There is no way to know the amount of gold shipped out, chiefly to China, but the fact that about 60,000 Chinese miners were at work there over about a century indicates that it must have been extremely large. As Dutch power advanced in the nineteenth century, most of the kongsis made their peace with it through a system of indirect rule, but the strongest Montrado kongsi remained defiant until conquered in the 1850s.

The Chinese Tin-Mining Frontier

A large proportion of the world's tin is concentrated in the chain of hills from eastern Burma in the north down through the Malayan Peninsula to the islands of Bangka and Belitung in the south. By the tenth century, the Peninsula was supplying most of Asia's tin needs. The trade boom of 1580–1640 witnessed a great increase in mining of this tin to supply the busy markets of India, China, Siam, and Java. Up until the seventeenth century, it was the ports of the western coast of the Peninsula—Junk Ceylon (Phuket), Perak, and Selangor—that supplied India, while Ligor (Nakhonsithammarat), Pahang, and other ports on the eastern coast supplied most of China's needs.

The miners appear to have been long-term Peninsula residents of various ethnicities, who attended to mining when the demands of rice growing or serving their rulers' requirements permitted. Mining sites were located and supervised by a *pawang* (shaman) who could mediate with the spirit of the tin. Men dug the ore and earth out of flooded pits, while women separated the tin ore with their fingers.[22] The method was first described in Perak by Eredia: "The earth is dug out of the mountains and placed on certain tables where the earth is dispersed by water in such a way that only the tin in the form of grains remains on the tables. It is then melted in certain clay moulds and by a process of casting is converted into . . . slabs."[23] The "casting" was a primitive form of smelting in which burning charcoal was mixed with the tin ore until the metal ran out into the mold. These slabs, of about twenty kilograms, were then floated down the rivers to port, where the port-ruler usually took the largest share of the profits of selling it.

Around 1500, the port-sultanate of Melaka controlled most of the tin of what is today Kedah, Perak, and Selangor, and sold most of it to passing Indian merchants to take back to their own South Asian markets. The amounts, however, appear to have been small. Pires gives figures for the tin rendered to Melaka as tribute by all the west-coast ports, which amounts to only 34 tons (36,000 calain), worth 1,000 cruzados.[24] Estimates of total exports around 1600 vary between 100–300 tons, mostly from Perak and Phuket. The largest estimate at the peak of the trade boom is a Dutch one of 1638, to be taken with caution, that Perak and Kedah could each produce up to 1,000 tons (6,000 *bahar*) a year.[25]

The Portuguese occupants of Melaka (1511–1641) had to contest the supply of tin with Muslim traders, and they lost out completely after their

great Muslim enemy Aceh conquered the Perak and Kedah fields in 1575. The Dutch, who in turn conquered Melaka in 1641, hoped to use the port to monopolize the supply of tin, and they were in a much stronger position to do so. The largest amount they ever succeeded in acquiring, however, was 380 tons, in 1650, and the effect of their heavy-handed "system of fixed prices, annual quotas and exclusive privileges" appears only to have been to drive the tin industry of the Peninsula into decline in the second half of the century.[26]

Verenigde Oostindische Compagnie (VOC) attempts to force the purchase of tin at unrealistically low prices from the Malay states it could control from Melaka drove the chief centers of production northward into Siamese and Burmese territory, so that Phuket (Junk Ceylon), Takuapa, and Tavoy were supplying much of the market in the early eighteenth century. Chulia (south Indian), Bugis, Chinese, and English traders paid higher prices and took the bulk of the supply.[27] The quantities remained modest (probably below 1,000 tons in total), however, until the systematic exploitation of tin discoveries on Bangka by Chinese miners in the middle of the century. China's demand for Southeast Asian tin expanded greatly during its prosperous eighteenth century, partly to make the tinfoil burnt as joss paper in offerings to the ancestors, but also for packaging the booming tea trade.[28]

The tin of Bangka was discovered around 1710 by Muslim Sino-Malays familiar with mines on the Peninsula. It came to the notice of Batavia in 1717, when a pretender to the Palembang throne in exile in Bangka offered some to the Dutch in an attempt to gain their support. In 1722, the VOC signed a contract with the sultan of Palembang for the delivery of all Bangka tin, and in the years 1723–1730 deliveries averaged 175 tons a year. Production continued at this modest level by traditional Southeast Asian methods until about 1750, when a Chinese known in Bangka tradition as Un Asing began systematically importing Chinese contract workers from Guangdong with their sophisticated sluicing techniques. Production increased rapidly, so that deliveries to the VOC averaged 1,037 tons a year in the 1750s and 1,562 tons in the 1760s.[29] Although the level of reported deliveries to the VOC dropped a little thereafter, the reason appears to have been that larger proportions of Bangka tin were evading Dutch control and being bought by English, Chinese, and other traders at independent ports such as Riau. European ships alone sold 1,611 tons of Southeast Asian (chiefly Bangka) tin in Canton in 1768 and an average of 2,162 tons a year in 1771–1774.[30] Presuming that an equal amount was being imported to China by Chinese vessels or being taken by Indian and Southeast Asian consumers, Southeast Asia's

tin production must have rivaled Cornwall's by the 1770s. Europe, however, was slow to realize the remarkable growth of this threat from the East.

Although some of the Chinese miners of Bangka were reported in a Malay history to have been brought from Siam and Vietnam, and links with the gold-miners of Borneo cannot be ruled out, most were certainly brought in directly from Canton through an exclusively Chinese network.

> Annually . . . a confidential and competent Chinese agent [went] by the junk returning from Palembang to China, to invite efficient and select men. . . . The expenses of their voyage and establishment was to be defrayed by the [local capitalist] who was to be reimbursed from their first profits at the mines. . . . Until they had liquidated the obligations they thus incurred . . . they were not permitted to relinquish the labours of the mines.[31]

There were probably over 6,000 Chinese miners there by the 1770s, chiefly Hakkas from the Meixian area of Guangdong. They were organized in teams (kongsi, pinyin *gongsi*) of about thirty men responsible to a headman representing the authority of the *tikos* (pinyin *dage*, elder brother), usually a Sino-Malay trader living in Palembang and providing the capital needed to open the mine and import the labor. The kongsis were relatively egalitarian: "The whole of the labourers work on terms of equality . . . while all share equally in the profits."[32]

The larger units of labor and capital, as well as techniques brought from China, made possible a much higher level of technology in both mining and smelting the tin. The Chinese used a chain-pallet pump common in Chinese irrigation to clear pits of 6–10 meters depth, and to wash the soil from the ore. In smelting, they introduced a superior furnace and bellows, with specialist teams of six or more men producing a high standard of purity that gave "Bangka tin" an unrivaled reputation worldwide.[33]

Bangka production declined in the 1790s because of the usual problem of insecurity. On the one hand, the essential function of the *tikos* in mediating between the Palembang court and Chinese miners broke down as Palembang aristocrats attempted to dominate the industry. On the other, Illanun and Malay marauders began raiding the island for tin and slaves, reducing mining communities to ruin and driving the surviving Chinese away. Production began to rise again when the British occupied Bangka, in 1812, and the restored Dutch in 1816 decided to rule the island directly. Although the miners and smelters remained Chinese, the autonomy of the kongsis was gradually replaced by a greater degree of Dutch control, even in the recruitment of

labor from Canton. Tin production recovered rapidly, from 1,250 tons a year around 1820 to 3,000 tons in the 1830s.[34] In addition, the production of the various centers on the Peninsula totaled 2,000 tons in 1835, according to a careful survey by P. J. Begbie.[35] Most of these centers, too, were worked by Chinese, with Sungei Ujong (around modern Seremban), Perak, and Trengganu the most productive.[36]

In the nineteenth century, industrial Europe and America surged ahead of Asia as importers of tin. Straits Settlements tin exports in the 1840s had been distributed between India (39 percent), China (10 percent), Europe (34 percent) and the United States (9 percent). By 1869–1873, the proportions had shifted to India 9 percent; China 18 percent, Europe 43 percent, and the United States 28 percent.[37] The reason for the shift was the manufacture of tin plate, in which rapid technical advances had been made throughout the century. Tin consumption in Britain grew from a thousand tons a year in the first decade of the century to 2,600 in the 1820s and 5,800 in the 1840s. From being the world's major exporter of tin, Britain became a net importer in the 1850s. Europe as a whole became a major importer of the tin first of Bangka and then of the Malayan Peninsula (see table 1).

Chinese mining gradually wrought the same transformation on the rich Peninsula tin fields as it had in Bangka, though with many initial setbacks due to the lack of security. Chinese had been involved in leasing the tin fields of Phuket from the Siamese king early in the eighteenth century, and were smelting there while Malays and Thais dug for the tin. Ambitious Malay rulers must periodically have introduced Chinese to boost the existing Malay production elsewhere in the Peninsula. The Sultan of Perak adopted a Dutch suggestion in the 1770s that he emulate the favorable Bangka experience by employing Chinese miners, finding some for the task in Dutch Melaka. The ruler of Selangor brought Chinese miners into Lukut around 1815, and there were more than 300 there by 1834, when fighting broke out and caused a collapse. The Penghulu of Sungei Ujong (now in Negri Sembilan) established 600 Chinese miners on the Linggi River in 1828, making use of a large advance from Melaka merchants to whom the tin was consigned. But after a conflict over a local woman in 1830, "great numbers" of the Chinese were slaughtered and the remainder fled, their property seized by the local chiefs.[38] In Perak, Chinese miners had begun work by 1818. Each time violence broke out, new miners were induced to return a few years later.[39]

The uneasy cooperation between Malay rulers, Chinese financiers from the Straits Settlements, Chinese smelters, and a mixture of Malay and Chinese miners opened up the forested peninsula and attracted a variety of mi-

Table 1 European Imports of Southeast Asian Tin, in Tons p.a.

	Total tin sold in Europe market	Imported from Southeast Asia (%)	Imported from Bangka (%)	Imported from the Peninsula (%)
1831–35	6,185	1,804 (29)	787 (12.7)	1,017 (16.4)
1836–40	7,704	2,403 (31)	1,575 (20.4)	829 (10.8)
1841–45	9,992	3,294 (33)	2,452 (24.5)	842 (8.4)
1846–50	11,793	4,875 (41)	4,066 (34.5)	809 (6.9)
1851–55	11,789	5,507 (47)	4,207 (35.7)	1,300 (11.0)
1856–60	14,647	7,773 (53)	5,978 (40.8)	1,786 (12.2)
1861–65	17,537	7,856 (45)	4,579 (26.1)	3,277 (18.7)
1866–70	18,277	8,515 (47)	4,956 (27.1)	3,559 (19.5)
1871–75	23,134	10,606 (46)	4,755 (20.6)	5,851 (25.3)

Source: Calculated from Wong Lin Ken, *The Malayan Tin Industry to 1914* (Tucson: University of Arizona Press, 1964), 14.

grants to it. Wong Lin Ken instances the system operated by the Dato Klana of Sungei Ujong in the 1820s. He received an advance of $2,500 every month from Chinese financiers in Melaka, in return for directing the tin output to them. The Dato provided supplies and opium to the Chinese kongsis that worked each mine, and also levied a monthly rent from them. He required each *bangsal* (shed) to provide him three *bahar* (540 kg) of tin at a favorable fixed price, which he then sold to the Melaka merchants.[40]

In the 1840s, production expanded rapidly in response to the increasing demand for and price of tin in Europe. New ore deposits were discovered in Lukut (in today's Negri Sembilan), along the Klang River in Selangor (including the area of modern Kuala Lumpur), at Kanching on the Selangor River, and above all at Larut in the Taiping area of Perak, where there were 5,000 Chinese miners working in 1861. Older workings in Melaka itself, in nearby Sungei Ujong, and in Phuket (southern Siam) were worked much more rigorously by Chinese miners than had been the case with the mixed and part-time labor of earlier periods. Phuket, where the ancient mines had been left to languish during the wars of the late eighteenth century and early nineteenth, revived spectacularly, to the point where Bradley claimed it had a population of 25,000 Chinese (and fewer than a thousand others) in 1870,

Table 2 Value of Penang Trade with Siam and
the Peninsula, in Thousands of Straits Dollars

	Siam	Peninsula
1845	345	69
1854	n.a.	572
1864	2,293	1,466
1872	5,669	4,120

Source: Anthony Reid, *The Contest for North Sumatra:
Atjeh, the Netherlands and Britain 1858–1898* (Kuala
Lumpur: Oxford University Press, 1969), 294.

producing 3,600 tons of tin per year.[41] As before, it was Chinese merchants
in the Straits Settlements who provided the capital and initiative for this
expansion, and who persevered in finding laborers for the booming mines
even when political instability and periodic massacres drove the original
miners out.[42]

Straits Settlements exports of Peninsula tin reached 2,446 tons per
annum in 1844–1848, 3,750 tons per annum a decade later, and 7,919 tons
per annum in 1864–1869, more than tripling in twenty years.[43] Bangka production grew much more slowly, and was overtaken by the Peninsula in the
1870s. For Penang, trade grew in the decade after 1851 "at a greater rate than
at any other period of her history," largely because it was a base for the tin of
Perak and of Phuket.[44] The value of Penang's trade with Siam and the Peninsula, fueled overwhelmingly by tin, rose more than tenfold in each case (see
table 2).

In the years after 1873, Britain was drawn to intervene in the crucial tin-
producing states—Perak, Selangor, Negri Sembilan, and Pahang—largely
by pressure from Straits merchants, Chinese and European, to end the cha-
otic instability that hindered commerce there. In the years after British control, Malayan tin production continued to increase rapidly, until 1895, as
did Bangka more slowly, though stabilizing or even stagnating thereafter.[45]
In 1879, Malaya surpassed Cornwall and Australia to become the world's
largest tin producer, and soon thereafter produced more than the rest of the
world combined, a position that Southeast Asian producers retain today.
Throughout that period of expansion, Chinese dominated the Malayan tin
trade, whether in terms of capital, labor, or technology. Peaceful conditions

and the beginnings of transport infrastructure helped after British intervention, but the pace of expansion on the Chinese mining frontier had been as great or greater during the thirty years *before* British intervention created those conditions.

The frontier levied a terrible toll on these Chinese miners. Tens of thousands arrived every year to work in the mines, and a substantial proportion of them died every year there. Many succumbed to the internal conflicts of the 1830s through the 1860s, initially at Malay hands but later overwhelmingly through secret-society conflicts, whereby the Cantonese of the so-called five districts were mobilized by the Hai San society, and those of the "four districts" by the Ghee Hin or Triad. Many more died of diseases, including malaria, cholera, and dysentery. Figures are not available until the late 1870s, by which time the ravages of beriberi made the Perak tin fields among the most lethal frontiers anywhere.[46] In the years 1879–1882, about 3,000 Chinese died every year in the Perak tin mines alone. From the 150,000 beriberi cases treated in the hospitals and clinics of the Federated Malay States in the 1880s and 1890s, and the assumption that only a third of total cases actually reached these clinics, a recent analyst has calculated that 100,000 miners may have died of beriberi in this period alone.[47]

Analysis

What was the effect of the Chinese mining frontier on the longer-term history of the region? Unquestionably, these Chinese miners brought capitalism, the global economy, and industrial-scale production techniques to areas that had previously been largely jungle. They provided some infrastructure, and survived the most dangerous disease regime before settled conditions were established. Their success made Malaya, Bangka, and West Borneo so productive and important that colonial power followed.

Reports are more mixed on the political effects. George Windsor Earl, like many other advocates of British intervention in the 1860s, regarded as a great evil the "unlimited extortion" that the Chinese capitalists, who typically also controlled the secret societies and hence the labor trade, could exercise over the miners. Mary Turnbull, while citing these views, argues that "the rapid expansion of the tin trade hastened the disintegration of traditional authority in the Malay states."[48] On the other hand, Wong Lin Ken sees the authority of the fifteenth-century Melaka sultanate as having well and truly disintegrated by the nineteenth century, to the point where any economic surplus local chiefs could extract was devoted to pursuing internecine conflicts rather than developing the land.[49]

In comparative terms, what was exceptional about the Chinese mining kongsis was their readiness to accept the fragile authority of established river chiefs, even including paying them substantial rents, provided their essential livelihood was not threatened. Had a male workforce of this scale entered the Peninsula under Bugis, Malay, Acehnese, Thai, or European auspices, it would immediately have changed the power balance and threatened the position of rulers. What attracted the local river chiefs, indeed, was the Chinese reputation for political docility, and for governing their own internal affairs through kongsi, secret-society, and religious means. When rival Chinese secret societies were drawn into Peninsula conflicts, they certainly exacerbated them by increasing substantially the scale of operations. However, the conflicts between the chiefs were already there, and inviting Chinese in was another weapon in the ongoing Malay struggles. In more unified political environments, as in Siam, Vietnam, or the Dutch sphere, such polarization seldom occurred.

Notes

1. Michael Montesano and Patrick Jory, eds., *Thai South and Malay North: Ethnic Interactions in a Plural Peninsula* (Singapore: National University of Singapore Press, 2008).

2. Charles Higham, *The Bronze Age of Southeast Asia* (Cambridge: Cambridge University Press, 1996). Anthony Reid, *The Lands below the Winds*, vol. 1 of *Southeast Asia in the Age of Commerce* (New Haven: Yale University Press, 1988), 106–19.

3. Paul Wheatley, "Geographical Notes on Some Commodities Involved in Sung Maritime Trade," *Journal of the Malayan Branch of the Royal Asiatic Society* 32.2 (1959): 117.

4. Tomé Pires, *The Suma Oriental of Tomé Pires*, trans. Armando Cortesão (1515; London: Hakluyt Society, 1944), 125.

5. Tom Harrison and Stanley O'Connor, *Excavations of the Prehistoric Iron Industry in West Borneo*, 2 vols. (Ithaca: Cornell University Southeast Asia Program, 1969).

6. Karl Hutterer, *An Archaeological Picture of a Pre-Spanish Cebuano Community* (Cebu: University of San Carlos, 1973), 34–37.

7. Cited in Harrison and O'Connor, *Excavations of the Prehistoric Iron Industry in West Borneo*, 1:199–200.

8. Reid, *The Lands below the Winds*, 111.

9. Cornelis Speelman, "De Handelsrelaties van het Makassaarse rijk volgens de Notitie van Cornelis Speelman uit 1670," *Nederlands historische bronnen*, ed. J. Noorduyn (1670; Amsterdam: Verloren, 1983), 113.

10. Wang Dayuan, *Daoyi Zhilue* [Island savages, 1349], translated in W. W. Rockhill, "Notes on the Relation and Trade of China," *T'oung Pao* (1915), 261.

11. Zhou Daguan, *The Customs of Cambodia by Chou Ta-Kuan (Zhou Daguan)* (c. 1310; Bangkok: Siam Society, 1993), 69.

12. *Encyclopedië van Nederlandsch-Indië*, 4 vols. (The Hague: Martinus Nijhoff, 1899–1905).

13. James Lee, "Food Supply and Population Growth in Southwest China, 1250–1850," *Journal of Asian Studies* 41.4 (1982): 742.

14. C. Patterson Giersch, *Asian Borderlands: The Transformation of Qing China's Yunnan Frontier* (Cambridge: Harvard University Press, 2006), 168.

15. Alexander Woodside, *Vietnam and the Chinese Model: A Comparative Study of Nguyen and Ch'ing Civil Government in the First Half of the Nineteenth Century* (Cambridge: Harvard University Press, 1971), 259–60; Nguyen Thanh-Nha, *Tableau économique du Vietnam aux XVIIe et XVIIIe siècles* (Paris: Cujas, 1970), 86–90.

16. William Dampier, *Voyages and Discoveries*, ed. C. Wilkinson (1699; London: Argonaut, 1931), 93; T. J. Veltman, "Geschiedenis van het landschap Pidië," *Tijdschrift van het Bataviaasche Genootschap* 58 (1904): 73–76.

17. Sharon Carstens, "Pulai: Memories of a Gold Mining Settlement in Ulu Kelantan," *Journal of the Malayan Branch, Royal Asiatic Society* 53.1 (1980): 50–67.

18. W. A. Graham, *Kelantan: A State of the Malay Peninsula: A Handbook of Information* (Glasgow: James Maclehose, 1908), 101.

19. Ibid., 103.

20. Mary Somers Heidhues, *Gold-diggers, Farmers, and Traders in the "Chinese Districts" of West Kalimantan, Indonesia* (Ithaca: Cornell University Southeast Asia Program, 2003), 51–52.

21. Wang Tai Peng, *The Origins of the Chinese Kongsi* (Petaling Jaya, Malaysia: Pelanduk, 1994); Heidhues, *Gold-diggers, Farmers, and Traders in the "Chinese Districts" of West Kalimantan, Indonesia*, 53–68.

22. Barbara Watson Andaya, *Perak, the Abode of Grace: A Study of an Eighteenth Century Malay State* (Kuala Lumpur: Oxford University Press, 1979).

23. Manoel Godinho de Eredia, "Eredia's Description of Malacca, Meridional India, and Cathay," trans. J. V. Mills (1613), *Journal of the Malayan Branch of the Royal Asiatic Society* 8.i (1930): 235 (repr., Kuala Lumpur: Malaysian Branch of the Royal Asiatic Society, 1997).

24. Pires, *The Suma Oriental of Tomé Pires*, 260–61.

25. G. W. Irwin, "The Dutch and the Tin Trade of Malaya in the Seventeenth Century," *Studies in the Social History of China and Southeast Asia*, ed. Jerome Ch'en and Nicholas Tarling (Cambridge: Cambridge University Press, 1970), 268–69.

26. Ibid., 287.

27. Dianne Lewis, *Jan Compagnie in the Straits of Malacca, 1641–1795* (Athens, Ohio: Ohio University Center for International Studies, 1995); Pierre Poivre, *Les Mémoires d'un voyageur*, ed. L. Malleret (1747; Paris: L'Ecole Française d'Extrème Orient, 1968), 75.

28. Paul Van Dyke, *The Canton Trade: Life and Enterprise on the China Coast, 1700–1845* (Hong Kong: Hong Kong University Press, 2005), 148.

29. Mary Somers Heidhues, *Bangka Tin and Mentok Pepper: Chinese Settlement on an Indonesian Island* (Singapore: Institute of Southeast Asian Studies, 1992), 2–9.

30. H. B. Morse, *The Chronicles of the East India Company Trading to China*, vol. 5 (Oxford: Clarendon, 1929; repr., Taipei: Ch'eng-Wen, 1966), 139, 155, 170.

31. M. H. Court (1821), cited in Heidhues, *Bangka Tin and Mentok Pepper*, 31–32.

32. John Crawfurd, *History of the Indian Archipelago: Containing an Account of the Manners, Arts, Languages, Religions, Institutions, and Commerce of Its Inhabitants*, 3 vols. (Edinburgh: A. Constable, 1820), 3:454.

33. Heidhues, *Bangka Tin and Mentok Pepper*, 10–18; Wong Lin Ken, *The Malayan Tin Industry to 1914* (Tucson: University of Arizona Press, 1965), 14–15.

34. Heidhues, *Bangka Tin and Mentok Pepper*, 17–37.

35. P. J. Begbie, *The Malayan Peninsula* (1834; Kuala Lumpur: Oxford University Press, 1967), 407–9.

36. Wong, *The Malayan Tin Industry to 1914*, 20.

37. Calculated from ibid., 12.

38. P. J. Begbie, *The Malayan Peninsula*, 407–9.

39. Heidhues, *Bangka Tin and Mentok Pepper*, 10; Wong, *The Malayan Tin Industry to 1914*, 17–20.

40. Wong, *The Malayan Tin Industry to 1914*, 19–20.

41. Jennifer Wayne Cushman, *Family and State: The Formation of a Sino-Thai Tin-Mining Dynasty, 1797–1932* (Oxford: Oxford University Press, 1991), 8.

42. Wong, *The Malayan Tin Industry to 1914*, 22–27; C. M. Turnbull, *The Straits Settlements, 1826–67: Indian Presidency to Crown Colony* (Singapore: Oxford University Press, 1972), 298–340.

43. Wong, *The Malayan Tin Industry to 1914*, 12.

44. Turnbull, *The Straits Settlements*, 160.

45. Wong, *The Malayan Tin Industry to 1914*, 246–47.

46. Anthony Reid, "Early Chinese Migration into North Sumatra," *Studies in the Social History of China and South-East Asia: Essays in Memory of Victor Purcell*, ed. Jerome Ch'en and Nicholas Tarling (Cambridge: Cambridge University Press, 1970), 300.

47. Ho Tak Ming, "Deaths in the Mines: On the Trail of a Killer Disease," *Heritage Asia* 4.2 (2007): 33; Wong, *The Malayan Tin Industry to 1914*, 74.

48. Turnbull, *The Straits Settlements*, 298.

49. Wong, *The Malayan Tin Industry to 1914*, 21–22.

COTTON, COPPER, AND CARAVANS

Trade and the Transformation of Southwest China

~~~~ C. Patterson Giersch

From the seventeenth through the nineteenth centuries, Southwest China experienced remarkable political, economic, demographic, and cultural changes. To fully understand these transformations requires coming to terms with a number of crucial variables, including geographical space. To date, however, our understanding of geography continues to be limited by long-standing conceptual and methodological approaches. Most notably, there are still too few studies that challenge the concept of "macroregions."[1] In a series of extraordinary articles in *The City in Late Imperial China*, William Skinner argued that by the late nineteenth century, China comprised nine separate urban systems, each occupying a major physiographic region of the country (see map 1). Each "macroregion" contained core and peripheral areas. Within a macroregion, each settlement—from marketing towns in the periphery to the great cities at the core—was linked in an interlocking marketing hierarchy. These urban systems developed along largely autonomous paths primarily because of high interregional transport costs.[2]

Over the years, the macroregion model has attracted both critics and defenders, but recently there have been well-articulated arguments that question the model's weakness in regard to long-distance trade and historicity.[3] In a particularly trenchant critique, Carolyn Cartier notes how the macroregion model emphasizes geography and distance over human agency, an approach now deemed problematic and potentially ahistorical by many geographers.[4] These findings are important for understanding Southwest China since the concept of macroregion has been used to shape our knowledge of early modern (Ming-Qing) developments there. In his brilliant work on southwest demography and economic transformation, James Lee drew from Skinner's conception to argue that migration helped transform the south-

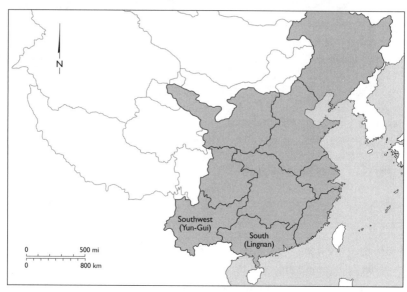

Map 1 G. William Skinner's macroregions of China. Sources: CHGIS Data [CD-ROM], Version 2.0 (Cambridge: Harvard Yenching Institute, 2003); ESRI Data and Maps [CD-ROM] 2004 (Redlands, Calif.: Environmental Systems Reasearch Institute, 2004). Available: Wellesley College Library.

west (Yun-Gui) macroregion from "congeries of small, fairly autonomous enclaves into an integrated regional hierarchy of central places and their hinterlands."[5] Lee includes long-distance trade analysis, but trade is envisioned primarily as a process of transferring resources from peripheries to cores, the implication being that historical transformations are best understood through the core-periphery model that is at the heart of the macroregion concept. As in Skinner's work, core and periphery were determined according to population density. In Lee's analysis of Yunnan Province, he created four categories—"inner core," "outer core," "near periphery," and "outer periphery"—to simplify the conception of space and emphasize the orientation of the province toward the macroregional core in Yunnan and Chengjiang prefectures (the Kunming metropolis).[6]

My own work has revealed a far messier landscape of human activity, particularly long-distance trade, which leads me to challenge the limitations of the macroregional approach to Southwest China. I begin with the assumption that the geographical patterns of human society and economy are shaped by human agency. Geography and climate do play a role, of course: a good harbor, a navigable river, plentiful rainfall, a strategic mineral deposit—any of these factors might prove advantageous for a location. How-

ever, as the literature on economic geography reveals, major events and the creation of human institutions to facilitate trade shape economic and social change.[7] In nonindustrial societies, the human ability to radically alter economic geography is perhaps weaker than in industrial ones, but it did have an impact. This is particularly clear in Southwest China, where human institutions, networks, and historical events shaped long-distance trade and radically altered economic geography.

To demonstrate these changes, I focus on the "circulation" of copper and cotton, two goods that were central to the Yunnan economy during the seventeenth through nineteenth centuries. The concept of "circulation" comes from a recent study of South Asia in which Claude Markovits, Jacques Pouchepadass, and Sanjay Subrahmanyam defined it as the "movement to and fro of men and goods between one part of the subcontinent and another." Circulation is more than mobility or trade, for circulation implies long-term relations of repeated flows that transform society. The goal of investigating circulation, then, is to gain new insights into forces that change a society.[8] As initially envisioned by Markovits et al., this approach emphasized the placement of society (India) in a larger global perspective in order to examine the connections and interactions of the subcontinent with the wider world. I adopt this approach in order to evaluate the circulation of goods between Yunnan Province and three other regions: South China, Tonkin, and Burma. The idea is to remove the concept of a Yun-Gui macroregion and to instead look at how miners, merchants, and others were linked through circulation to the You/Yu/West River basin, South China, and the Guangdong ports; to the Red River basin, Hanoi, and the port of Haiphong; and to the overland routes of Burma and Siam (see map 2).

These circulation patterns were intimately related to the great transformations of the eighteenth and nineteenth centuries. Long-distance circulation linked specific towns and mines to consumers and producers far away in China and Southeast Asia. Circulation was influenced by and changed according to demographic, political, economic, and technological changes, and not all of these changes emanated from China itself. Circulation shaped historical change, including remarkable population growth and urbanization in areas usually labeled "peripheral" in the macroregions model. Networks and institutions that facilitated circulation differed from place to place, but the overall tendency was for states and merchants to innovate and develop techniques for facilitating circulation across the long distances and rough topography of the regions discussed here. In the end, Southwest China's remarkable transformations are best understood not in terms of

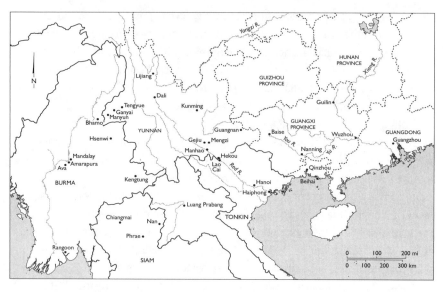

Map 2 South China and Southeast Asia. Sources: CHGIS Data [CD-ROM], Version 2.0 (Cambridge: Harvard Yenching Institute, 2003); ESRI Data and Maps Data [CD-ROM] 2004 (Redlands, Calif.: Environmental Systems Reasearch Institute, 2004). Available: Wellesley College Library.

autonomous macroregional growth alone but in terms of patterns of inter-regional circulation.

The period under consideration spans the seventeenth through the nineteenth century, when millions of settlers made Chinese the majority throughout Southwest China. Among those many migrants were merchants and miners, the central actors in this story of change. Others have noted the importance of these developments, including Victor Lieberman and Sun Laichen, who have linked Southwest China's population explosion and commercialization to profound transformations in mainland Southeast Asia.[9] I reverse their line of inquiry, asking not how Chinese developments affected Southeast Asia, but how commercialization throughout Eastern Eurasia (Southeast and East Asia) influenced Southwest China. While I build on the work of those who examined mining and copper transport, as well as those who examined the caravan trade between Yunnan and Southeast Asia, my approach nevertheless diverges from earlier work in several important ways.[10] First, I consider the trade from Yunnan to South China alongside Southeast Asia trade. Second, I provide an initial inquiry into the dynamics of merchant institutions and state policies that facilitated circulation. The level of state intervention into the Southwest China economy increased dramatically in the aftermath of the Three Feudatories rebellion (1673–1681). In a some-

what (but not entirely) related development, Chinese merchant practices in Southwest China and upland Southeast Asia seemed to change dramatically over the course of the eighteenth and nineteenth centuries, with the greatest growth and elaboration being from the early to late nineteenth century, a trend paralleling the expansion of the export fishing industry in Cambodia, in which Chinese were deeply involved (see Cooke, in this volume). Thus far it has proven challenging to clarify and analyze these transformations with precision, although they seem to reflect the extension of family and native place-based business practices at the heart of Chinese business structure since the early nineteenth century. Third, I argue that the important demographic and economic changes in Southwest China were not purely southwestern or even Chinese phenomena, meaning that southwest history *cannot be written* without reference to other parts of the Qing empire and Southeast Asia. The strong version of this argument therefore claims a central role for long-distance circulation in the major transformations of Southwest China.

Copper Circulation: Yunnan, Tonkin, and South China

From Tang and Song times, if not earlier, there were extensive exchanges between Yunnan, Tonkin, and South China.[11] In Ming and Qing times, the scale of trade increased dramatically, and four main routes connected Yunnan to a larger world. The routes to Tonkin went from Yunnan via Yuanjiang or Mengzi, down the Red River valley to Hanoi and Haiphong. A second set of routes connected Yunnan via Baise (Bo'se) and Nanning to Beihai (Pakhoi) and Qinzhou, two bustling ports on the "Dragon Gate Sea" (Beibu Gulf). By the Daoguang reign (1821–1850), Qinzhou had a dense population and was importing Vietnamese rice along with betel, pepper, sugar, and leather. It attracted merchants from Guangxi, Yunnan, and Guizhou.[12] A third set of routes to the maritime world also crossed overland from Yunnan's Guangnan Prefecture through Baise and Nanning before following the You River (右江) as it flowed into the Yu River (郁江) through Guangxi into the West River and on to the Guangdong delta. A fourth route, used to transport copper from Yunnan to China's prosperous eastern provinces, followed the You and Yu Rivers to Wuzhou city. The boats then turned north, going upstream to Guilin; eventually the copper was transhipped to the Xiang River and on to Changsha, Hankou, and Jiangnan.[13]

One of the key commodities that drove these circulation regimes was copper. It is well known that growth in marketing and commerce during the late Ming and Qing periods fueled Chinese demand for money, whether silver (imported from the Americas), copper (some imported, some mined

domestically), or, increasingly, paper money and credit. It is also known that the new Qing regime assumed that state control of copper coinage (bronze "cash," 錢) was central to maintaining order. Thus, the Qing created two metropolitan mints, the Baoyuan ju under the Board of Works and the Baoquan ju under the Board of Revenue, to oversee the casting of coins.[14]

The difficulties of managing the money supply were complicated by a number of factors. Before the 1680s, the Qing prevented coastal trade for strategic reasons, and the regime frequently experienced copper shortages because domestic supplies were weak. From 1684–1715, after coastal trade was permitted, the Qing relied on imported copper, mostly from Japan. However, China was not the only market for copper. By the late seventeenth century, demand for copper was high throughout Eastern Eurasia, much of this demand fueled by Chinese economic activity throughout the South China Sea (a phenomenon that has led Tony Reid to label the eighteenth century in Southeast Asia a "Chinese Century").[15] At this point, Southeast Yunnan mines increased output, and Tonkin merchants came to purchase copper at Lao Cai near Hekou.[16] Both China and Vietnam relied on copper imports, and both states' coinage was undermined when Japan began to limit copper exports in 1715. Copper became increasingly dear, and the eighteenth century was thus a period in which there was a copper coinage shortage in China and throughout the South China Sea trading world.[17]

Demand for copper was thus an important issue from the seventeenth century onward. From early on, the Qing and its agents sought to exploit Yunnan copper deposits, and Wu Sangui's Yunnan-Guizhou regime (1662–1681), nominally under Qing suzerainty, promoted mining and traded copper coins in a market just to the north of Hekou on the Red River. Cantonese merchants sailed up the Red River to purchase these coins, which went into circulation in the Southeast Asian trading networks and, presumably, can be counted among the coins exported from China to Cochinchina (Li, this volume). In 1682, immediately after the Qing destroyed Wu's autonomous government, Governor-General Cai Yurong initiated a program to expand Yunnan copper mining and coin minting in order to help pay for the conquest and reconstruction.[18] Cai encouraged merchants to open and administer mines, rewarding them with government titles; the state taxed the mines at a 20 percent rate, leaving merchants free to sell the rest on the market.

Cai's efforts marked the beginning of an era in which the central government tinkered with copper mining policies. In 1705, the state revamped its policies to make sure it captured the 80 percent of copper production that was previously sold on the open market. Local officials gained con-

trol over mines, which had to provide at fixed prices all copper to the state. Whereas the 1682 policies led to increases in copper production, the 1705 policies curbed production. In 1723, as copper imports declined, the Yong-zheng regime again permitted some private sales, and this helped ignite a major expansion of mining in Yunnan.[19] Although China never stopped im-porting Japanese copper, Yunnan copper came to supply all the needs of the central government mints by 1738. Provincial mints, meanwhile, still relied on some Japanese copper, but increasingly they too were turning to Yunnan. In general, as the circulation of copper from Japan declined, the state and consumers in China began to look elsewhere for copper and coin supplies, and Yunnan gradually became the biggest supplier.[20]

Qing China was not the only state to intervene in mining. Like China, Vietnam relied on copper (and zinc) imports to mint the coins that fed com-mercial growth (Li, this volume). When Japan curtailed copper exports, Tonkin's Trinh rulers also turned to the Sino-Southeast Asian borderlands, where veins of copper are found from the hills of Northeast Yunnan to those of northern Vietnam. The Trinh promoted mining in their territories and at-tracted tens of thousands of Chinese miners.[21] Victor Lieberman has argued that Chinese mining settlements in Tonkin were crucial to helping Southeast Asia's booming economy meet its needs for money. Chinese-run mines, in fact, may well have been the main non-agrarian industry in Vietnam.[22]

It was becoming a central industry in Southwest China, too. From the 1720s through the mid-nineteenth century, Yunnan provided almost all the copper for the empire's metropolitan and, later, the provincial mints, and the output was truly immense. In the 1720s, Yunnan was producing approxi-mately 650 short tons (1 million jin) of copper annually; by the 1740s, it was producing over 6,500 short tons (10 million jin). Those who have studied copper mining estimate that output peaked in the late 1760s, at nearly 9,500 short tons (about 14.57 million jin), but high production levels continued into the early nineteenth century. Approximately 4,000 tons annually were earmarked for the metropolitan mints, and much of this was shipped from the great Northeast Yunnan mines via Sichuan and then down the Yangzi.[23] The rest was kept for Yunnan provincial mints or shipped to other provinces. Since previous studies have emphasized the copper sent to the metropolitan Baojuan and Baoyuan Mints, I focus on the copper transported to the pro-vincial mints.

By the 1730s, provinces around the empire were reporting severe coinage shortages. Sufficient foreign copper was no longer available in the coastal markets, and provincial officials petitioned for access to Yunnan copper.

By 1740, ten provinces (Jiangsu, Zhejiang, Guangxi, Guangdong, Jiangxi, Shaanxi, Fujian, Hunan, Hubei, and Guizhou) had received permission to periodically send representatives to Yunnan to purchase copper (*cai mai* 採買 or *cai tong* 採銅), which would be used for minting coins in the provincial mints. These copper-buying missions were extremely important. Government-minted coins were used throughout the expanding commercial economy; people of all backgrounds and statuses needed coins. Thus, the copper purchases were vital to two government missions: providing for the people and paying the military. If the government could secure enough copper for casting coins, moreover, it could prevent the illicit casting of coins by private individuals, which was widespread in the mid-eighteenth century.[24] Illicit coin production was so lucrative at this time, in fact, that it fueled zinc exports to Vietnam, which were crucial for the counterfeit coins imported into Guangdong (Li, this volume).

When provincial officials purchased Yunnan copper, they sent representatives to both northern and southeastern Yunnan mines. Quite often they were directed to the Jincha mine (金釵廠) in Lin'an Prefecture's Mengzi County, a mine that was designated for cai mai. No matter where the copper was purchased, however, each province (except Guizhou) was required to ship it via Guangnan in Southeast Yunnan and on to Baise and Nanning in Guangxi.[25] These shipments were huge, the smallest being 10,000 jin (6.5 short tons) while most were about 40,000 jin. From 1740–1811, Yunnan's largest copper customer was Guizhou, but close on its heels were Guangxi and Guangdong, purchasing a minimum of 20 million jin (approximately 13,000 tons) over this seventy-two-year period.[26] All of this was transported via Southeast Yunnan and Nanning, Guangxi.

Mining was thus central to the circulation regimes that both linked and divided China and Southeast Asia. The Trinh and Qing sought to intervene to control circulation in ways that benefited their respective regimes. With a significant exception of ca. 1705–1723, Eastern Eurasia's growing commercial economy and state policies helped increase the copper supply. The significance of these findings lies not only in the fact that Yunnan's copper was exported first to Tonkin and then around the Qing empire, but also in the major transformations in demographics, urban landscapes, and indigenous (non-Chinese) livelihoods. To satisfy the demand for borderland copper, thousands of Chinese migrated to Southeast Yunnan (and Tonkin). To measure these changes, we can examine the mining areas of Mengzi County and the trade town of Guangnan.

Within Mengzi lay two important mine complexes: Jincha, a copper min-

ing area, and Gejiu, which produced silver, tin, and copper. Neither mine was new (there was mining near Gejiu as early as the Han dynasty), but early modern commercialization in Eastern Eurasia, followed by state promotion of mining, encouraged the opening of mines throughout Yunnan, and both Jincha and Gejiu mines expanded rapidly.[27] Expansion attracted an influx of miners, and by the late Qianlong period (1736–1795), an estimated 10,000 migrant miners worked these deposits; by the 1750s, the Gejiu sky was thick with smoke from the many smelting furnaces that contained their hard-won copper ore. As was so often the case, most migrant miners hailed from Huguang and Jiangxi, although some came from Shaanxi and Shanxi.[28]

Following patterns that existed elsewhere, Mengzi expanded its role as a trade entrepôt as the miners arrived. Migrant merchants from Jiangxi, Fujian, and Huguang established their associations (huiguan) in the county seat. Jiangxi was actually represented by three merchant associations, one established by merchants hailing from Ji'an, another by merchants from Fuzhou and Ruizhou, and a third by merchants from Nanchang. In the Gejiu mining area, these merchants established branch associations. The earliest date for any of these institutions belongs to the Shoufo Temple of the Jiangxi natives, first built in 1704.[29]

Merchant organizations and networks were directly linked to mining in four important ways. First, the state recruited investors and managers for copper mines, and often the recruits were merchants from outside the province. Second, both before 1705 and after 1723, private sales of copper were permitted, and merchants handled this trade.[30] Third, while the Qing government managed copper transportation, merchants handled the transport of tin, lead, and silver, often using the same Guangnan-Baise route.[31] Finally, the influx of miners to any site led to numerous opportunities to meet increasing local demand for clothing, food, and other goods.

This influx of miners and merchants transformed the landscape of Mengzi County. A town emerged at the foot of the Gejiu hills; meanwhile, nearby Mengzi town expanded in size and importance. The physical environment began to change as miners built elaborate tunnels and shafts, and smelting specialists erected furnaces and sought charcoal to help extract copper from ore. This need to fire the furnaces led to widespread deforestation. By the nineteenth century, most of the hills around Gejiu were bare, their trees turned into charcoal and thus sacrificed to commercial development in faraway places such as Hanoi, Hankou, Guangzhou, or Fuzhou.[32]

The demand for charcoal provided new, though limited, opportunities for local peoples. In surrounding villages, indigenous families, probably Yi,

Sha, Nong, and Tuliao (the latter three groups now classified as "Zhuang"), erected huts for preparing charcoal. To the northwest and north, in the areas around Lin'an and Amizhou, indigenous peoples, probably Yi and "Woni" (Hani or Akha), worked coal deposits, another fuel for the smelting furnaces of Gejiu.[33] By the 1870s, the Gejiu mines imported charcoal from indigenous producers who lived ten or more miles from the mines.[34] In addition to providing fuel for the smelters, indigenes often carried the copper on the gruelling overland transport legs.[35] This brief examination of Mengzi's Gejiu area demonstrates how mining was linked to demographic and environmental change, urbanization, and the integration of indigenes into production for the market. The promotion of copper, silver, and tin transport, however, touched more than just the mining towns.

The Jincha and Gejiu mines were linked to patterns of urbanization and change even further away. State interest in exporting Yunnan copper via Guangxi seems to have originated in 1728, and Kent Smith has reported that Governor-General E'ertai invested in roads and water transport in southeastern Yunnan.[36] This impacted towns such as Guangnan, which lay along the transport route. In the decade between E'ertai's initial investment and the time when copper began to be shipped, Guangnan underwent important changes. The Qing state increased the number of civil officials dedicated to Guangnan and also increased by four hundred (a significant number) the number of soldiers stationed in the region. With central government approval, moreover, the local government brought a local indigenous leader's revenue under imperial management.[37] Such a move was rare, and it provided the Qing state with tremendous control over the indigenous power structure in Guangnan. While the evidence is circumstantial, it seems that the Qing state was securing this region not only as part of E'ertai's general expansion of state power, but also because Guangnan would be the site where copper was stored during the shipping process.[38]

This expansion of the state presence in Guangnan was paralleled by a growing merchant and settler population. As an important stop on the caravan route that exported copper and other metals to South China, Guangnan attracted a diverse population of merchants and peddlers, who were soon followed by land-hungry migrants. These sojourners and settlers arrived during the same period in which the state promoted copper transport via Guangnan, and by the early nineteenth century, Guangnan boasted a local population that included people from Hunan, Sichuan, Guizhou, and Guangdong.[39] Many of these sojourners and settlers were involved in commerce with South China, but also with Tonkin.[40] As the migrant popula-

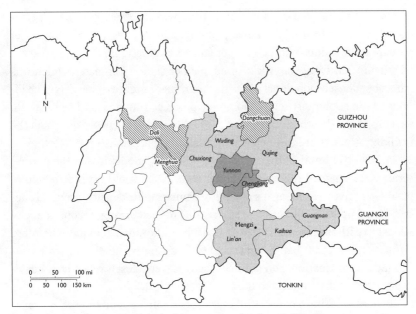

Map 3 Yunnan's "cores" and "peripheries." Sources: CHGIS Data [CD-ROM], Version 2.0 (Cambridge: Harvard Yenching Institute, 2003); ESRI Data and Maps [CD-ROM] 2004 (Redlands, Calif.: Environmental Systems Reasearch Institute, 2004). Available: Wellesley College Library.

tion increased, they had profound and unintended (from the state's point of view) impacts on indigenous societies. By the 1730s, Qing officials had become concerned that Chinese merchants were gaining ownership over indigenous lands.[41] This meant that local Sha and Nong peoples were simultaneously experiencing greater state control and competition from Chinese migrants who, increasingly, held the leases to their lands.

Places such as Mengzi and Guangnan were clearly experiencing tremendous changes as mining, the state, and mine-related commerce transformed their communities, landscapes, and livelihoods, but how should we understand the source of these changes? James Lee employed the macroregional core-periphery model to contextualize and analyze important changes in late imperial Yunnan (see map 3). For example, he argues that population growth in Lin'an (where Mengzi County was located) and Guangnan Prefectures led to a population density that placed them in the category of "near periphery," meaning that their population density relegated them to the third of four ranks within Yunnan Province. The first rank, boasting the highest population densities (129–52 people per square km), was the "inner core" and included Yunnan and Chengjiang prefectures in north-central Yunnan. Next in rank was the "outer core," including Dongchuan, Dali, and Menghua prefec-

tures (37–57 people per square km). Third was the "near periphery": Chuxiong, Guangnan, Kaihua, Lin'an, Qujing, and Wuding (15–28 people per square km). Kaihua's 15 people per square kilometer is, for some reason, distinguished from Tengyue's 13 people per square kilometer, which was the most densely populated of the next tier, the "outer periphery" (which included nine other districts). I do not dispute Lee's figures, and he is careful to emphasize that these categories are for "heuristic purposes only," but the ranking system implies a potentially misleading relationship.

A powerful implication of the core-periphery model is that the peripheries were oriented toward the "inner core." One would expect, therefore, that Guangnan's or Mengzi's changing demographic density, economic activity, and political infrastructures were due to their stronger economic relationship with the macroregional core in what is now metropolitan Kunming. However, it is clear that Mengzi's and Guangnan's population growth, economic transformation, and political changes were closely related to circulation patterns that connected these areas to South China and Tonkin.

Instead of using a core-periphery model to understand important transformations, one might do better to examine state policies, merchant networks, and the creation of circulation corridors linking Yunnan to South China and Southeast Asia (see map 2). Eastern Eurasian demands for copper were first met by exporting Yunnan coins via the Tonkin corridor. This provided the initial boost to mining in the seventeenth century. The Qing state then created transport and administrative infrastructures to capture copper resources for the empire; in the process they took advantage of and encouraged merchant activity along the Guangxi-Guangdong corridor. As Peng-Sheng Chiu has argued, imperial policies designed to expedite copper extraction helped merchants expand their businesses in Yunnan and elsewhere.[42] The economic activities promoted by the state and carried out in part by merchants contributed to the transformation of Yunnan. To build their networks, merchants often relied on the imperial state's power to protect communications routes. Merchants were not mere agents of empire. Neither were they limited by the territorial boundaries of the Qing realm, and their growing networks helped expand other circulation corridors, too.

Cotton Circulation: Yunnan and Burma

The circulation of goods, ideas, technologies, and religion between Yunnan and Burma can be found at least as early as the third century B.C.E. It was not until the eighteenth century, however, that bulk goods such as raw cotton began to be carried in large volumes. Responding to increasing demand

among the growing migrant communities in Yunnan, Chinese merchants imported tremendous amounts of raw cotton, kapok, and cotton textiles. They purchased cotton at the large markets in Burma's suzerain areas of Ava, Bhamo, or Hsenwi and pioneered relatively new routes to find cotton markets in Siam's suzerain territory.[43] At times, the Qing government sought to control or curtail the circulation of goods and merchants to Burma. The most important example was a postwar trade embargo placed on Burma after 1770.[44]

Once the embargo was lifted in 1790, merchants rapidly rebuilt the cotton trade. By the 1830s, Chinese mule trains transported large amounts of Chiangmai and Kengtung cotton into southern and central Yunnan. Some cotton merchants also went further in search of profits — to Luang Prabang, Nan, or Phrae. The Ava and Bhamo cotton markets sprang back to life as Chinese caravans returned. The caravans transported into Burma Chinese silk and manufactures, such as porcelain and bronze implements.[45] There are a few widely reported statistics that confirm the tremendous volume of the Yunnan-Burma trade. In the 1820s, John Crawfurd interviewed Chinese merchants in Burma and made the following estimates: Chinese raw silk exports to Burma totaled approximately 162,000 pounds annually. Burmese cotton imports to China ranged from about 7 million to almost 21 million pounds annually.[46] In 1855, Henry Yule visited Amarapura and learned that Yunnan's annual imports of Burmese cotton totaled approximately 14.6 million pounds while silk exports had increased to approximately 242,360 pounds. In addition, Yule estimated that Burma's suzerain Tai areas (Hsenwi, Bhamo, etc.) were exporting an additional 547,000 pounds of cotton annually to Yunnan.[47]

This remarkable trade volume could not have been produced without the merchants and caravaneers who plied the tracks between Burma and Yunnan. Of particular importance to this trade were the institutions and firms of Chinese merchants, for, in many cases, they reached from Kunming and Dali to Ava, Mandalay, and Amarapura. A particularly powerful set of institutions was the merchants' native place organizations, which proved successful in overcoming some of the disadvantages of the long distances. Elsewhere I have argued that they provided the Chinese with a tremendous advantage over local indigenous elites and Southeast Asian merchants who vied to control long-distance trade flows.[48]

The merchant's organization (huiguan) was created when Chinese from the same hometown or region pooled resources to purchase land, erect a lodging house, and build a temple housing a distinctive deity. Members

and new arrivals from the home region could use the organization's storage facilities and other services.[49] These organizations were found throughout China and overseas. They were particularly important to Southwest China. In mining towns, for instance, the merchant associations became critical local institutions. By the late eighteenth century, Mengzi and the Gejiu mines had a tremendous number of merchant associations. The high level of merchant organization can be seen by the fact that there were five different associations representing Jiangxi merchants alone.[50] These institutions would have been in contact with their brethren along important routes, whether to the Yunnan capital or to Guangxi Province, where each major trade town had merchant associations.

Merchant associations were therefore far more than local institutions. Their members could travel to other trade towns, where similar associations had been formed, thus linking trade areas together in networks based on native place. For example, in the late seventeenth century, migrant merchants from Jiangxi and Hunan established associations in the provincial capital, Kunming. The Jiangxi men built their Wanshou Temple while the Hunan merchants built their Shoufo Temple. These were the same temples that Jiangxi and Hunan merchants established in frontier towns such as Mengzi. One can trace the expanding reach of Jiangxi and Hunan merchants by the dates of the Wanshou and Shoufo temples throughout the region. Once established, the network could be used to manage long-distance trade.[51] Such links were extremely important to maintaining the networks into the mining regions and from Yunnan to Guangdong; they were also central for the cotton merchants who worked between Yunnan and Burma.

In Burma, Chinese merchants clustered in well-organized communities or neighborhoods, and they created networks to manage long-distance trade. At Ava and Bhamo, merchants built temples, much like the native place association temples in China. In Ava, for example, the Tengchong (Tengyue) merchants who dominated the Burma trade built a temple to Guanyin in the 1770s. This temple seems to have become a center for social and economic life in the Chinese community.[52] It provides further proof that Chinese merchants continued to operate in Burma even during the Qing embargo of Burmese trade.[53] When the Burmese capital was moved to Amarapura, moreover, a new temple was built. One of the few accounts we have that provides an insight into how these temple/merchant associations operated comes from Henry Yule. Yule visited Amarapura in 1855 and met with the chief Chinese merchants at a central Chinese temple, which served "not merely as a place of worship, but as a house of resort or club."[54] The temple

was therefore a central meeting location for Chinese commercial agents who represented merchant businesses based in Yunnan.

What Yule was observing was a set of business institutions that had become increasingly sophisticated and complex. Historians of Yunnan date the founding of Yunnan's first large-scale family-run firms (shanghao 商號) to the early nineteenth century. The earliest were founded by men from the major western trade towns, Dali and Tengchong, although there are also examples of them operating out of Guangxi and trading with Tonkin.[55] These family firms, however, still maintained important connections to the merchant associations. According to Yule, five or six of the "agency-houses" (the shanghao) dominated the Chinese trade with Amarapura, while there were an estimated two dozen smaller firms whose business amounted to about 10 percent of the big houses. All were linked through the temple and its affiliated businesses, including Amarapura's Chinese shopkeepers who sold imports purchased on credit from the major agency-houses.[56]

The merchant-agents in Southeast Asia were connected to Yunnan through a network of settlements along the trade routes. Representatives seem to have lived in Bhamo, Manyun, and other small towns on the caravan highways to Tengchong and Dali.[57] Even in the smaller towns, the role of the agent was to make money for the company. The permanent Chinese agents in Kengtung, for example, purchased and prepared cotton for the arrival of the caravans, thus speeding the turnaround time.[58]

Merchant organization seems to have originated in native-place organizations and family ties—a finding that is predictable both for China and for Chinese operating in Southeast Asia. As these institutions developed, though, they became more specialized, particularly in the transport industries that were so crucial to Southwest China and Southeast Asia. At Mengzi, for instance, merchant associations provided a base for men who then developed firms serving the local mining industry. The French adventurer J. Dupuis provides a few insights into how these businesses operated. Although he journeyed to Mengzi during the Panthay Rebellion (1856–1873) and found that trade had declined, Dupuis located merchants willing to do business. Local merchants, moreover, had developed specialized businesses for handling the challenges of shipping copper and tin over long distances. At Lao Cai, merchants had organized a system for transferring goods from Tonkin barges to Yunnan barges during the winter months when water levels were low. The Yunnan barges were smaller and more nimble for passing over the rapids above Lao Cai. Dupuis was also able to contract with a local merchant to help him procure copper and tin from the Gejiu mines; he concluded a

separate contract with another merchant to provide warehousing and shipping services.[59] Clearly the transport and service industries were fairly specialized.

The tendency toward increased specialization in transport was apparent throughout Yunnan, not just Mengzi. As time went on, the Yunnan-Burma caravan infrastructure became more elaborate as supporting businesses were developed. Dali, a major trade hub, expanded in the early to mid-nineteenth century as merchants built warehouses and shops to accommodate growing cotton commerce. In many caravan towns, enterprising merchants built inns to accommodate the mule trains. Whereas eighteenth-century caravaneers seem to have camped out, the nineteenth century saw an increasing number of caravanserai devoted to housing muleteers and their pack trains. In late-Qing Ganyai, for instance, there were seven inns with the capacity to house 2,000 people and their pack animals. Contemporary Manyun Market had five inns and four temples, which could accommodate 5,000 people. Lijiang town topped them all, with seventeen inns that catered to the tea caravans.[60]

Merchant organization through the family firm and association was the key to Chinese domination of the caravan trade. This does not mean that Chinese were alone in benefiting from the trade, for the Southeast Asian courts and local Tai rulers (tsaufas) could sell monopoly contracts or trade permits, collect caravan tolls, or even engage in some trade themselves. Nevertheless, it was Chinese merchants who developed and operated the most important business institutions that linked Yunnan, Southeast Asia, and South China across a terrain and in a climate that might generously be called "challenging." Through their firms and associations, they mobilized capital, created regulations for managing mines, cooperated with the Qing state at times, and developed new businesses to meet the challenges of topography and environment.

Under the influence of these changes in merchant institutions, southwest Yunnan underwent important transformations. As merchants knitted together networks that linked Southeast Asia and Yunnan, local Chinese and indigenes began to buy and sell products that circulated through Yunnan and Southeast Asia. Although the Yunnan-Southeast Asia trade connections were ancient, it was not until the late eighteenth and early nineteenth centuries that so many became incorporated into regional trade. By the early nineteenth century, indigenes throughout the borderlands—but especially those living in the circulation corridors—produced goods for sale in China or Burma. This economic geography, so dependent on copper and cotton, was changing Yunnan, but it was not permanent.

After Rebellion: Changing Circulation Regimes

In the mid-nineteenth century, regional and global events helped transform the circulation regimes described above. These changes included an initial obstruction of long-established circulation patterns and the rise of new patterns and routes under the influence of changing transport technologies and colonial relationships. These changes are important because they demonstrate how the economic geography of Southwest China could be transformed by historical developments, both within and outside China.

As the site where the Taiping uprising (1851–1864) originated, Guangxi Province's Yu River basin succumbed to banditry in the 1850s. This reduced traffic along the river, thus cutting off the trade routes. There were reports that only armed trading parties could conduct Nanning's trade with Beihai. There is also evidence of significant destruction. In the port of Hengzhou (橫州), for instance, the entire town was destroyed, including the powerful Guangdong merchant association (huiguan).[61] The destruction of the association deprived the town of a commercial institution that was crucial to maintaining the flow of goods between Yunnan and Guangzhou. Yunnan suffered even more from the Panthay (Hui) uprising of 1856–1873, a massive civil war pitting Muslims and non-Chinese against the Qing state and Chinese inhabitants. Centered in Dali, this massive rebellion interrupted the cotton and copper trades and left the province devastated.

After the rebellions, long-distance circulation from Guangdong to Yunnan was the first to revive. By 1880, Baise had regained some of its earlier prosperity. Its merchant associations recovered as Cantonese merchants regained their foothold as the most important of sojourner traders. Once again those living in Guangxi Province could buy Yunnan exports, including Pu'er tea, which was carried to Baise via the Guangnan route. To provide transport along these routes, boat operators and mule caravans went back into action.[62] Guangnan markets again entertained Cantonese and Hunanese sojourners. Marketgoers again had the option to purchase simple luxuries shipped from Guangzhou, including imported Tanstikkor matches and China-made mirrors.[63]

However, older circulation patterns were not simply restored. Before the Taiping and Panthay uprisings, Yunnan had exported cotton and copper to the Guangxi and Guangdong river basins. The uprisings first interrupted this trade, and then changes in the global trade patterns reversed the flow. By the 1880s, steamers transported cotton from Rangoon to Canton, where some of it was shipped upstream to Baise and then overland by horse to Yunnan.[64]

Merchants also began to import cotton via the ancient routes that linked the Beibu Gulf ports with Yunnan via Nanning, Baise, and Guangnan. Increasingly, the chief exports were not copper, but tin and opium.

The volumes of goods shipped were still very large. In 1889, Imperial Maritime Customs (IMC) officials estimated that 50 percent of Beihai's (Pakhoi's) imported piece-goods and 67 percent of its imported cotton yarn found their way inland to Yunnan's markets. In 1889, this meant that an estimated 62,000 piculs of imported Indian yarn were shipped via Nanning broker agents to Yunnan. The estimated value of this yarn was 1,180,000 haiguan taels or, based on the 1889 exchange rate of US$1.15 per tael, $1,357,000. One reason that the Beihai route was profitable, IMC officials and other observers believed, was that the post-Taiping domestic transit duty (lijin, likin) stations, operating along the Yu/West River, drove up costs, while the Beihai-Baise-Yunnan route was relatively free of transit duties.[65]

Rebellion and changing patterns of global trade and imperialism, combined with new shipping technologies, influenced the circulation patterns of Yunnan. Evidence suggests that the Yu/West River route from Guangzhou flourished initially, but then declined. Similarly, the Beihai to Nanning to Guangnan route initially became a major trade corridor. In the aftermath of France's conquest of Tonkin, both were eclipsed by the Red River route, which linked Haiphong to Mengzi. Although Beihai continued to be an important point of entry for some goods, most of the Hong Kong textile dealers moved their branches from Beihai to Haiphong—important evidence that the real action had shifted southwest toward Tonkin.[66]

Gradually, cotton shipped via the Red River from Tonkin increased in volume and began to dominate, a finding first reported by Chiranan.[67] This trade was managed from Lin'an, a small Yunnan port on the Red River. Lin'an merchants had agents or partners in Hong Kong who purchased cotton goods and arranged for shipping from Hong Kong to Haiphong and then up the Red River to Mengzi. French steamers carried the cotton to Lao Cai or Manhao; it was then off-loaded and shipped overland to Mengzi and on to Kunming via caravan. The transition to cotton imports via the Red River was an important transformation of Yunnan's relationship with maritime trade, and it represented a profound shift in merchant networks and cotton circulation.

In the aftermath of the Panthay uprising, the Burma cotton trade was slow to rebound. By the 1890s, overland cotton imports from Burma fell to an estimated 725,000 pounds annually. This was about 5 percent of the estimated volume for 1855.[68] A series of developments worked to diminish this

route of circulation. The Panthay uprising hit the west more seriously than it did southeastern Yunnan. Even a decade or more after the fact, travelers reflected on how many urban areas had not recovered their original populations or economic vitality. Particularly hard hit were some of the central trade entrepôts such as Tengchong, in western Yunnan, and Dali, which, along with Kunming, had been one of the province's two largest urban areas. In other words, the urban areas that had grown along with the circulation patterns of the eighteenth century and early nineteenth lost population; marginalized from the main circulation regimes of the post-rebellion era, they did not return to their previous population and trade levels.

This demographic disaster, however, was followed by other problems. Andrew Forbes has argued that the British seizure of Upper Burma and the French occupation of Tonkin resulted in these colonial powers seeking to redirect trade.[69] The Qing, moreover, subjected the overland routes from Burma to Dali to numerous lijin and prefectural tax stations, a fact that led some observers to believe that internal Qing levies, rather than the cost of transportation, caused the decline in overland routes from Burma. Merchants who transported Chinese cotton into Yunnan from Hubei and those who transported Indian, Burmese, or English cotton through Mengzi were subject to a single tax fee only, whether the lijin levied at the station on the Sichuan-Yunnan border or the import tariff levied at the Imperial Maritime Customs station in Mengzi.[70]

Thus, the remarkable decline of the Burma cotton routes resulted from major changes both within China (the Panthay Rebellion, the rise of the lijin revenue system) and in global patterns of colonialism and trade. The decline in trade directly affected the ability of certain urban areas to rebound from the economic and demographic losses during the Panthay Rebellion. The British missionary G. W. Clark, who lived in Dali during the 1880s, knew that the Burma trade was down because the British were redirecting cotton exports to Rangoon and, via steamer, to Guangzhou and Hong Kong. Clark met merchants who lamented their business losses, and he also reported that many local Minjia (Bai) men, who had once earned money as muleteers and peddlers in the Burma trade, were now left without livelihoods.[71]

Throughout the Qing period, Yunnan Province was involved in important patterns of circulation that linked it to coastal China, Tonkin, and Burma. As Li's and Cooke's papers demonstrate, if we are to understand the impact of Chinese merchants and the commodity flows they controlled, we must broaden our approaches to include inland circulation corridors and their connections to the coast, whether in South China or Southeast Asia. We must

also examine state policy and its impact on circulation.[72] For Yunnan, the circulation patterns of copper and cotton influenced migration, urbanization, and local economic changes. Yet these circulation flows were also subject to endogenous and exogenous events; once the circulation flows were transformed, moreover, they in turn transformed demographics and local economics. In order to understand fully the changes in Southwest China, therefore, we must place regional history within a larger global framework. The macroregional model may highlight some important aspects of regional society, but it lacks the type of dialectical analysis that David Harvey has found so necessary to the study of geography and perceptions of space.[73]

The rising demand for copper that affected all of Eastern Eurasia had a profound impact on Yunnan and northern Tonkin, where tens of thousands of Chinese miners migrated in the eighteenth century. Their arrival instigated important demographic and economic changes. Local urban areas attracted merchants who organized the long-distance transport of the precious metals. Local indigenous peoples sometimes reoriented their economies from subsistence to market production in order to sell grains or charcoal to the mining operations. The circulation of copper drew states into close relations with merchants and miners, leading to significant state activity in frontier regions, including the Qing mandate that nine provinces ship their copper via Guangxi. Networks and institutions were developed to make long-distance overland trade more efficient. Merchant associations helped orient and support migrant merchants who participated in transporting copper or cotton. Merchant associations and merchant houses began to place agents in key trade towns along major routes. Whether in Burma or, later, in Hong Kong, agents handled the purchasing and packaging of goods so that caravan leaders or ship captains could quickly load up and move on. Over time, industries became more specialized, and the number of businesses devoted to transport, servicing caravans, or storage increased.

In the aftermath of the great rebellions, there were fundamental transformations of Yunnan's circulation patterns. As new patterns emerged, they were shaped by both old and new conditions. Demand for cotton was a perennial condition, but this demand was met through new circulation corridors shaped by British and French colonialism, steamship technology, and the Qing internal tax regime. The goods that flowed out of Yunnan in exchange for these imports were changing, too; copper was replaced by tin and opium.

With these changes in circulation flows, western Yunnan was increas-

ingly marginalized. These were the areas that had once been central to the import of Burmese cotton and to the export of silks. After the destruction by the Panthay and then marginalization from the older circulation patterns, some of these towns did not fully recover in terms of population or trade, even decades afterward. Investigating Dali's population in the 1930s, C. P. Fitzgerald noted how the ruins on the town's southeast side attested to its former size and importance. According to James Lee's calculations, Dali had over 100,000 people by the 1820s, but government figures placed the population at 89,720 in 1939.[74] To understand this decline, as well as the rise that had preceded it, we cannot focus on intraregional or macroregional changes alone, for it was interregional circulation patterns, managed in part by the Chinese merchants who traded with South China and the Nanyang, that also shaped the destinies of so many people in Southwest China.

Notes

1. To the best of my knowledge, the first significant challenge came from Chiranan Prasertkul, *Yunnan Trade in the Nineteenth Century: Southwest China's Cross-Boundaries Functional System* (Bangkok: Institute of Asian Studies, Chulalongkorn University, 1989).

2. G. William Skinner, "Introduction: Urban Development in Imperial China," *The City in Late Imperial China* (Stanford: Stanford University Press, 1977), 8; Skinner, "Regional Urbanization in Nineteenth Century China," *The City in Late Imperial China*, 212–17.

3. For a notable challenge to the model, see Barbara Sands and Ramon H. Myers, "The Spatial Approach to Chinese History: A Test," *The Journal of Asian Studies* 45.4 (August 1986): 724–27; for a defense of macroregions, see Daniel Little and Joseph W. Esherick, "Testing the Testers: A Reply to Barbara Sands and Ramon Myer's Critique of G. William Skinner's Regional Systems Approach to China," *The Journal of Asian Studies* 48.1 (February 1989): 91–92. For a recent critique of the Southwest or Yun-Gui macroregion, see Bin Yang, *Between Winds and Clouds: The Making of Yunnan (Second Century BCE to Twentieth Century CE)* (New York: Columbia University Press, 2009), 225–31.

4. Carolyn Cartier, "Origins and Evolution of a Geographical Idea: The Macroregion in China," *Modern China* 28.1 (January 2002): 81, 85–86, 98–100, 102.

5. James Lee, "The Legacy of Immigration in Southwest China, 1250–1850," *Annales de Démographie Historique* (1982): 297.

6. James Lee, "Food Supply and Population Growth in Southwest China, 1250–1850," *The Journal of Asian Studies* 41.4 (November 1982): 731.

7. Paul Krugman, "Where in the World Is the 'New Economic Geography'?" *The Oxford Handbook of Economic Geography*, ed. Gordon L. Clark, Maryann P. Feldman, and Meric S. Gertler (Oxford: Oxford University Press, 2000), 52, 58; Andrew D. Mellinger, Jeffrey D. Sachs, and John L. Gallup, "Climate, Coastal Proximity, and Development," *The Oxford Handbook of Economic Geography*, 169–94.

8. Claude Markovits, Jacques Pouchepadass, and Sanjay Subrahmanyam, "Introduc-

tion: Circulation and Society under Colonial Rule," *Society and Circulation: Mobile People and Itinerant Cultures in South Asia 1750–1950* (Delhi: Permanent Black, 2003), 2–3.

9. Victor B. Lieberman, *Strange Parallels: Southeast Asia in Global Context, c. 800–1830* (Cambridge: Cambridge University Press, 2003), 47.

10. Good studies on mining and copper transport include Yan Zhongping, *Qingdai Yunnan tongzheng* (Beijing: Zhonghua shuju, 1957); E-Tu Zen Sun, "Ch'ing Government and the Mineral Industries before 1800," *The Journal of Asian Studies* 27.4 (August 1968): 835–45; Yunnan daxue lishi xi, *Yunnan yejin shi* (Kunming: Yunnan renmin, 1980); Kent Clark Smith, "Ch'ing Policy and the Development of Southwest China: Aspects of Ortai's Governor-Generalship, 1726–1731," Ph.D. diss., Yale, 1970, chap. 4. On the caravan trade between Yunnan and Southeast Asia, see Andrew D. W. Forbes, "The 'Cin-Ho' (Yunnanese Chinese) Caravan Trade with North Thailand," *Journal of Asian History* 21.1 (1987): 1–47; Ann Maxwell Hill, *Merchants and Migrants: Ethnicity and Trade among Yunnanese Chinese in Southeast Asia* (New Haven: Yale Southeast Asia Studies, 1998); Wang Mingda and Zhang Xilu, *Mabang wenhua* (Kunming: Yunnan renmin, 1993); C. Patterson Giersch, *Asian Borderlands: The Transformation of Qing China's Yunnan Frontier* (Cambridge: Harvard University Press, 2006), 168–86; Yang, *Between Winds and Clouds*, 29–58.

11. Lu Ren, *Yunnan dui wai jiaotong shi* (Kunming: Yunnan minzu chubanshe, 1997), 136–142, 240; Tu Yaojun and Lu Minsheng, "Qingdai Zhong Yue maoyi tongdao tanxi," *Guangxi difangzhi* no. 4 (2004): 38–40.

12. Lu Ren, *Yunnan dui wai jiaotong shi*, 213–16; Gu Yongji, "Ming-Qing shi Dian Gui diqu yu Yuenan guanxi shulun," *Yunnan shifan daxue xuebao* 37.2 (March 2005): 79–80.

13. Wu Qijun and Xu Jinsheng, *Yunnan kuangchang tulue*, juan 2:75b–76b, repr. in *Xuxiu sikuquanshu*, vol. 880 (Shanghai guji chubanshe, 1995–1999).

14. Yunnan daxue, *Yunnan yejin shi*, 31–32; Ramon H. Myers and Yeh-chien Wang, "Economic Developments, 1644–1800," *The Cambridge History of China, vol. 9, part 1: The Ch'ing Empire to 1800*, ed. Willard J. Peterson (Cambridge, UK: Cambridge University Press, 2002), 626–28.

15. Anthony Reid, introduction to *The Last Stand of Asian Autonomies: Responses to Modernity in the Diverse States of Southeast Asia and Korea, 1750–1900* (New York: St. Martin's, 1997), 1–26.

16. Lu Ren, *Yunnan dui wai jiaotong shi*, 213–16, 240–44.

17. Alexander Woodside, "Central Vietnam's Trading World in the Eighteenth Century as Seen in Lê Quý Đôn's 'Frontier Chronicles,'" *Essays into Vietnamese Pasts*, ed. K. W. Taylor and John K. Whitmore (Ithaca: Southeast Asia Program, Cornell University, 1995), 168–69.

18. Cai Yurong, "Chou Dian di si shu yi li cai," *Yunnan shiliao congkan*, ed. Fang Guoyu (Kunming: Yunnan daxue chubanshe, 2001), 8:428–31; Lu Ren, *Yunnan dui wai jiaotong shi*, 245.

19. Yunnan daxue, *Yunnan yejin shi*, 32–35, 49–55; Yan, *Qingdai Yunnan tongzheng*, 8; Smith, "Ch'ing Policy and the Development of Southwest China," 188–90; Sun, 'Ch'ing Government and the Mineral Industries," 840–41.

20. Peng-Sheng Chiu, "Shiba shiji dian tong shichangzhong de guan-shang guanxi yu liyi guannian," *Zhongyang yanjiuyuan lishi yuyan yanjiusuo jikan* 72.1 (March 2001): 60–61; for statistics on declining Japanese copper exports, see Helen Dunstan, "Safely Supping with the Devil: The Qing State and Its Merchant Suppliers of Copper," *Late Imperial China* 13.2 (December 1992): 43, 51–52.

21. Lieberman, *Strange Parallels*, 421–22, 435.

22. Ibid., 47, 436.

23. Smith, "Ch'ing Policy and the Development of Southwest China," 203–10; Sun, "Ch'ing Government and the Mineral Industries," 841.

24. See reports by the Board of Revenue and Huguang Governor-General Nasutu, cited in *Qing shilu you guan Yunnan shiliao huibian*, comp. Yunnan Provincial History Institute (Kunming: Yunnan renmin chubanshe, 1984–1985) (hereafter cited as QSL), 4:36–37.

25. Wu and Xu, *Yunnan kuangchang tulue*, 71a–76b; *Tongzheng bianlan*, juan 2:42a–b; juan 7:3a, repr. in *Xuxiu sikuquanshu*, vol. 880 (Shanghai guji chubanshe, 1995–1999).

26. Yan, *Qingdai Yunnan tongzheng*, 21.

27. Yunnan daxue lishi xi, *Yunnan yejin shi*, 1–6, 31–35.

28. *Xuxiu Mengzi xianzhi*, juan 3:45a–52b; *Mengzi xian zhi* (Kangxi 51), cited in Fang Guoyu, *Yunnan shiliao mulu gaishuo* (Beijing: Zhonghua shuju, 1984), 3:1268.

29. *Xuxiu Mengzi xianzhi*, juan 3:2b–5b.

30. Sun, "Ch'ing Government and the Mineral Industries," 845; Chiu, "Shiba shiji dian tong," 87.

31. Émile Rocher, *La Province du Yün-nan* (Paris: Libraire de la société asiatique de l'école des langues orientales vivantes, 1879, 1880), 1:247.

32. For official reaction to mining's environmental impact, see Helen Dunstan, "Official Thinking on Environmental Issues and the State's Roles in Eighteenth-Century China," *Sediments of Time: Environment and Society in Chinese History*, ed. Mark Elvin and Liu Ts'ui-jung (Cambridge: Cambridge University Press, 1998), 585–614.

33. For historical ethnic geography, see You Zhong, *Yunnan minzu shi* (Kunming: Yunnan daxue, 1994), 532, 555–58.

34. Rocher, *La Province du Yün-nan*, 1:224–29, 236; 2:234–35.

35. Wu and Xu, *Yunnan kuangchang tulue*, juan 2xia, 84a.

36. Smith, "Ch'ing Policy and the Development of Southwest China," 203–10.

37. QSL, 3:27.

38. Wu and Xu, *Yunnan kuangchang tulue*, 71a–72b.

39. *Guangnan fuzhi* (1966 reprint edition), juan 2 (Minhu): 1a–4a.

40. QSL 08 06 25 (14 August 1743), *Gaozong shi lu*, juan 195:20, cited in *Qing shi lu Yuenan Miandian Taiguo Laowo shiliao zhaichao*, comp. Yunnan Provincial History Institute (Kunming: Yunnan renmin chubanshe, 1986), 38–9.

41. QSL, 3:27.

42. Chiu, "Shiba shiji dian tong," 89–90.

43. Palace memorials (Zhupi zouzhe). Beijing Number One Archives. doc. 112–7, QSL 31 03 29, Yang Yingju; doc. 1733–2, QSL 11 05 09, Zhangbao; doc. 142–1 QSL 34 01 19,

Fuheng; Zhou Yu, *Congzheng Miandian ri ji*, 9a, in *Ming Qing shiliao huibian*, ed. Shen Yunlong, vol. 8 (Taibei: Wenhai chubanshe, 1967).

44. Giersch, *Asian Borderlands*, chaps. 4, 6.

45. Ibid., chap. 6.

46. John Crawfurd, *Journal of an Embassy from the Governor General of India to the Court of Ava*, 2d ed. (London: Henry Colburn, 1834), 1:160–61; 2:191–94.

47. Henry Yule, *A Narrative of the Mission Sent by the Governor-General of India to the Court of Ava in 1855* (London: Smith, Elder, 1858), 144, 148, 149.

48. Giersch, *Asian Borderlands*, chap. 6.

49. L. Eve Armentrout Ma, "Fellow-Regional Associations in the Ch'ing Dynasty: Organizations in Flux for Mobile People: A Preliminary Survey," *Modern Asian Studies* 18.2 (1984), 307–15.

50. *Xuxiu Mengzi xianzhi*, juan 3:2b–4a.

51. Lin Wenxun, "Ming Qing shiqi neidi shangren zai Yunnan de jingji huodong," *Yunnan shehui kexue* 1 (1991): 61; Fang Guoyu, *Yunnan shiliao mulu gaishuo* (Beijing: Zhonghua shuju, 1984), 3:1291–94; He Bingdi, *Zhongguo huiguan shi lun* (Taibei: Taiwan xuesheng shuju, 1966), 52.

52. Yi Wenhe, "'Sancheng hao': Yunnan zui gulao di Huaqiao shanghao," *Tengchong wenshi ziliao xuanji (di san ji)* (Tengchong, Yunnan: Tengchong xian yishua chang, 1991), 15–18.

53. For a discussion of the embargo and Chinese merchant activity, see Giersch, *Asian Borderlands*, 106–8, 176.

54. Yule, *A Narrative of the Mission Sent by the Governor-General of India to the Court of Ava in 1855*, 143.

55. Yi Wenhe, "'Sancheng hao'"; Luo Qun, *Jindai Yunnan shangren yu shangren ziben* (Kunming: Yunnan daxue chubanshe, 2004), 39–41; Gu Yongji, 'Ming-Qing shi Dian Gui diqu yu Yuenan guanxi shulun," 80.

56. Yule, *A Narrative of the Mission Sent by the Governor-General of India to the Court of Ava in 1855*, 144, 150.

57. John Anderson, *A Report on the Expedition to Western Yunan via Bhamo* (Calcutta: Office of the Superintendent of Government Printing, 1871), 51.

58. House of Commons Parliamentary Papers, 1868–69, vol. 46, sec. 420, Lieutenant W. C. McLeod's Journal, 36, 56–57, 59.

59. J. Dupuis, *A Journey to Yunnan and the Opening of the Red River to Trade*, trans. Walter E. J. Tips (Bangkok: White Lotus, 1998), 60–61, 71–73.

60. Hu Yangquan, *Yunnan mabang* (Fuzhou: Fujian renmin chubanshe, 1999), 92.

61. Archibald R. Colquhoun, *Across Chrysê: A Journey of Exploration through the South China Border Lands from Canton to Mandalay* (London: Sampson Low, Marston, Searle, and Rivington, 1883), 1:126–29.

62. G. W. Clark, *The Province of Yunnan* (Shanghai: Shanghai Mercury, 1885), 34–35; Colquhoun, *Across Chrysê*, 1:242, 266, 308–9.

63. Colquhoun, *Across Chrysê*, 1:370–77, 381–82.

64. Clark, *The Province of Yunnan*, 16–17.

65. China Imperial Maritime Customs, Returns of Trade and Trade Reports for the Year 1889 (Shanghai: Statistical Department of the Inspectorate General of Customs, 1890), part 1, 22; part 2, A. P. Happer Jr., "Trade Report on Mengzi," 533–34; part 2, H. B. Morse, "Pakhoi Trade Report for the year 1889," 510–15; Colquhoun, *Across Chrysê*, 1:56, 66–68, 158.

66. *Report on the Mission to China of the Blackburn Chamber of Commerce, 1896–1897* (Blackburn: North-east Lancashire Press, 1898), F. S. A. Bourne's report, 87, and Bell and Neville report, 54; China Imperial Maritime Customs, Returns of Trade and Trade Reports for the Year 1890 (Shanghai: Statistical Department of the Inspectorate General of Customs, 1891), part 2, "Pakhoi Trade Report for the Year 1890."

67. Chiranan, *Yunnan Trade*.

68. *Report on the Mission to China of the Blackburn Chamber of Commerce, 1896–1897*, Bourne report, 85–86.

69. Forbes, "The 'Cin-Ho' (Yunnanese Chinese) Caravan Trade with North Thailand," 40–44.

70. *Report on the Mission to China of the Blackburn Chamber of Commerce, 1896–1897*, Bell and Neville report, 54.

71. Clark, *The Province of Yunnan*, 16–17, 38–39, 64.

72. A finding reinforced by Yang's recent work. See *Between Winds and Clouds*, 225–29.

73. David Harvey, *Justice, Nature and the Geography of Difference* (Cambridge: Blackwell, 1996), 47.

74. C. P. Fitzgerald, *The Tower of Five Glories: A Study of the Min Chia of Ta Li, Yunnan* (London: Cresset, 1941; repr., Westport, Conn.: Hyperion, 1973), 45; Lee, "The Legacy of Immigration in Southwest China," 300–301; *Yunnan sheng zhi*, vol. 71 (renkou zhi), ed. Yunnan sheng difangzhi bianzuan weiyuanhui (Kunming: Yunnan renmin chubanshe, 1998).

THE SOCIAL LIFE OF CHINESE LABOR

~~~~ Adam McKeown

Was Chinese labor a commodity? This question should be hard to avoid in a discussion of Chinese traders and commodities, because the mobilization and exchange of labor were indispensable aspects of expanding markets and trade. Not only were migrant laborers important producers, consumers, and transporters of goods, but the trade in labor itself was a major source of profit for many merchants. But thinking about labor as a commodity quickly raises analytical difficulties. The rapid expansion of market- and commodity-based cultures over the past three centuries has included an insistence that people are free agents who exchange things, not things that can be exchanged. Imagining labor as a personal possession that can be separated from the body and voluntarily exchanged partly overcomes these difficulties. But the terms under which such exchanges should take place remain a major issue of contention, with deep implications for how we interpret the expansion of capitalism over the past three centuries.

Rather than get mired in debates over the definition of commoditization and free exchange, it is best to start by understanding the specific processes, politics, and meanings of labor exchange within concrete social and historical contexts. In the words of Arjun Appadurai, value does not generate exchange, but "economic exchange creates value. Value is embodied in commodities that are exchanged. . . . The link between exchange and value is politics, construed broadly."[1] Commodities have social lives, with values that change over time and space as they pass through and create different social relationships. The essays in this volume amply demonstrate how the meaning and value of objects like jade, birds' nests, opium, and coins have shifted through the complicated processes of exchange, in which market relations are important but hardly the only creators of value. Such an approach is even more relevant for the exchange of labor, suffused as it is with a high-stakes

vocabulary of slavery, freedom, dignity, self-determination, contract, obligation, indenture, protection, and development. Few things are more contentious, political, and value-laden than the conditions under which labor is exchanged.

A thorough history of the social life of Chinese migrant labor would be an immense undertaking. The aims of this essay are more modest: to introduce some of the complexities of the politics of Chinese labor exchange in the second half of the nineteenth century, and to give a sense of what is at stake. While many histories of Chinese labor migration have uncritically appropriated the vocabulary of the "coolie" trade, indenture, and the "pig" trade, a more careful awareness of the specific politics, interests, and incoherencies that surrounded the production of these categories is warranted. Ultimately, the very meaning of "freedom," the characterization of Chinese society, and the terms on which Asia is incorporated into world history are at stake.

Labor as Commodity

An attempt to think about labor as a commodity must contend with two pervasive conceptual anchors. The first is slavery, especially as exemplified in memories of the African slave trade to the Americas. The very body of a slave is under the power of others, treated as property, and subject to sale and exchange like any other thing. At the extreme, this commoditization can be seen as a form of "social death," but, in practice, slavery includes various levels of autonomy, subjection, and integration into families or society. Indeed, the biography of a slave can often be traced through periods of relative commoditization and social integration.[2] However, the legacy of abolitionist discourse, with its stark dichotomy between freedom and slavery, has come to dominate much of the global imagination and obscure the many possible variations of slavery.

The second conceptual anchor is labor as a service. Most economists speak of goods and services in the same breath, both subject to the laws of supply and demand that are grounded in the existence of free individuals making choices in their own best interests. Like any other good, labor is something that an individual can possess and should be allowed to dispose of as he or she chooses. Trading one's own labor is seen as an exercise of freedom that is quite the opposite of trading other people who are not free to dispose of their own labor. Indeed, the commoditization of labor is often situated as part of a grander world-historical narrative of progress through the liberation of markets and men.

Marxist political economy constructs a similar narrative with a different twist. Marxists share with other economists the concept of an evolution from slave to capitalist society in which labor is freed from other social bonds and commoditized in the context of an expanding market economy. But rather than understand this as the progressive realization of the natural laws of economics, they situate market relations as the manifestation of unequal power relations in the specific historical conditions of capitalism. Labor is not liberated but alienated and exploited. The value of labor and its products, previously determined by their specific use-values in the service of men and social relations, are now defined by market exchange-values far beyond the control of the laborer. Labor itself has become a commodity that can be quantified and made equivalent to things. The processes of production and exchange have become the masters of men rather than the other way around.[3] This diminishing control over the conditions and products of labor is sometimes referred to as "wage slavery." More nuanced analyses emphasize how the very process of "freeing" labor from other social obligations is a necessary step in its commoditization and alienation from the person who labors.

All of these approaches share a common belief in a historical trajectory from slavery to commoditized labor. They differ in their evaluation of the meaning of labor as a commodity. The same markets and property laws that can be seen to liberate human potential can also facilitate the subjection of people as property. The same process of commoditizing labor as service that can be described as the realization of free choice, consent, and the dignity of man can also be depicted as man's subjection to capital and alienation from the world that he produced.

These conceptual anchors have staked out a terrain of endless contention, not only because of the irreconcilable assumptions behind their evaluations, but also because none of them can adequately account for the myriad forms of labor exchange that actually have taken place in historical time. Debt, social obligations, family relations, adoption, rituals, job status, government regulation, legal requirements, and physical coercion all complicate the meaning and politics of labor exchange. Even the apparently straightforward institution of indenture, rooted in the capitalist values of contract and market, has generated over two centuries of inconclusive debate over whether it is a new form of slavery, "neo-slavery," or an effective exercise of personal consent that helps create labor markets and opportunities.[4] In a similar vein, scholars of commodity exchange find that a stark distinction between market and gift relationships is hard to uphold, and that taste, dis-

tinction, emotional bonds, obligations, and rational calculation pervade exchanges of all kinds.

These conceptual anchors need to be historicized themselves if they are to remain helpful. The first step is to excavate actual practices of labor exchange and mobility on their own terms. What are the conditions under which the value of labor is most likely to be shaped by market relations or embedded in social, family, or ritual obligations? How is labor mobility organized within and across social units, be they class, kinship dialect groups, or political entities? To what extent are common meanings shared by different participants in the process of labor exchange? How do the meaning and organization of labor change over time? In the nineteenth century, we quickly find that it is difficult, if not impossible, to answer these questions in "native" terms. Actual practices were entangled in the ideals, assumptions, and debates over the meaning and nature of free labor. These ideals and the institutions designed to enforce them often obscured the actual practices of migration.

One issue at stake in the understanding of Chinese migrant labor is the origins and meaning of capitalism. The conceptual anchors generally posit an evolutionary story in which capitalism developed in Europe and then diffused to incorporate the rest of the world. The essays in this volume all engage with this world-historical narrative to some degree, demonstrating the great extent, impact, and sophistication of Southeast Asian market economies both before and beyond the impact of Europeans, while simultaneously describing the specific regional contexts and meanings that cast doubt on attempts to project Western economic values as universal truths. It is a delicate balancing act, an attempt to recover the vitality of non-Western history while critiquing and modifying the Western narratives that have established the standards by which to evaluate vitality.

Discussions of Chinese labor have often failed to maintain that balance. The voluminous documentation surrounding indenture has suffused discussions of Chinese migrant labor with a vocabulary of "coolies," "abuses," "pig trade," and of corrupt Chinese officials and brokers. This vocabulary has marginalized Chinese migration from the main trends of world history. European migrants in the nineteenth century are routinely depicted as emblematic of the dislocations and entrepreneurialism of modernity, progressive and creative settlers who opened frontiers and created nations. Chinese migrants, in contrast, are routinely depicted as backward, earthbound peasants, unable or unwilling to participate in the sweep of modern migration history without the direct intervention, protection, and resources of Euro-

peans.[5] Causes of long-term migration patterns that have been discredited in European history, such as war, overpopulation, and despotism are still routinely used to explain Chinese emigration, as if the laws of supply and demand that shaped European labor migrations had to be imposed in Asia through political and economic domination.

In fact, when we look beyond indenture we find that Chinese migrations were qualitatively and quantitatively similar to European ones. Fewer than 4 percent of Chinese emigrants were directly indentured to Europeans. The bulk of the over 20 million Chinese who departed south China from the 1840s to 1930s traveled under their own resources and organization. Peak emigration rates from Guangdong and Fujian were similar to peak rates from Italy, Norway, and Ireland. The 35 million Asians (including Indians) who moved into Southeast Asia from 1870 to 1930 were comparable to the 39 million who moved into the United States. Despite their reputation as sojourners, Chinese return rates were only slightly higher than global averages. Chinese migration was part of an interconnected world on the move, flowing into factories, construction projects, mines, plantations, agricultural frontiers, and retail networks across the globe.[6]

However, this migration has not been remembered as part of world history. Most Western-language accounts of Chinese emigration only count 2 to 8 million migrants. The trail of footnotes shows these numbers were ultimately drawn from three studies by Chen Ta, Chen Zexuan, and Arnold Meagher, all of which were explicitly counting only contract labor and "coolie" migration.[7] The assumption that Chinese labor migrated only under conditions of direct European control has shaped the very collection of data. Chinese-language accounts often give a more accurate number of about 20 million. But they emphasize that the contemporary descendants of Chinese in the world do not even amount to the population of Canada, and interpret Chinese mobility as something other than a true migration of settlers.[8] While the basic insight that European power has critically shaped the social life of Chinese migration is accurate, it needs to be qualified with a more specific history of the social interactions that actually shaped mobility, labor exchange, and social relations.

Two entwined discourses had a deep impact on the social life of Chinese labor: the vocabulary of contracts and consent as a foundation of political and economic freedom; and the vocabulary of abolition, with its black-and-white dichotomies of freedom and slavery. These vocabularies proved entirely insufficient to describe, recruit, and understand Chinese migration. Attempts to do so were suffused with contradictions and incoherencies, con-

stantly undermined by the actual practices of migration. Despite this, the basic legitimacy of consent, freedom, and slavery as ways to frame labor exchange was never dislodged. One result of the continual attempts to reformulate these principles was to obscure the actual practices of migration under a haze of confusion. In the process, Chinese migration was largely erased from the historical memory as anything other than a collection of exploitative and uncivilized practices, reflective of Chinese society itself.

Indenturing Asians

British attempts to recruit Chinese contract labor in the 1850s were shaped by the experience and institutions of Indian indenture. These, in turn, were framed by the experience and debates of abolition.[9] Plans to bring indentured Indians to sugar colonies in the Indian Ocean and Caribbean regions materialized immediately after the abolition of slavery in the British Empire, in 1834. Criticisms of those plans emerged just as quickly. Both sides appealed to freedom, progress, and the greater interests of the empire. Anti-indenture activists drew on the ideals, personnel, and institutions of the antislavery movement to argue that the restrictions on personal liberty entailed in indenture contracts were actually a form of pseudoslavery. During the period of indenture, contracted laborers could be punished, exchanged, and confined by their employers, with no power over the conditions or location of their work. The empire had a responsibility to protect and assure the well-being of its colonial subjects. This was especially true for those who, whether due to ignorance or coercion, were unable to protect themselves against adventurers and self-interested capital.

Pro-indenture activists spoke of how indenture was essential for the progress and prosperity of all parts of the empire. Contracts and cash advances "freed" impoverished migrants to circulate throughout the empire to places where they could work most effectively for the benefit of themselves and their employers. Indenture alleviated poverty and overpopulation in India while alleviating labor shortages in the sugar colonies. To suppress the right of Indians to freely move and enter into contracts was to undermine British ideals. As one Calcutta firm wrote to the Bengal government in 1838, "It is a question involving the rights of British subjects (in principle, of all British subjects) to carry their manual labor to the most productive market. . . . Any other political doctrine, though practically extended for the present to only a particular class of men, must obviously be extensible to all classes alike; and to assert it, therefore, in this case, would be to establish a precedent of the most perilous nature to constitutional liberty."[10]

By the 1850s, however, both sides tended to agree that a "free" migrant was an independent, self-willed individual, and that most Indians were not inherently free but enveloped in networks of obligation and ignorance, unable to achieve their own natural liberty. They continued to debate whether indenture contracts could work to "free" them, but agreed that some level of government surveillance was necessary to maintain a level of free consent that could make the system acceptable, disagreeing only over the extent and effectiveness of that surveillance. As investigations and reports continued to reiterate the pro- and anti-indenture positions, the British government established an intermediary position of "benevolent neutrality" that could enact mild regulation to objectively mediate between the two extremes. In effect, the "free" migrant did not exist through a lack of government intervention but as a product of proper regulation. When abuses persisted, they could now be blamed on the activities of native recruiters, ignorance, and custom rather than on indenture itself.

This modus vivendi worked for Indian indenture within the British Empire until the rise of Indian nationalist sentiments in the the late nineteenth century, but its application to China was far from straightforward. Like India, China appeared to be a favorable site for labor recruitment because of a commercialized rural economy and dense population. Serious recruiting did not begin until the late 1840s, however, when the establishment of Hong Kong and the treaty ports helped ease many of the Chinese restrictions on European traders. But Chinese indenture remained a vexed and relatively unsuccessful enterprise throughout the 1870s, when abuses and scandal led the Chinese and American governments to suppress all but the most highly regulated recruitment. Britons and Americans blamed most of the abuses on the incompetence of the Chinese government and the schemes and greed of non-Anglophone recruiters. Ultimately, however, the biggest problem was that Chinese indenture did not take place within the surveillance of a single empire but across multiple frontiers. Migrants departed from China, Macau, Hong Kong, and Singapore to a variety of destinations, which included Hawaii, Peru, and British, Dutch, French, and Spanish colonies. Private recruiters could easily evade regulations and shop for favorable forums. From one perspective, this international market could have signified a truly free market beyond the controls of any single government. But in practice, British diplomats forsook "benevolent neutrality" in favor of a systematic campaign against the unregulated private organization of the "coolie trade."[11]

The transposition of Indian indenture was also difficult because mar-

ket relations with the Chinese were already on a different footing than with other Asian peoples. In European eyes, most native peoples were notable for their laziness and obstinate refusal to act according to the laws of economics by selling their labor at market rates. Indeed, indenture was often seen as one of the methods to assimilate Asians into the laws of the market. Chinese, on the other hand, were often noted for their commercial acumen, industriousness, and willingness to conform to the laws of the market. Reports from Penang, Melaka, and South China in the 1840s and early 1850s were aware of extensive Chinese-organized labor migration to mines and agricultural areas throughout Southeast Asia. Prevalent financing schemes in which the migrants' passages were paid in advance in return for one year of labor abroad were described in terms that made them appear little different than the indentured migration of Europeans to the Americas that had been prominent until the 1830s.[12] As late as 1876, U.S. Minister to China William Williams responded to questions posed by an investigation committee from California in a way that compared the freedom of Chinese emigrants favorably to that of European emigrants. Despite some reservations about the "heathenish influences" of Chinese emigrants, he asserted that the debts used to finance migration to the United States demonstrated the positive effect of the market forces and political restraint of China and the United States as compared to the aristocracies, serfs, and deportations of Europe.

> There is no caste among the Chinese, no privileged class or titled aristocracy on the one hand claiming rights over serfs, or slaves on the other; and, consequently, no power inheres in the hands of one portion of society to get rid of their drones, their criminals, their paupers, or their useless slaves, by shipping them to other lands. Those who arrive in California are free men, poor, ignorant, and uncivilized indeed, easily governed and not disposed to make trouble in any way, but hoping to get a good price for their labor. . . . The imperial government can no more control the movement of its subjects, or keep them within its territory, than the President can restrain those of our citizens; neither power can control or limit emigration or travel.[13]

All of these reports seemed to point to the ease of establishing contract relations with Chinese labor. In 1851, British officials began to collect information about the possibility of indenturing laborers from southern China to work in the Caribbean. A circular to South China consuls in 1853, asking if Chinese should be enticed through contracts and advances or left "wholly

free and unfettered," received unanimous agreement that a contract and cash advance was necessary to get Chinese to migrate to an unknown land.[14] The issue was not that Chinese were impoverished and ignorant of migration, but that they already had access to well-developed migration networks and could make well-informed, commercially astute choices. Recruitment for the West Indies would have to be competitive. However, these attitudes changed as soon as the British actually attempted to break into this market. It quickly became clear that indenture functioned best when it could be seen as a means of extracting natives from backward, nonmarket conditions, not in conditions of open competition.

Contracting Chinese

The first attempts at recruitment in Amoy (or Xiamen, chosen for its long-standing practices of labor migration to the outside world) not only failed to be competitive, but also caused riots against the Western companies that attempted them. The main complaints were that the Chinese recruiters engaged by the companies were outsiders who relied on kidnapping and deceit.[15] Indeed, such practices were probably necessary in order to recruit Chinese to unknown lands on terms much less favorable than those in Southeast Asia, although the effect of rumors generated by competing Chinese recruiters cannot be discounted. The British retreated to Hong Kong, where, despite repeated efforts over the next twenty-five years, they were never able to establish indenture recruitment on favorable terms and without "abuses."

To many Europeans, the Chinese state was a major obstacle against a smooth regime of free emigration. They saw it as excessively authoritarian and opposed to free intercourse, yet incapable of enforcing its own laws against emigration. It was indeed difficult to engage Chinese officials on this topic because of the embarrassment of discussing the regulation of a migration that was officially prohibited. After the withdrawal from Xiamen, the Colonial Office instructed Hong Kong governor John Bowring to notify consuls in China that they were not to aid in the recruitment of coolies; however, "if the Chinese subjects of their own free will should prefer to risk the penalty attached to the transgression of the law . . . you are not bound to prevent, or even ostensibly be cognisant of, such acts, for it is the duty of the Chinese government to enforce its own laws."[16] However, this attitude did not prove sufficient to channel labor away from competing recruiters in China or Macau. An 1853 report from the Colonial Land and Emigration Commissioners recognized, in reference to China, that "it would appear dif-

ficult to deal with abuses which take place in collecting foreign emigrants in a foreign country, having its own political and judicial organisation, and jealously alive to any interference with that organisation." But they also feared that increased regulations in Hong Kong would drive recruiters to Macau and migrants to destinations outside of the British Empire.[17] Indeed, the problem of obtaining a steady supply of "free" emigrants in an international sphere beyond the regulatory efforts of any single government would prove elusive.

Release from Chinese jurisdiction was also no guarantee that migrants themselves would become free. Rather, it only generated new ways to depict the migrants as unfree and the cause of their own abuse. As early as the 1840s, Hong Kong officials worried about their still tenuous control over the island argued that once Chinese were freed from the despotic control of the Chinese state, it could only be expected that a people with no habits of self-restraint would relapse into banditry and licentiousness. The very act of movement even selected for such people. As Chinese Secretary Charles Gutzlaff wrote in 1846, "It is very natural that depraved, idle, and bad characters from the adjacent mainland and islands should flock to the colony where some money can be made. They are a roving set of beings, and committing depredations wherever it can be done with impunity; they cannot be considered as domesticated, and are in the habit of coming and going according to the state of the trade."[18] Governor Bowring borrowed this image to explain the Amoy riots, explaining that emigration had become such a habit that the town was overpopulated by "the idle, vagrant and profligate," who, when stimulated by greedy Western recruiters, made it impossible to establish "a quiet, steady and progressing system of well-digested emigration, giving time for the fit selection and becoming organization of proper bodies of Chinamen."[19]

British officials also identified Chinese customs and economic practices as major obstacles working against a migration that was free from abuse, even when those customs seemed similar to the basic principles of free contracts. West Indian planters were adamant about the need for female emigrants to create a less "depraved" laboring population. James White, the emigration agent in China, argued that this would only be possible by offering bounties to men who traveled with their wives. This was based both on the perception of cultural restrictions against female emigration and on the sense that the sale of women and children was pervasive in Chinese society. White concluded that the distinction between marriage and a market transaction was trivial, and slavery was indistinguishable from the patriarchal

control over the household. Female emigrants could only be obtained by collaborating with local practices.[20] This led to some discussion and ethnographic reports on whether proper marriage even existed in China. The colonial land and emigration commissioners ultimately agreed with White, adding, "Whatever may be thought of the state of morality which renders this possible, we cannot but point out that, as far as the woman is concerned, the result will be to raise her from the state of slavery under Chinese, to that of freedom under British law. . . . We cannot help hoping that these considerations will be held to constitute a substantial difference between the proceedings recommended by Mr. White and the Slave Trade."[21] Hong Kong Governor George Bonham, however, objected that Mr. White's plan "would doubtless give rise [to] . . . a trade little different from the Slave Trade," arguing that "the offer of a premium, without some official check, is a dangerous experiment to try with so venal and money-grasping a people as the Chinese." He stated that if such a plan were to be implemented,

> The British authority should inquire carefully into every case of marriage so performed; should have the parties brought up before him, and the woman narrowly and strictly examined previous to shipment, and a declaration made and signed by her, to the effect that she was a free and voluntary emigrant, that she freely and voluntarily married her present husband, and that no compulsion or any other agency had been set at work to induce her to do so. Without some official control of this nature, the plan would be a bad one.[22]

A system similar to Bonham's was finally adopted as a solution that was "less abhorrent to our notions of freedom and less suggestive of abuse."[23] From all perspectives, the Chinese condition in the absence of British intervention was conceived as degradation and slavery. Indeed, the very commoditization of labor that framed the civilizing potential of indenture to free Asians from their traditional bonds and poverty was now seen as the source of Chinese corruption.

A series of Hong Kong regulations to limit recruiting and transportation abuses largely succeeded only in pushing recruitment activities to Macau and the Chinese mainland. The British military occupation of South China from 1858 to 1861, during the Arrow War (also called the Second Opium War), created an opportunity that officials believed would provide "great facilities for conducting emigration on fair and humane principles."[24] Europeans worked with local Chinese officials to develop a system of surveillance similar to India's. Governor-General Lao Chongguang issued orders to

local magistrates in April 1859, instructing them to punish all kidnappers, to make sure that emigrants were aware of all the conditions of their contract, and to reassure migrants that the government had no objection to their departing with the foreigners once both parties had given their consent. Emigration depots were established in October, requiring at least a forty-eight-hour stay during which migrants were subjected to a joint examination by Chinese officers and foreign emigration agents, and given a chance to think more carefully before signing a contract. A public proclamation from the governor-general that month described the regulations and explained of the migrants that "their emigration is voluntary, and wholly different from that which is conducted by the kidnapper who sells his fellow-man. In order that this villainy may be stopped, and the difference between it and the former made patent to the world, such means of investigation and of inspection should be provided as will plainly denote a distinction."[25]

During the negotiations, Prince Gong of the Zongli Yamen (the Chinese foreign-affairs office) had also distinguished labor emigrants from other migrants by insisting, "Although they are employed by foreigners and received monthly salaries, they are not selling their labor to foreigners, they should be considered as if China were loaning them to foreign countries to use. Therefore, even though they have left their homeland, they are still entitled to protection from the Chinese government."[26] This new surveillance, which for the Europeans meant a guarantee of the emigrants' freedom, was for the Chinese a means of asserting government jurisdiction in the face of other powers and over migrants themselves. Those who departed without surveillance were not entitled to protection.

The legitimacy of these arrangements was recognized in a provision of the Treaty of Beijing, signed between Britain and China in 1860, which declared that Chinese subjects "are at perfect liberty to enter into engagements with British subjects . . . and to ship themselves and their families on board any British vessels at the open ports of China." However, surveillance was difficult to maintain in the international conditions of the South China coast. Chinese depots were rarely used because recruitment via Macau circumvented this system altogether. By the late 1860s, Europeans and Chinese in Hong Kong frequently protested activities in Macau. As British ships were prohibited from carrying emigrants from Macau, the British had little interest in supporting the freedom of emigrants to depart from any port they wanted. In these conditions, accounts of Chinese indenture contracts grew overwhelmingly negative, depicting them as an abuse and infringement on individual freedom and calling for government suppression.

In 1867, Hong Kong Legislative Consul J. Whittall claimed that even the more rigorously monitored emigration from Hong Kong should be banned because it was a stain on the reputation of the colony. Indenture contracts should be made invalid in British courts, he argued, because "they shift the responsibility of the miserable coolie's detention from the shoulders of his kidnappers to those of official authority. . . . Let voluntary emigration, pure and simple, be as uncontrolled from China as from Ireland, but let it be made criminal for British subjects to aid, abet, or in any way subserve, contracts of servitude for a term of years."[27]

London officials, concerned with justifying Indian indenture, were somewhat dismissive of these objections. Acting Colonial Secretary Henry John Ball in London responded that under existing arrangements Chinese emigrants knew what they were getting themselves into. He blamed the problems on the severity of existing regulations and even hoped that "a uniform form of contract might perhaps be settled on terms more just to the planters than that adopted by the Peking Convention [of 1866], which has caused nearly all honest and open emigration to cease, and has thrown the trade into the hands of unscrupulous parties, who care nothing for the Chinese Government or their Convention, thus actually increasing the evils which it was intended to suppress."[28] In more moderate terms the colonial secretary added that the suspension of emigration from Hong Kong would cause difficult international complications. He insisted that the British government fulfilled its duty to the migrants merely by ascertaining that the emigrants signed their contracts voluntarily and understood their decision.[29] Opinions in Hong Kong were not so easily mollified. A series of scandals in the early 1870s resulted in British- and Chinese-led international pressure to stop the labor trade from Macau, especially to Cuba and Peru.

Between the accusations and counter-accusations, the vested interests, and the shifting of blame to crimps (local Asian recruiters) and subcontractors, the actual practices of migration were lost, never able to fit within the categories of voluntary or coerced. Both migrants and officials were even encouraged to obscure the modes of organization in order to fulfill the formal requirements of freedom. Migrants were easily trained to assert their voluntary adherence to the terms of a contract when undergoing inspection. On their part, Hong Kong officials found it in their best interest to deny knowledge of any local activities in their port that might be interpreted as a coolie trade, a silence similar to that they had once criticized among Chinese.

In 1854, the Hong Kong harbormaster wrote that the free emigrant and the coolie "are understood to be widely different, the former being a class of

persons who have paid their passage, while the latter are understood to be those who have had their passage paid for them under an agreement."[30] Such a categorization lumped kidnapped coolies into the same group as those who borrowed money from friends and family abroad, making it very difficult to make finer distinctions. By 1881, ignorance of alternatives to indenture and self-payment had become the official stance of Hong Kong officials. That year, in response to requests from Australia to report on the free or unfree nature of Chinese emigration, the attorney general of Hong Kong would only say that he had been consulted on the meaning of contract emigration and its relation to debt obligations many times. His answer was that he could only address concrete cases, not hypothetical ones.[31] Only in 1910 did Hong Kong formally admit that many Chinese engaged in "*kangany*" emigration, in which a returned migrant gave assistance to new emigrants.[32] These developments helped perpetuate an understanding of all Chinese labor migration as outside of legitimate social practice, something other than true, self-determined migration and free labor markets.

Chinese Labor in the Straits Settlements

Officials and planters in the Straits Settlements had a much more direct interest in the flow of Chinese labor. They remained fully aware of the activities of Chinese brokers, becoming entrenched in a long struggle over the control of Chinese labor. The consistently high labor demands and entrenched laissez-faire ideology of the late nineteenth century generated a firm opposition against most plans to regulate migration and labor markets. But regulation still found a ready audience when formulated in terms of suppressing the perceived abuses and underground government of secret societies, countering the perceived antimarket practices of Chinese brokers, and preventing the seduction of labor to places beyond British colonies.[33]

Secret-society riots of the 1860s and 1870s along with the wave of indenture scandals in Hong Kong set the stage for the discussion of migrant regulation in Singapore. In 1871 and 1873, groups of Chinese merchants and planters sent petitions to the legislative council requesting an inquiry into labor-recruitment practices that could lead to some sort of regulation. After praising the fame, paternal protection, and impartiality of English laws, the 1871 petition explained that "now-a-days we hear of ill-disposed people (vagabonds) that often make it their trade of the 'Singkeks' or new comers, who, on their first landing here, not happening to be acquainted with any one in the place, are by these vagabonds invariably deceived and cheated." They requested "a trustworthy officer to superintend all the new arrivals,

and ascertain from the 'Singkeks' themselves where they intend to go, those of them willing to stay to be apprised that they are at liberty to act as free agents, that these vagabonds may not have the opportunity of deluding these 'Singkeks.'"[34]

These complaints and suggestions resulted in the enactment of an 1873 law that required all incoming Chinese laborers to register with the authorities. At a public meeting held to protest the law, European employers and merchants complained that it was "impolitic because it interferes with the importation of free labour to this Settlement, and unnecessary, because it can never accomplish the object which it is supposed to secure."[35] In a petition to the legislative council, they explained that any abuses were surely the fault of the secret societies and their insistence on creating an *imperium in imperio*. Their suppression would help promote the establishment of a free market that could, by its very workings, offer the best protection against abuses.

> Once landed in Singapore, and apart from this influence [of the secret societies], the competition for labor is so great as to obtain for the newly arrived Immigrant perfect security from extortion or unfair labor bargains. The only danger which assails him is that he may be, either before landing or after, hurried and cajoled into engagements to work in countries outside of this Settlement, and in ignorance shipped away beyond the influence and protection of our laws.[36]

Enforcement of the 1873 law was delayed, and a committee was appointed in 1875 to investigate the conditions of Chinese labor migration. Its findings elaborated on those from the 1840s and 1850s, describing a system of brokers and agents that reached from Malayan plantations to Chinese villages and from European financiers to small headmen in charge of groups of ten to twenty migrants. Migrants who did not pay their own passage were distributed to local employers and obliged to work for six months or a year in order to pay off their passage, after which they were free to find employment on their own. The commission concluded that abuses were minimal and that "perhaps no stronger practical testimony could be borne to the respectability of the mass of Chinese immigrants who arrive here than the fact that the system described above works fairly well for the employers."[37]

Employer satisfaction was not entirely true. In their testimony before the commission, Chinese brokers and planters consistently called for a government depot and written contracts as a way to limit runaways. Europeans,

on the other hand, were more likely to complain about the unnecessary expense and obstructions of a depot and to imply that this would only further bolster Chinese control over the labor supply. Despite their satisfaction with the existing practices, the commission still found that a major source of abuse lay in the diversion of migrants to Penang and Sumatra against their will. They also agreed with Chinese brokers that the lack of legal recourse over runaway migrants was a problem. They argued that runaways should be treated as a police rather than a civil matter, because employers could rarely expect adequate compensation in civil proceedings, given that migrants owned little more than the clothes on their backs. The commission's most serious concern, however, was about the lack of government surveillance.

> The Government knows little or nothing of the Chinese, who are the industrial backbone of these Settlements; and the immense majority of them know nothing of the Government. We know that a certain number of Chinese arrive each year, and that a certain number go away; but how long they stay, how many come back a second time, what they think about and desire—as to all this we know nothing. . . . We believe that the vast majority of the Chinamen who come to work in these Settlements return to their country not knowing clearly whether there is a Government in them or not.[38]

As a consequence, whenever laborers got in trouble, they went to the secret societies rather than the government. Thus the commission proposed the establishment of a Chinese protectorate and government depot where labor contracts would be signed and direct contact with magistrates could be encouraged in case of trouble. A protectorate was duly legislated in 1877, along with a crimping ordinance that required all contracts signed by local residents to work outside of the colony to be signed at the protectorate. As in India, mild regulation would produce free migration and labor markets.

The government did not build the depot, but licensed it out to Chinese boardinghouse owners. A court case in 1890 also interpreted the protectorate law to say that the protectorate did not have the power to compel anybody to stay in a depot or sign a contract at its offices. These circumstances led, in 1890, to a new investigation into the conditions of migrant labor. By this time, the idea that the protectorate was designed to safeguard the interests of laborers rather than employers was already firmly entrenched. As the attorney general argued before the court in 1890, "The evil which the Ordinance was intended to meet was the virtual slavery which the immigrant

would be under to the man who had brought him down from China and paid his passage money, if he were free from the supervision of the Chinese Protectorate."[39] Such ideas helped frame new and more explicit attacks on the Chinese brokers as the main obstacle to free labor exchange.

The actual findings in 1890 about the organization of Chinese labor migration were again little different than previous reports, down to the conclusion that "the abuses of the current system are more sentimental than real." The report even promoted the further expansion of the credit-ticket system (the main source of trepidation among Hong Kong officials) as a way to create a more vibrant labor market.[40] However, in the spirit of the protectorate, it developed an extended and detailed critique of the Chinese brokerage system as the main obstacle to smooth and abuse-free labor exchange. It argued that brokers drove up prices, obstructed the free flow of labor, and contributed to the labor shortage by pocketing money, providing unnecessary services, speculating on labor contracts, and forming a ring that excluded outsiders.[41] Even the compensation paid by brokers to the families of lost coolies and for funeral expenses were criticized for driving up costs. The report complained that Chinese boardinghouse keepers were "generally of the most worthless class," unsupervised, and "free to obtain men where and how they can so long as they avoid the displeasure of the authorities."[42] Under existing conditions of minimal government surveillance, they could disrupt free markets by exerting undue influence over laborers through persuasion and deception.

> While the Sin-Kheh is in the depot it is the keeper to whom he must look as his government, and it is the servants of this man who bring him from the ship, guard him in the depot, and eventually remove him to the scene of his future employment. The power which is thus placed in the hands of the depot-keepers, who are agreed on all sides to be unscrupulous, appears to us greater than should be entrusted to private individuals, and we consider, therefore, that the system should not be perpetuated.[43]

The committee insisted that "it is important that the coolly should be a free agent, at liberty to choose the employment and country he prefers."[44] The means by which to create free agents was to suppress Chinese businessmen in favor of expanded government control. The committee recommended that the government directly operate depots in Singapore and China, and facilitate direct recruitment by employers that excluded middlemen and channeled each migrant from the very moment of recruitment to a

specific job in the straits. A free market in Chinese labor was to work for the benefit of consumers of labor, not traders or producers.

The Chinese government was held up as the other serious obstacle to a free labor market. Citing diplomatic correspondence in which the Chinese government opposed the emigration of laborers who had not paid their own passage, the commission insisted that this helped to push the credit and labor market underground. "From this cause doubtless springs much of the iniquity of which we have here, and there obtained a glimpse; the bringing of subordinates, purchasing the silence of parents, and tutoring of emigrants to lie to those in authority."[45] Nearly all the Chinese brokers who testified before the committee denied that the Chinese government in any way interfered with their activities. However, the commission insisted that even the limited efforts of the Chinese government, such as the public execution of a broker accused of kidnapping and attempts to hold brokers responsible for lost coolies, would dissuade more respectable Chinese from becoming involved in the traffic. Effective regulation must be put on a more systematic basis through depots and surveillance from departure to arrival. It was not the existence of regulation, but the form of regulation and the interests it served that made a market into one that was free or suffused with abuse.

Chinese Labor as Commodity

It is difficult to summarize these debates. Representations of a free and functioning market in Chinese labor varied across time, place, and even individuals, dependent on the immediate interests and circumstances involved. In Hong Kong, the topic of contracts and obligations became so embarrassing that officials ultimately avoided it altogether, relegating it to a hazy zone of vaguely illegitimate native practice. Singapore planters and officials managed to develop a somewhat more systematic critique of Chinese brokers for hindering the free market in labor, without adopting an abolitionist stance against labor contracts. In both cases, it is hard to determine the actual effects on migration flows. But one long-term legacy was to create a flexible and pervasive image of Chinese labor and society itself as somehow unfree and corrupt.

This legacy had a direct impact on global migration patterns. For example, in 1879 David Bailey, a former U.S. consul in Hong Kong, selected material from the extended local debates over Chinese indenture and the sale of women and children in Hong Kong to write a long treatise on Chinese slavery and concubinage. He forwarded it to the U.S. State Department

with the comment "If Chinese emigration to the United States is to continue and increase with slavery or *quasi* slavery, and concubinage, inbred and permeating its every feature and organisation, so that they may be said to be an indissoluble part of its present system, is it not a subject to which American statesmen should turn their attention with some degree of anxiety?"[46] His report was cited in congressional debates leading to Chinese exclusion, and in court decisions that validated exclusion. In 1884, in a reversal from earlier decisions that protected Chinese immigration under treaty agreements, Justice Stephen Field wrote that the actual practice of Chinese immigration did not live up to the "voluntary emigration" stipulated in treaties because it placed migrants "in the bond thralls of the contractor—his coolie slaves."[47] It was a kind of labor exchange appropriate for colonies and uncivilized peoples, but unsuitable for a free republic.

These decisions played an important role in the establishment of an exclusionary barrier that kept Chinese out of the white settler nations of North America and Australia. From the 1850s to the 1870s, nearly 40 percent of all Chinese migrants traveled to these locations, the majority under Chinese financing and organization.[48] By the end of the nineteenth century, however, this potential for a globally integrated system of migration was increasingly segmented into distinct regional migration systems. These exclusionary laws helped create a concrete geographic territory where labor was exchanged under conditions believed to be something other than freedom, and which could be relegated to a historical death at the margins of modern world history.

Notes

Thanks to the Asia Research Institute at the National University of Singapore for providing the support and time to write this essay. Thanks also to Eric Tagliacozzo for reading my paper at the conference on Chinese Traders and Commodities, Taipei, January 2007, and conveying helpful audience comments to me.
1. Arjun Appadurai, "Introduction: Commodities and the Politics of Value," *The Social Life of Things*, ed. Arjun Appadurai (Cambridge: Cambridge University Press, 1986), 3.
2. Igor Kopytoff, "The Cultural Biography of Things: Commoditization as Process," *The Social Life of Things*, ed. Arjun Appadurai (Cambridge: Cambridge University Press, 1986), 64–91; Orlando Patterson, *Slavery as Social Death: A Comparative Study* (Cambridge: Harvard University Press, 2005).
3. Karl Marx, *Capital*, vol. 1, part 1, and part 2, chap. 6. An excellent Marxist analysis of Chinese migrant labor can be found in Carl Trocki, *Opium and Empire: Chinese Society in Colonial Singapore, 1800–1910* (Ithaca: Cornell University Press, 1990).
4. Contributions to this debate include Tom Brass and Marcel van der Linden, eds.,

Free and Unfree Labor: The Debate Continues (Bern: Peter Lang, 1997); Pieter Emmer, "Was Migration Beneficial?," Migration, Migration History, History: Old Paradigms and New Perspectives, ed. Jan and Leo Lucassen (Bern: Peter Lang, 1999), 111–30; Hugh Tinker, New System of Slavery: The Export of Indian Labor Overseas, 1830–1920 (Oxford: Oxford University Press, 1974).

5. Sucheta Mazumdar, "Chinese and Indian Migration: A Prospectus for Comparative Research," Chinese and Indian Diasporas: Comparative Perspectives, ed. Wong Siu-lun (Hong Kong: Centre of Asian Studies, University of Hong Kong, 2004), 139–67.

6. Elaborations on arguments in this paragraph and the next are in Adam McKeown, "Global Migration, 1846–1940," World History 15 (2004): 155–89; Adam McKeown, "Chinese Emigration in Global Context, 1850–1940," Journal of Global History 5 (2010): 95–124.

7. Chen Ta, Chinese Migrations, with Special Reference to Labor Conditions (Washington: Government Printing Office, 1923); Chen Zexuan, "Shijiu shiji cheng xing de tiaoyue huagong zhi" [The nineteenth-century Chinese contract labor system], Lishi yanjiu 1 (1963); Arnold Meagher, "The Introduction of Chinese Laborers to Latin America: The 'Coolie Trade,' 1847–1874," Ph.D. diss., University of California at Davis, 1975.

8. Qiu Liben, Cong shijie kan huaren [Looking at Chinese from a world perspective] (Hong Kong: Nandao, 2000).

9. See Marina Carter, Servants, Sirdars and Settlers: Indians in Mauritius 1834–1874 (Delhi: Oxford University Press, 1995); Madhavi Kale, Fragments of Empire: Capital, Slavery and Indian Indentured Labor in the British Caribbean (Philadelphia: University of Pennsylvania Press, 1999); Radhika Mongia, "Regimes of Truth: Indentured Indian Labour and the Status of the Inquiry," Cultural Studies 18 (2004): 749–68.

10. Quoted in Kale, Fragments of Empire, 31–32.

11. On Chinese indenture, see also Persia Crawford Campbell, Chinese Coolie Emigration to Countries within the British Empire (London: P. S. King and Son, 1923); Robert Irick, Ch'ing Policy toward the Coolie Trade 1847–1878 (Taipei: Chinese Materials Center, 1982); Meagher, The Introduction of Chinese Laborers to Latin America; Wang Sing-wu, The Organization of Chinese Emigration, 1848–1888: With Special Reference to Chinese Emigration to Australia (San Francisco: Chinese Materials Center, 1978); Yen Ching-hwang, Coolies and Mandarins: China's Protection of Overseas Chinese during the Late Ch'ing Period (1851–1911) (Singapore: Singapore University Press, 1985).

12. "Annual Remittances by Chinese Immigrants in Singapore to Their Families in China," Journal of the Indian Archipelago and Eastern Asia (hereafter JIAEA) 1 (1847): 35–37; H. Crockwell, "The Tin Mines of Malacca," JIAEA 8 (1854): 112–33; Great Britain Parliamentary Papers (hereafter Parliamentary Papers), Correspondence Respecting Emigration from China (1852–53), 25–26; "Notes on the Chinese of Pinang," JIAEA 8 (1854): 1–27; "Notes on the Chinese in the Straits," JIAEA 9 (1855): 109–24.

13. Papers Relating to the Foreign Relations of the United States (Washington: Government Printing Office, 1876), 63–65.

14. Parliamentary Papers, Correspondence Respecting Emigration from China, 1–20.

15. Ibid., 71–72, 92–94.

16. Ibid., 31.

17. Parliamentary Papers, *Correspondence upon the Subject of Emigration from China* (1855), 2.

18. Quoted in Yiching Wu, "Prelude to Culture: Interrogating Colonial Rule in Early British Hong Kong," *Dialectical Anthropology* 24 (1999): 153–54.

19. Parliamentary Papers, *Correspondence Respecting Emigration*, 3.

20. Parliamentary Papers, *Chinese Emigration* (1853), 74, 79. On India, see Gyan Prakash, "Terms of Servitude: The Colonial Discourse on Slavery and Bondage in India," *Breaking the Chains: Slavery, Bondage, and Emancipation in Modern Africa and Asia*, ed. Martin Klein (Madison: University of Wisconsin Press, 1993), 64–82.

21. Parliamentary Papers, *Correspondence upon the Subject of Emigration from China*, 20.

22. Ibid., 25.

23. Ibid., 52–53.

24. Parliamentary Papers, *Correspondence Regarding Emigration from Canton* (1860), 127.

25. Great Britain, Confidential Print 894, *Correspondence Regarding Emigration from China* (1860), 21.

26. Quoted in Yen, *Coolies and Mandarins*, 106.

27. Parliamentary Papers c. 328, *Coolie Emigration* (1868), 8–9, 19.

28. Ibid., 13.

29. Ibid., 15.

30. Parliamentary Papers, *Correspondence upon the Subject of Emigration from China*, 62.

31. *Daily Press* (Hong Kong), 24 August 1881.

32. Campbell, *Chinese Coolie Emigration to Countries within the British Empire*, 2–24; Elizabeth Sinn, "Emigration from Hong Kong before 1941: Organization and Impact," *Emigration from Hong Kong: Tendencies and Impacts*, ed. Ronald Skeldon (Hong Kong: Chinese University Press, 1995), 32.

33. See also Anthony Reid, *An Indonesian Frontier: Acehnese and Other Histories of Sumatra* (Singapore: Singapore University Press, 2005), 194–225; Eunice Thio, "The Singapore Chinese Protectorate: Events and Conditions Leading to Its Establishment, 1823–1877," *Journal of the South Seas Society* 26 (1960): 40–80.

34. *Proceedings of the Legislative Council of the Straits Settlements* (hereafter PLC) 1871, app. 13. See also PLC 1873, app. 34, 124.

35. PLC 1891, app. 33, "Report of the Commissioners Appointed to Enquire into the State of Labour in the Straits Settlements and Protected Native States," 9.

36. PLC 1874, app. 33, 146.

37. PLC 1876, app. 22, "Report of the Committee Appointed to Consider and Take Evidence upon the Condition of Chinese Labourers in the Colony," 244.

38. Ibid., 244.

39. PLC 1891, app. 22, 8.

40. Ibid., 32.

41. Ibid., 17.

42. Ibid.

43. Ibid., 20.

44. Ibid.

45. Ibid., 17.

46. Parliamentary Papers c. 3815, *Correspondence Respecting the Alleged Existence of Chinese Slavery in Hong Kong* (1882), 58.

47. *Chew Heong v. United States*, 112 US 536, 568. See also Moon-ho Jung, *Coolies and Cane: Race, Labor, and Sugar in the Age of Emancipation* (Baltimore: Johns Hopkins University Press, 2006).

48. Adam McKeown, *Melancholy Order: Asian Migration and the Globalization of Borders* (New York: Columbia University Press, 2008).

OPIUM AS A COMMODITY IN THE CHINESE NANYANG TRADE

~~~~ Carl A. Trocki

The irresistible propensity of the inhabitants of these districts to the use of opium appears to have long afforded the government . . . the most effectual and easy means of bringing again into circulation, and of attracting to the capital of Batavia, the specie and ready money which . . . would have otherwise accumulated in the interior and been exclusively hoarded up in the treasuries of the native princes and regents.
—T. S. Raffles, lieutenant-governor of Java, quoted in H. R. C. Wright, *East-Indian Economic Problems of the Age of Cornwallis and Raffles*

The story of opium in Southeast Asia is a long one. It was traded to China and used as a medicine as early as the Song Dynasty, and, as the recent work of Zhang Yangwen documents, it was used as a recreational drug and an aphrodisiac in the Chinese court as early as the sixteenth century.[1] It was probably also by that time used by Southeast Asians, both as a work drug and as a recreational drug. Whether it was a true commodity may be debatable, but it was certainly an article of commerce that was manufactured in India and perhaps central Asia, then exported to the east and sold throughout the region. It was a luxury item, both as a medicine and as an indulgence, and its consumption was largely restricted to elites, but it was not yet fully commodified. At the time, it was probably considered to be in the same class of exotic, nature-based chemicals that China was obtaining from the Bornean rainforests.[2]

By the end of the seventeenth century, the picture of the opium trade in East and Southeast Asia had undergone some important changes, including the way in which opium was used. Europeans had brought tobacco to Asia, and with it came the habit of smoking.[3] Some of the first reports of opium smoking come from late-seventeenth-century Java, where opium was mixed

with tobacco and sold to the Javanese.[4] At that time, the drug was carried from India by the Dutch, who dominated the trade to the east.

The change or shift in the commercialization of Indian opium was instigated by the VOC [Verenigde Oostindische Compagnie] in the 1650's. After experimenting with exporting Malwa opium from Surat to Batavia, the Company began exporting Bengal opium in the mid-seventeenth century in increasingly larger quantities to Batavia for sale on Java and later in the Indonesian archipelago and the Malay world. The development and expansion of the sale of Bengal opium to Batavia for commercialization on Java by the VOC is well known. . . . The quantities exported from Bengal to Batavia by the Company rose from 1,300 *ponden* (one Dutch *pond* is equal to 0.4 kilo) in 1659 to an annual average of 120,000 *ponden* over the decade of 1707–1717 with a reported gross profit margin of 46%.[5]

According to Owen, it was probably the Dutch who spread the practice of smoking opium to Taiwan, and from there it became established in China. Somewhere along the way, however, the Chinese further refined the practice by dispensing with the tobacco and finding a way to smoke pure opium.[6] David Bello has noted that the first reports of smoking pure opium paste in China appear in the 1790s. The practice spread throughout the empire in the early nineteenth century.[7]

Until the Battle of Plassey, in 1757, the production and marketing of "Bengal" opium continued to be controlled by Indians, and was dominated by a group of merchants known as *pykars*. Once in control of Bihar, however, the British East India Company (EIC) servants in Patna quickly assumed monopoly control over the local opium crop.[8] By the 1760s, British country traders, together with their Parsi, Armenian, and Jewish affiliates, came to dominate the movement of opium from Calcutta to Southeast Asia and China. The country traders moved through Southeast Asia with variegated cargoes of Indian and European goods, mainly opium, cotton and cotton cloth, gunpowder, and arms. Their aim was to amass cargoes that would be saleable in China. This meant trading some of their cargoes for the products of Southeast Asia, usually tin, pepper, gold, and a range of other products from the jungles and seas of the region collectively known as "straits produce."

This trade brought the British traders into contact with the Chinese merchants who were settled in the main trading ports of the region. Some of them had already been buying opium from the Dutch for shipment to China.

Others, according to Kwee Hui Kian, were involved in revenue farming activities in north Java.[9] Although her work shows they were principally collecting the rice tax, James Rush shows that opium farms were already in existence by the mid-eighteenth century in Java.[10] Souza and Leonard Blussé, among others, have noted that during the mid-eighteenth century, the Dutch were focused more on the collection of primary agricultural commodities such as rice, sugar, indigo, coffee, pepper, and also metals such as tin and gold.[11] Much of the Asian trade had fallen to others, especially the Chinese and the country traders.

In the search for commodities, both the British and the Dutch entered the new production economy that the Chinese were developing in Southeast Asia. The junk traders who had been coming to Southeast Asia were a well-established phenomenon. Chinese traders, mostly based in Fujian, had been sailing to various parts of Southeast Asia since Song times.[12] The chaos that swept China during the Ming collapse and the Qing takeover disrupted this trade and the role played by maritime Chinese. When the dust settled and the Qing government permitted a resumption of trade with the region, there appears to have been a considerable demand for the products of tropical Southeast Asia. The demand could not be met by the production of Southeast Asian labor on its own, and as a result, Chinese labor was introduced into Southeast Asia for the purpose of producing those goods.[13]

This migration of "coolie labor" from China to Southeast Asia is a relatively recent phenomenon. There is no record of Chinese laborers coming to the region until the late seventeenth century or early eighteenth.[14] Some may have come as refugees a few decades earlier following the Qing conquest, but those who arrived after 1685 appear to have been sojourners who intended to work and then return home. It is also important to understand that this migration seems to have begun largely as a response to the growth of the Chinese domestic economy and an increasing demand in China for products such as tin, gold, pepper, and sugar. During the period from 1685 to 1720, there appeared in various parts of Southeast Asia the first settlements of Chinese laborers who went there expressly to produce commodities for shipment back to China.

By the 1780s, a number of similar settlements had appeared all around the Gulf of Siam, the coasts of the Malay Peninsula, Borneo, and Sumatra (see map 1). Of particular note were the pepper and gambier planters in Riau, tin miners in Bangka, gold-miners in Sambas and Pontianak, sugar planters in Kedah, and pepper planters in Brunei, Chantaburi, and elsewhere in the region. In addition to the production and export of these products, Chi-

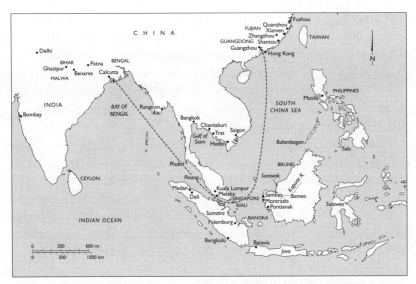

Map 1 Major Chinese settlement areas in Southeast Asia c. 1820, and major opium trading centers in South and East Asia.

nese traders were increasingly involved in developing the rice trade between Southeast Asia and China.[15]

These settlements of Chinese laborers represented a purely Chinese economy, a development that was unique in the region in that it was almost completely commercial. Laborers traveled to the various parts of Southeast Asia in Chinese ships for the sole purpose of producing specific commodities. They were supplied with food, provisions, and tools from outside sources. The laborers were essentially free, purchased their supplies from the market, and also exchanged their labor for cash or shares. The exchanges were managed by Chinese merchants who not only supplied the settlements of producers, but also purchased their products and sent them back to China.

This economic expansion seems to have been accompanied by a considerable upsurge of Chinese maritime activity. Chinese "pirates" were reported to be active, particularly along the coasts of Vietnam and in the Gulf of Siam. French missionary sources attest to the presence of Teochew pirates in the Gulf of Siam, and Dian Murray has written at length of the Cantonese seafarers in the Gulf of Tongkin in the late eighteenth century. Undoubtedly, some of them preyed on the settlers, while others attempted to manage their commerce.

Often burdened by debts for their passage and initial supplies (what in the language of American mining was called a "grubstake"), laborers were

commonly bound to monopoly arrangements with their suppliers and cus-tomers. Pepper and gambier planters in Singapore and Johor in the nine-teenth century were required to sell their products to specific merchants for a quarter of their value in the Singapore market. At the same time, they pur-chased goods priced at four times their market value. One would assume that most laborers were locked into "company store" type arrangements with their respective capitalists, or taukeh.

While these arrangements would have left the labor force in a completely dependent relationship, the workers were not without resources. The entire reason for their presence was the lack of labor in the first place. Labor was a valuable commodity and the taukehs were unable to police the settlements constantly, many of which were scattered in remote parts of the jungle. Far from being amenable to policing, the laborers were required to defend them-selves against pirates, bandits, and other Chinese like themselves, particu-larly in the mining areas. They were thus organized into kongsis, which not only provided defense but also served as economic partnerships allowing both laborers and taukehs to hold shares in their ventures. This organiza-tional pattern was widespread throughout the region, and variations of it were found in Pontianak, Sambas, Riau, and Bangka as early as the mid-eighteenth century. Similar patterns probably existed in places where they have not been formally documented, such as southeast Siam and on both sides of the Malay Peninsula. It is also likely that Chinese laborers gained a measure of solidarity through sworn oaths of brotherhood.

While such institutions may have been quite serviceable for pioneer settlements in the wilderness, they posed unique problems during the nine-teenth century, as Southeast Asia was bound into the global economy. The ritual and economic partnership between Chinese labor and Chinese capital came to be seen as a threat to both colonial and indigenous governments. Not only did the kongsi-type organization serve as a physical defense, it also served as a defense against economic exploitation. The kongsis could and did serve as institutions of governance and were, moreover, democratic, egali-tarian, and communal.

One might also argue they represented a kind of moral economy based on the ideas of justice embodied in the ideologies of the secret societies or triads. In a number of cases, these kongsis became virtually autonomous and waged organized warfare, defending themselves against outside forces, whether Southeast Asian or European. As such, they were an ideological, po-litical, and economic threat both to traditional autocratic and status-based

governments of Southeast Asia, and to the colonial-capitalist regimes that Europeans were then organizing in the region.

Despite the ability to occasionally invade, ravage, and destroy these settlements, outsiders could not easily control them in the long term. Both colonial and indigenous rulers came to realize that their own prosperity depended on Chinese laborers. They were the geese laying the golden eggs. Not only did they outproduce indigenous labor because of their more developed skills, but they also had greater incentives because they were in the cash economy. Conquest, slavery, and systems of ritual dependence were all counterproductive.

The key to capturing the fruits of both Chinese labor and Chinese capital was opium. In the eighteenth century, British country traders were in the habit of selling opium to the merchants who served the Chinese settlements. Opium was an ideal commodity for these laborers. Isolated in virtually all-male communities, they lacked most of the amenities of normal life: entertainment, families, women, and medicine. Opium filled these empty spaces, helping the laborers forget their loneliness and isolation, and easing the physical pain that accompanied long hours of heavy work in the tropical heat. In addition, it eliminated the symptoms of dysentery, malaria, and other tropical fevers, which allowed them to keep working.[16] Most important, the laborers, unlike their brothers in China, had the cash to buy opium. Thus, it was arguably in Southeast Asia, not in China itself, that opium use first took hold among lower-class Chinese, for as the British mass-produced opium in India, they found a mass consumer market among the Chinese laborers of Southeast Asia.

If opium was the "hook" that brought working-class Chinese into the opium economy, it was also the lever that pried open the kongsi brotherhoods, converting them into "secret societies" and shifting the Chinese taukehs and their wealth to the service of colonial and indigenous governments. In some respects, the wealthier Chinese had always worked with the local rulers and the colonial powers, in particular those Chinese who had established themselves and their families as residents in the towns and port cities of Southeast Asia, and whose descendants were the locally born Chinese known as *peranakan*, Baba, or mestizo, depending on the location.

A certain group of these men worked as tax collectors, or more correctly, as tax farmers. They were a species of entrepreneur who purchased from the government, usually at auction, the monopoly for the sale or collection of some item or the provision of some service. In the eighteenth century, under

the Dutch, they collected rice taxes and held other farms both for the colonial power and for indigenous rulers. They also held farms for the sale of opium to the population.[17] The opium farmers were often the only links between the local populations, whether Southeast Asian peasants or Chinese coolies, and the local government.

Opium farms became a widespread phenomenon throughout Southeast Asia and could be found in every state of the region during the nineteenth century. For this reason, and because Chinese capitalists almost exclusively dominated opium farming, it is useful to discuss the role of opium as a commodity in Southeast Asia in the context of the opium-farming system. It is also important to understand that the system was not static, but rather evolved with changes in the regional economy and in the development of European colonialism.

The Stages of Farm Development

Three stages can be discerned in the development of the opium-farming business in Southeast Asia, and in each phase the nature of opium's status as a commodity underwent significant changes. At the same time, the relations between Chinese labor, Chinese capital, and the local political units also changed. The first stage took place from about 1760 to about 1830, when British country traders supplied opium to settlements in Southeast Asia. The Chinese laboring kongsis remained relatively autonomous. Observers in the 1830s considered the Hakka gold-mining kongsis of western Borneo to be democratic, self-governing republics.[18] In about 1825, according to Munshi Abdullah's report, Singapore's Tiendihui was a largely autonomous organization dominating the pepper and gambier agriculture of the interior. Lee Poh Ping has styled it the "pepper and gambier society" to distinguish it from the "free trade society" of the town.[19] Taukehs held key positions in the kongsis, but were probably reliant on the members of the kongsi for their power and influence. There is little information about the level of opium use by members of the kongsis, but one can probably assume that it was not excessive. Certainly, opium-farming systems were rudimentary, and the taukehs who controlled the farms (most of whom were Babas) were, in many cases (Singapore, for instance), not the same taukehs who dominated the kongsis.

The second stage of opium farming development emerged between 1830 and 1880. During the 1830s and 1840s, colonial governments began to move against the kongsis. In Borneo and Bangka, the Dutch launched campaigns to dominate the mining kongsis, while in Singapore and Penang the British

took aim at the Ghee Hin (Tiendihui) and other "secret societies."[20] In Siam and Vietnam, indigenous governments undertook drastic military actions against the Chinese brotherhoods even when it required the massacre of the populations of entire towns.[21]

These governments formed strategic alliances with Chinese revenue farmers. It was not long before secret-society headmen, men who were not Babas or even Hokkiens, aspired to revenue-farming roles themselves. In 1846, a relative newcomer and a prominent secret-society leader, Lau Joon Teck, took charge of the Singapore opium farm in partnership with the Hokkien Baba, Cheang Sam Teo. By the 1850s, Lau was considered the "monied man" of the farms and the Ghee Hin had become his enforcement gang. The Dutch, too, found that opium farmers could subdue the kongsis.[22]

In Singapore, in the early years, the farms had been dominated by Babas, or locally born Chinese, many from Melaka families. They spoke English and were locally domiciled, and thus the British felt they could be trusted. As the farms came to be more dependent on pepper and gambier coolies as consumers, it became necessary for the Babas to form strategic alliances with the Teochew and Hakka taukehs who dominated the cultivation and who had contacts with the *kangchus* who ran the pepper and gambier settlements in the interior and in Johor. Many of these were either Tiendihui leaders or were closely associated with the other secret societies, as exemplified by Lau Joon Teck.

As the farms grew, they came to be managed by rather large cliques of the most powerful merchants in the various colonies and settlements. They financed their syndicates by breaking them up into shares and selling the shares to other Chinese in the community. These syndicates, or kongsis, as they were also called, often had an ethnic basis and competed for control of the farms in their settlement. In Singapore there was a Hokkien syndicate, led by Cheang Hong Lim, in the 1870s and 1880s and a Teochew syndicate, led by Tan Seng Poh, in the 1860s and 1870s. In Saigon, a Cantonese syndicate opposed the Hokkiens led by Banhap. In the absence of any other stable financial institutions (with the exception of European banks), the farms became the favored instruments of capital accumulation among the wealthier Chinese. The need to draw funds from the entire community, as well as the need to provide investment opportunities for all, likely influenced the trend toward consolidation and compromise between ethnic cliques.

Opium revenues soon became the major prop of the colonial states in Southeast Asia. In Singapore, the farm income varied between 40 and 60 percent of local revenues. Opium-smoking coolies literally paid for Singa-

pore's free trade. In Java and Siam, the farms brought in about 35 percent of total revenues throughout the nineteenth century. The farms also spared these governments the burden of expense needed to police the tax-collection regime and served to police the Chinese community in general. The alliance between revenue farmers, particularly the opium and spirit farmers, and the ritual brotherhoods gave them a ready-made police force.

At the same time, the heads of the opium farmers and their key investors took control of the economic enterprises developed by the kongsis. Thus, in Singapore between 1846 and 1880, the opium farmers also controlled the pepper and gambier business. In addition, since the cultivation covered British Singapore, Dutch Riau, the Malay state of Johor, and British Melaka, the farms of these same locales were also amalgamated under the same leadership.[23]

Similar constellations of opium-farming territories coalesced in other parts of the region. Each came to be grouped around a specific system of commodity production. Thus, in Penang and its vicinity, the revenue farms were largely focused on the tin-mining regions.[24] In areas such as Java and Siam, where there were large populations of opium-using Southeast Asian peasants, the economics of the farms were often structured around rice production and, especially in Siam, rice milling.[25]

In all cases, opium use was connected to a local productive economy. Farmers not only drew a profit from opium sales to peasants and coolies, but were also the primary investors in their respective industries. They thus profited from both the consumption and the production of these essentially captive populations. In addition to being habituated (if not actually addicted) to opium use, the coolies and peasants were frequently bound to the farmers and capitalists by debts. These chains of addiction and indebtedness, by insuring a captive labor force, guaranteed supplies of saleable commodities at the cheapest possible prices. It was during this period that Singapore became the key center not only for the opium trade, but also for the Chinese economy of Southeast Asia.

The Role of British Singapore

The British trading center of Singapore, which was founded in 1819 by Thomas Stamford Raffles, brought together all the elements of the new order in Southeast Asia. Protected by the Royal Navy, the British free port was a place where the British country traders could unload their precious cargoes of the Indian drug and where Chinese and other Asian merchants

could gather and amass their fortunes without fear of the depredations of "native" chiefs.

Singapore, in addition to lying beside the only clear, deep channel between the Indian Ocean and the South China Sea, was at the center of a line, running north and south, that linked Dutch Batavia and Bangkok (see map). Between those two capitals lay most of the major kongsi settlements in Southeast Asia. To the north were the two coasts of the Malay Peninsula, Sumatra, and the Gulf of Siam. Beyond that lay the populous mainland states of Burma, Siam, and Vietnam. The west coast of the Peninsula was then being settled by groups of adventurous tin miners from bases in Penang and Melaka. On a tangent to the west were the pepper gardens of Aceh. The east coast of the Peninsula was dotted with settlements of Chinese, Malays, and Siamese producing rice, pepper, tin, gold, birds' nests, and the vast range of forest produce always in demand in China. To the northeast were the pepper ports of Chantaburi, Trat, Chonburi, and Rayong, with sugar, tobacco, and endless supplies of dried and salted fish. Beyond those towns were Cambodia and Cochinchina and important supplies of rice, sugar, and timber.

To the south was Riau, the port that had set the pattern for Singapore in the previous century. It still housed a settlement of several thousand Chinese pepper and gambier planters that centered on the Sino-Bugis settlement of Tanjong Pinang. It had only recently been occupied by the Dutch in 1818. The islands to its south—Lingga, Bangka, and Belitung (Billiton)—were major tin-mining areas. Bangka had been the site of major mining kongsis since the early eighteenth century, and they continued to be productive throughout the nineteenth century. To the south was Java and to the east the Java Sea, Banjarmasin, Sulawesi, and the islands of the eastern archipelago. At either end of this axis were Siam and Java, which supplied foodstuffs to feed the burgeoning populations of miners and planters. This entire economic universe was dominated by Chinese opium farmers.

Singapore became the center of the Chinese economy of Southeast Asia and of the opium trade. Therefore, traders who serviced the settlements came to Singapore for their supplies, enabling Singapore traders to acquire the products of surrounding settlements. As the center of Chinese trade, Singapore was also where the junks from China landed, and it became the headquarters of Southeast Asia's Chinese labor exchange. Laborers and coolies first traveled to Singapore, then were shipped out to the various mines or plantations in the surrounding areas. Singapore was thus not only the head-

quarters of the opium trade, but also central to the labor trade, or the coolie traffic, as it was then known. This trade, too, was dominated by the taukehs who controlled the revenue farms, the secret societies, and the mines, plantations, rice fields. Opium was the key to the entire constellation.

Singapore was the source of capital and the source of labor. Naturally, the products of all Southeast Asia flowed back there. The port became the center of the region's commodity trade. As a trading port it did not really draw much trade away from other centers. John Crawfurd argued in 1824 that Singapore had, in fact, increased the overall trade of the region. In a matter of months after the founding of Singapore, Chinese junk traders, Bugis traders, and British merchants began to flock there. Within five years, Singapore's trade grew to a value of over $13 million annually.[26] Crawfurd argued that Singapore greatly contributed to an absolute increase in British trade in Asia. Answering critics who held that Singapore simply drew trade from Penang, he pointed out that in 1818 the whole of direct British trade with the Straits of Malacca, and generally with the eastern islands, excluding Java, centered at Penang, totaled $2,030,757 in exports. In 1824, however, the joint exports of Penang and Singapore were $9,414,464, of which $6,604,601 moved through Singapore.[27]

What was the basis of this sudden increase in British trade? Certainly an important share of it was opium. From 1823 to 1824, $8,515,100 of opium was shipped to China. Even though not all of this landed in the straits, much of it did. Singapore's location, moreover, was more advantageous than Penang's. In addition to serving as a base for British trade, Singapore was better able to tap into the very active trade carried on by Chinese junks in the South China Sea, the Gulf of Siam, and the Java Sea.

An important shift occurred in the middle of the nineteenth century in relation to the final destination of the products exported through Singapore. At the time of its founding, Singapore had been able to make a place for itself in the trade from Southeast Asia and the West to China. That was one of its great strengths. By midcentury, however, goods from Singapore, particularly those produced in Southeast Asia, began to flow increasingly to the West. As European and American industry developed, products such as gambier (for tanning leather) and tin were drawn away from China. This took place at a time when China's purchasing power was on the decline and when wealth was flowing out of China (mostly to pay for opium) faster than it was being replenished.

This shift did nothing to damage the trade of Singapore, which flourished throughout the middle years of the nineteenth century. In many ways this

was the high point of the Chinese economy of the region that had grown up around opium farming, labor control, and commodity production. The breakdown, or perhaps break-up, of the system may have been caused as much by its success as by anything else. Farm values had risen exponentially, making the Chinese capitalists who owned them among the richest and most powerful men in Asia. Their emerging power may have provoked the fears of the colonial elites, who began to tighten administrative controls on the opium economy and attempted to gain greater control over their own revenues. At the same time, the demand for tropical products in Europe, particularly raw materials, and the advance of colonial control and technology had brought other changes. Seeking investment opportunities, American and European corporations brought steamships, new mining technology, and new products such as rubber, all of which worked to diminish the importance of the old Chinese economy based on opium and control of Chinese labor.

The Decline of the Farming System

A number of trends became obvious during the 1880s, and it is significant that they were apparent throughout the region. The revenue farms continued to increase in value as populations expanded. While this meant that the farms could offer greater profits to the farmers, it also meant that they themselves needed deeper pockets and greater resources to obtain and manage the farms. It made economic sense for groups of local capitalists to combine into even larger syndicates to manage the farms. This offered them a double advantage: they could eliminate competition and thus strife within the Chinese community, and therefore, in turn, offer the colonial governments lower bids for the farms. Whereas these governments had previously depended on competition to keep up the price of the farms and to obtain an appropriate return from the farmers, by the 1870s, in places like Singapore, Hong Kong, and Cochinchina, the local farms had been subsumed into one large syndicate.[28]

In response to only minimal increases in the bids, the different colonial governments decided on a number of alternative strategies to regain a measure of control. One strategy was to invite investors from other settlements. Thus, in 1879, John Pope Hennessy, the governor of Hong Kong, invited Gan Tin Wee, otherwise known as "Banhap," the opium farmer of French Cochinchina and Cambodia, to form a syndicate to compete for the Hong Kong opium farm. Banhap (who had been born in Singapore) joined together with Cheang Hong Lim, one of the Singapore opium farmers, and

his Saigon partners, the three Tan brothers of Saigon.[29] They were success-ful in ousting the Cantonese syndicate which had controlled the Hong Kong farms for a number of years. Although Banhap and his associates were not particularly successful in holding and managing the Hong Kong farms, the colonial government had not only garnered an increase in the rent, it had actually strengthened its control over the farmers.[30]

The following year the Singapore government used a similar strategy to discipline the syndicate that had controlled the farms of Singapore and its vicinity since 1870. They sought bids from Penang merchants. As a result, Koh Saeng Tat, an established straits Chinese merchant from that settle-ment, took over the Singapore farms. The Singapore government gained an increase in rent, but Saeng Tat lost money due to smuggling and other acts of sabotage by members of the old syndicate. That did not discourage other hopefuls, however, and in the next auction another Penang taukeh, Chui Sin Yong, outbid the Singapore cliques and took the farms, giving the Singapore government yet another significant boost in rental income. He, too, faced difficulties in the form of smuggling and other problems. These events, how-ever, provided an opportunity for Governor Fredrick Weld to crack down severely on the Singapore farmers and to begin investigations into their operations.[31] In the end, the Singapore government gained much greater control over the farms.

In succeeding years, in Hong Kong and in British Malaya, governments adopted increasingly rationalistic approaches to the farming system and to colonial administration in general. The idea that the Chinese should be gov-erned under a system of indirect rule, with the opium farmers and secret-society leaders as the key agents of the state, came to seem anachronistic. The account books of the farmers came under closer scrutiny, and the prac-tices that led to the creation of permanent indebtedness among the coolies began to face calls for reform. While the measures by no means liberated the coolies immediately, they did begin to loosen the close ties that existed between opium farmers and the economy, a process made easier by the fact that the economy was becoming far more complex and the urban popula-tion more diversified. Finally, colonial police forces, particularly in the urban areas, were more capable of enforcing the laws without the cooperation of private gangs of "revenue peons" and secret-society thugs.

These measures did not destroy the profitability of the farms, nor did they prevent certain groups of wealthy Chinese from becoming even wealthier. Some farms remained in existence and continued to be profitable until the

early years of the twentieth century. It was at this point that a number of additional factors became pertinent. One was the increasing influence of the anti-opium movement in Britain and other colonial metropoles, which often focused on the farming system and on Chinese wealth. Then there was also the increasing instability of the farms. International syndicates bidding against one another for the farming concessions raised revenues, but the competition sometimes led bidders to overestimate their potential profits. If they overbid, or if the economic situation deteriorated, and commodity prices fell, opium consumption would likewise decline, and the farmers could be forced into bankruptcy. This is what happened in the mid-1880s and again in 1907. The result of pressures from metropolitan groups as well as threats to the stability of the revenue led colonial administrations to consider the possibility of taking the farms into their own hands.

The Creation of Government Monopolies

The final stage in the history of Chinese capitalism and opium farming came with the creation of government-controlled monopolies. There had always been a level of dissatisfaction with the farming system. The fact that it was a Chinese-dominated business led to jealousy on the part of European merchants and indigenous elites, as well as distrust on the part of European colonial governments. In 1880, when Banhap was in the midst of his difficulties with rival Cantonese cliques in Hong Kong, the Colonial Council in Saigon began a campaign to overthrow Banhap and his clique.[32] As a result of their discussions, the government took full control of the farms and ran them as a government-controlled monopoly after this time.

In 1881, the French colonial government set up the first government opium monopoly.[33] The organization was not particularly successful in its early years. In many respects it was simply a somewhat disguised opium farm, since it was largely run by Chinese. Most of the employees of the Régie, as it was called, seemed to be Cantonese associated with the syndicate that was the rival of Banhap's Hokkien clique in Saigon. By the 1890s, however, the French government had gained more complete control over the system and was able to extract a reasonable profit from the monopoly.

The farming system in Java came under closer government scrutiny during the 1880s as a result of the activities of Charles TeMechlen. When he was the Resident of Joana, in the early 1880s, he worked with the opium farmers to stop smuggling, organizing a naval task force to apprehend smugglers and ultimately devoting more and more of his time to antismuggling activities

and to strengthening the government's control over the farms. TeMechlen attracted a great deal of notice for his activities, but won few friends due to his abrasive personality and the fact that he was Eurasian.[34] While TeMechlen was a major voice pushing for the reform of the farming system in the Netherlands East Indies, other voices were calling for an abandonment of the farming system altogether. The anti-opium movement in Holland and a number of anticolonial novels turned Dutch opinion against the farms and built support for a government monopoly. Between 1894 and 1898, the opium farms of Java were replaced with a government-run monopoly.[35]

In British Malaya, colonial administrators seemed committed to the farming system despite the apparent success of the government-controlled monopolies in the Dutch and French colonies. By the middle of the first decade of the twentieth century, however, the same issues were beginning to influence them. The combination of moralistic pressures from the metropole, economic instability, a demand for rationalist administration, and growing concern about the economic and political power of the Chinese all led colonial administrators in Singapore and Penang to the same conclusions as the Dutch and French had come to before them. Following the collapse, in 1907, of a very large opium syndicate that had been organized by members of the powerful Khaw family of Penang, the colonial government decided to end the farming system in favor of a government monopoly. The farming system throughout British Malaya, as well as in Dutch Sumatra and Siam (many of whose farms had been held by Singaporean or Malayan Chinese syndicates), ceased, and government monopolies took over, in 1910, in all countries.[36]

The collapse of the Khaw syndicate is instructive of the relationship between Chinese capital and opium farming. Jennifer Cushman, whose work on this family is one of the classic studies of Chinese capitalism in Asia, has shown how the family reached a dominant financial position by the beginning of the twentieth century.[37] The Khaw clan had been founded by Khaw Soo Cheang, who came to Penang in about 1822 and began to trade in tin in southern Siam, particularly in Takuapa, Phang-nga, and ultimately Ranong. By the end of the nineteenth century, they had come to dominate the tin trade of the southern Siamese states and to hold most of the opium and gambling concessions of the region. The Khaws became the hereditary governors of the Siamese province of Ranong, taking the Thai family name of NaRanong.[38]

Under Khaw Sim Bee in the early twentieth century, the clan, organized as a large family kongsi based in Penang, attempted to create a major finan-

cial and industrial combination. Already controlling numerous mines and revenue farms, the family hoped to break through into the upper levels of the imperial economy. They organized a smelting company, an engineering company, steam dredges, an insurance company, and the Eastern Shipping Company. Part of the aim was to compete with major European firms such as the Straits Trading Company and the Peninsular and Oriental Shipping line, which then enjoyed a virtual monopoly of the long-distance trade of Malaya.[39] It appears that much of this rather hastily organized financial empire was rooted in the anticipated earnings of the extensive syndicate of opium farms controlled by another family member, Khaw Joo Choe. This was to be the cash cow of the entire enterprise. Unfortunately, when the economy went into a depression in 1907, Khaw Joo Choe went bankrupt, and the entire Khaw edifice began to disintegrate.[40]

It is also important to recall that in 1907 the Colonial Office had appointed a commission to study the opium-farming system in Malaya, and given its influence and that of the anti-opium crusaders, pressures were placed on the colonial government to abandon the farming system. In truth, the crusaders really wanted an end to all opium consumption in Malaya. They pointed to the Americans, who had banned opium altogether in their newly acquired colony in the Philippines, and to the treaty that Britain had just signed with China (in 1906) to gradually decrease imports of opium over the next decade with the aim of totally ending the opium trade. Unfortunately for the Southeast Asian colonies, the opium trade did not stop with the farming system.

With the collapse of the Khaw syndicate and the conclusion of their contract in 1909, the opium and spirit farms of British Malaya became part of the government monopoly in 1910.[41] This effectively marked the end of Chinese involvement with the legitimate side of Southeast Asia's opium economy. It is true that Chinese continued to use opium, which was now processed and distributed by the government. At the same time, Chinese secret societies and some of the groups retrenched by the monopoly system began to join the illegal trade, which included not only clandestine opium, but also the new injectable chemical derivatives and pills: morphine and heroin.

It is ironic that the anti-opium movement in the metropoles had such a decisive influence in bringing about the end of the farming system. The movement was launched and promoted by clergymen, missionaries, doctors, former civil servants, and some merchants. It struck a significant moral chord in Europe and America at a time when imperial governments were defending their global enterprises as projects that would improve the wel-

fare of the native peoples. Whether it was the Dutch "Ethical Policy" or the French "*mission civilisatrice*," or similar British or American policies, all of these discourses tended to characterize the Chinese as villains who were exploiting the native peoples. The colonial governments thus claimed they had a duty to protect their subjects from "foreign Asians."

They accomplished that end with the creation of government monopolies, which removed the farms from Chinese control. Henceforth the profits of opium sales to colonial subjects went directly into the coffers of colonial states. Despite the dire predictions of those who defended the farming system, the monopoly proved an almost embarrassing success. In 1909, the last year of the Singapore opium farm, the government collected $2,507,500 in rent. During 1910, the first year of the monopoly, the net profit to the government was only $1,785,387; by 1911, however, the net profit was $3,040,716, and by 1914, it had risen to $5,321,480. By 1920, the Straits Settlements as a whole (including Penang and Melaka) netted nearly $20 million from opium alone. Contrary to the wishes to the anti-opium lobby, the colonies continued to sell opium and to reap increasing and unprecedented profits from the monopolies until 1920, when the first attempts to actually reduce sales were put into practice. By 1928, the Straits Settlements netted only $14 million from opium sales, and due to the Great Depression, sales plunged to $9.7 million in 1929, and $8.8 million in 1930. Opium sales in Malaya were finally prohibited by the Colonial Office in 1943, after the colony had fallen into Japanese hands.[42]

Opium the Prime Commodity

For over a century, opium had been one of the major commodities of Southeast Asia's economy. It was an integral part of the colonial system in Asia, whether British, Dutch, French, or Spanish. Each colonial power, together with its Chinese allies, relied on opium for a major portion of their tax base and thus for their overall fiscal well-being. In Singapore and the Straits Settlements, opium regularly accounted for 40 to 60 percent of the local revenue. In other colonies, such as French Indochina and the Netherlands East Indies, it comprised 25 to 35 percent of revenues. If opium revenues had been subtracted from colonial budgets, it would likely have been fatal to the entire imperial structure, to say nothing of profits made by British India and in China itself.

More important, however, was opium's contribution to the overall economy of the region, particularly to the Chinese economy of Southeast Asia,

where it served three major roles. First, as what David Bello has called an "addictive consumable," it was one of the first mass consumer goods in the region. For Southeast Asian peasants as well as Chinese coolies, it served as one of the major incentives to enter the cash economy, to continue to work, and very often, to work until they dropped. Nothing kept a laborer working for a substandard wage more effectively than opium. And if the drug were made a part of his wages, he could be induced to work for practically nothing.

Opium was also the agency of capital accumulation for those Chinese who controlled the farms. All recognized opium's facility for concentrating capital and making it available to those who built the superstructure of the colonial economy. Opium capital financed the production of all of Southeast Asia's other major commodities: tin, pepper, gambier, gold, rice, and so on. As Wu Xiao An has shown in his essay on Kedah, the control of both opium and rice conferred great power on the Chinese allies of the sultan. Opium provided the foundation for the first great fortunes created by the Chinese taukehs. It backed fortunes that later created shipping lines, property empires, factories, banks, insurance companies, and all the other components of the Asian economy.

Finally, it helped to finance the accumulations of people and resources that became Asia's great cities. Singapore, Batavia, Bangkok, Saigon, Hong Kong, and Shanghai were all built on opium capital. The trading and exporting economies that centered on these cities all depended on opium. For a century, opium was the main business of Asia's great port cities.

Notes

1. Zhang Yangwen, *The Social Life of Opium in China* (Cambridge: Cambridge University Press, 2005).
2. See Tagliacozzo's essay in this volume.
3. Opium was generally eaten as pills, or drunk either as a kind of poppy-tea infusion, or dissolved in alcohol or mixed with milk. Ingestion of opium remained the preferred method of consumption among all users, except the Chinese and Southeast Asians, until well into the nineteenth century. Even then, the practice of smoking was generally seen as a peculiarly Chinese practice and was often considered to be an especially pernicious mode of consumption. Throughout the nineteenth century, most Europeans and South and Central Asian users continued to ingest the drug.
4. Engleberto D. Kaempfero, *Amoenitatum Exoticarum: Politico-Physico-Medicarum: Quibus continertur Variae Relationes, Observationes & Descriptiones: Rerum Persicarum & Ulterior's Asiae multa attentione in peregrinationibus per universum Orientem, collectae ab auctore Engleberto Kaemp-*

fero, D. (Lemgoviae: Henrici Wilhelmi Meyer I, 1712); Carl A. Trocki, *Opium, Empire and the Global Political Economy: A Study of the Asian Opium Trade* (New York: Routledge, 1999).

5. George B. Souza, "Trafficking Indian Opium to China: Portuguese and Chinese Trading Activities, ca.1750 to ca. 1830," paper presented at the Conference on Drugs and Empires: Narcotics, History and Modern Colonialism, University of Strathclyde, April 2003; (from Souza) Cf. Prakash, (1985) 145–56.

6. This was not necessarily an intuitive transition since it became necessary to refine raw opium further into what came to be known as *chandu* in Malay. It was also necessary to create a new kind of pipe, because chandu did not burn in the same manner as tobacco.

7. David A. Bello, *Opium and the Limits of Empire: Drug Prohibition in the Chinese Interior, 1729–1850* (Cambridge: Harvard University Asia Center, Harvard University Press, 2005).

8. David E. Owen, *British Opium Policy in China and India* (New Haven: Yale University Press, 1934).

9. Kwee Hui Kuan, *The Political Economy of Java's Northeast Coast, ca. 1740–1800: Elite Synergy* (Leiden: Brill, 2006).

10. James R. Rush, *Opium to Java: Revenue Farming and Chinese Enterprise in Colonial Indonesia, 1800–1910* (Ithaca: Cornell University Press, 1990).

11. Souza, "Trafficking Indian Opium to China," 13; Leonard Blussé, *Strange Company: Chinese Settlers, Mestizo Women and the Dutch in VOC Batavia* (Dordrecht: Floris, 1988). See also Blussé's essay in this volume.

12. Oliver W. Wolters, *Early Indonesian Commerce: A Study in the Origins of Srivijaya* (Ithaca: Cornell University Press, 1967); Wolters, *The Fall of Srivijaya in Malay History* (London: Lund Humphries, 1970).

13. Carl A. Trocki, *Opium and Empire: Chinese Society in Colonial Singapore 1800–1910* (Ithaca: Cornell University Press, 1990); Trocki, "Boundaries and Transgressions: Chinese Enterprise in Eighteenth- and Nineteenth-Century Southeast Asia," *Ungrounded Empires: The Cultural Politics of Modern Chinese Transnationalism*, ed. Aihwa Ong and D. M. Nonini (New York: Routledge, 1997), 61–85.

14. Leonard Blussé, "Batavia, 1619–1740: The Rise and Fall of a Chinese Colonial Town," *Journal of Southeast Asian Studies* 12 (March 1981): 159–78.

15. Trocki, "Boundaries and Transgressions."

16. Despite popular belief, opium does not automatically make one somnolescent and unproductive; it is quite possible to continue working while under its influence.

17. Rush, *Opium to Java.*

18. George W. Earl, "Narrative of a Journey from Singapore to the West Coast of Borneo in the Schooner Stamford in the Year 1834, with an Account of a Journey to Montradoh, the Capital of a Chinese Colony in Possession of the Principal Gold Mines," *Journal of the Royal Asiatic Society* 3.5 (1836): 1–24.

19. P. P. Lee, *Chinese Society in Nineteenth Century Singapore: A Socioeconomic Analysis* (Kuala Lumpur: Oxford University Press, 1978).

20. Mary Somers Heidhues, "Company Island: A Note on the History of Belitung," *Indonesia* 51 (April 1991): 1–43; W. Blythe, *The Impact of Chinese Secret Societies in Malaya:*

A Historical Study (London: Oxford University Press, 1969); James C. Jackson, "Mining in Eighteenth Century Bangka: The Pre-European Exploitation of a 'Tin Island,'" Pacific Viewpoint 10.2 (1969): 28–54; James C. Jackson, Chinese in the West Borneo Goldfields: A Study in Cultural Geography (Hull: University of Hull, 1970); Trocki, Opium and Empire.

21. Walter F. Vella, Siam under Rama III, 1824–1851 (Locust Valley, N.Y.: J. J. Augustin for the Association for Asian Studies, 1957); Chao Phraya Bodindecha Singasena, Annam Sayam Yut (Bangkok: Rong Pim Aksorn Borigan, 1971, BE 2514).

22. Jackson, Chinese in the West Borneo Goldfields; Trocki, Opium and Empire; Suehiro Akira, Capital Accumulation in Thailand, 1855–1985 (Chiang Mai: Silkworm, 1996).

23. Trocki, Opium and Empire.

24. Michael R. Godley, Mandarin Capitalists from Nanyang: Overseas Chinese Enterprise in the Modernization of China, 1893–1911 (Cambridge: Cambridge University Press, 1981); Jennifer W. Cushman, Family and State: The Formation of a Sino-Thai Tin-mining Dynasty, 1797–1932 (Singapore: Oxford University Press, 1991); Michael R. Godley, "Thio Thiau Siat's Network," The Rise and Fall of Revenue Farming: Business Elites and the Emergence of the Modern State in Southeast Asia, ed. John Butcher and Howard Dick (London: St. Martin's, 1993), 262–66.

25. Rush, Opium to Java; S. Akira, Capital Accumulation in Thailand.

26. John Crawfurd, Journal of an Embassy from the Governor-General of India to the Courts of Siam and Cochin China: Exhibiting a View of the Actual State of Those Kingdoms (Singapore: Oxford University Press, 1987).

27. Ibid., 549.

28. Lucy Cheung Tsui Ping, The Opium Monopoly in Hong Kong, 1844–1887 (Hong Kong: University of Hong Kong, 1986), 200; Trocki, Opium and Empire; Chantal Descours-Gatin, Quand l'opium finançait la colonisation en Indochine: L'elaboration de la regie generale de l'opium (1860–1914) (Paris: Editions L'Hartmann, 1992) (Ouvrage publié avec le concours du Centre National des Lettres).

29. The three brothers, Tan Keng Seng, Tan Keng Hoon, and Tan Keng Ho, were listed as contractors to the government and owned premises located on the Quai de Commerce in Saigon. The following year Tan Keng Hoon was listed as manager of the opium farm. The Tan brothers, like Banhap, were all Singapore-born Hokkien Babas. Chronicles and Directories for China, Japan and the Philippines 1872; Chronicles and Directories for China, Japan and the Philippines 1873. I am grateful to Dr. Li Tana for supplying me with these references.

30. Cheung, The Opium Monopoly in Hong Kong, 1844–1887, 200; Christopher Munn, "The Hong Kong Opium Revenue, 1845–1885," Opium Regimes: China, Britain and Japan, 1839–1952, ed. Timothy Brook and Bob Tadashi Wakabayashi (Berkeley: University of California Press, 2000), 105–26.

31. For the full story, see Trocki, Opium and Empire.

32. Descours-Gatin, Quand l'opium finançait la colonisation en Indochine: L'elaboration de la regie generale de l'opium (1860–1914) (Paris: Editions L'Hartmann, 1992) (Ouvrage publié avec le concours du Centre National des Lettres).

33. Phillipe Le Failler, "Le mouvement international anti-opium et l'Indochine, 1906–

1940," *History* (Provence: Université de Provence, 1993), 418, and appendices, 83; Hakiem Nankoe, Jean-Claude Gerlus, and Martin J. Murray, "The Origins of the Opium Trade and the Opium Regies in Colonial Indochina," *The Rise and Fall of Revenue Farming: Business Elites and the Emergence of the Modern State in Southeast Asia*, ed. John Butcher and Howard Dick (London: St. Martin's, 1993), 182–95.

34. Rush, *Opium to Java.*

35. Ibid.

36. Trocki, *Opium and Empire.*

37. Cushman, *Family and State.*

38. Ibid., 3–11.

39. Ibid., 62–87.

40. Trocki, *Opium and Empire*; Trocki, *Opium, Empire and the Global Political Economy.*

41. Other excisable drugs under the monopoly included *bhang*, a cannabis preparation, and coconut toddy, which was imbibed.

42. Trocki, *Opium and Empire.*

PART II ~~~ Precolonial

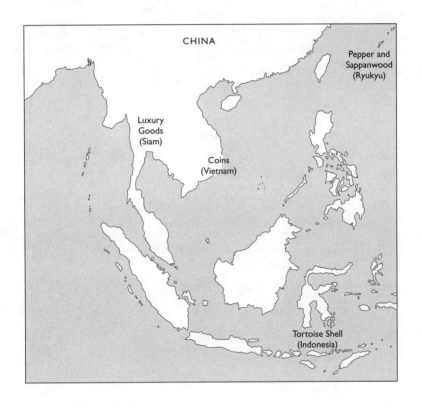

THE *LIDAI BAOAN* AND THE RYUKYU MARITIME TRIBUTARY TRADE NETWORK WITH CHINA AND SOUTHEAST ASIA, THE FOURTEENTH TO SEVENTEENTH CENTURIES

~~~~~ Takeshi Hamashita

The Ryukyu Kingdom (present-day Okinawa) was located at the intersection of the South China Sea and the East China Sea, facing South China and Kyushu. Long before the Ryukyu Kingdom period (1429–1879), the Ryukyu Kingdom was already alert to the advantages and opportunities offered by the sea and put them to use in its trade with East and Southeast Asia. Under the Ryukyu Kingdom, missions were sent to Southeast Asia to obtain goods for its tributary trade with China. Even after it was invaded, in 1609, by the Satsuma domain of Tokugawa-period Japan, Ryukyu continued to dispatch tribute envoys to Qing China. At the same time, it sent envoys to Tokugawa shoguns in Edo (present-day Tokyo) and maintained relations with Korea (see map 1).

The period from the late fourteenth century to the early sixteenth century was one of the most prosperous in the history of the Ryukyu Kingdom, due in large measure to the far-flung trading activities of its people, who traversed the East and Southeast Asian waters as enterprising agents of entrepôt trade for countries bordering those waters. Not only were the Ryukyuans in contact with China and Japan, but they also established and maintained relations with Korea and Southeast Asian countries. The story of the Ryukyu merchants' trading enterprises constitutes an important chapter not only in Ryukyuan history, but also in the history of the tributary trade system in East and Southeast Asia as a whole. This account draws on the primary historical source on the Ryukyus, the Lidai Baoan (Rekidai Hoan in Japanese), or "precious documents of successive generations."[1]

The current Lidai Baoan represents a fraction of the original archive compiled under the auspices of the Ryukyu Kingdom. While incomplete, the

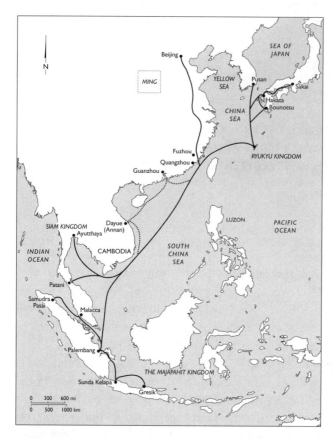

Map 1 Ryukyuan trade and tribute network. A redrawn map based on the general map outlining trade routes of the Ryukyu Kingdom, fourteenth century to mid-sixteenth century. *Source: The Rekidai Hoan: An Introduction to Documents of the Ryukyu Kingdom*, Okinawa Archives, Okinawa Prefectural Board of Education, March 2003.

surviving documents nevertheless provide a partial record of diplomatic correspondence exchanged between 1424 and 1867, encompassing a period stretching from the third year of the reign of the Ryukyu king Sho Hashi to the twentieth year of the reign of King Sho Tai, the last monarch to rule the Ryukyu Kingdom before its dissolution and incorporation into the Japanese state during the Meiji Restoration of January 1868. The collection thus spans the entire period from the twenty-second year of the reign of Emperor Eiraku (Yong Le) of the Ming Dynasty to the sixth year of Emperor Dochi (Tong Zhi) of the Qing Dynasty.

The *Lidai Baoan* is a compilation of manuscripts, written in Chinese, relating to Ryukyuan contacts with China, Korea, and eight Southeast Asian countries (or more precisely, port towns), covering a 444-year period, from 1424 to 1867 (see fig. 1). The countries are Siam, Malacca, Palembang, Java, Sumatra, Sunda-Kelapa, Patani, and Annam. *Lidai Baoan* documents shed new light on historical events and developments in all these countries (see

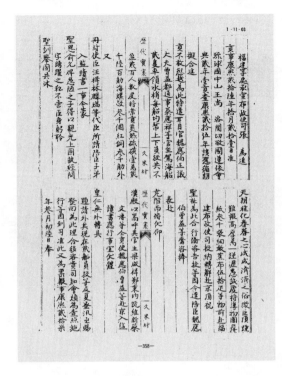

1 · 11 · 03

—358—

Figure 1 Letter from Lieutenant-Governor of Fujian to King of Ryukyu on 21st day, 12th month, 26th year of Kangxi. *Source: Lidai Baoan*, Okinawa Prefecture Library, 1992, 1:358.

table 1). In particular, they supplement and correct historical accounts relating to South Sea countries, where the activities of Ryukyu merchants have been entirely ignored in existing chronicles and historical records.[2]

The documents of the *Lidai Baoan* relate principally to the diplomatic relationship between the Ryukyu Kingdom and China, which developed from contacts initiated by Emperor Taizu in 1372. These initial contacts led to the subsequent development of an envoy-tribute relationship in which Ryukyu administrations offered loyalty and goods to the Chinese imperium in exchange for diplomatic recognition and external protection. As a result, the kingdom became a subordinate member of a regional security and trading alliance dependent on Chinese military and economic hegemony. In this essay, I explore the trading history between Ryukyu Kingdom and China and Southeast Asia.

Trading Relations between Ryukyu and Siam

Merchant ships (*manaban*) from Southeast Asia came to be a familiar sight in the Ryukyu Kingdom during the latter half of the fourteenth century (see fig. 2). In response, Ryukyuan traders began to engage in return expeditions.

Table 1 List of Ryukyuan Ships Dispatched to Southeast Asian Ports

Year	Xianluo	Palembang	Jawa	Melaka	Samudera	Patani	Annam	Sunda
				Destination				
1425	OO							
1426	O							
1427	OO							
1428	O	O						
1429	OO							
1430		O	O					
1431	O							
1432	OO							
1433	OOO							
1434	OO							
1435	O							
1436	O							
1437	OO							
1438	OO	O	O					
1439	O							
1440		O	O					
1441			OO					
1442	O		O					
* * * * * Lacunae in sources * * * * *								
1463				O	O			
1464	XO			O				
1465	O			O				
1466				O				
1467				O	O			
1468				O	O			
1469	O			O				
1470				O				
1471				X X				

Table 1 Continued

	Destination							
Year	Xianluo	Palembang	Jawa	Melaka	Samudera	Patani	Annam	Sunda
★ ★ ★ ★ ★ *Lacunae in sources (continued)* ★ ★ ★ ★ ★								
1472	X			OO				
1475				O				
1478	O							
1479	X			O				
1480	O			O				
1481	OO							
1490						O		
1492								
1498						O		
1503				X				
1509	OO			O			O	
1510				O				
1511				O				
1512	O							
1513	O							O
1514	O							
1515	O					O		
1516	O					O		
1517	O							
1518	OO							O
1519						O		
1520	O					O		
1521	O							
1522	X							
1526	O					O		
1529	O					O		
1530						O		

Table 1 Continued

				Destination				
Year	Xianluo	Palembang	Jawa	Melaka	Samudera	Patani	Annam	Sunda

★ ★ ★ ★ ★ Lacunae in sources (continued) ★ ★ ★ ★ ★

Year	Xianluo	Palembang	Jawa	Melaka	Samudera	Patani	Annam	Sunda
1533	O							
1536	O						O	
1537	O							
1538	O							
1540	O							
1541	O							
1543							O	
1550	O							
1554	O							
1564	O							
1570	O							

Number of ships sent

Xianluo	58	Melaka	20	Annam	1
Palembang	4	Samudera	3	Sunda	2
Jawa	6	Patani	11		

O: Ships that safely returned
X: Ships that wrecked

Source: Takara Kurayoshi, *Ryukyu no Jidai: Ooinaru Rekishizou wo Motomete* [Ryukyu's centuries: In quest of a new image of its history] (Tokyo: 1980), 116–17.

Records of these expeditions first appeared in the *Lidai Baoan* in the fifteenth century, during which time abundant references were made to contacts with Xianluo (Siam), Patani, Melaka (Malacca), Palembang, Jawa (Java), Samudera (Sumatra), Annam (Vietnam), and Sunda (see table 1). Pioneers of this trade with South Sea countries were accompanied on their voyages by letters containing the king's seal and gifts in anticipation of establishing formal trade relations with sister ports.

The entrepôt trade that subsequently developed involved the export of goods such as Japanese swords and gold, which were traded for ivory, tin,

Figure 2 Ryukyuan tributary ship at Naha Port. *Source: Tozen-zu* (Tributary Ship), Okinawa Prefectural Library.

jewels, pepper, spices, and caesalpinia sappan for medicine or dyes; such goods were often re-exported to China, Japan, or Korea. Many of the Ryukyu Kingdom's Southeast Asian trading partners shared a similar tributary relationship with the Ming Dynasty, and as a result Chinese became a lingua franca for official communication and trade negotiations.

The earliest document in the *Lidai Baoan* pertaining to Ryukyu-Siam relations is a dispatch dated Hongxi 1 (1425), but communication between the two territories is presumed to have begun in the late 1380s. The dispatch of 1425 states, "From our royal great-grandfather's time through the times of our grandfather and father down to this day, we have frequently dispatched our envoys." The great-grandfather referred to is King Satto, the grandfather of King Bunei and father of King Shisho. It was in Hongwu 4 (1371) that Siam sent its first tribute to China, after it had received the envoy and imperial rescript from Emperor Taizu of the Ming. This was in the reign of Somdet

Phra Baramarajadhiraj, the third ruler in the Ayutthaya dynasty of Siam. According to the Korean record, *Koryosa* (History of Koryo), a Siamese envoy, Nai Goung, came to Korea in the third year of the reign of King Kongyang (1391), having left Siam in the summer of 1388 and stayed in Japan for about a year before traveling to Korea. Again, in the second year of T'aejo of Chosôn (1394), another Siamese envoy, Nai Zhang Sidao, arrived in Korea. As he sailed home, Japanese pirates raided his ship, and he was obliged to return to Korea the following year. He left Korea the same year, accompanied by Korean envoys returning the Siamese courtesy.

Siamese interaction with Ryukyu must have begun about the same time that Siam established relations with Japan and Korea. For some time after King Satto of Chūzan began paying tribute to Ming China, sulphur and horses were taken as tribute, but from 1390, the tribute cargo included pepper, sappanwood, and other products of South Sea origin. It is presumed that these products were introduced as a result of Ryukyuan contact with Siam.

Judging from the documents in the *Lidai Baoan*, it appears that while Ryukyuan ships went to Siam, no Siamese ships came to Ryukyu during this period of early Ryukyuan-Siamese contact. The Siamese entrusted their messages to the Ryukyuan envoys coming to their country, and there was no envoy dispatched from Siam to Ryukyu. A Siamese ship visited Ryukyu in 1479, but this was under special circumstances and did not constitute a case of official relations.

Prior to the earliest *Lidai Baoan* documents from the third decade of the fifteenth century, however, there is evidence of a slightly different Ryukyuan-Siamese relationship. In 1404, the provincial government of Fujian wrote to the Chinese emperor about the accidental arrival of a Ryukyu-bound Siamese ship, whereupon Emperor Yongle replied that Siamese intercourse with Ryukyu was praiseworthy in relations among the barbarian countries. He ordered the provincial government to have the ship repaired and provided food for the Siamese, so that they could proceed to their own country or to Ryukyu, whichever they wished to do, after waiting for a favorable wind.[3] This episode indicates that Siamese ships were traveling to Ryukyu early on. As was the case with Siamese contact with Japan and Korea, Siamese contact with Ryukyu began as a result of the commercial activities of Chinese merchants living in Siam and other countries in the South Sea region. The influence of Chinese merchants living in these areas declined temporarily during the first half of the fifteenth century. With this decline, as ships from the south ceased coming, Ryukyuans headed toward the South Seas. The

decline of Chinese influence seems to have been a potent factor instigating Ryukyuan seafaring in Eastern waters.

The nature of Ryukyuan missions across the seas can be discerned from documents exchanged between Ryukyu and Siam.

Lidai Baoan, vol. 40, doc. no. 8
The King of Chūzan, Country of Ryukyu, declares with reference to tributary affairs.

This country has nothing that is appropriate as an article of tribute, and for this reason we are especially dispatching Chief Envoy Nanzatu and others to lead men and take ships with a cargo of porcelains, to proceed to your productive lands to purchase such goods as pepper and sappanwood, and then to return to our country to prepare our tributary needs.

They shall also take some presents we have specially prepared for presentation to you to convey our sincerity. We hope that you will accept them. We would like to request that the members of the mission now departing be allowed to obtain sappanwood and other goods through mutually satisfactory arrangements and return to the country speedily with the wind.

We desire that all within the four seas be regarded as brothers and that intercourse among us be maintained forever.

We list our presents below. Let this dispatch be given to the addressee.

The following goods:

[Woven-]gold satin	5 bolts
Ornamental satin	20 bolts
Swords	4 [5?]
Fans	20
Sulphur	2,500 jin
Big blue vases	20
Small blue vases	400
Small blue bowls	2,000

Dispatch to the Country of Siam
Xuande 4/10/10 [6 November 1429]

Lidai Baoan, vol. 39, doc. no. 1
The King of Chūzan, Country of Ryukyu, has received a dispatch from the Country of Siam in the sixth month of Xuande 5 [1430] [in which it was stated:]

We have read [the dispatch from Ryukyu, which stated:] "With reference to the matter of tribute to the Great Ming and other matters, we have few goods which are appropriate [as articles of tribute], and we still suffer great inconvenience. We are specially dispatching our envoy Nanzatu Utchi and others aboard a seagoing ship, with a cargo of porcelains and local products, to proceed to the country [Siam] and purchase such goods as pepper and sappanwood, and then to return to our country to prepare our needs. We have also prepared our presents for you."

We have received this dispatch. Heretofore, you have purchased goods to make [necessary] preparations. Your [present envoys] are now departing at this convenient time with a favorable wind. Therefore, we list our return presents below and inform you through this dispatch. Let this dispatch be given to the addressee.

The goods are as follows:

Sappanwood	3000 jin
Red oiled cotton cloth	20 bolts
Variegated velvet carpets	2
Soft Western silk	1 length

Dispatch to the King of Chūzan, Country of Ryukyu
Xuande 5/3/21 [13 April 1430]

Both the Ryukyuan and the Siamese king recognized each other very clearly and understood the purposes of trade. Both expected trading activities under tributary relations with Ming China, and the correspondences between the two kings were regular and formal.

Ryukyu ships searching for tributary commodities such as pepper and sappanwood in the South China Sea had to understand the changing networks of trade and had to find more lucrative and safer trade partners and trading ports.

Trading Relations between Ryukyu and Java

Chinese people had begun to reside in South Sea countries and to develop commercial enterprises there from about the late Yuan and early Ming periods. They settled in such places as Palembang and Siam, and probably also in Java. The time for Chinese settlement in Java may have been the latter part of the reign of Hayam Wurch (1350–1389), which was the golden age of the Majapahit dynasty in Java. The Chinese in South Sea countries were the driving force for the opening of trade relations. It is around the end of the four-

teenth century when trade started between those countries and countries in the north like China, Japan, Korea, and Ryukyu. As for Ryukyu, Chinese residents there also served as important trade and navigation personnel, and contributed greatly to the beginning and continuation of the country's intercourse with South Sea countries, as well as with China.

Ryukyuan contact with Java began in 1430. It is not apparent from the dispatch of that date that this was the first mission, but the Ryukyuan king's dispatch dated Chengtong 3 (1438) says that in Xuande 5 (1430), the Ryukyuan court sent its first contingent to pay courtesy to the country. A dispatch to Java dated Chengtong 5 (1440) mentions that in Xuande 5 presents were prepared and envoys dispatched to the said country for the first time.[4] The country named was Java.

In Ryukyuan history, King Shō Hashi of Chūzan is recorded to have subjugated King Tarumi of Sannan in Southern Okinawa in 1429 and thus effected the unification of the whole island under his control. In 1428, relations were opened with Palembang, which in the late fourteenth century became a vassal state of the Majapahit dynasty on the island of Java. Palembang was a port town where Chinese lived and carried on trade, and Chinese also lived and traded actively on the island of Java. The well-known prosperity of Palembang as well as of Javanese ports such as Gresik, Surabaya, and Tuban, located near the capital of the state of the Majapahit dynasty in Eastern Java, was largely the result of the business activities of many Chinese living in those places. It is easily understood that the Ryukyuan people voyaging to the South Seas took every opportunity to reach Java through Chinese trade networks.

There are six documents relating to Java in the *Lidai Baoan*, and they are all official dispatches from Ryukyu covering the period from 1430 to 1442. Chinese people were influential in maintaining relations between China and Java and other South Sea countries in which they resided, as well as in maintaining Ryukyuan relations with China. International relations in East Asia at this time were conducted around China based on the Chinese tributary system, and Chinese living overseas naturally played a significant role in this system.

The Javanese king at the time of the opening of Ryukyuan relations was a man mentioned in Chinese records as Yang Wei-xi-sha. It is recorded that in the ninth month of Hongwu 3 (1370), the Javanese king known in Chinese transcription as Si-li Pa-ta-la-p'u complied with the summons of Ming Taizu and sent his envoy to pay tribute to the Chinese emperor. Later, in Yongle 1

(1403), the "western" king of Java, by the name of Tu-ma-pan, sent a mission to offer felicitations on the enthronement of Emperor Yongle, and soon the "eastern" king of Java, Pen-ling-ta-hai, followed suit. Around this time there were two kings in Java, the eastern and western kings, who were rivals.

At the time of Zheng He's visit to Java in Yongle 4 (1406), a battle occurred in which the eastern king was defeated and his power destroyed. Some 170 soldiers under Zheng He's command, going ashore to do some trading, were killed by men of the western king. Later, probably at the time of Zheng He's departure from Java, the western king dispatched a mission to China, and it is recorded that the king offered apologies to the Chinese for the crime committed by his men.[5]

In Yongle 13 (1415), a tributary mission was dispatched in the name of the western king, Yang Wei-xi-sha, and this name is said to have been the new name adopted by Tu-ma-pan.[6] In Chengtong 8 (1443), Political Counsel Zhangyan of Canton wrote to the emperor that the almost yearly payment of tribute by Yang Wei-xi-sha was too burdensome because visits by Javanese incurred great expenses for receptions on the part of the Chinese. Accordingly, a decree was issued to the effect that Java, too, had to observe the rule of one tribute mission every three years like all other foreign countries sending missions to China.[7]

Formation of Tributary Missions to China

As a general rule, the upper echelon of a tributary embassy consisted of the following personnel: the envoy representing the king of a tributary state, his assistant or deputy envoy, interpreters, the general manager in charge of the ship's cargo (known in Chinese as *caifu* or *zhiku*; *zaifu*, *chokko*), the pilot of the ship (*huochong*; *kacho*), and his assistant.[8] As far as tributary states were concerned, this official and private trade in goods was likely to have been the core of the tributary system.[9] These goods were either those belonging to the king of the tributary state, those of the king and several powerful local chieftains of that state, or those traded by merchants of the state individually.[10] A similar structure of tributary mission existed from Ryukyu to other tributary countries such as Malacca. It should also be noted that the Ryukyu king issued a certificate with a similar form with it, and this exemplified the tally system from Ming China.[11]

> *Lidai Baoan*, vol. 42, doc. no. 3 (1509 Malacca)
> King Sho Shin of Chūzan, the Country Ryukyu, in reference to tributary affairs, now makes this known. This country, being deficient in products

and lacking tributary goods, still suffers great inconvenience. For this reason, we are now dispatching Chief Envoy Kamadu, Interpreter Ko Ken, and others aboard a seagoing ship bearing the designation K'ang, with a cargo of porcelain and other goods, to proceed to the productive land of Malacca to purchase such products as sappanwood and pepper through mutually satisfactory arrangements, and then to return to the country to make preparations for the presentation of tribute to the Celestial Court of the Great Ming in a subsequent year.

There is no special document, however, on which the members of this mission now departing can rely, and it is deeply feared that they may encounter the inconvenience of investigations and obstructions by officials along the way. Accordingly the Royal Court has now issued a certificate stamped with a seal bearing half each of the character Hsuan and the number 174, to be received and borne by Chief Envoy Kamadu and others in proceeding on their mission.

In the event of investigation by guards at landings and by coastal patrol officers in the course of the voyage, it is requested that the mission be released and that no obstacles that might cause delay and inconvenience be put in its way. Let this certificate be given to the envoys.

> It is now stated [that the mission consists of]:
> One chief envoy: Kamadu
> Two deputy envoys: Manyuku, Gurami
> Two interpreters: Ko Ken, Ko Ga
> Pilot: Ryo Jitsu
> General manager of the ship: Mabuta
> No. of personnel including crew: 150 persons

Cheng-te 4/8/18 [2 September 1509]
The above certificate has been issued for and received by Chief Envoy Kamadu, Interpreter Ko Ken, and others.
Certificate

According to the list of Javanese envoys, most of the chief envoys in the *Lidai Baoan* had the title of *alie*. In the intercalary sixth month of Chengtong 1 (1436), the Javanese king's envoy Ma Yongliang is said to have reported that previously he had been appointed *badi* and sent to China to present tribute, at which time he was given a silver sash; and that since he had now come to pay tribute again, this time in the capacity of *alie*, he requested a golden sash.[12] He also requested silver sashes for Badi Nan Wu and others in his company.

Emperor Yingzong granted all his requests.[13] The rank of badi (or *bazhe*) appears to have been below that of alie.

About this time, another envoy from Java, Gao Naisheng, came to China. He requested that ship carpenters repair his wrecked ship, while promising to take responsibility for providing necessary materials and provisions for the work. Also found is the name of another Javanese envoy, Man Yong, who had the title of caifu bazhe. Gao and Man may have come to China on a different ship than did Ma Yongliang, but the two missions arrived at the same time. The title caifu bazhe may indicate a badi acting in the capacity of caifu; that is, a general manager of the ship with the title of badi. Man Yong was a Chinese. He was originally known as Hong Mouzi and had been a resident fisherman of the district of Longqi in Zhangzhou Prefecture of Fujian Province, but was later taken prisoner by pirates, from whom he finally escaped and fled to Java. There he changed his name to reflect the Javanese style, and he was included as a member of the tributary embassy to China. In China, he requested permission to return to his original home and former occupation, whereupon Emperor Yingzong appointed him a civil servant, providing him with coolies and provisions and sending him back to his native district.[14]

Ma Yongliang came to China as a tributary envoy of Java again in Chengtong 3 (1438), also in the years 7 and 11 (1442 and 1446). In 1438, he was accompanied by the interpreters Liang Yin and Nan Wendan; they, like Ma, were men of Longqi in Fujian Province who had accidentally landed in Java during a fishing trip. In the sixth month of Chengtong 3, all three men, Ma, Liang, and Nan, were permitted to return to their native district, and Ma and Nan in particular were advised to build ancestral halls for the observance of ceremonies in honor of their ancestors.[15]

The Javanese tributary envoy of Chengtong 2 (1437), Ya Mizhe, had acted as interpreter in missions dispatched during the periods of Yongle and Xuande (1403–1435) and had been given a silver sash by the Ming court. Now, in Chengtong 2, he requested a golden sash by virtue of having been promoted to the rank of alie, and asked also for a silver sash for Huang Qi, his company's interpreter. Both requests were granted. Both Ya Mizhe and Huang Qi were also Chinese.[16]

In Chengtong 11 (1446), Bazhe Ma Mo and Chen Mawu came to China as Javanese envoys at the time of Ma Yongliang's visit. Also known are the names of Bianshi Bazhe, Li Fu, and the interpreter Li Ai.[17] Again, in Tianshun 4 (1460), in the suite of the Javanese envoy Alie Guoxin were the interpreter Bazhe Ma Mo and Caifu Bazhe Ma Wu.[18] All those mentioned here, possibly including Guo Xin, were Chinese.

Among the Javanese envoys coming during the periods of Yongle and Xuande, Bazhe Chen Weida, Li Qi, Li Tianshan, and others may have been Chinese, but it is difficult to ascertain the race of many of those chief envoys who had the title of alie. At any rate, many Chinese lived in Java and were appointed as chief envoys under the title of alie, and it appears that other important positions in a tributary mission, including interpreter, general manager, and pilot, were also held by Chinese.

In Hongchi 14 (1501), there came drifting to the coast of Tianbo District in Guangdong Province the ship of a Javanese envoy calling himself Naihe-dayamu. He and his men were sent to Guangzhou (Canton), where they were treated as members of a tributary mission and given provisions. A report was sent to the capital, and it was soon brought to light that Naihe-dayamu was a Javanese whose real name was Gengyisu, and that two men, named Li Zhaotie and Li Tingfang, both natives of Jiangxi Province in China, had conspired with a Fujianese by the name of Zhou Cheng and others to conduct secret overseas trade, for the purpose of which they had incited Gengyisu to load goods in Java to be taken to Canton. The false tally sheet carried by Gengyisu led to the disclosure of this conspiracy.

Gengyisu was the son of the Javanese chieftain Badi Niaoxin, who had given his son a tally bearing the Chinese character Zhao and the number 3 torn from the ledger book. This was the tally Gengyisu took for his voyage to China.

Under the tally system of the Ming as applied to Java, one hundred tallies were prepared, each bearing the designation Zhao, which was the first of the two characters for Java, and also two hundred tallies, each bearing the character Wa, the second of the characters for Java. Two copies each of two ledger books for the respective types of tallies were also prepared. One copy of the Zhao ledgers and one hundred Wa tally sheets were given to Java; another copy of the Zhao ledgers, one hundred Zhao tallies, one copy of the Wa ledgers, and one hundred Wa tallies were kept at the Board of Rites in Beijing; and another copy of the Wa ledgers was placed at the Provincial Office in Canton, which was the designated port of entry for Javanese ships. Each tally bore the stamp of a character and a number, each of which was split in half, and each ledger book contained one hundred tallies bound together. The tally brought by a Javanese envoy was to be checked against its ledger in China, and the tally carried by a Chinese against its ledger in Java, and in this way the authenticity of an embassy was verified. A new series of tallies and their ledger books were issued for the period of each reign in China. The fact that Gengyisu carried the tally bearing the character Zhao and the num-

ber 3 torn from the ledger naturally served to disclose the ruse. The Board of Rites held that the correct tally to be presented by the Javanese at this time was the one bearing the character Wa and the number 12. Hence it can be assumed that eleven of the tallies issued for use in the Hongchi period (1488–1505) had been used before that time. (The remaining tallies of the Chenghua period [1465–1487] had been returned to China by the first Javanese mission in the following period, Hongchi, according to the procedure stipulated by the Chinese for unused tallies.) On the back of each tally were entered the number and names of the men aboard the ship, the number of items in the ship's cargo, and the like.

The sham tally brought by Gengyisu bore the names of 109 Chinese and foreign people, together with a list of goods like pepper and garuwood. These names show that a Javanese tributary embassy in those days included people with Javanese names and those with Chinese names.[19] And yet, though carrying Javanese names, many persons occupying important positions were in fact Chinese.

Chinese and their descendants were important members of the tributary embassies of Ryukyu and South Sea countries, and the roles to which they were appointed had been more or less fixed since the middle of the fifteenth century. In the case of Ryukyu, the general manager of a tributary ship who took charge of its goods was appointed from among native Ryukyuans. In the case of Java, however, such an official seems to have been chosen from among Chinese, and in this sense it can be assumed that direct Chinese influence was considerable in the conduct of Javanese tributary relations with China, more so than in the case of Ryukyuan tributary relations. What has been described above generally holds true for tributary relations which other South Sea countries, like Siam, Malacca, and Palembang had with China, as well as with Ryukyu.[20]

Ryukyu Trade Networks: Tribute Trade and Private Trade by the Ryukyu King

According to the First Collection of the *Lidai Baoan*, Ryukyu engaged in commercial transactions with various parts of Southeast Asia such as Siam, Palembang, Java, Malacca, Sumatra, Annam, and Patani. It is likely that Japan, Korea, and China were added to these Southeast Asian countries, thereby linking Ryukyu in an extensive trade network.

The trade network, or what may be called the Ryukyu network, was founded on the Ryukyu tribute trade with China. Its trade with Southeast Asia was aimed at obtaining pepper and sappanwood, which were presented as tributes to China. This trade network had two distinctive features: that

trade with Siam and other Southeast Asian countries was vigorous between the early fifteenth century and the mid-sixteenth century; and that, as far as the records of Lidai Baoan show, the trade with Southeast Asia declined, while the trade with China and Japan increased.

This phenomenon prompts two questions. What happened to the trade with Southeast Asia after the mid-sixteenth century? And what was the nature of the trade with Manila and Luzon in the context of Ryukyu trade with Southeast Asia? In examining these questions, one must take into account that the Ryukyus were involved in two trade routes between South China and Southeast Asia. One route ran along the island chains on the eastern side of the South China Sea, from Luzon to Sulu, and the other stretched along the coast of the continent on the western side of the South China Sea, from Siam to Malacca.

The eastern route started from Quanzhou (or Fuzhou) and connected the Ryukyus, Taiwan, and Sulu. This route carried not only the trade with Southeast Asian tributary states, but also, from the sixteenth century onward, the trade with Spain centered at Manila—exchanging silk for silver—and the trade with the Dutch East India Company centered on Taiwan. At the same time, the route ran farther north from Fuzhou, connecting with soybean and soybean-meal trade from North China. Thus the Ryukyus mediated the north-south trade along China's eastern coast.

The western route, starting from Guangzhou, runs along the coast linking major Southeast Asian tributary states, including Siam, Malacca, and Sumatra. Major items traded on this route included rice, marine products, and spices. This route was therefore closely related to food production in the South China area, including Guangdong, Guangxi, and Hunan. Specifically, rice and sugar imported from Southeast Asia played a key role in supplementing such productions in South China. Related to this point, in 1666, ninety-six years after records of official trade with Southeast Asia stopped appearing in the Lidai Baoan, King Sho Shitsu applied for pepper, which was not produced locally, to be excluded from the list of tribute goods. The Chinese court approved. This suggests that over the preceding century, the Chinese were able to obtain pepper through non-official channels. Behind this development lay the increase in China's rice trade with Siam, which brought more merchants from the Chinese coast to Southeast Asia. As a result, the Ryukyuans had to obtain pepper and sappanwood either by competing with the Chinese merchants trading in Southeast Asia or by direct purchase from them (thus increasing their uncertainty and costs.)

This can also be explained by the record of annual extra export of pepper

and sappanwood by the Ryukyu king to China under the title of "attached commodities." To fulfill the demand for these so-called "attached commodities," the Ryukyu king continually needed to obtain pepper and sappanwood in ways other than trade missions to Southeast Asian countries.

Trading Relations between Ryukyu and Manila

In 1571, an expeditionary force led by the Spanish general Miguel Lopez de Legazpi entered Manila and made it the seat of government. At that time, Luzon and Sulu were already bound in tributary relationship with China, with their own Chinatown and Japanese-town. When Spanish galleons connected Manila with the American continents, large amounts of silver flowed into Asia. In return, the New World obtained Chinese raw silk, pepper, and other special products from Southeast Asia.

In 1494, as stipulated in the Treaty of Tordesillas, Spain and Portugal split the world in half. The whole of central south America, not including Brazil, came under Spain, while Asia was basically given to Portugal. After setting up base in Manila, Spain could not trade directly with Asia. But she recruited Chinese merchants to participate in China-Manila trade, exchanging silver for raw silk. It is likely that Ryukyu merchants also participated in this trade, transporting into China not the usual products from Southeast Asia, but silver transiting Luzon. Ryukyu was cited fifty-nine times in Spanish records over 220 years of trade with Ryukyu (from 1519 to 1738), including the name and location of Ryukyu; the locations of exchange and trade; the shapes and forms of the various islands and their living conditions; and Ryukyu's relations with Spain, Japan, and China. Besides these, the tributary relationship with China and the Satsuma invasion were also mentioned.

A number of records document the silver–raw silk trade between Ryukyu and Luzon. During the sixteenth century, the Spanish recorded on Ryukyu that every year six to eight Ryukyuan junks called at Luzon islands and that the Ryukyu people there were presumed to be Chinese. Depending on the situation, there may not have been a contradiction between Ryukyuan and Chinese because many Hokkien people were involved in Ryukyuan trade with South Sea countries. The Spanish, extending their influence (in competition with the Portuguese) by spreading Christianity, targeted the wealth of China, Ryukyu, Java, and Japan. Ryukyu became rich by selling Japanese silver for Chinese raw silk, and since Ryukyu was a small country, it could not possibly have had a vigorous external trade.[21]

From the above materials (though not necessarily immediately relevant), one gathers that in the latter half of the sixteenth century, Ryukyu secured

the conditions to expand its trade from one that was hitherto restricted to procuring tributary goods from Southeast Asia to a much bigger network with silver in Manila. Such conditions were created when a large amount of silver was supplied by Japan and the New World, turning East Asia into a silver-currency zone focused on China. The price ratio between gold and silver at that time was 1:13 in Spain, 1:6 in China, and 1:9 in Japan, thus making it profitable not only to trade with the Chinese for raw silk, but also to trade silver for gold.

In this way, when Ryukyu expanded to a more popular, silver-based exchange system, its trade network was no longer limited to the framework determined by the tributary system. The trade activities of Ryukyu became more versatile, at times getting closer to the network of the Chinese traders, at other times specializing in Japanese trade. However, the Ryukyu kingdom did not necessarily premeditate such an expansion.

Conclusion: Tribute System from Periphery

Under the tribute-envoy system, a tributary state sent periodic tribute missions to the Chinese capital, and each time the ruler of a tributary state changed, the Chinese emperor dispatched an envoy to officially recognize the new ruler. This tributary relationship was at the same time a political, economic, and trade relationship. Other than the exchange of tributes for silk products from the emperor, specially licensed traders accompanying the envoy engaged in commercial transactions at the Beijing Huitongguan (residence for tributary envoys). In addition, more than ten times as many merchants as these special traders were allowed to trade at the country's borders or at the ports of call. The specific direction and points on the sea routes for Ryukyuan tribute envoys were established, thus confirming their position in their voyage to the port of Fuzhou. Also, making use of seasonal winds, they were able to establish points and lines through navigational charts and by monitoring the coasts and the movements of the stars. This tribute trade was not limited to Chinese merchants from East and Southeast Asia; Indian, Muslim, and European merchants also participated, confirming the link among coastal ports.

A distinguishing feature of the Ryukyu Kingdom was the tributary trade in the East and South China Seas from the Ming to the Qing dynasties. The Ryukyuans obtained pepper and sappanwood, which were not produced locally in Southeast Asia, and presented them as tributes to China. This intermediary trade strengthened Ryukyu's relationship with Fuzhou on the opposite shore while also allowing its involvement in the migration network

from South China to Southeast Asia. Taking advantage of duty-free trading permitted under the tributary system, important trading ports were interconnected via coastal routes or pan-oceanic long-distance routes.

In 1839, it was decreed that the frequency of tributes from Siam, Burma, and Ryukyu would be reduced to once every four years, but this was not enforced in practice. An imperial edict issued by Emperor Daoguang on the sixth day of the fifth moon, 1839, states,

> Up until now, Vietnam has continued with biennial tribute missions and dispatched an envoy to Beijing once every four years. These two were conducted concurrently. Ryukyu sent tribute missions once every two years; while Siam once every three years. These countries submitted their good faith sincerely without complaining. Regardless of the long distances they had to travel or the bad weather that they have encountered, they have made great contributions showing their loyalty. From now on, Vietnam, Ryukyu, Siam will each dispatch tribute envoys once every four years. By so doing, they will demonstrate their will to be a vassal state.[22]

This was a major change for Vietnam, which was, beside Korea, the country closest to China politically; for Siam, China's stable source of imported rice; and for Ryukyu, which had continued with biennial tribute missions. The Ryukyu king opposed this edict and petitioned repeatedly to continue traditional tributary relations. For reasons related to the jurisdiction of the LiBu, tributes continued in the case of Ryukyu.

What could have triggered such a change in tribute policy as is evident in Emperor Daoguang's edict? The year 1839 was a significant date, just before the start of the opium war. Traditional studies have emphasized that the opium war was a result of the West's (Europe's and America's) need to fulfill their trade interests by forcing Asian nations to open up their markets. However, as seen in the change to tributary policy, the Qing court had become more sensible in relations with its traditional tributary states and was seen to attempt to adopt a policy of mercantilism in order to centralize its financial power. In other words, the central government had, by changing tributary regulations, refocused their attention on Guangdong so as to reap the profits from trade there.

One also cannot ignore the fact that in 1880, the Chinese Zongli Yamen (Foreign Affairs Office) took jurisdiction over all matters related to foreign relations. Thus, through consular offices, rather than the traditional interests in the king of a tributary state, the Qing foreign policy had shifted to

direct, cost-benefit relations with the parties concerned: overseas Chinese (huaqiao), overseas Chinese workers (huagong), and overseas Chinese merchant (huashang).

To summarize Ryukyu's foreign relations, the Ryukyu king's status was fixed by the tribute-envoy relationship with China; relationships with Korea and other Southeast Asian tributary states were maintained as equals; and while theoretically existing as an equal to Japan, Ryukyu was in reality regarded as a part of the Satsuma domain and thus expected to be subordinate to it. As the evidence suggests, the interrelationship among various Southeast Asian nations and regions was determined by the hierarchical ranking system.

Appendix: The Ryukyus and Java

1430 Java
Lidai Baoan, vol. 40, doc. no. 9
The King of Chūzan, Country of Ryukyu, with reference to matters of courtesy, sends this statement from afar.

You, the subject of China, are loyal, kind and broad-minded, and you look after the people of the country so that they enjoy their duties and live in peace. You give good treatment to [men coming from] all directions, and it is because of your great virtue that [people of] various countries come to you.

For a long time we have wanted to dispatch envoys bearing felicitations, but to our regret our small country lacked pilots well acquainted with the seaways, and thus we have been greatly remiss in showing courtesy.

We now have men who are well acquainted with the waterways, and we have prepared some trifling presents and are specially dispatching Chief Envoy Nan-zatu Utchi and others to proceed aboard a ship to your country, taking gifts with them to be offered as a small token of our sentiments. We shall be happy if you will accept them.

It would be our good fortune if you would facilitate trading for the men now being dispatched and let them depart as soon as possible to come back to the country with the wind. We hope that, by long maintaining intercourse, all men within the four seas will be united as brothers.

We list our gift items below. We now close this dispatch. Let this dispatch be given to the addressee.

The following goods:	
Gold satin	2 bolts
Golden gauze	3 bolts
White satin	20 bolts
Swords	5
Big blue vases	20

| Small blue vases | 400 |
| Small blue bowls | 2,000 |

Dispatch to the Country of Zhaowa [Java]
Xuande 5/10/18 [3 November 1430]

Notes

1. Kobata Atsushi, "Rekidai hōan ni tsuite" [On the Rekidai hōan], *Shirin* 46.4 (1968): 523–39; Sakamaki Shunzō, "The Rekidai hōan," *Journal of the American Oriental Society* 83.1 (January–March 1963): 107–13; Kobata Atsushi and Matsuda Mitsugu, *Ryukyuan Relations with Korea and South Sea Countries: An Annotated Translation of Documents in the Rekidai Hoan* (Kyoto: Kobata Atsushi, 1969); Editorial Committee of *Lidai Baoan*, Board of Education, Okinawa Prefecture, ed., *Lidai Baoan*, vols. 1–2 (first series), 1993; Takeshi Hamashita, *Okinawa Nyumon* [A history of Ryukyu-Okinawa] (Tokyo: Chikuma Shobo, 2000); Gregory Smits, *Visions of Ryukyu: Identity and Ideology in Early-Modern Thought and Politics* (Honolulu: University of Hawaii Press, 1999); Ng Chin Keong, *Trade and Society: The Amoy Network on the China Coast, 1683–1735* (Singapore: Singapore University Press, 1983).

2. The Rekidai Hoan is composed of three primary collections and one supplemental collection: the First Collection, originally 49 volumes, comprises 42 extant volumes (1424–1696), sorted according to style and nation; the Second Collection, originally 200 volumes, comprises 187 extant volumes (1697–1858), chronologically arranged; the Third Collection, originally 13 volumes, comprises 13 extant volumes (1859–1867), chronologically arranged; and the (Fourth) Supplement includes information on France, the United Kingdom, and the United States.

3. *Huang Ming shilu* [Veritable Records of the Ming Dynasty], Yongle 2/9/day of renyin (1404); Yoneo Ishii, ed., *The Junk Trade from Southeast Asia: Translation from the Tosen Fusetsugaki, 1674–1723* (Research School of Pacific and Asian Studies, Australian National University, Institute of Southeast Asian Studies, Singapore, 1998); Anthony Reid, *Expansion and Crisis*, vol. 2 of *Southeast Asia in the Age of Commerce, 1450–1680* (New Haven: Yale University Press, 1993); Hungguk Cho, "Early Contact between Korea and Thailand," *Korea Journal* 35.1 (spring 1995): 106–18; Sigeru Ikuta, "The Early History of the Kingdom of Ayutthaya Based on Foreign Sources with Special Reference to the Rekidai Hoan," *Sodai Ajia kenkyu* [Asia Studies on Soka University] 15 (March 1994): 122–47; Piyada Chonlaworn, "Relations between Ayutthaya and Ryukyu," *Journal of the Siam Society* 92 (2004): 43–61; Sarasin Viraphol, *Tribute and Profit: Sino-Siamese Trade, 1652–1853* (Cambridge: Harvard University Press, 1977).

4. See *Lidai Baoan*, vol. 40, doc. no. 9, as contained in the appendix to this essay.

5. *Huang Ming shilu*, under the date Yongle 5/9/day of Guiyu (1407). See also ibid., under the date Yongle 4/11/day of 1-chou (1406).

6. Ibid., under the date Yongle 13/3/day of wuwu (1415).

7. Ibid., under the date Zhengtong 8/7/day of Xinsi (1443).

8. Tributary protocol involved the following: presentation of gifts from the tributary state to the Chinese emperor, return of presents from the latter to the king and con-

sort of the tributary state, presentation of personal gifts from tributary envoys and "rewards" to them from the Chinese, and official and private trade in goods brought aboard the tributary ship. "T'aejong sillok" in the *Yijo sillok*, under the dates T'aejong 6/8/day of ting-yu (1406); T'aejong 12/4/day of i-hai (1412); and T'aejong 12/5/days of Guisi and wushen (1412).

9. Chang Hsiu-Jung, Anthony Farrington, Huang Fu-San, Ts'ao Yung-Ho, Wu Mi-Tsa, Cheng Hsi-Fu, and Ang Ka-in, ed. committee, *The English Factory in Taiwan, 1670–1685* (Taiwan: National Taiwan University, 1995); James Francis Warren, *The Sulu Zone 1768–1898* (Singapore: Singapore University Press, 1981); Dian H. Murray, *Pirates of the South China Coast, 1790–1810* (Stanford: Stanford University Press, 1987).

10. For instance, in the case of Ryukyu, general goods aboard a tributary ship belonged to the king, and the tributary trade was considered a royal monopoly. Tomiyama Kazu-yuki, *Ryukyu okoku no gaiko to oken* [Diplomacy and Sovereignty of the Ryukyu Kingdom] (Tokyo: Yoshikawa-kobunkan, 2004), 262–98.

11. With the Japanese, however, the tributary voyages conducted under the control of the *bakufu* (Tokugawa shogunate) took the form of joint ventures of the bakufu and some local feudal lords, and cargoes consisted mostly of goods belonging to individual merchants, who joined tributary voyages in great numbers. Thus, the membership of tributary embassies naturally varied, according to the types of trade. Ibid., 247.

12. Among thirteen envoys from Java to China between 1405 and 1429, the title of alie is 11 and title of badi, or bazhe, is 2.

13. See "Yingzong shilu" in the *Huang Ming shilu*, under the dates Chengtong 1/inter. 6/days of jichou and renchen (1436).

14. Ibid., under the date Zhengtong 3/6/day of wuwu (1438).

15. Ibid., under the date Zhengtong 2/3/day of bingwu (1437).

16. Ibid., under the dates of Zhengtong n/n/day of xinsi, and Zhengtong n/12/day of bingshen (1446). The title *bianshi* indicates a general manager, corresponding to the term *zongguan* (Japanese: *sōkan*), which is the same as *caifu* or *zhiku*.

17. Ibid., under the dates of Tianshun 4/8/days of xinhai and gengwu (1460).

18. This registration in the tally was called *tianxie*, meaning "to fill in."

19. "Gaozong shilu" in the *Huang Ming shilu*, under the date Hongzhi 14/3/day of renzi (1501).

20. For the case of Ryukyuan trade with Java, see the appendix to this essay.

21. E. H. Blair, *The Philippine Islands: 1493–1898* (Manila: Cachos Hermanos, 1973), 33:205, 33:207, 3:72, and 3:204; Robert R. Reed, *Colonial Manila* (Berkeley: University of California Press, 1978), 27–37.

22. "Xuanzong chenghuangdi shilu," vol. 320, in *Qing shilu* (Beiing: Zhonghua shuju, 1983), 37:37.

COCHINCHINESE COIN CASTING AND CIRCULATING IN EIGHTEENTH-CENTURY SOUTHEAST ASIA

~~~~~ Li Tana

While much has been written about Chinese business networks in modern Southeast Asia, there has been little discussion about the coins used in the various trade ports and their origins. Moreover, when they have been studied, coin casting and circulating have been examined mostly within specific local contexts, with only vague references to China and the Chinese.[1] In this essay I explore the links of the coin business between eighteenth-century Cochinchina and the different ports of Southeast Asia. The new evidence seems to indicate that close connections existed on this important front of Chinese business, particularly between mining in Tongking, copper and zinc importing from Japan and China, coin casting in Cochinchina, and circulation in the neighboring countries of China, Cambodia, and Siam, in the eighteenth-century archipelago.

China-Tonkin

A basic observation on the history of coinage exchange between Vietnam and China, up to the eighteenth century, is that traffic flowed in primarily one direction, from China to Vietnam. This direction reversed in the eighteenth century and early nineteenth. Both Dang Trong (Cochinchina, or southern Vietnam) and Dang Ngoai (Tonkin, or northern Vietnam) cast an enormous number of coins, and both types of coinage made their way to China. Although the coins from Tonkin were mainly of copper, and those of Cochinchina were of copper mixed with zinc, they shared two characteristics: first, coin casting was largely a Chinese affair; and second, in both areas it was a collaborative project between the Chinese and the local rulers and nobles.

Some historical figures hint at the magnitude of coin casting in Vietnam

and its impact on China's economy in the early nineteenth century. In 1829, the Guangdong governor reported repeatedly to the great council (*junji chu*) of the Qing court that 60 to 70 percent of coins circulated in Guangdong were Vietnamese, and that in Chaozhou (Teochiu) that percentage went even higher.[2] This was confirmed by an English source in 1836: "The Cochin-Chinese have a copper coin resembling the Chinese, and a great deal of it has been imported and circulated in the Province of Canton."[3] By 1840, 40 percent of coins circulating in Fujian were reportedly Vietnamese.[4] Vietnamese coins were also used in the cities of northern and western China, such as Jinan (Shandong Province), Chongqing (Sichuan Province), and even Beijing, in this period.[5] An archaeological dig in Huichang (Jiangxi Province) in 1985 unearthed 54 kilograms of coins, most of them Vietnamese. Huichang was the major junction of water traffic between Guangdong and hinterland China.

This information leads to a comment made by Do Van Ninh, an authority on Vietnamese coinage. He called the abundance of coin in Tonkin a "phenomenon of Canh Hung," that "the weakest king cast the most numerous coins."[6] Indeed, at least seventy-two types of Canh Hung coins were cast within a span of forty-six years (1740–1786), while all the previous Viet dynasties (from the tenth century to the seventeenth) cast a combined total of a dozen.[7] However, a closer examination reveals that 80 to 90 percent of the Canh Hung coins were cast not by the weakest king himself, but by the province officers or the Nung chiefs, and in collaboration with the Chinese. This was because province officers and the Nung chiefs could open mines, and these were predominantly copper mines. In the 1760s, according to Vietnamese records, "high officers, royal families, and provincial officers were encouraged to take the responsibilities of one or two mines each, invest their own money and choose the local chiefs to work with them, and recruit laborers. The mines would receive five years tax-free."[8] Some mines hired as many as 10,000 workers, most of them Chinese.[9]

Where did the copper go after being mined? Was it exported to other parts of Southeast Asia, particularly Java, by Chinese junks?[10] At present my sources indicate that Tonkin copper was for the most part consumed locally, a small percentage was exported to China, and only a minimum amount was exported to other parts of Southeast Asia, if at all.[11] The copper that remained in Tonkin contributed to the coin-casting boom that took place there from the 1740s to the 1780s, and it was mainly private-cast copper coins rather than raw copper that made it to China.

If coin casting in Dang Ngoai remained a story of the Gulf of Tonkin, that of Cochinchina and Cancao (Hatien) went much further in the South China Sea region and down to the Malay archipelago.

Up to the early eighteenth century, the coins that circulated in Cochinchina came from two sources: Japanese coins (old or counterfeited ones) during most of the seventeenth century and Chinese coins from the late seventeenth century to the early eighteenth.[12] From the late seventeenth century, however, the Tokugawa government put limits on the copper trade, and the China market was pressed by its own increasing demand for copper, both factors affecting the coin casting in their respective countries.[13] As the two sources dried up, Cochinchina was increasingly affected negatively. Between the late seventeenth century and 1770, the price of copper increased by 44 percent.[14]

At this important juncture of influences, zinc was first brought to Cochinchina, in 1745.[15] The Nguyen lord of Dang Trong, Nguyen Phuc Khoat, embraced this metal and cast 72,396 quan (string) of zinc coins between 1746 and 1748.[16] This quantity was not large, comprising only 70 percent of the quantity brought in by the Verenigde Oostindische Compagnie (VOC) alone in the seventeenth century.[17] Why was it, then, that unlike the seventeenth-century imports, the eighteenth-century castings led to a disastrous inflation?

The central similarity in coin casting between eighteenth-century Dang Trong and Dang Ngoai rested on two factors: ready and abundant casting material, and large numbers of Chinese in both regions. While Dang Ngoai used copper mined by the Chinese, however, Dang Trong employed zinc brought in by junks from Canton. This metal, cheap and abundant, met the requirement of the rapidly growing commercial economy of Cochinchina of the 1740s. Zinc soon made up the bulk of Sino-Cochinchina trade, as Pierre Poivre, a French merchant visiting Cochinchina, reported in 1749–51: "The huge profit they [the Chinese] make on this substance has led them to abandon or suspend trade in all other articles."[18] In 1767, for example, zinc formed the single most important cargo from Canton to Bassac (5,890 piculs), Cochinchina (9,868 piculs), Cancao (1,589 piculs), and Cambodia (1,014 piculs).[19] The total number of piculs could be cast into at least 616,929 strings of coins, even if no other material was added to the mix, which was usually the case with private casting.[20] The private cast in 1767 alone was

thus eight to ten times the three-year total of the Nguyen official cast in the 1740s.

The Importance of Canton Connections

Yunnan began to produce zinc in the late seventeenth century. Because of Canton's proximity and the convenience in transportation relative to Amoy, zinc prices differed remarkably between the two markets in 1737 (6.6 tael in Canton as opposed to 8.1 tael per picul in Amoy). Furthermore, merchants in Amoy had to wait for up to five months to receive the cargo they had ordered.[21] This trade imbalance elevated Canton's importance two decades before the Qing government made Canton the only official port open to overseas trade, in 1757. Zinc was thus an important stimulus for Canton trade and gave Canton an advantage in its competition with Amoy. This was particularly the case in terms of Sino-Cochinchina trade: zinc was the mainstay of trade between Cochinchina and Canton, as the figures on zinc exported from Canton in 1767 show.

A related trade between eighteenth-century Canton and Cochinchina was gold, but it contained an enigma. Before the 1760s, Western merchants consistently bought gold from China, as gold was about 60 percent cheaper there than in Europe.[22] As a result China exported gold and imported silver. However, at the same time, junks from Cochinchina were bringing gold into China. In fact, Cochinchina was one of the three gold sources (the other two being Suzhou and Nanjing) for the Hong merchants from the 1710s to the 1730s, according to Wen Eang Cheong.[23] This was because buying Chinese coins with Cochinchinese gold was more profitable, and at the same time fulfilled the country's acute need for gold.[24] As a result, Chinese coins were exported to Cochinchina in large quantities, particularly from Canton in the late seventeenth century, as Bowyear confirmed in 1695: "From Canton is brought cashes, of which they make a great profit."[25]

Chinese merchants, on the king's behalf, undertook gold speculation. When zinc coins flooded the Cochinchina market in 1750, for example, Lord Vo Vuong Nguyen Phuc Khoat used his zinc money power to "buy up all the gold in his kingdom," as recorded by Poivre.[26] Gold was then brought to China for speculation. In 1767 alone, some 386 gold shoes were brought from Cochinchina, a year when "gold from Cochinchina [was] extremely limited," according to H. B. Morse.[27] A contemporary Vietnamese source went as far as to estimate that no fewer than 1,000 gold shoes were brought to Cochinchina's port, Hoi An, every year to sell to the Chinese.[28]

There was a good reason, it now seemed, that the eighteenth-century historian Le Quy Don singled out Truong Phuc Loan, the most powerful and corrupt mandarin and the uncle of Vo Vuong, who monopolized the gold revenue of the country in the 1760s. The *Nguyen Chronicle* also pointed out that there was a Chinese merchant whose family name was Cai (Tsja in Hokkien), and who worked with Truong Phuc Loan on the main ports collecting revenues illegally.[29]

Truong Phuc Loan may or may not have participated in the forgery of the 1750s, but many Nguyen officials inarguably did. They eagerly took part in this profitable economic activity and gained the lion's share, according to the French merchant Poivre. In 1750, Poivre proposed to circulate "piastres to be marked with the stamp of the king . . . but the mandarins secretly opposed this edict's being issued. As they are all counterfeiters they would have forfeited a huge profit and would not have enjoyed the same ease in forging piasters as counterfeiting cash. They aroused suspicions in the king's mind, which became publicly known, and by an astonishing quirk the money fell into a state of disrepute."[30] That Nguyen officials actively participated in counterfeiting activities was also confirmed by Vietnamese sources: "Rich and powerful people competed to cast coins."[31] The same situation took place in Tonkin during the same period. The map of coin casting or counterfeiting in mid-eighteenth-century Cochinchina involved over one hundred furnaces around the capital area, most owned or sponsored by the Nguyen officials.[32] Further to the south, coin-casting permission had been given to the Mac in Hatien (Cancao) in the 1730s,[33] and thus a considerable number of coins were also cast there. The focus of coin casting in the 1760s to 1770s, however, seemed to be the Mekong Delta, particularly the Bassac area. The situation was so rampant in 1770 that the scholar Ngo The Lan wrote an urgent petition to the Nguyen lord, requesting that coin casting be prohibited in Bassac. Court officials retained his petition so that it never reached the king, according to the *Chronicle*.[34] Remarkably, the Tay Son rebellion broke out the following year, in 1771, which eventually brought the end to the Nguyen rule in Cochinchina.

Further Links: Canton, Cochinchina, and the Malay Archipelago

None of these coin-casting activities could have been possible without the raw material, the source of which centered on a group of leading Chinese merchants in Hoi An. According to the records of the Minh Huong community, there were ten such merchants, all of them called *laoye*. The term led Chen Chingho to speculate that these merchants served as government offi-

cials either in China or Vietnam, but more likely in the latter.[35] The top four Chinese families of the eighteenth century were Yan, Zhou, Huang (Oey in Hokkien dialect), and Cai (Tsia in Hokkien).[36]

When the list of Hoi An merchants was examined together with Paul Van Dyke's recent research on Canton, there emerged clear links in the individual business connections between Canton and Cochinchina in the eighteenth century. To begin with, the Yan family was one of the most prominent Hong merchants in Canton, and a major Hong that engaged in trade with eighteenth-century Cochinchina (see table 1). From the links shown between Canton, Cochinchina, and the Passiak, it is evident that a major associate of the family, Beau Khequa, traded extensively in Cochinchina's gold.[37] Another link that almost certainly could not have been incidental: an important associate of the Yan family was Tsia Hunqua, who shared the same family name with the Chinese who participated in monopolizing the gold revenue with Truong Phuc Loan.[38] More links seemed to have existed to the Huang in Canton, Hoi An, and the archipelago.

Simon (Huang Ximan, Oey) was the major partner of the Yan in the 1740s.[39] Incidentally, as was the case in Java in the same period, the Nguyen's coin mint was farmed out, to a Chinese named Huang (Oey in Fukien dialect), in 1746.[40] Although zinc was exported from China, Cochinchinese records stated that this man, surnamed Huang, suggested buying zinc from the Dutch to cast coins, and Vo Vuong accepted his proposal.[41] Thus the Nguyen record stated the earlier source of the zinc brought into Cochinchina, and pointed to a major link between zinc and the Chinese in the Dutch East Indies. It is remarkable that in the 1740s, both the Chinese *kapitains* in Tegal and Semarang were named Huang (Oey). According to Kwee, when the Oey in Tegal, a mint farmer himself, complained about the difficulties on the tax-farm of minting lead *picis*, the Semarang Chinese captain Oey Tjenkong helped him to pay the first three terms of the lease.[42] It is most likely that these Oeys (and other Chinese towkays) in the Dutch East Indies were behind the scenes, working through the mint farmer Oey of Cochinchina, when the VOC offered to cast coins for Cochinchina in 1754.[43] These links better clarify the existing but fragmented information on the trade between Cochinchina and Batavia in the eighteenth century. Le Quy Don, for example, mentioned casually that Cochinchinese tinsmiths were skillful in making fine wares and that tin was cheap in Cochinchina, a place that produced no tin.[44] When this information was viewed in combination with Poivre's report, it became clear that the tin came from the Dutch-controlled areas and was bought by the Chinese from the Dutch.[45]

Table 1 Canton Junks to Southeast Asia, 1762–1769

Year	Junk name	Chinese	Hong name	Destination
1762	Eckhing			
	Ecktay	益泰	Mantack Hang	Cochinchina
1764	Ecktay	益泰	Mantack Hang	Cochinchina
	Fongschyn	豐順	Fongzun Hang	
	Samjeck	三益	Fongzun Hang	
	Samkonghing	三廣興	Thatfong Hang	Batavia
	Sihing	瑞興	Mantack Hang	Batavia
	Tainganschyn			Caucong
1765	Eckhing			Cochinchina
	Ecktay	益泰	Mantack Hang	Batavia
	Fongschyn	豐順	Fongzun Hang	Siam
	Hingtai	恆泰	Wu Heguan	Cochinchina
	Quim Contay			Passciak
	Samjeck	三益	Fongzun Hang	Cambodia
	Samkonghing	三廣興	Thatfong Hang	Cochinchina, Batavia
	Sihing	瑞興	Mantack Hang	Cochinchina, Batavia
	Tainganschyn			
	Wansun	源順	Mantack Hang	Siam
1766	Eckhing			Cochinchina
	Ecksun	益順	Mantack Hang	Passicak, CC, Cambodia
	Ecktay	益泰	Mantack Hang	Batavia
	Kimfong			Cochinchina, Siam
	Quim Contay			Passiak, Manila
	Samjeck	三益	Fongzun Hang	Cambodia, Passiak
	Samkonghing	三廣興	Thatfong Hang	Batavia
	Wansun	源順	Mantack Hang	LO: Cambodia
	Winghing			

Table 1 Continued

Year	Junk name	Chinese	Hong name	Destination
1767	Eckhing			Cochinchina
	Ecktay	益泰	Mantack Hang	Batavia
	Quim Contay			Passiak
	Samjeck	三益	Fongzun Hang	Passiak
	Samkonghing	三廣興	Thatfong Hang	Cochinchina
1768	Ecktay	益泰	Mantack Hang	Cochinchina
	Kimfong			LO: Cochinchina
	Quim Contay			
	Samjeck	三益	Fongzun Hang	Passiak
	Samkonghing	三廣興	Thatfong Hang	Batavia
	Tayli	泰利	Tayschoen Hang	Cochinchina
	Tayon	泰安	Tayschoen Hang	Cochinchina
	Wansun	源順	Tayschoen Hang	Batavia, Cochinchina
1769	Ecktay	益泰	Mantack Hang	Batavia
	Samjeck	三益	Fongzun Hang	Passiak
	Santay	新泰	Tayschoen Hang	Cochinchina
	Tayon	泰安	Tayschoen Hang	Passiak

Source: Paul Van Dyke, "The Yan Family: Merchants of Canton, 1734–1780s," *Review of Culture*, International Edition 9 (2004): 73.

More strikingly, Cochinchinese coins could have been directly circulated in Java from the 1750s. As in Cochinchina, there appeared in this period a notable need for small currencies in Java. As Peter Klein points out, "The process of economic penetration, extension and innovation was accelerated by about 1750. . . . It had a rising need of small currencies which would serve this purpose."[46] As a result, some semi-lead (zinc?), semi-copper coins (picis or *kepengs*) were used as small change in central and east Java. Because the Mataram court had forsworn its minting rights in the 1743 treaty with the VOC, these kepengs were all imported, and appeared as coins of China, Japan, and Tonkin.[47]

A closer examination, however, suggests that many of the so-called China, Japan, and Tonkin coins were in fact forgeries of eighteenth-century

Cochinchina. According to Ta Chi Dai Truong, the authority on coins of Cochinchina, molds of coins of the Tang and Song dynasties arrived from China, Japan, and Tonkin in the eighteenth century.[48] There were many coin specimens to copy, which private coin casters in Cochinchina then further developed, multiplying the number of coin types. There were fifty-three types identified as Dang Trong coins, but the list of "unidentified species" unearthed in Saigon and the western part of the Mekong Delta (Mien Tay) area was even longer.[49]

Cochinchina Coins in the Malay Archipelago

A recent book on coins found in Bali provides a chance to test the theory of connections between Cochinchinese coins and the archipelago. This book contains photos of three coins, each of which was Cochinchinese cast. One is Thieu Binh phong bao.[50] Thieu Binh was the title of Le Thai-ton during his reign (1434–1441), but the coin Thieu Binh phong bao did not exist in fifteenth-century Tonkin; it was one of the private casts of Cochinchina in the eighteenth century.[51] Another coin was the Khoan Vinh thong bao, supposedly a Japanese coin cast between 1624 and 1643, but again it was in fact an eighteenth-century Cochinchinese imitation.[52] Even more obviously Cochinchinese was the An Phap nguyen bao, which was cast of good quality copper in Cancao in the eighteenth century.[53]

It was most likely the Canton junks that brought the coins cast in Cochinchina, Bassac, and Cancao to the archipelago. Cochinchina's, Bassac's, and Cancao's connections with Batavia are now evident, with the detailed reports on the destinations of Canton Hong merchants from 1762 to 1772. Thanks to Paul Van Dyke, we now know that while some junks visited Cochinchina, Bassac, or Batavia alternately in different years, other junks visited Cochinchina and Batavia within the same year (see table 1).[54] This meant that the junks stopped in Cochinchina before heading for Batavia, and Cochinchinese coins would have been used for purchasing Canton goods, while some were brought to Batavia.

In particular, Cochinchina, Bassac, and Cancao were the most important coin-casting bases that provided coins to southern Vietnam as well as to Batavia and Canton. They could do so because of the specific water frontier nature of the Lower Mekong Delta in the eighteenth century.[55] Two important elements existed in the region: ready and abundant casting material, and large numbers of Chinese. As many Chinese were active either in upstream and downstream trade or in coastal trade, and the individual capital

and trade volume were never large, coins were the most useful intermediary in such trade.

The newly found and published *Kung kuan* (*Gongan bu*, or Minutes of the board meetings of the Chinese Council) material in Batavia provides further evidence that coins were widely used among the Chinese in Batavia as small change, for donations and on gambling tables.[56] They were sometimes also used for large spending; one of the minutes, for example, stated that a Chinese spent 189,000 cash to buy eleven slaves in Bali in 1788.[57] Remarkably, coins circulated in Bali were made of zinc, according to John Crawfurd in the early nineteenth century.[58] A considerable proportion of these coins would have been from Cochinchina and Cancao.

Circulation among Neighbors

The largest percentage of the Cochinchinese cast went to China, although Chinese sources of the eighteenth century did not record much about them as they did in the early nineteenth century. It is clear, however, that Cochinchinese cast contributed 80 to 90 percent of the coins recorded as "unidentified" in one of the Chinese sources, if one compares the descriptions of them with the photos and descriptions made by Ta Chi Dai Truong on the coins cast in eighteenth-century Cochinchina.[59]

As Singapore's second most significant trade partner (the first being Bangkok) in its earlier years, Saigon must also have imported some coins into Singapore. According to William Milbourne, the Spanish dollar was the principal coin, while Chinese cash was used in small payments.[60]

In Cambodia, too, which was increasingly under the control of Cochinchina from the late seventeenth century, the coins of Cochinchina circulated widely, although Battambang coinage circulated throughout the country until the early eighteenth century.[61] One Cambodian coin, a small silver coin stamped with a chicken, was most likely the "chicken silver" recorded in eighteenth-century Cochinchinese records and used in exchange with Chinese and Vietnamese.[62]

Cochinchinese coins were used in Cambodia from the eighteenth century to the late nineteenth. A Vietnamese manuscript entitled "Tran Tay phong tho ky" (Customs of Tran Tay, i.e., Cambodia in the early nineteenth century) stated that Cambodia's silver was not pure and thus one tien of silver (3.5 grams) was worth only 40 Vietnamese cash.[63] A French observation in 1867 gave further details on Khmers using Vietnamese coins: "The commonest [coin] is made of a brittle composition, whereof the chief ingredient is

antimony. . . . 2,400 of these little coins made up the value of one Siamese tical. They are universally in use among the people of Cambodia, who may be seen carrying them in cumbrous bundles from place to place. In Bangkok the same coins are employed as counters at the public gaming tables."[64]

It was at the gambling table that copper coins were introduced to Siamese society. Besides the gambling function, these pieces often served as small change in outlying provinces. Chantaburi must have been one such place, as gambling tax collected from Chantaburi was the highest in southeast Siam in 1809.[65] It was also where Chinese and Cochinchinese were concentrated in the eighteenth and early nineteenth centuries. "Ever since the counters made their first appearance—about 1760—there existed in circulation some bronze coins of the value," one scholar noted.[66] In the 1760s, too, copper coins began to circulate in Siam, and large numbers of private coins began to be cast in Bassac.

Close relations existed between eighteenth-century Chantaburi, Cancao, and Cochinchina. Chan Bon (Chantaburi) and Thungyai appeared frequently in the Vietnamese sources of the eighteenth and early nineteenth century.[67] Such traces can also be found in Siamese chronicles. In 1782, for example, Nguyen Anh, the future king of Gia Long, and his followers were on the edge of starvation on an island when a Chinese junk saved them. According to Siamese chronicles, this junk was owned by a Chinese married to a Vietnamese woman from Chantaburi. They were carrying rice to sell to Ca Mau and Rach Gia.[68] A similar event had been observed a decade earlier in Siam, with Taksin and his followers. With more people having died of starvation than had died in the war, in 1768 Taksin "bought rice from ships coming from Pontameas (Cancao or Ha Tiên) at the high cost of three to five baht per thang to distribute to the people."[69] It thus appears that both baht and Cancao coins were accepted at the markets.

Reflecting the rather frequent economic intercourse in the region, Vietnamese coins and currency of the early nineteenth century were used as tenders in Siam and Laos, and were submitted by Thai or Lao people as taxes. According to Puangthong Rungswasdisab,

If the suai ngoen (tax in money/silver) came straight from the northeast and Lao towns, it also contained Thai baht but mixed with various kinds of local monies, including Lao coins and others called ngoen naentu and ngoen naenrang that originated in Vietnam. . . . The value of local silver coins was usually reduced by the smelting fee. Local officials in Battambang and Siemreap, however, made no difficulty in accepting other currencies that

seem to have been in common use among the local people. This suggests that the cross-border trade between Siam, Cambodia, Laos, and Vietnam was long established.[70]

The regular exchanges of coins and currencies between Vietnam and her neighbors must have had some impact on the prices of commodities in the region. We can find one such example in the inflation of the price of rice in Siam in 1803, after the Nguyen started casting coins in that year. According to Junko Koizumi,

> Causes of price increases were not always natural disasters. In 1803/4, a brisk trade in rice with provincial officials and merchants who came by boat to buy rice to trade with other countries, and the increased consumption for official purposes in the capital, resulted in a shortage of rice and its price increase in the capital. The king, in this case, coped with the problem by prohibiting the sales of rice to junks and sailboats, except for the case in which royal permission was granted.[71]

One wonders whether this tightening rice trade in Siam was a response to the large-scale coin casting under the new emperor Nguyen Anh, in 1802–1803.[72] Between 1789 and 1799, Anh granted 27,000 quan of cash to his troops; on his ascension to the throne, in 1802, he rewarded them with 65,000 quan, and in 1803 he awarded another 56,800 quan.[73]

Thus one sees an almost instant jump of the price of rice in 1803. According to the *Nguyen Chronicle* of February 1803, "Rice price is high in Gia Dinh and people are hungry. [The court] ordered soldiers at different passes to not let merchant junks to carry rice out."[74] The same situation occurred in Bangkok, although 1803 was a good year of harvest, and there was no record of drought or flood.

Further Connections?

The large scale of coin casting in present northern and southern Vietnam happened in the greater context of the eighteenth-century Chinese migration to southwest China and Southeast Asia. If the contact points between China and Southeast Asia were limited to the few ports before this period, when tens of thousands of Chinese miners were employed in the same mine in northern Vietnam, and the same number of Chinese were settled in the Mekong Delta, the old contacting points were a hundred times multiplied. Cochinchina cast coins were useful not only in that they circulated in Cochinchina and were brought to China, but also in that they were used as

small change in ports of such locations as Batavia, Palembang, Cambodia, and Laos, and in that they were used as gambling money among the Chinese settlements. In short, they were used predominantly where there were sizeable Chinese communities in Southeast Asia.

It was not unimaginable that a kind of Chinese network existed in mid-eighteenth-century Southeast Asia, which interwove the matrix of mining, export and import of the metals, minting, and exports of coins for circulation, if one notes that coin casting existed in eighteenth-century China.[75] According to a report made by the deputy minister of industry (gongbu) in 1739, there were two official casting sites, at Bao Yuan and Bao Quan, in Beijing, with seventy-five heads of furnaces, who were nonetheless from but a dozen families.[76] In other words, only a few families controlled the business of coin casting of about one million strings per year.[77] (It would be illuminating, if one had the details of families who controlled the copper and zinc mining in eighteenth-century Yunnan, to see the extent to which they were connected to the merchants in Canton.)

To be sure, the huge span of mining activities spread out from eighteenth-century Yunnan to Tonkin, and the zinc trade and coin casting by the Chinese were not controlled by only a few Chinese families. What I am interested in and what I have been trying to illuminate are the connections between the events that happened in this region, which seemed to be individual, incidental, and local, but were in fact connected to a larger context, and moreover, in what manner they may have been connected. As Hans-Dieter Evers points out, the peddling trade, though carried out by individuals on a small scale, was not anarchic. Van Leur stresses, quite rightly, the flexibility of this kind of trade, but neglects the systematic aspects of the trading networks that made its persistence possible.[78]

Whoever controlled the finance sector also dominated the mercantile economy. The lucrative trade between eighteenth-century Canton and Southeast Asia, both of which stretched to their respective hinterlands, could not be removed from the aspects of cash flow surveyed above. One note on private casting in Cochinchina and the Mekong Delta observed that in China, forgery was most widespread in the areas near copper- and zinc-producing areas such as Sichuan, Yunnan, and Guizhou.[79] However, neither Cochinchina nor Cancao produced copper or zinc. This implies active trading of the mineral material in the region and thus that connections overseas (Canton and Batavia) might have decided the status of the Chinese families in Hoi An, and vice versa.

Notes

1. My own work on the Nguyen Cochinchina is such an example. Li Tana, *The Nguyen Cochinchina: Southern Vietnam in the Seventeenth and Eighteenth Centuries* (Ithaca: SEAP, Cornell University, 1998).

2. *Ming qing shiliao* (Taipei: Academia Sinica, 1960), Gengbian, 243. As many such coins were cast privately and mixed zinc with sand, the Qing court was forced to buy and destroy them, which cost no small fortune. Since Guangdong suffered the most, the governor suggested a dramatic measure against Vietnamese coins, that all the arriving ships from overseas should be checked in Canton, and that if any such coins were found, the ship would not be allowed to trade and had to return to its port of origin.

3. *Canton Press* 1.35, 7 May 1836.

4. Fifteen types of Canh Hung and Quang Trung coins can be found in Fujian. Xu Xinxi, "Qing zhong houqi yuenan tongqian zai min yue de liutong yu guanfu de duice" [Vietnamese coins circulated in Fujian and Guangdong in the late Qing period and the government's policy], *Haijian shi yan jiu* [Journal of Overseas Communication], no. 1 (2001): 118.

5. Peng Xinwei, *Zhongguo huobi shi* [A history of Chinese currency] (Shanghai: People's Press, 1988), 884.

6. Personal communications. Canh Hung was the reign title of the king Le Hien-ton (r. 1740–1786).

7. Ed Toda, "Annam and Its Minor Currency," *Journal of the North-China Branch of the Royal Asiatic Society* 17.1 (1882): 106–12.

8. Phan Huy Chu, *Lich trieu hien chuong loai chi* [Accounts on the institutions of successive dynasties] (Repr., Hanoi: Nha xuat ban khoa hoc xa hoi, 1992), 2:262. Tax regulation—regarding trading copper to the mining sites made in 1720—was quite heavy, 30 percent over the copper traded (4.5 quan for every 15 quan), a fee and gift money for the certificate which could cost over 100 quan, plus 16 quan for each passing boat going through.

9. See Li Tana, "Vietnamese Mint and Chinese Miners in the Eighteenth Century Northern Vietnam," paper presented at the International Convention of Asian Studies 3, Singapore, August 2003.

10. Kwee Hui Kian, "Colonialism Creeping In: The Dutch East India Company's Promotion of Petty Coins in Central and East Java, 1740s–1790s," paper presented at the fourth Euroseas Conference, Sorbonne University, Paris, 1–4 September 2004.

11. According to a 1750 English source: "There is no trade by junks, only overland, and by boats and small coasters. The Chinese carry thither, drugs, a little green tea, and Nankeen cloth, and the returns are copper and fine cinnamon" (R. Kirsop, "Some Account of Cochinchina," in Alexander Dalrymple, *Oriental Repertory* [London: East-India Company, 1808], 2:286.

12. Between 1633 and 1637, the Verenigde Oostindische Compagnie brought 105,834 strings of Japanese coins into Cochinchina. Chinese merchants also brought large quantities of Japanese coins to Cochinchina. See Li Tana, *The Nguyen Cochinchina* (Ithaca: Southeast Asia Program, Cornell University, 1998), chap. 4, "Money and Trade."

13. The zinc to copper ratio in Chinese coins was 30:70 in 1550–1650; 40:60 in 1684; 50:50 in 1727; and 41.4:50:6.5:2 (zinc:copper:lead:tin) in 1740. See Yang Duanliu, *Qingdai huobi jinrong shigao* [A draft on the history of currency and finance of the Qing dynasty] (Beijing: Sanlian Press, 1962), 59.

14. Copper in Cochinchina was 20 string (quan) per picul in 1695, doubled by 1750, and reached 45 *quan* per picul in the 1770s. See A. Lamb, *The Mandarin Road to Old Hue: Narratives of Anglo-Vietnamese Diplomacy from the Seventeenth Century to the Eve of the French Conquest* (London: Chatto and Windus, 1970), 52; Pierre Poivre, "Memoires sur la Cochinchine," *Revue de l'Extrême Orient* 2 (1884): 336; and Le Quy Don, *Phu bien tap luc* [A compilation of the miscellaneous records when the southern border was pacified] (Saigon: Phu quoc vu khanh dac trach Van Hoa, 1973), j.4, 21a.

15. On the term *tutenague* (zinc) see Li Tana, *The Nguyen Cochinchina*, "Annex Four," where the problem is considered in more detail. Here I refer to zinc coins, as *tutenague* was essentially that metal.

16. *Dai Nam thuc luc Tien Bien* [The Nguyen Chronicle, premier period] (Tokyo: The Oriental Institute, Keio University, 1961), vol. 1, j. 10, 141.

17. Merchants in Macau also brought large numbers of Chinese coins into Cochinchina in the seventeenth century. Phan Khoang, *Viet su Xu Dang Trong* [A history of Cochinchina, 1558–1777] (Saigon: Khai Tri, 1969), 573.

18. Pierre Poivre, "Description of Cochinchina," *Southern Vietnam under the Nguyen: Documents on the Economic History of Cochinchina (Dang Trong), 1602–1777*, ed. Li Tana and Anthony Reid (Singapore: Institute of Southeast Asian Studies, Singapore / ECHOSEA, Australian National University, 1993), 85.

19. Dalrymple, *Oriental Repertory*, 1:286–87.

20. This calculation is based on the Nguyen official cast of zinc coins in 1814. *Dai Nam thuc luc Tien Bien*, vol. 1, j.49, 274. Private casting always used less zinc; labor cost was also much lower.

21. In 1734 at Chincheu, immediately available stocks of zinc totaled only 70 piculs, at an extravagant price, and delivery took up to five months. George Souza, "Ballast Goods: Chinese Maritime Trade in Zinc and Sugar in the Seventeenth and Eighteenth Centuries," *Emporia, Commodities and Entrepreneurs in Asian Maritime Trade, c.1400–1750*, ed. Roderich Ptak and Dietmar Rothermund (Stuttgart: Franz Steiner, 1991).

22. Gold to silver ratio in China: 10:105 in 1731; 10:115 in 1733; 10:103–7 in 1735; 10:124 in 1737; 10:116 in 1738; 10:125 in 1740; 10:149 in 1751; 10:152 in 1775 (for 93 touch, so it was 1:16.15); 10:180 in 1779, when many types of gold were imported to China; and 10:130 in 1780, as China was flooded with an oversupply. Yang Duanliu, *Qingdai huobi jinrong shigao*, 302–3.

23. Wen Eang Cheong, *The Hong Merchants of Canton: Chinese Merchants in Sino-Western Trade* (Richmond, Surrey: Curzon, 1997).

24. In the late seventeenth century, there was a remarkable depreciation of the lighter Kangxi coins in China. In 1688, one tael of silver was worth 1,400 to 1,500 copper coins, but by 1697 it was valued at 3,030 of the lighter coins. Peng Xin Wei, *Zhongguo Huobi Shi*

[A history of Chinese coinage] (Shanghai: People's Press, 1958), 567. Those 3,030 coins would then have been worth over five quan coins in Cochinchina, where gold was worth about thirteen quan for a tael, or even less. Pierre Poivre said that before 1750 gold was valued at 130 *quan* for 10 taels, in an expensive year 150 quan ("Voyage de Pierre Poivre en Cochinchine," *Revue de l'Extrême Orient* 3 [1885]: 430. Thus, when the ratio of gold to silver in China was 1:10, it would bring 288 percent profit. Before 1710, the official proportion of gold and silver was 1:10, but in reality the English bought gold at 9.85 tael silver of 94 touch, in 1700. See H. B. Morse, *The Chronicles of the East India Company Trading to China, 1635–1834* (Oxford: Clarendon, 1926), 1:69.

25. Bowyear cited in Lamb, *The Mandarin Road to Old Hue*, 52.

26. Poivre, "Description of Cochinchina," 86–87.

27. Equaled 136.8 taels of silver in each. Morse, *The Chronicles of the East India Company Trading to China, 1635–1834*, 4–5:562.

28. Le Quy Don, *Phu bien tap luc*, j.4, 27b. While there is likely exaggeration in this estimate, as the production from the gold mines of Cochinchina was limited, it is possible that the Chinese from Cochinchina bought gold from the Malay Peninsula, particularly from Terengganu, and brought it to Canton. Captain Light, in a report written in June 1789, states: "'Tringano': Malay port, chief trade with China. Produces pepper, gold and some tin. Yearly exports 30,000 Spanish dollars" (quoted in Koo Kay Kim, *Malay Society: Transformation and Democratisation: A Stimulating and Discerning Study on the Evolution of Malay Society through the Passage of Time* [Petaling Jaya, Malaysia: Pelanduk, 1991], 88–89).

29. *Dai Nam thuc luc Tien bien*, vol. 1, j.11, 152.

30. Poivre, "Description of Cochinchina," 87.

31. Le Quy Don, *Phu bien tap luc*, j.4, 22a.

32. Ibid.

33. *Dai Nam thuc luc Tien Bien*, vol. 1, j.9,132.

34. *Dai Nam thuc luc Tien Bien*, vol. 1, j.11, 156–57.

35. Chen Chingho, *Historical Notes on Hoi-an (Faifo)* (Carbondale: Center for Vietnamese Studies, Southern Illinois University, Monograph series 4, 1974), 43.

36. On top of the list was Kong (Tianru, or Khong Tien Nhu in Vietnamese), but he was referred to as *tai laoye*, which indicates that he was a generation older than the other nine Chinese merchants in Hoi An. Kong died in 1695, according to his tombstone in Hoi An.

37. On Beau Khequa's trade in gold, see Cheong, *The Hong Merchants of Canton*, 56–57. His Hong was called Tzu-yuan Hong (Ziyuan Hang) (Cheong, *The Hong Merchants of Canton*, 43; Paul Van Dyke, "The Yan Family: Merchants of Canton, 1734–1780s," *Review of Culture*, International Edition 9: 66).

38. Van Dyke, "The Yan Family," 68.

39. Ibid., 65.

40. On the case in Java, see Kwee, "Colonialism Creeping In." On the Nguyen coin mint, see *Dai Nam thuc luc Tien Bien*, 140.

41. Le Quy Don, *Phu bien tap luc*, j.4, 21b.

42. Kwee, "Colonialism Creeping In."

43. The deal they made with Vo Vuong was that 12 percent of profit would go to the king, and 2 percent to the mint farmer. However, the VOC gave up the contract in 1755 because the profit was too little. W. J. M. Buch, "La compagnie des Indes neerlandaises et l'Indochine," *Bulletin de l'École Française d'Extrême-Orient* 37 (1937): 257; also Ta Chi Dai Truong, "Tien kem va cuoc khung hoang tien te o Dang Trong vao hau ban the ki XVIII" [Zinc coin and the monetary crisis in Dang Trong in the second half of the eighteenth century], *Nhung bai da su Viet* [Articles on unofficial history] (California: Thanh Van, 1996), 361.

44. Le Quy Don, *Phu bien tap luc*, j.6, 216b.

45. "Calin [tin], which they buy from the Dutch" (Li and Reid, *Southern Vietnam under the Nguyen*, 86).

46. Peter W. Klein, "Dutch Monetary Policy in the East Indies, 1602–1942," *Money, Coins and Commerce: Essays in the Monetary History of Asia and Europe*, ed. Eddy H. G. Van Cauwenberghe (Löwen: Studies in Social and Economic History 22, 1991), 430.

47. Kwee, "Colonialism Creeping In."

48. Ta Chi Dai Truong, "Tien duc o Dang Trong: phuong dien loai hinh va truong quan lich su" [Coin casting in Dang Trong: The types and their relations to history], *Nhung bai da su Viet*, 313. Many coin types were found in Ha Tien in 1874, and many remained to be seen in the western part of the Mekong Delta (Mien Tay) (ibid., 297).

49. Ibid., 298. Archaeology findings around the Saigon area indicate that the Hatien and Bassac areas produced mostly Ming coins, while Thuan Hoa, the capital area, produced Song coins. The coins that Mac cast were Jianwen (Kien Van), Hongxi (Hong Hi), Xuande (Tuyen Duc), Tianshun (Thien Thuan), Shenghua (Thanh Hoa), all the reigns of the Ming, and all with larger holes at the center and smaller characters at the edge.

50. Sartono Kartodirdjo, *Nilai histories Uang Kepeng* (Ida Bagus Sidemen dan Larasan-Sejarah, 2002), 127.

51. Ta Chi Dai Truong, "Tien duc o Dang Trong," 292–93.

52. Over fourteen types were cast in Hatien (seven were Thai Binh and An Phap coins), plus seven Ming coins (ibid., 298).

53. Kartodirdjo, *Nilai histories Uang Kepeng*, 139. An Phap nguyen bao was cast in Hatien in 1736 of good-quality copper, clear and thin (Ta Chi Dai Truong, "Tien duc o Dang Trong," 277, 297. The one cast in Hatien had signs to signify the character "Minh" (298). For An Phap nguyen bao, see also Masahiro Okudaira, *Dongya qianzhi* [A list of coins in East Asia] (Tokyo: Iwanami Shoten, 1938), 16:40.

54. Van Dyke, "The Yan Family," 73–74.

55. Nola Cooke and Li Tana, eds., *The Water Frontier: Commerce and the Chinese in the Lower Mekong Region, 1750–1880* (New York and Singapore: Rowman and Littlefield / Singapore University Press, 2004).

56. Leonard Blussé and Wu Fengbin, collated and annotated, *Gongan Bu* (Xiamen: Xiamen University Press, 2002), 60–61 (on donations), 69–70 (on gambling), and 63 (on buying male and female slaves).

57. This price would match the slave price of the eighteenth century given by Barbara Andaya, who puts the price of a slave between 8–40 reals (To Live As Brothers [Honolulu: University of Hawaii Press, 1993], 96–97). If one string (quan) were 600 cash, as it was in Cochinchina, 29 quan per slave would be equivalent to 572 grams of silver and thus to 22.5 real. If one quan were 1000 cash, 17.2 quan would be equivalent to 344 grams of silver and thus to 13.48 reals per slave. According to Zhang Xie, 1000 cash would form one quan in the seventeenth century (Dongxi yangkao [Beijing: Zhonghua shuju, 1981], 48).

58. "A great variety of small coins of brass, copper, tin and zinc are in circulation throughout all the islands. . . . The small coins of Palembang, Achin, Bantam, and Queda are of tin. . . . In Bali and Lomboc the currency consists of Chinese zinc coins with a hole in the middle for filing them on a string, each string having 200, and five of these called a siah, that is 'one thousand.' . . . [T]heir value rises and falls in the market according to the supply . . . so that a Spanish dollar will sometimes buy 800 of them, but often as few as 500 only" (John Crawfurd, A Descriptive Dictionary of the Indian Islands and Adjacent Countries [Kuala Lumpur: Oxford in Asia Historical Reprints, 1971], 285–86).

59. Jin Xichang, 晴韻舘收藏古銭述記 (compiled 1825, first print 1834; repr., Shanghai: Zhongguo shudian, 1930), j.7, 3–18; Ta Chi Dai Truong, "Tien duc o Dang Trong," 267–335.

60. William Milbourne, Oriental Commerce (London: Black, Parry, 1813), 2:320.

61. Robert Wicks, "A Survey of Native Southeast Asian Coinage, circa 450–1850: Documentation and Typology," Ph.D. diss., Cornell University, 1983, 191.

62. Le Quy Don, Phu bien tap luc, Hanoi edition, in Le Quy Don toan Tap [A complete collection of Le Quy Don's works] (Hanoi: Nha xuat ban khoa hoc xa hoi, 1977), 1:236.

63. "Tran Tay phong tho ky" [Customs of Tran Tay], a manuscript housed in the Han Nom Institute, Hanoi, trans. Li Tana.

64. H. C. Kennedy, "Report of an Expedition in Southern Laos and Cambodia in the Early Part of the Year 1866," Journal of Royal Geographical Society 37 (1867): 311–12.

65. Baas Terwiel, Through Travelers' Eyes (Bangkok: Editions Duang Kamol, 1989), 190.

66. Wicks, "A Survey of Native Southeast Asian Coinage, circa 450–1850," 174–75.

67. Dai Nam thuc luc Tien Bien, year 1767, j.11, 153; Dai Nam thuc luc Chinh Bien [The Chronicle of Greater Vietnam, period of Gia Long], I, year 1785, 329; Tong Phuc Ngoan, Duong Van Chau, and Nham Van, eds., Xiemla quoc lo tinh tap luc [A collection of routes to the Kingdom of Siam], introduced by Chen Chingho (Hong Kong: New Asia Institute, Chinese University of Hong Kong, 1966), 71.

68. The Dynastic Chronicles, Bangkok Era, the First Reign, revised for publication by Kromluang Damrongrachanuphap, trans. and ed. by Thadeus Flood and Chadin Flood (Tokyo: Centre For East Asian Cultural Studies, 1978–1990), 135–37; Chính Biên says it was a woman from Hatien, who came to Ánh to "donate" rice to him (see Dai Nam thuc luc Chinh Bien, I, j.2, 323).

69. Hong Lysa, Thailand in the Nineteenth Century: Evolution of the Economy and Society (Singapore: Institute of Southeast Asian Studies, 1984), 40.

70. Puangthong Rungswasdisab, "Siam and the Contest for Control of the Trans-

Mekong Trading Networks from the Late Eighteenth to the Mid-Nineteenth Centuries," *The Water Frontier: Commerce and the Chinese in the Lower Mekong Region, 1750–1880*, ed. Nola Cooke and Li Tana (New York and Singapore: Rowman and Littlefield / Singapore University Press, 2004), 114.

71. Junko Koizumi, "Some Observations on the Economic Administration of King Rama 1," paper presented at International Association of Historians of Asia, 13th conference, Tokyo, 5–9 September 1994, 12–13.

72. "1803: start casting 'Gia Long thong bao' coin" (*Dai Nam thuc luc Chinh Bien*, I, j 21, 336).

73. *Dai Nam thuc luc Chinh Bien*, I, j.17–22, 568–632.

74. *Dai Nam thuc luc Chinh Bien*, I, j.20, 325.

75. Kwee, "Colonialism Creeping In."

76. Yang Duan Liu, *Qing dai huobi jinrong shigao*, 42.

77. 1751–1773: 914,480–1,043,280 strings. Man-houng Lin, "Jia-Dao qianjian xianxiang chansheng yuanyin 'qianduo qianlie lun' zhi shangque: Haishang fazhan shenru yingxiang jindai Zhongguo zhi yi shili" 嘉道錢賤現象產生原因「錢多錢劣論」之商榷——海上發展深入影響近代中國之一事例, *Zhongguo Haiyang fazhanshi lunwenji diwuji* 中國海洋發展史論文集第五輯, Maritime History Series (Taipei: Academia Sinica, 1993), 404–5.

78. Hans-Dieter Evers, "Traditional Trading Networks of Southeast Asia," *Archipel* 35 (1988): 91.

79. Yang Duanliu, *Qingdai huobi jinrong shigao*, 56; Man-houng Lin, "Jia-Dao qianjian xianxiang chansheng yuanyin 'qianduo qianlie lun' zhi shangque," 388.

IMPORT OF PROSPERITY

Luxurious Items Imported from China to Siam during the
Thonburi and Early Rattanakosin Periods (1767–1854)

~~~~~ Masuda Erika

The Chinese used to do their hair in topknot style but they switched to the pigtail
    style to obey the orders of the Lord of Tartar.
They wore elegant coats and hats, and also shoes wrapped with leather.
There are countless cities full of people where it is possible to travel freely as one
    wishes.
Kungtang [Guangzhou] is an exciting city incomparable to any other.
People are enchanted to watch the variety of products.
Numerous ships line up on the surface of water even during the night.
—Verses engraved on the walls of pavilions in the Pho temple (Wat Pho) to explain
the presence of foreigners during the latter half of the third reign

This Siamese verse about China was composed during the latter period of the
reign of Rama III (r. 1824–1851).[1] Previous studies on the rise and fall of the
Sino-Siamese junk trade demonstrate that after the trade reached its peak
within the framework of the Chinese tributary system in the early 1830s, it
started to decline gradually, and Siam reacted keenly to its decay and finally
seceded from the trade.[2] These studies give the misleading impression that
Siam abruptly stopped paying attention to China and that the latter disappeared entirely from the former's external perspective.[3] However, Siamese
documents show that the degradation of China's political prestige due to
the opium war and the loss of the economic privilege of trade in Guangzhou
under the tributary system did not soon change the prosperous image of
China, or of Guangzhou, although Siam gathered information concerning
political turmoil in East and Southeast Asia, in the middle of intense human

Figure 1 Map of Guangzhou drawn in Siam during the nineteenth century. *Source*: Santanee Phasuk and Philip Stott, *Royal Siamese Maps: War and Trade in Nineteenth Century Thailand* (Bangkok: River Books, 2004), 182–83.

communication between Guangzhou and Bangkok (see fig. 1). Moreover, the Siamese rulers' fondness for Chinese artwork continued even after Siam stopped sending tributary missions to China in the middle of the nineteenth century.

In order to analyze these cultural preferences and the underlying values, I focus on the Siamese ruling class's taste for luxurious or ornamental items, which were exported from China to Siam during the early Rattanakosin period.[4] Not only did the Siamese ruling class enjoy these items, but the latter sometimes embellished the Siamese monarchs' power.[5] While these imported items did not represent a substantial amount of the trade between the two countries, they nevertheless preoccupied the minds of the Siamese ruling class. These commodities were a small window into the Siamese rulers' understanding of China and their relationship with the Chinese courtiers and traders who acted as go-betweens. Examining how the Siamese ruling class related to Chinese luxury items may also clarify Siam's indigenous perception of her external relationships and diplomatic practices, which have been overlooked since the advent of western diplomacy.

The Fall of Ayutthaya in 1767: The Turning
Point of Siam's Understanding of China

The distinctive nature of Sino-Siamese interaction during the Thonburi era (1767–1782) merits observation, given that the kings of the early Rattanakosin dynasty perpetuated the basic pattern of King Taksin's external relationships, which emphasized Siam's interactions with China. The reign of King Taksin stands out in its peculiarity within the nature of Sino-Siamese relations in comparison with former ages. Since the tributary order was disrupted by the fall of Ayutthaya, in 1767, China was aware of the extinction of the royal line of the kingdom of Ayutthaya. Detailed descriptions of Siamese political turmoil in Chinese documents reflect China's interest in the aftermath of the Burmese destruction.[6] This Chinese response was the first case in the history of Sino-Siamese interaction. In the beginning, King Taksin's endeavour to reopen tributary relations was hindered by the obstructionist efforts of Mac Thien Tu of Hatien, who had thorough knowledge of Chinese diplomatic practices and alleged that King Taksin was a usurper.[7] This situation forced Siam to seek investiture from China in an effective and achievable way that would not stir up problems either in the Siamese or in the Chinese courts.

A notable example of Siam's effort to overcome a critical moment in its contacts with China can be found in a misleading piece of correspondence between the two courts. Having acceded to the throne, Rama I (r. 1782–1809) sent his letter to China on 15 May 1782, approximately two months after he had executed King Taksin, in early April in the same year. In this letter he said: "On 23rd of the second month in the 47th year of Qianlong [5 April 1782], as a great misfortune befell my father, Zhao, he perished from a disease. In his last moments, he admonished Hua, 'Be prudent in administration and do not change the old regulation. Attend to the country with devotion and obey the Celestial Court.'"[8] Rama I, who had been a military commander under King Taksin, referred to himself as Taksin's son in his letters, which were written in Chinese. It is noteworthy that in Chinese documents there are no references to King Taksin's fall from power, which was characterized in contemporary Siamese and Western sources as having resulted from his mental derangement. This ruse was never exposed, and eventually Rama I received investiture from China, in 1787.[9]

A letter written by the governor-general of Liangguang and presented to King Taksin's last mission in 1781 illustrates the same kind of distortion, which occurred when the Siamese court received a letter from the Chinese side.

A letter of the governor-general of Liangguang to the great Phra Khlang of Ayutthaya.[10] The gist of the matter is as follows. This time <Ayutthaya> appointed envoys to carry a royal letter and royal gifts for *chim kong*.[11] In Guangzhou, Hu iau and Hai iang were ordered to send the envoys, the royal letter and the royal gifts from Guangzhou to Beijing on 21 August in 1781. Personnel to carry the letter and gifts by forming a procession on the land route and the waterway were prepared according to custom. After the envoys finished the official mission in Beijing, they returned to Guangzhou. [We] let the envoys go back to report the course of the official mission on 3 March 1782. However, the envoys said that the monsoon was too severe to go against the wind and in December a tail wind would come. Then Luang Phakdi Wanit, a captain of a junk, came to receive the envoys by a Husong junk. Luang Aphai Chonthi and Khun Phakdi Kanlaya bore a letter whose contents are as follows. The old King passed away already. The new King ascended the throne. This was reported to Somdet Phra Chao Munpi already.[12] He knew this matter and thought as follows. The old King did not love his subjects and was apt to oppress them unjustly. Thus, he deserved death. As for the new King, he is adored by the subjects. Please accept royal gifts.[13]

It is important to note the evaluations given by the Chinese emperor to the Siamese kings. It is clear that "old king" and "new king" indicate King Taksin and Rama I. Although the Chinese side initially regarded King Taksin as a usurper, they gradually acknowledged his efforts to restore the country. Thus, negative valuations such as "he deserved death" must have resulted from the translation process.

Although the remarkable ascendancy of Chinese courtiers during the last period of Ayutthaya has already been demonstrated, it is worth emphasizing that the Siamese ruling class's concern with the nature of tributary relationship with China is hardly reflected in Siamese and Chinese source materials, even during a Chinese courtier's service of Phra Khlang, the highest executive of foreign affairs.[14] On the contrary, contemporary Chinese sources reveal that in the period following Ayutthaya's destruction, the Siamese court started to take into consideration the Chinese diplomatic practice of paying tribute, as they wanted to maintain smooth relations with China to find a way out of political turmoil after the Burmese destruction. Without going into detail about the extent to which King Taksin's personal intentions in contacts with China are reflected in the Chinese documents, it can be noted that during the premodern period, the Siamese

ruling class and the Chinese intermediaries, who negotiated directly with the Chinese officials in Guangzhou and Beijing, represented Siam's contacts with China.

During the early Rattanakosin period, the intentions of the Siamese kings in interaction with China gain greater clarity in Siamese sources.[15] Yet, the possibility of cover-ups should not be overlooked, since Siam was victorious in its competition with Hatien for dominance of the trade with China in the Gulf of Siam. Once Siam's disrupted tribute to China was restored, China no longer attempted to intervene in the domestic affairs of Siam.[16] In other words, despite the frequent dispatch of tributary missions to China, the Siamese rulers did not have to adapt themselves to the ideology of the Chinese tributary system. The Siamese ruling class started to show significant interest in imported commodities from China under these conditions of external negotiation with the Chinese, and given a greater understanding of the diplomatic contacts than in former ages.[17]

Imported Commodities from China in the Mind of the Siamese Ruling Class

In analyzing the pattern of imports and exports between Siam and China during the late eighteenth century and early nineteenth, Jennifer Wayne Cushman observed that Siam's imports from China were composed of "manufactured items for popular consumption."[18] On the other hand, Cushman also mentions briefly the high-quality goods ordered by the king and nobility.[19] Dhiravat na Pombejra provides, in his study on Siamese court life during the seventeenth century, many examples of luxury goods and rarities ordered by the Siamese king and nobles in their contacts with foreign countries.[20] During the early Rattanakosin period, it seems reasonable to suppose, the frequent dispatch of tributary missions to China offered the Siamese elites the means to acquire those varieties of commodities. Phraya Mahanuphap, one of the envoys of King Taksin's mission to China in 1781, portrays rich and abundant merchandise sold in various shops in Guangzhou.

> After making consultations, the governor-general came to pay respect to the royal letter and all the Siamese envoys.
> The envoys went by wagons carried by men along a wide street.
> Beautiful stones paved the street.
> Countless strange-looking stores elaborately made of rain trees stood along both sides of the street.
> There were golden boards engraved with the names of products in vermilion in front of the shops for customers to know what was on offer.

Censers and candles were painted with golden patterns, and beautiful bedsteads were arranged in rows.

As for merchandise for decoration, there were so many sundry riches.

There were dazzling silk clothes in various colors and the materials of which the clothes and curtains were made were luxurious.

There were countless bowls, earthen jars, plates, and chan-ap.[21]

Some people carried goods on their shoulders and drew the attention of customers skilfully, while others tried to do so by beating on pieces of wood.[22]

Siamese kings and nobility often ordered tributary missions or merchants, who in many cases were Chinese, to purchase or request rare and high-quality goods in China. A list of merchandise ordered by a Siamese noble in 1844 provides an insight into the pattern of desired goods ordered (see table 1).

This list is excerpted from the documents concerning the import and export of commodities by ships sent to China, outfitted by Siamese nobles from 1843 to 1845. Although further discussion is needed if the catalogued goods indeed represent the general pattern of Siam's imports from China during the early Rattanakosin period, most items in the list correspond to products cherished by the Siamese elites during the same era, which can be found in contemporary Siamese, Chinese, and Western language sources.

The testimony of a tributary mission in 1843 describes how Cantonese Ratkot-silk was ordered. On their return from the imperial audience in Beijing, while waiting in Guangzhou for the ship bound for Bangkok, the envoys received an order from the king to purchase the silk. The first envoy, with the mahatlek Mr. Phu, the captain and the lata of the Chinda Duangkaeo, spent two days locating a shop that could provide the requested item.[23] It is safe to assume that the cloths were first sent to Chamun Waiworanat, a Siamese noble who was the ship-owner, and then offered to the king.[24] F. A. Neale, who stayed in Siam less than a year, in 1840, remarked while enumerating a list of imported goods from China to Siam: "In such a place as Bangkok, where the fashion is to wear as little clothing as one possibly can, and where such a thing as a tailor's bill was never heard of, silks and satins are of course in small requisition."[25] However, as Cushman refutes this view by utilizing Western sources on Siamese external economic activities, it is important to say that Neale's judgment is totally unsound.[26] Silk cloth was in demand in the Siamese court as an item to bestow on nobles as rewards.[27]

The second noteworthy group of commodities in the catalogue was that

Table 1 Commodities Imported from Guangzhou by the Thepphakosin Outfitted by Chamun Waiworanat on 2 June 1844[i]

Captain	Mr. Kaeo,
Lata[ii]	Chin[iii] Nu,
88 crews	

1) 10 blocks of rectangle-shaped stone.
2) 10 blocks of round or rectangle-shaped stone.
3) 1 rectangle-shaped stone for a column with lotus-shaped decoration. There is an example. Length: 1 wa 3 khup. Made according to a sample.
4) 20–30 blocks of big marble. Buy as much as it would be possible.
5) 5,000 plates of rectangle-shaped marble for paving. Length: 18 niu.
6) 2 blocks of white stone, big enough to make 1 sok-high stone image.
7) Loy-Stone [?], big enough to make 2 or 3 beautiful round-shaped incense pots in Chinese style. 2 or 3 square ones are also needed if possible.
8) Branch or log-shaped red stone big enough to carve 2–3 niu-high's Buddha image is needed if possible.
9) Stone with pattern for handrail of a staircase 8, for column 8 total: 16.
10) Tung-stone [?] as much as they could buy.
11) 5 blocks of marble.
12) [Statue of] cow, water buffalo in life-size. 5–6 for each. Similar to those at pillar of the round shaped pagoda in the Phrakaeo temple.
13) [Statue of] middle sized hog deer and pig, 5–6 for each. [Statue of] peafowl 2–3. [Statue of] chicken, egret, 5–6 for each. Made of glazed ceramic, some stand up, sleep or fall face down.
14) A model of a junk ship, made of glazed ceramic, with sailor, green or red head. length:1 wa 1 sok.
15) 2 models of a cart, made of glazed ceramic, with a driver with harness. Length: 1 sok.
16) 4 glazed ceramic images of male, female, child, nobles, and commoners. 1 wa 6 khup high. Poses of standing up, sitting, sleeping.
17) 20 different models of Chinese pavilion. Made of ceramic. The same size as it was ordered last time.
18) Tiles with small holes. Dark yellow 1000, white 1000, dark blue 1000, green 1000, pale yellow 1000, total 5000, all in the same design.
19) 100 brass lanterns in hexangular shape.
20) 20 brass lamps.
21) 10 big brass lanterns. Diameter 1 wa 1 sok.
22) 20 flag of yellow tiger with wings, with no edge. Flags of dragon, centipede in 5 colors (dragon 200, centipede 100, total 300), total 320.
23) 300 bolts of Cantonese Ratkot-silk[iv] in good quality, 100 percent silk.
24) 40 bolts of silk in Chinese design of gardenia.

Table 1 Continued

Captain	Mr. Kaeo,
Lata[ii]	Chin[iii] Nu,
88 crews	

25) Cantonese gold brocade with no pattern. Yellow color 100, different colors 50, total 150. Cantonese gold brocade with pattern in different colors 50. Total 200.
26) Kin-silk [?] in different colors. Red and green are much needed while navy blue is less needed. Total 80 bolts. White is not needed.
27) Kalamphak,[v] as much as can be purchased.
28) Black horns to make snuff pipe [?], as much as can be purchased.
29) Your Lordship ordered to make 4 old style silver trays. Diameter 4 sun. Each should weight 9 tamlung.
30) Silver tray with high stand. Diameter 6 sun: 1. 15 sun: 1.Total 2.
31) Copper alloy tray with high stand. Weight: 8 tamlung 3 bat 1 fuang. Teapot shape. Large: 1, small: 1, Total: 2. There is an example.
32) 1 silver altar. Length of a side: 1, 3 chia.
33) A pair of glasses with golden-coated frame. Strong enough for a 60-year old person.

i. The noble Chamun Waiworanat was Chuang Bunnak, who played a dominant role in the government in the mid-nineteenth century.
ii. The clerk in Chinese seagoing junks of that time.
iii. The title Chin is used to signify that the person is of Chinese origin.
iv. The term ratkhot refers to cloth used to tie up one's body.
v. Kalamphak is a kind of herb.

Source: Records of the Third Reign, CS 1206–49, Manuscript Division, National Library of Thailand.

of stones, tiles, and Chinese-style stone images. These materials were used in the construction of royal palaces and residences of nobles, especially during the second and third reign when Chinese-style architecture and gardens decorated the homes of the nobles who resided in the capital. The royal chronicle tells of Suan Khwa (The garden of the right), a garden in the Chinese style built in the Grand Palace by Rama II. In 1818, when tributary envoys returned from China, they reported to the king that in China, even wealthy commoners laid out palatial gardens. After this report, Rama II ordered Prince Chetsadabodin (Rama III) to construct a magnificent garden on the right side of the royal palace.[28] Boat races that took place on the artificial ponds of the garden among the king's concubines, who wore beautiful silk dresses, are vividly described in the chronicle. Court officials

and palace ladies of the inner court took royal orders to compete with each other in adorning Chinese pavilions and floating houses on the ponds. "Life-size stone images in sitting or standing poses," altars, and lanterns were among the decorations.[29] Kanthika Sriudom suggests that courtiers sought those decorative items chiefly from China.[30] These materials were also used in temples. Ordered in the same year as the Thepphakosin was dispatched were a Chinese pavilion made of stone for the Pho temple and tiles to decorate the round pagoda of the Arun temple.[31]

Ceramic constitutes the third cluster of import merchandise from China during this period. The ruling elite ordered not only ware for decorative purposes, but also a large quantity of functional ware such as bowls and jars. Wares characterized by the most distinctive features of this period were *bencharong*, multicolored enamelled porcelain with Siamese-style motifs, and *lainamthong*, gold-washed ware. They were exclusively for export from China to Siam and used only by royalty and nobles. *Bencharong* started to be produced in China in the seventeenth century, and the early Rattanakosin period is known as the greatest period of their production, while lainamthong were mostly made during the early Rattanakosin period.[32] Occasionally, Siamese craftsmen were sent to China to supervise the production of these enamels.

It is well known that members of tributary missions were given individual rewards from the Chinese emperor in Beijing and Guangzhou, as well as in cities en route (see table 2). Some of these gifts may have been used as offerings to the court or sold to the nobility and the king. Furthermore, envoys spent around nine months in Guangzhou before and after their trip to Beijing. It is possible that this period was used to purchase goods that were ordered by the ruling class. When Rama IV (r. 1851–1868) dispatched a tributary mission to China in 1852, he required the envoys to order or buy merchandise in Guangzhou.[33] In a letter to the second envoy of the mission in January 1853, Rama IV reproached Kham, one of his trusted mahatlek, very harshly on the grounds that the envoys sold him inferior merchandise because they thought he could not offer high prices.[34] What infuriated him all the more was that they sold merchandise of better quality to nobles who belonged to the front palace of the second king, whom he saw as his formidable opponent.[35]

> He made people in the king's palace look much more impoverished than in another person's palace. Mr. Nak and Mr. Sombun do not serve me from the start. Thus they can be excused. But Kham, a fool, though he is

Table 2 Gifts Given to the Siamese Mission in 1843–1844[1]

January 1844 in Jiangxi
For each envoy: Fur clothing 1, kin-silk [?] 1 bolt, box of tea 4, Chinese orange 1.
For each attendant: clothes stuffed with cotton 1.

February 11, 1844 at the guesthouse for envoys in Beijing
For each envoy: Flower vase made out of glass 1, glass bottle for snuff 1, cup made out of glass 1, tea cup 1, saucer 1, box of tea 2, big box for a bag [?] 1, small box for a bag [?] 1, Chinese orange 5.

February 16, 1844 at the guesthouse for envoys after seeing the emperor at Wu Men in Beijing
For each envoy: phayun fish [?] 1, fur wrap 1, satin surfaced fur clothes 1, clothes stuffed with cotton 1, socks stuffed with cotton made of satin 1 pair, shoes made of black satin 1 pair.
For each attendant: fur hat 1, fur wrap 1, belt 1, cloth surfaced fur clothes 1, clothes stuffed with cotton 1, trousers 1 pair, socks 1 pair, shoes 1 pair.

February 19, 1844 at Zi Guang Ge palace in Beijing
For the first envoy: satin 14 bolts, pao [?] 3 pairs.[2]
For the second and third envoy and the manager: satin 10 bolts, pao [?] 3 pairs. Each item was given to each.

March 14, 1844 at Wu Men in Beijing
For the whole mission: silk 575 bolts, other varieties of cloth 360 bolts.

March 13, 1844 in Jiangxi
For each envoy: Box of tea 4, gauze 4 bolts, cup with a lid 10, folding fan 10.

---

1. Departing from Bangkok, the mission arrived in Guangzhou on 1 June 1843. They stayed in Beijing from 6 February to 27 March of the following year. They returned to Guangzhou on 20 June and left for Bangkok on 8 November, reaching Bangkok on 29 November. The Siamese tributary mission to China was usually composed of the first, second, and third envoys, a manager, an interpreter, and attendants.
2. In contemporary Thai, "pao" means "to blow" or "to perform on wind instrument"; however, I am not able to determine its meaning here.

Source: Phra Sawat Sunthon Aphai, "Khamhaikan thut ruang chamthun phraratchasan ok pai krung pakking cho. so. 1205" [A testimony of a mission which brought a royal letter to Beijing in 1843], *Thalaenggan prawattisat* 14.1 (1980): 88–109.

my personal attendant, when he came back this time, saw me as an unfortunate person who lost a wife. He showed great disrespect! He let the server women, royal concubines, and wives of nobles in the front palace possess higher quality articles than those of the king's palace. He made the king's palace into the palace of a thief. He thinks only about profit.[36]

On the other hand, when the king proclaimed Siam's secession from the Chinese tributary system, in 1868, he reproached the Siamese kings and nobles for their behavior in the past, when they had allowed themselves to be subordinate to the Chinese emperor, dazzled as they were by luxurious merchandise and gifts brought by Chinese traders in their contacts with China.[37] "[Chinese who acted as go-betweens] chose rarities of the best quality in Guangzhou as an offering to the Siamese king and praised craftsmanship in Guangzhou to the skies. The king received those gifts and nobles received bribe from the Chinese. They were very much pleased, as they were blind with greed."[38] Rama IV historically reviews the Sino-Siamese commercial relationship under the tributary system of China in the proclamation. He repeatedly mentions the treasures brought to the Siamese elites by Chinese traders and courtiers, who acted as intermediaries in Siam's contacts with China, yet he never refers to manufactured consumer products, which represented the largest percentage of Siam's imports from China. This may reflect the fact that Rama IV himself shared with his Siamese contemporaries a taste for the abundant riches from China, as was shown in his letter to the second envoy.

During the early Rattanakosin period, luxurious goods and rarities from China were often purchased by Chinese traders, and by tributary envoys in some cases. Mahatlek were among those sent to China.[39] This may reflect one aspect of the interests, especially the commercial interests, of the court in the early Rattanakosin period, where the king, nobles, foreign courtiers, and merchants were linked by very personal interconnecting ties, often developed through the gift-giving practice. In these circles, high-quality goods from China played a significant role in developing human relations.[40] At the same time, while these luxury commodities enhanced the court, members of the nobility and temple residents also played a part in forming a prosperous image of China, especially Guangzhou.

Siam's Sinicization: Visible but Undocumented

Taking the translation of Chinese literature and Chinese influence in architecture and decorative arts as examples, David K. Wyatt suggests identifying

the early Rattanakosin era as the period of "Sinicization" of Siam's intellectual life.[41] Chinese political influences were certainly more noticeable during this era than in previous times. Did the eagerness of the Siamese elites to decorate their court with imported items from China reflect their effort to adapt themselves to the Chinese tributary ideology?

In comparison with other East Asian kingdoms such as Korea, Japan, and Ryukyu, Siam seems to be indifferent to the influence of the ideology of the Chinese tributary system, since Siam did not belong to a cultural area where Chinese characters played a role in the process of communication. Toby finds that Siam followed the tributary convention of China in order to attain commercial profit and rejected the ideology of tribute when she was away from China.[42] However, the Siamese ruling class did not have to "reject" the ideology of the Chinese tributary system, since Chinese political ideology did not exercise direct influence over actual political and social scenes within the political sphere of Siam. In other words, they could choose what they wished to gain from China according to their "Siamese-centric" worldview. Maurizio Peleggi points out that before the latter half of the nineteenth century, especially after the foundation of the Rattanakosin dynasty, the Siamese elite recognized the social and symbolic meanings of Sinic civilization, namely "imperial recognition" from the Qing court and "material wealth" from maritime trade with China.[43] If one uses the term "imperial recognition" in the Chinese sense, it would be more appropriate to state that the value was appreciated by Chinese courtiers, who played an intermediary role between Siam and China, and had an affinity with China's ruling ideology. Another group of subjects who could have been sensitive to the political implications of Chinese investiture was the Chinese population of the kingdom, particularly residents in Bangkok, the kingdom's center of communication with China.

This raises the question of the values the Siamese ruling class acknowledged in their junk trade and relations with China. Rama II's intention in constructing Suan Khwa provides a hint on this point: "Even wealthy commoners are able to construct a garden to enjoy. If we, the monarch of a vast country, cannot have a place to glorify honor of the country, foreigners would disdain us as a small country. Thus, we should build one to entertain people from foreign countries and our tributary states, and let them say unanimously that the Siamese king has such a fantastic place."[44] This statement reveals the Siamese ruler's keenness to demonstrate the kingdom's glory to both its subjects and foreign visitors. John Crawfurd, who visited Siam during the second reign, describes the Siamese as a "ceremo-

nious people" and the importance they attached to ceremonies as "undue and ridiculous." According to him, breaches of ceremonial rules in Siam are "rather considered in the light of political crime than offences against mere etiquette."[45] However, for the Siamese during that period, the importance attached to ceremonies such as coronations, funerals of the king and nobles, and the reception of envoys sent by foreign monarchs was hardly "undue and ridiculous," as the grandeur of these ceremonies promoted a prosperous image of the ruling class to subjects and foreign visitors alike.[46]

Naturally, the ceremony of sending tributary missions to China was also included in those occasions, since the royal letter, an engraved golden missive to the Chinese emperor, was an important part of the ceremony.[47] Processions of envoys were dispatched from the royal palace and marched along the city of Thonburi/Bangkok to the Chao Phraya River once a year, from King Taksin's last mission to China in 1781 to Siam's last tributary mission to China, in 1852. These impressive scenes enhanced the king's power by stressing a close relationship with China, which brought wealth to Siam via the junk ships of tribute to China. In particular, Guangzhou, from which the busy seaborne traffic transported various merchandise and passengers to Bangkok, embodied prosperity (see fig. 2).[48]

Consequently, the Siamese adulation of China or Siam's Sinicization can be more obviously observed in the rarities and luxury goods imported from China and in the adornment of Siamese courts, palaces, and temples with these products, rather than in the recorded documents that recount Siamese efforts to adapt to the Chinese tributary order.[49]

In addition, the impact of Chinese fashions on the Siamese elite during the early Rattanakosin period has been passed down in the form of oral recollections and family images, for example, that of the Kanlayanamit family, one of the few Chinese families whose genealogy can be traced back to before the third reign. Kanlayanamit, the founder of the family, was born in Siam in 1784, the third year of the first reign. This ennobled Fujian merchant mandarin is known as a trusted subject of Rama III, with whom he shared the profits of the junk trade with China.[50] A scene with Chinese-style persons and ships in mural paintings of the Kanlayanamit temple, built on the riverside of the Chaopraya by To's fund in 1825, implies a shared image of the family's connection to China (see fig. 3).[51]

A portrait of Rama III in Chinese costume found in a book of Kulap Kritsanon, an author of various articles and essays on the history of Siam during the late nineteenth century, is another curious example (see fig. 4).[52] This picture does not necessarily imply the king adopted the costume accord-

Figure 2 Mural of the Suthat temple (Bangkok, the third reign). *Source:* Santi Leksukhum, *Chittakam thai samai ratchakan thi sam* [Thai mural paintings during the third reign] (Bangkok: Muang Boran, 2005), 164.

ing to his liking for Chinese fashion.[53] Rather, it could be considered one of the visual images of the past shared by people in the late nineteenth century regarding Chinese cultural elements in early Rattanakosin court life.

Well-known portraits of Rama IV, Rama V, and two nobles in the Chinese imperial robes should be evaluated in the political context in addition to the cultural one.[54] During the late period of the third reign, when the court started to obtain news on the political and economic disadvantages China was facing from defeat in the opium war, the king of Siam started to assess the nature of the Chinese world order critically for the first time in the history of Sino-Siamese relations.[55] Moreover, the court also had to be cautious about how the Chinese in the kingdom responded to the Siamese ruler's diplomatic policy toward China. Social disturbances caused by the increase in the Chinese population since the late period of the third reign made the rulers realize that the well-organized groups of Chinese could be hazardous to the security of society.[56] It could be said that the king, not Chinese go-betweens, had to come to terms with China's ruling ideology after the

Figure 3 Mural of the Kanlayanamit temple (Bangkok, the third reign). *Source*: Santi Leksukhum, *Chittakam thai samai ratchakan thi sam* [Thai mural paintings during the third reign] (Bangkok: Muang Boran, 2005), 172.

Figure 4 Portrait of Rama III. *Source*: Muang Boran, ed., *Suan Khwa* [The garden of the right] (Bangkok: Muang Boran, 1997), 69.

middle of the nineteenth century, when Siam stopped laying stress on inter-action with China in her external relationships.[57]

At the same time, even after Siam cut off the tributary relationship with China, Rama IV and Rama V (r. 1868–1910) continued to admire the cul-tural aspects of their relation with China as their predecessors had done.[58] This continuity has been overlooked by prior studies on the Sino-Siamese junk trade, which characterize Siam's view of China by the middle years of the nineteenth century as being determined only by commercial profit, and which portray an oversimplified picture of bilateral communications between the two countries. There is still a need for a careful examination of the various aspects of Siam's indigenous diplomatic view of China and its historical background before the conclusion of the Bowring Treaty with Britain in 1855, a view that may change over time. This view may provide a better understanding of the many characteristics of Siamese society during the Thonburi and early Rattanakosin periods.

Notes

1. The author of the verse is Kromma Mun Decha Adisorn, one of the princes who had the right of succession when Rama III passed away. The prince is said to have con-sulted Dan Beach Bradley, an American missionary, on the subject of knowledge of various races in the world. Thawisak Phuaksom, *Khon plaek na nana chat khong krung sayam* [Strangers from various countries in Siam] (Bangkok: Matichon, 2003), 120. Other races mentioned in the Wat Pho verses are Singhalese, Siamese, Karen, African, Dutch, Italian, French, Egyptian, Saracen, Japanese, Arab, Turk, Pathan Indian, Chulia (pre-sumably Chola) Indian, Petersburg Russian, Tartar Russian, Mon, Krasae, Ngiao (Thai yai), Burmese, Hindu, Malay, Hindu Brahman, Ramhet Brahman, Cham, Lao, Huihui, Korean, Vietnamese, Cambodian, and Ryukyuan (see ibid., 31–44). There is also an ex-ample of the prosperous image of China held by a Siamese noble during the reign of Rama II (r. 1809–1824). John Crawfurd, an envoy dispatched by the governor-general of British India, was sent to Bangkok to prevent Siamese interference with British com-mercial activities in the Malay Peninsula. He refers to a conversation between a Siamese minister and the commander of the mission ship, in which the minister states that China is a very populous nation and that the emperor regards himself as "the great-est King on earth" (Vajiranana National Library ed., *Crawfurd Papers: A Collection of Offi-cial Records Relating to the Mission of Dr. John Crawfurd Sent to Siam by the Government of India in the Year 1821* [Farnborough: Gregg, 1971], Org. pub. 1915, 95). Such images of China were occasionally introduced by members of tributary missions dispatched to China. For example, the 1843 tributary mission describes a crowded street in Beijing as fol-lows: "Around eleven in the morning, this street started to become very crowded, and this never ceased all day and night. We walked along trying to avoid the people passing through" (Phra Sawat Sunthon Aphai, "Khamhaikan thut ruang chamthun phraratcha-

san ok pai krung pakking cho. so. 1205" [A testimony of a mission which brought a royal letter to Beijing in 1843], *Thalaenggan prawattisat* 14. 1 [1980]: 88–109, 106).

2. Two landmark studies on the subject stress this point. See Jennifer Wayne Cushman, *Fields from the Sea: Chinese Junk Trade with Siam During the Late Eighteenth and Early Nineteenth Centuries* (Ithaca: Cornell University Press, 1993), chap. 7; Sarasin Viraphol, *Tribute and Profit: Sino-Siamese Trade, 1652–1853* (Massachusetts: Harvard University Press, 1997), chap. 11.

3. I have already pointed out that Siam's sending tributary missions to China during the early Rattanakosin period had political and cultural significance and implications, and that contemporary Siamese acknowledged these values even after Siam stopped sending tributary missions to China. See Masuda Erika, "The Last Siamese Tributary Missions to China, 1851–1854, and the 'Rejected' Value of *Chim Kong*," *Maritime China in Transition 1750–1850*, ed. Wang Gungwu and Ng Chin-keong (Wiesbaden: Harrassowitz Verlag, 2004), 33–42. In the current essay, I wish to extend the observation into more concrete examples in order to show the characteristic liking of the Siamese ruling class for Chinese culture during the era, the historical background of which can be traced back to the Thonburi period.

4. Yoshikawa Toshiharu has already enumerated the Chinese cultural products imported to Siam during this era. See Yoshikawa Toshiharu, "The Development of Chinese Culture within the Urban Formation of Nineteenth Century Bangkok," *The Formation of Urban Civilization in Southeast Asia* 2, ed. Tsubouchi Yoshihiro (Kyoto: Center for Southeast Asian Studies, Kyoto University, 1991), 52–73.

5. The fondness of the Siamese ruling class for Chinese luxury or ornamental items, especially porcelain, can be observed from the Ayutthaya period. This tendency was most noticeable during the early Rattanakosin period, when Siam's junk trade with China reached its peak.

6. China was involved in a campaign against Burma along the Yunnan–Burma border since 1766, which is one reason behind China's attempts to seek information on the political situation in mainland Southeast Asia, including Siam.

7. However, after Mac failed in attacking Chanthaburi in September 1769, China gradually changed her attitude and in 1771 became completely supportive of the king. China's favorable attitude persisted even when King Taksin sent his last mission to China in 1781. It may have been assumed that the Chinese emperor was going to give him an investiture. I have developed the subject of King Taksin's diplomatic contacts with China thoroughly in "The Fall of Ayutthaya and the Disrupted Order of Tribute to China, 1767–1782," *Taiwan Journal of Southeast Asian Studies* 4.2 (2007): 75–128.

8. Copies of Palace Memorials for the Reference of the Grand Council, Foreign Affairs, 03–164–03, First Historical Archives, Beijing, no. 7785–43. "Zhao" refers to King Taksin, who was known in China as Zheng Zhao. "Hua" refers to Rama I. The first five kings of the Rattanakosin dynasty had Chinese names, used exclusively for their communication with China. As is well known, they adopted "Zheng" as their Chinese surname, the same surname by which King Taksin was known.

9. Masuda Erika, "Rama I's Diplomacy toward China," paper presented at the Thirteenth Conference of International Association of Historians of Asia, Tokyo, 1993, 9.

10. The words *Phra Khlang* literally mean "national treasury." However, in this case "Chaophraya Phra Khlang," a title in the administrative system of premodern Siam, has been shortened. This title could be translated as the "Ministry of Financial Affairs." Ishii Yoneo analyzes the historical role and function of Phra Khlang in "Purakuran ko" [On Phra Khlang], *Tai kinseishi kenkyu josetsu* [An introduction of the history of Thailand during the fourteenth and eighteenth centuries] (Tokyo: Iwanami Shoten, 1999), 95–115.

11. The term *chim kong* is certainly a transliteration from the Chinese word *jingong*, whose meaning is "to go to pay tribute." The royal letters presented by the Siamese envoys were written usually in both Siamese and Chinese. In the Chinese version, the Siamese king would state clearly that he came to pay tribute as a subject, but in the Siamese version the term used for paying tribute, *chim kong*, could be ambiguously interpreted. Thus, it would be possible for those who used this term to claim that in the eyes of Siamese subjects, *chim kong* simply meant "to visit China to deliver royal gifts and a letter," thus allowing the Siamese to retain their honor as sovereigns of an independent country, while the Chinese construed Siam's *chim kong* as the vassal homage of Siam. It could be said that the term *chim kong* began appearing in Siamese royal letters to the Chinese emperor during the late Ayutthaya or Thonburi eras as mutual communication between the two countries intensified. See Masuda, "The Fall of Ayutthaya and the Disrupted Order of Tribute to China, 1767–1782," 117–18.

12. The term *Mun pi* means "ten thousand years" in Siamese. In this case, the title Somdet Phrachao Munpi presumably designates the Chinese emperor.

13. Records of the First Reign, CS 1143–3, Manuscript Division, National Library of Thailand.

14. For detailed argument on this topic, see Dhiravat na Pombejra, "Princes, Pretenders, and the Chinese Phrakhlang: An Analysis of the Dutch Evidence Concerning Siamese Court Politics, 1699–1734," *On the Eighteenth Century as a Category of Asian History*, ed. Leonard Blussé and Femme Gaastra (Aldershot: Ashgate, 1998), 107–30.

15. The most outstanding example is the fact that the convention of *hong* (transliterated from the Chinese *feng*), investiture from the Chinese emperor, is described as a very important Siamese royal tradition in the dynastic chronicles and the Siamese version of royal letters of the early Rattanakosin kings. This is an exceptional feature from the Ayutthaya period, when the only evidence confirming this tradition is found in Chinese documents. For further details on this point, see Masuda, "The Last Siamese Tributary Missions to China, 1851–1854," 41–42.

16. China sent investigators three times during the reign of King Taksin to gather information on the outcome of Ayutthaya's destruction. However, once Siam's disrupted order of tribute to China was recovered, China lost interest in Siamese politics and stopped sending investigators. It would be proper to say that the fall of Ayutthaya was not an occasion for China, or more precisely for the Qing court, to look at Siam in a new light.

17. Maps recently discovered in the Princess Abbhantri Paja Mansion in the Grand Palace are an outstanding informative source that illustrates the rise of knowledge of China by Siam. See Santanee Phasuk and Philip Stott, *Royal Siamese Maps: War and Trade in Nineteenth Century Thailand* (Bangkok: River Books, 2004), 162–89.

18. Cushman, *Fields from the Sea*, 66.

19. Ibid., 83.

20. Dhiravat na Pombejra, *Siamese Court Life in the Seventeenth Century as Depicted in European Sources* (Bangkok: Chulalongkorn University, 2001), chap. 8.

21. Chinese mixed candy usually eaten with Chinese tea.

22. Fine Arts Department, ed., *Wannakam Samai Thonburi, lem nung* [Literature of Thonburi era, vol. 1] (Bangkok: Fine Arts Department, 1996), 377.

23. Phra Sawat Sunthon Aphai, "Khamhaikan thut ruang chamthun phraratchasan," 104. A *mahatlek* was a royal page, an officer of a royal or princely household. Since the mahatlek served the king or other princes directly, the position was deemed a gateway to political ascendancy in the court.

24. Silk cloths were the main items among goods used to reward Siamese kings who paid tribute to the Chinese emperor. For example, the mission of 1843 was granted 575 bolts of the cloths. Ibid., 102.

25. F. A. Neale, *Narrative of a Residence at the Capital of the Kingdom of Siam* (Bangkok: White Lotus, 1997), Org. pub. 1852, 175. Neale's examples for imported Chinese goods are as follows: elegantly wrought China silks and satins, nankeens, grass cloth, tinsel, exquisitely carved ivory fans, fine painted feather fans, rice paper, and colourings upon rice paper, Japanese trays and tea-caddies, boxes of ivory worked puzzles, elegant Mosaic cut silver card-cases, bales of Chinese writing paper, boxes of watercolours, cakes of the finest Indian ink, and a vast deal of bird's nests, glues, gums, pickles and endless preserves, with a few straw hats and Chinese slippers (ibid., 173–74).

26. Cushman, *Fields from the Sea*, 73.

27. It is likely that silk cloth bestowed on nobles was used to make costumes to be worn when they served at the court. A picture of a court costume worn by Mom Rachothai, a noble during the fourth reign, depicts such an outfit. See Anake Nawigamune, *Kan taeng kai samai rattanakosin* [Thai costume in the Rattanakosin period] (Bangkok: Maung Boran, 2004), 43. The king awarded not only fabric, but also clothing to nobles. Anake presents a document from the third reign (1839) that concerns granting clothing to nobles, including a piece with a dragon pattern that might have been imported from China (ibid., 38).

28. Chaophraya Thiphakorawong, *Phraratcha phongsawadan krung rattanakosin ratchakan thi 2* [Royal chronicles of the Rattanakosin dynasty, the second reign] (Bangkok: Ongkankha Khrusapha, 1961), 93–94. The 1852 tributary mission testified that during their stay in Beijing, envoys led by Chinese officials visited natural landscape gardens in the palace. They recounted their observations of miniature mountains, small hills, ponds, streams, Chinese-style pavilions, and so on, stating, "It was so delightful to visit there beyond description" ([Phraya Sanphakon], "Raya thang ratchathut thai pai krung

pakking prathet chin" [A journey to Beijing in China of a royal mission of Thailand], *Thalaenggan prawattisat* 8 [1974]: 16–44, 27).

29. Thiphakorawong, *Phraratcha phongsawadan krung rattanakosin ratchakan thi 2*, 97–106.

30. Kanthika Sriudom, "'Phon' khong phranakhon nai samai ratchakan thi ha" [King Chulalongkorn's blessings for modern Bangkok], *Muangboran* 32.1 (2006): 36–49, 38.

31. Records of the Third Reign, CS 1206–49, Manuscript Division, National Library of Thailand.

32. Besides bencharong, Dawn F. Rooney mentions blue-and-white ware and brown ware as examples of imported Chinese ceramics of this period ("Chinese Export Ware in Thailand," *Siam in Trade and War: Royal Maps of the Nineteenth Century*, ed. Narisa Chakrabongse, Henry Ginsburg, Santanee Phasuk, and Dawn F. Rooney [Bangkok: River Books, 2006], 65–73). Natalie V. Robinson's *Sino-Thai Ceramics: In the National Museum, Bangkok, Thailand and in Private Collections* (Bangkok: Fine Arts Department, 1982) offers the most extensive discussion of bencharong, based on the examination of the collection of the ware. Rooney's forthcoming book examines bencharong's trading network historically within the context of the lucrative trade route between China and India. Dawn F. Rooney, *Bencharong: Royal Thai Porcelain* (Bangkok: River Books, 2010).

33. This was the last tribute that Siam paid to China. For a detailed account of this mission and its significance in Siamese history, see Masuda, "The Last Siamese Tributary Missions to China, 1851–1854," 34–38.

34. Rama IV dispatched Kham to Guangzhou to buy merchandise and to collect political information, while he himself stayed in China during the 1852 mission. According to Rama IV's letter, Kham and envoys jointly purchased merchandise such as a box and tray for betel nuts, a box for tobacco, silverworks, golden bracelets, cups made of jade, and so on to sell to the king and nobles in Bangkok.

35. For Rama IV's rivalry with his younger brother, the second king, see Junko Koizumi, "From a Water Buffalo to a Human Being: Woman and the Family in Siamese History," *Other Pasts: Woman, Gender and History in Early Modern Southeast Asia*, ed. Barbara Watson Andaya (Honolulu: Center for Southeast Asian Studies, University of Hawaii at Mānoa, 2000), 254–68, 264–65.

36. National Archives of Thailand, Document of Department of His Majesty's Principal Private Secretary, Fourth Reign No. 1, Ko/3.

37. For evaluation of this proclamation and its influence on Thai historians' perceptions of the premodern Sino-Siamese relationship, see Masuda, "The Last Siamese Tributary Missions to China, 1851–1854," 38–42.

38. Chomklaochaoyuhua, Phrabat somdet phra (King Rama IV), *Prachum prakat ratchakan thi 4 pho. so. 2408–2411* [Collected proclamations of the fourth reign, 1865–1868] (Bangkok: Ongkankha Khrusapha, 1961), 159–60.

39. A large number of mahatlek were included in King Taksin's 1781 mission to China. See Kromma Luang Narintharathewi, *Chotmai khwam songcham khong phrachao paiyikathoe kromma luang narintharathewi chao khrok watpho* [Memoirs of Kromma Luang Narintharathewi, Royal Princess of the Pho Temple] (Nonthaburi: Ton Chabap, 2003), 232.

40. Siamese sources reveal that before visiting Bangkok in 1855 to negotiate a trade treaty, John Bowring made contact with Kham and the Siamese tributary envoys who visited in 1852. Bowring helped Kham issue instructions to Chinese craftsmen to make high-quality products according to Rama IV's orders. In addition, Bowring handed to Kham a golden clock with a diamond-decorated cover, an English-style writing tool, and a golden container with legs and a pointed cover as gifts to Rama IV. Bowring's effort seemed likely to bring good results in building good relations with the king. Records of the Fourth Reign, CS 1216–109, Manuscript Division, National Library of Thailand.

41. David K. Wyatt, *The Politics of Reform in Thailand: Education in the Reign of King Chulalong-korn* (New Haven: Yale University Press, 1969), 25. As introduced in Lucille Chia's essay in the current volume, the translation of *San guo yanyi* (The romance of the three kingdoms) in the first reign is often referred to as an example of Siam's absorption or reconceptualization of Chinese cultural products. For detailed arguments on this topic, see Craig J. Reynolds, "Tycoons and Warlords: Modern Thai Social Formations and Chinese Historical Romance," *Sojourners and Settlers: Histories of Southeast Asia and the Chinese,* ed. Anthony Reid (Sydney: Allen and Unwin, 1996), 115–47.

42. Ronald P. Toby, *State and Diplomacy in Early Modern Japan* (Stanford: Stanford University Press, 1991), 202.

43. Maurizio Peleggi, *Lords of Things: The Fashioning of the Siamese Monarchy's Modern Image* (Honolulu: University of Hawaii Press, 2002), 164.

44. Thiphakorawong, *Phraratcha phongsawadan krung rattanakosin ratchakan thi 2,* 93. Chao Anu, king of Vientiane, was invited to the garden by Rama II. Naengnoi Saksi, *Phra aphinaoniwet, phraratcha niwet nai phrabat somdet phra chomklao chaoyuhua* [Phra aphinaoniwet: A palace of Rama IV] (Bangkok: Matichon, 2006), 77–78.

45. John Crawfurd, *Journal of an Embassy to the Courts of Siam and Cochin China* (Singapore, New York: Oxford University Press, 1987), org. pub. 1828, 349.

46. Prince Damrong explains that one of Rama II's intentions in building the garden was to demonstrate to neighboring countries Siam's restoration after the devastation of Ayutthaya. Damrong Rachanuphap, Somdet Phrachao Borommawongthoe Krom Phraya, ed., *Phongsawadan krung rattanakosin ratchakan thi 2, lem 2* [Royal chronicles of the Rattanakosin dynasty, the second reign, vol. 2] (Bangkok: Ongkankha Khrusapha, 1962), 25–27.

47. Rama II's letter to the Daoguang emperor, preserved in the Late Palace Museum of Taiwan, is one of very few extant golden missives of the Siamese monarchs. I wrote a brief introduction to this letter in "Phraratchasan charuk nai phaen suphannabat phraratchathan chakraphat chin" [A royal golden missive sent to the Chinese emperor], *Sinlapa Watthanatham* 29.10 (2008): 46–49. According to Dhiravat, translation of foreign monarchs' letters was also regarded as part of the ritual of the reception (*Siamese Court Life in the Seventeenth Century as Depicted in European Sources,* 105–6).

48. We can be fairly certain that the Chinese junk, a common motif of temple murals in early Rattanakosin Bangkok, impressed residents of the city. A mural painting of the

Suthat temple portrays wealth from China brought by junks (see fig. 2). In examining the meaning of the rituals of receiving Siamese tributary envoys in Guangzhou during the Qing periods, Murao Susumu points out that the ritual was a familiar scene for residents of the city ("Kaieneki" [Guesthouse for foreign envoys], *Chugoku bunka kenkyu* 16 (1999): 1–21, 9–10). In analyzing how and by whom these rituals, including diplomatic receptions and gift giving, were recognized, scholars should give greater attention to the intensified human exchange between Bangkok and Guangzhou in busy seaborne traffic after the fall of Ayutthaya. Moreover, as Koizumi Junko emphasizes, it is important to extend the sphere of observation about the meaning of the Chinese emperor's bestowal of silk cloth on the Siamese king, from the Sino-Siamese bilateral relationship to the interrelationship among China's tributary states or Siam's neighboring states ("Choko to joyaku no aida' [Between tribute and treaty], *Rekishi jojyutsu to nashonarizumu: Tai kindaishi hihan josetsu* [Historiography and nationalism: Reflections on modern Thai history] [Tokyo: University of Tokyo Press, 2006], 161–97, 163).

49. Nidhi points out that unlike in the Ayutthaya period, opportunities to gain wealth from overseas trade and to demonstrate power by displaying it were no longer the exclusive possession of the king, but fully enjoyed by new bourgeoisie in Bangkok, specifically nobles and Chinese merchants who formed a successful partnership in the pursuit of economic interests. Eoseewong Nidhi, *Pak kai lae bai rua* [Pen and sail] (Bangkok: Amarin, 1984), 226–27.

50. To's life history as presented here is derived from a book compiled by his descendants. Chan Kanlayanamit and Phenphan Kanlayanamit, *Sakun kanlayanamit* [The Kanlayanamit family] (Bangkok: Suan Thonthin, 1993). A recollection of the Chinese import merchandise is found in an account of Tha Phra Palace, Rama III's residence when he was crown prince in the early nineteenth century. The storyteller is M. R. W. Nat Chumsai, a descendant of Kromma Khun Ratcha Sihawikrom, the founder of the Chumsai family, who resided in the palace during 1835 and 1868. Nat Chumsai refers to Chinese stone images and the shards of Chinese ceramics scattered and buried in the ground of the palace in his childhood in the late nineteenth century. See Sumet Chumsai na Ayutthaya, *Wang Tha phra* [The Tha Phra Palace] (cremation volume of M. R. W. Thawilapha Puranasukhon, Makutkasattriyaram temple, 1985), 16–17. Craig J. Reynolds also provides examples of Chinese culture at the court as reflected in the memories noblemen handed down to their offspring ("Tycoons and Warlords," 123–25).

51. Santi Leksukhum surmises that a person in yellow Chinese dress on the left side of the painting could be To himself, while Malenee Gumperayarnnont infers that the same figure could be the Chinese emperor in the imagination of Siamese painters. Santi Leksukhum, *Chittakam thai samai ratchakan thi sam* [Thai mural paintings during the third reign] (Bangkok: Muang Boran, 2005), 172; Malenee Gumperayarnnont, "Chittakam faphanang phra ubosot wat kanlayanamit: Ruang ching ru chintanakan" [Mural paintings at the ubosot of Wat Kanlayanamit: Imagination or nonfiction], *Muangboran* 32. 3 (2006): 88–101, 96.

52. Kulap Kritsanon, *Ayatiwat* [On civilization and culture] (Bangkok: Amarin, 1995),

99. On the contrary, Kulap placed pictures of Rama IV and Rama V in Western costume in the same book (13, 40).

53. The king's portrait was painted from the fourth reign. See Peleggi, Lords of Things, 62.

54. One of the nobles is Kromma Khun Ratcha Sihawikrom. The pictures can be seen in Samniang Khanthachawana, "Thian moeng toei: Wehatchamrun" [Tianmingdian: Wehatchamrun Palace], Sengthang setthakit chabap phiset: Khon chin 200 pi phai tai phraborommaphothisomphan phak 2 [Special volume of route of economy: The Chinese during 200 years under the royal patronage, part 2], Senthang setthakit (Bangkok: Senthang Setthakit, 1983), 20–23, 21. More detailed discussion of the political background during the latter half of the nineteenth century and the early years of the twentieth as reflected in those portraits is demonstrated in Koizumi, "Choko to joyaku no aida," 161–97. Samniang Khanthachawana also refers to this point in "Thian moeng toei," 23.

55. On the subject of political information on China that Siam gained during the period, see Masuda, "The Last Siamese Tributary Missions to China, 1851–1854," 40–41, and Masuda, "The Domestic Opium War of Rama III: Siamese Ruler's Perception of the Chinese Population during the Late Period of King Rama III's Reign," South and Southeast Asia Culture and Religion 2 (2008): 129–50, 130–36.

56. Masuda, "The Domestic Opium War," 130–43.

57. Reynolds stresses the impact of Chinese ideology on the Siamese elite after the late eighteenth century in his analysis of the process of translating San guo yanyi in the political context of Siamese history after the fall of Ayutthaya. While his suggestion is thought-provoking, there is room for argument on this point since the paucity of Siamese contemporary documents obstructs attempts to explain in a straightforward manner how and by whom the novel was read. See Reynolds, "Tycoons and Warlords," 119–27.

58. Kanthika Sriudom explains that when Rama V built the Suan Dusit Palace, he named various buildings, roads, and bridges after motifs of Chinese tableware, the collection of which was popular among the ruling elite and inspired competition during the fourth and fifth reigns (" 'Phon' khong phranakhon," 38–41).

A SINO-INDONESIAN COMMODITY CHAIN
The Trade in Tortoiseshell in the Late Seventeenth and Eighteenth Centuries

~~~~~ Heather Sutherland

We usually analyze the social structure of early modern long distance trade in Asia in terms of ethnicity, seen as the basis for merchant networks, or, with a more cultural emphasis, as expressed in diaspora.[1] This emphasis also fits the categories used by our main sources, whether they are the archives of the great European trading companies or Chinese annals.[2] Given, however, that trade is driven by the search for profit, it would be more logical to use primarily economic models. Relationships can then be located within political economies, rather than seen as expressions of (essentialized) socio-cultural entities. This is easier said than done, as in societies where there is a relatively low level of institutionalization, both legal and bureaucratic, security is sought through personal relationships (from kin to patronage), and hence poorly documented. We usually only glimpse aspects of complex transactions (often as recorded by European competitors or regulators), and there is little quantitative information, let alone long series of data.

Chinese traders in Indonesia were once commonly defined in terms of their relationships with European powers, as facilitators of VOC (Verenigde Oostindische Compagnie, or Dutch East India Company) expansion, or as "middlemen" in the service of (pre-, post-) colonial political elites. De-colonization, the resulting shifts in historiography, and the development of Asian early modern history have discredited this view. An emphasis on the deterritorialized Chinese community of the diaspora has become more popular. But this homogenizing emphasis on an assumed fixed, even static, ethnic identity ignores both the dynamic of ethnogenesis in migrant societies, and differentiation within the category "Chinese."[3] It also underestimates the instrumentalist use of both ethnic and trans-ethnic ties, and the pliable nature of boundaries.[4]

The idea of "diaspora" reflects current preoccupations, including a simplified Sinocentrism implicit in the idea of the "Han civilizational state," the influence of modern identity politics, including that of long-distance nationalism, and fears of Chinese economic competition, as manifested in a "bamboo network."[5] This concept also encourages the dissolution of specific identities into "the Chinese" and excessive emphasis on connections with China. Furthermore, it tends to suggest that all overseas Chinese are the same, underestimating both the range of available identities (various "Chinese," mestizo, and local) and the institutionalized roles that negotiated difference among "Chinese" and indigenous communities. At least in trading ports, both these categories—indigenous and Chinese—could be subdivided into localized, floating, and "homeland-based" groups, with the caveat that individuals were geographically and socially mobile.

Identity was relatively flexible, and a major factor in ensuring access to resources. Social capital (trust, norms, networks) was mobilized through personal ties, which were often—but by no means always—organized around ideas of cultural identity.[6] It is essential that the distinction between categories of analysis and categories of practice be clear. Social actors may use "ethnic" labels to construct their own frames of reference, reflecting social norms, but this is not to say that ethnicity was actually decisive in determining behavior. Class, for example, might prove to be a more productive analytic tool. Moreover, the different communities were hierarchical; intra- and intercommunal vertical patron-client ties and horizontal instrumental friendships were fundamental to success. In immigrant communities, dependent for security and income on exploiting and developing niche opportunities, self-interest and (limited) trust created essential bonds. These alliances pooled the resources, such as knowledge, capital, technology, and access to labor, which were essential to maintaining commodity chains, the sequence of transactions moving goods from producers to consumers.[7]

Commodity chain analyses are often used to highlight inequalities, for example, between cores and peripheries in world-systems theory. In Wallerstein's classic formulation the typical exchange of manufactured goods from the center for raw materials from the periphery always benefited the core, as in (neo)colonial exchange.[8] At first glance, much early modern trade also appears exploitative, as prices paid in the production zones are extremely low compared to those in the areas of consumption.

However, as Michael Pearson has shown in his discussion of the trade between India and East Africa, what appears to be a malign, unequal exchange can actually be of mutual benefit if the commodities have a significantly dif-

ferent use-value in the two zones. This was so in the case Pearson discusses: ivory and gold were cheap in East Africa, where wealth was measured in terms of cattle and women, but worth a great deal in India.[9] In such circumstances all may benefit, particularly if needs are complementary and dependence reciprocal or even exclusive. Contemporary commodity-chain models stress the role of transnational capital and knowledge-based activities, such as management, technology, or marketing.[10] At different levels in the chain, different forms of knowledge are appropriate and profitable, often forming the basis for a division of labor. This also applies to trade in the early modern period.

In this essay I consider the traffic in sea products between eastern Southeast Asia and China, specifically the tortoiseshell trade between Makassar and Amoy (Xiamen) in the seventeenth century and the eighteenth. Documentation is fragmentary, but contextualization enables me to extract the maximum possible information. While "ethnicity" was a basic category in organizing and describing the marine-products commodity chain, transcommunal interdependence was exemplified in complementary forms of social capital, knowledge, and access to finance (in particular credit). Shifts in business practice also indicate that ethnic specialization was not inherent, but contingent, as location within the chain changed over time.

The Context: Makassar and Trade

The geographical facts of an excellent site determined Makassar's location, a sheltered harbor on the southwest peninsula of Sulawesi (Celebes), facing the Makassar Straits between Borneo and Sulawesi.[11] However, the timing of Makassar's rise was due to politicoeconomic developments in Europe, China, and the region—particularly in the strategic Straits of Melaka and Maluku (the Moluccas or "Spice Islands"). South Sulawesi had participated in trade with China and India since before the thirteenth century, but only indirectly, via the southern Philippines and the northeast coast of Java.[12] Makassar itself lay on a commercial backwater and produced few commodities, so its traders had to tap into trading flows at other locations, where local and transit goods were accumulated and exchanged (see map 1).

The main sea lanes linking China to Melaka, Java, and Maluku bypassed the Makassar Straits, running down through the Sulu Sea, or past the north Borneo sultanate of Brunei, or via Java.[13] Makassar's own exports were not rich enough to attract traders when more valuable cargoes (notably Maluku spices) could be picked up elsewhere. In the early sixteenth century, before Makassar became a major commercial player, the Portuguese Tomé Pires

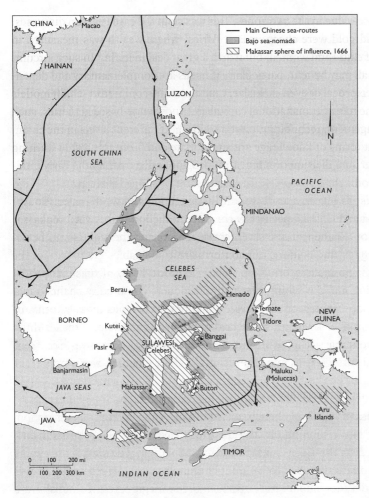

Map 1 Makassar's sphere of influence before 1669.

noted that it exchanged rice, foodstuffs, and gold for Gujarati, Bengali, and Coromandel textiles. Vessels from Makassar sailed to Java, Melaka, Borneo, and Siam, and "all the places between Pahang and Siam."[14] Most of these ships may have been owned and crewed by Makassar-based traders of outside origin, such as Malays or Javanese, rather than by local Sulawesians.[15] Commerce was probably of less importance to local elites than control of the wet-rice fields that had provided the basis for centralizing power.

However, during the first half of the sixteenth century, various imperial ambitions combined to make Makassar an attractive trading center. The galleon link between Manila and Acapulco (1565), Central Javanese Mataram's

conquest of the north Java ports (1625), and, in the 1620s, campaigns to establish a spice monopoly in Maluku by the voc all drew traffic toward the Makassar Straits. By the 1630s Makassar was receiving one junk a year from Macau and two or three from Maluku.[16] After the Dutch took Melaka, in 1641, some Indian Muslim, Portuguese, and Malay merchants left to seek friendlier harbors, and Makassar benefited. These men brought their contacts, capital, and market knowledge with them, as well as their ambition.[17]

The exchange of Indian textiles for "smuggled" Maluku spices became Makassar's main attraction for European and Indian merchants, but it was by no means the only commerce. Makassar transhipped eastern archipelago commodities like wax, tortoiseshell, slaves, gold, and sandalwood, as well as ironware and textiles. Certain consumption goods, including sugar, tobacco, horses, and textiles were destined for internal use, while some locally produced textiles, coins, rice, and iron were exported.[18]

Merchants focused on distant markets found many of these items uninteresting, either because of cost-profit calculations, or because they could be more easily obtained elsewhere. But after the 1620s, as the relative availability of spices attracted more traders, the resulting opportunities drew other profitable commodities to Makassar, such as Chinese goods from Macau and Manila. The once peripheral harbor emerged as an important port of call. By the mid-seventeenth century, Makassar had joined Brunei and Sulu as a central link in the regional trade in sea and forest products.[19]

Makassar may have benefited from the voc's military expansion in Maluku, but it soon had to pay the price. The company's obsession with safeguarding the spice monopoly required strong action against "smuggling," so Makassar had to be brought under control. After a series of ultimata, blockades, and military campaigns, the Portuguese and English were expelled, and it was decreed that Chinese and Indian goods could be obtained only from Dutch Batavia. The company finally conquered Makassar, in 1666–1669, generating a wave of refugees who settled throughout the Malay world, creating networks that were to help shape later political and commercial trends.[20] However, a Chinese trading presence remained in Makassar and was able to tap into the energy released with the dramatic expansion of Chinese trade and migration following the consolidation of Qing control in the 1680s.

The Chinese, the voc, and the Bugis

We know little of Makassar's Chinese community before Dutch documentation began in the early seventeenth century, although we do know that they

had their own residential area, and some acted as trading partners and incidental advisers to the ruler and the company. Chinese identified with VOC patrons were vulnerable to political tides before the conquest, but benefited after the war; conversely, those closest to the court were more likely to move on once the Dutch took over in 1669.[21] After the conquest, the victorious Admiral Speelman listed nineteen Makassar Chinese, noting that about half had been resident in the town before the war, and the rest had arrived subsequently.[22]

It might be assumed that the Chinese community would expand rapidly under the VOC, but growth was slow in the seventeenth century.[23] A casual reader of the 1688 census might have been impressed by a "Chinese" community said to number 627, but few (perhaps only the men) would have been of full Chinese descent, as the category included not only 52 men, 52 women, and 112 children, but also 342 slaves and 69 debt-bondsmen.[24] It is true that Ongwatko (captain of the Chinese, 1669–1701) was one of the two most prominent traders of the postwar years (the other being the Indian Muslim Mapule), but when he was succeeded by his son Ongieko, in 1701, the VOC referred disparagingly to the "small handful" of Chinese.[25] A *peranakan* group of locally born creoles had developed, of mixed ancestry, but in 1701 the VOC did not yet rate them as Chinese, hence the dismissive "handful."[26] In 1724, the company reckoned there were just forty Chinese inhabitants of Makassar.[27]

The Makassar Chinese community seems to have been smaller and less stable than some other comparable groups, such as that of Ambon, which was also active in agriculture.[28] Indeed, VOC officials hoped that it might be possible to eliminate Chinese trade in the waters around Sulawesi and Maluku; in 1727 they restricted traffic in the hope that Chinese commerce around the Spice Islands would "die out."[29] In 1731 Chinese trade east of Makassar was banned.[30] This had the unexpected effect of making Makassar more attractive as an entrepôt, and it seems that just as the Dutch were becoming optimistic about the decline of their competitors, the fundamental changes that were to lead to the "Chinese century" were gathering momentum.[31] In Makassar, the origins of these changes lay in an increasing Chinese appetite for trepang, the unprepossessing sea slugs known also as *bêche-de-mer*.[32]

Trepang fishermen are first mentioned in the Makassar archives in 1710, but such references quickly became common. In 1732 the VOC decided to appoint a lieutenant of the Chinese to assist the captain, because Chinese commerce was increasing, driven by growth in the trepang trade.[33] Although

at first this was primarily routed through Batavia, the establishment of an (initially) erratic direct junk trade with Amoy after 1746 initiated a further expansion of the Chinese community.[34] In 1759 Chinese immigration was subjected to supervision, but restrictions seem to have become serious only in the 1780s, when the economic power of the Chinese created problems for Makassar's Dutch administration.[35]

For the VOC, trade control was a priority; some products, such as spices, were subject to monopoly, others were restricted, while ship movements were channeled through systems of passes.[36] This was more difficult in some regions, and for some commodities, depending on the geographical distribution of production and markets. Forest and marine commodities (except pearls) were particularly difficult to manage, with their dispersed collecting zones and multiple potential exchange sites, while highly localized spice production was particularly amenable to monopoly.[37] Local Dutch officials were often less interested than Batavia in limiting commerce, perhaps because they themselves, and the communities they administered, derived such benefits from it. Already in 1695, Makassar indignantly rejected Batavia's suggestion that tortoiseshell was being smuggled into the port.[38]

VOC bases were few, and their patrols easily evaded. Much trade went underground, developing connections beyond Dutch control. Sulawesi Bugis and Makassarese, Chinese and, particularly after 1760, country traders operating out of India were all, in varying degrees, in competition with the company. For the trade in sea products, this was particularly true in the waters around Borneo, the Sulu Sea, southern Maluku, and the arc of islands further south known as Nusa Tenggara.[39]

Chinese and "Bugis" (that is, anyone from South Sulawesi) were crucial to the integration of local networks into long-distance commerce. Following Bugis dispersal at the end of the seventeenth century, their trade became focused on an axis centered on Johor-Riau to the west and Makassar to the east. Indeed, despite the company's attempted stranglehold, Bugis activity increased.[40] Chinese traders, the second major integrating factor, were regarded by the Dutch with profound ambivalence. They may have played an essential role in VOC settlements, but the company was deeply suspicious of their role in competitive trading systems.[41] The sultans of both Ternate and Tidore, however, were hostile to Dutch attempts to limit the lucrative Chinese presence.[42] Geography, profit incentives, and the resilience of Asian networks ensured that the newcomers from the north remained marginal to entire economic sectors, despite the military dominance of the VOC.

The Trade in Marine Commodities

Sea products such as tortoiseshell, pearls, coral, and seaweed had been valued imports into China from at least the time of the Sung. Tortoiseshell came from Champa, the Philippines, Java, Borneo, Sumatra, Malaya, and Thailand; Borneo and Sulu, easily accessed from Makassar, were specifically listed in the early fifteenth century.[43] Apart from an occasional reference to India, tortoiseshell is given as coming from Southeast Asia. Late Ming tax lists include Indonesian products such as aromatic woods, resins, plants, spices, seeds, rhinoceros and deer horn, ivory, skins, feathers, birds' nests, and sea products. The most important marine commodities were agar-agar (seaweeds) and tortoiseshell, of which the most valuable came from the hawksbill turtle. The plates that comprise the shell were described as being yellowish brown with black streaks, and were known to the Dutch as karet, a word of West Indian origin.[44]

Eastern Indonesia first joins Sulu and Borneo as a supplier of tortoiseshell in the late sixteenth century, with turtle populations being reported at north and west Sulawesi, particularly the Gulf of Tomini; Menado was the site of a major trading center. Roderich Ptak believes most of this trade was in local hands: "The Chinese, if they took part in it, certainly came to eastern Indonesia by way of Java, as private merchants from Fujien or Kwangtung or as settlers from the western part of Indonesia. Few, if any, seem to have sailed the 'eastern route' that travelled down from the Sulu archipelago via Minahassa, the Moluccas and Banda islands."[45]

The catchment areas and collecting markets for turtles and trepang overlapped, but trade in the former was much older, smaller, and more diffuse. If trepang virtually all went to China, tortoiseshell was a desirable product in many markets; moreover, the differences between hunting turtles and gathering trepang meant karet could not develop into a bulk commodity like trepang. Nevertheless, the expansion of fishing fleets and markets would have intensified the trade in turtles. As was the case with trepang, the tortoiseshell commodity chain involved skippers and fishermen, intermediate traders, wholesale merchants, and shippers. Chinese generally provided marketing and product expertise, and most of the capital; Sulawesians and Malays were prominent traders, although peranakan Chinese gained ground in the late eighteenth century, while Buginese and Makassarese did much of the gathering and fishing.[46] But one particular group specialized in turtle-catching: the "sea nomads" or "sea gypsies," or Bajo, as I will call them hereafter.[47]

Turtle-favored environments are characterized by shallow seas offering seagrass beds for feeding and access to sandy beaches which serve as nesting sites; the Sulu Sea in the southern Philippines and the coastal waters of eastern Indonesia met such needs, and consequently were rich in turtles.[48] So it is not surprising that Brunei, in northeast Borneo, and the southern Philippine sultanates of Sulu and Maguindinao were early centers of the turtle trade. They also claimed hegemony over Bajo communities' home waters. Although these groups were widely distributed throughout Southeast Asia, major concentrations were to be found around the Riau-Lingga archipelago, east and northwest Borneo, the coasts of south, east, and north Sulawesi, the Sulu Sea, and Nusa Tenggara. Typically, these were shallow waters dotted with coral reefs and islands.

The eastern archipelago Bajo was described by François Valentijn at the end of the seventeenth century, and then by J. N. Vosmaer over a hundred years later.[49] Vosmaer, a trader who spent months in Sulawesi, was familiar with the tortoiseshell trade and the Bajo. Like modern biologists, the Bajo distinguished four sorts of turtle; the most sought after was the hawksbill, the source of karet, the thirteen or more plates of which the shell was composed. The Chinese preferred a shell with regular markings in black and white; they were prepared to pay extraordinary prices for such "white turtles."[50] The VOC labeled this white and transparent shell "Japanese"; the other top-quality type, "Surat," was clear and well "flamed," but much less valuable.[51] The Chinese would also pay up to fifty guilders for the hind feet of turtles, if they weighed more than half a kati which was, however, very rare.[52] The combined karet from one turtle rarely exceeded 3 kati (nearly 2 kg.) in weight, although it was said that occasionally 4 to 5 kati could be taken from one animal.[53]

By the early seventeenth century, the VOC was already interested in tortoiseshell as a cargo to be exchanged in Japan and India for, respectively, metals and textiles. In fact, the first reference to tortoiseshell in the company's *Generale Missiven* refers to the latter; in 1614 it was reported that there was great potential for ambergris and tortoiseshell sales in India. In 1617 the Dutch estimated that they could dispose of 4,000 to 5,000 pounds in Surat each year, while Cambay and Masulipatnam were other promising markets. However, before they could sell their karet, they first had to buy it, in increasingly fierce competition with other merchants, including the English and the French. The former, by far the most important, had established their Makassar lodge in 1614 primarily to access foodstuffs, but by the mid-1620s

they were increasingly interested in high-value commodities such as spices and tortoiseshell.[54]

The local royal courts also benefited from the expansion of trade: in 1638 VOC officials recorded that the ruler of Makassar drew taxes from rice, tortoiseshell, cloves, wax and pepper, copper and iron.[55] By the mid-seventeenth century, the Dutch were emphasizing the strong grip of the Makassar Chinese on the tortoiseshell trade, noting in 1657 that they could only obtain karet "through our Chinese creatures."[56] The English experienced similar difficulties in obtaining supplies, and in 1665 they complained that the VOC was giving 5 percent commission to their Chinese agents, who then used credit to monopolize imports.[57] After the Dutch conquest, in 1669, the English were expelled, but the key Chinese role in Makassar's tortoiseshell trade actually increased, in parallel with the early-eighteenth-century boom in the China-focused trepang industry. Consequently, the VOC was always frustrated in its efforts to develop regular access to karet.

Throughout the seventeenth and eighteenth centuries, the company repeatedly tried to tap into marine-commodity circuits by using a combination of naval and political pressure to open up areas of supply, particularly in the Southwest and Southeast Islands (Zuidwestereilanden and Zuidoostereilanden) of southern Maluku.[58] These were a source of spices as well as of sea products, and consequently irresistible to traders the Dutch called "smugglers." As early as 1645, they complained that small seasonal fleets and occasional vessels, primarily from Sulawesi, were collecting ambergris and tortoiseshell there, and making handsome profits on sales in Makassar: 700 percent in the case of tortoiseshell.[59] Buyers in Makassar would have re-exported the shell to markets such as that in Surat.[60]

Batavia wanted more of this valuable shell and was always dissatisfied with the efforts of their Makassar merchants to obtain it; they in turn complained that they could not compete against Bugis and Makassarese "smugglers" on the one hand, or Chinese commercial networks, credit, and pricing on the other. In October 1696 Makassar's VOC officials wrote to Batavia: "It is certain the Noble Company here will never get one pound [of tortoiseshell], because the Chinese know how to secure their advantage, by collecting it secretly from the Turijene fishermen, called Bajo in Ternate, and carrying it without paying duty, which we call smuggling, but that is by no means the case with the above mentioned fishermen or natives, who bring it to market here."[61]

In 1697 the Makassar governor was more specific, complaining that while

in theory they could expect to obtain tortoiseshell and birds' nests, in reality the Chinese Captain Ongwatko controlled this traffic "almost on his own and ruin[ed] it for other, small traders, by providing goods a year in advance against the supplies for the following year."[62] A year later, when Batavia demanded extra vigilance against turtle smuggling, Makassar's officials replied they could only do more if they carried out extremely rigorous searches of Chinese sloops just before they sailed. They warned that this would be seen as an unreasonable violation of custom and would ruin trade, so they would rather continue as before. The Dutch could never replicate Chinese success, the Makassar governor continued, as "it [would] not be practicable for us . . . to obtain tortoiseshell like the Chinese do, who send small boats with their slaves or hired men to the surrounding islands . . . to exchange old iron, or lengths of cloth with the Turijene [Bajo] or fishermen, scraping together the tortoiseshell two or three at a time . . . against commodities which are put out on long-term credit."[63]

The amount of time and effort that it took to collect a cargo is illustrated by the journey of a Chinese ship en route to Mindanao that was seized in 1693. The cargo of wax, tortoiseshell, and tobacco was only worth 1,076 rds (rijksdaalders), but had taken the captain forty-three months to assemble.[64] For the Dutch, such small-scale scouring of the seas was out of the question. Moreover, they complained, their Chinese "vrunden" (friends) grabbed many a juicy cargo by offering higher prices for "smuggled" goods.[65] All the company servants could do was to try friendly persuasion on the fishermen, because the private traders always outbid them, and no amount of vehement protest helped.[66]

That sweet-talking was less effective than high prices was hardly surprising. So the following year the Makassar authorities advanced captain Ongwatko 400 rds to deploy as credit on their behalf, hoping to obtain more tortoiseshell, but the results remained poor. Neither fishermen nor merchants could be persuaded to sell for less. When the captain's "blacks" came back to Makassar with two piculs (about 124 kg.) he offered them to the company officials at the going price of 100 rds, but they did not dare exceed the VOC limit. Moreover, the law-abiding company—if not officials acting on their own behalf—always ended up paying 10 percent more than the "smugglers," so the governor proposed that all goods in which the company itself traded should be freed of duty.[67]

The VOC was thus advancing money to the Kapitan China, who used it to outfit his "blacks" voyages to fish and barter with locals lower down the commodity chain, such as (Bajo) gatherers or petty part-time traders. Typi-

cally, there were several intermediate levels between the company and producers. A description from February 1703 confirms this complexity. Tjako, a Chinese trader from Makassar, told the Dutch in Ternate that sixty Buginese had established a settlement in Banggai, and twenty or thirty Buginese vessels were sailing through the islands, even to the inner coasts of the Gulf of Tomini and Gorontalo, exchanging textiles for wax and tortoiseshell. Consequently, the people of Banggai now put such a high value on the shell (one *salempuris*—an Indian cloth—per turtle) that Tjako himself did not dare buy on behalf of his master. He added that he had heard that all these vessels belonged to the Kapitan China of Makassar, Ongwatko. When these Buginese brought the goods to Makassar, they would be stored in private houses, and no duty was paid.[68] Presumably the Buginese obtained their stock for barter from Ongwatko, who then had privileged access to their cargoes.

Besides the local Chinese, Buginese, particularly the efficient traders from Wajoq, were also outperforming the company.[69] In 1715 the Makassar governor wrote that Wajorese were able to buy all the locally available tortoiseshell (more than 20 picul) for sale in Batavia, as they were willing to pay 110 to 115 rds per picul. This made it impossible for the inhibited company to fulfill its quota. The governor was as impatient with his subordinates as Batavia was with him, accusing them of laxity. He complained that Wajorese boats from Selayar, without Dutch passes and laden with textiles, were being allowed to sail past Buton to Southeast Sulawesi. These smugglers from Wajoq, noted the governor, avoided VOC restrictions by claiming to be Bajo: "They pass themselves off as fishermen, sail the Banda and Ternate seas and with their petty trade make themselves master of all the tortoiseshell." This could not be stopped unless the smaller VOC outposts blocked such activities; however, their efforts would no doubt have been as ineffective as those of Makassar itself, and for the same reasons.[70]

Other regional markets were also active in the tortoiseshell trade, including the old centers round the Sulu Sea, or, more locally, at Kutei and Berau on the east Borneo coast, where Chinese and Malays exchanged textiles for karet; these ports were still regarded as too "perilous" for the Dutch to visit.[71] Banjarmasin was also a wealthy market offering tortoiseshell, as well as pepper, gold, and aromatic woods, while the ruler of Brunei offered to provide gold, pearls, wax, tortoiseshell, birds' nests, and other attractive commodities to the company in 1719.[72] But Ternate remained the main port shipping tortoiseshell to Batavia, collecting it from southern Maluku, the Gulf of Tomini and, later, from new if equally unreliable sources such as Mindanao. It is clear that the company's main competitors here were "Bu-

ginese" (including Makassarese, Wajorese, and, particularly in the Gulf of Tomini, Mandarese), many of whom would have been supplying Chinese merchants.[73]

The VOC was unable to break into the commodity chain at any level: they were ineffective in controlling production zones and could not compete in the various markets, ranging from beachside barter to wholesale deals in the ports. Holding to the principle of buying cheap and selling dear, the company capped the amounts officials could offer, so the Chinese regularly outbid them. However, bowing to reality in 1704, Batavia allowed its Ternate and Tidore agencies to raise the tortoiseshell price to 70 rds per picul in the hope of attracting Gorontalo karet to Dutch Maluku, while urging that Chinese be discouraged from buying the shell.[74] Company attempts to expand their supplies over the next few years followed a familiar pattern, combining intimidation with adjustments in prices and permitted trading zones.

Despite all these efforts, the indications are that marine commodities continued to flow through primarily Chinese circuits outside VOC control. A spike in supply occurred in 1730, when the Ternate governor threatened to search all Chinese houses; suddenly karet stocks were discovered in many forgotten storerooms. Chinese and Sangirese sold the officials an impressive 851 lbs. of tortoiseshell, while Menado provided 62 lbs. and Gorontalo 22 lbs.; the result — 935 pounds of karet — exceeded the total collected in the preceding fifteen years. This energetic governor brought in 3,597 pounds weight of tortoiseshell in the course of his four-year tenure.[75] As a result of this squeeze on the Chinese, Batavia was reasonably satisfied with sea-product supplies in the early 1730s, but this was to prove the high point of the company's trade in tortoiseshell.[76,77]

The Dutch lacked the knowledge and contacts needed to work with the dispersed populations who provided karet, and the company was unwilling to match prices in the port itself. From the mid-seventeenth century, at least, Chinese in Makassar and Batavia had cornered tortoiseshell supplies by providing credit to intermediate traders who were able, in turn, to connect with fishermen and Bajo. The rapid development of the trepang business from the early eighteenth century onward led to further commercialization of such networks. Producing areas were drawn into the market as exports of trepang created the opportunities and provided the means to buy imports, many of which were of Chinese origin.[78] One result was an ongoing Sinification of the middle levels of the marine-products trade in the second half of the eighteenth century.

Until the mid-1700s the trade between Makassar and China had been indirect. The most important and best documented of the intermediate ports was naturally VOC Batavia, though other independent rendezvous, such as Banjarmasin, must not be discounted; even in Batavia the buyers were Chinese, not the company. In 1746 an intermittent direct junk connection between Makassar and Amoy was established, but Dutch policy vacillated.[79] In 1769, however, strong pressure from the local VOC and the ruler of Bugis Bone finally forced a reluctant company to allow annual visits. Soon after 1770 Amoy passed Batavia as Makassar's main trading partner. The junk brought in large quantities of tobacco, tea, silk, pans, and linen; on the return voyages the cargo was more uniform, dominated by trepang, accompanied by small amounts of wax, birds' nests, and tortoiseshell; this last was by far the most valuable sea product per unit. Other marine commodities were much less important. Seaweed (agar-agar) exports did become significant by the 1770s, but not via the Amoy junk. The seaweed was exported through Batavia, probably because the junk was fully loaded with trepang.[80]

With the massive growth of the trepang trade, Makassar's economy became clearly China-centered, as can be seen in the local VOC's shipping registers.[81] Exchanges with Nusa Tenggara also surged, as Makassar became the central entrepôt in a south-north traffic exchanging trepang for commodities like porcelain, tobacco, or textiles.[82] If in the 1720s the main items traded in Makassar were Indian cloth, Javanese tobacco, rice, and salt, by the 1760s the main imports were arrack from Batavia, rice, raw cotton, coconut oil, and trepang, while the dominant (re)exports were trepang and seaweed to Batavia (to meet the Chinese junks), and cash being sent to pay for imports. The pattern in the 1770s was the same, but now much trepang was going straight to Amoy in addition to Batavia. The 1780s showed a similar, but more intense pattern.

The Makassar harbormaster's registers also provide more detailed insights into the tortoiseshell trade, enabling us to locate the sources of shipments and the ethnicity of captains. In the 1720s the dominant points of origin for Makassar's karet were Solor, a small island to the east of Flores (with 81 percent), and Barru, on the central west coast of south Sulawesi (19 percent); both had become politically and hence economically subject to the Dutch after 1669.

However, by the 1760s tortoiseshell came from two quite different areas, both politically independent of the VOC: the sultanate of Buton, off the southeast arm of Sulawesi (94 percent), and the Bugis territories of the

southwest peninsula (6 percent). The volume of tortoiseshell traded had grown, riding the intensification of trepang fishing. Such independent areas chose to trade at Makassar, despite Dutch regulations and fees, because of the direct junk link with Amoy. This trend is confirmed by the data from the 1780s, with Banda producing 30 percent, Bugis 23 percent, Buton 20 percent, Ternate 19 percent, and Bonerate 8 percent of Makassar's karet. The emergence of Maluku as a major source of supply is striking. Banda and Ternate had traditionally shipped their tortoiseshell to Batavia, but the junk connection drew supplies away from the Dutch center and into exports to China via Makassar. This was a significant realignment.

There were also important shifts in the proportions of tortoiseshell-carrying skippers as classified by ethnicity. In the 1720s all were of Sulawesi origin (44 percent Wajorese, 41 percent Makassarese, and 15 percent Buginese). Dutch policy confined their voyages to a zone stretching from Batavia through Nusa Tenggara, so the marine products available in these seas represented a significant remaining opportunity for Sulawesians; the previously important Straits of Melaka and Maluku waters had become forbidden territory.[83] Chinese, however, were still permitted to sail to the east, and they played an important role in exchange between Makassar and Maluku. By the 1760s the category "Wajorese" had disappeared from Makassar's trade register.[84] Their role was taken over by the ill-defined "Company Subjects" (which probably included many Wajorese) who were bringing in 83 percent of tortoiseshell. Chinese were responsible for a further share, with peranakan logging an impressive 14 percent and Chinese 3 percent of the total.[85]

The Chinese proportion of tortoiseshell imports had soared by the 1780s; peranakan had maintained their 14 percent, but Chinese now claimed 66 percent, so together they were responsible for 80 percent of karet coming into Makassar. It is unlikely that Chinese hunted turtles; the dramatic growth in their import share reflects commercialization in once-peripheral islands, as increasing market penetration made it easier for them to buy tortoiseshell. In 1787 more than half the Chinese captains were peranakan (13 of 24 skippers), most of whom (12) arrived from Buton. The non-peranakan Chinese, on the other hand, were more wide-ranging, importing karet from various sources (Bugis, 3; Banda, 2; Ternate, 1), or exporting to Batavia (4) and Amoy (1). Unfortunately, 1787 is the only year for which there is a breakdown between Chinese and Chinese peranakan, but it suggests that the latter concentrated on short-haul imports, while the former were more diversified importers (from South Sulawesi and Maluku) and exporters.[86] Malays were also quite significant in this later period.[87]

Conclusion

The advantage of a commodity-chain approach is that it places relationships within an explicitly commercial context, in which a complementary search for profit transcends divisions between political entities and ethnic groups. The exploitation of comparative advantages enables participants to benefit from the difference between expenses incurred and receipts generated as they pass products on to the next link in the chain. The trepang business sustained an ongoing integration, involving financiers, outfitters, and various levels of merchants and traders, as well as fishermen. It was so important to the economy of eighteenth-century Makassar that the VOC, the Chinese Captain, and major traders cooperated to stabilize prices.[88] Tortoiseshell was a much more valuable commodity, but supplies were also less predictable. Diving or dredging for trepang in appropriate waters guaranteed a result, whereas the only reliable opportunity for finding turtles was during the west monsoon nesting season (December, January, and February).[89] This was also the time the trepang fleets were out accumulating their cargoes, and those sailing near known nesting beaches probably hunted turtles as a profitable sideline. Increased killing would have intensified pressure on turtle populations and might explain the disappearance of the hawksbill from Sulawesi's Togian islands, famous for their karet in the seventeenth and eighteenth centuries.[90]

In the seventeenth century, local rulers and Chinese merchants supported tortoiseshell-seeking trading and collecting expeditions, manned by motley crews that probably included slaves, clients, free men who had taken goods on credit in order to trade, traditionally subaltern Bajo, or simply fishermen who sought the protection of their lord before sailing. It remains very difficult to know to what extent such relationships and activities were economically based, either as a business partnership or a calculated investment.[91] But the development of the trepang industry seems to have further commercialized the tortoiseshell trade, and as fishing groups became more aware of the value of their products, they demanded higher prices.[92]

The Dutch failed to gain a foothold in the marine-products market. Their attempts to control the production zones were ineffective, and they were unable to compete in trading centers like Makassar. If in the late 1600s and early 1700s the company was castigating its servants for their failure to provide tortoiseshell, by the mid-eighteenth century the VOC in Makassar was no longer interested in the issue. There was a clear dwindling in Batavia's tortoiseshell imports in the second half of the eighteenth century, while Makas-

sar's imports and exports grew.[93] But East Indonesia's karet increasingly went straight to China, bypassing the company completely. This position as outsider seems to have been readily accepted for trepang, which was a specifically Chinese product, but had earlier been a source of great frustration to the Dutch, anxious as they were to obtain tortoiseshell for exchange in Japan and Surat. However, by the mid-eighteenth century they had given up on tortoiseshell as well as trepang. Despite the need for cargoes that could be used in China to obtain tea (a major reason for the country traders' interest in marine products), the VOC seems to have become resigned to its own nonparticipation.

This Dutch failure reflected their inability to operate effectively in the fine channels of commerce, where small numbers of commodities were slowly collected from diffuse and unpredictable sources. Outposts on forsaken beaches, like that in Aru, proved incapable of building the necessary relationships and were too expensive for a company operating on tightly controlled calculations of profit and loss.[94] This precluded paying the prices Asian merchants were willing to offer. The Chinese in Makassar drove prices upward, because they knew the market could sustain their purchasing policy. Before 1750 most of the tortoiseshell that passed through their hands may have been bound for Batavia, but it was destined for Chinese traders accumulating junk cargoes, not for the VOC. This Chinese-dominated complex operated under the company umbrella, but may have been linked to other, independent and hence less-documented markets where Makassar karet could be sold. Such harbors would have included Kalimantan ports and Sulu, established points of rendezvous for the China trade.

Tortoiseshell must have remained an important commodity in Bugis, Chinese, and country trader networks that avoided the VOC. In this respect the Wajorese are intriguing. In the 1720s, these efficient traders had been the major importers of tortoiseshell into Makassar (44 percent) and dominated exports to Batavia (83 percent), only to disappear from the harbormaster's administration after the 1730s. This shift parallels two other trends: the decline in Batavia's tortoiseshell imports, and the growing Chinese domination of Makassar's sea-product trades after the Amoy link was established in 1746. Two, by no means exclusive, hypotheses might explain this. According to the first, Wajorese "smugglers" left VOC-controlled circuits and operated out of areas under Buginese rule, entering "Bugis" networks trading to Sulu, Brunei, and various Borneo, Sumatra, and Melaka Straits ports, notably Riau.[95] These links, supported by scattered Bugis settlements, helped reconstitute Makassar's old east-west trading connection, broken by the VOC

in 1666. Insofar as Wajorese remained in Makassar, they probably became "Company Subjects." This might have had the advantage of freeing them from intervention by the Bone kings, who were prone to meddle in the community's affairs.[96] The second hypothesis is that this east-west link remained insignificant, that the Wajorese, like other Indonesian peoples, had lost their commercial capacity, and that the picture presented in Makassar's shipping register shows the new reality: a Chinese-dominated commercial world.

A compromise scenario, with less emphasis on ethnic segregation, seems most likely, that there were cross-cutting relationships connecting the circuits avoiding Dutch restrictions with those making use of company ports. The former were exemplified by Sulu, where Bugis, Chinese, and European country traders accessed commodities, including those proscribed by the voc, such as guns and opium, as well as textiles, sea products, and China goods. It is possible that there were Bugis (or other) chains that chose, for political or religious reasons, to isolate themselves from Chinese or European networks, but their extent is impossible to judge. However, since the exploitation of different commercial environments offered complementary advantages, the search for profit probably created links between apparently separate systems of exchange.

Uneven documentation makes it impossible to know how far Makassar merchants may have participated in commercial circuits not sanctioned by the company. It is quite possible that capital accumulated by Makassar Chinese was also invested in "smuggling" circuits operating out of other ports. This raises the interesting point of why it was Makassar that became the center of the trepang trade. Geography was important, but voc policy must have been crucial, as the company jealously restricted the junk trade to a few select ports, including Makassar. Company fleets may have been unable to shepherd the movement of small *perahu*, but a junk of up to 200 tons burden with several hundred men on board was much easier to police. But other factors might also help explain why neighboring harbors, notably Banjarmasin, could not compete effectively with Makassar in the trepang trade.

Banjarmasin was a port of comparable size and shipping activity to Makassar, but independent until the voc established a supervisory trading post there, in 1747. If for some reason the Amoy junk did not come to Makassar, as happened occasionally in the mid-eighteenth century, trepang traders took their cargoes to Banjarmasin or Batavia in the hope of connecting with a China-bound vessel. Pepper had always drawn Chinese merchants to the Borneo port, but nonetheless Makassar proved more attractive as a transit point for trepang. One possible reason for this is that the Borneo junks left

fully laden with pepper and had no room for trepang, just as Makassar's agar-agar was carried to China via Batavia, as vessels leaving the Sulawesi port preferred to use their holds for trepang. But another explanation may be more relevant.

The success of a commodity chain depends on efficient movement between different stages, including shifts from one place to another, or to another organizational level (retail to bulk, or vice versa), or alterations due to (semi) processing. Each mutation required certain types of knowledge, technology, and coordination that, in early modern times, were closely linked to social capital. In the case of the commodity chain of marine goods, Bajo, Bugis (that is, Sulawesian), and Chinese all brought specialist skills to their various but not static points in the chain.

Makassar's trade in sea products was probably shaped by patterns developed earlier in Sulu or perhaps Brunei, areas familiar to the Bajo, who also frequented Sulawesi waters. Skills and contacts acquired there became increasingly valuable in Makassar as the availability of spices attracted more traders after 1620. The Dutch conquest initiated several decades of stagnation, until the explosion of the trepang trade in the early eighteenth century, when experience in the tortoiseshell trade enabled some key players to connect Chinese demand with local supply.

The Chinese Captains were such players; the central role Ongwatko played in the late seventeenth century was neither unique nor temporary. In 1742 Captain Lianko petitioned the VOC for the traditional captains' privilege of sending a vessel to the Gulf of Tomini for tortoiseshell and trepang.[97] But the Bajo were also crucial, and while they were numerous in Sulu, North Borneo, the Sulawesi seas, and around Ternate and Nusa Tenggara, they were not common west of Pulau Laut, off the Borneo coast. So in contrast to the Sulawesi courts, Banjarmasin had no tradition of working with Bajo, which would have limited its direct access to karet. In Makassar, on the other hand, Dutch permission (and perhaps protection) for the junk traffic; Chinese credit, purchasing, and marketing networks (in Southeast Asia and China itself); Bajo maritime expertise; and Bugis links to Bajo and their own skills in shipping, fishing, and trading all combined to create the trepang industry, building on the established tortoiseshell trading network. This is an example of the "organizational learning" that underpins complex commodity chains.

Cooperation between Southeast Asian knowledge and technology (of fishing sites and techniques, shipping) and Chinese expertise (in marketing, finance, and credit) was fundamental to the marine-commodities trade. In

the case of trepang, the difference in use-value was absolute: only Chinese ate trepang, and while tortoiseshell was used in local handicrafts, the profits in overseas trade were considerably more attractive. Ethnic differentiation was important in that it related directly to relevant knowledge about production and consumption, and to social capital embodied in networks of trust. However, these networks were not, and could not be, limited to any one community. The very basis of the successful trade in sea products lay in transcommunal transactions.

In the course of the eighteenth century, however, there was a growing appetite for imported goods in once-peripheral regions, which, because of trepang, now had commodities they could export. Chinese earthen- and metalware were popular, so traders with easy access to this merchandise acquired a commercial edge. There was a partial "Sinification" of the sea-products trade, as the Chinese expanded their role from that of wholesale purchasers of trepang into shipping and direct trade with the producers. Upstream levels of the trade, once dominated by Sulawesians, were successfully penetrated by the Chinese, perhaps aided by an effective use of local knowledge by the peranakan.

Over a period of a century and a half, changes in commodity chains moved Makassar from the periphery of commerce to the center. For several hundred years, Makassar's skippers had sailed out to connect with long-distance trade in other harbors, as the main shipping routes bypassed South Sulawesi. After the sixteenth-century rise of Gowa-Talloq, Makassar became a more useful source of foodstuffs, particularly rice, but was not, in Michelin terms, worth a detour. From the 1620s, however, political distortion of the spice trade redirected these extremely attractive goods to Makassar, drawing more merchants to the port. This increased the number of potential purchasers for other commodities, including Borneo pepper and tortoiseshell. The arrival of Portuguese and English, Spanish from Manila, and, in the mid-seventeenth century, a new wave of Portuguese and Indian Muslim merchants fleeing Dutch Melaka all added to the international synergy driving commerce. The VOC conquest put a stop to that, but from the beginning of the 1700s trepang emerged as a new staple product, generating rapidly swelling commodity flows from Makassar to China, and creating feeder routes for importing trepang and distributing exchange cargoes throughout eastern Indonesia. The ramifications of new sources of credit and trade opportunities linking many small settlements transformed the commercial landscape of the region.

Notes

1. Sanjay Subrahmanyam, ed., *An Expanding World: The European Impact on World History 1450–1800*, vol. 8 of *Merchant Networks in the Early Modern World* (Aldershot: Variorum, 1996); Ina Baghdiantz-McCabe, G. Harlaftis, and I. P. Minoglou, *Diaspora Entrepreneurial Networks: Four Centuries of History* (Oxford: Berg, 2005).

2. Geoff Wade, "The Ming-Shi Lu as a Source for Southeast Asian History," *Southeast Asia in the Ming Shi-lu: An Open Access Resource* (Singapore: Asia Research Institute and the Singapore E-Press, National University of Singapore, 2005), http://epress.nus.edu.sg/msl.

3. Nola Cooke and Li Tana, eds., *Water Frontier: Commerce and the Chinese in the Lower Mekong Region, 1750–1880* (Oxford: Rowman and Littlefield / Singapore University Press, 2004); Roderich Ptak, "Ming Maritime Trade to Southeast Asia, 1368–1567: Visions of a 'System,'" *From the Mediterranean to the China Sea*, ed. Claude Guillot, Denys Lombard, and Roderich Ptak, *South China and Maritime Asia* (Wiesbaden: Harrassowitz Verlag, 1998), 157–92; Ronald Skeldon, "The Chinese Diaspora or the Migration of Chinese Peoples," *The Chinese Diaspora: Space, Place, Mobility and Identity*, ed. Laurence J. C. Ma and Carolyn Cartier (Oxford: Rowman and Littlefield, 2003), 51–66.

4. Stathis Gougouris, "The Concept of Diaspora in the Contemporary World," *Diaspora Entrepreneurial Networks: Four Centuries of History*, ed. Ina Baghdiantz-McCabe, G. Harlaftis, and I. P. Minoglou (Oxford: Berg, 2005), 383–90.

5. Susan Debra Blum and Lionel M. Jensen, eds., *China Off Center: Mapping the Margins of the Middle Kingdom* (Honolulu: University of Hawaii Press, 2002); Benedict Anderson, *Long-Distance Nationalism: World Capitalism and the Rise of Identity Politics*, Wertheim Lezing lecture (Amsterdam: Centre for Asian Studies Amsterdam, 1992); Murray Weidenbaum and Samuel Hughes, *Bamboo Network: How Expatriate Chinese Entrepreneurs Are Creating a New Economic Superpower in Asia* (New York: Free Press, 1996).

6. Alejandro Portes, "Social Capital: Its Origins and Applications in Modern Sociology," *Annual Review of Sociology* 24 (1998): 1–24.

7. For examples of commodity-focused analyses, see Leonard Blussé, "In Praise of Commodities: An Essay on the Crosscultural Trade in Edible Birds'-Nests," *Emporia, Commodities and Entrepreneurs in Asian Maritime Trade, c. 1400–1750*, ed. Roderich Ptak and Dietmar Rothermund (Stuttgart: Franz Steiner Verlag, 1991), 317–35; David Bulbeck et al., *Southeast Asian Exports since the Fourteenth Century: Cloves, Pepper, Coffee and Sugar*, Data Paper Series no. 4, Sources for the Economic History of Southeast Asia (Singapore: Institute of Southeast Asian Studies, 1998); W. G. Clarence-Smith and Steven Topik, eds., *The Global Coffee Economy in Africa, Asia and Latin America, 1500–1989* (Cambridge: Cambridge University Press, 2003).

8. Immanuel Wallerstein, *The Modern World System: Capitalist Agriculture and the Origins of the European World Economy in the Sixteenth Century* (New York: Academic Press, 1974).

9. M. N. Pearson, *Port Cities and Invaders: The Swahili Coast, India and Portugal in the Early Modern Age* (Baltimore: Johns Hopkins University Press, 1998).

10. Gary Gereffi and Miguel Korzeniewicz, eds., *Commodity Chains and Global Capitalism* (Westport, Conn.: Praeger, 1994).

11. In the sixteenth century, the small, sea-oriented kingdom of Taloq merged with more agrarian Gowa to form a polity generally known as Makassar after the dominant ethnic group and language. Anthony Reid, "The Rise of Makassar," *Review of Indonesian and Malayan Affairs* 17 (1983): 117–60.

12. David Bulbeck and Ian Caldwell, *Land of Iron: The Historical Archaeology of Luwu and the Cenrana Valley: Results of the Origin of Complex Society in South Sulawesi Project (Oxis)* (Hull: Centre for South-East Asian Studies, University of Hull / School of Anthropology and Archaeology, Australian National University, 2000).

13. Roderich Ptak, "The Northern Trade Route to the Spice Islands: South China Sea-Sulu Zone—North Moluccas (Fourteenth to Early Sixteenth Century)," *Archipel* 43 (1992): 27–56; John E. Wills, "China's Further Shores: Continuities and Changes in the Destination Ports of China's Maritime Trade, 1680–1690," *Emporia, Commodities and Entrepreneurs in Asian Maritime Trade, c. 1400–1750*, ed. Roderich Ptak and Dietmar Rothermund (Stuttgart: Franz Steiner Verlag, 1991), 53–80.

14. John Villiers, "Makassar: The Rise and Fall of an East Indonesian Maritime Trading State, 1512–1669," *The Southeast Asian Port and Polity: Rise and Demise*, ed. Jeyamalar Kathirithamby-Wells and John Villiers (Singapore: Singapore University Press, 1990), 145.

15. B. J. O. Schrieke, "The Shifts in Political and Economic Power in the Indonesian Archipelago in the Sixteenth and Seventeenth Century," *Indonesian Sociological Studies* (The Hague: W. van Hoeve, 1955): 1–82.

16. NA VOC 1127, 577r. Citations in this form refer to the Netherlands National Archive in The Hague, specifically the VOC "General series of letters from Batavia to Amsterdam" (Overgekomen Brieven en Papieren uit Indië aan de Heren XVII en de Kamer Amsterdam, 1607–1794, inv. nrs. 1053–3987), with the inventory and folio (page) number.

17. Heather Sutherland, "Trade, Court and Company: Makassar in the Later Seventeenth and Early Eighteenth Centuries," *Hof en Handel: Aziatische Vorsten en de VOC 1620–1720*, ed. Elsbeth Locher-Scholten and Peter Rietbergen (Leiden: KITLV Press, 2004), 85–112.

18. J. Noorduyn, "De Handelsrelaties van het Makassaarse Rijk Volgens de Notitie van Cornelis Speelman (1669)," *Nederlands Historische Bronnen* ('s-Gravenhage: Martinus Nijhoff, 1983), 97–123.

19. D. K. Bassett, "English Trade in Celebes, 1613–1667," *Journal of the Malayan Branch of the Royal Asiatic Society* 31 (1958): 1–39; John Villiers, "One of the Especiallest Flowers in Our Garden: The English Factory at Makassar, 1613–1667," *Archipel* 39 (1990): 159–78. See also Roderich Ptak, "China and the Trade in Tortoise-Shell (Sung to Ming Periods)," *Emporia, Commodities and Entrepreneurs in Asian Maritime Trade, c.1400–1750*, ed. Roderich Ptak and Dietmar Rothermund (Stuttgart: Franz Steiner Verlag, 1991), 195–229.

20. Leonard Y. Andaya, "The Bugis-Makassar Diasporas," *Journal of the Malaysian Branch of the Royal Asiatic Society* 68.1 (1995): 119–38.

21. Sutherland, "Trade, Court and Company." Loquo, or Loquin, the Chinese captain (head of the community) before the conquest in 1669, received considerable advances

from the Dutch company and was clearly a trusted trading partner, but died in poverty (NA VOC 1220, 833; NA VOC 1267, 350).

22. Cornelis Speelman, "Notitie Diendende voor Eenen Korte Tijd en tot Nader Last van de Hoge Regering op Batavia voor den Ondercoopman Jan van Oppijnen," typescript held in the KITLV, Leiden, from the 1669 original, D H 802, 744. For information on the manuscript, see Noorduyn, "De Handelsrelaties van het Makassaarse Rijk Volgens de Notitie van Cornelis Speelman (1669)."

23. Chinese numbers (and trade networks) may have been strengthened if some of the fifty Chinese who arrived in 1685, fleeing religious restrictions in the Philippines with a cargo of wax, sugar, and tortoiseshell, chose to stay in Makassar, but most probably moved on (GM 4:797). Citations in this form refer to the twice yearly reports, or *Generale Missiven*, sent by the VOC administration in Batavia to the Netherlands; those covering the years up to 1761 have been published by several editors—W. Ph. Coolhaas, J. van Goor, J. E. Schooneveld-Oosterling, and H.K. s'Jacob—as *Generale Missiven van Gouverneurs-Generaal en Raden aan Heren XVII der Verenigde Oostindische Compagnie*, 13 vols. ('s-Gravenhage: Nijhoff, 1960–2007). The published volume number is followed by the page reference.

24. NA VOC 1437, 296.

25. Speelman lists a "Watko" or "Wanco" who arrived after the conquest and immediately set off for Mandar. On the VOC-created Chinese-officer system, see Mona Lohanda, *The Kapitan China of Batavia 1837–1942* (Jakarta: Djambatan, 1996). The officers were usually wealthy merchants who could use their influence with both company and community to further their commercial ambitions. On Mapule, see Sutherland, "Trade, Court and Company," 89–92. For the VOC perspective on Ongwatko, see NA VOC 1647, 223.

26. I have discussed elsewhere the blurred ethnic lines in the port, particularly those between peranakan Chinese and Malays. See Heather Sutherland, "The Makassar Malays: Adaptation and Identity," *Journal of Southeast Asian Studies* 32.3 (2001): 397–421.

27. GM 7:755.

28. Gerrit J. Knaap, "A City of Migrants: Kota Ambon at the End of the Seventeenth Century," *Indonesia* 51 (1991): 105–28.

29. GM 8:100.

30. NA VOC 2345, 73.

31. Carl A. Trocki, "Chinese Pioneering in Eighteenth-Century Southeast Asia," *The Last Stand of Asian Autonomies: Responses to Modernity in the Diverse States of Southeast Asia and Korea, 1750–1900*, ed. Anthony Reid (London: Macmillan, 1997), 83–102.

32. Heather Sutherland, "Trepang and Wangkang: The China Trade of Eighteenth Century Makassar," *Authority and Enterprise among the Peoples of South Sulawesi*, ed. R. Tol, K. van Dijk, and G. Acciaioli (Leiden: KITLV Press, 2000), 73–94.

33. NA VOC 2238, 119.

34. Gerrit Knaap and Heather Sutherland, *Monsoon Traders: Ships, Skippers and Commodities in Eighteenth Century Makassar*, Verhandelingen 224 (Leiden: KITLV Press, 2004), 145–49.

35. NA VOC 2694, 28; on the proclamation of 1785, see NA VOC 3673, 29–30, and on its renewal in 1796, see the archive of the successor to the VOC, the Comité Oost-Indische handel no. 95, para. 68. On the relationship between Chinese economic power and Makassar's Dutch administration, see Heather Sutherland, "Money in Makassar: Credit and Debt in an Eighteenth Century VOC Settlement," *Credit and Debt in Southeast Asian History*, ed. David Henley and Peter Boomgaard (Singapore: Institute of Southeast Asian Studies, 2009), 102–23.

36. Els M. Jacobs, *Koopman in Azie: De Handel van de Verenigde Oost-Indische Compagnie Tijdens de 18de Eeuw* (Zutphen: Walburg, 2000); Knaap and Sutherland, *Monsoon Traders*.

37. Heather Sutherland, "Review Article: The Sulu Zone Revisited," *Journal of Southeast Asian History* 35.1 (2004): 133–57.

38. NA VOC 1568, 255.

39. The Lesser Sundas; early-eighteenth-century Dutch sources had noted the strong turtle trade around southern islands including Lomblen, Alor, Roti, Savu, Solor, Timor, and Flores. On Sulu, see Ruurdje Laarhoven, *Triumph of Moro Diplomacy: The Maguindinao Sultanate in the Seventeenth Century* (Quezon City: New Day, 1989); James Francis Warren, *The Sulu Zone: The Dynamics of External Trade, Slavery, and Ethnicity in the Transformation of a Southeast Asian Maritime State* (Singapore: Singapore University Press, 1981), 5–11; Knaap and Sutherland, *Monsoon Traders*.

40. Leonard Andaya, "Local Trade Networks in Maluku in the Sixteenth, Seventeenth and Eighteenth Centuries," *Cakalele* 2.2 (1991): 71–96. Heather Sutherland, "Kontinuitas dan Perubahan Dalam Sejarah Makassar: Perdagangan dan Kota di Abad Ke-18," *Kontinunitas Dan Perubahan Dalam Sejarah Sulawesi Selatan*, ed. Dias Pradadimara and Muslimin A. R. Effendy (Makassar: Ombak, 2004), 3–40.

41. Leonard Blussé, *Strange Company: Chinese Settlers, Mestizo Women and the Dutch in VOC Batavia*, vol. 122, *Verhandelingen van het Koninklijk Instituut voor Taal-, Land- En Volkenkunde* (Dordrecht: Foris Publications, 1986); Hendrik E. Niemeyer, *Batavia: Een Koloniale Samenleving in de 17de Eeuw* (Amsterdam: Balans, 2005).

42. Andaya, "Local Trade Networks"; Leonard Y. Andaya, *The World of Maluku: Eastern Indonesia in the Early Modern Period*, 1st ed. (Honolulu: University of Hawaii Press, 1993).

43. Ptak, "China and the Trade in Tortoise-Shell (Sung to Ming Periods)."

44. Stephen Tseng-Hsin Chang, "Commodities Imported to the Chang Chou Region of Fukien during the Late Ming Period: A Preliminary Analysis of the Tax Lists Found in Tung-Hsi-Yang K'ao," *Emporia, Commodities and Entrepreneurs in Asian Maritime Trade, c. 1400–1750*, ed. Roderich Ptak and Dietmar Rothermund (Stuttgart: Franz Steiner Verlag, 1991), 179–94; *VOC-Glossarium: Verklaringen van Termen Verzameld uit de Rijks Geschiedkundige Publicatien die Betrekking Hebben op de Verenigde Oost-Indische Compagnie* (Den Haag: Instituut voor Nederlandse Geschiedenis, 2000).

45. Ptak, "China and the Trade in Tortoise-Shell (Sung to Ming Periods)," 221.

46. Sutherland, "Trepang and Wangkang."

47. The specialists in marine commodities were Sama speakers known as Orang Laut

(sea people) in the Western archipelago, and Samal, Badjau, or Bajau Laut in the southern Philippines and along the northeast Borneo coast, while the Bugis and Makassarese called them Bajo or Turijene (water people). See Leonard Andaya, "Historical Links between the Aquatic Populations and the Coastal Peoples of the Malay World and Celebes," *Historia: Essays in Commemoration of the Twenty-fifth Anniversary of the Department of History, University of Malaya,* ed. Muhammad Abu Bakar (Kuala Lumpur: Department of History, University of Malaya, 1984), 34–51; Clifford Sather, *The Bajau Laut: Adaptation, History and Fate in a Maritime Fishing Society of South-Eastern Sabah* (Kuala Lumpur: Oxford Univerity Press, 1997); David E. Sopher, *The Sea Nomads: A Study of the Maritime Boat People of Southeast Asia,* 2nd ed. (Singapore: National Museum, 1977).

48. The current status of turtles in the region can be found on various turtle websites.

49. François Valentijn, *Oud en Nieuw Oost-Indiën, Vervattende een Naaukeurige en Uitvoerige Verhandelinge van Nederlands Mogentheyd in die Gewesten, Benevens eene Wydlustige Beschryvinge der Moluccos, Amboina, Banda, Timor, en Solor, Java en alle de Eylanden Onder Dezelve Landbestieringen Behoorende: Het Nederlands Comptoir op Suratte, en de Levens der Groote Mogols: Als ook een Keurlyke Verhandeling van 't Wezentlykste, dat Men Behoort te Weten van Choromandel, Pegu, Arracan, Bengale, Mocha, Persien, Malacca, Sumatra, Ceylon, Malabar, Celebes of Macassar, China, Japan, Tayouan of Formosa, Tonkin, Cambodia, Siam, Borneo, Bali, Kaap der Goede Hoop en Van Mauritius . . . ,* vol. 1 ('s-Gravenhage: H. C. Susan, 1856).

50. J. N. Vosmaer, "Korte Beschrijving van het Zuid-Oostelijk Schiereiland van Celebes, in het Bijzonder van de Vosmaers-Baai of Van Kendari: Verrijkt met Eenige Berigten Omtrent den Stam der Orang Badjos, en Meer Andere Aanteekeningen," *Tijdschrift van het Bataviaasch Genootschap* (1839), 135. For extensive information on Chinese use of tortoiseshell, see Ptak, "China and the Trade in Tortoise-Shell (Sung to Ming Periods)."

51. GM 1745, 9:245.

52. A kati is 617 grams.

53. Ptak gives the Chinese and European names for the four turtle types ("China and the Trade in Tortoise-Shell [Sung to Ming Periods]," 197.)

54. F. W. Stapel, *Het Bongaais Verdrag* (Leiden: University of Leiden, 1922); Villiers, "One of the Especiallest Flowers in Our Garden."

55. NA VOC 1127, 577v.

56. NA VOC 1221, 353.

57. Villiers, "One of the Especiallest Flowers in Our Garden."

58. So called because of their location relative to the VOC base on the nutmeg island of Banda. The former group included the lesser archipelagos of Babar, Damar, Luang, Leti, Tomang, and Wetar; the latter included Tanimbar, Timor Laut (a subcluster of the Tanimbar archipelago), Aru, Kai, Watubela, and Goram. For an early-eighteenth-century description, see Valentijn, *Oud en Nieuw Oost-Indiën,* 2:32–43.

59. P. A. Tiele and J. E. Heeres, *Bouwstoffen voor de Gescheidenis der Nederlanders in den Maleischen Archipel,* 3 vols. (The Hague: 1886–1895), 3:245. This would mean, roughly, that tortoiseshell could be bought for 0.31 guilders a pound in southern Maluku, and sold for 2.4 guilders a pound in Makassar.

60. GM 5:62. Ptak notes that the British were making 40 to 50 percent on the trade there in 1632, and repeats a contemporaneous estimate that Gujarat absorbed 12,854 pounds of shell between 1638 and 1645. It is possible that the price for tortoiseshell was by this stage higher in India than in China, as there are indications that China had become an exporter of tortoiseshell. Ptak, "China and the Trade in Tortoise-Shell (Sung to Ming Periods)."

61. NA VOC 1579, 154; see also NA VOC 1556, 255 (1695). Issues of jurisdiction also complicated "smuggling." The Bajo were protected by local rulers; until 1726 the Bajo were able to sail using a pass from the king of Gowa and were thus exempt from Dutch restrictions (GM 8:75).

62. NA VOC 1595, 215. As well as these typically Chinese products, Ongwatko also traded in slaves, including at Banggai and Tobunku, and had trade connections in Manila and Timor, NA VOC 1414, 348.

63. NA VOC 1595, 298.

64. GM 1693, 5:583. The rijksdaalder, c.2.5 guilders, was the VOC money of account.

65. When particularly irritated by competition, be it Portuguese, English, or Chinese, the company tended to fall into heavy irony, referring to their "friends."

66. NA VOC 1663, 92–93.

67. NA VOC 1676, 180–81. A picul equaled c. 62 kilograms.

68. NA VOC 1676, 281.

69. Knaap and Sutherland, *Monsoon Traders*.

70. NA VOC 1867, 49–50.

71. GM 1718 7:373; GM 1719 7:398; GM 1706 6:418; GM 1720 2:51; GM 1722 7:633; GM 2:679; GM 3:844; GM 4:336. In May 1831 the *Singapore Chronicle* described how raiders along the coast prevented the development of exports of tortoiseshell and trepang from Kutei; pirates took most of the shell ("Remarks on the Exports of Coti," reprinted in J.M. Moor, *Notices of the Indian Archipelago* [London: CASS, 1968], 57).

72. GM 4:279, 408; GM 1719 7:398.

73. On the Eastern Indonesian marine-products trade in general, see also R. F. Ellen, *On the Edge of the Banda Zone: Past and Present in the Social Organization of a Moluccan Trading Network* (Honolulu: University of Hawaii Press, 2003); David Henley, *Fertility, Food and Fever: Population, Economy and Environment in North and Central Sulawesi, c. 1600–1930* (Leiden: KITLV Press, 2005); Sutherland, "Review Article,"; Esther Velthoen, "'Wanderers, Robbers and Bad Folk': The Politics of Violence, Protection and Trade in Eastern Sulawesi 1750–1850," *The Last Stand of Asian Autonomies: Responses to Modernity in the Diverse States of Southeast Asia and Korea, 1750–1900*, ed. Anthony Reid (London: Macmillan, 1991), 367–88.

74. Knaap and Sutherland, *Monsoon Traders*. Prices had clearly risen: Ongwatko had offered the VOC 2 picul for 100 rds.

75. Governor Jacob Pielat left Ternate in 1732 to continue a promising career in Ceylon, GM 1731 9:234; GM 8–9; Andaya, *The World of Maluku*, 207–8.

76. During the financial year 1731–1732, VOC purchases of tortoiseshell from Portu-

guese, Chinese, and native traders amounted to 2,093 pounds, and in October 1731 Ternate sent 1,983 pounds to Batavia. In 1735 the VOC obtained a total of 1,030 tortoiseshells worth 2,769 guilders, and 5,972 pearlshells (for mother-of-pearl), weighing 6,568 pounds and worth f.985.5 (GM 1734 9:625; 1731 9:234; 1735 9:630).

77. Value in Guilders of Tortoiseshell Passing through VOC Batavia from Makassar: Years 1711–12: From Banda, 1,400; From Ternate, 1,200; To Japan, 2,800; To Surat, none. Years 1712–13: From Banda, 1,000; From Ternate, 900; To Japan, 2,400; To Surat, none. Years 1730–31: From Banda, none; From Ternate, 4,300; To Japan, 5,300; To Surat, none. Years 1731–32: From Banda, 500; From Ternate, 1,200; To Japan, 4,600; To Surat, none. Years 1752–53: From Banda, none; From Ternate, 400; To Japan, none; To Surat, 1. Years 1771–72: From Banda, 300; From Ternate, 800; To Japan, none; To Surat, 600. I am very grateful to Dr. Els Jacobs for this information. The original sources were the archives of the company's general accountant, held in the National Archives in The Hague, inventory numbers BGB 10.758, 10.767, 10.777, 10.791.

78. For example, in the mid-eighteenth-century Buton became the main collection port channeling trepang from southeastern waters to Makassar; in the early days this exchange was limited in range and value. But by the 1780s Buton was able to absorb an impressive range of manufactured goods (textiles, porcelain, axes, etc.). Heather Sutherland, "Power, Trade and Islam in the Eastern Archipelagos, 1700–1850," *Religion and Development: Towards an Integrated Approach*, ed. Philip Quarles van Ufford and Matthew Schoffeleers (Amsterdam: Free University Press, 1988), 145–66. See also Sutherland, "Review Article."

79. Knaap and Sutherland, *Monsoon Traders*.

80. Sutherland, "Trepang and Wangkang." Knaap and Sutherland, *Monsoon Traders*, 98–102, 145–49.

81. Knaap and Sutherland, *Monsoon Traders*. The registers, introduced in 1713, were the primary source for this analysis. For sources and methodology, see ibid., 5–9. The data can be consulted by arrangement with the Nederlands Instituut voor Wetenschappelijke Informatiediensten, an institute of the Netherlands' Royal Academy of Sciences. The following paragraphs draw on this data, referred to hereafter as "Data base of the Makassar's harbormasters register."

82. Knaap and Sutherland, *Monsoon Traders*; Noorduyn, "De Handelsrelaties van het Makassaarse Rijk Volgens de Notitie van Cornelis Speelman (1669)."

83. Travel restrictions were always changing, and sometimes ignored, but nonetheless were an important constraint for those wishing to trade in VOC ports.

84. Toward the end of the 1720s the ruler of Buginese Bone prohibited Wajorese trade with Batavia; Wajorese withdrawal accelerated in the 1730s, during the war between the Wajorese rebel Arung Singkang and the VOC; in 1735 they left Makassar. Despite their return in 1742 the community vanished from the trade statistics, probably because of classification changes. J. Noorduyn, "The Wajorese Merchants' Community in Makassar," *Authority and Enterprise among the Peoples of South Sulawesi*, ed. Roger Tol, Kees van Dijk, and Gregg Acciaioli (Leiden: KITLV Press, 2000), 95–120. See also Knaap and Sutherland, *Monsoon Traders*.

85. Ibid.

86. "Data base of the Makassar's harbormasters register"; see Knaap and Sutherland, *Monsoon Traders*.

87. "Data base of the Makassar's harbormasters register"; Sutherland, "The Makassar Malays."

88. Sutherland, "Trepang and Wangkang."

89. C. F. H. Campen, "De Visscherij op Halmahera," *Tijdschrift voor Nijverheid en Landbouw in Nederlandsch-Indie* 28 (1884); Ellen, *On the Edge of the Banda Zone.*

90. On the contemporary situation, see Anthony J. Whitten, Muslimin Mustafa, and Gregory S. Henderson, *The Ecology of Sulawesi* (Yogyakarta: Gadjah Mada University Press, 1987).

91. For fundamental criticism of Warren's influential emphasis on coercion in the sea-products trade of Sulu, see Sutherland, "Review Article."

92. Sutherland, "Trepang and Wangkang."

93. See note 77.

94. GM 6:144; GM 8; GM 16:417, 532.

95. Andaya, "Local Trade Networks."

96. Noorduyn, "The Wajorese Merchants' Community in Makassar."

97. NA VOC 2568, 696.

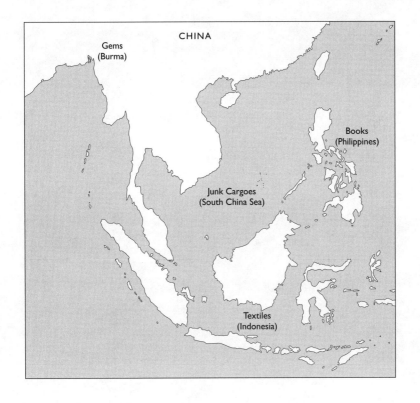

FROM *BAOSHI* TO *FEICUI*

Qing-Burmese Gem Trade, c. 1644–1800

〰〰〰 Sun Laichen

"A base [*feicui*] stone wastes so much money; it is indeed a monster thing (*wuyao* 物妖)."
—Xu Zhongyuan, *Sanyi bitan* 三異筆談 (1920)

"The price [of *feicui* jade] far exceeds the genuine jade (*zhenyu* 真玉) [from Xinjiang]!
—Ji Yun, *Yuewei caotang biji* 閲微草堂筆記 (2001)

As a preliminary inquiry into an understudied but significant topic in Sino-Southeast Asian economic history, this essay has two goals. First, it intends to clarify some issues surrounding the spread of Burmese jade (*feicui*) to China.[1] With the increasing consumer interest in Burmese gems (jade in particular) since China's economic reforms in 1978, academic interest in the history of Burmese jade exports to China has also surged. Two issues have been hotly debated: when did Burmese jade spread to China? And when did the Chinese first apply the term *feicui* to Burmese jade? The first issue will be dealt with in a separate paper in greater detail (mentioned in passing below).[2] As for the second issue, the earliest use of the term *feicui*, this paper points out that all the available studies have tackled the problem outside the Yunnan context, thus making it difficult to reach a correct conclusion. Carefully sifting through the many hitherto ignored Chinese sources and examining the feicui issue within the Yunnan context, one is on safe ground to say that in 1719 the term *feicui* was first applied to Burmese jade.

Second, a better understanding of the gem trade during the Qing period requires comparison with that of the Ming dynasty. For half a century, the scholarly inclination to lump together Ming and Qing trade has hidden critical differences between the two eras.[3] Careful comparison of the two eras

reveals that an important change took place: while the baoshi (including rubies, sapphires, and tourmaline, but excluding jade and jadeite, according to the Chinese usage)[4] dominated the gem trade during the Ming, during the Qing, especially from the eighteenth century on, jadeite or feicui (as a type of jade or yu 玉) started to overtake the baoshi. This change can be traced to shifting fashions in the Chinese court, for often it was the taste of the Chinese emperor and his consorts that dictated the mining and trading of gems in northern Burma.

This research concludes with the argument that China was (and still primarily is) the driving force behind the whole gem business, particularly jade mining and trade. In other words, one can say that from its inception through the first half of the twentieth-century trade in gems was a "Chinese business" as it was instigated by Chinese demand. Using the example of the Qing-Burmese gem trade, I highlight China as an external stimulus on the development of Southeast Asian history.

Burmese Gems and Yuan-Ming China

Although Burmese jade and rubies were discovered at some Pyu sites (from the third to the eighth centuries), gemstones from Burma did not appear in China until the late thirteenth century, with the invasion of Burma by the Mongols, who had introduced gemstones from Western Asia to China not long before. It is likely that the growing demand for gems in China gave rise to the relatively large-scale mining of Burmese gemstones. Although Chinese sources still do not specify the gems, they probably included jade, rubies, and amber. In other words, it was the Mongols who jump-started gem mining in Upper Burma and the gem trade with China.

Despite the distaste of the (Han) rulers of the Ming dynasty (1368–1644) toward Mongol culture, they not only inherited the Mongol craze for gemstones, but dramatically popularized them across China. Particularly from the mid-fifteenth century, a "gem fever" (more for baoshi than for jade) started by Wan Guifei, the favorite consort of the Ming emperor Xianzong (r. 1465–1487), spread quickly throughout the country. This intensified the mining and export of Burmese gems and precipitated the emergence of two Shan principalities in Upper Burma—Mongmit and Mohnyin—which controlled gem sources and benefited from the trade.[5] Again, China acted as a primary mover for the Asian gem trade in general and the Burmese gem trade in particular.

An end to Ming court procurement of gems in 1599 in Yunnan cooled but

did not extinguish the gem fever. As late as 1639, when the famous Ming traveler Xu Xiake was in western Yunnan, he witnessed Burmese gems on sale in the market and local gem traders being harassed by gem searchers sent by local officials, which suggests that gems were still prized and sought by the Chinese. For example, in Dali, he saw gem merchants from Yongchang (modern Baoshan) selling "baoshi, amber, and jade" from Burma, while in Tengyue (modern Tengchong) he himself was offered jade.[6] The Chinese fascination with baoshi in particular did not end with the dynastic transition from the Ming to the Qing in 1644.

The Transition of the Gem Trade (c. 1644–1719)

The earliest account of the Qing-Burmese gem trade was written by Liu Kun in 1680.

> Merchants collect the stones and return to the frontier passes. Those rubble-shaped ones are called "rough stones" [huang shi 荒石]. The workmen in Tengyue grind them with shellac [zigeng 紫梗] and smooth them with small stones [baosha 寶砂], and then they start to shine [baoguang 寶光].[7] The red-[colored] ones are the best, such as "rose-water" [meigui shui 玫瑰水], "pigeon-blood" [gezi xie 鴿子血], and "garnet color" [shiliu hong 石榴紅]. All these are good ones, whereas those called "old red" [lao hong 老紅] are valueless. The blue ones are called yaqut [yaqing 鴉青], the white ones cat's-eye [maoeryan 貓兒眼], the green ones zumurrud [zumulü 祖母綠].[8] But only the extremely shiny ones are excellent pieces. Those as big as peas are called "hat top" [maoding 帽頂], those as big as soybeans and mung beans are called "precious stones" [baoshi 寶石], while the smallest ones are called "ghost eyelash" [gui jieyan 鬼睫眼].[9]

This account reveals precious information on the classification of gems and the gem trade in the late seventeenth century. Far more effectively than the descriptions of Song Yingxing (1587–1666) and Gu Yingtai (1620–90), Liu Kun contributes to the terminology of gemstones in general and of Burmese rubies and sapphires in particular.[10] For example, he uses, for the first time, gezi xie and gui jieyan to describe gemstones, and applies meigui (hong) and shiliu (shui) to Burmese rubies and sapphires, illustrating that Chinese knowledge of these gems had deepened. Indeed, either the Chinese or, more possibly, the Arabs invented the term "pigeon's blood" and the Burmese borrowed this term (kuiswe) to refer to the best kind of ruby.[11]

During the early Qing, the gems from Burma desired by the Chinese were

still dominantly baoshi (as during the Ming times), not jade (*yu*). This is seen from the fact that Liu Kun writes with elaborate detail on baoshi, despite the fact that his *zumulü* may refer to jade. Three other accounts written in or concerning Yunnan between 1687 and 1694 reinforce the view that the Chinese were still primarily fascinated with baoshi, not jade. All of them mention Burmese baoshi, and two have relatively detailed descriptions, while only one mentions jade (*biyu* 碧玉).[12]

The Chinese probably could not purchase the best baoshi, including rubies and sapphires, as the Burmese king had monopolized the mines since the late sixteenth century.[13] Many Chinese sources of the seventeenth and eighteenth centuries, including the one by Liu Kun, attest to this.[14] For example, Liu Wenzheng stated in 1625, "Now it is up to the barbarians (the Burman and the Shan) to provide [baoshi], whereas in the past [the Chinese] could choose at will and set the price. Thus the prices are getting increasingly high, while the good ones are harder to obtain."[15]

Xu Jiong, who was sent to Yunnan as an inspector, wrote around 1688 on Burmese baoshi. He first quotes Liu Wenzheng's observation above, then provides his own comments.

> Also, in the barbarian land there is much poison, and on the way the bandits are rampant. [Baoshi traders] who take shortcuts to avoid custom duties suffer heavily [from these dangers]. I hear that in recent years the barbarians guard baoshi even tighter; those who take [baoshi] out of [Burma] will be immediately executed. There are big baoshi, [but they have to be] broken into smaller pieces and then smuggled out [to China]. Even the small ones are not cheap! At present these [gem] stones in the capital (Beijing) are from Yunnan, but in Yunnan they are not as good as those in the capital (Beijing). This is because [in Yunnan] females do not use them as decorations, and the Luoluo [Yi people] favor black color. Thus beautiful stones mostly reach the capital while it is difficult to obtain locally [within Yunnan].[16]

The last sentences of this passage suggest huge demand for Burmese gems in the capital Beijing, while the demand in Yunnan was small.

Unlike Burmese jade which was solely exported to China up to the twentieth century, rubies, sapphires, and other gemstones were in demand among Chinese and Burmese, as well as among Indians and Europeans. By the end of the sixteenth century, the Chinese were the largest buyers, but after the Burmese court took control of the mines the quantities and quality of baoshi exported to China must have dwindled.

The Debut of *Feicui* (c. 1719–1763)

Up to the mid-eighteenth century, it appears, baoshi still dominated the Qing-Burmese trade. Nonetheless, Burmese jade was gaining momentum. As Burmese jade increased in popularity, soon to replace baoshi as the primary export to China, the term *feicui* was introduced.

The transition from baoshi to feicui can be observed in the writings of the historian Ni Tui, who arrived in Yunnan in 1715. In his 1719 work, *Dian xiao ji*, he wrote a lengthy passage entitled "Baoshi," which not only includes important information on the historical development of baoshi in China and baoshi trade during the Ming times, but also lists various types of Burmese baoshi.

> The green ones: luzi 瓐子 and zumulü; the blue ones: soft blue [ruanlan 軟藍] and *feicui*; the white ones: diamond [*jin gang* 金剛], and *tan yangjing* 賧羊精 [literally "(color of) goat semen"]; the yellow ones: cat's eyes 貓睛, and *jiuhuang fen* 酒黃粉 [literally "(color of) powder of yellow Chinese chives"]; the red ones: tourmaline or garnet [*biyaxi* 比牙洗]; and so on, which cannot be all enumerated.[17] It is unknown whether they are from the same mine or not.[18]

This is a valuable account. First, Ni Tui provides new classifications of baoshi, including *tan yangjing*, which had never before appeared in Chinese records, while jin'gang and biyaxi are applied to Burmese baoshi for the first time. Biyaxi is a loan word from the Arabic bijādī, with its Persian form being beejād.[19] The Chinese transliteration of bijādī is various, with the earliest one being bizheda 避者達 in Tao Zongyi's 陶宗儀 *Nancun cuogeng lu* 南村輟耕錄, written in 1366.[20] The Tengyue prefect Tu Shulian provides the most detailed description on bixiaxi: "Besides baoshi there is bixiaxi. It has five colors, with the crimson and clear [toushui 透水] ones being the best, and purple, yellow, green, and moon white colors being inferior, while the worst ones are white and black colors. They are also produced in Mongmit, perhaps belonging to the baoshi type."[21]

Second and more important, Ni Tui used the term *feicui*, probably for the first time, to refer to Burmese jade, albeit lumped under the rubric of baoshi. This creative use of the word *feicui* was influential, as it would soon be employed to refer to Burmese jade exclusively. Looking at the Chinese terminology for Burmese jade from the mid-Ming times, one realizes that the Chinese, the Yunnanese in particular, had been trying to find a suitable term for Burmese jade for a long time (see table 1).[22]

Table 1 Burmese Gems in Chinese Accounts (c. 1455–1890s)

Ming Dynasty

1455	Hupo 琥珀 (produce of Mohnyin/Mengyang 孟养)
c. 1475	Yudai 玉帶, Lüyu 綠玉, Zumulü 祖母綠
1488	Yushi 玉石 (presented by Yixi or Mohnyin natives 迤西夷人)
1510	Hupo 琥珀, bitian 碧瑱 (produce of Mohnyin)
1583	Baoshi 寶石, cuisheng wenshi 催生文石, hupo 琥珀, baiyu 白玉, biyu 碧玉
	Lüyu 綠玉, heiyu 黑玉
1619	Yunnan biyu 雲南碧玉
1621	Baoshi 寶石, baosha 寶砂, cuisheng shi 催生石, shuijing 水晶
	lüyu 綠玉, moyu 墨玉, bitian 碧瑱, biyu 碧玉
1632	Baoshi 寶石, hupo 琥珀, lüyu 綠玉, heiyu 黑玉, cuisheng shi 催生石
	Moyu 墨玉, biyu 碧玉
1639	Baoshi 寶石, hupo 琥珀, cuisheng shi 翠生石, biyu 碧玉
1611–71	Yunnan bi 雲南碧

Qing Dynasty

1680	Hongzhu 紅珠/baoshi 寶石: meigui shui 玫瑰水, gezi xue 鴿子血, shiliu hong 石榴紅, yaqing 鴉青, maoeryan 貓兒眼
	Zumulü 祖母綠, maoding 帽頂, baoshi 寶石, guijieyan 鬼睫眼
1687–88	Baoshi 寶石
1688	Hupo 琥珀, biyu 碧玉, zhenbao 珍寶
1691	Caiyu 菜玉, moyu 墨玉, cuisheng shi 催生石
1694	Hupo 琥珀, biyu 碧玉, zhenbao 珍寶, baoshi 寶石
1702	Hupo 琥珀, shuijing 水晶, caiyu 菜玉, moyu 墨玉, cuisheng shi 催生石
	Baosha 寶沙, baoshi 寶石
1719	Baoshi 寶石: luzi 瓐子, zumulü 祖母綠, ruanlan 軟藍, feicui 翡翠, jingang 金剛
	Tan yangjing 賧羊精, maojing 貓睛, jiuhuang fen 酒黃粉, biyaxi 比牙洗
1733	Yongchang biyu 永昌碧玉
1736	Hupo 琥珀, shuijing 水晶, caiyu 菜玉, moyu 墨玉, baosha 寶砂,
	Baosha 寶砂, haijinsha 海金砂, baoshi 寶石, cuishengshi 催生石, ziyingshi 紫英石
1741–53	Baoshi 寶石: meigui 玫瑰, yinghong 映紅, yingqing 映青
c. 1763	Baoshi 寶石, hupo 琥珀, feicui 翡翠, manao 瑪瑙
1764	Yunnan yu 雲南玉
1769	Bixiya 碧石砑
c. 1769	Yushi 玉石, baoshi 寶石, biyaxi 碧牙西
1769	Hupo 琥珀, baoshi 寶石
1769	Bixiaxi 碧霞璽
1771	Yunnan yu 雲南玉

Table 1 Continued

Qing Dynasty (continued)

1771	Feicui 翡翠
1772	Yunnan yu 雲南玉
1772	Feicui 翡翠
1772–82	Dianyu 滇玉, baoshi 寶石, bi(xia)sui 碧(霞)髓, feicui shi 翡翠石, cuisheng shi 催升石
1777	Bixia? 碧霞玊, feicui yu 翡翠玉, yushi 玉石
1777	Dianyu 滇玉
1779	Feicui 翡翠
1780	Feicui 翡翠
1782–95	Yu 玉, baoshi 寶石
1790	Baoshi 寶石, bixia 碧霞, yinhong 印紅, zhubao 珠寶, baiyu 白玉, cuiyu 翠玉, moyu 墨玉, hupo 琥珀, bixiaxi 碧霞璽, baosha 寶沙
c. 1790	Baoshi 寶石: yinghong 映紅, yinglan 映藍, bixiaxi 碧霞洗
1793	Feicui yu 翡翠玉, lüsongshi 綠松石, biyaxi 碧鴉犀
1795	Feicui 翡翠
1799	Yu 玉, feicui 翡翠, baiyu 白玉, cuiyu 翠玉, heiyu 黑玉, baoshi 寶石 Bixiaxi(pi) 碧霞璽(批), bixi 碧洗, kulani 苦剌泥, bitian 碧瑱, yinhong 印紅, haozhu ya 豪猪牙, ruanyu 软玉
1802	Feicui 翡翠
1804	Feicui yu 翡翠玉
1816	Feicui yu 翡翠玉
1827	Boashi 寶石, feicui 翡翠, bixi 碧璽, Yunnan yu 雲南玉
1839	Feicui 翡翠
1848	Yushi 玉石, hupo 琥珀, baoshi 寶石, lihong 瓈玬
c.1852	Hupo 琥珀, baoyu 寶玉
mid-1900s	Feicui 翡翠
mid-1900s	Feicui 翡翠, bixi 碧璽
mid-1900s	Feicui 翡翠
1862	Feicui 翡翠
1864	Cuishi 翠石, feicui shi 翡翠石
1871	Yu 玉, ruanzan 軟瓚, baoshi 寶石, bixi 玭璽, feicui 翡翠, cuiyu 翠玉
1875	Yushi 玉石, hong baoshi 紅寶石, yaqing 鴉青
1875	Yushi 玉石
1879	Yushi 玉石
1886	Yu 玉, hupo 琥珀, baoshi 寶石, bixia(xi) 碧霞(犀)
1887	Jade category 玉屬: bixia baoshi 碧霞寶石, yinhong baoshi 印紅寶石 Hongla baoshi 紅剌寶石, yushi 玉石, hupo 琥珀, manao 瑪瑙, shanhu 珊瑚
1890	Biyu 碧玉, Yunnan yu 雲南玉, feicui 翡翠
1890	Feicui 翡翠, yushi 玉石, baoshi 寶石, maojing shi 貓睛石, hupo 琥珀
1890s	Yushi 玉石, baoshi 寶石, cuiyu 翠玉

The history of Burmese jade in China can be traced according to the evidence presented in table 1, for which the abundant information on Burmese baoshi for the Ming period has been omitted in order to highlight the Burmese jade. Burmese jade possibly started to reach China in the late thirteenth century, but the "gem fever" of the mid-Ming gradually lent it visibility and importance. For example, prior to 1475, jade from Burma was not recorded, and the 1455 gazetteer of Yunnan mentions only that Mohnyin (Mengyang) produced amber (which had entered Yunnan centuries before). Around 1475 appeared hard written evidence showing that Burmese jade was prized and sought (and even sent to Vietnam as gifts) by a Ming eunuch. No doubt, some amount of Burmese jade had arrived in Beijing and other places in China with large quantities of baoshi. Interestingly, it was already called yu 玉, lüyu 綠玉, and zumulü 祖母綠 by the Chinese, emphasizing, correctly, the green color of the Burmese jade, as the word lü 綠 indicates. An account of 1488 even records that people from Mohnyin presented jade (yushi 玉石) to the Ming court. The 1510 gazetteer of Yunnan accordingly updated the produce of Mohnyin by adding green jade (bitian 碧瑱), referring to the Burmese jade and stressing its green color (bi 碧). The firsthand account of 1583 suggests that western Yunnan and Upper Burma (particularly Mohnyin) produced many kinds of jade: cuisheng wenshi 催生文石, baiyu 白玉, biyu 碧玉, lüyu 綠玉, heiyu 黑玉. Actually, they should have all come from Mohnyin.[23] The 1621 account states, "Foreign-produced amber, crystal, green jade (biyu), Gula (Assamese) brocade, Western Ocean cloth, and drugs such as asafoetida and opium are gathered and distributed [by Yunnan merchants], and walk to the four directions without legs."[24]

The green jade no doubt came from Mohnyin. This suggests that jade from Upper Burma circulated in China to a certain degree, and the earliest archeological find of jade in fact testifies to this circulation.[25] One hastens to add that, comparatively speaking, the amount of Burmese jade in China was still small (vis-à-vis the much larger quantities of baoshi), hence it is not surprising that archaeological finds are still very rare.

However, from around 1475 to the end of the Ming dynasty (and later), the Chinese had been searching for a better name for Burmese jade. During this relatively long period (about 170 years), about ten different names (yu 玉, lüyu 綠玉, zumulü 祖母綠, bitian 碧瑱, yushi 玉石, cuisheng wenshi 催生文石, cuisheng shi 催生石, cuisheng shi 翠生石, biyu 碧玉, heiyu 黑玉, moyu 墨玉, and even possibly baiyu 白玉 [for non-green color Burmese jade]) were used. Even Xu Xiake himself used two names (cuisheng shi 翠生石 and biyu) to refer

to the same thing, showing the fluidity of the Chinese terminology for Burmese jade.

Despite these various terms, most accounts emphasize the green color or shade, indicated in words such as lü, cui, bi, and even mo and hei. The word cui 催 is apparently a mistake for cui 翠 (which means "green," greener than ordinary lü), as Xie Zhaozhe, using the term cuisheng shi 催生石 in 1621, explained that the gem had "green color with white spots" (secui er jianbai 色翠 而間白).[26] Xu Xiake makes clear that people in Yunnan favored the pure cui ones (chuncui zhe 純翠者). This demonstrates that the Yunnanese had, from the very beginning, noticed the special green color in Burmese jade and applied the word cui to it. This usage of the word cui led eventually to the term feicui for the Burmese jade in the eighteenth century, starting from Ni Tui in 1719.

Burmese jade was not known to the Qing court until 1733, when the Yunnan governor Zhang Yunsui presented a piece of "Yongchang green jade" (Yongchang biyu 永昌碧玉) to the Qianlong emperor. The possible origins of the Burmese word for jadeite, kyok' cim' (literally "green stone") are worth examining. Such a popular usage in modern Burmese actually has a relatively short history. It first appeared in the early seventeenth century, around 1637–1638, and probably did not become popular until the nineteenth century.[27] Prior to the seventeenth century, at least in the Burmese chronicles, mra or mra kyok' were used for jadeite (or green-colored gems).[28] This Burmese usage is corroborated more by the Burmese-Chinese dictionaries compiled by the Chinese for official translation by the sixteenth century (and updated in the early eighteenth century). In these dictionaries, the Burmese word mra was transliterated as 比呀 (biya) or 麥剌 (maila) and translated as "玉 (yu)," while mra kyok' was transliterated as 哶繳 (miejiao), 麥剌繳 (mailajiao), or 麥賴繳 (mailaijiao) and translated as "玉石 (yushi)."[29] In view of the long emphasis by Chinese from the late fifteenth through the early seventeenth century on the "green" (lü, cui, and bi, etc.) color or shade of the Burmese jade, and the appearance of the Burmese word kyok' cim' in 1637–1638, one may speculate that the coining of this Burmese new word was due to Chinese influence. This should not be surprising, as the terminology and classification of Burmese jade have been dictated by the Chinese. Moreover, up to the early eighteenth century, the term feicui had not entered the official Chinese usage, and it still took more time to popularize it.

The Triumph of Feicui (c. 1763–c. 1800)

From the 1760s on, feicui start to appear more frequently in Chinese records. Indeed, Burmese jade, quite literally, began to show its true colors to the Chinese people.

Zhang Yong, in his work *Yunnan fengtu ji* (c. 1736), described the bustling market in Dali, western Yunnan: "Precious and exotic goods are bought and sold, such as *baoshi*, amber, *feicui* . . . Burmese tin, Burmese brocade. . . . Entering the market, [one sees] all kinds of precious and exotic things, goods and people are as many as ten thousand everyday."[30]

This was indeed a huge market for Burmese commodities, especially gems. Though it seems that baoshi still dominated as it is listed first, *feicui* (third on the list) clearly refers to Burmese jade. It must be that the Yunnanese had adopted Ni Tui's word *feicui*, which had first appeared in 1719. From 1764 to 1772, in Chinese records, including Qing palace archives, Burmese jade is much more frequently mentioned than baoshi under the names *Yunnan yu*, *yushi*, and especially *feicui* (in 1771). After that, the Yunnan official Wu Daxun wrote extensively on gems and other minerals based on his personal experiences during 1772–1782, referring inter alia to "Yunnan" (actually Burmese) jade ([Dian] yu [滇] 玉), baoshi 寶石, tourmaline (bixiasui 碧霞髓), feicui stone (feicui shi 翡翠石), and cuisheng shi 催升石. This account is significant because it indicates that the previous emphasis on Burmese baoshi had now shifted to Burmese jade, which received enormous attention. Burmese jade now was divided into three categories and classes: yu, feicui shi, and cuisheng shi. The first and the third, according to Wu Daxun, were of inferior quality and hence not worth much, while the green type of feicui shi was worth as much as baoshi: "Regarding the quality of *feicui* stone, the whiter the better; as for its *cui* 翠 [green], the deeper the better. There are two types of *cui*, *qing* 青 [darkish green] and *lü* 綠 [yellowish green], while the *qing* kind is even better, and its value equals to *baoshi*."[31]

This emphasis on the cui color is typical for Burmese jade. During the 1770s–1780s the value of feicui soared, and the best feicui could even compete with baoshi. Another decade or two witnessed feicui's overtaking China's traditional type of jade (nephrite) in price. Moreover, Wu Daxun was the last person who employed the term *cuisheng shi*; after him, it completely disappeared. After two centuries in circulation—it had been coined in 1583—*cuisheng shi* was abandoned partially because the Yunnanese had a better term: *feicui*, which was on the rise in China, both in popularity and quantity.

Indeed, during the second half of the eighteenth century, Burmese jade made a great leap forward in China, in two senses. First, the term *feicui* crystallized. From its debut in 1719 up to 1799, the usage of the word *feicui* became more widespread. It was mentioned in 1771, between 1772 and 1782 intermittently, and again with exactitude in 1777, 1779, 1780 (twice), 1796, and 1799, and then even more frequently in the nineteenth century. From this period on, though other names were still used for Burmese jade, *feicui* became most popular, and has remained so to the modern times. Second, the volume of Burmese jade exported into China must have increased dramatically. The *Tengyue zhouzhi* by Tu Shuliang reflects the situation by 1790. It first points out that because gems gathered in Tengyue, their collective street name was changed from *Babao jie* 八保街 to *Baibao jie* 百寶街 (meaning "street of 100 kinds of gems"). Then the account states,

> Today the commodities purchased [from Burma] by merchants to Tengyue include, first, gems [*zhubao*] and, second, cotton. Gems [*bao*] come in their uncut form [*pu* 璞], while cotton is carried in bales. [These are] transported on mules and horses which crowd the roads. Currently at the provincial capital there are many jade-cutting shops [*jie yu fang* 解玉坊], the noise of cutting goes on day and night. [The jade] is all from Tengyue, while the cotton bales travel to Guizhou.[32]

Apparently, *zhubao* and *bao* mainly refer to Burmese jade as the word *pu* is used exclusively for jade, while jade-cutting shops are clearly mentioned. It is notable that this source lists jade before cotton, demonstrating the crucial role of jade in the Qing-Burmese trade during this period.

Another source also demonstrates the large-scale jade trade between Burma and China. By the 1790s the price of feicui had surpassed the age-old conventional type of jade from Xinjiang. In 1793, the famous scholar Ji Yun 紀昀 (1724–1805) wrote,

> The value of things is dependent on the fashion of their time and [hence cannot be] fixed. [I] recall when I was young, ginseng, coral, and lapis lazuli were not expensive, [but] today [they are] increasingly so; turquoise and tourmaline were extremely expensive, [but] today [their prices are] increasingly reduced; *feicui* jade [*feicui yu* 翡翠玉] of Yunnan at that time was not considered as jade . . . [but] at present it is seen as precious curio [*baowan* 寶玩], [and its] price far exceeds the genuine jade [*zhenyu* 真玉] [from Xinjiang]. . . . Prices of goods are so different in fifty to sixty years, let alone in several hundred years![33]

Table 1 contains some post-1800 information in order to show the triumph of feicui. Despite the records of baoshi, the term *feicui* overwhelmingly dominates the picture. The 1887 edition of the gazetteer of Tengyue arranges all the gems under the rubric of yu, or jade, in a sharp contrast to Ni Tui's 1719 arrangement, which includes all the gems under the baoshi category. This demonstrates that baoshi and feicui had switched places, with the latter dominating, if not monopolizing the export trade. Statistics are lacking for the gem trade between China and Burma for the period prior to 1800, but large quantities of jade were exported to China during the nineteenth century and the early twentieth.[34] Jade consumption in China in these two centuries had reached a new high.[35] By contrast, there are no statistics on baoshi, which implies that, relative to jade, it was far less important.

Conclusion: The Gem Trade as a Chinese Business

The first written Chinese record of Burmese jade appeared around 1475, while the term *feicui* referring to Burmese jade appeared in 1719. However, the appearance of the term *feicui* is significant not only in itself, but also in that it registers a transition from an "age of baoshi" to an "age of jade" in the history of Sino-Burmese gem trade. Its emergence demonstrates that Chinese tastes in gemstones had shifted. Behind this shifting were deeper social and cultural forces at work.

Feicui's trajectory in China coincides with the trend of jade consumption in Qing China as described by Yang Boda. The first 115 years (1644–1759) comprised the first, or slow-growth, phase. This was a transitional period from the Ming to Qing, when style was still dominantly Ming and few jade works were made. The next fifty-two years (1760–1812) comprise the second phase, or the booming period, which witnessed the socioeconomic recovery of China. Many jade-cutting shops were opened, especially after the Qing started to control the sources of jade in Xinjiang, after the rebellions there were suppressed. Hence, in terms of raw jade supply, places of jade works, procedures of jade-cutting, the distribution of jade craftsmen, classifications of Qing jade, techniques of jade carving, as well as the size of jade works, this was a peak period in the history of jade in premodern China.[36]

In particular, the Qianlong emperor (r. 1736–1795) was an especially ardent jade lover and connoisseur, and his personal hobby became the most important driving force behind the "jade mania" in Qing China. One modern scholar states that Qinglong "*shiyu chengpi* 嗜玉成癖" meaning his being obsessed with or addicted to jade, and he composed 848 poems altogether on jade (though none on Burmese jade).[37]

China's impact on Southeast Asian history is exemplified by the Sino-Burmese gem trade. One probably can say with justification that it was the Chinese who gave life and history to Burmese gem mining and exports, particularly jade. It started with the Mongol invasion of Burma in the thirteenth century, and the Mongols' search for local gemstones. The Mongols taught the Han Chinese people to appreciate gemstones, including those from Burma, and the Chinese after the Mongols indeed followed that teaching. The huge demand in Ming times, especially from the mid-fifteenth century, created a fever for gemstones, particularly baoshi, across China and thus influenced Burmese history (the rise of the Shans in the fifteenth and sixteenth centuries) in a significant way.

If Burmese baoshi benefited from a mix of Burmese, Indian, and European stimuli, then Burmese jade was a thoroughly Chinese business (hardly surprising, as the Chinese have been jade-lovers since prehistoric times). Indeed, Burmese jade had nothing to do with Indians and Europeans. The Europeans had been fascinated by Burmese rubies since the fifteenth century and left with numerous accounts.[38] But they did not mention jade and the jade mines in Upper Burma until the early nineteenth century, when unfamiliarity led them to call it "noble serpentine."[39] As late as the nineteenth century, one Chinese source commented that "[Burmese] green jade [cuiyu 翠玉] is only exported to China, whereas Westerners prize rubies."[40]

This is true to this day, as the Chinese people within China and overseas continue to dominate the jade market. Important events and consumption waves in China have substantially influenced Burma's gem business in the past, and do so still. For instance, for the wedding of the Qing emperor Tongzhi, in 1872, four lakhs (400,000) of rupees were expended at Guangzhou in buying Burmese jade, and "a great impulse was thereby given to the jade trade in Burma." The total cost of Guangxu's (Tongzhi's successor) wedding, in 1889, was 5,500,000 liang of silver, with 80 percent on purchasing dowries, clothes, gold and silver vessels, pearls, jade, and jadeite, and so on.[41] Chinese consumers since the Reform Era in the twentieth century, especially in recent decades, have been driving the mining of and trade in jade in northern Burma. Even now, the terminology and classification of feicui follow the Chinese convention.[42]

Even the Burmese demand had little to do with the jade business by the eighteenth century and thereafter. The long title of the Burmese king throughout history—such as "Proprietor of all kinds of precious stones, of the mines of Rubies, Agate, Lasni, Sapphires, Opal; also the mines of Gold, Silver, Amber, Lead, Tin, Iron, and Petroleum . . ."—which in slightly vari-

ous forms frequently appears in Burmese chronicles and other historical sources, never includes jade.[43] It was not until the late eighteenth century that the Burmese king started to realize the value of jade and thus to regulate it.[44] From around the 1820s the Burmese king added "jade" to the numerous possessions in his title ("possessor/owner of mines of gold, silver, rubies, amber and noble serpentine [jade]"), and meanwhile also presented jade to the Chinese emperor and some European monarchs.[45]

The Chinese gave life and history to Burmese gems, particularly jade. Thus the history of Burmese jade well illustrates how China, in its desire for luxuries, has been a driving force behind the discovery and export of exotic goods from Southeast Asia, and by extension, this region's economic growth and state formation.[46]

Notes

I thank Michael Aung-Thwin, Sylvie Pasquet, Wu Yongping, Liu Zhen'ai, Liu Shiuh-feng, Wang Chunyun, Yamazaki Takeshi, and Koizumi Junko for help with sources, and Wen-Chin Chang and Eric Tagliacozzo for comments. Special thanks go to Victor Lieberman for his meticulous reading of the draft of this essay and for his extensive and constructive comments. The Visiting Fellowship from the Center for Southeast Asian Studies of Kyoto University in 2008 allowed me to complete this paper.

1. Burmese jade is technically called "jadeite" (yingyu 硬玉 in Chinese), while conventional jade (Hetian yu 和田玉) from Xinjiang is called "nephrite" (ruanyu 軟玉). Mineralogically speaking, these two have different chemical composition and crystalline structure. The former is a silicate of sodium and aluminum, consisting of an aggregate of minute crystal grains, while the latter is a silicate of calcium and magnesium with a structure of closely interlocked fibers of microscopic size (S. Howard Hansford, "Jade and Kingfisher," Oriental Art 1.1 [1948]: 15). In addition, the hardness of jadeite is mol 7, while nephrite is 6–6.5. For convenience, I use the term jade for Burmese jadeite, except on several occasions.

2. Sun Laichen, "The Mongols and the Asian Gem Trade" (forthcoming).

3. For example, Xia Guangnan, Zhong Yin Mian dao jiaotong shi 中印緬道交通史 (Shanghai: Zhonghua shuju, 1948); Lan Yong, Nanfang sichou zhilu 南方絲綢之路 (Chongqing: Chongqing daxue chubanshe, 1992).

4. This is because jade had penetrated into and become entrenched in Chinese cultural life to such a degree that it became a separate category in Chinese gemological classification, and the juxtaposition of baoshi and yushi 玉石 (jade) in modern Chinese classification reflects this division. In the Western usage, however, "precious stones" include jade and jadeite as well.

5. Sun Laichen, "Shan Gems, Chinese Silver, and the Rise of Shan Principalities in Northern Burma, c. 1450–1527," Southeast Asia in the Fifteenth Century: The Ming Factor, ed. Geoff Wade and Sun Laichen (Singapore: Singapore University Press, 2010), 169–96.

6. Xu Xiake, *Xu Xiake youji jiaozhu* 徐霞客遊記校注, annotated by Zhu Huirong (Kunming: Yunnan renmin chubanshe, 1999), 1020, 1106, 1113–34.

7. This is better known as *jieyu sha* 解玉沙 and other names in Chinese texts. See Zhang Hongzhao, *Shi ya* 石雅 (Shanghai: Shanghai guji chubanshe, 1993), 132–34.

8. *Ya(hu)qing* and *zumulü* are derived from Arabic or Persian *yaqut* (meaning "ruby") and *zumurrud* (literally means "emerald," a beryllium aluminum silicate, the most valuable of the beryl group; but in this context it should refer to a greenish ruby or sapphire, or more possibly jadeite), respectively. See Aḥmad ibn Yusuf Tifashi, *Arab Roots of Gemology: Ahmad ibn Yusuf al Tifaschi's Best Thoughts on the Best of Stones* (Lanham, Md.: Scarecrow Press, 1998), 182, 192. Two late Ming sources—Gu Yingtai, *Bowu yaolan* 博物要覽 (Changsha: Shangwu yinshuguan, 1941), 6:44, and a poem included in Xuan Shitao, *Yongchang fuzhi* 永昌府志 ([S.1.: s. n.,] woodblock print, 1785), 25:33a—use *yahu qing* 鴉鶻青 and *yaqing* 鴉青, respectively, for Burmese rubies.

9. Liu Kun, *Nanzhong zashuo* 南中雜説 (Taibei: Yiwen yinshuguan, 1970), 18a–20b.

10. Song Yingxing, *Tiangong kaiwu* 天工開物 (Changsha: Yuelu shushe, 2004), 394–95; Gu Yingtai, *Bowu yaolan*, vol. 6.

11. Richard W. Hughes, *Ruby & Sapphire* (Colorado: R. W. H. Publishing, 1997), 329.

12. Xu Jiong, *Shi Dian zaji* 使滇雜記 (Shanghai: Shanghai guji chubanshe, 1983), 14a; Shitongkui 釋同揆, *Erhai congtan* 洱海叢談, in Fang Guoyu, *Yunnan shiliao congkan* 雲南史料叢刊 (Kunming: Yunnan daxue chubanshe, 2001) (henceforth YSC), 11:371; Chen Ding, *Dian youji* 滇遊記, in YSC, 11:380–81. Chen Ding also mentions *biyu*, but it is a verbatim copy from Shitongkui, and thus does not count.

13. E. C. S. George, *Ruby Mine District A* (Rangoon: Superintendent, Government Printing and Stationery, 1961), 30–31; Than Tun, *The Royal Orders of Burma*, A.D. 1598–1885 (Kyoto: Center for Southeast Asian Studies, 1983), 1:9, 165.

14. Xu Jiong, *Shi Dian zaji*, 14a; Ni Tui, *Dian xiao ji* 滇小記, in YSC, 11:127; Wu Daxun, *Diannan wenjian lu* 滇南聞見錄, in YSC, 12:28; Zhao Yi, *Yanpu zaji* 簷曝雜記 (1810; repr., Beijing: Zhonghua shuju, 1997), 57–58; Tan Cui, *Dianhai yuheng zhi* 滇海虞衡志 (Taibei: Yiwen yinshuguan, 1967), 2:5a–7a.

15. Liu Wenzheng, *Dian zhi* 滇志 (Kunming: Yunnan jiaoyu chubanshe, 1991), 212.

16. Xu Jiong, *Shi Dian zaji*, 14a.

17. According to one Chinese treatise on jade—Chen Xing's *Yu ji* 玉記 (prefaced in 1864; repr., Mantuoluo Huage congshu 曼陀羅華閣叢書, 1902)," "Yuse 玉色," 2a—"those that are as green (*lü* 綠) as *cui* feather (*cuiyu* 翠羽) are called *lu* 璷 (綠如翠羽曰璷)." "Jin'gang" should be *jin'gangzuan* 金剛鑽 (see table 1 in this essay).

18. YSC, 11:127.

19. Tifashi, *Arab Roots of Gemology*, 204; Song Xian, "'Huihui shitou' he Alabo baoshixue de dongchuan 回回石頭和阿拉伯寶石學的東傳," *Huizu yanjiu* 回族研究 3 (1998): 59; Fuge, *Tingyu congtan* 聽雨叢談 (Beijing: Zhonghua shuju, 1997), 143. Zhang Shizhao in the *Shi ya* (77–79, 83, 108) discusses this term and its variations, but says nothing about its etymology. In modern usage it has been called *bixi* 碧璽. For other transliterations of this term, see table 1 in this essay.

20. Tao Zongyi 陶宗儀, *Nancun cuogeng lu* 南村輟耕錄 (1366; repr., Beijing: Zhonghua shuju, 1980), 84.

21. Tu Shulian, *Tengyue zhouzhi* 騰越州志 (Taibei: Chengwen chubanshe, 1967), 3:33.

22. Sources for table 1 include Chen Wen, *Jingtai Yunnan tujing zhishu* 景泰雲南图經志書 (prefaced in 1455; repr., Kunming: Yunnan minzu chubanshe, 2002), 346; *Ming Xianzong shilu* 明憲宗實錄 (Taibei: Zhongyang yanjiuyuan yuyan lishi yanjiusuo, 1967), 168:4b, 174:8a; Zhang Zhicun, *Nanyuan manlu* 南園漫錄 (prefaced in 1515; repr., Beijing: Shumu wenxian chubanshe, 1988), 7:1; Tian Rucheng, *Xingbian jiwen* 行邊記聞 (prefaced in 1560), in YSC, 4:605; Chen Zilong et al., *Ming jingshi wenbian* 明經世文編 (Beijing: Zhonghua shuju, 1962), 1:665; Zhou Jifeng 周季鳳, *Zhengde Yunnan zhi* 正德雲南志 (Shanghai: Shanghai shudian, 1990), 14:4a (vol. 2 also mentions that *bitianzi* 碧瑱子 was produced in Anning 安宁 nearby Kunming, Yunnan, but this is no doubt not jadeite, but rather a kind of green stone [2:9b]); *Xinanyi fengtu ji* 西南夷風土記, in YSC, 5:493; Shen Defu, *Wanli yehuo bian* 萬曆野獲編 (Beijing: Zhonghua shuju, 1997), 907; Xie Zhaozhe, *Dian lue* 滇略, in YSC, 6:690; Liu Wenzheng, *Dian zhi*, 115, 212, 748 (115, records that it was made into cups to cure dystocia); *Xu Xiake youji jiaozhu* 徐霞客遊記校注 (Kunming: Yunnan renmin chubanshe, 1999), 1020, 1106, 1113–14; Fang Yizhi, *Wuli xiaoshi* 物理小識, *Xu baizi quanshu* 續百子全書 (Beijing: Beijing tushuguan chubanshe, 1998), 14a; Liu Kun, *Nanzhong zashuo*, 18a–20b; Xu Jiong, *Shi Dian zaji*, 14a; Shitongkui, *Erhai congtan*, in YSC, 11:371; Fan Chengxun and Wu Zisu, *Yunnan tongzhi* (prefaced in 1691; repr., Beijing: Shumu wenxian chubanshe, 1988), 12:8; Chen Ding, *Dian youji*, in YSC, 11:380–81; Luo Lun and Li Wenyuan, *Yongchang fuzhi* 永昌府志 (Beijing: Shumu wenxian chubanshe, 1987), 10:7–8; Ni Tui, *Dian xiao ji*, 126–27; *Qing dang* 清檔, *Gong dang* 貢檔, and *Zalu dang* 雜録檔, cited in Yang Boda 楊伯達, "Cong wenxian jizai kao feicui zai Zhongguo de liuchuan" 從文獻記載考翡翠在中國的流傳, *Gugong Bowuyuan yuankan* 故宮博物院院刊 2 (2002): 14–15; Ertai and Jin Daomo, *Yunnan tongzhi* 雲南通志 (prefaced in 1736; repr., Taibei: Taiwan shangwu yinsshuguan, [1983]), 27:13; Zhang Hong, *Diannan Xinyu* 滇南新語 (Taibei: Yiwen yinshuguan, 1968), 12a–13b; Zhang Yong, *Yunnan fengtu ji* 雲南風土記, in YSC, 12:50; Fu Xian, *Miandian suoji* 緬甸瑣記, in Yu Dingbang 余定邦 and Huang Zhongyan, *Zhongguo guji zhong youguan Miandian ziliao huibian* 中国古籍中有关缅甸资料汇 (henceforth *huibian*) (Beijing: Zhonghua shuju, 2002), 1161; Wang Chang, *Zhen Mian jilue* 征緬紀略, in *huibian*, 1103; Zhou Yu, *Congzheng Miandian riji* 從征緬甸日記 (Taibei: Yishi chubanshe, 1968), 4b; *Qing shilu* 清實錄, vol. 899, Qianlong 36/12, 1125b; *Qing shilu*, vol. 1031, Qianlong 42/4, 819b; *Qing shilu*, vol. 1484, Qianlong 60/8, 840; *Qing shilu*, vol. 134, Jiaqing 9/9, 822b; *Qing shilu*, vol. 320, Jiaqing 21/7, 240b; *Qing shilu*, vol. 328, Daoguang 19/11, 1160a; *Qing shilu*, vol. 22, Tongzhi 1/3, 596a (for the *Qing shilu* references, see the Academia Sinica website, http://www.sinica.edu.tw/); Wu Daxun, *Diannan wenjian lu*, 18, 27–29; Xie Qinggao, *Hai lu* 海録, in *huibian*, 1081; Tu Shulian, *Tengyue zhouzhi*, 3:26–29, 33; Zhao Yi, *Yanpu zaji*, 57–58; Ji Yun, *Yuewei caotang biji* 閱微草堂筆記 (Beijing: Zhonghua gongshang lianhe chubanshe, 2001), 1:427; Tan Cui, *Dianhai yuheng zhi*, 2:5a–7a; Guifu, *Dianyou xubi* 滇游續筆, in YSC, 12:82; Xu Zhongyuan, *Sanyi bitan* 三異筆談 (Shanghai: Jinbu shuju, 1920), 2:14b; Peng Songyu,

Mian shu 緬述, in huibian, 1193; Gong Chai, Miandian kaolue 緬甸考略, in huibian, 1184; Yu Yue, Chaxiangshi congchao 茶香室叢鈔 and Jiang Chabo, Nanru kuyu 南潃楛語, both cited in Deng Shupin, "Feicui xutan" 翡翠續談, Gugong wenwu yuekan 故宮文物月刊 2.5 (1984): 41; Xie Kun, Jinyu suosui 金玉瑣碎, cited in Deng Shupin, "Tan feicui" 談翡翠, Gugong wenwu yuekan 2.3 (1984): 4; Chen Xing, Yu ji, "chuchan" 出産, 1b; Wang Zhi 王芝, Haihe riban 海客日譚, in huibian, 1215, 1223, 1234, 1237; Cen Yuying, Cen Xiangqingong zaogao 岑襄勤公奏稿, in huibian, 416; Huang Maocai, Xiyou riji 西輶日記, in huibian, 1201; Wu Qizhen, Miandian tushuo 緬甸圖説, in huibian, 1171, 1177, 1181; Chen Zonghai and Zhao Ruili, Tengyue tingzhi 騰越廳志 (prefaced in 1887; repr., Taibei: Chengwen chubanshe, 1967), 3:3–4; Tang Rongzuo, Yu shuo 玉説, cited in Yang Boda, "Cong wenxian jizai," 20–22; Xue Fucheng, Chushi Ying Fa Yi Bi siguo riji 出使英法意比四国日記, in huibian, 1307, 1310, 1312, 1326; Yao Wendong, Jisi guangyi bian 集思廣益編, in huibian, 1401, 1403–4, 1409.

23. Xinanyi fengtu ji, 493.

24. Xie Zhaozhe, Dian lue, 700.

25. A Burmese jade bracelet was found in a tomb in Tengchong whose owner lived from 1586 to 1646. Yang Boda, "Feicui chuanbo de wenhua beijing jiqi shehui yiyi" 翡翠傳播的文化背景及其社會意義, Gugong xuekan 故宮學刊 1 (2004): 131–32.

26. The term cuisheng shi 催生石 is also used in other Chinese texts and contexts such as India and Tibet (Zhang Hongzhao, Shi ya, 82–83, 111, 180–81). However, it seems to be that the 1583 instance in the Upper Burma context is the earliest record.

27. J. S. Furnivall and U Pe Maung Tin, eds., Cambu' di pa u" chon'" kyam'" (Yangon: Mran' ma nuin" nam su te sa na 'a san,'" 1960), 48; Than Tun, English translation of the Cambu' di pa u" chon'" kyam'" (manuscript), 58; Khin Maung Nyunt, "History of Myanmar Jade Trade till 1938," Traditions in Current Perspective: Proceedings of the Conference on Myanmar and Southeast Asian Studies, 15–17 November 1995, Yangon (Yangon: Universities Historical Research Centre, 1996), 283–85.

28. Mhan' nan'" maha rajavan' to' kri" (Yangon: Sa Tan'" nhan' Ca Nay' Jan'" Lup' Nan,'" Pran' Kra" Re" Van' Kri" Thana, 1992–1993), vol. 1,204, passim.

29. Nishida Tatsuo 西田龍雄, Mentenkan yakugo no kenkyu: Biruma gengogaku Josetsu 緬甸館譯語の研究: ビルマ言語學序説 [A study of the Burmese-Chinese vocabulary Miandianguan yiyu: An introduction to Burmese linguistics] (Kyoto: Shokado, 1972), 135, 140–41 (the term feicui appears on p. 102 but refers to kingfisher); Miandian fanshu 緬甸番書 (unpublished manuscript at Fu Sinian Library, Academia Sinica, Taibei, A437.774.v.1).

30. In YSC, 12:50.

31. In YSC, 12:27–29.

32. Tu Shulian, Tengyue zhouzhi, 3:26, 28.

33. Ji Yun, Yuewei caotang biji, 1:427.

34. W. A. Hertz, Myitkyina District (repr., Rangoon: Superintendent, Government Printing and Stationery, 1960), 121–23; Khin Maung Nyunt, "History of Myanmar Jade Trade till 1938," 277.

35. Wang Chunyun, "Guangzhou Yuqixu he feicui wenhua lishi chutan" 广州玉器墟

和翡翠文化历史源流初探 (available at Guoying Keji Wangzhan 国英科技网站 http://www.guoying.com.cn/); Qiu Zhili 丘志力 et al., "Qingdai feicuiyu wenhua xingcheng chutan" 清代翡翠玉文化形成探释, *Zhongshan Daxue Xuebao* 中山大学学报 47.1 (2007): 46–50.

36. "Qingdai gongting yuqi 清代宫廷玉器," *Gugong Bowuyuan yuankan* 1 (1982): 49–52.

37. Yin Zhiqiang, *Guyu zhimei* 古玉至美 (Taibei: Yishu tushu gongsi, 1993), 30; Deng Shupin, "Tan feicui," 10.

38. Hughes, *Ruby & Sapphire*, chap. 12; Khin Maung Nyunt, "History of Myanmar Jade Trade till 1938," 255–56.

39. John Crawfurd, *Journal of an Embassy from the Governor General of India to the Court of Ava* (London: R. Bentley, 1834), 2:194; Henry Yule, *A Narrative of the Mission to the Court of Ava in 1855* (Oxford: Oxford University Press, 1968), 146, 265; Khin Maung Nyunt, "History of Myanmar Jade Trade till 1938," 261–63.

40. Yao Wendong, *Jisi guangyi bian*, in *huibian*, 1404.

41. Hertz, *Myitkyina District*, 130; Li Pengnian, "Guangxu di dahun beiban haoyong gaishu" 光緒帝大婚備辦耗用概述, *Gugong bowuyuan yuankan* 2 (1983): 80–86, 79.

42. Khin Maung Nyunt, "History of Myanmar Jade Trade till 1938," 270–21; Kyi" sai Ññvan" Nuin', *Kyok' myak' ratana abhidhan'* (Yangon: A mran' sac', 1989), 64, 85–89; U" Ñan' San,'" *Mran' ma' kyok' cim'*" ([Yangon]: Pan'su Bhumibeda Lup' nan'" mya' Chon' rvak' mhu Samavayama A san,'" 1993), 195, 197.

43. Mhan' nan'" *maha rajavan' to' kri*"; U" Mon' Mon' Tan', Kun'" bhon' chak' *maha rajavan' to' kri*" (Yangon: Lay' ti Manduin' Pum nhip' tuik', 1967–1968) (hereafter as Kun'" bhon' chak'), 3 vols. The quote is from Michael Symes, *An Account of an Embassy to the Kingdom of Ava, Sent by the Governor-General of India, in the Year 1795* (Westmead, Hants., England: Gregg International, 1969), 487.

44. Khin Maung Nyunt, "History of Myanmar Jade Trade till 1938," 260–66, 283–85.

45. Kun'" bhon' chak', 2:361, 3:30, 3:34; Henry Burney, "Some Accounts of the Wars between Burma and China, together with the Journals and Routes of Three Different Embassies Sent to Pekin by the King of Ava; Taken from Burmese Documents," *Journal of the Asiatic Society of Bengal* 6.2 (June–July 1837): 437, 542; Henry Burney, "Embassies between the Court of Ava and Peking: Translated from Burmese Chronicles," *Chinese Repository* 9.4 (November 1840): 469. With regard to the Burmese king offering jade to the Chinese emperor and certain European monarchs, see Kun'" bhon' chak', 2:362, 3:35; Burney, "Some Accounts of the Wars between Burma and China," 438, 543; Burney, "Embassies between the Court of Ava and Peking," 470; Cen Yuying, *Cen Xiangqingong*, in YSC, 9:416; U" Ñan' San,'" *Mran' ma' kyok' cim,'*" 127–28; Khin Maung Nyunt, "History of Myanmar Jade Trade till 1938," 254.

46. For the Chinese search for jadeite in modern times, see Wen-Chin Chang's piece herein; for the impact of Chinese demand for forest produces on Borneo's ecology, see Eric Tagliacozzo's piece, also in this volume.

JUNKS TO JAVA

Chinese Shipping to the Nanyang in the Second Half of the Eighteenth Century

~~~~~~ Leonard Blussé

The sea is the most extensive of all things. In the southeastern islands barbarians live in great numbers, infinitely far away between the clouds and the waves. Therefore men of letters did not go there in the past. Now that the virtue and splendor of the emperor has spread everywhere, the maritime world is tranquil. Every year ships sail to faraway barbarian lands, stable and safe on the waves, as if they were coming and going over flat land.

—Phan Huy Chu, "Hai trinh chi luoc 海程誌略" [Summary of a sea voyage], *Recit sommaire d'un voyage en mer* (1833)

These idyllic lines open the travel account by the mandarin Phan Huy Chu, who departed in 1833 from the Vietnamese port of Hoian on a diplomatic mission to Batavia for the emperor of Vietnam. He sailed on a Chinese junk in an era when the predominance of these ships as carriers of the South China Sea trade was being challenged by the Western square-riggers that frequented these tropical waters in ever greater numbers. His poetic words are quite revealing. Because Confucian men of letters, that is to say writers of flowery travel accounts, hardly ever hazarded their lives on the stormy seas, Phan felt an urge to commit his own adventures to paper. It turned out not to be a hair-raising peregrination but actually quite a comfortable trip, "stable and safe" as if passing over land. By these words, the Vietnamese mandarin not only meant that the sea route was as trodden as a footpath—a *wagenspoor*, as the Dutch sailors used to call the oceanic route from Holland to Java in those days—he was also alluding to the peaceful conditions in the coastal waters of Vietnam since imperial peace had been restored after the chaos of the Tay Son rebellion.

The notable lack of written evidence about Chinese shipping amounts to a formidable obstacle for the historian who wants to restore life to China's maritime past. "Lack of surviving evidence" and "well-trodden paths": this almost amounts to a contradiction in terms. Yet it cannot be denied that, unlike Western long-distance navigation, which has produced a wealth of travel writing by sailors and adventurers high and low, the Chinese maritime tradition has left us very few useful travel accounts. Chinese sailors themselves may have been so accustomed to life at sea that they saw little use in writing up experiences that they took for granted, assuming they could write at all. In 1821, an Englishman who met the crew of the first junk visiting Singapore that year was surprised to discover that the sailors possessed neither maps nor ship's papers, nor any log book about the course they had steered.[1]

Thanks to a number of Chinese rutters (sailing directions) dating as far back as the Song dynasty, we do know exactly what navigational trunk routes Chinese shipping took toward the tropical regions. Overseas traffic to Vietnam, Cambodia, Siam, the Malay Peninsula, and the Indonesian archipelago skirted the western rim of the South China Sea along the so-called Xi Yang 西洋, or Western Ocean route. Chinese junks heading for Luzon, Mindanao, and onward in a southern direction to the Spice Islands in the eastern Indonesian archipelago would choose the Dong Yang 东洋, or Eastern Ocean route, island hopping along the eastern side of the South China Sea. For centuries, these two beltways served as umbilical cords connecting the islands in the "Southern Seas," the Nanyang 南洋, with the mountains of Tang, Tang Shan 唐山, as the Chinese sailors used to call their mother country. Both sailing routes have been well documented in the Chinese rutter Zhinan Zhengfa 指南正法 of 1720, which painstakingly records the sailing distances between promontories, islands, shoals, and other natural hazards that the junks passed.[2]

Time and Space

In terms of time perspective, the Chinese junk trade to the Nanyang in the second half of the eighteenth century has some very interesting features. During the reign of the Qianlong emperor (1736–1796), the overseas trade of China's southeastern coastal provinces expanded as never before. Propelled by the northeastern monsoon, year after year Chinese junks carried tens of thousands of people abroad, thereby creating pockets of Chinese settlement all around the rim of the South China Sea. If under the preceding reigns they had mainly delivered "guest workers" such as artisans, peddlers,

and horticulturalists to the commercial hubs of Ayutthaya, the Siamese capital, and of Manila and Batavia, the Spanish and Dutch headquarters in the east respectively, they now began to carry large numbers of laborers to tin- and gold-mining camps on the Malay Peninsula and West Kalimantan (Borneo), gambier plantations on the Riau archipelago and *panglong* or lumber operations on Sumatra. Swarming out on the northern monsoon, Chinese traders and fishermen also connected with the intra-archipelago networks of the marauding Iranun bands from the Sulu archipelago or the Bugis traders and Makassar fishermen of Sulawesi (Celebes), who roamed the Indonesian waters as far as Sumatra in the west and New Guinea and Australia in the east, and who could provide all kinds of maritime products for the Chinese kitchen, such as sea cucumbers, swallows' nests, turtles, and so on. To the two main thoroughfares to the Indian Ocean, the Sunda Strait and the Melaka Strait, junks from China brought finished commodities such as tea, paper umbrellas, iron utensils, and ceramics of all kinds to exchange for what came to be known as "straits products," that is, "raw" commodities like tin, rattan, pepper, and of course also sea cucumbers and edible birds' nests. At these crossroads the Chinese sailors also began to meet with interloping English country traders who increasingly challenged the hegemony of the Dutch East India Company (VOC) in the archipelago by bringing in opium and textiles from the Indian Ocean.[3] This period of formidable Chinese trade expansion toward Southeast Asia, which reached well into the nineteenth century, has sometimes been characterized as the "Chinese century."

During the seventeenth century, the Dutch East India Company had been the most powerful trading power in the Eastern Seas, but in the second half of the eighteenth century it was confronted with increased competition from European rivals in the China trade and their intrusion in the seas of Maluku, which the company had successfully sealed off from foreign competition for more than a century. It revamped the routes of its own shipping to and from the Middle Kingdom while trying to protect its Maluku spice monopoly, and attempted to force the Chinese junk trade to continue sailing to its headquarters at Batavia, on Java. In retrospect, VOC documents referring to the dogged efforts by Chinese junk skippers to dodge Dutch regulations help us understand how and why the Chinese junk traders ultimately chose destinations other than Batavia. The shifting patterns of trade made it far more attractive to sail to new ports rather than to continue sailing to malaria-infested Batavia.

Some twenty years ago I hinted at these late developments in a chapter

about the administrative problems the VOC had in controlling the junk trade to Batavia during the two hundred years of its existence.[4] Based on newly discovered material, I shall presently focus on the period between 1750 and 1800, and deal in greater detail with the changing fortunes of Chinese shipping to the Indonesian archipelago. This will enable me to rephrase some earlier conclusions or to underline them in greater detail. Why begin in the 1750s, and why draw a seemingly abrupt dividing line at the end of that century? Both periods are significant in the decline of the Dutch East India Company as the hegemonic playmaker in Indonesian waters and the concurrent rise of the Iranun pirates, the Bugis traders, and Western country traders — in short, in the shifting balance of maritime trade in the Eastern Seas.[5]

These developments were not yet apparent in 1755, when the management of the VOC, the Gentlemen XVII, decided to establish a direct shipping link between the Netherlands and Canton at the expense of its headquarters in the Orient, Batavia. This change of policy had a big impact on the existing trading link between Canton and Batavia, which had hitherto been an inherent part of the company's intra-Asian trading network. Fifty years later, in 1800, when the bankrupt VOC was dissolved as a trading organization and all connections with the Dutch Republic were broken off as a result of the Napoleonic Wars, the rules of the game in the trade between China and Java changed fundamentally again. American ships moved in to save the Dutch on Java and in Canton and Nagasaki, and what was left of the junk trade to Batavia continued to hold its own, although not without undergoing important changes in organization and management. In the two decades that followed, the so-called ocean guilds, *Yanghang*, which had been running the Chinese shipping business with Batavia for almost one hundred years, went into decline and were replaced by independent shipping companies, the *Shang Hang*. Why the Chinese overseas security merchants were replaced by independent traders on the shipping lanes to the Nanyang is an interesting question that begs an answer, but basically the same developments were taking place in European shipping, where independent shipping firms were replacing the chartered East India companies, the dinosaurs of the ancien régime.

Now that the scene and the time period of this essay have been fixed, let us join again our learned Vietnamese voyager and follow him on his way to Batavia. Phan Huy Chu's ship sailed the centuries-old course that all Chinese junks used to steer toward overseas destinations in the Nanyang, once they had crossed over from China's southernmost island, Hainan, to the Vietnamese coast. Propelled by the northeastern monsoon, the vessel sailed

southward, coasting the Indochinese Peninsula, "plowing through the wild waves that roared like ten thousand galloping horses," as Phan put it. This particular stretch of the sea route is indeed known for its choppy seas because of its shallow waters. The crew of Phan's junk plumbed the sea bottom to be no deeper than twenty to thirty fathoms and at shallower spots only five to ten fathoms.

A few days later, Cape Varella was passed and a new course was plotted to Pulau Condor (Con Lon), lying just below the southernmost point of Vietnam. Once this island had been passed in the night, the junk arrived in the "converging waters," marking the interface between Vietnamese waters and the Java Sea. Here the author meant the dark seas of the Gulf of Siam, the greater depth of which, as he remarked, soon produced a much gentler and longer wave pattern. After two more days and nights, Phan and his crew sighted the island of Tioman, near the southern tip of the Malay Peninsula and a traditional rendezvous where passing ships used to fetch fresh water.

From Tioman, the junk pursued its course via Riau and Lingga and headed for Selat Bangka, the strait between the mountainous island of Bangka and Sumatra. On passing these narrows, the junk headed south straight for Pulau Seribu (Thousand Islands), which stretched along the horizon in an emerald line, "like a flock of green birds floating on the water." The ultimate destination was almost in sight, because these isles formed the perimeter of the Bay of Kelapa (Sunda), or Batavia. On the outer roads, European square-riggers rode at anchor; closer inshore was the anchorage for Indonesian craft and the large trading junks from Amoy.

The indefatigable George Windsor Earl, who roamed the Eastern Seas in the early 1830s, describes in vivid detail how thrilling the yearly arrival of the junks from China was for those living abroad.

> The first junk, which arrives generally a little before Christmas, is most anxiously looked for, and when its approach is notified by the crew of a Malay sampan which has been on the look out to the eastward, the greatest bustle pervades the Chinese community: some running along the streets to communicate the important intelligence to their friends, come in contact with others rushing from the opposite direction, and many hasten off to the vessel to learn the news from China, every thing that will float, from a sampan to a cargo boat, being put in requisition.
>
> The first boat reaches the junk when she is still several miles distant, and as she nears town, she gains an accession of bulk at every fathom, until at last the unwieldy mass slowly trails into the roads, surrounded by

a dense mass of boats, having the appearance of a locust which has inadvertently crossed an ant's nest, and is dragging after it countless myriads of the enraged inhabitants attached to its legs and feelers. As the decks of the junk are always crowded with emigrants, the greater proportion of the visitors are obliged to remain in the boats, and these endeavour to gain as much information as they can by shouting out questions to the people on board.

The Chinese sailing-master, who struts about on the top of the thatched habitation on the quarter deck, with all the importance of a mandarin with a peacock's feather, endeavours in vain to make himself heard above the noise, so that the junk is generally brought up in the outer roads until sufficiently cleared of its visitors to render it safe for it to enter into the inner anchorage.

Other junks soon arrive, and although these do not excite quite so much interest as the first, the same scene is acted over in each. For a day or two after their arrival there is little business transacted, as the crews are all engaged in building roofs over the vessels to shelter the wares which are exposed for sale on the decks. When these arrangements are completed, the fair commences and the junks are surrounded from morning till night by the boats of the Chinese traders from the shore.[6]

Lack of Quantitative Data

Not much precise serial source material has been preserved about the Chinese shipping figures along the eastern and western trunk routes, but there are a few notable exceptions. Throughout the eighteenth century, the arrival and departure of all junks that sailed along the western route to Batavia were duly noted by the shahbandar, or harbormaster, of Batavia. The shipping lists give the port of departure in China, the approximate tonnage of the vessel, and the total number of crew and passengers on board. These data on the Chinese junk trade have been entered into a database that is now available on the Internet. Some of this has also been published in the form of graphs and diagrams.[7]

In the late 1970s, a team from Leiden University fed into a computer all quantitative data about outgoing and returning VOC shipping during the two hundred years of the company's existence, and then made these data available to the general public.[8] A similarly detailed database cannot be created for the Chinese junk trade because there is (with a notable exception) no precise serial information available under headings like the names of the junks, duration of voyage, names of nachodas (Chinese supercargoes), num-

Table 1 Redemption Fees on Total Cargo According to the Size of Vessels and the Port of Origin

	Amoy (Xiamen)	Canton (Guangzhou)	Ningpo (Ningbo)
Large junks	2200 rds	3000 rds	3600 rds
Small junks	1680 rds	2800 rds	3000 rds

Source: Zhou Kai, *Xiamen zhi* (Xiamen: 1832), chap. 7 on taxes, 关赋略·关税科则.

bers of people on board, ports visited en route, and total value of the cargo, to say nothing of the home voyage and the occasional shipwreck.

What is more, almost no serial data are available about the cargoes of the junks that sailed annually from China to Batavia, because as early as 1644 the Collectors of Revenue in this Dutch emporium gave up inspecting the merchandise carried by the Chinese vessels as this caused too much haggling and quarreling with the nachodas and the many itinerant peddlers on board. An entry in the *Nederlandsch-Indisch Plakaatboek* describes in detail how the Chinese merchants complained: "They always arrived in the midst of the rainy season and were forced to have their vessels examined by the tax farmer and his servants and have everything which was in the hold of the ship piecemeal fashion noted down, before they were allowed to bring the merchandise under a shelter. During these procedures part of the merchandise was either broken or got wet and rotted away owing to the recurrent rain showers."[9]

The Batavian harbor authorities therefore decided to slap a "redemption" fee on the total cargo according to the size of the vessels and their port of origin. As time passed, these fees were adjusted. In the period under study the redemption fees were levied as shown in table 1.[10]

The cargoes from Amoy were considered less valuable than those from Canton and Ningpo. The levies were intended to be equal to about 5 percent of the cargo's actual value. This would mean that the value of a large Amoy junk was about 40,000 rijksdaalders (rds). The junks from Canton generally carried large cargoes of tea (estimated value 60,000 rds), while those from Ningbo were said to bring large quantities of Japanese copper (estimated value 70,000 rds). The junks from Xiamen primarily served the Fujianese settlements overseas by furnishing all sorts of ceramics and utensils, and more important, they brought to the Batavian labor market large numbers of itinerant workers and settlers whose actual "value," of course, cannot be expressed in terms of money.

Owing to these tariff regulations, which continued until the end of the junk trade, hardly any data are available about the quantities or value of the commodities imported into and exported from Batavia.[11] We find occasional references to the quantities of tea that were brought in the ledgers of the VOC factory in Canton. The company also enumerated the commodities they sold to foreign ships calling at Batavia, including the junks. However, these were aggregate lists, and it is impossible to figure out what share of the goods was sold to the junks.

Paroles, Paroles, Paroles

Throughout the eighteenth century, a discussion dragged on between company officials in the Dutch Republic and Batavia about the significance and the utility of the Batavian junk trade to the treasury of the company. Nobody denied that the Chinese connection was of enormous economic importance to the prosperity of the company's headquarters in Asia, in particular its Chinese population, and also Batavia's trade with its satellite ports in the archipelago. The junk trade attracted Bugis and other Indonesian traders and fishermen, who collected the bulk of the forest and marine export commodities for the China market and transported them to Batavia where they could barter their wares for Chinese commodities as well as textiles or opium from the Indian subcontinent. All this was an asset to the company because most of the ceramics and utensils imported into the archipelago by the Chinese were of little value to Europeans and came from ports where the latter were not admitted.[12]

The stockholders of the VOC in the Low Countries nonetheless could not help wondering how this trade with Chinese bottoms actually benefited the company, which made a great deal of money on the profitable tea trade with China. The question of whether it would be preferable to establish a direct shipping link between the Netherlands and China without having to involve Batavia in these operations was posed over and over again. Throughout the seventeenth century, the company had persistently sought openings in the direct trade with China and sent VOC ships from Batavia to Guangzhou, Xiamen, and Fuzhou. The continuous problems regarding the China trade eventually became a nightmare for the management, as the company's executive director, Pieter Van Dam, remarked.[13] The Gordian knot was cut through in the 1690s when the high government at Batavia decided to give up trading in China using its own vessels. The transactions there yielded such meager profits and were so hindered by the local mandarins that the same ships could ply more remunerative routes in the Indian Ocean.[14] At the time, this

conclusion was natural and sensible because Chinese junks from Xiamen were already serving Batavia, which provided Batavia with most of the commodities it needed from China.

To prove the wisdom of his decision, in 1694 Governor-General Willem van Outhoorn reported to the Gentlemen XVII in the Netherlands that in that year, twenty-one Chinese junks and one Portuguese vessel from Macau had sold to the company 108,498 rds of imported merchandise from China but had purchased from the company more than double that amount, 230,581 rds, in export wares. In addition to this, the junk trade yielded 17,665 rds in customs fees, poll taxes imposed on the crews while they were in Batavia, safe-conduct fees (for the protection of the junks against pirates), and so on.[15]

The discussion flared up again in the 1720s, when the conditions in the China trade had changed considerably for a few reasons. Several years earlier, in December 1716, the Yong Zheng emperor had suddenly issued a proclamation forbidding any Chinese shipping from sailing to the Southern Ocean. Recurrent piracy along the coast and illegal shipments of rice to overseas destinations so irritated the Son of Heaven that he ordered an end to all relations with Manila and Batavia, "asylums for the Chinese outlaws, and headquarters of Chinese pirates."[16] This sudden halt in China's long-distance navigation played havoc with the Batavian economy, and although the traffic was stealthily resumed, the Dutch authorities drew the lesson that in the future such a dependence on the Chinese network had to be avoided at all costs. The imperial *Haijin*, or maritime prohibitions, were not formally lifted until 1727, after persistent requests by the Fujianese provincial authorities.

There was yet another reason why the Gentlemen XVII in the Dutch Republic were eager to reconnect with the China market. Facing increasing competition in the tea trade from European rivals, they felt a need to establish a direct shipping link between Europe and China. The English East India Company and the Oostende Company of the Spanish Netherlands were already sending ships to Canton, where they could select and purchase tea on their own terms, whereas the Dutch in Batavia were completely dependent on the quality and quantities selected and shipped in Chinese junks.

J. de Hullu has described in detail how the Dutch China trade with VOC ships to Canton was resumed in 1727, showing that between the 1730s and 1750s this new trade connection did not reap the expected profits owing to organizational problems. The ongoing trade in Chinese tea via the Amoy junk network to Batavia also remained a formidable competitor.[17] Indeed,

Table 2 Number of Junks Visiting Batavia, with Ports of Origin, per Five-Year Period

	Total	Xiamen	Ningbo	Guangzhou	Others
1751–55	37	26	4	6	1
1756–60	39	33	1	5	0
1761–65	34	23	2	9	0
1763 missing					
1766–70	33	27	1	5	0
1771–75	21	20	1	0	0
1772 missing					
1776–80	25	25	0	0	0
1781–85	33	22	0	11	0
1786–90	52	13	0	11	28

Source: Leonard Blussé, *Strange Company: Chinese Settlers, Mestizo Women, and the Dutch in VOC Batavia* (Leiden: Foris, 1986), 146.

the Batavian authorities were unhappy with the initiatives taken by the VOC management in Holland because they feared that Batavia's economic position would be undermined if the company's ships began competing with the junks and bypassed Batavia. One member of the Council of the Indies in particular, Wijbrand Blom, showed himself a vocal advocate of the junk trade and a vociferous opponent of the directors' new policies, which he dismissed as nothing less than a nightmare.[18] His forebodings turned out to be wrong because the Canton-bound ships from Holland continued to call at Batavia on the round trip and did not seem to impinge on the activities of the junks from Xiamen. The junk traffic continued at the same pace with an average of about seventeen junks a year until the year of calamity, 1740, when almost all the Chinese living within the walls of Batavia were slaughtered.[19] After an initial slump, the number of annual visits soon picked up and varied between five to eight junks a year until the collapse of the company in the 1790s (see table 2).

In November 1752, Governor-General Jacob Mossel sent his "Considerations over the Intrinsic State of the Company" to the Gentlemen XVII, in which he voiced his concerns about the marked decline in the company's trade within Asia.[20] He believed that the company's establishment in Canton could play an instrumental role in redressing this unfortunate situation, because of the enormous profits then being made in the tea trade between China and Europe. He conceded that many other European nations were also sending ships to Canton, but hastened to add that the position of the VOC

was much more advantageous than that of its rivals, who did not command such an extended intra-Asian trading network as the Dutch. Batavia could send local products—tin, pepper, cotton, wax, spices, and other goods—to Canton, but their competitors in the China trade who were sending their ships directly to Canton from Europe had to pay for Chinese tea with precious metals.

In March 1754, the Gentlemen XVII responded to Mossel, whose basic arguments they agreed with.[21] However, they differed fundamentally with his proposals on the China trade. They announced that they envisaged a complete reorganization of the Canton trade. Not only did they believe that many of the commodities Mossel proposed to sell in China could be sold in Europe as well and perhaps at even better prices, they also complained about the company vessels idling on the Batavia roads before they proceeded to China or returned to Patria. They pointed out that because Dutch ships called at Batavia, their European rivals were able to ship their cargoes of the new tea harvest much faster to Europe, where they consequently arrived on the market in better shape. One year later, the Gentlemen XVII emphatically determined that the tea trade should henceforth bypass Batavia. In 1755, they decided to assert full control over this domain of trade and set up the "China Committee," which from then on was authorized to manage the direct trading link between the Netherlands and Canton. By 1757, the high government in Batavia had effectively lost its grip on the company's trade with China.[22] This time the reforms made an impact on Batavia, the receiving end of the junk trade.

Chinese reforms

No less important than the changing attitudes toward the junk trade to Java were the sweeping institutional reforms introduced on the Chinese side on the lifting of the maritime prohibitions in 1727. It is really against the background of the Qing imperial court's new rules about the overseas trade that we should look at the developments in junk shipping in the following decades. According to the *Qingchao Wenxian tongkao* (1747), new regulations were introduced that applied to the securities given by the merchants participating in a commercial venture, the ownership of the junks, the composition of the crews, and the enforcement procedures concerning the return of those who went abroad. Under the new regulations, there was a considerable difference in the duties imposed on the ocean junks leaving from Guangzhou and Xiamen. The Cantonese ships were measured according to length and beam and subdivided in four categories of size (charters). Junks of the first and largest charter had a length of 7.3 zhang and a beam of 2.2 zhang

Table 3 Import Taxes on Overseas Commodities

品名	单位	通用税率	厦关税率	备注
嗶嘰缎 Biji satin	丈 3.3 meter	一钱五分	一钱五分	厦关一丈五尺为一身，每匹作五身，每身例一钱五分
嗶嘰纱/绒 Biji yarn	身（二丈为一身）	一钱五分		
鹿皮 Deerskin	百张 100 pieces	五钱		
牛皮 Cow-hide	百张	五钱		
牛马皮条 Strips of Ox- and horse- hide	百斤 100 jin (half kilo)	一钱		
藤（洋藤芯） Rattan	百斤	八分		
靴鞋底 Shoe soles	百双 100 pairs	六分		
鹿脯 Dried venison	百斤	一钱五分		
鹿筋/腿 Deer sinews	百斤	二钱		
燕窝 Birds' nests	百斤	三两四钱		三两四钱，红者征二两

or more. One zhang being approximately 3.3 meters, this meant in effect a vessel of 25 meters long by 7 meters wide, measuring about 400 tons. The Fujianese vessels were measured likewise by taking different dimensions.

The Yanghang or "authorized ocean firms" that were introduced as a new form of overseas trading guild under the new regulations consisted in effect of *ya hang*, or brokers, whom the authorities provided with brokerage certificates allowing them to manage the foreign trade. Henceforth the Yanghang purchased the cargo of the junk, assessed its total value, paid the export tariffs, and stood surety for the traveling merchants and were held responsible for their behavior abroad.[23] These Chinese junks also had to pay on their return to China the usual import taxes on various overseas commodities. These taxes are presented in table 3, which describes the taxes in the thirteenth year of the Yongzheng reign (1735).[24]

Table 3 Continued

虾干 Dried prawns	百斤	一钱		
虾壳/皮 Dried small 　shrimps	百斤	三分		虾壳（多属洋船回 　日，税免征）
白糖 White sugar	百斤	一钱		
黑糖/乌糖 Brown sugar	百斤	三分		
胡椒 Pepper	百斤	八钱		
壳珠 Pearls	千粒	四分		
锡/番锡 Tin	百斤	六钱		
铅 Lead	百斤	二钱五分		
檀香 Sandalwood	百斤	一两	九钱一分	
丁香 Nutmeg	百斤	二两		
苏木 Sappanwood	百斤	二钱	一钱六分	惟暹罗者一钱八分

Source: Zhou Kai, *Xiamen zhi* (Xiamen: 1832), chap. 7, on taxes, 关赋略·关税科则.

Inevitably there was plenty of pilfering by the provincial and military personnel, who did not care much about the official rules. In 1768, a coastal defense commander, Huang Shijian, complained in a report to the throne that local officials had extorted from the crews of returning ships 500 to several thousand yuan (Mexican dollars). Informed of this matter, the Qian Long emperor ordered an investigation. The results were shocking. According to the secretary of the Ministry of Punishments, the Yanghang had to bribe local mandarins with gifts like edible birds' nests, silver, camlets and other cloths to a value of no less than 36,900 dollars per year. All echelons of the provincial hierarchy from the governor-general all the way down to the county officials thus profited from the overseas trade to the Nanyang.[25]

The Economic Importance of the Junk Trade

The importance of the junk trade to China's domestic economy is illustrated by the following discussion, which took place at the Chinese imperial court in the aftermath of the massacre at Batavia in 1741. The debate focused on the issue of whether to continue trading with Batavia or to prohibit it. Among the defenders of the trading system, the voice of Qing Fu, the governor of Guangxi and Guangdong, was without doubt the most stridently insistent. This high-ranking mandarin declared that the promulgation of another overseas trading ban should be out of the question. According to him, more than one hundred vessels from the southern coastal provinces annually plied the waters of the Nanyang, providing 500,000 to 600,000 people in South China's coastal provinces with export and import trade-related jobs. A new prohibition would cut off an annual inflow of 10 million taels of silver coins: "The resulting situation would render people homeless and cause them to wander from place to place, as there would be no food left for thousands of persons, because neither would the merchants have merchandise, nor would the farmers have produce."[26]

A spectacle similar to the roaring reception of the first Chinese junk to reach Singapore or Batavia at the beginning of the wet monsoon could be seen elsewhere. The visits of the junks in Southeast Asian port principalities were likened to annual fairs, where people from all walks of life came flocking in to gape at the articles displayed, to spend their money, or to steal what they could not afford or were unwilling to pay for.

This was the case in the port of Banjarmasin on the south coast of Borneo, where every January one or sometimes two *wangkang* (a junk of about 250 tons) from Amoy would arrive at the mouth of the Barito River. Sixty to eighty small *prahu* towed the junk upriver until it reached the temporary abode of the sultan in Tatas. On being informed of the junk's arrival, the sultan would come down from his *kraton* at Kota Inten with a large troupe of two to three thousand followers, including *ronggeng* dancers, clowns, and children in fancy dresses. A great number of prahu decorated with flags and pennants carrying princes and princesses in their most beautiful garb would also welcome the Chinese junk. Aboard the wangkang, ashore and in the Chinese quarter, hundreds of stalls were set up displaying silks, glassware, earthenware and iron pans, and sweet delicacies. The local people came in flocks to purchase these exotic articles on credit, giving goods and even people as securities for their outstanding debts.

A Dutch commissioner who happened to be visiting Banjarmasin when a

junk arrived and tried to maintain some order among the buyers and sellers promptly drew the ire of the local ruler.[27] In Banjarmasin as well as in Makassar, on the island of Sulawesi, where the ruler of Bone, a staunch ally of the VOC, insisted on the yearly visit by a Chinese junk, the local nobility were esteemed by their people because of the annual visits of the junks, which attracted many visitors from the surrounding regions.

Attempts at Batavian Intervention

On various occasions the high government at Batavia tried to discourage or even to forbid outright Chinese junks from trading in Banjarmasin, Makassar, and Melaka, but each time it had to relent in the face of local opposition or because the junk skippers simply chose to risk arrest and stubbornly continued to come.

On 28 January 1746, the Batavian administration forbade navigation to Makassar and Banjarmasin, because the Chinese tax farmer of Chinese-cut tobacco in Batavia had complained about the "illegal" import to Java via these two ports. Nonetheless, on 25 November of the same year, a Chinese junk showed up in the Makassar roads feigning distress and actually got away with it, so happy was everybody about its unexpected appearance.[28] On 9 July 1754, one Chinese junk was allowed into Makassar (despite a prohibition of 8 May 1753), and one or two sailed to Banjarmasin. In the latter case, this was done in order to "cajole" the sultan into cooperation.[29] In 1765 and 1766, the high government again tried to close down the junk trade to Malacca and Makassar but Chinese shipping to Makassar was reopened in 1769 on the insistence of the ruler of Bone. It was not hard to acquiesce to the wishes of this ruler, because in retrospect the Batavian Chinese agreed that one junk a year to Makassar could hardly make a dent in their own business. Many Chinese in Batavia partook in this Makassar venture. The annual public auction (in Batavia) of the pass allowing the navigation from Amoy to Makassar and vice versa actually contributed a hefty sum of money to the company treasury.[30]

Probably the most enlightening policy statement on the junk trade and the limited power of the company to curtail it was that of 9 April 1778, when Governor-General Reinier de Klerck and the Council of the Indies spoke their minds about the navigation and trade of Chinese junks in the archipelago. Only in those regions where the company reigned as *heer en meester* could it afford to prohibit this navigation. Elsewhere, in places like Trengganu, Patani, Sangora (Sonkhla), or even Johor, where Chinese junks used to sail to purchase pepper, the company simply could not prohibit such

trade. Of course, it was suggested the sultan of Banjarmasin be bought off by promising him 2,000–3,000 rds a year if he would surrender his rights to the visits by junks from China, but the latter had no intention of doing so.

The evidence produced by Gerrit Knaap and Heather Sutherland on the importance of the junk trade to the local economy of South Sulawesi, and the fascinating monograph by Jim Warren on the links between the Chinese junk trade and the prosperity of the Sulu sultanate at the end of the eighteenth century, leave no doubt about the relative importance of the visits of the junk vessels to Southeast Asian regional economies.[31]

The selling of commodities and the purchase of tropical products from the hinterland of course required resident Chinese all over Southeast Asia, but the Chinese junk trade also connected with other circuits of trade and shipping such as the Bugis network, in which the Chinese themselves played little or no direct role. Using information about shipping movements derived from harbormasters' registrations, Gerrit Knaap has cogently illustrated this aspect in his study on the Pasisir trade of Java, *Shallow Waters, Rising Tide*. He discerns a three-level hierarchy, with Batavia serving as the international emporium. Pasisir ports like Surabaya, Gresik, Semarang, and Cirebon functioned as small emporia linking Java to other islands in the Java Sea, and finally Banten, Tegal, Jepara figured as gateways to the production centers of agricultural products in the hinterland. Knaap makes the point that the flourishing economy of Java's northeast coast produced a marked increase in coastal shipping. This VOC "granary" and "timber yard" underwent considerable growth after coming under company control in 1755, and it contributed a great deal to the growing importance of Batavia as the hub of local shipping networks.[32] Knaap's optimistic assessment, however, does not tally well with the pessimistic opinions of contemporary Batavian authorities, who, without exception, spoke about the rapid decline of Batavia as a trade emporium.[33]

Even if the attempts of the VOC to concentrate in Batavia the Chinese junk trade serving Java were quite effective, there was no way in which the company could deal with junks sailing to Malay ports that fell outside its control. When increasing numbers of junks started to sail to previously peripheral ports like Pahang, Johor, Siak, Riau, and Trengganu, the Dutch could do little but watch control of the Chinese trade in the archipelago slip out of their hands. Haphazard measures were the result: the easily policed Melaka Straits were temporarily closed to junks, a move that drew justifiable protests from the Chinese community in Melaka itself, which now saw all trade go to neighboring Johor and the Riau archipelago.

A few general remarks about the shifting balance of trade at the end of the eighteenth century seem necessary here. It is easy for a contemporary historian to throw out observations on "increasing numbers" of junks, "flourishing and declining" economies, the "rise of the country trade," the "expansion of the Bugis and Iranun networks," and so forth, as though we are dealing with developments that were plainly visible and clear to contemporary observers when they occurred. The contrary is true, however. These were all phenomena that occurred over a period of several decades, and although they were indeed noted with alarm when they became apparent, the causes remained very difficult to point out, insofar as it makes sense to speak about "causes" in history.

Anyone who has lived through the last few decades, when we are much better informed about global economic developments, will agree that even nowadays it is very difficult to develop farsighted policies within the constraints of the sociopolitical environment in which we are living. It was no different in the eighteenth century for the directors of the VOC or the high government in Batavia, who had to guarantee a continuous flow of goods from a complex and diffuse network in Monsoon Asia to Europe. In that context, the decision in 1755 of the Gentlemen XVII to reform the tea trade with China and the establishment of the largely autonomous "China Committee" should be seen as a dramatic step, and one they knew would deal a heavy blow to the prosperity of Batavia.

The Trading Figures of 1750–1759

Once the die was cast, the directors tried to find out how the direct shipping link between Canton and Holland might affect the imports and exports of the Chinese junk trade to Batavia.[34] Thanks to that question, we have a rare glimpse behind the scenes. At the request of his superiors, the shahbandar of Batavia, Christiaan Elsevier, drew up a list of all Chinese shipping to and from Batavia in the years 1750–1759.[35] In his report Elsevier regretted that he was unable to give detailed information about imports because of the regulation of 22 September 1752, which stipulated that incoming junks only had to pay redemption fees. On the other hand, he was able to provide data on the ships, their size, the names of the nachodas, and the cargoes they exported from Batavia to three different destinations in China, not forgetting the number of passengers they carried. However, the data on the passenger traffic were totally false and unreliable.

What does table 4 tell us? Between 1750 and 1759, some forty junks visited Batavia one or more times. A few came quite frequently: *Thaij Assien*

Table 4 Accounted for in *Rijksdaalders* (rds) and *Stuivers* (st)

1750   13 junks

10 FROM EIJMUIJ (XIAMEN)

Name of the junk	Name of nachoda
Hok Eeng	Oen Tyeko
Soemie	Lie Honko
Jaenne	Oeij Loengko
Tengoan	Lim Hoaijko
Sienkiomhien	Oeij Tohsko
Am-pho	Tan Ganho
Soehoengoan	Kan Inko
Oijee Sientjioen	Po Pieko
Jonghien	Que Ti Ecko
Gansoen	Que Quanko

10 junks, cargoes unknown, each junk 100 last
[1 *last* is approx. 1,500kg], people on board 3,066 men,
each junk paying in import and export levies

2,200 rijksdaalders: in total	rds	22,000
3,066 men pay 12 stuivers each: in total	rds	766:24
(Taxes in) total	rds	**22,766:24**

3 FROM CANTON (GUANGZHOU)

Kengoan	Ang Siequa
Hapsoen	Nio Hapko
Sonhonkien	Ang Sonquan

3 junks, each junk 100 last, crew 548 men, 3,000	rds	9,000
548 men pay 12 st. each	rds	137
total	rds	**9,137**

1751   8 junks

5 FROM XIAMEN

Soehoengoan	Kan Engko
Hok Eeng	Swa Ki-Ecko
Khidie	Lim Phouwko
Ouwpo	Que ti Ecko
Cai-asien	Que Maseeng

3 junks, each junk 110 last, 2,200 rds each	rds	6,600
2 junks, each junk 60 last, 1680 rds each	rds	3,360
1,913 men 12 st each	rds	478:12
total	rds	**10,438:12**

Table 4 Continued

1751　8 junks (continued)

2 FROM GUANGZHOU

Inaangtijauw	Kinjoeko
Kenwantjouw	Ang Siequa

2 junks of 80 last 2,800 rds each	rds	5,600
329 men 12 st each aboard	rds	82: 12
total	rds	**5,682: 12**

1 FROM NIMPHO (NINGBO)

Japoentjouw	Tyan Tjiecko

1 junk, 100 last, 3,600 rds	rds	3,600
166 men	rds	31: 24
total	rds	**3,631: 24**

1752　8 junks and 1 brigantin

4 FROM XIAMEN

Tay Assies	Aque Kanko
Opho Kouw	Kouw Heijonko
Hock Eng	Lim Phoko
Toea Sieeng	Ong Eng Sioeng

4 junks, each junk 100 last, 2,200 rds	rds	8,800
793 men	rds	198: 12
total	rds	**8,998: 12**

3 FROM GUANGZHOU

Sun Thaij	Eauw Jak
Tian Tjoen	Tjoa Pinko
Koe Kieauw	Kung Tjoequa

3 junks, each junk 100 last, 3,000 rds	rds	9,000
631 men	rds	157: 36
total	rds	**9,157: 36**

1 FROM NINGBO

Soenghap	Tan Tyapko

1 junk 80 last	rds	3,000
101 men	rds	25: 12
total	rds	**3,025: 12**

Table 4 Continued

1752 8 junks and 1 brigantin (continued)

1 FROM TONQUIN (TONKIN)

Brigantin *De Hoop*	Lieutenant Chinese Tan Wanseeng of Batavia

Ship arrived new and empty from Java, and paid export duties on:

50 piculs powdered sugar à 12 st	rds	12,24
40 piculs candy sugar à 24 st	rds	20
Pass and seal money	rds	20
total	rds	**52:24**

1753 7 junks and 1 brigantin

6 FROM XIAMEN

Kede	Kau Hijongko
Hok Eeng	Swa Ki Etko
Tagasien	Lim Hooijko
Soenhoengaan	Lim Thimko
Soenhapsoen	Que Gonko
Ton Sonhie	Tan Tjenkyko

6 junks, each junk 100 last	rds	13,200
1,513 men	rds	378: 12
total	rds	**13,576: 12**

1 FROM NINGBO

Consie	Tan Siqua

1 junk, 80 last	rds	3,000
110 men	rds	27: 24
total	rds	**3,027: 24**

1 FROM TONKIN

Brigantin *De Hoop*	Lieutenant Chinese Tan Wanseeng of Batavia

Paid import fees on commodities from Tonkin
50,000 salted eggs
20,000 porcelain bowls
1,000 nests of lacquered boxes
100 iron pans

In total 16000 rixdollars import taxes at rate of 6/100	rds	960
Export taxes on 50 piculs candy sugar à 24 stuiver per picul	rds	25
Pass and seal money	rds	20
total	rds	**45**

Table 4 Continued

1754 6 junks and 1 brigantin

5 FROM XIAMEN

Tona Kientsien	Lim Houko
Opo	Kouw Himgko ?
Kiedje	Que Ti Etko
Soehoengoan	Lim Timko
Taij Assien	Lim Oeijko
Hapsoen	Que Kanko

5 junks, each junk 100 last, a 2,200 rds	rds	11,000
1 junk, 60 last, 1680 rds	rds	1,680
80 coyang export rice à 2 rds	rds	160
1,781 men	rds	445: 12
rotal	rds	**13,285: 12**

1 FROM NINGBO

Souw Haptjauw	Ang Pacqua

1 junk, 100 last	rds	3,600
147 men	rds	36: 36
total	rds	**3,636: 36**

1 BRIGANTIN FROM 1754 TONKIN

Brigantin De Hoop	Lieutenant Chinese Tan Wanseeng of Batavia

Bringing from Tonkin		
1,000 pieces lacquered boxes		
3,000 bowls		
300 piculs tin		
300 pots with salted eggs		
10 pieces of cloth		
In total 22,500 rds taxed at 6/100 in total	rds	**1,350**

1755 6 junks and 1 chaloupe

6 FROM XIAMEN

Thee Kienhien	Ong Pacqua
Thoa Hongoan	Kan Hinko
Taij Assan	Lim Hoeijko
Tjaij Thien	Tan Tijellon
Kioe	Giet Kanko
Hoopho	Kouw Hiongko

6 junks, each junk, 100 last	rds	13,200
3,916 men	rds	979
total	rds	**14,179**

Table 4 Continued

1755   6 junks and 1 chaloupe (continued)

Chaloupe *Catharina* (150 last)	Lieutenant Chinese Tan Wanseeng of Batavia

Paid export duties on:		
150 piculs powder sugar à 12 st per picul	rds	37: 24
80 piculs candy sugar à 24 st per picul	rds	40
Pass and seal	rds	20
total	rds	**97: 24**

1756   5 junks

5 FROM XIAMEN

Tan Tyeeko	Thoa Ongoan
Thoa Kienghien	Lim Phouko
Khiedie	Que Kanko
Soen Hoengoan	Lim Oeijko
Taij Assien	Que Kienhien

5 junks, each junk 100 last	rds	11,000
2,399 men	rds	599: 36
total	rds	**11,599: 36**

1757   9 junks

7 FROM XIAMEN

Kiem Tjikseeng	Lim Pouko
Tjoa Hoengam	Lim Koenko
Teassen	Lim Panko
Khiedie	Que Tynhoen
Tan Tjapsoen	Que Lanijong
Sie Tjongsiem	Tsoa Teenko
Siang Losien	Lim Oeijko

7 junks, each junk 100 last	rds	15,400
2,671 men	rds	667: 36
Total	rds	16,067: 36
690 piculs of powdered sugar à 12 st	rds	**172: 24**

1 FROM GUANGZHOU

Kim Kaijtijon	Ong Katko

1 junk of 100 last	rds	3,000
151 men	rds	37: 36
100 piculs powdered sugar	rds	25
total	rds	**3,062: 36**

Table 4 Continued

1757 9 junks (continued)

1 FROM NINGBO

Samphan	The Binko		
1 junk of 100 last		rds	3,600
99 men		rds	24:36
total		rds	3,624:36

1758 10 junks

5 FROM XIAMEN

Kiem Tijikseeng	Tan Tyecko		
Teekseng Tjauw	Lie Trjongko		
Tay Assien	Liem Oeijko		
Soen Hongoan	Ong Tijamko		
Tjoa Kinhing	Lim Koenko		
Khiedie	Que Ganglong		
6 junks, each junk 100 last		rds	13,200
3764 men		rds	941
1,350 piculs powder sugar a 12 st		rds	337: 24
total		rds	**14,478: 24**

3 FROM GUANGZHOU

Toa Soenie	The Ingko		
Ojoe Poen Tyauw	Tyong Koko		
Soey Hiena	Lim Houko		
3 junks, each junk 100 last, 3,000		rds	9,000
373 men		rds	93: 12
500 piculs powder sugar a 12 st per picul		rds	125
20 coijang rice a 2 rds per picul		rds	40
total		rds	**9,278: 12**

Table 4 Continued

1759   8 junks

6 FROM XIAMEN

Toa Kienghiem	Tijan Tjoeko
Thoa Hongoan	Lim Kamko
Kinghiam	Soa Tjetko
Khidie	Que Ganglong
The Singtyauw	Que Tayko
Thaij Assien	Lim Koenko

6 junks, each junk 100 last	rds	13,200
1,145 men	rds	286: 12
total	rds	**13,486: 12**

2 FROM GUANGZHOU

Soenian	Lie Thehoe
Souhin Jauw	Lim Hoanko

2 junks, each junk 100 last	rds	6,000
421 men	rds	105: 12
total	rds	**6,105: 12**
SOMMA	**rds**	**200,904: 12**

Source: VOC 4387, Batavia, 15 August 1760.

visited eight times; *Khidie*, seven times; *Soen Hongoan*, six times; *Thoa Hongoan* and *Tjoa Kinhing*, three times; others only once. Fifty-one different nachodas sailed on these ships; one person, Liem Oeijko, sailed quite frequently (seven times), the rest at most twice, but generally only once. This is a striking observation. Some persons may have sailed along the Batavia corridor as private merchants before they served as a nachoda, but even then it is noticeable that they were not necessarily appointed to this responsible position based on their prior experience of Batavia.

The size of the junks was very similar. They were all middle-sized wangkang, measuring about 200 tons. The tonnage of the junks increased dramatically around the turn of the century, when the number of junks declined and the Batavia administration, instead of curtailing large numbers of immigrants as it had done in the past, actually encouraged the Yanghang to bring more people. This is borne out by the fact that junks were then built with two decks, making it possible to transport more people. In addition to a crew of 250 persons, these two-deckers were allowed to bring 500 passengers.[36]

Because the pre-emption fees due on arrival remained unchanged, it made sense to build bigger ships once a large number of passengers was allowed.

People on Board

The numbers of people on board noted in table 2, which are based on the data provided by Elsevier, are unreliable. This came to light in 1760, when it was discovered that traders were smuggling people. According to the official data, eight junks were supposed to have brought 1,527 people, but one ship that had reported 220 crew members was found to have carried 700 persons.[37] In the following year, four junks were supposed to have brought 1,509 persons, but the junk *Soe Ongoan*, a frequent visitor to Batavia, was rumored to have carried between 600 and 700 men instead of the 425 passengers it had reported. According to the regulations it was not supposed to carry more than 110 crew members.

When large fines were imposed, the Chinese supercargoes complained that they dared not face the shipowners in Xiamen. Their argument is interesting because it explains how the shipping network was run. These supercargoes pleaded that they were newcomers, which, given the above data, is quite probable. They also confessed that their superiors had forced them to transport a multitude of passengers under the express condition that all these people would return to China with the same junk. They asserted that the transportation of passengers was a very lucrative business, especially when trading transactions were less profitable owing to the arrival of too many junks in town.

The Chinese officers of the Council of Batavia, the Kong Koan, who were responsible for enumerating the newcomers and for the distribution of permits to those who wished to remain in Batavia, added that every Chinese merchant needed to be accompanied on his voyage by at least two assistants. If these traders were not allowed to bring the necessary personnel, they would back out of the voyage and refuse to load their wares, with disastrous results for the shipowners, who would be unable to load their vessels fully.

They also described another interesting feature of the junk trade. Sailing south along the Chinese coast, the junk was continually boarded by people from the port towns who sought either to deliver letters or to take them personally to Batavia. These letter carriers actually made a living from this long-distance commute. Anybody who has ridden long-distance buses in China will immediately recognize a system of delivery that is still practiced nowadays.

The outcome of the discussions with the nachodas and the Chinese officers was that henceforth the junks were allowed to carry more passengers
in addition to their already enormous crews: 200 passengers instead of 140
passengers for smaller junks, and 250 instead of 160 for larger junks.

Commodities

Apart from certain goods such as tin, cloves, and pepper, which the Chinese
supercargoes had to purchase from the company itself, all the other commodities were products destined for the China market that could not possibly have found any customers in Europe. In other words, the Chinese junk
trade generally tapped different sources than the VOC. Also notable is that
each of the markets of Canton (Guangzhou), Amoy (Xiamen), Ningbo, and
Tonkin sought its own particular products. The goods shipped to Canton
were used partly as payment for cargoes of tea and porcelain or for packaging purposes (rattan). The primary demand in Amoy was for commodities
used for local consumption. How the various commodities were consumed
in China still awaits further analysis.

Not included in shahbandar Elsevier's lists are the doubtless sizeable
sums of silver money that overseas sojourners sent as remittances to family
and business relations at home. Thanks to the Batavian Chinese population's
resistance to the colonial authorities' attempts to stem this outflow whenever the urban economy ran short of cash, we know that this money was sent
in small bags and letters often amounting in total to no less than 50,000
rds.[38] The governor-general and council of the Indies agreed that the dispatching of remittances was "an old custom" on which many thousands of
people in China depended. Nevertheless, in 1798, when the treasury really
threatened to become totally depleted, the export of silver dollars to China
was limited to 20,000 rds.

The figures in table 5 show the composition of the cargoes that the Chinese junks carried home. Almost everything had been brought to Batavia
by VOC ships or native and Chinese shipping from all quarters of the Indonesian archipelago.

Decline

After the 1750s, the junk trade gradually declined. By the end of the 1770s,
the Batavian authorities became thoroughly worried about the prospects of
the junk trade "which in the past was very considerable [in size] but now has
gone into steep decline to the detriment of the local inhabitants." They again

ordered the Chinese navigation to Melaka to be halted and wrote about this to the Yanghang in Amoy, requesting that junks should no longer be sent to the Melaka Straits, but directly to Batavia. The answer they received was telling. The Chinese shipping guilds wrote that, although it was a big blow for them to be shut out of Melaka, they were willing to accept that situation. But they made it clear that they could not afford to stay away from neighboring Johor on the Malay Peninsula. If forced to do so, they would have to give up their shipping enterprise itself for the simple reason that it was the only place where they could find all the timber necessary for repairing their junks and for making new rudders and masts. That was, of course, only part of the story. The navigation to Johor and other ports near the straits had fundamentally changed the flow of Chinese trade.[39]

Chinese tobacco and many other wares from China were now transported straight to Johor and from here distributed all over the archipelago, even to places as far away as the east coast of Java, thereby undermining the VOC tariff system. As Batavia lost its position as the terminus of Chinese trade to the free ports on the Malay Peninsula, the Batavia Chinese sought other lines of work and moved out of town into the hinterland. This trend was observed by Councillor of the Indies Isaac Titsingh in an address he handed over to the governor-general and his fellow councillors on 24 September 1793. He claimed that the decline in the economy due to the virtual disappearance of the junk trade afflicted all business in town and forced Chinese inhabitants, who had previously made a living from the trade with China, to close their doors and move out into the countryside to start a new life there.[40]

Conclusion

Having begun with an idyllic ride aboard the junk of a Vietnamese mandarin, let us now end with the last trip of the *Tek Sing*, which ended in a tragic disaster.

In the early morning of 14 January 1822, as the ebb tide started to flow out of the bay of Amoy, the nachoda Io Tau Ko ordered the heavy ironwood anchors of the gigantic two-deck junk *Tek Sing* (True Star) to be raised. A few hours later this majestic vessel of more than a thousand tons could be seen sailing past Da Dan island with all its sails set, heading for the sea.[41] In all respects, this promised to be another swift voyage along the western ocean route, a trip that this same ship had made five years in a row to Batavia, "calm and smooth like overland." The junk was well ballasted with a load of tombstones, stone sugar millstones, and a large cargo of earthenware and porce-

Table 5 Commodities Exported in 1750–1759, According to Christiaan Elsevier

AMOY PICULS	1750	1751	1752	1753	1754	1755	1756	1757	1758	1759
(Company) Bangka tin	3,100	950	800		120		30	400	500	1,200
(Company) Black pepper	1,000				200					
Trepang	3,340	1,150	1,350	2,610	2,820	3,250	4,200	3,400	2,500	8,500
Agar-agar	4,400	1,900	1,440	2,400	4,320	4,200	1,200	2,500	2,450	4,400
Sandalwood	1,000	250	203	1,100	120	300	500	750		900
Sappanwood				700	3,400	4,500		1,800	400	
Aguilwood	300									
Black ebony wood	550		430	750	70					
Birds' nests	440		6.5	13	16	11	233		41	90
Dried apostles	50									
Buffalo leather	400									
Buffalo sinews		240	65	200	200	410	150	800	80	150
Scraped buffalo hides	2,500	340	550	300	500					
Deer meat	350									
Areca	200	650	1,600	1,000	200	24,050	1,000	2,100	300	2,300
Unrefined oil	1,500	1,500	1,200	300	3,120	5,550	1,500	1,500	500	
Dried meat	635	640	100		150		100		300	
Wax		40				150		20		
Deerskins			120	50						
Dried shrimp			115							
Lead				100	900	400	50	480		
Mother-of-pearl shell				200					450	
Putchuk				30						

(Company) Cloves					3			16	10
(Company) Nutmeg					1			9	2
Dried fish					100				
Camphor						1			19
Capok							50	1,350	1,100
(extra ballast) Powdered sugar							690		
Saltpeter									
Buffalo dinding (dried meat)									700
Deer dinding (dried meat)									200
Extra ballast rice (coyang)				80					
Camphor (catties)			50						
Piece goods			10						
Buffalo hides	9,000	6,100	12,300	7,100	500	1,200	3,300	3,700	3,900
Assorted woolen cloth	25	2	10		25			50	35
Hand canes	50,000	10,200		24,000	16,500	18,200	23,000	3,450	
Binding canes	1,000	1,200	500				2,000		
Sole leather			4,500	2,060					
Camlet									20
Deerskins		330	20						

Table 5 Continued

CANTON PICULS	1750	1751	1752	1753	1754	1755	1756	1757	1758	1759
(Company) Bangka tin	100									
(Company) Black pepper	300								596	500
Trepang	1,700	600	1,800					200	4,500	2,600
Agar-agar	1,200	800	700					500	1,200	900
Sandalwood	1,400	800						300	400	
Sappanwood									300	
Ebony wood	300		250						500	
Birds' nests	55.5	8	1.5						78	30
Apostles		150								
Buffalo sinews	30	30	15							
Deer meat									300	
Areca	1,900	850	1,400					1,500	1,000	500
Unrefined oil									500	1,500
Dried meat	60									
Wax		50								
Deerskins			120							
(Company) Cloves	4								10	2
(Company) Nutmeg									2	5
Capok									1,000	500
Powdered sugar								100	500	
Blue dye		3								
Dragon blood		7								

	1750	1751	1752	1753	1754	1755	1756	1757	1758	1759
Incense									300	
Rice									20	
Piece goods										
Buffalo hides	2,100	10,000	2,300							
Assorted (woolen) fabrics		10							35	
Hand canes									500	
(Bundles of) binding canes		5,000							11,500	
Sole leather									500	

NINGBO PICULS	1750	1751	1752	1753	1754	1755	1756	1757	1758	1759
Tin (Bangka)	1,000		800	50			700			
Black pepper	500		1,000	1,250			1,000			
Trepang	700	400	1,000				200			
Agar-agar	800	200	500	800			200			
Sandalwood		100	500				200			
Sappanwood		100								
Aguilwood		100		300						
Black ebony										
Birds' nests							50			
Deer meat	20									
Deer sinews		25	100							

Table 5 Continued

NINGBO PICULS	1750	1751	1752	1753	1754	1755	1756	1757	1758	1759
Areca	300	100	300				100			
Putchuk			30							
Cloves				14						
Nutmeg				2						
Blue dye	1	5								
Dragon blood		30								
Piece goods										
Buffalo hides										
Assorted woolen fabrics	10	10								
Hand canes	5,000									
(Bundles) binding canes		200	1,000	1,000			100			
Straw mats		100	200							
(Laxa) Jennangs canes		10								

TONKIN Export Piculs	1750	1751	1752	1753	1754	1755	1756	1757	1758	1759
(Company) Bangka tin			200	300			50			
Black pepper			200	600			200			
Trepang			20							
Sandalwood			150	60			50			
Sappanwood				100						
Birds' nests			1							
Candy sugar			40	50			80			
(Company) Lead (Siam)			400	200			200			
Putchuk			5							
(Company) Cloves			2	5			2			
(extra ballast) Powdered sugar			50				150			
(Company) Saltpeter			150							
Blue dye			1							
Dragon blood			5							
Gantie			50							
Piece goods										
Porcelain bowls				10,000			2,000			
Buffalo hides				1,500						
Oil in barrels							40			
Caret				1						
Medicine				70						

Table 5 Continued

TONKIN Imports	1750	1751	1752	1753	1754	1755	1756	1757	1758	1759
Salted eggs				50,000						
Bangka tin piculs					3					
Pieces porcelain bowls				20,000						
Nests of lacquerware boxes				1,000	4,000					
Pieces iron pans				100						
Pieces crude bowls					3,000					
Urns with salted eggs					300					
Chinese armosins					2					
Pieces cloth					10					

Source: VOC 4387, Batavia, 15 August 1760.

lain down the holds. Porcelain was an ideal cargo in the age of sail because, stowed below, not only did its weight serve as ballast, but it was also a commodity that did not smell. Therefore, it was safe to stow a load of tea on top of it, and on top of that the usual array of trinkets needed for Batavia's local community: writing paper, ink, umbrellas, axe heads, iron pans, and other miscellaneous items.

The Tek Sing was extraordinarily large, a sea castle towering high above the waves. No doubt the crew and passengers on board felt safe on such a ship. Its high bulwarks provided a fine defense against pirates. In addition to the normal crew of about 400 sailors and merchants traveling with their wares, no less than 1,600 passengers were aboard this vessel, which must have looked like a floating stadium, as most of the passengers slept on deck, save those who had secured a bunk in the reed-matted cabins high on the poop of the ship. One reason why there were so many people aboard was that it was by now the only junk sailing from Xiamen for Batavia.

After passing the Riau archipelago, instead of heading straight for the Bangka Straits, Io Tau Ko decided to pass through the less well-known and still uncharted thoroughfare between Bangka and the island of Billiton, the so-called Selat Gelasa or Gaspar Straits. There disaster struck: on the evening of 5 February, the Tek Sing hit a shoal and sank almost immediately. An English merchantman, the Indiana, which happened to be sailing nearby, managed to save about a hundred survivors drifting on wooden rafts and other floatable materials. More people perished in this disaster in tropical waters than died after the Titanic hit an iceberg, in 1912.

In April 1999, Captain Mike Hatcher, the diver who made a fortune from his discovery of the porcelain-filled VOC East Indiaman Geldermalsen, discovered the wreckage of the Tek Sing near the Belvidere Reef north of Selat Gelasa, while looking for another Dutch ship. In the following months, he was able to salvage some 350,000 pieces of porcelain and earthenware from the sea bottom.[42]

The wreck of the Tek Sing closed the book on a long era of sea transport in which Batavia was served by the large Yanghang junks. Smaller junks continued to sail in the years that followed, but they were completely replaced by square-riggers after the opium war, when the southeastern Chinese ports that traditionally traded with the Nanyang were forced open to Western shipping.

Notes

1. Li Jinming, *Xiamen hai wai jiao tong* 厦门海外交通 (Xiamen: Lujiang chubanshe 厦门鹭江出版社, 1996), 65.

2. In Xiang Da, ed., *Liang zhong Haidao Zhenjing* [Two rutters] (Beijing: Zhonghua shuju, 1961).

3. James. F. Warren, *Iranun and Balangingi: Globalization, Maritime Raiding and the Birth of Ethnicity* (Singapore: Singapore University Press, 2002).

4. Leonard Blussé, "The VOC and the Junk Trade to Batavia: A Problem in Administrative Control," *Strange Company: Chinese Settlers, Mestizo Women and the Dutch in VOC Batavia* (Leiden: Foris, 1986), 97–155.

5. Warren, *Iranun and Balangingi*; Reinout Vos, *Gentle Janus, Merchant Prince, the VOC and the Tightrope of Diplomacy in the Malay World, 1740–1800* (Leiden: KITLV Press, 1993).

6. George W. Earl, *The Eastern Seas* (London: Allen and Co., 1837), 365–66.

7. For the database, see the Data Archiving and Networked Services website, http://dans.knaw.nl. Leonard Blussé, Jan Oosterhoff, and Ton Vermeulen, "Chinese Trade with Batavia in the Seventeenth and Eighteenth Centuries: A Preliminary Report," *Asian Trade Routes*, ed. Karl Reinhold Haellquist, Scandinavian Institute of Asian Studies, Studies on Asian Topics 13 (London: Curzon, 1991), 231–45. For graphs, see Blussé, *Strange Company* and also George Bryan Souza, *The Survival of Empire: Portuguese Trade and Society in China and the South China Sea, 1630–1754* (Cambridge: Cambridge University Press, 1986).

8. Jaap R. Bruijn, Femme S. Gaastra, and Ivo Schöffer, *Dutch-Asiatic Shipping in the Seventeenth and Eighteenth Centuries*, vol. 1 (The Hague: Martinus Nijhoff, 1987).

9. J. A. van der Chijs, *Nederlandsch-Indisch Plakaatboek 1602–1811*, 17 vols. (Batavia 1885–1900), 29 June 1750, 6:68.

10. Ibid., 26 June 1751, 6:68.

11. These special tariffs for the junk trade may have persisted until as late as 1865 when the first general tariff act was introduced, according to P. H. van der Kemp in *Oost-Indië's Geldmiddelen: Japansche en Chineesche Handel van 1817 en 1818* ('s-Gravenhage: Martinus Nijhoff, 1919), 14.

12. P. H. van der Kemp, *Oost-Indie's Inwendig Bestuur van 1817 op 1818, Falck als Minister, Weduwefonds, Onderwijs, Wetenschap, Kunst, Kerk en Zending Slavernij, Verblijfrecht, Handel, Scheepvaart* ('s-Gravenhage: Martinus Nijhoff, 1918), 282.

13. F. Stapel, ed., *Beschrijvinge van de Oost-Indische Compagnie* ('s-Gravenhage: Rijksgeschiedkundige Publicatien, 1931), 2–1:698.

14. "No Boats to China: The Dutch East India Company and the Changing Pattern of the China Sea Trade, 1635–1690," *Modern Asian Studies* 30.1 (1996): 51–76. See also Chang Pin-tsun, "Shiji shijimo Helan DongYindu Gongsi weishemma bu zhai bao quan dao Zhongguo?," *Zhongguo haiyang fazhanshi lunwenji* [Essays in maritime history], ed. Liu Shiuh-feng (Taipei: Academia Sinica, 2005), 9:139–68.

15. Blussé, *Strange Company*, 127.

16. Fu Loshu, *A Documentary of Sino-Western Relations 1644–1820* (Tucson: University of Arizona Press, 1966), 122.

17. J. de Hullu, "Over den Chineschen Handel der Oost-Indische Compagnie in de Eerste Dertig Jaar van de 18e Eeuw," *Bijdragen Koninklijk Instituut Taal-Land-en Volkenkunde van Nederlandsch Indië* (BKI), ('s-Gravenhage: Martinus Nijhoff, 1917): 32–154, p. 73.

18. For Blom's objections to the policies, see Blussé, *Strange Company*, 135–37.

19. Ibid., 73–96.

20. Nationaal Archief, 's-Gravenhage. VOC 172, 28 November 1752.

21. VOC 172, written answer of the Gentlemen XVII to Jacob Mossel, 28 March 1754.

22. See J. de Hullu, "De Instelling van de Commissie voor den Handel der Oost-Indische Compagnie op China in 1756," *Bijdragen Tot de Taal-, Land-, en Volkenkunde van Nederlandsch Indië* ('s-Gravenhage: Martinus Nijhoff, 1923), 79: 529–33, and Liu Yong, *The Dutch East India Company's Tea Trade with China, 1757–1781* (Leiden: Brill, 2007).

23. Li Jinming, *Xiamen hai wai jiao tong*, 42.

24. See Zhou Kai, *Xiamen zhi* (Xiamen: n.p., 1832), chap. 7, on taxes，关赋略·关税科则.

25. Qing Gaozhong shilu (The Veritable Records of the Gaozhong era of the Qing dynasty) *juan* 714, Qianlong 29, 7th month.

26. T'ien Ju-k'ang, "Shiqi shiji zhi shijiu shiji zhongye Zhungguo fanquan zai Dongnan Yazhou hangyun he shangye shandi diwei" [The position of Chinese sailing vessels in the shipping and trade of Southeast Asia from the seventeenth until the mid-nineteenth century], *Lishi yanjiu* 8 (1956): 19.

27. Van der Kemp, *Oost-Indië's Geldmiddelen, Japansche en Chineesche Handel*, 295. For the description of Commissioner Boeckholtz's visit, see van der Kemp, "Het Afbreken van onze Betrekkingen met Bandjermasin onder Daendels en de Herstelling van het Nederlandsh Gezag Aldaar op den 1en Januari 1817," BKI 49 (1898): 1–168.

28. Van der Chijs, N.I. *Plakaatboek V*, 323, 426.

29. Van der Chijs, N.I. *Plakaatboek VI*, 689.

30. Van der Chijs, N.I. *Plakaatboek VIII*, 28, 90, 519.

31. Gerrit Knaap & Heather Sutherland, *Monsoon Traders, Ships, skippers and commodities in eighteenth-century Makassar* (Leiden: KITLV Press, 2004). The authors do not mention, however, that this trade was largely financed by the Chinese of Batavia. James F. Warren, *The Sulu Zone, The World Capitalist Economy and the Historical Imagination*, Comparative Asian Studies No. 20 (Amsterdam: VU University Press, 1998).

32. Gerrit Knaap, *Shallow Waters, Rising Tide: Shipping and Trade in Java Around 1775* (Netherlands: KITLV Press, 1996), 3–16.

33. See, for instance, the gloomy views expressed in April 1778, *Plakaatboek X*, 232.

34. VOC 790, resolutiën Gouverneur Generaal en Raden 1760, 509: Batavia, dinsdag 10 juni 1760, [In margin:] Bezoigne over de Patriase missive van den 10: oct. 1759 rakende de directe vaart en handel op China.

35. VOC 4387, Batavia, 15 August 1760.

36. Van der Chijs, N.I. *Plakaatboek XIV*, 27 April 1804, 35.

37. Van der Chijs, N.I. *Plakaatboek VII*, 23 May 1760, 409.

38. Van der Chijs, N.I. *Plakaatboek X*, 18 July 1785, 791.

39. "Voorschriften op de Vaart en Handel der Chinese Jonken," *Plakaatboek X*, 9 April 1778, 227.

40. Adres Isaac Titsingh in 24 September 1793, *Plakaatboek* XI, 618.

41. Nigel Pickford and Michael Hatcher, *The Legacy of the Tek Sing, China's Titanic: Its Tragedy and Its Treasure* (Cambridge: Granta, 2000).

42. The recent legal tug-of-war about the cargo partly reclaimed from the wreck of this ill-fated junk by Michael Hatcher has contributed to the revived interest in the junk trade to the Nanyang. So enormous was the quantity of the salvaged cargo that it was decided to auction the booty on the Internet.

CHINESE BOOKS AND PRINTING IN THE EARLY SPANISH PHILIPPINES

〰〰 Lucille Chia

By the mid-seventeenth century, the first sizeable Chinese diaspora had resulted in settlements throughout Southeast Asia, some with inhabitants in the thousands. The most dramatic growth occurred in the Spanish Philippines, chiefly around Manila, where the number of Chinese (known there as *Sangleyes*) increased from perhaps 100 just before the Spanish established control to approximately 20,000 by 1603. The figure never dropped below a few thousand, even after the largest expulsion in the 1760s. In the second half of the nineteenth century, the number of Chinese immigrants peaked at about 100,000 in the 1880s and 1890s.[1] Trade and the search for a better livelihood motivated the sojourners and settlers, nearly all of whom came from southeast China, specifically the coastal area of southern Fujian (Minnan).

The arrival of both humans and goods led to the introduction of many elements of Chinese culture into Southeast Asia: religious practices, foodways, languages, architecture, performing arts, as well as a variety of social organizations and practices. What is striking is that so little of Chinese culture was introduced through print. Indeed, of the myriad commodities carried by Chinese junks in the Nanyang trade, books may have been the one item that was largely missing. Moreover, except briefly between about 1593–1607 in the early Spanish Philippines, books in Chinese were not printed in Southeast Asia until the early nineteenth century. Reasons for this centuries-long lacuna include the generally low educational level of the Chinese sojourners and settlers in the Nanyang, whose motives for going overseas, in any case, had little to do with books, and the restrictions imposed on them by the different regions' ruling powers, both indigenous and European. Such a void meant not that Chinese literary culture did not spread at all to Southeast Asia

in the early modern period, but that we cannot attribute the dissemination mainly or directly to the Chinese who went to the Nanyang.

This essay explores such issues by looking at the anomalous phenomenon of book-printing and the availability of Chinese books in the early Spanish Philippines—topics whose treatment by previous scholars has suggested some of the questions posed here. For example, how might Chinese books and the way they were printed have changed as a result of encounters with Western religious, linguistic, and bibliographic ideas? In addition, could there have been an overseas market for books printed in China? Because the sources are few and not very forthcoming, my answers remain necessarily speculative, but they should help us to appreciate the complexities of the circumstances that allow books and book culture to be exportable commodities, and to think of ways to study these questions in greater detail in the future.[2]

Chinese Books in the Early Spanish Philippines

About a year after arriving in the Philippines in 1588, Juan Cobo, the Dominican missionary, remarked in a letter that most of the Chinese in the Philippines were literate. Supposedly, out of a thousand of these Sangleyes, only ten did not know many Chinese characters, in contrast to the peasants in his native Castile, where literacy rates were far lower.[3] As one of four Dominican friars assigned to minister to the Chinese, Cobo made a serious effort to learn Chinese; at one point, he was reputed to have mastered some 3,000 characters. Like so many other early Spanish missionaries, Cobo saw his missionary work among the Chinese in the Philippines as preparation for the much greater goal of converting China. Thus, in addition to learning the language, he also collected Chinese books and tried to translate books from Chinese into Castilian or the other way around.[4]

Of Cobo's own works, two are extant: a Confucian anthology that he translated into Castilian, and a book that he wrote in Chinese.[5] The latter, entitled *Xinke sengshi Gaomu Xian zhuan Wuji tianzhu zhengjiao zhenchuan shilu* 新刻僧師噶呣羨撰無極天主正教真傳實錄 [A printed edition of the Veritable record of the authentic tradition of the true faith in the Infinite God, by the religious master Gao Muxian (Juan Cobo)] (henceforth *Shilu*), was one of the first two books blockprinted (i.e., using xylography) in the Philippines in 1593.[6] Cobo's remark about the literacy of the Sangleyes was most likely a great exaggeration, but his impression may have spurred his own literary efforts as part of his missionary activities.

The publication date of Cobo's *Shilu* indicates that he had been learning

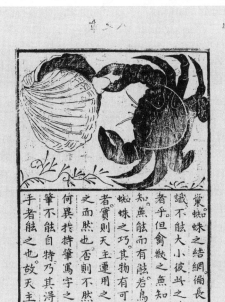

Figure 1 *Xinke sengshi Gao Muxian zhuan Wuji tianzhu zhengjiao zhenzhuan shilu* 新刻僧師喎哶羨撰無極天主正教真傳實錄, by Juan Cobo. Illustration from the eighth zhang 章 ("How animals know what they should eat and drink") showing a crab using a stone to keep open the shell of an oyster. Convento de San Gabriel, Manila, 1593. Source: Biblioteca Nacional (Madrid), R/33.396.

Chinese—certainly the southern Fujian dialect, or Minnanese, in order to minister to his Chinese parishioners—for about four years when he wrote this work.[7] Since it is in classical Chinese, however, Cobo almost certainly could not have written it without a great deal of help from educated Chinese, most probably the interpreters assigned to work with the Dominicans.

Cobo's *Shilu* largely resembles in appearance books produced in China at that time: the blockframe surrounding the text, the ruled columns, and the arrangement of four of the illustrations above the text on the page (fig. 1)—not at all surprising, given Cobo's examination of books from China, and that the text was written by a Chinese scribe and the blocks engraved by Chinese carvers.[8] Several features do depart, however, from the usual Chinese imprints: most significant are that the text is printed on both sides of the sheet and that the work has several fold-out sheets containing diagrams demonstrating Western ideas of geography and astronomy.[9] This would have been an innovation among Chinese books, in which there were illustrations, diagrams, and tables spread over an entire leaf. But since each leaf was often folded in half, the image had to be viewed either in two parts by turning the page or as the facing sides of two consecutive leaves. Such a modification

may seem trivial, but has great implications for clarifying and thus further empowering the presentation of information through images.

Certainly much effort was put into the production of Cobo's *Shilu*, but for whom was it meant? In his postface, Cobo said that he edited several chapters and had them engraved on blocks to disseminate them for those joining the faith to study deeply the meaning of this book [. . . 校正數章梓以廣傳 為冀從教者深習此書之旨]. His phrase *guangchuan* 廣傳 is found in numerous prefaces of Chinese imprints and claims that a book was being printed to disseminate it. But since the work was written in classical Chinese, few of the Chinese in the Philippines — even those who knew many characters — would have been able to understand much of it, not only because they lacked the necessary education, but also because nearly all of them spoke exclusively Minnanese. Perhaps his fellow missionaries who knew some Chinese could have read it to improve their language skills, but they would also have been primarily concerned with mastering spoken Minnanese to minister to their parishioners. Finally, the price of the book was officially set at four reales, making it a rather expensive item, as Governor Dasmariñas admitted, and probably not something that many Chinese, even catechumens, would have bought. As a rough comparison, four reales would have bought four arrobas (about sixteen gallons or sixty litres) of palm wine, or one buffalo, or twelve hens, or thirty fine porcelain dishes.[10]

Without rejecting Cobo's expressed purpose for publishing the work, however, one can also argue that the *Shilu* was written to show what the Dominicans were capable of in their task of converting the Chinese. Thus, although Cobo wrote that he did not presume to compare his Chinese to that of other Frankish priests, he probably did want to demonstrate his progress in the language. The "Frankish" priest that he almost certainly had in mind was the Jesuit Michele Ruggieri, who had already published his *Tianzhu shilu* 天主實錄 in China in 1584.[11] In addition, as van der Loon argues, when the governor of the Philippines sent to the Spanish court in 1593 a catechism in Castilian and Tagalog and another in Chinese, the latter was most probably Cobo's *Shilu*, rather than a later work. There may not have been very many copies of the *Shilu* printed if its chief purpose was to show off the Dominicans' achievement rather than to be distributed broadly to potential converts. It may also explain why another Dominican, Diego de Nieva, could already in 1605 mistakenly claim that his own book was the first to be printed in Chinese in the Philippines.

As for the *Mingxin baojian*, which Cobo and his Chinese assistants translated into Castilian, it was apparently never printed. However, how the origi-

nal Chinese work came to the Philippines tells us something about the book trade in Fujian and its likely market in Manila. One late Ming edition of the work lists (quite possibly fictitiously) Li Tingji 李廷機 (js 1583, d. 1616) as the collator.[12] Li was a native of Jinjiang in southern Fujian who had placed first in the provincial and metropolitan examinations and second in the palace examination of 1583, and he became a grand secretary in the early seventeenth century. Because of his high status, his spectacular success in the government examinations, and his Fujian origin, Li has been credited as the compiler or annotator of many Fujian commercial editions of examination essays, commentaries to the classics, and collections of sayings culled from the classics. One in the last class of works was the *Mingxin baojian*, which had been reprinted several times and was highly popular in Fujian. As a collection of short passages from Confucian works rather than a scholarly work replete with lengthy commentaries, it appealed widely to readers other than the highly educated, such as merchants and tradesmen, and was brought over to the Philippines, where it attracted Cobo's attention. Indeed, some sixty years later, another Dominican, Domingo Navarrete, made his own translation of this same work, the first he had read on arriving in China.[13]

Cobo's *Shilu* and another work, the *Doctrina christiana* in Castilian, in Tagalog in the native baybayin script, and in romanized Tagalog, were printed in 1593 by the Dominicans in their monastery of San Gabriel, making them the first publications in the Philippines.[14] The latter (fig. 2) was not a surprising choice, since *doctrinas* were the first work printed in several parts of Spanish colonial America, including the 1539 edition in Castilian and Nahuatl in Mexico City. The Philippine edition, however, was unique in that it was an entirely blockprinted book, showing that xylography was technologically adequate for printing in three very different scripts. Nevertheless, perhaps the technical challenges of engraving a polyglot text meant both longer production times and greater labor costs than finishing a blockprinted book in one script. Hence economic considerations may well have figured in the switch to movable-type printing. Evidence from slightly later imprints shows that while a few more works were blockprinted in Chinese and Tagalog, no more were thus produced in Western languages. Books in Castilian, Latin, as well as later ones in Tagalog and other Filipino languages were printed in movable type beginning around 1604.

One of the remaining blockprinted books in Chinese, a *Doctrina christiana en letra y lengua china* (fig. 3), was printed c. 1605 by a Chinese, Keng Yong, in the Parián, the Chinese quarter just outside of Manila.[15] On the title page, which is in Castilian, the authorship of the work is attributed to the Domini-

los çielos. fanctificado sea el tu
nombre. Venga a nos el tu reyno.
hagase tu voluntad, asi en latier
ra como en el çielo. El pan nuef
tro de cada dia danoslo oy. y per
donanos nueftras deudas. asi co
mo nofotros las perdonamos a
nueftros deudores. y no nos de
xes caer en la tentaçion. Mas
libranos de mal. Amen.
  Eng ama namin..
  ma namin nasa langit ca
ypafamba mo ang ngala
mo, mouifaamin ang pagcabari

mo. ypafono: mo ang loob mo.
dito falupa para sa langit, big ya
mo cami ngaion nanga min caca
nin. pata nang sa amoarao. atpa
cavalin mo ang amin cafalana,
ya rang vinapalan babala namit
sa loob ang cafala nan nang
nagcafasala sa amin. Houag
mo caming oevan nang dicami
matalo nang tocfo. Datapo
uat yadia mo cami fadilan ma
fama. Amen. Jefus.

Figure 2 *Doctrina Christiana, en lengua española y tagala, corregida por los Religiosos de las ordenes Impressa con licencia, en S. Gabriel, de la orden de S. Domingo En Manila, 1593.* Pages showing the text of the Lord's Prayer in Castilian, Tagalog romanization, and then Tagalog baybayin script (last two lines of page on the right). Source: Library of Congress Lessing J. Rosenwald Collection.

Figure 3 *Doctrina christiana en letra y lengua china.* Published by Keng Yong in the Parián, Manila, c. 1605. *Source*: Vatican Library, Riserva, V, 73.

3a Title page.

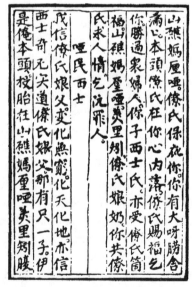

3b Part of the Hail Mary and part of the Apostles' Creed. Each prayer ends with phrase "Yamin Shixi" (Amen, Jesus), which also serves to separate the texts.

cans ministering to the Sangleyes, although again, the Chinese interpreters working with the Spanish missionaries were probably responsible for much of the actual translation. Moreover, unlike Cobo's *Shilu*, the text was clearly composed for Minnanese readers and listeners. The physical appearance of the imprint, as well as the notable difference in language styles between the first and second parts of the work, suggest that this was a commercial publication by a printer aware of the potential of a book market in Manila and who was not associated with, or at least not supervised by, the missionaries.[16] Indeed, this potential market was not limited to the Sangley residents in the Philippines but included the hundreds or thousands of Chinese who annually came on the junks and returned to China.[17] We do not have a price for the Chinese *Doctrina*, but being smaller in size than Cobo's *Shilu*, containing about only half as many leaves, and lacking illustrations, it probably was a cheaper book, probably even cheaper than the *Doctrina* in Castilian and Tagalog that had about the same number of leaves and sold for two reales.

Despite the success of these early xylographic imprints, the Spanish missionaries seemed uncomfortable with blockprinting for Western and Filipino languages and were anxious to perfect movable-type printing, which they considered to be the proper technology. Around 1604, another Dominican friar, Francisco Blancas de San José, had printed, using movable type, his *Libro de las quatro postrimerías del hombre en lengua tagala y letra española* [Book on the last four years of man's life, in Tagalog in roman letters]. In his dedication, Blancas wrote,

> We now have in these our islands complete and perfect printing for a more perfect fulfilment of our ministry. For we shall now be able, not only verbally by preaching but also in writing, to teach these our brothers, and write for them, either in Spanish characters for those who know how to read them, or in their own Tagalog script, everything which will seem to us to further the progress of this mercy which the Lord has done to them in making them Christians. I have prepared other works before this one . . . but the new craftsman has not dared begin his business except with this smaller work.

Blancas, after learning Tagalog in order to preach and write religious works in that language, had found a Chinese Christian named Juan de Vera ("the new craftsman") to produce the movable type. And if the descriptions in the two Dominican histories are reliable, then Juan de Vera practically "reinvented" the technique, cutting the punches, striking the metal matrices, and casting the metal type. In his admiring account, Diego de Aduarte wrote,

Since there was no printing in these islands, and no one who understood it or who took it up as a trade, he [Blancas] planned to have the printing done by means of a Chinese, a good Christian, who, seeing that the books of Father Fray Francisco were sure to be of great use, bestowed so much care upon this undertaking that he finally (aided by some who told him some details they knew) achieved everything necessary to do the printing; and he printed these books.

Indeed, there is no historical evidence that any equipment or craftsmen for movable-type printing technology were brought over from Spain, the Americas, or even Macau. The Jesuits, who began movable-type printing in Goa in 1556, in Macau in 1588, and in Japan around 1590, apparently did not expend any effort on such activities in the Philippines until 1610 at the earliest. Nevertheless, Juan de Vera could not have developed his types in a vacuum, and it may be that he and his workmen learned enough about typographic technology from the Chinese on the mainland or from the Westerners from Macau or from Mexico.[18]

Even the front matter in Castilian for the few blockprinted Chinese books after 1605 utilized movable type, including the *Memorial de la vida christiana en lengua china* by yet another Dominican friar, Domingo de Nieva. Ironically, Nieva's argument in his preface, that converts should be taught in their own language, was written in Castilian. The printer responsible for both the typesetting and the block engraving was Pedro de Vera, the younger brother of Juan de Vera, who also produced Tomás Mayor's *Símbolo de la Fé, en lengua y letra China* (1607), in which the front matter in Castilian was also set in movable type.[19]

Nieva's *Memorial* and Mayor's *Símbolo* had another thing in common—they were both adaptations into Chinese of the works of the Spanish preacher and mystic Luis de Granada (1504–1588), one of the best-selling authors in Europe in the second half of the sixteenth century and the seventeenth. By the late sixteenth century, all his works had been published and translated into a number of European languages; the *Memorial* alone had been reprinted 124 times before 1600. Granada's works figured prominently and frequently in the reading materials of passengers on ships from Spain to the Americas, in the booksellers' consignments to the Spanish colonies, and in the personal libraries of not only clerics but also lay readers there.[20] Thus it was no surprise that both the missionaries in Asia would so quickly choose to translate Granada's works into Chinese and Japanese.[21]

Blockprinting continued to be utilized where it was convenient and eco-

nomical, for images rather than for text, as suggested by one recorded instance. For All Saints' Day (1 November) in 1602, pictures of the saints of the year in the form of slips were printed in the Jesuit college and distributed to the people of Manila.[22] Such a use of woodblock images was well known in Europe and predated the development of movable type in the mid-fifteenth century. During the fifteenth and sixteenth centuries, stock woodcut illustrations were used repeatedly, within a single work, or in different imprints from the same publisher, or loaned by one printer to others.[23] That both the text composed in movable type and the images carved in woodblock could be printed together made this the most economical combination of illustrated imprints that was employed until the late sixteenth century. In Tomás Mayor's *Símbolo*, at least one of the illustrations in the Chinese main text was copied from the 1584 edition of Luis de Granada's work, *Introducción del símbolo de la fé*. Both pictures were woodcuts.[24]

For texts, however, the missionaries in the early Spanish Philippines very quickly chose to print books using exclusively movable type and mostly roman letters. For works in Western languages, such as Castilian and Latin, this trend simply conformed to what the Spanish understood printing to be. For works in Tagalog and other Filipino languages, printing in roman letters together with or in place of the original baybayin script served several purposes. First, missionaries felt that the baybayin graphs did not convey with sufficient precision the pronunciation of the words, a task better served by roman letters. For this reason, Blancas, in his later work *Memorial de la vida christiana en lengua tagala*, advocated the use of romanized script.[25] Second, Hispanization was part of the conversion of native Filipinos to Christianity, a process facilitated by using the roman alphabet for reading as many different languages as possible. Consequently, after the first decade of the seventeenth century, doctrinas and other religious works in the various Filipino languages were printed using romanized scripts.[26]

Chinese, however, was a language for which the Philippine missionaries were reluctant to use in print the romanization they had been developing, so that all works in Chinese were xylographically produced.[27] On the other hand, competent blockcarvers were available. Thus the question remains why no Chinese books were printed by any method after the beginning of the seventeenth century, either by missionaries or commercial publishers in the Philippines, for another three centuries. Records show that a number of the missionaries who sought to convert and minister to the Chinese continued learning at least to speak Minnanese, and some became highly proficient in the language. Their enduring interest in Chinese is supported by

the grammars and vocabularies that they produced, of which we have manuscript but no print copies, suggesting that such works circulated among a limited readership. But did the missionaries in the Philippines lose interest in providing the Chinese with catechisms, confessionals, and other religious works? If so, did commercial printers in the Parián, Binondo, or another area with a sizeable Chinese population take up the publishing of these books? But other than the *Doctrina christiana* of Keng Yong in 1605, we know of no imprint in Chinese other than a few more produced by the Dominicans. It is possible, of course, that the missionaries wished to maintain control over the production of such texts and prevented commercial publishers from obtaining the needed license for publication.

It is also possible that by 1632, when Dominicans finally gained a foothold in Fujian, religious books were printed there and exported to the Philippines.[28] We have, however, neither extant samples of such works nor mention of such shipments. Moreover, since the Dominicans established themselves first in northeast Fujian (Mindong), where the language differed greatly from the Minnanese spoken by the Chinese in the Philippines, and where the missionaries made contact with the local literati elite, who preferred using classical Chinese, it is unlikely that suitable doctrinas and other religious works in Minnanese would have been produced for the Philippines, at least until the Dominicans also founded missions in Zhangzhou 漳州. In fact, as the vocabulary for translating religious terms became more standardized, the later Dominicans suppressed the earliest imprints from the Philippines, such as those by Cobo, Nieva, and Mayor.[29] Perhaps the Dominicans in Mindong imbued their colleagues in the Philippines with a disdain for the latter's poorly educated and not very pious parishioners, so that the friars increasingly settled for teaching the converts simply to memorize the basic tenets of their faith.[30] As a result, there was no large market for religious works in Chinese in the Philippines. In fact, despite the two book prices we have, for Cobo's *Shilu* and the *Doctrina christiana* in Castilian and Tagalog, the early Dominican publications were not commodities; quite possibly shorter imprints were treated as religious tracts to be given away rather than sold, much as later Protestant missionaries distributed their materials in Asia.[31]

Thus, to consider Chinese books as commodities, we must explore the possible import of traditional kinds of works from China, including popular works of entertainment and literature (collections of songs and plays, illustrated novels and stories, joke books), medical texts (such as *materia medica* or *bencao* 本草, and simple manuals for lay readers), general household refer-

ences, almanacs, the Confucian classics, and school primers. After all, a realistic estimate of the number of Chinese in the early Spanish Philippines who could read to some extent must fall between Cobo's starry-eyed assessment and the highly negative opinion of other Spaniards. Sources record the existence of Chinese booksellers (*libreros*) in the Manila area, who probably sold books from China and possibly Spanish books as well. One whom we know by name was a pagan Chinese by the name of Zunhu, who had a shop in the Parián around 1606.[32]

Of the Chinese books that could have been exported to the Philippines, at least three likely publishers were located conveniently in the chief port for the China-Nanyang trade during the late sixteenth century and early seventeenth: Haicheng 海澄 in Zhangzhou prefecture in southern Fujian. Among other works, these publishers produced collections of popular dramatic acts, operatic arias, and songs of the time, works that would have greatly appealed to the southern Fujianese in the Philippines, who staged theatrical performances on a variety of different occasions, including the safe arrival of a junk, Christian religious festivals, and the Chinese New Year.[33]

Juan Cobo viewed these theatricals quite unfavorably, considering them full of superstition and idolatries. Not only the Chinese but also the Filipinos and Spanish flocked to the performances, where they, "covered by the dark cloak of night, did many things which ought not to be done in Christian lands." Cobo persuaded his vicar-general to threaten with excommunication those who went to the plays, but it is hard to know how successful their efforts were. The Spanish Inquisition did not have jurisdiction over the Chinese or the Filipinos, and its commissar in the Philippines limited himself to inspecting Western-language books brought over by ships from Mexico.[34] Consequently, any effective censorship of Chinese books could only come from the vigilant efforts of the missionaries themselves—a task made immensely difficult by the very few clergy able to read Chinese trying to inspect any books they could find in the junks that came from China, as well as the offerings of the Manila booksellers. As for banning theatrical performances, the vicar-general might have had some success temporarily, but apparently one of the added attractions of the highly popular gambling houses in Manila run by the Chinese and frequented by non-Chinese as well, including prominent and high-ranking Spaniards, was the performance of acts from plays. Over two hundred years later, the Augustinian friar Martínez de Zúniga voiced much the same complaints.[35]

For the Chinese who could read or listen to texts of plays and songs, commercial publishers in late Ming China offered a wealth of plays, dra-

Figure 4 *Xinkan xianguan shishang zhaiyao ji* 新刊絃管時尚摘要集 [Newly engraved selection from fashionable melodies for string and wind instruments]. Late Ming-early Qing. Source: Sächsische Landesbibliothek, Dresden.

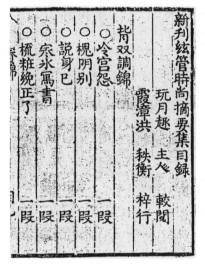 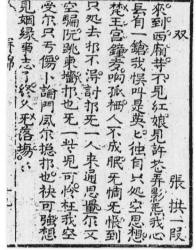

4a Page from the table of contents stating, "Published in Xiazhang (Zhangzhou) by Hong Zhiheng" 霞漳洪秩衡梓行. Many song collections were printed in this chapbook format, for which we have extant examples from the late Ming onward.

4b Apparently, this particular song in Minnanese for Zhang Gong 張拱, the male lead in the play Xi xiang ji 西廂記 [Story of the western chamber], has no corresponding version in the standard speech.

matic arias, and popular songs.[36] The format of two of the three extant collections of songs and dramatic arias in Minnanese resembles that of similar works published in the same period (late sixteenth century to the early seventeenth) in Nanjing and Jianyang (northern Fujian), then the two largest book centers in China, and of the later chapbooks from all parts of the country, for which we have examples from the seventeenth century onward.[37] Such cheaply printed chapbooks have always appealed to fans of theatre and popular songs regardless of their educational level, so works like the two Zhangzhou imprints shown in figure 4 may well have made their way from Fujian to the Philippines.

Moreover, the oldest extant work in Minnanese (a play) and at least one of two surviving song collections in Chaozhou speech were printed in Jianyang by commercial publishers, whose own dialect was very different, but who knew what would sell, suggesting that such books were quite popular.[38] Furthermore, evidence from the imprints published in Haicheng mentioned above—the design of the printer's colophon (fig. 5) and the name of one

Figure 5 Printers' colophon blocks. The lotus-leaf design was a universally recognized trademark of Ming Jianyang printers, so that its use in an imprint from Haicheng in Zhangzhou suggests connections with Jianyang.

5a *Xinke zengbu xidui jinqu daquan mantian chun* 新刻增補戲隊錦曲大全滿天春 [All-embracing Spring: Newly engraved comprehensive collection of dramatic acts and operatic arias] (Hanhai [Haicheng]: Li Bifeng and Chen Wohan, 1607). Cambridge University Library.

5b *Xuke Wenling si taishi pingxuan gujin ming wen zhuji* 續刻溫陵四大太史評選古今名文珠璣 [Supplemental edition of the gems of famous writings of the past and present, chosen by and with commentaries by the Four Great *Taishi* of Wenling] (Jianyang: Yu Liangmu (Shaoyai) Zixin zhai, 1595). National Central Library, Taiwan.

of the printers—suggests that these men might have moved from Jianyang to Haicheng, hoping to take advantage of the opening of a new book market overseas. Haicheng was not known as a printing center in the late Ming and Qing periods, and when it was displaced by nearby Xiamen as the chief port for the Nanyang trade, its publishing business probably disappeared as well.[39]

It is also useful to consider books in Chinese that the Spanish thought worth acquiring, primarily through the efforts of missionaries in China or the Philippines. For example, on his first journey to Fujian in 1575, the Augustinian friar Martín de Rada bought copies of Chinese books in Fuzhou, the provincial capital where, according to Rada's Fujianese hosts, the best imprints were produced.[40] The governor of Fujian, who had been quite curi-

5c *Fengyue jin nang* 風月錦囊 [Brocade satchel of lyric arias] (Jianyang: Zhan family Jinxian tang, 1553). The sole extant copy is held in the Royal Library of San Lorenzo de El Escorial.

ous about European books and received a breviary from Rada's party, originally had offered to provide his visitors with as many books as they wanted, but then failed to deliver on his promise, perhaps out of concern that the Spaniards were intent on gathering information about China that would have strategic military value. According to a surviving list, Rada managed to obtain gazetteers (descriptions of the entire country, the provinces, and neighboring countries, as well as tributes and taxes owed to the government); histories; technical works on shipbuilding and military technology; works on building and architecture; medical works; agricultural manuals; works on astronomy; Confucian classics; law codes; general household encyclopedias; divination texts (on geomancy, oneiromancy, chiromancy, almanacs, etc.); and manuals on musical instruments and songs.

Rada and his fellow travellers brought these books back to Manila, but they probably did not survive for long the hot humidity and insects of the islands.[41] Nevertheless, some of the Chinese books acquired by Rada and other missionaries probably ended up in collections such as that of the royal library in San Lorenzo de El Escorial and others in Spain and throughout Europe. Thus the holdings of Chinese rare books in European (and Japanese) libraries have copies of Chinese books not extant in China, including a number of popular (that is, nonscholarly) works, such as household encyclopedias, cheap writing manuals, and illustrated fiction and drama.[42]

Figure 6 Excerpts from songs about Liang Shanbo and Zhu Yingtai.

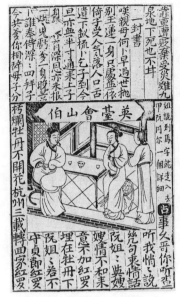

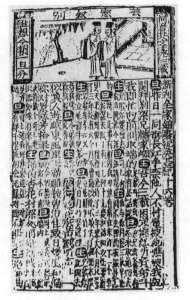

6a The lower register is the first page of excerpts from a play in Minnanese about Liang Shanbo and Zhu Yingtai. *Source: Xinke zengbu xidui jinqu daquan mantian chun* 新刻增補戲隊錦曲大全滿天春 [All-embracing Spring: Newly engraved comprehensive collection of dramatic acts and operatic arias] (Hanhai [Haicheng]: Li Bifeng and Chen Wohan, 1607). Cambridge University Library.

6b The song is in standard speech (*zhengyin* 正音). *Source: Fengyue jin nang* 風月錦囊 [Brocade satchel of lyric arias] (Jianyang: Zhan family Jinxian tang, 1553). The sole extant copy is held in the Royal Library of San Lorenzo de El Escorial.

Such imprints have survived in part because of the broader or more tolerant interests of European collectors who acquired imprints that Chinese bibliophiles of the time would have disdained to buy either because of their perceived shoddiness or because of their frivolous contents. Unlike the missionaries in Asia who originally amassed the works, most of the earlier European buyers and collectors were probably quite ignorant of Chinese culture and bought a work for its pictures or for its exotic value. When such books reached Europe, some would be split up, with different fascicles of a single work going to different collectors. Today, different libraries may own portions of the same imprint, a minor inconvenience compared to the good fortune of the work's survival.[43]

The survival of the Philippine incunabula discussed above is attributable

to similarly fortuitous circumstances. All extant copies of the blockprinted books from the Philippines and the few collections of songs and plays in Minnanese are found in Europe.[44] Given the unfavorable conditions for the survival of such books in the Philippines, it is a wonder that we have any extant copies, even had printing of Chinese books continued after the first decade of the seventeenth century.

Some Concluding Remarks

Of all the areas in Southeast Asia where there were sizeable Chinese settlements in the early modern period, it is ironic that books in Chinese were printed only in the Philippines—ironic because in studying the history of the Chinese in the Nanyang, the Philippines have generally proven to be the most difficult area of study due to the scarcity and recalcitrance of the sources. Through the interest and determination of the Spanish missionaries, both xylography and typography were introduced into the Philippines soon after it was colonized, and the print quality of these incunabula from the late sixteenth century through the first decade of the seventeenth shows the potential for a book-publishing industry that was not realized for books in Chinese.

For instance, while books in Filipino languages continued to be printed using romanized script that the Spanish missionaries developed, no corresponding attempt was made for Chinese. One important reason was that in the colonial Philippines, the civil and religious authorities, as well as the non-Chinese population, including the native Filipinos, the creoles, and even the Chinese mestizos (the children of Chinese fathers and Filipina mothers and their descendants), harbored economic and social resentment against the Chinese and saw them as a foreign group that required constant control. During most of the Spanish occupation, the colonial government viewed the Chinese as unassimilable—efforts to Christianize and Hispanize them were far less successful than with the native Filipinos and the Chinese mestizos. In fact, the Spanish authorities consistently attempted to drive a political, economic, cultural, and religious wedge between the Chinese and all other ethnic groups in the Philippines. This resulted in a low-conscious receptivity to Chinese written culture, certainly less than in some other parts of Southeast Asia. Thus until the Philippine Chinese themselves began looking to China for diplomatic and political support, until the Chinese government grew more responsive to the needs of overseas Chinese, and until reformers and revolutionaries began to instill nationalistic feelings among Chinese living abroad, there was little interest in Chinese learning. Even at

the end of the nineteenth century, there were no Chinese schools in the Philippines and early Chinese newspapers did not survive for long.[45] In fact, after the early sixteenth century, the Philippines became more like other regions of Southeast Asia, none of which showed any inclination among its Chinese population to publish books or newspapers before the late nineteenth century.

Concerning Chinese books, another comparison among Southeast Asian areas is worth noting. By the early seventeenth century, Spanish missionaries in the Philippines appeared to have given up proselytizing among the Chinese there through the printed word. Thus, their early publishing efforts in the Philippines are dwarfed by those of the British and American Protestant missionaries of the nineteenth century. It was the Protestants who systematically investigated the comparative cost-benefit aspects of various printing technologies (xylography, typography, lithography) as they geared up for ambitious large-scale publishing projects. Various Protestant missionary societies considered the translation and retranslation of the Bible into Chinese and other Asian languages a matter of great urgency, and mounted a campaign to print a million copies of the New Testament in the mid-nineteenth century.[46] Perhaps it was the Protestant missionaries' fervent belief in the power of the written word that led them to distribute religious tracts for free and Bibles for low prices—to the point of saturation, by walking the streets and visiting ships in harbors, and even chartering boats to cruise along the coast of China and throughout insular Southeast Asia, undaunted by the low literacy rate of many, if not most of the recipients of their literature.

The Catholic missionaries in the early Philippines and the later Protestant ones in Southeast Asia, however, shared one important objective—their desire to proselytize in China. Once they could enter China—the Dominicans in 1632, and the British Protestants after the 1842 Treaty of Nanjing—they largely lost interest in the overseas Chinese as linguistic and cultural informants. Indeed, the London Missionary Society closed down its Chinese stations in Penang, Malacca, Singapore, and Batavia, and moved its resources (including printing presses) to China. Thus, in Southeast Asia the printing of books in Chinese and of Chinese works in translation would occur chiefly when the overseas Chinese themselves or interested readers and writers of the host cultures assumed the work of publishing, starting in the late nineteenth century. Ironically, in that later stage, the Philippines would be the least receptive of all the areas in Southeast Asia. Just as the Spanish missionaries' first efforts at proselytization led to the production of a few Chinese

books, the eventual success of Christianity also meant Hispanizing both the natives and Chinese mestizos and turning both groups away from Chinese culture. The result was the formation of a modern Filipino culture that diverged in essential ways from those of other regions of Southeast Asia.

Notes

1. Estimates for the populations of Chinese in Southeast Asia in the early modern period are far from precise. For the Philippines, see Edgar Wickberg, *The Chinese in Philippine Life 1850–1898* (repr., Manila: Ateneo de Manila University Press, 2000), esp. 16, 22, 24, 53, 58, 61, 147–48, and 169–70.

2. Claudine Salmon, ed., *Literary Migrations: Traditional Chinese Fiction in Asia (Seventeenth–Twentieth Centuries)* (Beijing: International Culture, 1987). This is the only work that has attempted comparative studies of the dissemination of Chinese literary culture throughout northeast and southeast Asia. Linguistic challenges and the dearth of sources for periods prior to the mid-nineteenth century render such research particularly difficult, but not impossible, as demonstrated by the works cited in this essay.

3. For the literacy of the Chinese in Manila, see Antonio de Remesal, *Historia de la provincia de S Vicente de Chapaya y Guatemala de la orden de nro glorioso padre Sancto Domingo* (repr., Madrid: Ediciones Atlas, 1964–1966), bk. 10, chap. 10, 413. For Cobo's knowledge of Chinese characters, see Diego de Aduarte, *Historia de la Provincia del Santo Rosario de la Orden de Predicadores en Filipinas, Japón y China* (repr., Madrid: Consejo Superior de Investigaciones Científicas, 1962–63), bk. 1, chap. 23, 219. On the subject of the Dominicans being assigned to the Chinese parishes in the Manila area, see Domingo de Salazar, "Carta-relación de las cosas de la China y de los chinos del parián de Manila, enviada al Rey Felipe II . . . desde Manila, á 24 de junio de 1590," Archivo General de Indias (henceforth AGI), Filipinas 47, N38, ff. 183r–190v. This report has been reprinted in numerous works and translated into English in E. H. Blair and J. A. Robertson, *The Philippine Islands, 1493–1898* (Cleveland: Arthur H. Clark, 1907), 7:212–38.

4. In his letter, Cobo talked of guidebooks in Chinese ("libros de itinerario") that he was translating with the help of his Chinese neighbors. See Remesal, *Historia de la provincia*, 412. These works may well have been the merchant route books that were a popular offering of commercial publishers in China in the late Ming.

5. This work, originally compiled in the early fifteenth century by Fan Liben 范立本 of Hangzhou, was translated from classical Chinese, probably with much assistance from Cobo's Chinese interpreters. The book's original title, *Ming xin baojian* 明心寶鑑 [Precious mirror of the clear heart], was romanized in Spanish as *Beng sim po cam*, following the Minnanese pronunciation. Indeed, the Minnan versions of over a hundred personal names and book titles in this work confirm that the translators were speakers of this dialect. See Piet van der Loon, "The Manila Incunabula and Early Hokkien Studies," pt. 1, *Asia Major* n.s. 12 (1966), 19–20; and Liu Limei, *Espejo rico del claro corazón* (Madrid: Letrúmero, 2005). Piet van der Loon's two-part study of the early books printed in the Philippines through 1607 ("Manila Incunabula," *Asia Major*, n.s. 12 (1966): 1–43

and 13 (1967): 95–186) is meticulous and his analysis generally more convincing than most other secondary works on the subject. Throughout this paper, I shall refer to his articles rather than repeat his arguments in detail. But because other copies of some of the books van der Loon discusses have been discovered since his articles appeared, it is worth consulting more recent works like Albert Chan, *Chinese Books and Documents in the Jesuit Archives in Rome: A Descriptive Catalogue: Japonica-Sinica 1–4* (Armonk, N.Y.: M. E. Sharpe, 2002).

6. Reduced facsimile reprints of the 1593 edition are available in Carlos Sanz, *Primitivas relaciones de España con Asia y Oceania: Los dos primeros libros impresos en Filipinas, más un tercero en discoria* (Madrid: V. Suárez, 1958); and Juan Cobo, *Pien Cheng-Chiao Chen-Ch'uan Shi Lu* 辯正教真傳實錄, ed. Fidel Villarroel (Manila: University of Santo Tomás Press, 1986). Cobo's *Shilu* is discussed in van der Loon, "Manila Incunabula," pt. 1, 2–8. A number of recent studies focus on the ideas in Cobo's work, such as Liu Dun, "Western Knowledge of Geography Reflected in Juan Cobo's Shilu 实录," *History of Mathematical Sciences: Portugal and East Asia*, ed. Luís Saraiva (Hackensack, N.J.: World Scientific, 2004), 45–58; and José Antonio Cervera Jiménez, "Spanish Friars in the Far East: Fray Juan Cobo and His Book Shi Lu," *Historia scientiarum* 7.3 (1998): 181–98.

7. Cobo had intended to continue writing this work but was interrupted when he went on an embassy mission to Japan. While returning, in 1592, he was shipwrecked and drowned. Consequently, the incomplete work came out posthumously, in 1593. Even today, nearly 80 percent of the Filipino Chinese come from or have ancestors from Minnan. Yet more specifically, long-term settlers tended to be natives of Zhangzhou prefecture, while merchants and other short-term sojourners were more likely to be from the Quanzhou area. This situation lasted until the late eighteenth century. See van der Loon, "Manila Incunabula," pt. 2, 132, where he concludes that early Spanish missionaries in the Philippines studied the Zhangzhou version of Minnanese. See also Lucille Chia, "The Butcher, the Baker, and the Carpenter: Chinese Sojourners in the Spanish Philippines and Their Impact on Southern Fujian (Sixteenth–Eighteenth Centuries)," *Journal of the Economic and Social History of the Orient* 49.4 (2006): 521.

8. As noted by van der Loon and others who have studied this work, there probably was a title page in Castilian that would also have been blockprinted, but has been lost. Judging from the title pages of the other incunabula from the Philippines, such a title page would have had a lengthy full title, the name of the author, place and date of publication, and that the work was printed with license (by the colonial government) and approbation of the Dominican order. Some of this information has been written in on the first page of the main text. For title pages of early Philippine imprints, see W. E. Retana y Gamboa, *Orígenes de la imprenta Filipina* (Madrid: Librería General de Victoriano Suárez, 1911), 138–77; and Sanz, *Primitivas relaciones de España con Asia y Oceania*, 198–203.

9. The title of the *Shilu* implies that it is a religious work, but only the first three sections (*zhang* 章) discuss strictly theological matters, and the later six zhang discuss astronomy, geography, and natural science. As Jiménez argues in "Spanish Friars in the Far East" and Matthew Chen in "Unsung Trailblazers of China-West Cultural En-

counter" (paper presented at the International Conference on Western Chinese Studies, 12–14 September 2003, Beijing, available online http://staff.feweb.vu.nl/ppeverelli/ Chen.html), the presentation of such topics was very much in keeping with the "God-through-nature approach" that has a long tradition among Catholic thinkers, including popular Spanish mystics such as Teresa of Ávila, John of the Cross, and Luis de Granada (1504–1588). Several works of the last author were adapted by several Dominicans and printed in early seventeenth-century Philippines.

10. On the bottom of page 1a of the *Shilu* is handwritten "Tassada en cuatro reales" and signed "Juan de Cuellar" (the governor's notary). Governor Dasmariñas, in his letter of 20 June 1593 to the king, Felipe II, noted that things were generally more expensive in the regions of the Indias (overseas from Spain), and so he set the price of the imprint at four reales until the king made his own decision (AGI, Filipinas, 6, R. 7, N. 104). Indeed, being printed on Chinese (bamboo) paper, the *Shilu* was cheaper than if the very costly Castilian paper had been used (four or five pesos per quire, or twenty-five sheets according to Juan Arze de Sadornel's deposition in 1584 [Blair and Robertson, *The Philippine Islands, 1493–1898*, vol. 6:52]). Both kinds of paper had to be imported, either from China or Mexico. The prices for the various goods are given in Fr. Juan González de Mendoza, *Historia de las cosas mas notables, ritos y costumbres del Gran Reyno de la China* (Rome: A costa de Bartholome Grassi: En la stampa de Vincentio Accolti, 1585), *Itinerario*, chap. 8, 373.

11. Chan, *Chinese Books and Documents in the Jesuit Archives in Rome*, 90–99 and references therein. Chan's catalogue is a good starting point for the sizeable literature on Jesuit publishing in China (including Macau) and Japan.

12. Ibid., 180–83.

13. For Li Tingji, see L. Carrington Goodrich and Chaoying Fang, eds., *Dictionary of Ming Biography 1368–1644* (New York: Columbia University Press, 1976), esp. 329. See Chan, *Chinese Books and Documents in the Jesuit Archives in Rome*, 180–83, for an edition that was probably printed in Jianyang 建陽 in northern Fujian, one of the largest commercial publishing centers in late Ming China. Although Chan credits the publication to a publisher in Jiangsu, the edition was more probably an imprint of the Yugeng tang 與耕堂 of the Zhu 朱 family in Jianyang, who also published one of the very few extant plays in Minnanese. See Piet van der Loon, *The Classical Theatre and Art Song of South Fukien: A Study of Three Ming Anthologies* (Taipei: SMC Publishing, 1992), 3.

14. Derived probably from the Javanese kavi script, the baybayin script was a syllabary that was used for various Filipino languages, including Tagalog from perhaps the fourteenth century onward. For an introduction to the baybayin script, see Paul Morrow, "The Ancient Script of the Philippines," http://www.mts.net/~pmorrow/ (accessed 27 March 2007). The information given on the title page of the *Doctrina christiana* reads: "Doctrina Christiana, en lengua española y tagala, corregida por los Religiosos de las ordenes Impressa con licencia, en S. Gabriel, de la orden de S. Domingo En Manila, 1593." The only known copy is held in the Library of Congress, but facsimile reprints are easily available, including the edition with an introductory essay by Edwin Wolf II

(Washington: Library of Congress, 1947), the text of which is available online at the Project Gutenberg website, http://www.gutenberg.org/. In general, doctrinas consist of basic prayers and tenets of Catholicism, such as the sign of the cross, the Lord's Prayer, the Hail Mary, the Apostles' Creed, the Confiteor, a catechism, lists of the Ten Commandments, the seven sacraments, the works of mercy, the capital sins, rules for attending mass, days of fast and abstinence, and so on. Even though a doctrina was read and used as a reference, the missionaries could use it to help converts commit to memory the basics of their faith.

15. For photofacsimile reprints of this entire work, see Jesús Gayo Aragón, *Doctrina christiana: Primer libro impreso en Filipinas* (Manila: Imprenta de la Real y Pontificia Universidad de Santo Tomás de Manila, 1951); and Sanz, *Primitivas relaciones de España con Asia y Oceania*, 464-01 (pages in reverse order following the original; reduced images).

16. Van der Loon notes that the first part of this Chinese *Doctrina* "is distinguished by its consistent use of characters that are peculiar to Hokkien [Minnan] colloquial in the Ming period, whereas the second part . . . has very few such special characters" ("Manila Incunabula," pt. 1, 11). More recent scholars have modified and elaborated on van der Loon's analysis: see Anne O. Yue, "The Min Translation of the *Doctrina christiana*," *Chinese Linguistics* 14 (1999): 42–76; and Henning Klöter, *Written Taiwanese* (Wiesbaden: Harrassowitz Verlag, 2005), 41–58. The imprint is also smaller than the two 1593 publications from the Dominicans, and the name of the printer, Keng Yong, is Chinese rather than Spanish, suggesting that he was not a Christian.

17. Alonso Fernández, *Historia eclesiastica de nvestros tiempos* (Toledo: Por la viuda de P. Rodriguez, 1611), 318, mentions that Domingo de Nieva's *Memorial* and Tomás Mayor's *Símbolo* were both distributed to the passengers who sailed back to China (cited from a different edition in van der Loon, "Manila Incunabula," pt. 1, 40).

18. The original edition of Blancas's book, which is not extant, was probably printed in 1604, and information about the work comes from the surviving 1734 reprint. The two Dominican histories are Aduarte, *Historia de la Provincia del Santo Rosario*, bk. 1, chap. 27, 176 and bk. 2, chap. 2, 28 (from which the quote is taken, with the translation by van der Loon, "Manila Incunabula," pt. 1, 37–38); and Juan López, *Quinta parte de la Historia de santo Domingo* (Valladolid, 1621), 251. See also Retana, *Orígenes de la imprenta Filipina*, 94–102, and van der Loon, "Manila Incunabula," pt. 1, esp. 25–28, who speculates but admits that there is no evidence that Juan de Vera might have known about the movable type that was used in China.

19. See van der Loon, "Manila Incunabula," pt. 1, 31–37, and Chan, *Chinese Books and Documents in the Jesuit Archives in Rome*, 229–31.

20. See Irving A. Leonard, *Books of the Brave* (Cambridge: Harvard University Press, 1949) for passengers' books (161–62) and for the book market in Lima and booksellers' shipment lists (220, 287). Like many other readers in the Spanish Americas, Antonio de Morga (1559–1636), the Spanish official and author of the *Sucesos de las islas Filipinas*, left works of Granada among his books (Morga, *Sucesos de las islas Filipinas*, trans. and ed. J. S. Cummins [Cambridge: Cambridge University Press, 1971], 15). Certain nonreligious

works were as popular as those of Granada among readers of Spanish—for instance, *Don Quixote*. However, lacking the missionaries' interested efforts, these books were not translated into Asian languages in the early modern period.

21. For example, an abridged version of Granada's most popular work, *Guide for Sinners*, was translated from the Portuguese and published by the Jesuits in Japan in 1599. See Chan, *Chinese Books and Documents in the Jesuit Archives in Rome*, 260–61.

22. Horacio de la Costa, *The Jesuits in the Philippines, 1581–1768* (Cambridge: Harvard University Press, 1961), 202–3.

23. See, for example, David Bland, *The Illustration of Books* (London: Faber and Faber, 1962), 49–51.

24. Reproduced in van der Loon, "Manila Incunabula," pt. 1, 34 and 35.

25. Information about the *Memorial* comes from a second-generation reprint from Mexico. See Retana, *Orígenes de la imprenta Filipina*, 72–75; and van der Loon, "Manila Incunabula," pt. 1, 38–39. For a discussion of the missionaries' rejection of the baybayin script and adoption of romanized Tagalog, see Vicente L. Rafael, *Contracting Colonialism* (Ithaca: Cornell University Press, 1988), 44–54.

26. How the Spanish missionaries, despite their admiration for (some of) the Filipino languages, changed them in their discourses, and how the native speakers resisted such changes are briefly discussed in T. H. Pardo de Tavera, *Una memoria de Anda y Salazar* (Manila: La Democracía, 1899), 58–59n12, which is translated in Blair and Robertson, *The Philippine Islands, 1493–1898*, 50:147–48.

27. Extant manuscripts from the early seventeenth century show that missionaries like Miguel de Benavides and Juan Cobo had worked hard at developing romanization for Minnanese, as well as vocabularies and grammars. See van der Loon, "Manila Incunabula," pt. 2, esp. 95–100; Yue, "The Min Translation of the *Doctrina christiana*"; and Klöter, *Written Taiwanese*, 41–58.

28. At the end of the sixteenth century, few Spanish missionaries except the Jesuits had succeeded in entering China to proselytize, but in 1632 the Dominican friar Angelo Cocchi arrived in Fuzhou and was invited to Fuan where he began his missionary work. For the first years of the Dominicans' presence in (north)eastern Fujian (Mindong), see Eugenio Menegon, "Ancestors, Virgins, and Friars: The Localization of Christianity in Late Imperial Mindong (Fujian, China), 1632–1863," Ph.D. diss., University of California, Berkeley, 2002, esp. 57–59 and 102–15.

29. Chan, *Chinese Books and Documents in the Jesuit Archives in Rome*, 230–31, cited in Menegon, "Ancestors, Virgins, and Friars," 59n101. Before the suppression, however, two of Mayor's works so impressed Dominicans in China that they reprinted them (Domingo Fernández Navarrete, *Controversias antiguas y modernas de la mission de la Gran China* [Madrid: 1679], 56, cited in van der Loon, "Manila Incunabula," pt. 1, 36). On the other hand, it is interesting that the Jesuits chose to preserve their earlier authors' works in circulation, even by making substantial revisions where they felt necessary. Thus Michele Ruggieri's work first published in 1584 was printed as a heavily revised edition toward the very end of the Ming. It is uncertain what happened to the blocks of the original edition (Chan, *Chinese Books and Documents in the Jesuit Archives in Rome*, 95–96, 97–99).

30. Menegon describes a scholar from Mindong who visited Manila and came away with a highly unfavorable impression of the Chinese Christians there ("Ancestors, Virgins, and Friars," 59n102).

31. See Su Ching's "The Printing Presses of the London Missionary Society among the Chinese" (Ph.D. diss., University of London, 1996) for a detailed account of the Protestant publishing efforts, and Jean de Bernardi's essay in this volume for the distribution of the Bible in China in the nineteenth century.

32. "Testimonio sobre las casas y tiendas que se han construido en el Parián de los sangleyes después del alzamiento, con declaración de los nombres de los que en ellas habitaban. Manila 27 de Mayo de 1606," contained in AGI Filipinas 19 R7 N105. We know nothing about the bookselling activities of another librero, Pablo Hechiu, who was mentioned only in reference to his Christian piety (Aduarte, *Historia de la Provincia del Santo Rosario*, bk. 1, chap. 32, 209–10; Blair and Robertson, *The Philippine Islands, 1493–1898*, 30:263–64). Chinese booksellers might also have sold books in Spanish. In the 1590 report of Domingo de Salazar, archbishop of Manila, he recounts the story of a Sangley who learned the craft of bookbinding from a Spaniard who came from Mexico. The former mastered the skill so quickly that he set up shop for himself and quickly drove his former employer out of business. See AGI Filipinas 47 N38.

33. See Piet van der Loon's *The Classical Theatre and Art Song of South Fukien* for photo-facsimile reproductions of several Ming and Qing imprints of collections of Minnan songs and dramatic acts.

34. See José Toribio Medina, *El Tribunal del Santo Oficio de la Inquisición en las islas Filipinas* (Santiago de Chile: Imprenta Elzeviriana, 1899) and Blair and Robertson, *The Philippine Islands, 1493–1898*, 5:256–73, which has a translation of the instructions dated 1583 for the commissar sent to the Philippines by the inquisitors in Mexico. For a glimpse into "One Man's Library, Manila, 1583," see Leonard, *Books of the Brave*, 226–40.

35. Fr. Joaquín Martínez de Zúñiga, *Estadismo de las islas Filipinas* (Madrid: Imprensa de la viuda de M. Minuesa de los Rios, 1893), 320.

36. Such extant works in Minnan and Chaozhou speech are rare, but many more survive in the standard speech (*zhengyin* 正音) and in the Wu dialect of the Jiangsu area.

37. In addition to a number of collections with examples dating mainly from the nineteenth and twentieth centuries, there are studies on the works in Minnanese, known as *gezi bu/ce* 歌仔簿/冊. See Klöter, *Written Taiwanese*, 71–87 and the references therein. A larger secondary literature in Chinese and Western languages focuses on corresponding chapbooks in Cantonese (*muyu shu* 木魚書) and in Chaozhouese.

38. Van der Loon, *The Classical Theatre and Art Song of South Fukien*, 2–4.

39. One of the Haicheng publishers, Chen Wohan 陳我含, may have been related to contemporary Jianyang publishers, such as Chen Hanchu 陳含初 of the Cunren tang 存仁堂, which published at least one play, a rhyming dictionary, two household encyclopedias, and two story collections. The possibility of such a relationship is strengthened by the lotus design of the printer's colophon box (fig. 5), which was a well-known trademark of Jianyang publishers.

40. See the translation of Rada's own account and a critical discussion of related

sources in C. R. Boxer, ed., *South China in the Sixteenth Century* (London: Hakluyt Society, 1953). How Rada obtained the books is briefly described in González de Mendoza's *Historia de las cosas mas notables, ritos y costumbres del Gran Reyno de la China*, pt. 1, bk. 3, chap. 17, and the detailed list of some these imprints is given in chap. 18. Neither González nor Rada himself indicated how many books were acquired.

41. The words used in Juan Cobo's own and far less detailed description of Chinese books are very similar to those in González, and even if Cobo did not see any of Rada's books, he probably read either Rada's report or González de Mendoza's *Historia*, which was published in 1585, three years before Cobo's arrival in Manila.

42. It seems that the current tiny collection of pre-Qing Chinese imprints (eleven titles, six of them by early Jesuits) in the royal library at El Escorial are the survivors of culling, either deliberate or accidental (Gregorio de Andrés, "Los libros chinos de la Real Biblioteca de El Escorial," *Missionalia Hispanica* 26 [1969]: 115–23). Out of the non-Jesuit works, two are unique copies, the first of a *Sanguo zhizhuan* 三國志傳 and the second of a collection of plays and lyrics published in Jianyang, which has been described in James J. Y. Liu, "The *Fêng-Yüeh Chin-Nang* 風月錦囊 : A Ming Collection of Yüan and Ming Plays and Lyrics Preserved in the Royal Library of San Lorenzo, Escorial, Spain," *Journal of Oriental Studies* 4.1–2 (1957–58): 79–107.

43. In addition to those presented in van der Loon's *The Classical Theatre and Art Song of South Fukien* and Liu's "The *Fêng-Yüeh Chin-Nang*," see Hartmut Walravens, ed., *Two Recently Discovered Fragments of the Chinese Novels San-kuo-chih yen-i and Shui-hu chuan* (Hamburg: C. Bell Verlag, 1982); and Li Fuqing and Li Ping, eds., *Haiwai guben wan Ming xiju xuanji san zhong* 海外孤本晚明戲劇選集三種 (Shanghai: Shanghai guji, 1993). For books that were apportioned in sections to different collectors, see, for instance, the discussion on the possible customers for the Chinese works offered by a leading Dutch bookseller in the early seventeenth century in Bert van Selm, "Cornelis Claesz's 1605 Stock Catalogue of Chinese Books," *Quaerendo* 13 (1983): 247–59.

44. Including the *Doctrina christiana en lengua española y tagala* now in the Library of Congress, which was bought from a bookseller in Paris.

45. Wickberg, *The Chinese in Philippine Life 1850–1898*, 188–89. The first school for Chinese in the Philippines was the Anglo-English school, established at the Chinese embassy in 1899.

46. As described in Jean DeBernardi's essay in this volume.

THE END OF THE "AGE OF COMMERCE"?

Javanese Cotton Trade Industry from the
Seventeenth to the Eighteenth Centuries

⎯⎯⎯ Kwee Hui Kian

Studies on cotton textiles have inspired many theories on the rise of Industrial Europe and the concomitant underdevelopment of Asian societies. Economic historians working on South Asia are at the forefront in discussing how the English manufacture of fine cotton yarns and textiles using steam-run machinery (and the dumping of these products in India) resulted in the failure of Indian society to advance from proto-industrialization to full mechanization. Along similar lines of argument, Hiroshi Matsuo also explains that the Dutch imitation of English technology and subsequent exports to Java interrupted the development of Javanese cotton textile production in the nineteenth century.[1] Anthony Reid proposes that signs of underdevelopment were already at play in Southeast Asia prior to the Industrial Revolution. In view of the thriving Southeast Asian import trade of Indian cotton cloth in the period from the 1500s to the 1680s, Reid has argued that the drastic fall in the demand for Indian textiles from the late seventeenth century marked the beginnings of poverty, or the end of the "Age of Commerce" in the Southeast Asian region.[2]

With regard to Matsuo's theory, more up-to-date research by Alfons van der Kraan and Peter Boomgaard has shown that dwindling domestic production did not necessarily connote deindustrialization. Instead, they consider yarn-spinning and textile-weaving to be laborious, time-consuming tasks. The decline of the industry would thus enable the "restructuring of the island's economy," as such releasing labor for other purposes, like producing food and commercial crops for sale.[3] Experts on textile history also argue that European cotton imports helped the Javanese batik textile industry to take off. Due to the shorter fiber and climatic conditions, the types

of yarn spun from cotton varieties in Java were coarse in quality. Dutch-produced yarns were much stronger; textiles woven from these yarns were thus smoother in texture. As such, more intricate batik patterns could be drawn.[4] In other words, use of European cotton products enabled batik art to ascend to the prime of its development. Very beautiful north Javanese textiles were created and produced in this period.

This chapter offers an alternative explanation to Reid's observation of the falling demand for Indian textiles in early modern Southeast Asia. Using Dutch archival materials, it first discusses the development of the Javanese cotton textile industry and intra-Asian trade, and how Indian cloth came to occupy a niche in the Southeast Asian markets. Emphasis is placed on how Chinese merchants and Javanese rulers and lords came to assume key roles in the production and circulation of these commodities. In contrast to Reid's argument, the essay also shows how the fall in demand for Indian textiles was more a function of switching back to domestic and regional production with the price inflation of the Indian supplies, than it was a sign of poverty on the part of Southeast Asian consumers. Furthermore, it looks at how the Dutch East India Company (Verenigde Oostindische Compagnie, VOC), which began to participate in the textile trade in Java from the seventeenth century, could only gain a share of the market after collaborating with the existing interest groups in the manufacture and commerce of these commodities.

Javanese Textile Production and Trade: Developments from
the Ninth Century to the Eighteenth

Manufacturing cotton textiles involves the following processes: cotton growing, spinning, yarn preparation (washing and dyeing), winding and warping of threads, weaving, and finishing. For the famous Javanese painted cloth or batiks, an additional process is required before the finishing, namely, ornamenting the cloth using the wax-resist method. Patterns are drawn on the plain cloth with wax, and subsequently dipped into dye solutions. Repeated sequences of waxing, dyeing, and drying eventually yield the desired motifs and colors.[5] These multiple processes can generally be divided into three primary categories: yarn-spinning, textile-weaving, and batikking.

In terms of the origins, weaving was probably first introduced to Indonesia by bronze- and iron-using peoples, who brought with them a simple back-tension loom.[6] Through her analysis of the Javanese court *kakawin* literature and the *sima* charters, J. Christie has shown that Javanese textile weaving dated back to the first millennium.[7] Although Indian textiles were

exported to central and east Java, most Javanese households appeared to produce the majority of the cloth they consumed, utilizing a type of body-tension loom still in use in some parts of Indonesia in the recent period. By the eleventh century, there were also professional dye processors (*mangapus*), weavers (*acadar*), and other textile support industries in most Javanese villages, as well as peddlers (*atukel, abasana, amalanten, amananten*) who specialized in cotton yarns and other textile products.[8] Materials needed for manufacturing textiles, like cotton, and also various kinds of dyestuffs, such as indigo, *mengkudu* or Indian mulberry, safflower, and so on, had become taxable trade items as well. In other words, the production of cotton yarn and textile in early Java was not confined to the subsistence sector, but formed a commercial operation as well.[9] Chinese sources from the Sung dynasty (960–1279) have also listed cotton cloth and cotton piece goods among the export items from Java.[10]

Meanwhile, the first forms of batikking apparently developed in Java in the twelfth century. During this period, this method was known as *tulis warnna* or "decorated with drawings in colour." The term *batik* entered the Javanese vocabulary only in the seventeenth century.[11] Whether this method was generated locally or introduced from outside is far less clear. Nevertheless, Indonesian textile experts, citing local myths and legends, are quite convinced that it was foreign, and more specifically, that the method came either from China or India.[12]

Textiles in Java were used for clothing, decorative hangings, screens, cushion covers, covering-cloths for containers, and ritual receptacles, as well as to sit upon.[13] In fact, they did not function only as clothing or accessories but had socio-religious import. By the tenth century, distinctions in terms of types and colors of textiles, as well as who was allowed to wear and use them, had also emerged. Those presented to the royal family and high officials were of a finer weave, like the *cadar* cloth and *bananten* cloth, and of much higher value compared to those used by commoners. Furthermore, the latter would normally wear cotton textiles of red (*rangga*) and blue (*angsit*), while aristocrats could don a wider range of colors such as pinks, ruby red, vermilion, orange, and saffron pink.[14] Cloth bearing patterns like *nagasari* flowers, split lotus, yellow seeds, vegetal patterns, and rock motifs in specific colors were also worn during certain ritual occasions such as making offerings (*wali*) and life-crisis rituals (*pras*).[15] From fourteenth-century Javanese records, the *gringsing* design, in particular—which subsequently became an important batik motif—is said to have been used by the king's entourage in the annual royal procession.[16] This tradition of demarcating social differentia-

tion through colors and patterns of textiles persisted into the early modern period. Dutch company sources recorded that, in 1786, Yogyakarta sultan Hamengkubuwana I confiscated textiles with the *larangan* motif sold on the market, as these were to be worn only by Javanese courtiers.[17] Under the proprietary decree of 1769, the *jelamprang* motif—an eight-rayed rosette set in a modified square, circle, or hexagon—was also reserved for the *susuhunan* of Surakarta and his family.[18]

In early modern Java, high-quality cotton textiles served as a form of property, and luxury textiles conferred prestige and were used as gifts and dowries or at funerals.[19] Javanese rulers would also present gifts to their subordinates and vassals during ceremonial occasions such as the annual Garebeg day, when vassals would travel to the *kraton* (palace) of their overlord to pay homage.[20] By the sixteenth century, besides locally produced luxury textiles, those produced in the Coromandel coast, Surat, Bengal, and other parts of the subcontinent were also highly sought after in Java and the Indonesian archipelago as a kind of wealth and status symbol. Indian traders would sometimes acquire decorative designs from their Southeast Asian buyers and commission Indian producers to manufacture textiles following these patterns.[21] Thus, for many centuries, these cloth products were among the main commodities brought by South Asian traders to exchange for the fine spices produced in the Indonesian archipelago.

High-quality textiles, whether locally made or imported from India, have been regarded as markers of wealth and status not only in central and east Java, or Mataram Java, but also in many parts of the islands of Borneo, Sulawesi, Sumatra, as well as the eastern Indonesian archipelago.[22] Together with the imports, textiles produced in the region were also traded in different parts of the archipelago. Some specialized regions had also appeared by the seventeenth century. From the little that is known, central and east Java imported raw cotton and cotton yarn from Bali and occasionally also from Palembang, which converted to growing cotton and spinning cotton yarn when pepper prices fell.[23] Moreover, by the early modern period, there was a high degree of market specialization. European merchants found that Malay traders would not buy the Coromandel cottons they brought as these had "a little narrow white edge" when there should be none.[24]

The importation of Indian textiles to maritime Southeast Asia decreased in the late seventeenth century, however. From about 40,000 rijksdaalders (rds) worth of Indian textiles brought to central and east Java in the late 1670s, these imports diminished by a staggering 90 percent to about 4,000

Table 1 Exports of Indian Textiles from Batavia to Java's Northeast Coast by Private Traders, in Dutch Rijksdaalders

year	quantity (rds)	year	quantity (rds)	year	quantity (rds)
1672	37,893	1695	26,923	1720	14,043
1675	38,857	1700	8,440	1725	8,820
1680	41,234	1705	4,838	1730	7,635
1685[i]	57,970	1710	7,844	1735	3,015
1690	41,143	1716	4,635	1740	1,919

i. The rise in private import amounts of Indian cloth in 1685 reflects the fact that from that year on, the company withdrew from the direct sales of the commodity on the Pasisir and sold cloth to Chinese traders at the company's auctions in Batavia (Nagtegaal, *Dutch Tiger*, 147–48).

Source: L. Nagtegaal, *Riding the Dutch Tiger: The Dutch East Indies Company and the Northeast Coast of Java, 1680–1743* (Leiden: KITLV Press, 1996), 148, table 12.

rds thirty years later.[25] The re-export of Indian textiles from Batavia to the north coast of Java by private traders also declined substantially, from 41,234 pieces in 1680 to fewer than 10,000 pieces twenty years later (see table 1). This phenomenon was accompanied by a simultaneous increase in cloth production in Java. In the early 1680s, the Batavia high government—the company's highest administrative body in Asia—noted that the Javanese had begun to prefer the batiks manufactured in their own region to those imported from the Coromandel coast.[26] The Pasisir, or the north coast of Java, exported not only batik textiles, but also plain cloth. Javanese textiles were exported predominantly to Sumatra, Kalimantan, the Melaka Straits, and also China.[27] By 1695, there was a noticeable increase in weaving activities, causing a Dutch resident to comment that there were as many looms as there were households.[28] A similar phenomenon occurred in other polities as well. Palembang and Jambi also drastically reduced their purchase of Indian textiles and turned to those produced locally and also in Cambodia, Siam, and Java instead.[29]

Reid has interpreted this late-seventeenth-century phenomenon as a sign of impoverishment of the island Southeast Asians during this period. More specifically, he has argued that indigenous traders gradually lost out in the economic competition against the Europeans who had appeared in the region in the sixteenth century. By the late seventeenth century, the local

peoples had become so impoverished that they could afford only cloth made in the region instead of the luxurious ones manufactured in the Indian subcontinent and elsewhere.[30]

However, Reid's explanation is questionable since the textiles produced in the region were of comparable quality to those of Indian origin and included very luxurious ones too. Reporting to their superiors in the Netherlands in the early 1680s, company administrators for Java wrote that Javanese batik was scarcely inferior in its dyeing to that of the Coromandel cloth, and in terms of durability it was actually superior.[31] In her study of the cloth trade in the southeastern part of Sumatra, B. Andaya also shows that, from the late seventeenth century, Palembang court ladies began to import much raw silk and gold thread to weave high-quality luxury fabrics.[32] The reason was that these court ladies were unhappy that for the same price, Indian textiles were poorer in quality compared to those produced in the earlier decades.[33]

Furthermore, the prices of Indian textiles had markedly increased in the last two decades of the seventeenth century. War on the Coromandel coast, whose textiles were among the most coveted among Southeast Asian consumers, drove up the prices of the commodity.[34] More importantly, after about 1680, Indian calicoes became very popular not only among Asians, but in Europe as well. As the various European companies competed fiercely for the textiles on the subcontinent, the prices of the commodities became inflated.[35] The cost of Indian textiles in Jambi and Palembang, for instance, rose by 8 to 10 percent in the 1690s.[36]

In contrast to Reid's impoverishment thesis, it seems more probable that the consumers of the Indonesian archipelago, who had the technology to manufacture textiles, including very fine ones, had considered it more cost-effective to undertake the production themselves. Unhappy that they were not getting value for money in the purchase of Indian products, Southeast Asians began to weave their own or get textile supplies from within the region. Figures from Dutch shipping lists show that regional centers of textile production began to increase their output and their manufactures were widely traded in the Indonesian archipelago in the eighteenth century. In 1719, only one *corge*—cloth measurement unit of twenty pieces—of Cambodian cloth was exported to Palembang between January and April. However, during the same period in 1759, 515 corge of Cambodian cloth and 255 corge of Siamese ones arrived in Sumatran port towns.[37] In the 1720s, an annual average of 5,100 pieces of the cloth produced in the Bugis, Selayar, and other Sulawesian areas were exported to the archipelago, a figure that climbed steadily to about 130,000 pieces in the 1770s.[38] The actual numbers

were possibly greater, since smuggling activities were rife in the Indonesian archipelago as traders sought to evade the customs at the ports controlled by the Dutch East India Company in the eighteenth century.[39]

Central and east Java featured most prominently among these centers of textile manufacture. There had been production prior to the seventeenth century, with Madura and Tuban as two of the better-known production areas since the early sixteenth century.[40] When Batavia demanded its residents on the Pasisir acquire indigo from 1693, it was noted that virtually every coastal regency grew the indigo plant in modest quantities for the local textile industry.[41] Javanese textiles were sold to neighboring polities in Sumatra and Borneo as well.[42] Palembang, for example, had been buying rough cloth from Java since the early seventeenth century to cater to the commoners, but increased its imports of Javanese textiles in the eighteenth century. In 1719, 64 corge of Javanese cloth are listed. By 1758, the amount had reached 728 corge. Over 400 corge were registered for the October shipments of that year. The pattern continues through the century so that, from September to October 1793, it was noted in the Dutch shipping lists that 2,745 corge of Javanese cloth had reached Palembang.[43]

By the 1760s, it was common for vessels, be they manned by Chinese, Bugis, Javanese, Malays, or Dutch burghers, leaving from the Pasisir to other ports to carry some Javanese textiles with them. The quantity each brought along ranged from fewer than ten to as many as one hundred corges.[44] In general, from the 1720s to the 1770s, exports had increased by about five times. For example, in the first nine-and-a-half months of 1720, 16,360 pieces of cloth were exported from Semarang to Borneo and the areas surrounding the Melaka Straits. From 1774 to 1777, during the same period, the average quantity of Javanese textile exports to these places had risen to 75,853 pieces of cloth.[45]

Dutch Intervention in Javanese Cotton Textile and Yarn Production

The Dutch East India Company considered the development of the Javanese cotton textile industry a threat. In the seventeenth century, it had been imitating South Asian and other regional traders in importing Indian textiles and opium to exchange for fine spices and other commodities from the Indonesian archipelago. Following their treaties with the rulers of the north coast of Java, as well as south Sulawesi in the 1670s and 1680s, the Dutch company administrators could quite successfully drive away all the Indian and Arab traders from the Indonesian archipelago region.[46] However, almost simultaneously, the Javanese cloth practically priced the company imports of

Indian textiles out of the market in Sumatra, Borneo, and the Melaka Straits region. Company administrators tried to stop this trend. In 1684, they commissioned weavers on the Coromandel coast to make batik cloth in the Javanese style so as to undercut the Javanese producers. Much to their dismay, however, the Coromandel batik textiles not only were five times as expensive as the Javanese ones, but also proved to be less durable. In 1686, the high government in Batavia even considered prohibiting imports of beeswax into Java, as this product was indispensable to the production of batik cloth. It gave up the idea when the coastal personnel reported that the strategy was impossible to implement.[47]

By 1683, the company warehouses in Batavia lay overstocked with unsold Coromandel textiles. Hopes that the demand would again improve were not given up. In fact, the Batavia high government continued to import Coromandel cloth to Java in the next few years. However, by 1687, the high government had lost its optimism and instructed the personnel at the South Asian port town not to send any cloth above the specified quantity.[48] By 1685, the Batavia high government also decided to withdraw from the direct sales of Indian textiles on the Pasisir. It did not give up the monopoly on Indian textiles, however. Instead, the high government sold these imported cotton goods to private traders, most of whom were Chinese, at the company's auctions in Batavia.[49]

Javanese textile production was largely left to develop on its own after the 1690s, but only for a few decades. By the 1740s, the Dutch company had begun to interfere in the Javanese textile trade again, this time because of its interest in acquiring cotton yarn from the region. From this period on, there was a reasonable market for the commodity in India and the Netherlands.[50] Factories in the Netherlands kept up their demand for cotton yarn from the Indies through the rest of the eighteenth century.[51] In 1761, the governor-general noted that the popularity of the product there had generated a 237 percent profit for the company, and that the supplies thus far were insufficient to satisfy demand.[52]

Hence, it is no wonder that when the Dutch East India Company administrators gained governance over the north coast and eastern part of Java in 1743, a region they called "Java's Northeast Coast," they lost no time in utilizing their political supremacy to acquire the desired commodities. In the contract signed with the Batavia high government that year, besides cession of his rule over the Pasisir, the Mataram ruler was also obliged to deliver some products yearly to the company. Among them were 300 piculs of cotton yarn. In more concrete terms, the Javanese ruler had to arrange for his *bupatis*, or

his vassal lords on the north coast, to deliver annually to the company the first, second, third, fourth, and "dispense" (*dispens-soort*) qualities of cotton yarn at the fixed prices of 40, 30, 20, 16 and 10 rds per picul respectively.[53] These prices were certainly much cheaper than what the company had to pay in the Batavia market, namely, 45, 35, 24, 18 and 12 rds per picul for the respective grades of yarn.[54] Furthermore, to discourage the use of cotton yarn among the Javanese, Java's Northeast Coast government also imposed a high export tax of 25 percent, compared to the usual 8 percent on most goods, on the Javanese textiles.[55]

This was not to say that the company employees managed to acquire the products as they had planned. Though the regents were obliged to send 300 piculs of cotton yarns to the company yearly, they continued to be deficient in the deliveries.[56] As Batavia saw it, these regents were unhappy with the low price and would do the deliveries "more out of pressure than willingness."[57] Faced with the unsatisfactory deliveries, the Batavia high government resorted to ordering their residents to buy the yarn from market.[58]

When the Batavia authorities tried to use bans in the trade in cotton yarn to ensure that they could acquire the product, they also noted that private traders resorted to chicanery to beat the rule. For example, in the early 1740s, the high export toll of 25 percent was imposed only on white cotton textiles. What some Chinese traders did was to dye the cloth and wash the dye out after exporting them, such that the Batavia high government had to impose a similar heavy tax on colored fabrics.[59] Despite the placards announcing the bans in cotton-yarn trade in 1761 and 1766, the high government observed that cotton yarn was imported from Palembang to Batavia in 1768.[60]

Organization of Textile Production and Trade in Java

It is thanks to the Dutch company's keenness in competing against the Javanese textile trade, and subsequently in the yarn trade, that we can gain some insight into the organization of trade and production of these cotton goods. By comparison, the Javanese *babads* are silent about these details, as is often the case with regard to the economic workings of the society. From Dutch documents, it appears that various ports on the northeast coast of Java had become key export centers of Javanese textiles by the 1770s. The most preeminent among them were Semarang, Gresik, and Surabaya, where exports were mostly sent to the Borneo and Melaka Straits regions (see table 2).

Tegal, Pekalongan, and Sumenep could each export about 1,500 to 2,000 pieces annually.[61] Notably, even in these towns of middle-range production, the export value could be substantial. In Pekalongan in the late 1740s and

Table 2 Exports of Javanese textiles from Semarang, Gresik, and Surabaya to the Named Areas, in Pieces

		pieces	%
Semarang	Total	90,800	100
	Java	8,465	9
	Melaka straits	57,160	63
	Kalimantan	24,735	27
	Other	440	1
Gresik	Total	9,250	100
	Java	905	10
	Melaka straits	4,755	51
	Kalimantan	3,075	33
	Other	515	6
Surabaya	Total	32,100	100
	Java	1,930	6
	Melaka straits	20,445	64
	Kalimantan	7,885	24
	Other	1,840	6

Source: G. Knaap, *Shallow Waters, Rising Tide: Shipping and Trade in Java around 1775* (Leiden: KITLV Press, 1996), 132, table 20.

early 1750s, the average annual export value of Javanese textile was 20,000 Spanish reales.[62] Notably, these port towns served not only as centers of textile manufacture, but also as points of collection of textiles from smaller port towns and more inland areas. Goods exported from Gresik and Tegal were mostly from the core Mataram realm, located at the south central part of the island of Java. The former was connected by the Solo River with the heartland of the Mataram realm, while the latter was easily accessible to the south-central region of Java via land routes.[63]

While every Javanese town apparently had weaving villages that produced cloth for domestic consumption, it is difficult to discern from the Dutch documents the precise centers of textile production for export purposes. One main center of the textile industry was Kartasura, where company employees had noted since the mid-seventeenth century that the susuhunan and other courtly nobles set thousands of women to do spinning, weaving, embroidery, sewing, and "painting"—probably batikking—in their various *dalem*, or residence and compound of a Javanese lord, producing textiles in relatively large weaving mills.[64] With the shift of the susuhunan's court from Kartasura to Surakarta in the late 1740s, the textile manufacture center was duly relocated. Surakarta and Bagelen were big textile production centers

in the early nineteenth century.[65] Sumenep was another place where weaving was done for export purposes. It was in this port town that the so-called Banda type of textile was produced, presumably for sales in Banda in the eastern Indonesian archipelago. The "Madurese cloth" brought to Palembang was probably from Sumenep, which was located on the eastern end of the island of Madura.[66] Production of yarn was also concentrated in the interior of Java until the 1760s, when the Dutch company encouraged spinning activities in the coastal region.[67]

While the higher-quality textiles were manufactured in the dalems, coarser types of textiles were made through household production, or "cottage industry." That is, commoners did the spinning and weaving in the off-peak seasons of agricultural activities and sold the surplus textiles to peddling traders.[68] From nineteenth-century reports, it appears that there also existed a "putting-out system," wherein although the work was done at home, spinners and weavers produced cotton goods for the market. Their materials and equipment were often provided by an engrosser (bakul), who would also decide on the size and quality of the product, and paid the producers wages. This indicates that there were professional weavers in the Javanese cotton industry during this period.[69]

As for the main players involved in the organization of production and trade of cotton textiles in eighteenth-century Java, while the Javanese ruling class and nobility were involved in providing and organizing the labor, Chinese merchants appeared to be the main dealers of the cotton goods. When the Dutch company gave up competing against the Javanese textiles, it sold its imports of Indian textiles to Chinese traders. On the north coast of Java, Chinese merchants were also dominating the export trade in locally produced cotton goods. Since the seventeenth century, Chinese commercial operators were also the ones who usually become the tax farmers on "branding" (tjap, sjap) the textiles in the Mataram realm. Only with these authorized labels could the textiles be released for trade circulation.[70]

Chinese merchants also tended to win the bids to gain privileges as syahbandar, who had rights to collect taxes at the port areas, and as toll-gate keepers, who collected taxes at various points in the main land and riverine routes of transportation. In effect, this meant that they could collect taxes on the textiles brought from interior Java to the coast for sales and export. By winning these revenue farms, merchants could also have access to the commodities before the latter reached their final port of destination. Some tax collectors would also coerce traders to sell the textiles to them, as noted in the complaints of various Javanese bupatis to the Dutch residents.[71]

Besides buying up textiles available in the markets and using tax farms to gain earlier access to these goods, some Chinese traders also began to supply credit to peasant households in exchange for guaranteed deliveries of textiles at a later date. The first signs that this credit system was at work appeared in the last years of the seventeenth century, when Javanese cotton textiles became increasingly popular in the Indonesian archipelago.[72]

Hence, when the Dutch East India Company employees sought to participate in the Javanese textile trade, they had to depend on the mediation of both the Javanese ruling elite and Chinese merchants to acquire cotton textiles. This happened in the early 1750s, when the Batavia high government, having observed the popularity of Javanese cotton textiles for some years, ordered its Semarang subordinates to purchase Javanese textiles for sales in the company's trading offices at Banda, Basra, and also back in the Netherlands.[73] In 1752, it also used the service of a European textile trader on the Pasisir, Christiaen Mente, to buy textiles made in Java and other parts of the region.[74] In July 1754, the high government also ordered the Semarang authorities to seek out inhabitants of Banyumas, Bagelen, and Kedu and arrange with them to produce textiles for the company in order to get the best textiles in the fastest way possible.[75]

The plan did not work out well. Supplies were not readily available, which the company employees saw as a factor of the state of unrest in the early 1750s, when the Javanese princes Mangkubumi and Mangkunegara were rebelling against the Mataram susuhunan.[76] Having signed reconciliation treaties with both princes in 1755 and 1757, the company administrators were hopeful that peace would be restored and more commodities could be acquired. Although it did become easier to acquire Javanese textiles, the purchase could only be made at very high prices and many were "not well-made."[77] There was also another problem: as a result of household production, those that were bought up were of varying lengths and widths. Hartingh, the governor of Java's Northeast Coast, reported in August 1758 that it was extremely difficult to get textiles of the same length and width, because of the method of household production.[78] Governor Hartingh also reported that, "despite all efforts," the Javanese remained "reluctant" to alter their style of working. As such, he asked to be excused from the procurement of the commodity.[79]

Some success in buying up Javanese textiles in large quantities was finally achieved thirty years later, in the late 1780s. Notably, this was accomplished only with the help of Chinese towkays. In 1787 and 1788, the Company signed

a contract with the toll-gate keeper (*bandar*) in Yogyakarta, Que Tjinsing, and the Chinese captain of Surakarta, Sie Sokliang, who promised to deliver 350 corges of Javanese textiles and 30 corges of bunting of the sizes and quality stipulated by the company every year.[80]

Concluding Remarks

At this point in history, the Dutch mainly contented themselves with the amounts they could buy from the market or collect through obligatory deliveries from the Javanese bupatis. In the latter case, the company residents generally cared that the quota had been met. Since Javanese cotton yarn and textiles were not key items of trade for the Dutch company, especially in comparison to rice, their superiors also generally kept an eye closed. The Javanese bupatis could mostly get away with deficient deliveries of cotton yarn if they claimed that pressuring the commoners too much would affect rice yields. As the Dutch did not attempt to organize manufacture of the cotton products themselves in the eighteenth century, we cannot get a clear sense from the Dutch sources of what went on in Javanese textile production at the village level.[81]

It is evident however that Chinese merchants played a prominent role in the trade of Javanese cotton goods. Yet, although the names of the individual merchants are made available at times, we do not know how far the Chinese merchants who gave credit to local producers as advance payment for the cotton textiles were linked with those who sold Indian textiles in the local markets. From the Dutch company materials, it is also not possible to discern the relationship between the Chinese merchants and the Javanese rulers and lords. Both groups must have cooperated, given the way in which the former provided credit to the producers while the latter controlled the production labor.

What was clear is that, by the early nineteenth century, Javanese cotton textile production had developed both in magnitude and specialization. Boomgaard notes that in nineteenth-century Java, not only was there production of coarse cloth for home consumption, but also, in areas like Cirebon, Tegal, Bagelen, Yogyakarta, and Surakarta, "specialization in one or several stages of cotton processing had occurred," "whence considerable quantities of cloth were exported to other Residencies or even outside Java." In 1808, there were 22,628 spinning wheels and 17,641 weaving looms in a total of 45,093 families in Surabaya and Gresik, or one spinning wheel for every two families and one loom for every two-and-a-half. In the same

year, Bagelen was said to have 10,000 weavers, or almost 11 percent of all the families. There were 36,000 weavers in Besuki, a relatively small north-eastern Javanese port town, in 1836, or 50 percent of all households. However, hemmed in by his conception that Java had, at most, "cottage industry" and moderate textile production, Boomgaard judges the archival figures to be "extreme" and best left "out of consideration."[82] Yet, these figures were probably accurate, considering the expansion in exports of Javanese cotton textiles in the eighteenth century.

Although textile manufacture went into decline with the arrival of European imports after the mid-nineteenth century, the Javanese batik industry took off and reached one of its peaks of development in its long history. The development of Javanese cotton textile production witnessed another interesting twist of fate in the early 1930s, when the dying industry experienced an upswing as the Dutch textile export trade to Southeast Asian markets faced competition from the Japanese. To compete against the Japanese, the colonial government decided to conduct weaving in Java, using Dutch cotton yarns. In this historical context, Majalaya, where the bupatis and residents had maintained a small weaving industry, emerged as the center of textile production, accounting for almost 90 percent of all weaving enterprises in Java by 1938. Two groups of people, in particular, jumped on the opportunity and set up textile-weaving industries in the town. The first were members of a landowning class among the Muslim Sundanese in Majalaya, who also had a commercial background, particularly in the trade of textiles. The second group was the Hokchia (pinyin: Fuqing) Chinese, who came from the Fuqing region in the northeastern part of Fujian, China. The Hokchia Chinese, who had specialized in money-lending services, decided to invest in the weaving business when the colonial state imposed an anti-usury ruling in 1936.[83] These two groups of people continue to dominate the industry in the region up to the present day.

Notes

I thank the Asia Research Institute and the Royal Netherlands Institute of Southeast Asian and Caribbean Studies for the fellowships that supported me during the period of writing and revising this essay. I also thank Heather Sutherland, Nola Cooke, and the editors for their comments on an earlier version of the essay.
1. H. Matsuo, *The Development of Javanese Cotton Industry* (Tokyo: Institute of Developing Economies, 1970).
2. A. Reid, *Southeast Asia in the Age of Commerce 1450–1680*, vol. 2 (New Haven/London: Yale University Press, 1993).

3. P. Boomgaard, "The Non-Agricultural Side of an Agricultural Economy: Java, 1500–1900," In the Shadow of Agriculture: Non-farm Activities in the Javanese Economy, Past and Present, ed. Paul Alexander, P. Boomgaard, and Ben White (Amsterdam: Royal Tropical Institute, 1991); A. van der Kraan, Contest for the Java Cotton Trade, 1811–40: An Episode in Anglo-Dutch Rivalry (Hull: Centre for South-East Asian Studies, University of Hull, 1998), 54.

4. P. Keppy, "Hidden Business: Indigenous and Ethnic Chinese Entrepreneurs in the Majalaya Textile Industry, West Java, 1928–1974," Ph.D. diss., Vrije Universiteit, 2001, 34; M. Gittinger, Splendid Symbols: Textiles and Tradition in Indonesia, 2d ed. (1979; Singapore: Oxford University Press, 1990), 115.

5. For a good description of the batikking method and its development through the centuries, see M. Gittinger, Splendid Symbols, 115–22; R. Heringa, "Appendix 3," Fabric of Enchantment: Batik from the North Coast of Java, ed. R. Heringa and H. Veldhuisen (Los Angeles: Museum of Art, 1996), 224–30.

6. Gittinger, Splendid Symbols, 13. Gittinger has also convincingly argued against scholars who suggest that the weaving technique was introduced by migrants from China, India, and the Middle East. For details, see ibid., 13–15.

7. J. Christie, "Texts and Textiles in 'Medieval' Java," Bulletin de l'École française d'Extrême Orient 80 (1993): 181–211. "Sima charters" are documents dating back to the period from the ninth century to the fifteenth which record the transfer of tax and labor rights by a ruler or highly placed taxing authority to a specified beneficiary.

8. The dye processors were subjected to taxation, which indicates that their products were considered commodities.

9. The roots from the mengkudu shrub are used to produce a bright red dye often used on Pasisir batik.

10. Information in this paragraph is obtained from Christie, "Texts and Textiles in 'Medieval' Java."

11. Christie, "Texts and Textiles in 'Medieval' Java," 191–92. Comparison should be made with Gittinger, who considers that batikking began only after the fourteenth century. See Gittinger, Splendid Symbols, 15–16, 116–17.

12. R. Heringa is inclined to believe that the origins of the batikking method came from the Chinese, and she rejects a Javanese myth that dates the origin of batik on Java to A.D. 700, when a princess from Coromandel and her retinue were credited for teaching weaving, batik, and dyeing to the Javanese on the northeast coast of Java ("The Historical Background of Batik on Java," Fabric of Enchantment: Batik from the North Coast of Java, ed. R. Heringa and H. Veldhuisen [Los Angeles: Museum of Art, 1996], 31–34). For other theories of the origins of batikking, see Gittinger's introduction to Splendid Symbols (13–16).

13. Christie, "Texts and Textiles in 'Medieval' Java," 190; D. Gluckman, "Introduction," Fabric of Enchantment: Batik from the North Coast of Java, ed. R. Heringa and H. Veldhuisen (Los Angeles: Museum of Art, 1996), 16.

14. For a good ethnographic account on the traditional method of dyeing, see R. Heringa, "Dye Process and Life Sequence: The Coloring of Textiles in an East Javanese Village,"

To Speak with Cloth: Studies in Indonesian Textiles, ed. M. Gittinger (Los Angeles: Museum of Cultural History, 1989), 107–29.

15. Unless otherwise stated, the information in this paragraph is from Christie, "Texts and Textiles in 'Medieval' Java."

16. Gittinger, Splendid Symbols, 14–15. See also A. Forge, "Batik Patterns of the Early Nineteenth Century," To Speak with Cloth: Studies in Indonesian Textiles, ed. M. Gittinger (Los Angeles: Museum of Cultural History, 1989), 91–105. See especially 103–4 for the batik patterns worn by individuals of different status during the early nineteenth century.

17. VOC 3738, Siberg to Batavia high government, 3 March 1786, 49–50. Larangan is the Malay word for "prohibition," and the motif mentioned here was probably that of the parang rusak, or "broken knife." Refer to Gittinger, Splendid Symbols, 125–26 for the design.

18. Gittinger, Splendid Symbols, 123–24.

19. See example of susuhunan Pakubuwana II, textiles among cash, gold rings, and so on. VOC 2767, dagregister of governor on his trip to Surakarta, 1749, 81–82.

20. L. Nagtegaal, Riding the Dutch Tiger: The Dutch East Indies Company and the Northeast Coast of Java, 1680–1743 (Leiden: KITLV Press, 1996), 148–50.

21. John Guy, "Commerce, Power and Mythology: Indian Textiles in Indonesia," Indonesian Circle 42 (1987): 57–75; and "Indian Textiles for the Thai Market: A Royal Prerogative," Textile Museum Journal 31 (1992): 82–96.

22. R. Maxwell, Textiles of Southeast Asia: Tradition, Trade and Transformation (Melbourne: Oxford University Press, 1990). Historically speaking, the western part of Java is not considered to be under the rule of Javanese, but under that of the Sundanese and Bantenese people. The early Mataram, Singasari, and Majapahit empires, which held sway from the eighth century to the fifteenth, were basically composed of areas in central and east Java. As a result of lesser interaction, the Javanese people also speak a different language from the Sundanese and Bantenese people.

23. Batavia high government to Gentlemen XVII, 5 March 1750, Generale missiven van gouverneurs-generaal en raden aan Heren XVII der Verenigde Oostindische Compagnie [hereafter GM] ('s-Gravenhage: Martinus Nijhoff, 1971), 11:849.

24. Cited in Guy, "Indian Textiles for the Thai Market," 82.

25. Nagtegaal, Riding the Dutch Tiger, 148, table 12.

26. T. Raychaudhuri, Jan Company in Coromandel 1605–1690: A Study in the Interrelations of European Commerce and Traditional Economies ('s-Gravenhage: Martinus Nijhoff, 1962), 162.

27. Boomgaard, "The Non-Agricultural Side of an Agricultural Economy: Java, 1500–1900," 20–21; Nagtegaal, Riding the Dutch Tiger, 135–36.

28. B. Andaya, "The Cloth Trade in Jambi and Palembang during the Seventeenth and Eighteenth Centuries," Indonesia 48 (1989): 39.

29. Ibid., 27–46.

30. A. Reid, "The Origins of Poverty in Indonesia," Indonesia: Australian Perspectives, ed. J. J. Fox et al. (Canberra: Australian National University, Research School of Pacific Studies, 1980), 441–54.

31. Batavia high government to Gentlemen XVII, 31 December 1683, GM 4:621.

32. The imports of these items to Palembang expanded through the eighteenth century, from negligible amounts in the late seventeenth century to 275 tubs of gold thread and 35 tubs of raw Chinese silk in 1759. In 1821, the trade in Chinese raw silk was valued at around 9,940 guilders, and 75 containers and 25 packs of gold thread worth more than 583 guilders were also imported.

33. Andaya, "The Cloth Trade in Jambi and Palembang during the Seventeenth and Eighteenth Centuries," 41–43.

34. S. Arasaratnam, "The Coromandel-Southeast Asia Trade 1650–1740," *Asian History* 18 (1984): 129–31.

35. K. Glamann, *Dutch-Asiatic Trade 1620–1740* (Copenhagen: Danish Science Press / 's-Gravenhage: Martinus Nijhoff, 1958), chap. 7; E. Jacobs, *Koopman in Azie: De Handel van de Verenigde Oost-Indische Compagnie Tijdens de 18de Eeuw* (Zutphen: Walburg, 2000), chap. on "The Competition for Indian Textiles." Jacobs has described how the English and French East India Companies came to dominate the European market for Indian textiles in the period from 1730 to 1760. The VOC came in third place, because the directors preferred to trade in more profitable commodities such as spices.

36. Andaya, "The Cloth Trade in Jambi and Palembang during the Seventeenth and Eighteenth Centuries," 39.

37. Ibid., 41.

38. G. Knaap and H. Sutherland, *Monsoon Traders: Ships, Skippers and Commodities in Eighteenth-Century Makassar* (Leiden: KITLV Press, 2004), 111–16.

39. In the eighteenth century, besides being a trading company, the Dutch East India Company had also gained much income by acting as a territorial power, that is, by earning through taxation at the ports it controlled in the eastern seas. For more details, see J. van Goor, "Introduction," *Trading Companies in Asia 1600–1830*, ed. J. van Goor (Utrecht: HES Uitgevers, 1986); and "A Hybrid State: The Dutch Economic and Political Network in Asia," *From the Mediterranean to the China Sea: Miscellaneous Notes*, ed. C. Guillot, D. Lombard, and R. Ptak (Wiesbaden: Harrassowitz Verlag, 1998), 193–214.

40. Boomgaard, "The Non-Agricultural Side of an Agricultural Economy: Java, 1500–1900," 20.

41. Nagtegaal, *Riding the Dutch Tiger*, 168.

42. K. Hall, "The Textile Industry in Southeast Asia, 1400–1800," *Economic and Social History of the Orient* 39.2 (1996): 126–28.

43. Andaya, "The Cloth Trade in Jambi and Palembang during the Seventeenth and Eighteenth Centuries," 40–41.

44. See, for instance, VOC 3247, list of private vessels leaving Semarang from 1 September 1767 to 31 August 1768; VOC 2706, Semarang authorities to Batavia high government, 20 May 1747, 123–25.

45. Nagtegaal, *Riding the Dutch Tiger*, 136.

46. S. P. Sen, "The Role of Indian Textiles in Southeast Asian Trade in the Seventeenth Century," *Southeast Asian History* 3.2 (1962): 92–110.

47. Nagtegaal has not explained why the company personnel at the coast found it impossible to ban the imports.

48. Raychaudhuri, *Jan Company in Coromandel 1605–1690*, 162. His comment was probably right. Note in 1691, a Dutch observer in Palembang who described the varieties of Javanese cloth had remarked that these were rarely washed; Andaya commented that this was probably because of the tendency of dyes to fade ("The Cloth Trade in Jambi and Palembang during the Seventeenth and Eighteenth Centuries," 43).

49. Nagtegaal, *Riding the Dutch Tiger*, 147–48.

50. Batavia high government to Gentlemen XVII, 5 March 1750, GM 11:849; Nagtegaal, *Riding the Dutch Tiger*, 136; Jacobs, *Koopman in Azie*, 187.

51. Batavia high government to Gentlemen XVII, 5 March 1750, GM 11:849.

52. J. A. van der Chijs, ed., *Nederlandsch-Indisch Plakaatboek 1602–1811*, 17 vols. (Batavia: Landsdrukkerij / 's-Gravenhage: Martinus Nijhoff, 1885–1900) [hereafter *Plakaatboek*], 7:475.

53. Batavia high government to Gentlemen XVII, 31 December 1744, GM 11:191; see articles 14 to 18 in the 11–13 November 1743 contract between the company and susuhunan (F. Stapel, ed., *Corpus Diplomaticum Neerlando-Indicum: Verzameling van Politieke Contracten en Verdere Verdragen door de Nederlanders in het Oosten Gesloten, van Privilegiebrieven aan hen Verleend* ['s-Gravenhage: Martinus Nijhoff, 1938], 370–71). The quantities were fixed by 1744 (VOC 2633, Sterrenberg to Batavia high government, 5 October 1744, 558–61). "Dispense" quality refers to the lowest grade of cotton yarns. The high government mainly bought these yarns as provisions for the company personnel.

54. 15 August 1747, *Plakaatboek* 5:471–72.

55. 25 November 1751, *Plakaatboek* 6:97.

56. VOC 2655, Tegal resident Breekpot to Batavia high government, 13 October 1745, 383–85.

57. Batavia high government to Gentlemen XVII, 31 December 1745, GM 11:316.

58. Hartingh's memorandum of transfer (*memorie van overgave*), *De Opkomst van het Nederlandsche Gezag in Oost-Indië: Verzamelingen van Onuitgegeven Stukken uit het Oud-koloniaal Archief* [hereafter *Opkomst*], ed. J. K. J. de Jonge and M. L. van Deventer (Amsterdam: Martinus Nijhoff, 1862–1909), 10:354–55; VOC 3247, Semarang resolution, 31 August 1768, 88–89. For more details on the Dutch company's attempts to acquire cotton yarn from Java, see Kwee Hui Kian, *The Political Economy of Java's Northeast Coast, c. 1740–1800: Elite Synergy* (Leiden: Brill, 2006), chaps. 3, 10.

59. Batavia high government to Gentlemen XVII, 31 December 1748, GM 11:713.

60. 20 May/15 June 1768, *Plakaatboek* 8:449–50.

61. G. Knaap, *Shallow Waters, Rising Tide: Shipping and Trade in Java around 1775* (Leiden: KITLV Press, 1996), 131.

62. VOC 2886, Semarang government to Batavia high government, 26 February 1756, 66; 25 November 1751, *Plakaatboek* 6:95–100.

63. Instructions by Governor-General Van Imhoff to Semarang authorities during his visit to and departure from Java's northeast coast, 9 June 1746, *Opkomst* 10:90; Siberg's memorandum of transfer, *Opkomst* 12:109–10.

64. H. de Graaf, ed., *De Vijf Gezantschapsreizen van Ryklof van Goens Naar het Hof van Mataram 1648–1654* ('s-Gravenhage: Martinus Nijhoff, 1956); Nagtegaal, *Riding the Dutch Tiger*, 135.

65. P. Boomgaard, *Children of the Colonial State: Population Growth and Economic Development in Java, 1795–1880* (Amsterdam: Free University Press, 1989), 127–28.

66. Batavia ordered Semarang to send forth some samples of this Banda-type textile in 1752 (VOC 2804, Semarang government to Batavia high government, 18 September 1752, 73–74). See also Andaya, "The Cloth Trade in Jambi and Palembang during the Seventeenth and Eighteenth Centuries," 40–41.

67. Hartingh's memorandum of transfer, *Opkomst* 10:354–55. More discussion on the yarn production is given in a later section.

68. Boomgaard, *Children of the Colonial State*, 125–30; Nagtegaal, *Riding the Dutch Tiger*, 135–36.

69. Boomgaard, *Children of the Colonial State*, 125–30; Matsuo, *The Development of Javanese Cotton Industry*, vii–viii.

70. See Ruurdje Laarhoven, "The Power of Cloth: The Textile Trade of the Dutch East India Company (VOC) 1600–1780," Ph.D. diss., Australian National University, 1994, 258–61.

71. VOC 2681, Semarang commandership to Batavia high government, 24 September 1746, 149–50; VOC 2706, Semarang commandership to Batavia high government, 28 February 1747, 40–41.

72. Nagtegaal, *Riding the Dutch Tiger*, 135. Nagtegaal did not quite spell out the exact years, but his citations, dated 1698 and 1713, point to the beginning of the eighteenth century.

73. VOC 2766, Semarang government to Batavia high government, 28 December 1750, 34; VOC 2766, Semarang government to Batavia high government, 16 January 1751, 57–58; VOC 2787, Semarang government to Batavia high government, 29 February 1752, 4; VOC 2824, Semarang government to Batavia high government, 31 January 1753, 11–12; VOC 2843, Semarang government to Batavia high government, 13 July 1754, 148–49.

74. VOC 2804, Semarang government to Batavia high government, 18 September 1752, 73–74.

75. VOC 2843, Semarang government to Batavia high government, 13 July 1754, 148–49.

76. VOC 2864, Tegal resident Falk to Batavia high government, 4 April 1755, 48.

77. VOC 2968, Semarang government to Batavia high government, 28 December 1758, 6–7.

78. VOC 2938, Semarang government to Batavia high government, 15 August 1758, 80–81.

79. VOC 2938, Hartingh to Batavia high government, 20 October 1758, 20–21.

80. VOC 3763, Siberg to Batavia high government, 13 July 1787, 387–88; VOC 3861, Semarang government to Batavia high government, 22 December 1788, §448; VOC 3861, Semarang government to Batavia high government, 14 March 1789, §17.

81. In the early 1800s, company employees set up two textile factories with hundreds

of looms in Semarang. The looms were not for commercial purposes but to produce coarse cottons for the army. At this point in time, the supply of military clothes from the Netherlands had ceased as a result of the Napoleonic Wars. Boomgaard, "The Non-Agricultural Side of an Agricultural Economy: Java, 1500–1900," 22.

82. Boomgaard, *Children of the Colonial State*, 127–30.

83. Keppy, "Hidden Business," chaps. 1–3.

PART IV ~~~ High Colonial

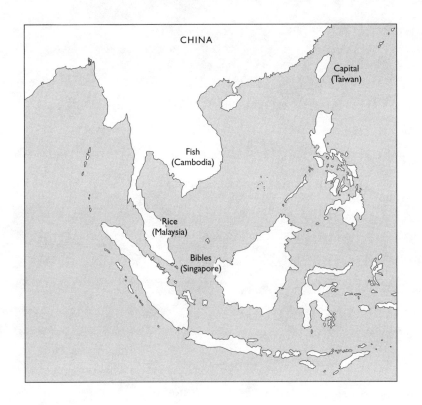

THE POWER OF CULTURE AND ITS LIMITS

Taiwanese Merchants' Asian Commodity Flows, 1895–1945

—— Man-houng Lin

Since the 1990s, newspapers and journals have been using terms such as "Greater China Economic Zone" and "Global Chinese Network" to describe how Chinese cultural ties facilitate economic relations. Scholars such as Leo Suryadinata, Wang Gungwu, and others depict Chinese oscillation between the affirmation of their specific ethnic identity and assimilation into other cultures.[1] Other scholars, such as Marie-Sybille de Vienne, stress that the total gross domestic product (GDP) owned by the ethnic Chinese population around 2004 is barely the GDP of Germany, and the diasporic rate of Chinese is only 3 percent of the Chinese population, while the Greeks have more than half.[2]

In this chapter I take up the question of the effect of cultural ties on establishing economic relations by looking at Taiwanese merchants' Asian commodity flows during the period of Japanese colonial rule over Taiwan (1895–1945). By "cultural ties" I refer specifically to ethnicity, customs, languages, and personal relations, and in the phrase "commodity flows" I include goods and capital traded. Taiwanese merchants' East Asian commodity flows denote their trade with and investment in South China, Manchukuo, and Southeast Asia.[3] The data for this study derive from archives or libraries in Taiwan, Japan, the United States, Singapore, and the People's Republic of China (PRC), and consist of Japanese Foreign Affairs archives, investigations published by the Taiwanese general government and the Bank of Taiwan, and newspapers in overseas Chinese communities, in Manchukuo, and in Taiwan.

Culture and Immigration

Following Shibaoka Hisashi, who defined overseas Chinese as settlers rather than sojourners who merely stayed abroad for less than three months, immigration here refers to settlers rather than to sojourners.[4] Immigration is a prerequisite for direct investment.[5] Statistics on overseas immigration of Taiwanese during the period of Japanese rule are scattered. One 1926 document offers a basis for understanding the distribution of Taiwanese who moved abroad. Like other sources for immigration statistics, this document sometimes excludes nonregistered people or dependents and thus provides numbers that are lower than the real numbers. Nonetheless, this document does effectively illustrate the geographical distribution of Taiwanese immigration: South China had the greatest number (4,118), followed by Southeast Asia (522), other areas of China (118), Guandongzhou (19), Qingdao (4), Australia (3), and Chile (1) (see map 1).[6] In contrast to Japanese immigrants, who moved out of East Asia and Southeast Asia in greater numbers than moved within this area from 1904 to 1935, Taiwanese migration was mainly restricted to East Asia and Southeast Asia (see map 1, fig. 1).

Taiwanese immigration remained largely within South China, especially within south Fujian, as well as within the overseas Chinese communities from this region across Southeast Asia. According to the registered number published by the Taiwan general government, the total number of Taiwanese in China was approximately 335 in 1907, and 12,900 by 1936.[7] If we include the estimated 7,000–8,000 who did not register, the number of Taiwanese in China in fact reached nearly 21,000 in 1936. Of this number, around 20,000 resided in Fujian Province alone; the distribution within Fujian put 18,000 of these in Xiamen, 2,000 in Fuzhou, and several hundred within the Zhangzhou and Quanzhou regions.[8] An estimated 80 to 90 percent of the ancestors of the Taiwanese had arrived within the previous three hundred years from Xiamen, Quanzhou, and Zhangzhou, and they often retained family, property, and friends in their ancestral homes.[9] Guangdong was somewhat further from Taiwan than south Fujian was, and the dialects spoken there were quite different from Fujianese. But their dialects were similar to the Hakka Taiwanese, whose population is about one-fifth of the Fujianese in Taiwan in 1928.[10] While the number of Taiwanese in Guangdong increased in the later period of Japanese rule in Taiwan, overall their numbers were far less than those in Xiamen.[11]

In the early twentieth century, Taiwanese made up the greatest proportion of Japanese nationals in South China, especially in Xiamen, Fuzhou, and

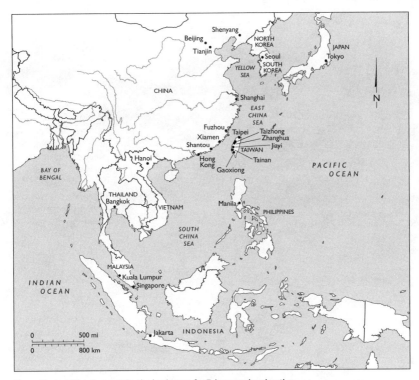

Map 1 East and Southeast Asia, the basic area for Taiwanese immigration.

Shantou. Immigrants from Japan proper began to expand into South China only in the late Meiji period (1868–1912), comprising but a tiny proportion by the beginning of the twentieth century. There were virtually no Koreans in South China in this period. By 1936, when 12,900 Taiwanese were registered in South China, only 2,783 migrants had come from Japan proper.[12] According to a survey from 1 April 1937, of the 2,100 Japanese nationals in Fuzhou, 1,700 were Taiwanese; of the 10,678 Japanese nationals in Xiamen, 10,000 were Taiwanese.[13] Based on the results of a Japanese consular survey from 1 January 1942, the number of Japanese nationals in China indicates that Japanese and Koreans clearly outnumbered Taiwanese in north and central China, but the opposite was true in South China (see figs. 2, 3, 4, and 5). This data corroborates the trend of Taiwanese immigrants settling more in South China than in other parts of China.

According to article 4 of the 1896 Treaty of Commerce and Navigation between China and Japan, Japanese nationals were only allowed to rent or purchase houses, and rent or lease land for residence, doing business, or engag-

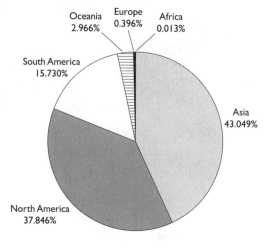

Figure 1 Distribution of overseas Japanese proper in various continents, 1904–1935. *Source*: Summed up and chart made from Gaimushō chōsabu, *Kaigai kakuchi zairyū honpōjin jinkōhyō* [A population table of the Japanese overseas] (Tokyo: Tsushokyoku, 1935), 103–6.

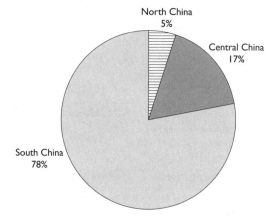

Figure 2 The distribution of Taiwanese in China, 1942. *Source*: Chart derived from the table in Komekura Jirō, *Manshū, Shina: Sekai chili seiji taikei* [Manchuria and China: The great series of world geography and politics] (Tokyo: Hakuyōsha, 1944), 392. I am grateful to Xu Xueji for kindly providing me with this material.

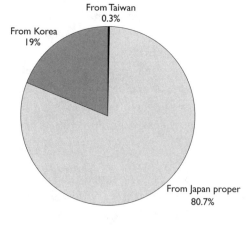

Figure 3 The distribution of Japanese nationals in North China, 1942. *Source*: Chart made from the table in Komekura Jirō, *Manshū, Shina*, 392.

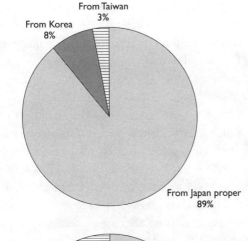

Figure 4 The distribution of Japanese nationals in Central China, 1942. *Source: Manshū, Shina*, 392.

From Taiwan 3%
From Korea 8%
From Japan proper 89%

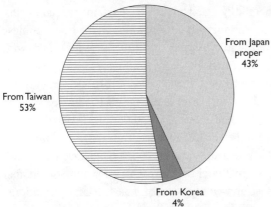

Figure 5 The distribution of Japanese nationals in South China, 1942. *Source: Manshū, Shina*, 392.

From Japan proper 43%
From Taiwan 53%
From Korea 4%

ing in industry at the international concessions or settlements of the treaty ports.[14] Article 4 stipulated that they could also carry Japanese passports with Chinese officials' agreement, which were valid for thirteen months, to travel among the treaty ports. If travel extended beyond the treaty ports, it had to remain within 100 Chinese li (189,412 ft) from the treaty ports, and it could not extend for a period of more than five days (article 6).[15] The distance between Xiamen and Zhangzhou is 45 kilometers. As one kilometer is 3,280.83 ft, and one Chinese li is 1,894.12 ft, 45 kilometers is 78 Chinese li. The distance between Xiamen and Quanzhou is 100 kilometers, which is 173.12 Chinese li. However, several hundred Taiwanese had inhabited or done business in Zhangzhou and Quanzhou. As Japanese nationals, the Taiwanese could live with the local Chinese.[16] They were not required to live with Japanese from Japan proper in the treaty ports.[17] As China did not have a

well-established household-registration system, the Taiwanese could claim themselves as local people in order to do business or attend school.[18] Some Taiwanese went so far as to sign contracts with local governments to cultivate opium, leveraging familial relations in inland areas. In the years around 1920, the Taiwanese merchant Li Zhongyi, for example, could send money to a relative in Xiamen to purchase a farm of several thousand mou (0.1647 acres) and over 400 head of plow-oxen; and set up the Zhannan Company, which, in addition to farming livestock, grew lychees, longans, mangos, and chestnuts.[19] Taiwanese merchants could use their relatives to deeply penetrate into Fujianese society.[20]

At the same time, because China's Nationality Law, issued in 1909 (remaining effective with revisions through 1957), was based on the bloodline principle and insisted that any revocation of Chinese nationality required the state's consent, even for people living on territories ceded to other countries, the Taiwanese were able to claim legally to be Chinese. Like other Chinese with other nationalities in the early twentieth century, the Taiwanese with Japanese nationality were able to retain their Chinese nationality and enjoy its considerable economic benefits.[21] They were not restricted in employment or excluded from landowning rights as foreigners in China.[22]

Taiwanese migrating to Southeast Asia also had the advantage of sharing a subculture with overseas Chinese already there. In Japanese colonial Taiwan, classes for Taiwanese to learn Southeast Asian languages were available. The Chengyuan School in Taipei began teaching Malay in September 1913.[23] Yet, when Taiwanese arrived at their Southeast Asian destinations, they rarely had problems communicating; whether in Singapore or Bangkok, they were able to call for a cab in the Taiwanese dialect to get to hotels and restaurants, and local residents could employ overseas Chinese to serve as translators in dealing with Taiwanese.[24] In 1941, a Taiwanese merchant in Indonesia said, "It is common here to hear radio broadcasts from Taiwan, and since eighty percent of the overseas Chinese here are from Fujian, Minnan dialect is used in radio broadcasts."[25] In 1936, when a trade-oriented special program was opened to Taiwanese students in Taipei Commercial College, Taiwanese who could not speak Minnan dialect had to take related courses.[26] In this school, Malay, Thai, Filipino, Burmese, Vietnamese, Cantonese, Fuzhou dialect, Minnan dialect, Santou dialect, spoken and written Chinese, Dutch, French, German, and English were offered at a minimum of two choices in one semester with two hours a week.[27]

By the end of Japanese colonial rule, approximately 3,000 Taiwanese had

migrated to Southeast Asia.[28] This suggests that cultural affinity could explain why the number of Taiwanese in Southeast Asia was second only to the number of Taiwanese in South China.

The Taiwanese situation in Manchuria was different. Unlike in South China, where Taiwanese immigrants far outnumbered Japanese, in Manchukuo it was not until 1938 that the Taiwanese approached one thousandth of the immigrants from Japan proper and one thirty-fifth of the number of Taiwanese in South China. According to the *Shengjing Shibao*, the largest newspaper in Manchukuo, the number of Taiwanese in Manchuria rose from about 60 in 1911, to 500 in 1932 at the establishment of Manchukuo, to 600 by 1938.[29] Furthermore, according to Liang Jinlan, a Taiwanese whose father operated a medical practice in Manchukuo, about 1,000 Taiwanese lived in Manchukuo on the eve of 1945.[30] The number of Japanese immigrants in Manchuria was already 100,000 in 1911, 270,000 by 1932, and 600,000 by 1938 (excluding military personnel and their dependents).[31]

Before the outbreak of the Sino-Japanese War in 1937, the passport application procedure for Taiwanese traveling to Southeast Asia or to the Republic of China was not as simple as going to Manchukuo, since the latter was under greater Japanese influence than the former.[32] Still, far fewer Taiwanese migrated to Manchukuo than South China or Southeast Asia. One reason was the rather high linguistic barrier in Manchuria. According to a 1919 article in the *Taiwan Nichinichi Shinpo*,

> People from Jiayi (in south-central Taiwan) who have traveled to Fuzhou, Xiamen, and all over Southeast Asia have had no difficulties in travel, but as their prospects would be constricted by not being well versed in Mandarin Chinese, young people in this town thought deeply about the problem and formed the Tu'nan [Breaking through the South] Institute to study the spoken and written Mandarin.[33]

In 1917, the Dongyang Association's Taiwan Commercial and Industrial School also began teaching Mandarin to facilitate trade across the Taiwan Strait.[34] In 1938, the Jiayi Commercial School in Tainan Prefecture, complying with Japan's national policy, began actively cultivating merchant talents to expand business in China, Southeast Asia, and Taiwan. By the fifth academic year, students had to study written Chinese every Wednesday, and it was hoped they would all take up spoken Chinese courses.[35] From these examples, it is clear that moving outside of South China or Southeast Asia required surmounting the linguistic barrier of Mandarin, even in Manchukuo.

It was, of course, possible for Taiwanese to speak Japanese in Manchukuo. As Liang Jinlan recalled, "In Manchukuo, I mostly spoke Japanese, and after being away from Taiwan for some time, I was not able to speak Taiwanese."[36] However, Japanese people were the only people who could not communicate with the Mandarin-speaking people in Manchuria.

Taiwanese immigration was 22,935 in South China, 7,045 in Central China, 1,442 in North China, 1,000 in Manchuko, and 3,000 in Southeast Asia on the eve of 1945.[37] Cultural ties certainly provide an explanation for this clear trend in migration.

Culture and Investment

Most Taiwanese immigrants during the period of Japanese rule were merchants who made large and important investments in South China. Southeast Asia and Manchuria ranked next in sequence.

According to the *Tongji nianjian* [the statistics almanac] published by the Fujian provincial government's statistics office in 1937, 81.18 percent of the Taiwanese in Xiamen were merchants, 4.51 percent were doctors, and 7.85 percent were prostitutes.[38] In Fuzhou, 68.18 percent were merchants, 8.36 percent were doctors, 7.48 percent were government employees, and 5.28 percent were teachers.[39] According to a 1926 article in the *Taiwan Nichinichi Shinpo*, "Some Taiwanese merchants and doctors are moving to Manchuria."[40] In 1941, the Taiwan Association in Thailand had 76 members (including 8 Japanese), and if we include 10 others who had not become members and 65 family members, the total number of Taiwanese there was 150; of these, only 3 were not engaged in commercial activities.[41]

Even doctors often made investments as a side business. Dr Huang Shunji from central Taiwan's Zhanghua county moved to Manchukuo and made purchases in real estate and farmland.[42] Cai Shixing from Lugang of central Taiwan, who with his uncle's help was able to attend medical school, graduated and worked for the Sanwu [J. Sango] Company as a doctor. After ten years in Xiamen, by managing with small capital, he was able to rent pastureland to sell milk, his family was involved in the sugar business, and he was fast gaining respect.[43] Wang Jingqiu, who spent twenty-two years in Thailand, engaged in several enterprises in addition to running a successful medical practice.[44]

In addition to their work as company and store employees, these Taiwanese merchants' commercial activities extended to investments ranging from individual stores to large-scale industries such as factories, farms, mines, and banks.

Categories of Taiwanese Investment

In 1929, Taiwanese in South China engaged in a wide range of commercial activities. They opened businesses that dealt in foodstuffs (rice, tobacco, tea, wine, ginseng, fruit, candy, and seafood); clothing (cloth, dyes, leather, rubber shoes, jewelry, and lace); everyday products (coal, medicine, timber, antiques, incense, writing implements, printing, toys, porcelain, and furniture); modern products (clocks, fertilizer, machinery, chemicals, drugs, glasses, cement, alcohol, bicycle parts, medical implements, ship repair items, ship materials, and dry-cell batteries); factories (incense, wine, staples, ice, drugs, soda, gas refining, batteries, and mining); and services (hotels, restaurants, real estate, and finance).[45] In September 1926, the occupations of Taiwanese in Xiamen included the operation of opium dens, grocery stores, restaurants, hospitals, pharmacies, and distilleries. In 1941, service trades dominated their business.[46]

From 1935 to 1940, Taiwanese in Southeast Asia had food-related stores for bread, coffee, tea, vegetables, rice, tobacco, and seafood; and for general products including western medicine, ship sail fabric, mosquito nets, exercise equipment, and porcelain. They also invested in factories that produced canned fruit, ice, drinking water, iron, lime, and hats; or in factories for machine repair. In addition, they had plantations, fishing, and husbandry. In the service sector they had investments in finance, hotels, and real-estate agencies. In addition, Taiwanese in Southeast Asia included a fair number of doctors and actors. Taiwanese in Thailand, the Philippines, and Vietnam tended to work in Japanese companies or to own grocery stores, hardware stores, pharmacies, and tea stores. In Indonesia, more Taiwanese owned production industries, including weaving, dying, charcoal, iron, soy sauce, candy, canvas, and cold beverages. They also had more extensive financial power and a longer and closer relationship with the local overseas Chinese than Taiwanese did in other Southeast Asian countries. Taiwanese in Malaya and Singapore, being mostly of the laboring classes and weak in economic power, formed a great contrast with those in Indonesia.[47]

The scale of the factories of Taiwanese merchants in South China and Southeast Asia was comparable. From 1935 to 1940, the businesses operated by Taiwanese in Southeast Asia had mostly ten or fewer employees, but there was also a factory employing over 600 workers. In terms of capital and operating expenses, the range was from 200 guilders to 280,000 guilders. Factory employees included Chinese, Japanese, and locals.[48] One Taiwanese business in Xiamen had ten or fewer employees in July 1941.[49]

In the field of manufacturing, a Taiwanese merchant in Fuzhou in about 1914 operated a shoe factory with 32 employees, capital expenses of 45,000 yen, and an annual profit of 26,000 yen.[50] In Xiamen, a Taiwanese merchant opened the Guangjian Leather Factory with a local Chinese in 1920 on the Gulangyu international settlement with 62,500 yen as capital. In May 1928, another merchant opened the Huang Chengyuan Ice Factory with 22 employees, and a daily production average of 5 tons of ice. The Jiaji Yanghang Distillery had 80 employees and an annual gross profit of 110,000 yen, capital of 650,000 yen, and a net profit of 50,000 yen. Xinji Yanghang Crystal Sugar Factory, using sugar from Java and selling to Tianjin and Shanghai, was established in about 1917 with capital of 10,000 yen. With 60 employees and 12,000 crates of crystal sugar produced per year, the factory netted a profit of 120,000 yen.[51]

Taiwanese Investment in Public Works

The largest investments were made by the prominent Lin family of Banqiao, Taiwan. Lin Erjia (the son of Lin Weiyuan, who helped Governor Liu Mingchuan in Taiwan to build the wall of Taipei in the 1880s) established the Xiamen Telephone Company.[52] In 1907, Lin Erjia assisted the Xiamen Guild to establish the Common Electrical Appliance Company and install street lamps. Over half of the Xiamen-based Electric Lamp Company's capital of 120,000 yuan was provided by Lin Erjia.[53] In 1909, Lin Erjia answered the call of his relative through marriage, Chen Baochen (the teacher of Puyi, the last Qing emperor), to begin planning a railroad for Fujian province.[54] In 1918, when the Xiamen Merchant Affairs Bureau was established, Lin Erjia was asked to repair the road from Anhai to Quanzhou. Lin Erjia also contributed to the development of the Quanzhou Electric Company.[55] In 1913, Sun Yat-sen called for the development of modern industry, and the Quanzhou region began planning for electrification, but the 10,000 yuan of capital collected by nine well-known locals was insufficient. Since the Lins of Banqiao were related by marriage to the Gong family of Quanzhou, the Lin family entered into the investment, contributing over 80,000 yuan, with an 85 percent share of the total investment. It was only through this arrangement that it was possible to purchase generators to provide light for Quanzhou in 1916. Throughout 1913 to 1921, a relative of the Lin family managed the Quanzhou Electric Company.[56] Furthermore, Lin Erjia's nephew, Xiongzheng, and his uncle, Cai Faping, a merchant in Fuzhou, each contributed 500,000 yen to establish the Ri-Hua Joint Stock Company to mine in Anxi.[57] In 1935, the manager of the Lin family of Banqiao, Xu Bing, carried out three surveys of

Tieshan Mountain in Anxi, Fujian province.[58] Lin Xiongxiang (the grandson of Lin Weirang, Lin Weiyuan's brother) ran a lumber business in Fuzhou and set up the Fuma People's Car Company.[59]

In soliciting investments to establish a sewer system in Fuzhou, Fujian's construction bureau hoped to raise 500,000 yuan from overseas Chinese and 1,000,000 yuan from the provincial government. The bureau guaranteed a return of 5 percent interest every year for three years, and they allowed Taiwanese and foreigners to join in; they solicited a loan from Lin Xiongxiang. In order to pay off old loans and encourage industry and commerce, the bureau borrowed 2,000,000 yuan, and the Fujian finance bureau also sought a loan from Lin of 300,000 yuan to consolidate the province's finances and to encourage industry and commerce. Lin Xiongxiang's loans to the Fujian provincial government for public works in Fujian in 1921–1922 totaled 2,600,000 yen, 120,000 yuan of Fuzhou money, and 410,000 of the Taiwan Bank's yen. They took place about every three weeks.[60]

Another prominent family, the Lins of Wufeng in central Taiwan, made extensive investments in public works as well. Lin Jishang, the son of Lin Chaodong (a general merchant who had helped Liu Mingchuan to defeat the French in Taiwan and who monopolized Taiwan's camphor industry), operated a canal from Longyan to Huating in Zhangzhou, Fujian, establishing it with a capital of 150,000 yen and jointly operating it with Lin Ruiteng, Jishang's brother. In 1911, Lin Jishang's firm received permission from the Chinese government to extend the canal by 80 li. Lin Ruiteng and Lin Jishang set up three steam-powered pumps in Changle County, irrigating 2,000 jia of land. They invested about 30,000 yen in Zhangpu, Zhangzhou, to reclaim over 980 jia of farmland, and they also owned 1,500 jia of forested land in the mountains. Zhangzhou's merchants once asked Lin Jishang to purchase a steamship that could service Zhangzhou and Xiamen. Lin Jishang and Lin Ruiteng also jointly ran a light rail between Quanzhou and Anhai. They also started the Jingkou Cultivation and Herding Company, in 1909, with a capital of 50,000 yen, purchased about 500 jia of land, then an additional 100 jia of farmland and 200 jia of dry farmland, which they reclaimed and used to raise cattle and grow fruit. Lin Jishang, Lin Ruiteng, and Lin Erjia started the Fujian Mining Company in Longyan of Zhangzhou with a capital of 400,000 yen. In 1913, Lin Jishang obtained the Chinese government's permission to mine and sell smokeless charcoal; they produced about 10,000 tons of coal per year, an amount that rose during times of war with increased demand.[61]

By contrast with the previous two Lin families, whose ancestors both came from Fujian and invested heavily in Fujian, the Xiao family, whose an-

cestors were Hakka from Guangdong, invested in Guangdong. Xiao Xindong from Pingdong, in southern Taiwan, went to Shantou, in 1916, to begin a joint venture with a local merchant; they established the Yonghe foreign firm on 80,000 yen of capital, with Xiao and his cousin Xiao Enxiang providing 20,000 yen.[62] Xiao's younger brother Xiao Ranzhao moved to Shantou to serve as consultant to the firm. The firm purchased a mine in the Longfeng region of Guangdong province and began digging. Xiao also provided capital for the Shanzhang Light Rail Company, which purchased ten li of track produced in Osaka from Mitsui Company. The ten-li light-rail line they built connected Shantou and Chenghai.[63]

The extent to which Taiwanese merchants invested in public works ranging from telephone, electricity, and rail to canals, automobiles, steam-powered pumps, and mining in South China was simply not found in Southeast Asia or Manchukuo. Other than the big families, Taiwanese in general played a decisive role in Xiamen and Fuzhou relative to Shantou and Guangzhou in South China.

The Role of Taiwanese Merchants in South China

According to the *Maritime Customs Annual Report* from Xiamen in 1903, "They [the Taiwanese with Japanese nationality] have larger shop signs, and by being able to use the title of 'foreign firm,' they are able to thrive off Chinese merchants and contend for the business [of] other foreign firms. . . . In the same year, Xiamen had 254 foreign firms, 230 of which were owned by Chinese with foreign nationality, and 150 of whom were Taiwanese."[64] A survey by the Taiwan general government in 1929 also reveals that Taiwanese merchants in Xiamen were very influential in political and financial circles; financially, they owned altogether 7,000,000 yen of real estate, and 12,000,000 yen in liquid assets. Twenty of the Taiwanese merchants collectively owned over 100,000 yen, far more than any local Chinese.[65] In 1941, during the Japanese occupation of Xiamen, the major companies and trading firms were run by Taiwanese. Among these major firms, 76 were Taiwanese, while 29 were Japanese, 4 were Fujianese, 2 were Korean, and 2 were non-Fujianese Chinese. In terms of the number of employees, Taiwanese firms had the most; three Japanese firms had over 8 employees, two had 8, and one had 17. Five Taiwanese firms had over 8 employees (10, 11, 12, 22, and 29 employees, respectively). Thus, in terms of scale, Taiwanese firms were larger than Japanese firms.

In Fuzhou, the Taiwanese were fairly powerful in Fuzhou's politics and economy from 1918 to 1921, but their power decreased markedly after 1933

as Chinese overseas students grew more powerful and after the 18 September Incident (also known as the Mukden Incident, which gave Japan the pretext to invade and occupy Manchuria) sparked anti-Japanese sentiment.[66] In Shantou, fourteen Taiwanese firms owned over 10,000 yen in capital in 1934.[67] In Guangzhou, quite a few of the Taiwanese in Guangzhou were laborers, servants, miners, and factory workers; transport workers were particularly common. While prostitution was common, fewer Taiwanese than Japanese joined this trade. Likewise, fewer Taiwanese than Japanese were company employees or workers involved in finance. In addition, quite a few Taiwanese were professionals such as doctors, artists, and reporters. Lastly, some Taiwanese were in the field of industry and commerce, in sundries, foodstuffs, clothing, printing, transport, and trade.[68]

Modest Taiwanese Investment Activities in Manchukuo

Japan wanted to develop Manchukuo on the model of Taiwan, and Taiwan's capital had flowed to Manchukuo. Yet most of it came from the Taiwan general government or from merchants from Japan based in Taiwan.[69] When Taiwan's Lin family of Banqiao visited Manchuria in 1910 and 1932, they were cautious in investing here.[70] This was very different from the situation in Xiamen, where Taiwanese merchants including the Lins of Banqiao made major investments. In 1935, the native banking industry in Fujian, dominated by Taiwanese capital, provided about 70 percent of capital for trade between Fujian and Taiwan, leading even the Bank of Taiwan.[71] This was also the opposite of the situation in Manchukuo, where Japanese capital led Taiwanese resources.

Not only did linguistic and cultural similarities cause Taiwanese to migrate and invest more in South China, but trade between the two countries was also quite developed.

Cultural Networks and Trade

Quite a few Taiwanese merchants were engaged in trade between Taiwan and South China. For example, in 1924 Gu Xianrong operated a 161-ton Japanese-registered ship, the Jinzhou Hao, between Fuzhou and Quanzhou.[72] Jian Shiyuan, who was born in 1898 and lived in the Taiping street area in Taipei, built Guangshengtang in Xiamen in 1932; he was elected six times as president of the Taiwanese Association in Xiamen. He set up a branch of his company in Guangdong, dealing in medicine and trade.[73] Shi Tianshou, born in Tainan city in 1892, set up the Heyu Shipping Company in 1910, went to Xiamen to work for the postal service in 1920, and in 1927 set up the Yiquan

Yanghang, a trading firm. In addition, he served as head of the Xiamen Export Union's fourth section, the director of the Xiamen Import and Export Union's Federation, a member of the Xiamen residents' association's assembly, a director of the Xiamen finance union, and a council member of the Xiamen trade hall.[74]

With trade networks like this, the value of Taiwan's trade with south Fujian actually comprised an average of 72.72 percent of all of Taiwan's trade value with China between 1902 and 1912. After 1913, the percentage gradually dropped: by 1931 the average was 51.3 percent, and between 1932 and 1937 the average was 50.6 percent.[75] Taiwan's volume of trade with South China was twice that with Southeast Asia in 1922 and eight times that in 1935.[76] This somewhat describes the effect of cultural relations on trade, because Taiwan's cultural relations with South China were closer than those with Southeast Asia. However, in Taiwan's case, we see the influence of Japanese policy and power manifesting itself in increased immigration to, investment in, and trade with South China.

Japanese Policy and Power

When Taiwanese engaged in economic activities out of Taiwan, legally, they had to apply for the Japanese passport. This passport allowed Japanese people to enjoy extraterritorial rights while they were in China or some Southeast Asian countries, and it also gave them closer access to Manchukuo.

PASSPORT SYSTEM

Article 2 of the Treaty of Shimonoseki, signed between Qing China and Japan in 1895, reads: "China cedes to Japan in perpetuity and full sovereignty, the following territories together with all fortifications, arsenals, and public property thereon." The "following territories" denote the island of Formosa and the Pescadores. Article 5 of the same treaty conveys, "The inhabitants of the territories ceded to Japan, who wish to take up their residence outside the ceded districts, should be at liberty to sell their property and retire. For this purpose a period of two years from the date of the exchange of the present Act [5 May 1895] shall be granted. At the expiration of that period those of the inhabitants who shall not have left such territories shall, at the option of Japan, be deemed to be the Japanese subjects."[77]

As Japanese subjects, the Japanese from Japan proper (naichijin 內地人) were not required to carry Japanese passports when they entered China. Article 4 of the Treaty of Commerce and Navigation between China and Japan had allowed Japanese nationals to move and reside freely in China's

treaty ports. As the passport was aimed at ensuring that Japanese subjects in China could gain protection from their consuls in the destination country, no passport was needed unless going inland. However, Taiwanese with Japanese nationality, hontojin 本島人, had to apply for a passport to enter China. Since Taiwan had been China's territory before its cession to Japan, the movement of people across the Taiwan Straits had been controlled after cession.

For the general population to travel from China to Taiwan for business or personal matters, a certificate from the government on the China side was required as regulated in September 1895. Before 1898, to prevent anti-Japan violence from being fanned, laborers from China were prohibited. Between 1898 and 1905, desperately needed tea workers from China were allowed in. From 1905 to 1937, all laborers from China were required to come with the agency of a Japanese-run Nanguo gongsi (Nankoku kaisha), which provided certificates allowing them to enter Taiwan or return to China. Between 1937 and 1945, people from China were generally not allowed to enter Taiwan.[78]

People moving from Taiwan to China had to go through a more thorough passport system. In 1878, the Japanese government issued its Passport Act. In April 1897, as the deadline for the Taiwanese to decide whether to stay as Japanese nationals or to leave drew near, the Taiwan governor-general ordered that those who stayed and registered in each district and prefecture could follow the 1878 Passport Act when traveling to China or other countries. However, those going to China still required special investigation. Before 1907, the attachment of photographs to certificates was encouraged, but not enforced, because many Taiwanese still feared to have their photograph taken due to the belief that their soul would thereby be stolen. The submission of certificates for household registration was also flexible, as the system was not established until 1907. From 1907, certificates were required. In Japan, photographs were not required until 1918, while in Taiwan the requirement was introduced in 1907. In special cases, a guarantee from a local notable was required. Japanese nationals from Japan or Korea could also apply for a passport in Taiwan via a similar process, but applicants who were financially better-off could proceed faster. After Japanese nationals arrived at their destination, they had to register with the Japanese consul there. The passport application had to be made at the prefecture. The passport application section of the local government had moved from the general affairs section to the police section in 1901. On the application form, applicants had to provide information on their name, native place, birth date, current residential address, profession, title, travel destination, and purpose of travel.

Taiwanese who went directly to China from Japan without applying for a passport could be fined, depending on the circumstances: a Taiwanese in Japan who made an urgent visit to his dying father in China without applying for a Taiwanese passport in Japan could be pardoned; but an anti-Japan Taiwanese on the same route would be fined.[79] The discretionary nature of the fine opened loopholes for smuggling criminals or anti-Japanese Taiwanese into China.[80] Of the sixty to seventy Taiwanese who sneaked into China from the ports of Japan through Shanghai to Fujian, fewer than 10 percent used the cross–Taiwan Strait junks, and 30–40 percent bribed sailors of Osaka Steamship Company to hide them in cabins while passing through the Taiwan Strait.[81]

The Japanese passport illustrated in figure 6 lists the holder as belonging to the category of merchant (merchant category no. 6776). The passport notes his Taiwan address (17, Chome 2, St North Gate, Taipei, Taipei district), age (42), business (antiques), and the port (Tamsui) and date of departure (29 April 1900). A photo of Li Zhishan, wearing a mandarin robe, is attached. "Passport of the Japanese empire" was stamped by the Minister of Foreign Affairs. The main text asks protection for the bearer of the passport. The bearer filled out the destination of his travel (Xiamen and Fuzhou of the Qing empire and Hong Kong under the British rule). On the left fold of the passport, there are Chinese, English, and French translations of the main elements on the right fold. In addition, a handwritten addendum given by the Taipei prefect claimed that this passport could be renewed when it expired three years after issuance.

The Japanese passport, though troublesome to obtain, provided Taiwanese in China with the advantage of not having to pay local taxes or be molested by local bullies as the Japanese consuls protected them. Like overseas Chinese from Southeast Asian countries who had taken up French, British, Dutch, or Spanish nationalities, the Taiwanese could now hold a foreign passport to open "foreign firms" (yanghang 洋行) in China.[82] Even the local notables in South China attempted to obtain this kind of passport in order to be one of Taiwan's registered people.[83]

Japan took Fujian as its sphere of power after 1898, just as France had taken Southwest China; England, the Yangtze Valley; Germany, Shandong; and Russia, Xinjiang, Mongolia, and Manchuria. Taiwanese or Fujianese notables could serve as intermediaries for the penetration of the Japanese empire into South China. By contrast with the Chinese immigrants in Japanese colonial Taiwan, who were poorer than Taiwan's notables, the Taiwanese in Fujian were better off than the locals.[84] In Xiamen, Japanese nationality

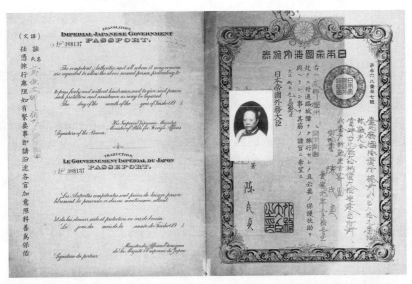

Figure 6 Overseas passport of the Japanese empire. A passport issued by the imperial Japanese government in 1917 for use by Taiwanese people for travel to China. Reproduced courtesy of Chang Tun-chih.

was preferred over that of the European countries as the latter would have involved military conscription and the inheritance taxes exempted by the Japanese nationality.[85] The Dutch assimilation law issued in 1907 required a familiarity with spoken Dutch, the possession of wealth, the obligation of military service, and the equal division of property among sons and daughters in accord with Western, and not Oriental, ideas of justice.[86] By contrast, Japanese naturalization in the early twentieth century required no racial or geographical condition of birth. Those who had lived in Japan for more than five years, were more than twenty years of age, of good morals, possessing property or the ability for self-maintenance, and had no other nationality could be naturalized. Marriage and adoption were two other routes to becoming a Japanese national.[87] The Taiwanese in the Dutch East Indies paid fewer taxes than the Chinese there, and overseas Chinese often tried to gain Japanese nationality.[88] For the latter, doing business in Taiwan was one avenue to achieving Japanese nationality.[89] As Japan's southern advance policy took the alliance of Taiwan and South China as the basis for the further alliance with Southeast Asia, the Japanese government generally welcomed the naturalization of these overseas Chinese in Southeast Asia.[90] The overseas Chinese from Southeast Asia received more advanced technology for investment from their association with the Taiwanese. For example, when overseas

Chinese from Java, Penang, and Hong Kong invested in the railway construction in Shantou, they obtained Japanese technology through the introduction of a co-investor from Taiwan.[91]

This period witnessed a series of boycotts against the Japanese goods, as these movements often drove up the prices of the Japanese goods sought after by the market and eventually earned the Taiwan-Japanese profit.[92] The power or policy of the Japanese government also made South China lose out relative to Manchuria as Taiwan's main trading partner after Manchukuo was set up, in 1932. The Sino-Japanese War put the Taiwanese in opposition to the Chinese under the rule of Chiang Kai-shek.

POLITICS-ECONOMICS TRUMPED CULTURE

Before 1932, the entire Chinese mainland was governed by the Republic of China. Between 1932 and 1944, Manchuria fell out of China's de facto control. During the period between 1902 and 1932, the value of Taiwan's trade with Fujian made up the greatest portion of the value of Taiwan's trade with the Republic of China.[93] Between 1925 and 1927, the value of Taiwan's trade with South China was greater than its trade value with Manchuria, but from 1928 to 1939, the value of trade with Manchuria quickly surpassed the value of trade with South China. Although there was more smuggling between Taiwan and South China than between Taiwan and Manchukuo, the value of Taiwan's legal trade with Manchuria increased rapidly between 1932 and 1939 and made up 67.6 percent of Taiwan's total value of trade with the Chinese mainland, while during the same period, that with South China only comprised 11 percent on average.[94] During this period, the value of Taiwan's trade with Manchukuo was six times that of Taiwan with Fujian and eight times that of Taiwan with Southeast Asia (see fig. 7). Taiwan's trade with Manchuria generally fluctuated around the level between that of 1938 and 1939 until 1941, and then declined after 1943 when Japan increasingly lost control of Manchuria with the increasing threat from Russia and the Chinese communists.[95]

Taiwanese who participated in the Taiwan-Manchuria trade include notables such as Liu Xinshui, born in 1897 in Luliaokeng, Qionglin Village, Zhudong County, Xinzhu Prefecture, who worked to expand the marketing network for Taiwanese citrus fruits in Manchukuo, Korea, and Tianjin; and Liu Zongmiao, born in 1880 in Sanxia Town, Haishan County, who became a tea master (who graded the quality of tea) for the Mitsui Tea Company in 1927, and set up the Nanxing Yanghang in 1932 to export tea. In 1941,

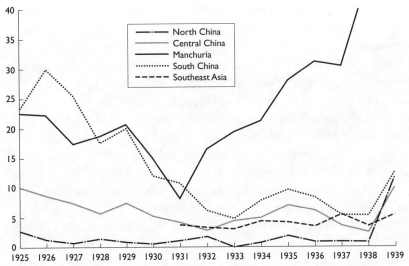

Figure 7 Changes in the value of trade between Taiwan and various regions of mainland China, and Southeast Asia, 1925–1939. *Source*: Calculated and combined from the following trade records: for 1925–1926, Taiwan sōtokufu kanbō chōsaka, *Shina no jikyoku to Shina bōeki no shōchō*, 170; for 1927–1936, Taiwan sōtokufu kanbō gaijika, *Taiwan to Minami Shina (bōeki)*, 43; for 1937–1939, Taiwan Sōtokufu zaimukyoku zeimuka, *Taiwan tai nan-Shi nan'yō bōekihyō (tsuki chū-Shi, hoku-Shi, Manshūkoku, Kantōshū)*, 1.

Liu Zongmiao began serving as a council member in the Taiwan Tea Export Union for Manchukuo and China.[96]

An important factor for the more dominant Taiwan-Manchuria trade was Manchukuo's advantage over South China and Southeast Asia of being compatible with Taiwan in terms of a regional division of labor. In agricultural production, both Taiwan and Southeast Asia were at the development stage: Taiwan produced sugar, rice, and tea, the major products of Southeast Asia, and besides several fruits that could not be grown in China due to the climate, Taiwan's products were also grown in China in large amounts.[97] Other industries, such as fishing, timber, or mining, were "identical" with resources on the Chinese mainland; very few products were unique enough to find a profitable niche.[98] Thus, the economies of South China, Southeast Asia, and Taiwan did not share complementary functions. In contrast, there was a great demand for Taiwan's abundant fruits and vegetables in the cold climate of Manchukuo, and Manchukuo's bean-cakes could be used as fertilizer in Taiwan. Thus, even though Taiwan's distance from Dalian was far greater than the distance between Dalian and mainland China, it came to be

that the tonnage of freight transported between Taiwan and Dalian was second only to that of Dalian freight with Japan, far outweighing the tonnage of freight between Dalian and any other place in China.[99]

Relations between Taiwan and Manchukuo were also encouraged by the Japanese government, as evidenced by the establishment of a branch of the Bank of Taiwan and the increase in shipping. After the 18 September 1931 Incident, the surge in anti-Japanese sentiment in South China and Southeast Asia harmed Taiwan's trade position there.[100]

The 18 September Incident led to the establishment of Manchukuo, and the 7 July Incident of 1937 put Manchukuo under even greater influence from Japan. These two incidents led Taiwan to replace China as the major provider of tea to Manchukuo, especially after Taiwan's tea market in Southeast Asia dried up due to anti-Japanese sentiment. These two incidents, in which Japan invaded China and earned the enmity of the Chinese people, actually received a positive appraisal in Taiwan. Chen Rongsen, of the Dadaocheng-based Rongxing Tea Company, was quoted in the *Taiwan Nichinichi Shinpo*, during his 1933 inspection tour of Manchukuo, as having said, "As tea sales have slumped, the tea farmers who grew tea for me deem the addition of the Manchukuo market as a lucky star."[101] When Japan invaded China, in 1937, prominent tea merchant Chen Qingpo was deeply moved by the "valiance" of the "imperial army," calling it a "holy war" (*sheng zhan*). When Chen visited Mongolia to work on developing the market for Taiwanese tea, he said, "The untrustworthiness of Chinese merchants has earned the hatred of the Mongolians." Further, he said, "Now, the Japanese empire is leading these peoples to establish a great East Asian union."[102]

In 1938, when the Japanese army occupied South China, the power of Taiwanese merchants in South China expanded greatly. They provided running water, electricity, banks, hospitals, newspapers, food cans, marine products, garments, ships, intelligence, and even opium for the Japanese army.[103] In the process of the Sino-Japanese War, the Chongqing government planned to take Xiamen as "a base from which airfields could be used to bomb Japan and Taiwan."[104] When Japan started to invade China after 1937, many local students acquiring a Japanese education at a Japanese-sponsored school in Xiamen withdrew, while several Taiwanese students at the school celebrated the victory of the imperial army.[105] Even though both Taiwanese and the Fujianese shared the same culture, they now belonged to two nation-states in conflict.

Conclusion

In view of the overseas migration of Taiwanese merchants during the period of Japanese rule, the Taiwanese diasporic rate is less than 1 percent, even including those who had migrated to Japan.[106] It is less than the 16 percent of Japanese from Japan in 1935.[107] However, the size of Taiwanese immigration and investment was still big when compared with other internationals. Yang Duanliu's and Hou Houpei's *Statistics of China's Foreign Trade during the Last Sixty-five Years* has listed the annual number of people from various countries in China between 1872 and 1928. The peak years for each nationality in China were as follows: Russia had 148,170 nationals in China in 1919; the United States had 9,356 in 1923; England had 15,247 in 1925; and Japan had 239,180 in 1928.[108] The presence of around 20,000 Taiwanese in China in the 1930s and 1940s was more than the number of American or British people in the 1920s. Yang also had statistics of international firms in China. Using the 150 Taiwanese firms in Xiamen in 1903 as a basis for comparison, the various internationals had the following firm numbers in China in the same year: England had 420; Japan had 361; the United States had 114; Portugal had 45; Spain had 29; Russia had 24; and Norway had 7.[109] The Taiwanese had 171 firms in 1938 in Xiamen.[110] In 1941, Taiwanese commercial power in Xiamen was stronger than that of the Japanese from Japan in terms of firm number and employment rate. Japanese foreign-affairs records indicate that there were approximately 171 Taiwanese firms in Southeast Asia from 1935 to 1940.[111]

These Taiwanese firms were involved in various trades, from salty fish to cameras. In general, their scale was small, but they could be involved with big enterprises such as factories, plantations, mining, banks, and even public works such as telephones, electric power, canals, and railroads. When the American robber barons such as Leland Stanford, Cornelius Vanderbilt, Andrew Carnegie, John D. Rockefeller, and J. P. Morgan invested in railroads, mines, telephones, telegrams, and finance and industry at home and abroad, including China between the 1880s and 1930s, the Taiwanese joined this investment fever in South China.[112] Overseas Chinese from Southeast Asia also invested in Fujian's urbanization. An example was Huang Yizhu (1868–1945), a Fujian-born merchant in Indonesia who was the most important real-estate investor among the overseas Chinese in Fujian from 1927 to 1935, and who was described as the biggest investor among the overseas Chinese merchants in modern China by Lin Jinzhi, an overseas Chinese his-

torian in the PRC. Huang was vice chairman of Xiamen's chamber of commerce in 1920, while the Taiwanese Lin Erjia was its chairman.[113]

By contrast with other internationals, the Taiwanese had the advantage of speaking the same dialect with some people in Fujian and Guangdong Provinces. They could also rely on the bloodline-based Chinese nationality law to acquire Chinese nationality. Relatives and friends could help them to find work and invest in the interior area, which legally excluded foreigners, including Japanese, and to which the Taiwanese now legally belonged. In Southeast Asia, the Taiwanese also shared the same dialects or ethnic traits with the overseas Chinese communities there, whereas the Mandarin used in Manchuria was a foreign language to the Taiwanese under Japanese colonial rule. The cultural affinity certainly explains the greater immigration and investment of the Taiwanese in South China and Southeast Asia as compared with that in Manchuria.

On the other hand, the Taiwanese, considered Japanese subjects according to the Treaty of Shimonoseki, carried the status of foreigner in China. In the late nineteenth century and early twentieth, many Chinese people tried to obtain foreign nationality in the treaty ports of China so as to avoid lijin and other political harassment from the unstable Chinese government.[114] Even in Southeast Asia, some overseas Chinese coveted Japanese nationality.[115] The legal identity of Taiwanese cast them as intermediaries for the Japanese southern advance policy in South China and Southeast Asia, demonstrating the cross-fertilization of the cultural affinity of the Taiwanese and Japanese policy and power.

Yet, when Japan set up Manchukuo, in 1932, Taiwan traded more with the latter than with South China or Southeast Asia, due to its Japanese infrastructure and the comparative advantage that Taiwan gained through selling tropical agriculture products in exchange for Manchurian soybean, coals, and fertilizer. In particular, when Japan was at war with China, the Taiwanese found that their status as Japanese subjects overrode their cultural affinity with the Chinese.

Unlike the Chinese in Malaya under British rule, whose rice trade was replaced by the British, as described by Wu Xiaoan, Taiwanese indigenous capital under Japanese colonial rule had the chance to develop overseas.[116] Through the passport system, the Japanese government had actually screened Taiwanese merchants abroad through the legal process.

As with the overseas Chinese in Southeast Asia, the Taiwanese merchants had legal investments as well as investments in opium or other illegal businesses. Carl Trocki describes the relationship between Southeast Asian

opium development and the European imperialist powers, particularly the British Empire.[117] John Jennings had depicted the Japanese government's opium policy in Japan proper and in its colonies without mentioning its relationship to the Taiwanese merchants' overseas opium trade.[118] In Taiwanese investment in Manchukuo, even the Lins of Banqiao, the Lins of Wufeng, and the Lius of Liuying had cooperated with Manchurian people in setting up an opium factory in Manchukuo.[119] In Thailand and South China, the Taiwanese used their extraterritorial privileges to sell opium or to engage in terrorist activities, and they left a terrible impression on locals.[120] Liang Huahuang had pointed out the Japanese consul's guidance of Taiwanese opium cultivation and marketing to cooperate with local warlords.[121] Zhong Shumin provided evidence of the Japanese consul's tolerance, elimination, and encouragement of the sale of Taiwanese opium.[122] Wu Lingjun's study reveals an institutional background to the link between extraterritorial rights and crime. It was not because the foreign powers intended to nurture crime in the treaty ports, but because the foreign powers tended to lack the manpower to police and enforce laws overseas. Wu's study is based on an American case in the 1850s–1860s, when the American consuls' prisons in China's treaty ports had been so full that they were forced to borrow the British consuls' prisons, from which some criminals escaped.[123]

The Taiwanese selling opium in Thailand in 1919, for example, had little contact with the Japanese consuls, and were reluctant to make known their Japanese nationality.[124] However, that the Taiwanese tea traders had declared of "Holy War" because Japan had opened a bigger market for them through the Mukden and Marco Polo Bridge incidents fully reveals the Taiwanese identification with Japan. With Japan having ruled over Taiwan for about fifty years, the governmentality and subjectivity had become deeply entrenched. The process of Taiwanese "becoming Japanese" was a process that put both the Taiwanese and the Japanese government in the same boat. The Taiwanese were not only ready to die for the Japanese emperor, as Leo T. S. Ching notes, but were also seeking their own benefit while staying with the Japanese empire.[125]

In PRC scholar Lin Jingzhi's history of overseas Chinese investment in China, the chairman of the chamber of commerce and a leading Taiwanese in South China, Lin Erjia, was described as a "Taiwan compatriot," while the vice-chairman, Huang Yizhu, was categorized as overseas Chinese because he was from the Dutch East Indies.[126] In fact, however, all of Lin Erjia's sons carried Japanese nationality, and Lin's family endorsed many businesses in Xiamen promoted by the Japanese government.[127] Lin Erjia's family, which

carried multiple nationalities, including French, British, Japanese, and Chinese, was similar to the overseas Chinese merchant Guo Chunyang, who was from the Dutch East Indies but adopted Dutch, British, Japanese, and Chinese nationalities.[128] Neglecting the fact that the Taiwanese, under Japanese colonial rule, were in fact also overseas Chinese prevents greater reflection on the concepts of the "Greater China Economic Zone" and the "Global Chinese Network." The ways in which the Japanese government utilized Taiwanese cultural traits to promote its southern advance policy and Japan's war with China illustrate the extreme power of culture, as well as its limits.

Notes

I would like to thank Joseph Wicentowski for helping to edit preliminary drafts of this paper.

1. Leo Suryadinata, ed., *Ethnic Chinese as Southeast Asians* (Singapore: Institute of Southeast Asian Studies, 1997); Leo Suryadinata, *Chinese Adaptation and Diversity: Essays on Society and Literature in Indonesia, Malaysia and Singapore* (Singapore: Singapore University Press, 1993); Wang Gungwu, *Community and Nation: China, Southeast Asia and Australia* (Sidney: Allen and Unwin, Asia Studies Association of Australia, Southeast Asia Publications series, 1992).

2. Marie-Sybille de Vienne, "For a Tentative Modelization of the Economic Weight of Overseas Chinese at the Beginning of the Third Millennium," Fifth International Conference of the International Society for the Study of Chinese Overseas, 10–14 May 2004, Copenhagen, available at the Nordic Institute of Asian Studies website, http://www.nias.ku.dk/.

3. The trade statistics for Manchukuo in this period sometimes include Guandongzhou, which was leased territory (zujiedi 租借地) in Dalian and Lushun transferred to Japan from Russia after the Russo-Japan War. Leased territory denotes areas in the treaty ports leased to foreign powers for their absolute military, judicial, and administrative rule. The leasing countries set military commanders there, and even the passage of the Chinese army through this territory required the permission of the leasing country. Chinese nationals or subjects of the leasing country and other internationals in this territory were subject to the judicial rule of the leasing country rather than Chinese judges or consuls of related countries, as in concessions or settlements (zujie 租界). In the concessions or settlements, the government or private foreigners had to pay rent or taxes for the land they rented. The leased territory in some sense meant territory ceded temporarily. Russia's leased territory in Lushun and Dalian was obtained from Qing China in 1898 with a lease of twenty-five years. Russia set a governor-general there as the highest official and named this area Guangdong Province, in 1899. After taking the province, in 1905, Japan set the commander-in-chief office of its Guangdong army there, where it remained until 1945, and changed the name to Guandongzhou. Fei Chengkang, *Zhongguo zujieshi* [A history of China's concessions or settlements] (Shanghai: Shanghai shehui kexueyuan chubanshe, 1991), 312–18, 432.

4. Shibaoka Hisashi, *Saishin nanpō tokō an'nai* [Information on recent immigration to the south] (Taipei: Sanseidō, 1943), 20.

5. In this essay, I use "investment" to mean direct investment, not absentee security or bond investment.

6. Ihara Suekiti, *Seikatsujy ō yori mitaru Taiwan no jissai* [Taiwan as seen from its daily life] (Taipei: Shinkōto, 1926), 77–78.

7. Taiwan sōtofuku kanbō gaijika, *Taiwan to Minami Shina (bōeki)* [Taiwan and southern China (trade)] Minami Shina oyobi nan'yō chōsa, dai 236 shū (Taipei: Taiwan sōtofuku, 1937), 13.

8. Lin Zhen, "Kangzhan shiqi Fujian de Taiwan jimin wenti" [The problem of registered Taiwanese in Fujian during the war of resistance], *Taiwan yanjiu jikan* [Bulletin for Taiwan Study] 2.44 (February 1994): 71.

9. Yoshikawa Hiroshi, "Amoy shōhin chinretsukan setsuritsu shuisho" [Purpose and plans explanation note for the establishment of Amoy's commodity exhibition center], *Minami Shina kenkyūshi* (Osaka: Osaka keizai shinbunsha, 1920), 372.

10. Taiwan sōtokufu kanbō chosaka, *Taiwan zaiseki kan minzoku gyokanbietsu chosa* [An investigation of the native place distribution of the Han people registered in Taiwan] (Taipei: Taiwan sōtokufu kanbō chosaka, 1928). This source lists 586,900 Hakka and 3,000,900 Fujianese.

11. See Man-houng Lin, "The Taiwanese Merchants' Taiwan-China Economic Ties, 1895–1937," *China in the Growth of the Asian International Economy, 1850–1949*, ed. Kaoru Sugihara (Oxford: Oxford University Press, 2005), 217–43, 222–26.

12. Calculated from Taiwan sōtofuku kanbō gaijika, *Taiwan to Minami Shina*, 13.

13. Ide kiwata, "Taiwan to Minami Shina" [Taiwan and southern China], *Tōyō* [Asia] 40.41 (1938): 135. Of the 741 Japanese nationals in Shantou, 605 were Taiwanese.

14. Cheng Meixiang, "A Comparative Study of the Foreign Settlements at Tamsui of Taiwan and Inchon of Korea (1858–1913)" (in Chinese), master's thesis, department of architecture, Zhongyuan University, 2002, 8–9, cited the Taiwan general government's archive to point out the difference between concessions and settlements in the treaty ports. The former rented whole pieces of land to the foreign government, which leased or sold part of that land to its own subjects. The latter allowed foreigners to rent land piece by piece from private owners in the zone of treaty ports.

15. Gaimusho joyakukyuku, *Nihonkoku oyobi kaku kuni aida no joyaku* [Treaties between Japan and various countries] (Tokyo: Gubisu shuppansha, 1936), 51–52. The distance of Chinese li is obtained from Herbert A. Giles, *A Chinese-English Dictionary* (Taipei: Ch'engwen Publishing, 1978), 864, entry 6870.

16. Bian Fengkui, trans., *Zhongcun xiaozhi jiaoshou lunwenji: Riben nanjin zhengce yu Taiwan* [Collected essays of Professor Nakamura Koshi] (Taipei: Daoxiang chubanshe, 2002), 205.

17. In the treaty ports in Fujian such as Fuzhou and Xiamen, no particular concession or settlement for the Japanese nationals was set up. Fei Chengkang, *Zhongguo zujieshi*, 431.

18. Bian Fengkui, *Zhongcun xiaozhi jiaoshou lunwenji*, 150.

19. Fujiansheng dang'anguan and Xiamenshi dang'anguan, eds., *Min-Tai guanxi dang'an*

ziliao [Archival materials on Fujian-Taiwan relations] (Xiamen: Lujiang chubanshe, 1992), 11–12, 635.

20. Taiwan sōtofuku kanbō gaijika, Taiwan to Minami Shina, 18–19.

21. Harley Farnsworth MacNair, The Chinese Abroad: Their Position and Protection: A Study in International Law and Relations (Shanghai: Commercial Press, 1933), 121–27. See also Man-houng Lin, "The Multiple Nationality of Overseas Chinese Merchants: A Means for Reducing Commercial Risk," Modern Asian Studies 35.4: 985–1010.

22. Taiwan sōtofuku kanbō gaijika, Taiwan to Minami Shina, 18–19. Fujiansheng dang'anguan and Xiamenshi dang'anguan, Min-Tai guanxi dang'an ziliao, 18–20.

23. Taiwan Nichinichi Shinpo (abbreviated as Nichi hereafter), Taisho (abbreviated as Thereafter) 2.8.26. The nightly courses were taught by an instructor who had lived in Java and Singapore for many years, and who was fluent in the languages spoken and well-versed in the local situations in each location. Regular and rapid-pace courses were offered, each six months in duration.

24. Ōta Shūkichi, 'Taiwan sekimin no nan'yō ni okeru katsudō jōkyō' [The activities of Taiwan registered people in Southeast Asia], Taiwan keizai nenpō [Annual report of Taiwan economics] (Tokyo: Taiwan keizai nenpō kankōkai, August 1942), 671–94.

25. Nichi, Showa (abbreviated as S hereafter) 16.10.7.

26. Kurozaki Zunichi, "Taibei gaodeng shangye xuexiao yu nanzhi nanyang yanjiu," master's thesis, department of history, National Taiwan Normal University, 2002, 25.

27. Ibid., 29, 33, 43.

28. Yang Jiancheng, "Erci dazhan Riben qiye liyong Riji Huaqiao shentou Nanyang qiaoshe miwen" [Secret information about Japanese enterprises' utilizing overseas Chinese with Japanese nationality to penetrate into Southeast Asia], Hongguanbao, 28 January 1994.

29. Shengjing Shibao (abbreviated as Sheng hereafter), S13.8.9.

30. Zhongyang yanjiuyuan jindaishi yanjiusuo [The Institute of Modern History, Academia Sinica], Koushu lishi (Oral history), no. 5 (ed. Xu Xueji), 1994, 318.

31. Sheng, S13.8.9.

32. Taiwan Jihō Hakkōjo, "Nanshi nan'yō ni okeru Hontōjin" [Taiwanese in South China and Southeast Asia], Taiwan jijō (Taipei: Taiwan Jihō Hakkōjo, 1944), 164–68.

33. Nichi, T8.3.22.

34. Nichi, T6.1.21.

35. Nichi, S13.3.17.

36. Zhongyang yanjiuyuan jindaishi yanjiusuo, Koushu lishi, no. 5 (ed. Xu Xueji), 1994, 318.

37. Man-houng Lin, "'Greater East Asia Co-Prosperity Sphere': A New Boundary for Taiwanese People and Taiwanese Money, 1940–1945," paper presented at the Eighteenth International Asian History Association Conference, 8 December 2004, Academia Sinica, Taipei.

38. Lin Zhen, "Kangzhan shiqi Fujian de Taiwan jimin wenti," 72.

39. Teki shusei, "ZaiKō Taiwan jin no kinkyō" [The recent situation of the Taiwanese in Shanghai], Taiwan jihō (Taipei: Taiwan jihō hakkōsho, May 1938), 159.

40. Nichi-Japanese version (abbreviated as J hereafter; not specifying Nichi as Japanese version means it is the Chinese version), T13.7.6.

41. Nichi, S16.6.5 and Nichi, S17.7.4 show that most of the two hundred Taiwanese living in Bangkok were in business.

42. Zhongyang yanjiuyuan jindaishi yanjiusuo, *Koushu lishi*, 206.

43. Yoshikawa Hiroshi, *Minami Shina kenkyūshi*, 376.

44. Nichi, S16.6.5.

45. Man-houng Lin, "The Taiwanese Merchants' Taiwan-China Economic Ties, 1895–1937," 222–26.

46. As the original documents reproduced show, in Fujiansheng dang'anguan and Xiamenshi dang'anguan, *Min-Tai guanxi dang'an ziliao*, 8–9, 31–34, 640–46.

47. Nihon Gaimushō (Ministry of Foreign Affairs of Japan), *Kaigai zailiu honbojin chosa* [Investigation of the Japanese nationals], Showa 10, Showa 11, Showa 15.

48. Ibid.

49. Fujiansheng dang'anguan and Xiamenshi dang'anguan, *Min-Tai guanxi dang'an ziliao*, 640–46.

50. Taiwan sōtokufu kanbō chōsaka, *Taiwan, Nanshi nan'yō, dai ni bu: Nanyō* [Taiwan, southern China, and Southeast Asia, 2d part: Southeast Asia] (Taipei: Taiwan sōtokufu, 1935), 16. The monetary unit this paper uses will follow the sources cited. The exchange rate between the British pound and the currencies of the United States, France, Germany, India, Japan, Russia, and Mexican silver dollars between 1868 and 1928 refers to Yang Duanliu and Hou Houpei, *Liushiwu nian lai Zhongguo guoji maoyi tongji* [Statistics of China's foreign trade during the last sixty-five years] (National Research Institute of Social Sciences, Academia Sinica, 1931), 151. One Japanese yen equals 1.2 yuan (silver dollars) in 1927. Also, by 1927 one yuan (silver dollar) was about 0.50 US$ and it was 0.30 US$ after 1927. See Lin Jinzhi, *Jindai huaqiao touzi guonei qiye gailun* [A sketch of the overseas Chinese investment in China in the modern period] (Xiamen, Fujian: Xiamen daxue chubanshe, 1988), 56n1.

51. One crate equals forty catties (units of weight used in Southeast Asia equal to 500 grams, approximately 1.1 pounds).

52. Lin Benyuan jisi gongye, *Banqiao Linbenyuan jiazhuan* [The family biography of the Lins of Banqiao] (Taipei: Lin Benyuan jisi gongye, 1985), 55.

53. Taiwan sōtokufu, *Nettai sangyō chōsa: Nanshi nanyō ni okeru shinbun: Nanshi nan'yō ni okeru hōjin no keizai no katsudō jōkyō* [Survey of the production of the tropical areas, newspapers, Japanese nationals' economic activities] (Taipei: Taiwan sōtokufu, 1935), 19.

54. Lin Benyuan jisi gongye, *Banqiao Linbenyuan jiazhuan*, 55.

55. Chinese Maritime Customs, *Decennial Report, 1912–21, Amoy* (Shanghai: Chinese Maritime Customs, 1921), 159.

56. Zhongguo renmin zhengzhi xieshang huiyi, *Quanzhou wenshi ziliao* [Literary and historical materials collected by Quanzhou committee] (Quanzhou: Quanzhou wenshi ziliaoshi, 1987), 3:5–6.

57. Nakamura Takashi, *Nihon no nanpō kanyo to Taiwan* [Japan's southern involvement and Taiwan] (Nara: Tenrikyō dōyūsha, 1988), 264.

58. Nihon Gaimushō, Gaimushō kirōku: From General Consul Usomi to Prime Minister Hirota Kōki about Taiwanese investment in Fujian heading by Lin Xiongxiang (24 January 1935).

59. As Mr. Lin Hengdao recalled.

60. Nihon Gaimushō, Gaimushō kirōku: From General Consul Usomi to Prime Minister Hirota Kōki about Taiwanese investment in Fujian heading by Lin Xiongxiang (24 January 1935).

61. Nichi, M37.10.9; Nichi, T6.1.7.

62. The Xiao family from Pindong of Taiwan are Hakka from Chaozhou of Guangdong.

63. Yoshikawa Hiroshi, *Minami Shina kenkyūshi*, 399; Yoshikawa Seima, *Sengo no Nanshi nan'yō to Taiwan* [Postwar Taiwan, southern China, and Southeast Asia] (Taipei: Taiwan jitsugyō sha, 1925), 45.

64. Guoshiguan shiliaochum, *Zhonghua minguo haiguan huayang maoyi zongce, 1903, Amoy* [Chinese maritime customs: Trade reports and returns] (Taipei: Guoshiguan shiliaochu, 1982), 759.

65. Taiwan sōtofuku kanbō gaijika, *Taiwan to Minami Shina*, 21–22.

66. Nakamura Takashi, " 'Taiwan Sekimin' ni kansuru sho mondai" [Various problems relating to the "Taiwan registered people"], *Nanpō bunka* [Southern culture] 17 (November 1990): 134.

67. Taiwan sōtofuku kanbō gaijika, *Taiwan to Minami Shina*, 24–25.

68. Tanaka sen, "Minamishina (Kanton) to Taiwan renkei no hōto" [Approaches for the liason between southern China (including Guangdong province) and Taiwan], *Taiwan jihō* (Taipei: Taiwan jihō hakkōsho, December 1943), 49–50.

69. Huang Qiongyao, "Riju shiqi de Taiwan yinhang, 1899–1945" [The Bank of Taiwan during the Japanese colonial period], master's thesis, National Taiwan Normal University, 1991, 93; *Sheng*, S11.6.25, S11.10.2.

70. *Sheng*, M43.5.24; Nichi, S7.7.26.

71. Ide Kiwata, "Tai Shi bōeki no fushin to Taiwan bōeki no shinkōsaku" [The slump in trade with China and the policy to promote Taiwan's trade], *Taiwan Jihō* (Taipei: Taiwan jihō hakkōsho, October 1931), 52.

72. Nihon Gaimushō, Gaimushō kiroku: nanyō ryōji kaigi [Records of: Consulars' meeting], 6 May 1924, Mitaku Tetsuichirō Jimukan.

73. Kōnan Shimbunsha, ed., *Taiwan Jingzhi kan* [Almanac of Taiwan's notables] (Taipei: Shinnan Shimbunsha, 1943), 103.

74. Ibid., 181.

75. Man-houng Lin, "Taiwan yu dongbei jian de maoyi, 1932–1941" [Trade between Taiwan and Manchuria, 1932–1941], *Zhongyang yanjiuyuan jindaishi yanjiusuo jikan* [Bulletin of the Institute of Modern History, Academia Sinica] 24 (June 1995): 653–96; Man-houng Lin, "Qiaoxiang Ties versus Japanese Maritime Power: Trade between Taiwan and Manchuria, ca. 1932–1939," *Chinese Diaspora, Since Admiral Zheng He, with Special Reference to Maritime Asia*, ed. Leo Suryadinata (Singapore: Chinese Heritage Center, May 2007), 137–59.

76. Tamiya Ryōsaku, "Minamishina to Taiwan" [Southern China and Taiwan], *Taiwan*

jihō (Taipei: Taiwan jihō hakkōsho, March 1938), 10. It cites *Taiwan bōeki yonju'nen hyō*, *1896–1935* [40 years of tables on Taiwan's trade, 1896–1935] (Taipei: Taiwan sōtokufu, 1936) and mentions that Taiwan's volume of exports to major cities in South China was 11,083,000 yen in 1922, and 16,687,000 yen in 1935; in comparison, Taiwan's volume of exports to Southeast Asia was 5,034,000 yen in 1922 and 2,861,000 yen in 1935.

77. Gaimusho joyakukyuku, *Nihonkoku oyobi kaku kuni aida no joyaku*, 20–21.

78. Wu Wenxing, *Riju shiqi zaiTai huaqiao yanjiu* [A study of the Chinese nationals in Taiwan in the Japanese colonial period] (Taipei: Taiwan xueSheng shuju, 1991), 1–17.

79. Liang Huahuang, *Taiwan zongdufu de "duian" zhengce yanjiu: Riju shidai TaiMin guanxi shi* [The cross–Taiwan Strait policy of the Taiwan governor-general: The Taiwan-Fujian relation in the period when Taiwan was occupied by Japan] (Taipei: Daoxiang, 2001), 131–82.

80. Bian Fengkui, *Rizhi shiqi Taiwan jimin zai haiwai huodong zhi yanjiu (1895–1945)* [A study of Taiwan registered people's overseas activities, 1895–1945] (Taipei: Lexue shuju, 2006), 142–46.

81. Bian Fengkui, *Zhongcun xiaozhi jiaoshou lunwenji*, 94.

82. Ibid., 75.

83. Liang Huahuang, *Taiwan zongdufu de "duian" zhengce yanjiu*, 184–90.

84. Ibid., 51–58, 184–90; Man-houng Lin, "The Taiwanese Merchants' Taiwan-China Economic Ties, 1895–1937."

85. Bian Fengkui, *Zhongcun xiaozhi jiaoshou lunwenji*, 107.

86. MacNair, *The Chinese Abroad*, 107.

87. Ibid., 127.

88. Detailed in Man-houng Lin, "The Multiple Nationality of Overseas Chinese Merchants," 985–1010. Also, see Bian Fengkui, *Zhongcun xiaozhi jiaoshou lunwenji*, 89.

89. Man-houng Lin, "The Multiple Nationality of Overseas Chinese Merchants."

90. Liang Huahuang, *Taiwan zongdufu de "duian" zhengce yanjiu*, 40.

91. Bian Fengkui, *Zhongcun xiaozhi jiaoshou lunwenji*, 111; Lin Jingzhi, *Jindai huaqiao touzi guonei qiye gailun*, 167–68.

92. Bian Fengkui, *Zhongcun xiaozhi jiaoshou lunwenji*, 173–74.

93. Taiwansheng wenxian weiyuanhui, *Taiwansheng tongzhi* [A comprehensive history of Taiwan province], jingjizhi (economy), shangye pian (chapter on commerce) (Taipei: Taiwansheng zhengfu yinshua chang, 1971), 4:174.

94. Man-houng Lin, "Taiwan yu dongbei jian de maoyi, 1932–1941," 690–91.

95. Taiwan sōtokufu, *Taiwan tōsei gaiyō* (Taipei: Nantian shuju, 1997), 459–60.

96. Shimbunsha, *Taiwan Jingzhi kan*, 444.

97. Danan, "Taiwan jingji yu nanyang," [Taiwan's economy and the Southeast Asia], *Taiwan yinhang jikan* [Quarterly of the Bank of Taiwan], 1st issue (Taipei: Taiwan yinhang jingji yanjiushi, June 1947), 155.

98. Ye Lizhong, "Taiwan jingji zai Zhongguo" [Taiwan economy in China], *Taiwan yinhang jikan* [Quarterly of the Bank of Taiwan], 1st issue (Taipei: Taiwan yinhang jingji yanjiushi, June 1947), 132.

99. Man-houng Lin, "Taiwan yu dongbei jian de maoyi, 1932–1941," 663, 672–87; Man-houng Lin, "Qiaoxiang Ties versus Japanese Maritime Power."

100. For detailed discussion on Taiwan and Manchuria, see Man-houng Lin, "Taiwan yu dongbei jian de maoyi, 1932–1941," 665–69; for Taiwan and Southeast Asia, see Danan, "Taiwan jingji yu nanyang," 151–152; and Man-houng Lin, "Culture, Market, and State Power: Taiwanese Investment in Southeast Asia, 1895–1945," International Economic History Congress, 20–25 August 2006, Helsinki; for Taiwan and South China, see Man-houng Lin, "The Taiwanese Merchants' Taiwan-China Economic Ties," 229–31.

101. Nichi, S8.4.12.

102. Nichi-J, S12.12.27.

103. Detailed in Man-houng Lin, " 'Greater East Asia Co-Prosperity Sphere.' "

104. Disan zhanqu JinXia hanjian anjian chuli weiyuanhui, Mintai hanjian zuixing jishi [An account of the criminal actions of the Fujian and Taiwan traitors] (Xiamen: XiamenjiangSheng wenhua chubanshe, 1947), 14.

105. Liang Huahuang, Taiwan zongdufu de "duian" zhengce yanjiu, 192–94.

106. The nonsoldier Taiwanese emigration was about 60,000 by 1945 (see Man-houng Lin, " 'Greater East Asia Co-Prosperity Sphere' "); the population of Taiwan in this year was six million (see Chen Shaoxing, Taiwan de renkou bianqian yu shehui bianqian [Taiwan's population change and social change] [Taipei: Lianjing chubanshe, 1979], 18).

107. The number of immigrants from Japan in 1935 (1,151,462) is obtained from Gaimushō chōsabu, Kaigai kakuchi zairyū honpōjin jinkōhyō. [The population of Japan in 1935] (69,254,148) is obtained from http://www.stat.go.jp/data/kokusei/2000/kako/danjo/zuhyou/dao2.xls by the instruction of Hori Kazuo.

108. Yang Duanliu and Hou Houpei, Liushiwu nian lai Zhongguo guoji maoyi tongji, 143–48.

109. Ibid., 143–48.

110. Nichi-J, S12.12.27.

111. Nihon Gaimushō, Kaigai zailiu honbojin chosa, Showa 10, Showa 11, Showa 15.

112. Walter LaFeber, The American Search for Opportunities, 1865–1913, vol. 2 of The Cambridge History of American Foreign Relations (Cambridge: Cambridge University Press, 1993), esp. chap. 2, "The Second Industrial Revolution at Home and Abroad," 21–44. Thanks to Wu Lingjun for this reference.

113. Lin Jingzhi, Jindai huaqiao touzi guonei qiye gailun, 80.

114. MacNair, The Chinese Abroad, 112–120.

115. Man-houng Lin, "The Multiple Nationality of Overseas Chinese Merchants."

116. See Wu Xiao An's essay in this volume.

117. See Carl A. Trocki's essay in this volume.

118. John M Jennings, The Opium Empire: Japanese Imperialism and Drug Trafficking in Asia, 1895–1945 (Westport, Conn.: Praeger, 1997).

119. Nichi, S8.3.10; Nichi, S8.11.7.

120. Oda Shūkichi, "Taiwan sekimin no Nanyō ni okeru seidō jōkyō," Taiwan keizai nenpō (Tokyo: Taiwan keizai nenpō Kankōkai, 1942), 682.

121. Liang Huahuang, Taiwan zongdufu de "duian" zhengce yanjiu, 110, 114, 116, 117, 220–22.

122. Zhong Shumin, "Taiwan zongdufu de duian zhengce yu yapian wenti" [Taiwan

general government's opium policy in South China], *Taiwansheng wenxianweiyuanhui, Taiwan wenxian shiliao zhengli yanjiu xueshu yantaohui lunwenji* [Conference proceedings on Taiwan historical materials and its arrangements] (Nantou Taiwansheng wenxian weiyuanhui, 2000), 223–54, 229, 248–51.

123. Wu Lingjun, "Tiaoyue guanxi yu Qingmo Meiguo zaihua shangwu: Yi lingshi bude jian shangren yu tongshang kouan she gongchang liangan wei li" [Treaty relations and American business in China: To take consuls not being supposed to do business and setting factories at treaty ports as examples], *Guoli zhengzhi daxue lishi xuebao* [Historical journal of National University of Political Science], no. 26 (November 2006): 29–64, 40.

124. Nihon Gaimushō Kiroku 3–8–6–34 (kō [public] no. 130): A document sent from acting Japanese consul at Xiamen, Ishikawa Noboruya, written on 5 May 1919 to Japanese Minister of Foreign Affairs Baron Uchida Kōsai, received on 13 May 1919, regarding the situation of Koreans and Taiwanese in Bangkok.

125. Leo T. S. Ching, *Becoming "Japanese"* (Berkeley: University of California Press, 2001), 97.

126. Lin Jingzhi, *Jindai huaqiao touzi guonei qiye gailun*, 80, 209.

127. Liang Huahuang, *Taiwan zongdufu de "duian" zhengce yanjiu*, 188n12.

128. Man-houng Lin, "Riben zhimin shiqi Taiwan yu Xianggang jingji guanxi de bianhua: Yazhou yu shijie guanxi diaodong zhong zhi ti fazhan" [The change in economic relations between Japanese colonial Taiwan and Hong Kong: A chapter in the structural change in the relationship between Asia and the world], *Zhongyang yanjiuyuan jindaishi yanjiusuo jikan* (Bulletin of the Institute of Modern History, Academia Sinica) 36 (December 2001): 47–115, 66. Regarding the merchant Guo Chunyang, see Man-houng Lin, "The Multiple Nationality of Overseas Chinese Merchants"; Guo Chunyang is listed as overseas Chinese in Lin Jingzhi, *Jindai huaqiao touzi guonei qiye gailun*, 301.

RICE TRADE AND CHINESE RICE MILLERS IN
THE LATE-NINETEENTH AND EARLY-TWENTIETH CENTURIES
The Case of British Malaya

~~~~ Wu Xiao An

Rice is currently the second-largest-produced cereal in the world, and about 90 percent of the world's rice production and consumption, 50 percent of imports, and 72 percent of exports are concentrated in Asia. The global rice-export market is also very concentrated, although it consists of only 5 percent of total rice production. In line with postwar political and economic changes, many Asian countries have implemented rice self-sufficiency policies, while China and the United States have emerged as the two most important rice exporters. Over the last decade, Thailand was the largest exporter, accounting for around 25 percent of global trade. Vietnam ranked second (around 17 percent), and the United States was third (around 12 percent). China (4th), India, Pakistan, and Myanmar (10th) were also major exporters.[1] Within Southeast Asia, among the top rice-importing countries currently are Indonesia (1st), Philippines (8th), and Malaysia (9th).[2]

Historically, mainland Southeast Asia has been the major world rice exporter, with the rice-export market centered on three delta areas—the Irrawaddy in Burma, the Chao Phraya in Thailand, and the Mekong in Vietnam. As with other agricultural products such as pepper and other spices, regional and long-distance trade in rice and other commodities has always existed.[3] However, it was not until the 1850s that these delta areas started to emerge as major world rice-export centers, driven by the colonial expansion, the increasing demand (initially from Europe and later from India and Japan), the flows of immigrant labor, infrastructure improvement, and technological advancement. Besides faster demographic growth, one outstanding feature of Southeast Asia is that domestically, a clear division of labor was organized in line with ethnic boundaries. The indigenous people of Burma, Thailand,

and Vietnam became farmers while Indians migrated to the Irrawaddy delta to become wage laborers, moneylenders, and small businessmen, as did the Chinese in the Chao Phraya and Mekong deltas. Regionally, a clear division of labor was organized in line with national boundaries. The mainland Southeast Asian countries of Thailand, Burma, and Indochina functioned as the major rice exporters, accounting for four million tons each year (prior to the First World War), more than 90 percent of the world rice export and half the value of their total exports.[4] While the maritime Southeast Asian countries of British Malaya, the Dutch Indies, and the Spanish and American Philippines were the major rice importers, where the colonial economy depended on the tin-mining, rubber, and other cash-cropping plantations and immigrant Chinese, capital and labor also played a leading role.[5]

"Rice production and supplies have always ranked as a problem of first importance with the government because the rice situation dominates all other industries and it is necessary to the progress of the country," as one prominent Chinese rice miller in Penang insightfully observed.[6] If rubber and tin were the two main props for the colonial economy of British Malaya, then rice and opium were another two main sources for maintaining labor and government. The prosperity of both the opium and rice economies resulted from the expansion of the tin and rubber economies. The immigrant labor was the core link between the production (rubber and tin) and consumption (rice and opium) economies. The prosperity of tin and rubber brought into Malaya a large number of immigrants, who came not as paddy producers, but as wage labor and rice consumers. This large new immigrant community not only provided an indispensable labor force for the colonial production economy, but also provided a huge new profitable market for the immigrant consumption economy.[7] As Carl Trocki's research has shown, opium not only provided the main revenue source for the colonial government and for Chinese towkays, but also became a daily necessity for Chinese labor. Therefore, opium formed an integral part of the colonial social order and a capital accumulation for the beginnings of Chinese capitalism.[8] Just as labor was the mainstay of the colonial rubber, tin, and opium economies, so was rice. Cheap rice means cheap food; cheap food means cheap labor; while cheap labor means cheap costs, more profits, and continued economic prosperity for the interests of rubber planters, tin miners, and the government. The depressive tin and rubber market in turn also influenced the rice and labor situations, which brought social instability and even crisis. These could be the dynamics of the colonial political economy.[9]

However, although the rice-milling industry was a prosperous and profit-

able business in British Malaya, the Chinese did not engage in the commercialization of rice cultivation, which was left to the Malays. The colonial government did encourage Chinese capitalists for such commercial cultivation in the 1890s and 1930s, but was not successful. This is not only because tin-mining and rubber and other cash-crop plantings, such as sugar and coconut, were more profitable and attractive than rice cultivation itself, but also because cheap and good-quality rice from mainland Southeast Asia was usually available. Interestingly, besides rubber planting, the established rice millers in Penang—such as the Lim brothers, Cheng Teik and Cheng Law, and the Choong brothers, Lye Hock and Lye Hin—were also among the most important coconut-oil millers in early-twentieth-century Malaya. Of course, the founding fathers of established rice millers in Penang, such as Lim Leng Cheak and Choong Cheng Kean, were also the most important opium farmers in Kedah, which again confirms that the development of the Chinese rice-milling industry and of rubber planting was based on the capital accumulation of the revenue (opium) farms.[10]

Prior to the Second World War, British Malaya mainly depended on rice imports, which comprised over 60 percent of its total consumption. In the early 1950s, efforts were made, and British Malaya's domestic production of rice accounted for 55 to 60 percent of total requirements.[11] The production peaked around 90 percent in the late 1970s and about 85 percent in the early 1980s due to the Green Revolutions.[12] However, the Malaysian domestic rice supply was steadily declining, and Malaysia was becoming "the Asian country most reliant on rice imports."[13] Malaysian rice imports were projected to rise marginally from 1998 to 2005, as continued small declines in rice area were more than offset by rising yields resulting from the higher productivity.[14] These days, the Malaysian government targets 65 percent self-sufficiency in rice production, and it is believed that Malaysia remains dependent on rice imports for 30–40 percent of its supply. This is attributed to the impact of more profitable industrial crops such as palm oil and coconut, competition arising from the trade liberation driven by globalization and the implementation of the ASEAN Free Trade Agreement (AFTA), and urbanization.[15] It is no wonder that the Malaysian government deems rice a security issue, not only because it is the staple food for most Malaysians, but also because of their high dependence on international imports, which exposes the state's vulnerability in case of international political, economic, and nature-based turmoil. In fact, Malaysia has experienced such lessons many times in history due to wars, depressions, and natural disasters.

Rice Trade

For a long time, the world rice trade was dominated by the three mainland Southeast Asian countries of Siam, Burma, and Indochina.[16] Around 20 percent of world rice production originated in Southeast Asia from 1920 to 1990, but the region dominated the world market up to the Second World War with 80–90 percent of world rice exports.[17] Throughout most of Southeast Asia, the rice trade was dominated by the Chinese, and mostly by one clan, the Teochieu. They handled exports to Hong Kong, mainland China, Singapore, Malaya, and other Asian markets.[18] Although Indian and European merchants initially dominated this field in Burma, Chinese rice millers made substantial inroads during the 1930s.[19] The rice trade in British Malaya was no exception, and it was largely monopolized by Chinese merchants, who formed a close-knit trading network linked by credit, kinship, and guild associations. However, the Chinese rice traders were largely Hokkien and Teochieu.[20]

Malaya was the largest single rice importer among Southeast Asian countries. In 1920, for example, 69.9 percent of Malaya's total rice supply depended on imports; it was 66.7 percent in 1931, and 62.5 percent in 1941. Malaya imported 50 percent of its total rice imports from Siam, 43 percent from Burma, and 5 percent from Indochina.[21] Between 1918 and 1929, Malaya produced an annual average of 197,000 tons of rice, while it imported 408,000 tons of rice each year over the same period.[22] Singapore was the most significant entrepôt in the rice trade. Rice was imported from three mainland Southeast Asian countries and re-exported from Singapore to the Malay Peninsula and the Dutch Indies, from Hong Kong to Japan and the Philippines, as well as mainland China. Singapore handled up to 40 percent of Siam's exports. Over half the rice import, up to 80 percent in some years between 1871 and 1939, was re-exported from Singapore.[23] Prominent Singapore-based Chinese merchants such as Tan Kim Ching, Khoo Cheng Tion, and Tan Kah Kee owned large rice interests in Bangkok, Saigon, or Singapore.[24]

Within the Malay Peninsula, Penang, Malacca, and Kuala Lumpur were another three subregional distributing centers that functioned as secondary nodes. Unlike Singapore, Penang mostly imported rice from Rangoon, as well as very small quantities from other countries. Compared to Siamese rice, Rangoon rice was much cheaper and consumed by Hokkien Chinese, Malays, and some Tamils, which was in contrast with the other Chinese consumers in Singapore and the Dutch Indies, who preferred Siamese-quality

rice. The rice was exported from Burma to Penang and re-exported to Sumatra and the hinterlands of the Malay Peninsula. However, in 1920, due to the improvement of port facilities in Belawan (Deli), the greatest changes in Penang trade occurred when the Dutch took to shipping rice directly from Rangoon instead of importing through Penang as before. The Federated Malay States not only imported rice from Penang, but also got it by rail from Siam and Perak.[25]

Rice Milling

The other pattern of rice trade concerned the local rice-milling business in northern Malaya.[26] These millers dealt mainly in local rice milling, rather than rice from mainland Southeast Asia. These millers were situated in or near the large rice-producing districts of Kedah, Province Wellesley, Penang, and north Perak (Krian). The local rice millers also sold rice to the rice dealers and merchants categorized above. However, there were usually two different systems of rice trade that functioned in their own respective areas without much direct interaction, with each influencing, complementing, and even competing with the other through market forces, such as supply and price elements. Unlike the rice industry in mainland Southeast Asia, where the expansion of rice cultivation and export was driven by the demand from the world market, both in Southeast Asia and beyond, the commercialization of the rice industry in Malaya was mainly due to the tin and rubber boom and immigrant labor, and oriented to the local market in the Malay Peninsula, although a small portion was exported to outside markets such as Sumatra and China.[27] Moreover, unlike mainland Southeast Asia, where the commercialization of rice cultivation and export was the predominant source of revenue, in the premier paddy-cultivation state of Kedah, rubber also became another important revenue item.

Except for their own local paddy, Penang and Perak depended mainly on Kedah for their paddy supply. Paddy was imported from Kedah, and milled in Penang, Perak, and Province Wellesley. Besides a certain proportion consumed locally, the milled rice was exported to other Federated Malay States, northern Sumatra, even to Ceylon, and sometimes to Hong Kong and mainland China. At the local level of Kedah, the rice millers were concentrated in northern Kedah, centering on the Kota Star district. The rice and paddy trade route followed a course from west to east, then moved south to Penang and the southern state of Perak. The port of Kuala Kedah, near Alor Star, was the major loading point in the Muda region. Ports at Kuala Perlis, Langkawi, and Yen formed the hinterland collections of Kuala Kedah.[28] The rice miller

made both white rice and parboiled rice, with the latter especially prepared for the consumption of Indian estate labor.[29]

There were three types of commercial rice mills. The first comprised large and medium-sized commercial mills in Penang, Kedah, Province Wellesley, and Perak, which were controlled by a few Penang Chinese. The second type comprised small and medium-sized commercial mills, situated mainly in Kedah, partly in Penang, Province Wellesley, and Perak. Most of these mills were still dominated by Chinese, but with some Malay participation in Kedah, particularly in the 1930s. The third type comprised the government mills, namely Bagan Serai mill (built in 1919) and Kuala Kurau mill (acquired in 1924) in Perak, and Anak Bukit mill (built in 1940) in Kedah. The latter two types of mills mainly operated independently to compete with the first type of mill.

In communal terms, Chinese, mostly Hokkien and a few Hakka, dominated the rice milling, while Malays were mainly involved with rice cultivation. One prominent Penang Hokkien Chinese miller disclosed that rice milling was "almost entirely in the hands of the Chinese, who were originally pioneers in the trade. And in former years good profits were made by millers and the partners. Some of the Chinese rice-milling firms in Penang [had] acquired large fortunes in times past."[30] In marketing terms, the rice-milling structure included two stages and seven channels. The rice mill was a core linkage between the production and consumption. The first stage of the paddy-collecting and rice-manufacturing process was from production to the mills. The second stage of the rice sale was from the mills to consumption. The Chinese shopkeeper usually advanced money to the Malay paddy farmers so that he could have their crops after harvest. The Chinese shopkeeper would be associated with a Chinese miller, from whom he got credit to finance the paddy.

Rice Combine

The history of the rice-milling industry and community in northern Malaya (1880s–1941) features the following characteristics. First, there had been a rice-milling hierarchy that was controlled by a few Penang Chinese families. Second, Chinese rice millers made endless efforts to form a combine to coordinate the regional trading networks. Third, parallel to the rice combine was the change of the rice-milling community and its leadership. At the regional level, the hierarchy was controlled by a few of the interrelated Penang Chinese families, who formed a top layer of the Chinese rice millers' pyramid. They were the Phuah (Lim) Hin Leong family, the Lim Leng Cheak

Table 1 The Penang Chinese Families Controlling Regional Milling Interests, 1880s–1941

No.	The First Generation	The Second Generation
1.	Phuah Hin Leong	Lim Cheng Teik
		Lim Cheng Law
2.	Lim Leng Cheak	Lim Eow Hong
		Lim Eow Thoon
3.	Choong Cheng Kean	Choong Lye Hock
		Choong Lye Hin

Source: Wu Xiao An, *Chinese Business in the Making of a Malay State, 1882–1941: Kedah and Penang* (London: RoutledgeCurzon, 2003), 128.

family, and the Choong Cheng Kean family.[31] These families' control over the rice-milling networks continued through the second generation, namely the brothers Lim Cheng Teik and Lim Cheng Law, of the Phuah (Lim) Hin Leong family; the brothers Lim Eow Hong and Lim Eow Thoon, of the Lim Leng Cheak family; and the brothers Choong Lye Hock and Choong Lye Hin, of the Choong Cheng Kean family (see table 1). The rice-milling business history of northern Malaya before the Second World War was basically their family history.[32]

The establishment of pioneer rice mills can be traced back as far as the 1880s. The first rice mill in Penang was Khie Heng Bee, which was jointly established by Phuah Hin Leong, Lim Leng Cheak, and Chuah Yu Kay. Some years later, the partnership was dissolved. Phuah Hin Leong took over the entire shareholdings of Khie Heng Bee. Lim Leng Cheak built up his own rice mill, Chop Chip Hong Bee, around the late 1880s. In 1889, Lim Leng Cheak had another rice mill, Chop Chip Bee, in Kedah. These two families controlled the regional rice-milling and -trade markets in the 1890s. In the late 1900s, Chuah Yu Kay built another rice mill in Penang, named Sin Khie Bee. In 1909, their scions brought together four Penang rice mills—Phuah Hin Leong's Khie Heng Bee, Lim Leng Cheak's Chop Chip Hong Bee, Chuah Yu Kay's Sin Khie Bee, and another mill named Joo Cheang Company—to form the Tai Chuan Company rice-milling ring.[33]

Tai Chuan Company may be considered the predecessor of the Rice Milling Agency, the regional milling organization that was formally opened in January 1913. There were altogether seven mills in the rice combine: four in Penang, one in Kedah, one in Parit Bundar (Perak), and one in Prai, Province Wellesley (see table 2).[34] Its Chinese name was Tai Yu Company, and it

Table 2 Mills Controlled by Rice Milling Company, 1913

Mill	Principal Owner	Place
Chip Hong Bee	Lim Eow Thoon	Penang
Khie Heng Bee	Lim Cheng Teik	Penang
Ban Hock Bee	Choong Lye Hock	Penang
Joo Cheang and Company	Khoo Sin Hoh	Penang
Chip Bee	Lim Eow Hong	Alor Star/Kedah
Kwong Mee	n/a	Prai/Province Wellesley
Kwong Jin	Heah Swee Lee	Parit Bundar/Perak
	Leong Fee	

Source: Wu Xiao An, *Chinese Business in the Making of a Malay State, 1882–1941: Kedah and Penang* (London: RoutledgeCurzon, 2003), 129.

held capital of \$1,000,000, which was divided into twenty shares. Its main purposes were to avoid competition and reduce risk on the one hand, and to monopolize the northern Malayan rice-milling and -trading market, on the other. Indeed, there were three other rice mills outside the combine that belonged to the same families in the milling syndicate. These were Choong Lye Hin's Ban Hin Bee and Lim Cheng Law's Cheng Law and Company in Penang, and the Kwong Hin Mill in Parit Bundar (Perak). This arrangement may have been a strategy to deal with public opinion and the government, as there was strong public debate in the local newspapers.[35] As one commentator observed, "It would appear to be a sort of family arrangement to work for mutual profit while keeping up a semblance of competition."[36]

The partnership agreement of the rice combine covered five years, till 1918. During this period, the combine closed three mills: one on Penang Island and two in Province Wellesley, of which two of the Penang mills had been put out of action by fire.[37] Therefore till the end of 1918, there were a total of eight large rice mills in the region. Another important development was the decision of the government to build mills in Kedah and Krian, which finally broke up the combine. In 1918, the partnership agreement terminated and the partners carried on business independently until 1919. In January 1919, the Rice Milling Company was again formed. In September 1919, the partners entered into a supplementary agreement and changed the name to the Central Milling Agency, with capital of \$1,650,000. The seven mills were controlled by the Central Milling Agency (see table 3). Former key member Lim Eow Thoon ceased to be a partner.[38] Another important member, Lim Cheng Teik, left in 1919 to take up the management of the government mill

Table 3 Mills Controlled by Central Milling Agency, 1920

Mill	Owner	Place
Ban Hock Bee	Choong Lye Hock	Penang
Cheng Law and Company	Lim Cheng Law	Penang
Ban Hin Bee	Choong Lye Hin	Penang
Ban Hin	n/a	Alor Star/Kedah
Kong Foh	n/a	Kuala Kurau/Perak
Kwang Hang	Tan Lo Heong	Parit Bundar/Perak
Kong Mee	n/a	Prai/Province Wellesley

Source: Wu Xiao An, *Chinese Business in the Making of a Malay State, 1882–1941: Kedah and Penang* (London: RoutledgeCurzon, 2003), 148.

at Bagan Serai, Perak. At this point, Choong Lye Hock and Choong Lye Hin started to play an important role in the milling ring, although there were other new members such as Cheng Law and Company.

The Central Milling Agency continued to operate until 1925, when it ceased to be registered in the Singapore and Malayan Directory.[39] Now the firm controlling the Chinese milling and buying ring in Kedah and Penang was Messrs. Hock Hin Bros., although there was no formal name for the combine organization (see table 4). The mills paralleled or competed with two government mills, one in Bagan Serai and one in Kuala Kurau.[40] In 1934, the daily capacity of the Choong family mills was 2,000 bags, with each bag weighing 170 katis, or 225 lbs., and this daily capacity equaled the total amount produced by all fourteen large and medium-sized mills in the state of Kedah at that time.[41] In 1938, the rice millers in Kedah, Penang, and Province Wellesley were again formally amalgamated and formed into a company with a capital of $500,000. The primary object was "to buy paddy economically and to sell rice at a moderate and fair profit," as the local press stated.[42] The rice combine referred to the controlling firm, Hock Hin Bros. Company.

Government Policy on Paddy Cultivation

In British Malaya, the government policy on paddy cultivation was determined by two main interrelated factors: the availability of cheap rice on the international market, on the one hand, and the continued prosperity of the rubber and tin-mining economy on the other. If this situation remained unchanged, any criticism of the government's prewar food policy would be useless. There were two conflicting schools of thought on the subject of rice production during the colonial period. One held that rice production should

Table 4 Rice Mills Belonging to the Choong
Family in the 1930s

Name	Place
Ban Hock Bee	Penang
Ban Hin Bee	Penang
Ban Heng Bee	Alor Star / Kedah
Ban Kean Bee	Parit Bundar / Perak
Ban Eng Bee	Nibong Tebal / Province Wellesley

Source: Wu Xiao An, *Chinese Business in the Making
of a Malay State, 1882–1941: Kedah and Penang*
(London: RoutledgeCurzon, 2003), 158.

be encouraged by all possible means so as to reduce dependence on external sources of supply. The other maintained that agricultural prosperity had been built on a foundation of rubber and tin exports, and that with the availability of cheap rice on the international market, large-scale effort and expenditure on domestic rice production could possibly lead to a loss of prosperity.[43] The government policy prior to 1930 generally followed the latter view, although there were some government efforts to promote paddy planting in the late 1890s and early 1910s. However, the government reconsidered its position after 1930, and the former view was subsequently pursued. The 1919 food crisis, the 1931 slump, and the Second World War no doubt contributed to this change of view.

As far as the local paddy-producing state of Kedah was concerned, two basic factors had to be taken into account in government policymaking. First, Kedah was the premier state for paddy cultivation in Malaya. Second, unlike other Unfederated Malay States (UMS), rubber planting in Kedah was the number one agricultural revenue source. Kedah government policy hence had to find a balance between the two crops. Two aims were consequently established: first, the Kedah government had to serve British strategic interests by supplying cheap food for the Straits Settlements and Federated Malay States (FMS); and second, it had to promote its own state interests of increasing state revenue, guaranteeing the food supply for its rubber-planting population, and ensuring the welfare of the Malay peasantry. Reflected in the paddy-cultivation policy was the role of the government in encouraging and supporting paddy cultivation, and the increase in the acres and amount of paddy crop. Reflected in the policy on rice milling and trading was its care-

ful watch and effective control over the movement of paddy and rice, and the issue of price and export duty.

Government and Chinese Rice Millers

The government policy on Chinese rice millers had two targets: one was the Penang rice combine, and the other, Chinese rice millers in general. In dealing with the former, the Kedah government cultivated competition by encouraging the Kedah Chinese milling industry to be independent of the Penang Chinese. The government tackled the Penang Chinese regional rice-milling monopoly by declaring the rice combine illegal, by getting a Chinese from Kedah to open a new mill, and by breaking up the rice-mill monopoly—previously granted by the sultan—of Lim Leng Cheak in Kedah. However, the government found itself in a conflict of interest where Malay paddy farmers were concerned.[44] The issue of price control was an irreconcilable problem between the state government and Chinese rice millers. The latter tried to enhance the price of rice and depress the price of paddy; while the state government, on the contrary, aimed to depress the price of rice and enhance the price of paddy. In order to achieve their respective aims, both state government and Chinese rice millers clashed in a showdown of control and anti-control. Chinese millers organized themselves as regional milling networks to coordinate the milling and trading market, reduce competition, and maximize profit. In competition with the Chinese millers, the state carried out a series of measures by establishing government mills, encouraging internal Chinese competition, setting up a credit society for the Malay peasantry, and initiating cooperative movements.

Central to the issues of price and export duty, the interaction between the state and Chinese millers had been subject to the interchanges between the government's administrative and political intervention, on the one hand, and the competition and free play of market forces on the other, with each influencing the other. These elements, which influenced the price of rice and paddy in Kedah and Penang, were subject to fluctuations in the international rubber and tin markets in general, and the rice market in particular. The price was also greatly influenced by natural and political conditions, including pests, cattle disease, and war. Whenever they occurred, paddy supplies decreased sharply, while demand rose. These special circumstances, in turn, further affected the government policy of liberal trade, which was replaced by market intervention in terms of food restriction and control (see table 5). In theory, prices eventually depended on the changing relationship of production and consumption, or supply and demand. But, as the

Table 5 The Natural and Political Situations in Kedah for the Rice-Trading Policy, 1910–1940

Year	Cause	Policy
1910–1911	Cattle disease	Restriction
1911–1912	Failure	Prohibition
1914–1915	War	Prohibition
1919–1920	Food crisis	Food control
1920–1921	Food crisis	Food control
1923–1924	Drought	Restriction
1925–1926	Drought and pest	Restriction
1927–1928	Drought	Restriction
1929–1930	Drought	Restriction
1936–1937	Flood and stem rotting fungi	n/a
1939–1940	War	Food control

Source: Wu Xiao An, "Chinese Family Networks in the Making of a Malay State: Kedah and the Region, 1882–1941," Ph.D. diss., University of Amsterdam, 1999, 268.

demand or consumption in Malaya had been certain and instant, the price of paddy, therefore, was mainly subject to one-sided change in the production and supply market. Basically, under normal circumstances, the price of paddy depended on two main factors: one was the cost of imported rice into Malaya; and the other was the abundance of local crops that influenced supplies of paddy for the mills in Kedah and Penang.

The Price

The government also attempted to compete with the rice combine by erecting a government rice mill at Alor Star. The state council invited J. Reid, a managing partner in a very large rice mill in Rangoon, to visit Alor Star and report on the situation there. In February 1914, Reid submitted a detailed report, recommending the erection of a government mill and expressing confidence in its success.[45] However, the preparations and discussions took a long time.[46] In 1918, the high commissioner informed the British adviser in Kedah that he should advise the state council to take over management of the Alor Star rice mill at once. Legislation was then passed giving the government power to take over the mill. The scheme was estimated to cost $368,600 and would take eighteen months to complete. However, the problem was how to get access to the relevant experienced management and trading networks. In particular, if the object was "to reduce the cost of rice

to the consumer, the most detailed elaboration is required," as the British adviser reported.[47] This scheme was eventually set aside. It was only in 1939 that the government rice mill was put into action at Anak Bukit. Once it was completed on 23 July 1940, the Kedah government took it over.[48] The Perak government made a similar attempt, between 1917 and 1920, to oppose the Chinese rice combine through the establishment of government rice mills in the Krian district. Two mills were built: one at Bagan Serai and the other at Kuala Kurau. The Bagan Serai mill was erected by the government, while the Kuala Kurau mill was formerly owned and operated by Chinese. From 1 September 1924, the Kuala Kurau mill was taken over by the government, but it was closed down in 1926 for lack of paddy supply.[49]

As the establishment of government rice mills was to influence the paddy price, both the governments of Kedah and Perak maintained good coordination on this issue. In discussing a food-decontrol proposal in the beginning of 1921, the government mill in Perak was prepared to offer $4.30 per picul for Kedah paddy delivered at Bagan Serai railway station, while the Central Milling Agency would not commit to any statement as to price. Four Chinese shops were appointed agents for the government mill with a total paddy supply of 18,000 piculs.[50] However, in March 1921, the Kedah Agent Food Control requested the sum of $10,000 for the purpose of buying from the *raiats* [peasants] through the medium of *penghulus* of *mukims* [heads of villages] and forwarding it to the Bagan Serai government mill. The principal object was to eliminate the "middleman," who bought paddy from the raiats and sold it to the mills at a good profit. They said that the middleman made a profit of about $5 per kuncha when exporting to the Perak government mill. Before long, a further $10,000 was again requested by the Agent Food Control.[51] After the Kuala Kurau mill was acquired by the government in 1924, the manager immediately wrote to the British adviser in Kedah, requesting that the penghulus and paddy planters be informed that government mills in Perak were prepared to purchase any paddy. The paddy might be delivered either at Bagan Serai by rail or at Kuala Kurau by junk.[52] Under the arrangement of both governments, the prominent Kedah Chinese merchant Goh Soon Leong was appointed the buying agent, serving between 1924 and 1928.[53]

In order to raise the price in Kedah, H. W. Jack, economic botanist of the Straits Settlements and the FMS, suggested in his report of 1928 that the Kedah government should "have an arrangement with the FMS government mills in Krian, whereby whenever the price of paddy fell below a certain figure, they would purchase paddy in large quantities at an agreed fair

Table 6 Paddy and Rice Export in Kedah, 1913–1939

Year	Paddy	Percentage (%)	Rice	Percentage (%)
1913–1914	11,915.3*		2,308.3*	
1914–1915	13,290.4		2,171.2	
1915–1916	15,968.8		2,854.4	
1916–1917	17,156.8		2,672.0	
1919–1921	—		—	
1931–1932	19,204**	42.8	25,662**	57.2
1932–1933	20,627	40.5	30,298	59.5
1933–1934	20,998	44.2	26,553	55.8
1934–1935	23,858	38.9	37,486	61.1
1935–1936	20,027	34.8	37,520	65.2
1936–1937	12,880	26.1	36,451	73.9
1937–1938	9,513	24.3	29,625	75.7
1938–1939	15,923	41.0	22,910	59.0

* unit = gantang
** unit = ton

Source: Wu Xiao An, "Chinese Family Networks in the Making of a Malay State: Kedah and the Region, 1882–1941," Ph.D. diss., University of Amsterdam, 1999, 268.

price and thus create the necessary competition."[54] A special rate by railway transportation was also arranged on rice and bran between Alor Star and Taiping in 1931–1932. Nevertheless, according to a local Kedah official, the government mills in Perak did not affect the prices in Kedah too much.[55] For example, it was disclosed that in 1933–1934, all the millers in Kedah agreed among themselves that they would not buy paddy above a certain price. Hence the Kedah paddy planters were forced to sell their produce to the government mills in Perak at a lower price, instead of to their local mills.[56]

The Export Duty

With regard to paddy and rice export, there was structural change in Kedah probably from the late 1920s (see table 6). For a long time, Kedah had been exporting much more paddy than rice to Penang and the FMS. In the normal years prior to 1922, the export of paddy and rice averaged the equivalent of 10,200,000 gantangs of rice. Of this quantity, 15 percent was exported as rice and the remaining 85 percent as paddy.[57] At least from 1930 on, the export of rice outstripped that of paddy. This development was attributed to the government policy of encouraging the rice-milling industry in Kedah since

1910, which led to the emergence of many new rice mills in Kedah, particularly from the late 1920s.[58]

Long discussions took place between the Kedah government and Chinese millers with regard to export duty. The export duty of paddy and rice in Kedah was fixed by the Treaty of 1869, and had been maintained for a long time. Paddy was $4 per koyan and rice $8 per koyan (see table 7). In 1911, the state council decided to raise the duty beginning in 1912. However, the right to collect export duty on paddy and rice was given to the Penang farmer Lim Cheng Teik, the eldest son of the pioneering miller Phuah Hin. It was initially intended that the government should collect all the duty itself and pay the farmer his due portion, but this was strongly opposed by Lim Cheng Teik. An agreement was later reached to the effect that, first, the state council would allow Lim Cheng Teik to collect the duty, but any duty in excess of the amount fixed in the old farm contract should be handed over to the government; second, Lim Cheng Teik should appoint Malay clerks and keep all accounts in Malay at every place; and third, all clerks and revenue officials should be selected and placed under the control of the harbormaster.[59] The export duty was raised to $5 per koyan for paddy and $10 per koyan for rice.[60] However, owing to paddy failure, the government exerted an export-restriction policy for 1912, out of which there was five months' absolute prohibition. This caused Lim Cheng Teik a great loss. With the intervention of the high commissioner, the state council acceded to Lim Cheng Teik's request for a remission of the farm rent for five months.[61]

With the expiry of the rice and paddy farm at the end of 1918, the government undertook the collection of the export duty itself. The government also abolished the system of collecting measure, and introduced a system of collecting by weight. The duty was increased with the rice-to-paddy ratio of 2:1. During the food-control period, from 1919 to 1921, no paddy was allowed for export without special permission from the state council. A duty of 100 percent would be charged if such special permission was obtained.[62] When the food control was removed in 1921, the old rate of 1919 was resumed. The rate was 20 cents per picul on paddy and 50 cents per picul on rice. The difference between the paddy and rice duties constituted a serious setback to the Kedah rice millers in their competition with the millers of the Straits Settlements and the FMS. On the petition of the Kedah rice millers in March 1923, the government approved a reduction of the duty by 10 cents, to 40 cents, in order to encourage the milling industry in Kedah.[63] When the Kedah rice millers continued to petition for a reduction of export duty for the same concern in 1924, the government refused their claims on the

Table 7 The Export Duty of Paddy and Rice in Kedah, 1869–1934

Year	Rice	Paddy	Unit	Rate: Rice:Paddy
1869–1913	8	4	$/K[i]	2:1
1913–1919	10	5		2:1
1919–1921	—	100	C/P[ii]	—
1923–1927	50	20		2.5:1
1927–Dec. 1930	40	20		2:1
Dec. 1930–Feb. 1931	35	20		1.75:1
Feb. 1931–1934	25	20		1.25:1
1934	10	10		1:1

i. $/K = $/koyan
ii. C/P = cent/pikul

Source: Wu Xiao An, "Chinese Family Networks in the Making of a Malay State: Kedah and the Region, 1882–1941," Ph.D. diss., University of Amsterdam, 1999, 269.

grounds that the duty rate was "substantially fair."[64] The higher duty on rice as opposed to that on paddy continued to place Kedah rice millers at a disadvantage in competition with external millers. In 1927, the Kedah rice millers again petitioned Tunku Ibrahim, regent of Kedah, to reduce the rice export duty. According to the going rate at the time, it was estimated that the export duty for 100 piculs of paddy was $20, while the total export duty on rice and by-products from 100 piculs of paddy amounted to $29.22. It was suggested that the rice millers in Kedah were paying about $10 more to export rice and by-products manufactured from 100 piculs of paddy than to export paddy itself for manufacture by millers outside Kedah, but the state council refused to change its stance after consulting with the Perak government mills.[65]

However, the situation regarding the rice market changed before long. In the international market, supplies of cheap Rangoon rice were available, and local rice could be purchased at $7.50 per bag. Many estates had already made six- to twelve-month contracts, chiefly with Messrs. Mohamed Kassim and Company for Rangoon parboiled rice at prices of about $8.40 per bag. The 1930–1931 season witnessed the largest harvest in Kedah in ten years, with a yield of 73,446,000 gantangs (compared to 69,280,000 gantangs in 1920–1921).[66] But the prices of paddy and rice were very low, in fact the lowest for many years. As they were afraid that they could not compete with the low-priced Rangoon rice, all the Penang buyers, the large mills, and the government rice mills were holding back from buying. The price of the

new paddy crop was \$1.70 to \$1.80 per picul and \$10 per kuncha (160 gantangs). Paddy at \$1.80 per picul could be landed in Penang at \$2.10 per picul. It cost 84 cents to ship a bag of rice from Kedah to Penang, of which 59 cents was export duty.[67]

Under these circumstances, the state council had to reconsider the export duty, which was reduced twice in the space of a few months. From 21 December 1930 onward, the state council decided to temporarily reduce the rice export duty from 40 cents to 35 cents.[68] The reduction of export duty had the desired effect, causing the Penang Hock Hin Bros. Company to immediately arrang a large rice-supplying contract with a well-known Indian rice-importing company and the local estates as well. Nevertheless, paddy prices fell further, with the millers offering about \$1.40 per picul. In order to encourage mills to reopen and to keep up the prices of paddy, the state council again reduced the export duty by 10 cents, to 25 cents, and paddy from 20 cents to 10 cents.[69] This reduction came into effect on 18 February 1931. However, in half a month, a petition was again submitted to the state council asking for a further reduction of the export duty on paddy. The request was made through the Choong family agent in Alor Star and manager of Ban Heng Bee, Kang Cheng Wan.[70]

The Malay Peasantry

To enhance the paddy price and depress the rice price, the government also attempted to break the Chinese rice millers' financial ties with the Malay peasantry, who were predominantly rice cultivators, through the commonly practiced advance sale of paddy, known as "paddy *kunca*." The majority of the paddy planters had fallen into the clutches of Chinese paddy dealers owing to their debt relationship with the latter. At the beginning of every planting season, through paddy dealers, the rice miller advanced loans to most of the Malay cultivators. The miller would provide the cash loans in exchange for paddy at harvest time. The practice was heavily criticized for its exploitative nature, as the Malay cultivators were required to pay back their loan to the miller in paddy at a price under market rates, and at exorbitant interest rates.[71]

The original idea of paddy kunca was to help and encourage poor Malay paddy cultivators on behalf of the sultan, and to guarantee the paddy supply market for the miller. In 1891, there was a debate over Lim Leng Cheak's rice mill in Kedah. The *Straits Independent and Penang Chronicle* charged Lim Leng Cheak with exploitative conduct for having entered into a contract with

the cultivators in advance, while the *Pinang Gazette and Straits Chronicle* argued that it saw "nothing particularly immoral" in it. On the contrary, the *Pinang Gazette and Straits Chronicle* argued that the result was that many more Malays were going into paddy planting, paddy cultivation was rapidly expanding, and Kedah was being developed. In 1893, when discussing a scheme to encourage paddy planting, the British were very interested in Lim Leng Cheak's experience in providing monetary advances to the Malay peasantry. The colonial secretary W. E. Maxwell suggested that "some such system might with advantage be introduced in connection with the development scheme."[72] When there was a famine and failure of paddy crops, Phuah Hin Leong took over from Lim Leng Cheak. At the request of the sultan, the new farmer pursued the same practice of giving cash advances to the cultivators. The same *Straits Independent and Penang Chronicle* admitted that the new farmer should assist the cultivators, otherwise the situation of the latter would become worse than before. Also, in his report to the Kedah government in 1928, H. W. Jack, the economic botanist of the Straits Settlements and the FMS, admitted that "the practice of borrowing cash from Chinese Milling Agents and others is a necessary one under prevailing conditions, for the cultivator must have some cash for the purchase of implements, matting, tongs, etc., while on the other side the Chinese must have paddy to keep their mills running and so competitive buying forces them to obtain a hold on the crops before they are cut."[73]

An important consideration for government policy centered on the rivalry with Chinese rice millers for the control of the Malay peasantry. Measures such as the government loan scheme of 1910–1916, the credit society for paddy planters in the late 1910s and early 1920s, the Cooperative Movement in the 1920s, and the Week Fairs in the 1930s were aimed at destroying the Chinese intermediary roles with regard to the Malay peasantry. It was claimed that the government policy's object was to "keep the Malay paddy-planters out of indebtedness to the Chinese paddy-dealers," to "release them from the ditches of the 'Rice Combine.'"[74] However, all these efforts failed in the end, although the government had boasted of its great success. As early as 1917, even the British district officer in Perak thought the government loan scheme was "a failure although it . . . gave some temporary relief." The most serious defect was its fixed time for repayment in harvest. It made the paddy market situation even worse, as the paddy planters had to repay their loans in paddy crop to the government, Chinese paddy dealers, and native moneylenders (*chetties*) at the same time.[75] In the 1920s, there were

many reports that Malay paddy planters were unable to repay their government loans even by selling cattle.[76] Many of them were prosecuted by the government.[77] In 1935, a cooperative rice mill was formed with capital of $50,000 authorized by the government. That mill was built in 1936 with a total membership of 1,081. Due to the strong monopolistic structure of the Chinese corporate business, it failed after a few years. That mill worked for only eighty-eight days per year. The British adviser to Kedah, J. D. Hall, admitted that its failure was due to the price-cutting strategy of the Chinese businessmen, sustained for a long period and facilitated by large capital support.[78]

In a word, the situation remained unchanged and most of the Malay peasantry continued to be indebted to Chinese paddy dealers, a fact that was confirmed in 1938 by the local Malay agricultural official H. H. Tunku Yaacob.[79] The Chinese continued to dominate the rice-milling industry and trading networks. As long as the government could not solve the issue of Malay poverty, the financial ties between the Chinese paddy dealers and the Malay paddy planters could not be broken up. Furthermore, as long as Malay participation in the dominant colonial economy continued to be marginal, the issue of Malay poverty could not be solved.

Conclusion

As with the opium business, the commercialization of the rice industry in Southeast Asia, both in terms of production and consumption, was closely related to the colonial economy of tin and rubber and other cash crops, all of which were tied up in the world capitalist economy. Southeast Chinese capitalism was a feature of colonial expansion and the colonial economy, such that Chinese capital, labor, and trading networks were able to penetrate all essential aspects of the Southeast Asian colonial transformation. In Malaya, the large-scale commercial rice milling business emerged with the large influx of immigrant labor and the colonial Southeast Asian transformation in the late nineteenth century and early twentieth. If the rice-trade and -milling industries were interdependent with the tin-mining and rubber-planting economies on the one hand, then the international rice trade influenced and complemented the domestic rice milling trade. The Chinese dominated the rice milling business and trading networks, of which Penang, Kedah, Perak, and Province Wellesley comprised an integral chain. On the top level of the milling hierarchy were a few Penang Chinese families that had formerly been prominent revenue farmers. Centering on the rice-milling

business had been strong economic competition between the state and the Chinese millers on the issue of price. As the Malay peasantry were also brought into the struggle, this economic competition took on a political and ethnic dimension. Eventually, however, market forces prevailed in the form of the international and local rice markets, and the finance, management, and trading networks. Hence, under the complex economic, political, and ethnic circumstances of the time, the interaction between the state and Chinese milling society was a struggle that alternated between conflict and compromise, dependence and cooperation.

Notes

This paper was finished when the author was a visiting research fellow (2005–2006) at Asia Research Institute, National University of Singapore. The author is grateful to Anthony Reid and Alan Chan for providing such an excellent research environment.

1. G. Selvaraju, Singapore Rice Trade (Singapore: International Enterprise Singapore Resource Centre, 2004), 5–6.

2. See Jemmimah Jewel R. Canoy and Cesar S. Belangel, "Asian Farmers Fight for Survival and Control of the Rice Industry," AFA and AsiaDHRRA Issue Paper 1.1 (December 2004), available from the Asian Partnership for the Development of Human Resources in Rural Asia website, http://www.asiadhrra.org/.

3. P. A. Coclanis, "Southeast Asia's Incorporation into the World Rice Market: A Revisionist View," Journal of Southeast Asian Studies 24.2 (1993): 251–67; C. Hirschman, "Population and Society in Twentieth-Century Southeast Asia," Journal of Southeast Asian Studies 25.2 (1994): 381–416.

4. Paul H. Kratoska, "The British Empire and the Southeast Asian Rice Crisis of 1919–1921," Modern Asian Studies 24.1 (1990): 117; A. J. Latham and Larry Neal, "The International Market in Rice and Wheat, 1868–1914," Economic History Review, New Series, 36.2 (1983): 262.

5. R. Barker, R. W. Herdt, B. Rose, The Rice Economy of Asia (Washington: Resources for the Future, 1985), 185–88.

6. The Pinang Gazette: Centenary Number 1833–1933, 32.

7. Wu Xiao An, Chinese Business in the Making of a Malay State, 1882–1941: Kedah and Penang (London: RoutledgeCurzon, 2003), 186.

8. Carl A. Trocki, Opium and Empire: Chinese Society in Colonial Singapore 1800–1910 (Ithaca: Cornell University Press, 1990); Carl A. Trocki, "Opium and the Beginnings of Chinese Capitalism in Southeast Asia," Journal of Southeast Asian Studies 33 (2002): 297–314; Carl A. Trocki, "A Drug on the Market: Opium and the Chinese in Southeast Asia, 1750–1880," Journal of Chinese Overseas 1.2 (November 2005): 169–83.

9. Wu Xiao An, Chinese Business in the Making of a Malay State, 1882–1941, 31–38.

10. Trocki, "Opium and the Beginnings of Chinese Capitalism in Southeast Asia," 297–314; Wu Xiao An, Chinese Business in the Making of a Malay State, 1882–1941, chap. 7.

11. Wu Xiao An, *Chinese Business in the Making of a Malay State, 1882–1941*, 252.

12. J. Overton, *Colonial Green Revolution? Food, Irrigation and the State in Colonial Malaya* (Wallingford, Oxon: Cab International, 1994), 208; L. J. Fredericks and R. J. G. Wells, *Rice Processing in Peninsular Malaysia: An Economic and Technical Analysis* (Kuala Lumpur: Oxford University Press, 1983), 7.

13. International Rice Research Institute, *Rice Today* (April 2004): 37.

14. Rip Landes, Paul Westcott, and John Wainio, *International Agricultural Baseline Projections to 2005*, Agricultural Economic Report no. 750 (Washington: Commercial Agriculture Division, Economic Research Service, U.S. Department of Agriculture, 1997), 4. See also http://www.ers.usda.gov.

15. Julian Roche, *The International Rice Trade* (Cambridge: Woodhead, 1992), 79. See also http://www.agobservatory.org; Wong Sook Yeen, "Modelling the Rice Supply in Malaysia," unpublished master's thesis, department of transportation, Malaysian University of Science and Technology, 2004.

16. See, for example, James C. Ingram, *Economic Change in Thailand 1850–1970* (Stanford: Stanford University Press, 1971); Sompop Manarungsan, *The Challenge of the World Economy* (Groningen: University of Groningen, 1989); Michael Adas, *The Burma Delta: Economic Development and Social Change on an Asian Rice Frontier, 1852–1941* (Madison: University of Wisconsin Press, 1974); Norman G. Owen, "The Rice Industry of Mainland South-East Asia 1850–1914," *Journal of the Siam Society* 59.2 (1971): 75–143.

17. Pierre van der Eng, "Productivity and Comparative Advantage in Rice Agriculture in South-East Asia since 1870," *Asian Economic Journal* 18.4 (2004): 345–70. However, in Paul Kratoska's opinion, the three major rice-exporting countries accounted for 67 percent of the world rice trade in 1930. See Paul H. Kratoska, "The Impact of the Second World War on Commercial Rice Production in Mainland South-East Asia," *Food Supplies and the Japanese Occupation in South-East Asia*, ed. Paul H. Kratoska (New York: St. Martin's, 1998), 9.

18. Latham and Neal, "The International Market in Rice and Wheat, 1868–1914," 274.

19. Paul H. Kratoska, ed., *Food Supplies and the Japanese Occupation in South-East Asia* (New York: St. Martin's, 1998), 13.

20. Cheng Siok-Hwa, *The Rice Trade of Malaya* (Singapore: University Education Press, 1973), 14.

21. Ding Eing Tan Soo Hai, *The Rice Industry in Malaya, 1920–1940* (Singapore: Malaya Publishing House, 1963), 4–5.

22. Paul H. Kratoska, "Malayan Food Shortages and the Kedah Rice Industry during the Japanese Occupation," *Food Supplies and the Japanese Occupation in South-East Asia*, ed. Paul H. Kratoska (New York: St. Martin's, 1998), 104.

23. Overton, *Colonial Green Revolution?*, 69–71; Latham and Neal, "The International Market in Rice and Wheat, 1868–1914," 262–67.

24. A. J. Latham, "From Competition to Constraint: The International Rice Trade in the Nineteenth and Twentieth Centuries," *Business and Economic History*, 2d series, 17 (1988): 91–102.

25. Trade Commission, *Report of the Commission Appointed by His Excellency the Governor of the*

Straits Settlements to Enquire into and Report on the Trade of the Colonies, 1933–1934 (Singapore: Singapore Government Printer, 1934), 2: 429; 3:329–30.

26. Belated interest in the rice industry in Malaysia has focused mainly on the postwar period, especially on the Green Revolution. See A. M. Thomson, Report to the Government of the Federation of Malaya on the Marketing of Rice (Rome: Food and Agriculture Organization, 1954), 1–68; E. H. G. Dobby et al., "Paddy Landscapes of Malaya," Malayan Journal of Tropical Geography 6 (October 1955): 1–94; Otto Charles Doering III, "Malaysian Rice Policy and the Muda River Irrigation Project," Ph.D. diss., Cornell University, 1973; R. D. Hill, Rice in Malaysia: A Study in Historical Geography (Kuala Lumpur: Oxford University Press, 1977); Afifuddin bin Haji Omar, "Peasants, Institutions, and Development in Malaysia: The Political Economy of Development in the Muda Region," Ph.D. diss., Cornell University, 1978; Diana Wong, "Rice Marketing in Kedah, Malaysia," working paper no. 6, Faculty of Sociology, University of Bielefeld, 1981; Diana Wong, Peasants in the Making: Malaysia's Green Revolution (Singapore: Institute of Southeast Asian Studies, 1987); Rodolphe De Koninck, Malay Peasants Coping with the World: Breaking the Community Circle? (Singapore: Institute of Southeast Asian Studies, 1992); Mario Rutten, "Business Strategy and Life-Style: Owners of Combine-Harvesters in North Malaysia," Kajian Malaysia [Journal of Malaysian studies] 14.1–2 (1996): 112–50.

27. Owen, "The Rice Industry of Mainland South-East Asia 1850–1914," 79, 81, 139, 141.

28. Ahmad bin Sa'adi, "The Development of Malaya's Rice Industry 1896–1921," (Singapore: University of Malaya, 1960); Ding Eing Tan Soo Hai, The Rice Industry in Malaya, 1920–1940; James C. Jackson, "Rice Cultivation in West Malaysia," Journal of the Malaysian Branch of the Royal Asiatic Society 45.2 (1972): 76–96; Cheng Siok-Hwa, "Pre-War Government Policy for the Rice Industry of Malaya," Journal of the South Seas Society 27.1–2 (1972): 26–40; Cheng Siok-Hwa, The Rice Trade of Malaya, 1–44; Lee Say Lee, "A Study of the Rice Trade in Kedah Before and During the Japanese Occupation," Malaysia in History 24 (1981): 109–16; Paul H. Kratoska, "Rice Cultivation and the Ethnic Division of Labor in British Malaya," Comparative Studies in Society and History 24 (1982): 280–314; John Overton, "The State and Rice Production in Malaya in the Later Colonial Period," Review of Indonesian and Malaysian Affairs 23 (1989): 16–34; Paul Kratoska, "The British Empire and the Southeast Asian Rice Crisis of 1919–1921," 115–46. See also Paul Kratoska, "Malayan Food Shortages and the Kedah Rice Industry during the Japanese Occupation," 101–34.

29. Trade Commission, Report of the Commission Appointed by His Excellency, 2:362; The Pinang Gazette: Centenary Number 1833–1933, 32.

30. The Pinang Gazette: Centenary Number 1833–1933, 32.

31. For details about these families, see Wu Xiao An, "Chinese Family Business Networks in the Making of a Malay State: Kedah and the Region, 1882–1941," Ph.D. diss., University of Amsterdam, 1999, 53–66, 79–111.

32. Wu Xiao An, Chinese Business in the Making of a Malay State, 1882–1941, 127–31.

33. Pinang Sin Pao, 1 June 1909.

34. Malaya Tribune, 3 February 1915.

35. Pinang Gazette and Straits Chronicle, 29 December 1912, 14–15 January 1913; The Malaya Tribune, 3 February 1915.

36. High Commissioner's Office (hereafter HCO) 880/1917, Maxwell's Memorandum on the Rice Mills.

37. *Pinang Gazette and Straits Chronicle*, 10 February 1919.

38. *Straits Echo*, 20–21 November 1922.

39. Chualeeporn Pongsupath states that it ceased to operate before 1930, while Rajeswary Brown mentions that it collapsed in the early 1930s. See Chuleeporn Pongsupath, 1990, 220; Rajeswary Brown, 1994, 130.

40. Trade Commission, *Report of the Commission Appointed by His Excellency*, Minutes of Evidence, 2:359–65.

41. *Pinang Sin Pao*, 31 July 1934.

42. *Straits Echo*, 16 February 1938.

43. H. A. Tempang, "The Economics of the Rice Situation," *Malayan Agricultural Journal* 18.5 (1930): 229–31.

44. Wu Xiao An, *Chinese Business in the Making of a Malay State, 1882–1941*, 148–51.

45. HCO 550/1914, Erection of a Government Rice Mill at Alor Star in Opposition to the Rice Combine's Mill.

46. See, for example, HCO 1578/1915, Special Terms for Titles for Paddy Cultivation in Kedah; HCO 880/1917, Memorandum on the Erection of a Rice Mill.

47. HCO 600/1918, Proposal that Kedah Government Take Over and manage the Alor Star Rice Mill.

48. Kedah Secretariat Files (hereafter SUK/K) 1242/1358, Proposal to Erect a Government Rice Mill at Alor Star. The statement by Ahmad bin Sa'adi might be wrong that a government rice mill was built at Anak Bukit in 1921, which was cited by Otto Charles Doering III and Afifuddin bin Haji Omar. See Sa'adi, "The Development of Malaya's Rice Industry 1896–1921"; Doering, "Malaysian Rice Policy and the Muda River Irrigation Project," 13; Omar, "Peasants, Institutions, and Development in Malaysia," 104.

49. *Report of the Rice Cultivation Committee*, 1: 40, 2:173–75; HCO 585/1918, Krian Rice Mills: Government to take over control.

50. SUK/K 930/1339, Paddy Harvest 1339.

51. SUK/K 1595/1339, Purchase of Paddy by Government Rice Mill, Bagan Serai, 1921.

52. SUK/K 511/1343, The Government Mills in Perak were prepared to buy paddy, 18 September 1924.

53. SUK/K 1861/1346, Goh Soon Leong, Alor Star: That he has been appointed buying agent for the FMS Government Rice Mill at Bagan Serai.

54. SUK/K 2122/1346, Brief report on paddy in Kedah by H. W. Jack, 26 January 1928.

55. *Report of the Rice Cultivation Committee*, 1:118.

56. *Report of the Trade Commission*, 2:333.

57. SUK/K 930/1339, Memorandum on Rice Position in 1922, by J. J. Fleury, Agent Food Controller, 15 December 1920.

58. As the Kedah trade statistics during the 1920s include one item of paddy and rice together, rather than under separate items, the data concerned are not available during that period.

59. Colonial Office Files (hereafter CO) 273/384, The Minutes of Kedah State Council Meeting, 21 Zilkaedah 1329 (13 November 1911), 8 Zilhijah 1329 (30 November 1911).

60. CO 273/385, The Minutes of Kedah State Council Meeting, 13 Muharram 1330 (3 January 1912).

61. HCO 663/1912, Petition of Lim Cheng Teik, 7 May 1912, Penang; CO 273/387, The Minutes of Kedah State Council Meeting, 19 Shaaban 1330.

62. SUK/K 1388/1338, The Minutes of Kedah State Council Meetings, 13 Jemadilakhir 1338 (4 March 1920).

63. SUK/K 1732/1341, Rice Millers in Kedah ask that the export duty on rice be reduced, 19 March 1923.

64. SUK/K 21/1343, Rice Millers in Kedah: Reduction of the Export Duty on Rice, 4 and 9 August, 29 October, 25 November 1924.

65. SUK/K 535/1346, Kedah Rice Millers, Alor Star: Regarding Rate of Export Duty on Paddy and Rice, 15 August 1927.

66. Kedah Annual Report, 1930–1931.

67. SUK/K 2427/1349, Report on the Present Position of the market for Kedah Paddy and Rice, 15 August 1927.

68. SUK/K 1965/1349, Revision of Export Duty on Paddy and Rice.

69. SUK/K 2620/1349, Export Duty on Paddy and Rice: Proposed to Reduce.

70. SUK/K 2957/1349, Ask for Further Reduction of Export Duty on Paddy, 15 Shawal 1349.

71. Wu Xiao An, Chinese Business in the Making of a Malay State, 1882–1941, 132–33.

72. Proceedings of the Straits Settlements Legislative Council, 1893, c176.

73. Straits Independence and Penang Chronicle, 15 January 1891, 18 July 1894; Pinang Gazette and Straits Chronicle, 24 January 1891; Legco, 1893, c176; and SUK/K 2122/1346, Brief Report on Paddy in Kedah by H. W. Jack, 26 January 1928.

74. CO 273/411/311, The Minutes of the Kedah State Council Meetings, 27 Jemadilawal 1332 (23 April 1914); Kedah Annual Report, November 1913–November 1914.

75. HCO 880/1917, Loans to Paddy Planters by R. Clayton, District Officer, Krian, Perak.

76. SUK/K 1377/1340, Postponement of Payment of Loans of Paddy Planters by Assistant Adviser, Land Office, North Kedah, 11 March 1922; SUK/K 1325/1340, Saad bin Haji Hassan bin haji Md. Salleh and Others, Pengkalan Kundur: Ask for Time to Pay Their Loans to Government.

77. SUK/K 186/1343, Permission to Sue Debtors in Connection with Loans for Paddy Planning, Harbour Master, Alor Star, 11 Muharram 1343.

78. Omar, "Peasants, Institutions, and Development in Malaysia," 124; SUK/K 571/1355, 528/1356, Annual Report on the Co-operative Societies Department, Kedah, for the Years 1354 and 1355.

79. SUK/K 3381/1357, Rice Mills in Kedah.

TONLE SAP PROCESSED FISH

From Khmer Subsistence Staple to Colonial Export Commodity

~~~~ Nola Cooke

The Tonle Sap Great Lake and River in central Cambodia together form one of the environmental wonders of the world, driving a unique natural regulatory system without which the Mekong Delta region would be entirely submerged for nearly half the year. As the Mekong rises, from May to June, fed by snowmelt in Tibet and then by monsoon rains, a huge volume of water hurtles downstream. At Phnom Penh, where the Mekong meets the Tonle Sap, the pent-up pressure overwhelms the smaller river, reversing its flow and pushing billions of cubic meters of water back up to its headwaters to create a huge inland sea. The dry season lake surface expands fourfold, to well over one million hectares, while its volume rises from about five billion cubic meters to an immense eighty billion cubic meters. Flooding twenty to thirty kilometers beyond the dry season shoreline, the rising waters inundate a highly adapted forested floodplain, taking with them innumerable fish eggs and fingerlings that fatten on its decomposing vegetation and algae. In the dry season, as the waters seep away, the fish follow, first toward the permanent lake bed and then later down the Tonle Sap River toward the Mekong. From December to June, fishermen from floating lakeside villages and neighboring provinces alike converge on the dwindling lake and river. Some seek only to secure their family's off-season protein staple and a small excess to trade for other necessities, but others labor for months in large-scale intensive fishing operations that range from the deployment of seine nets several kilometers long to an ingenious array of traditional bamboo fish traps, great and small.[1]

Cambodia is the fourth largest freshwater fish producer in the world, with an annual catch conservatively estimated at 400,000 tons.[2] Fish from

the Tonle Sap Great Lake alone currently account for about 60 percent of the total yield.[3] While the vast bulk of the Tonle Sap catch is now consumed within the lower Mekong basin, especially by Khmer who live in nearby provinces, this was not always the case.[4] From the late nineteenth century, fishing on Tonle Sap Great Lake and its river was transformed into a major export industry, only slightly less valuable than rice in the early twentieth century. Chinese played key roles at every level of the new export industry, whether as local traders, international exporters, or financiers who supplied the essential capital that funded large-scale operations. Without their input, it is unlikely that bulk commodity production of processed fish would ever have attained the scale that it did by the end of the nineteenth century. By then, fishing on the lake had been transformed. Although Khmer peasant subsistence producers had dominated Cambodian inland fisheries for centuries, by the early twentieth century they formed only "a tiny minority" on Tonle Sap Great Lake, where Vietnamese fishing masters using "Chinese, Vietnamese and Malay" laborers produced a cheap protein staple that was then exported by downstream Chinese firms to Southeast Asia and China.[5] In the high-colonial era, Indochinese dried fish, overwhelmingly from Cambodia and thus from the Tonle Sap system, became a key commodity import that helped to feed the coolie masses of Java, Singapore, and Hong Kong: by the mid-1930s, Chinese businessmen in Cambodia were shipping 15,000 tons of dried fish annually to the Dutch East Indies alone.[6] Newly emergent bulk commodity production in inland Cambodia thus played a silent but nonetheless significant role in sustaining the contemporaneous European colonial system in Southeast Asia.

In the following discussion I chart the remarkable career of Tonle Sap processed fish and fish products over the century in which they were transformed from a Khmer subsistence staple to an important colonial commodity consumed by tens of thousands of people beyond Indochina, in China and throughout the colonial Malayo-Indonesian world. I begin with what we know of the emergence and growth of market-oriented fishing in the nineteenth century, until about 1880, before considering the industry's transformation in the new economic environment created in Cambodia by the royal revenue farming system. I conclude by outlining the disastrous impact on fish stocks of the essentially unregulated industry after revenue farming was abolished, and the 1920 establishment of the regulatory system that controlled fishing for the rest of the colonial era.

Fish has always formed the main protein component in the Cambodian diet. Over millennia, Khmer fishermen had devised an ingenious array of traps, nets, rods, and bamboo barrages designed to secure a good supply of this precious staple. So locally well adapted was this equipment that much of the traditional gear remains in use today. Cambodians also learned to preserve their catch by drying, salting, or smoking it, and to exploit even the tiniest fish by processing them into the national condiment, a thick, salted fish paste called *prahoc*. As Ian Mabbett and David Chandler recognized, "the technology of fishing, the taxonomy of species, the craft of fish cuisine and the science of garnishes and seasoning for fish dishes" had all long ago reached "a high pitch of refinement" among the Khmer.[7]

Traditionally, however, fishing and fish processing were seasonal peasant sideline activities, with only a comparatively small number of long-resident Islamic (Malay and Cham) fishing villages engaged in it all year round.[8] Every year, large numbers of Khmer families, even whole villages, would trek to the lake at low water, build temporary homes, and spend about six weeks catching and processing their subsistence protein for the coming year, as well as rendering fish oil for cooking and lighting.[9] These perennial activities were undoubtedly identical to those witnessed in 1878 by the French official Jean Moura, who described these Khmer groups as living cooperatively, with individuals joining short nets to boost a catch that was later shared out according to long-established customary rules.[10] By the late eighteenth century to the early nineteenth, however, things were starting to change.

In the nineteenth century, access to the Great Lake was free to all. Chinese junk crews, for instance, regularly went there to hunt marabouts for their feathers during the breeding season and paid only the customary 10 percent royal levy in kind on circulating commodities when taking their cargo back to China.[11] According to a handful of early Vietnamese sources, another seasonal industry with regional ramifications was also taking shape there. From at least the early nineteenth century, if not before, itinerant fishermen from the Nguyễn realm were taking their boats upstream to catch and process fish for markets downstream. A late 1830s Vietnamese account of eastern Cambodia, for instance, noted that "Khmer boats and those from Lục Tỉnh [southern Vietnam] all gather [at the lake], often in their thousands. The fishermen dry the fish and boil the oil."[12] We also know from the 1901 recollections of a highly successful Vietnamese fishing entrepreneur, Lê Thượng Tiếng, that his father's 1840s–1850s operation, the biggest mid-nineteenth-

century exploitation on the Great Lake, was averaging about 60 tons of fish per season.[13] If Khmer peasant producers smoked much of their catch at the time, as many still do, to dry fish for export itinerant Chinese, Vietnamese, and Sino-Vietnamese commodity producers needed the greater preserving power of salt (as did Khmer who wanted to make prahoc).[14] Lê Thượng Tiếng reported that it took one picul (60 kilos) of salt to process 2.5 piculs of fish (although later French observers cited one picul of salt per three to four piculs of fish), so that his father's midcentury operation alone would have required about 400 piculs (or 24 tons) of salt, if all the catch was salted.[15] Ready access to large quantities of salt was thus crucial for both commercial operators and subsistence producers alike. From a Vietnamese source of the 1820s we also know that a flourishing salt trade had long existed between the old "salt province" of former lower Cambodia—the Bassac region (modern Sóc Trăng and Bạc Liêu) at the mouth of the Hậu Giang or lower Mekong branch—and the rest of the Khmer kingdom.[16] Chinese, Vietnamese, and Khmer in the Bassac area manufactured a red salt which, when sold upriver by Chinese and Vietnamese junk traders, realized good profits for all involved.[17]

When French materials become available in the 1860s, we can infer the continuing growth of the inland fishing industry from the economic importance of salt in French Cochinchina, both in terms of its soaring production and the vast quantities being imported into Saigon for distribution throughout the local region, including to Cambodia. From the mid-1860s, cheaper white salt from other sources, especially from Bà Rịa in French Cochinchina, began outstripping traditional red salt in fish processing. After the 1862 cessation of hostilities between the Huế court and the French, salt production at Bà Rịa developed quickly. By 1868, its salines had expanded to 371.4 hectares, from a mere 13.2 hectares in 1836, soaring past Sóc Trăng's 200 hectares in 1868.[18] The real breakthrough came in 1865, however, when 2,504 seagoing junks traded between Bà Rịa and Saigon at the same time that thousands of other junks imported over 100,000 piculs of salt there from several small ports in the nearby Vietnamese provinces of Bình Định, Bình Thuận, Phú Yên, and Quảng Nam.[19] According to one French source, salt imports in 1865 exceeded those of 1864 by a staggering 233,193 piculs (or nearly 14,000 tons).[20]

It is hard not to connect the great local increase in salt production and its bulk importation with an expansion of the inland processed-fish industry around that time. From an estimated average total catch of about 30,000–40,000 piculs in the 1840s, Tonle Sap Great Lake's estimated annual yield

had risen to around 60,000 piculs by the early 1860s, while important fishing and prawning industries were also emerging elsewhere, especially in the three western Cochinchinese provinces that remained under Vietnamese rule until 1867.[21] Evidence of Cambodia's share in a growing export-oriented fish-processing industry appears in early French records: according to one 1862 French observer, all 2,430 tons of dried fish exported from Saigon that year derived from the Great Lake, with access to more salt the main restraint on increased productivity.[22] Between 1862 and 1865, the value of processed fish exports from Saigon doubled, from 1.2 million to 2.48 million francs, although the actual quantity fell to 1,358 tons.[23] This might indicate that more valuable fish were being targeted by larger operators, who salted them for export to distant markets like Java, the Malay states, and Singapore.[24] Certainly, the data show that the proportion of processed-fish cargoes transported by the large commercial ships that serviced such ports was rapidly rising at the time, from around 50 percent in 1863 to 70 percent by 1865.[25]

By 1865, customs records show that bulk salt imports into Saigon had solved the problem of inadequate supplies downstream, and Chinese junk traders were quick to ensure this essential commodity reached Cambodia. Indeed, the trafficking of salt from Cochinchina was one of the earliest Chinese economic niches in the developing Cambodian fishing industry. Although Chinese fishermen worked in Cambodia, and Chinese businessmen also owned fishery operations there, the most common Chinese involvement in fishing during this period was as the indispensable commercial middlemen supplying the needs of the fishing communities.[26]

By the mid-1860s, Louis de Carné of the 1866 Mekong expedition reported seeing "some thousands" of Vietnamese boats working the Great Lake.[27] Vietnamese had been returning to Tonle Sap in increasing numbers from the mid-1860s, encouraged by the protectorate treaty with Cambodia that allowed all French subjects free access and settlement rights. In effect this opened the country to any Vietnamese or locally born Chinese from Cochinchina after 1867. However, of the thousands de Carné saw, only a handful of large-scale, well-financed operations could have hoped to take their whole season's requirements with them to the uninhabited lake; the vast majority of fishermen had to rely on junk traders, overwhelmingly Chinese but also occasionally Malay, for daily necessities and vital industrial inputs like salt and net preservative. They were also often the main source of start-up capital for many fishermen.[28] In 1869, almost all the vessels Jean Moura encountered heading upriver to the lake were chartered by Chinese, who took salt, rice, areca, betel nuts, tobacco, alcohol, and ritual items (fire-

crackers, paper money, joss sticks) to exchange directly for fish.[29] Even Cambodian subsistence producers needed some salt, so profits were high in this classic sellers' market. Other benefits were also available. In 1879, on his second tour of the lake, Moura reported that most fishermen were "generally" forced to sell their catch to itinerant traders at the lake, in many cases without even being able to add value by preserving it first. Only larger professional fisheries could afford to process their own catch and then wait to sell it, in order to benefit directly from post-seasonal rises in prices.[30] Thus, even before Chinese financiers took control of the industry generally, the Chinese junk traders and middlemen who acquired fish cheaply at the lake, whether in return for loans on catches or in exchange for expensive imported items, were already making profitable inroads into small producers' returns.[31] But without these circulating junk traders the industry could never have expanded as it later did, since no other means existed to supply the 30,000 (or more) people, mostly Vietnamese, who worked the lake by the early 1880s.[32]

In an industry marked by large seasonal fluctuations, the perennial scarcity of operating capital left the great mass of small to medium producers highly vulnerable. Fishing was an expensive business. At the time, only a few comparatively large-scale operations existed, employing about twenty-five men to operate a seine net averaging only about 1.5 kilometers in length, and with twelve women to process the fish, among a mass of subsistence and small-scale producers.[33] (By the end of the century, in comparison, the largest operators employed seventy to one hundred men to deploy nets up to six kilometers in length, with forty women processing the catch.)[34] These early professional operations were almost entirely Vietnamese. In 1859–60, Henri Mouhot had recorded a few "enterprising Cochinchinese" who were taking "literally miraculous" catches at the lake each year.[35] The most successful of them was Lê Thượng Tiếng's father. However, his miraculous results required a huge capital investment of about 3,000 piasters per season on hired help, nets, boats, salt, and so on, for a profit of 1,000 to 1,500 piasters. If this represented a fortune at the time, high start-up costs meant new operators effectively needed a fortune in order to make one.[36]

In 1878, Moura calculated that a large operation employing forty men with a single big net (and excluding the cost of women to process the fish) would cost nearly 21,000 Vietnamese quan (or approximately 3,800 piasters).[37] This figure was later confirmed by a Vietnamese fishing boss who reported spending 20,000 quan in his first year. He employed only men, and his busy workers threw away fish heads and entrails from which female em-

Table 1 Customs Data at Phnom Penh for Fishing Products, in Piculs

	Dried/ salted fish	Fish bladders	Fish oil
1873	128,628	83	233
1880	93,200	849	—
1882	183,266	787	—
1887	158,000	—	—

Source: For the 1873 figure, see A. Bouinais and A. Paulus, *L'Indo-Chine contemporaine* (Paris: Challamel, 1884), 1, 549, citing Étienne Aymonier; for 1880 and 1882, see the customs figures in CAOM GGI, FA 11867; and for 1887 see the report of Resident General de Champeaux, dated 30 June 1888, in CAOM GGI, A 20 (27), carton 6.

ployees might have extracted oil worth several thousand quan at comparatively little additional expense. But as it was considered too uneconomical to interrupt the fishing for any reason, the heads were cast into the lake to rot. So common was this practice that in 1869 Moura saw Vietnamese from Châu Đốc collecting the discarded heads, which they processed for their own profit.[38] Although fish oil fetched 1.5 piasters per 30 liters in Phnom Penh in the early 1860s, undercapitalization restricted its production to a comparatively small area along the Tonle Sap River and the Mekong between Phnom Penh and Oudong.[39]

Open access to the Great Lake was protected by the Franco-Siamese convention of 1870, but elsewhere (including on Tonle Sap River) a patchwork of commercial fishing leases operated in traditional royal or apanage waterways. These leases were either auctioned annually to the highest bidders (usually Chinese), who might re-let them to others or operate them with their own equipment and crews, or they were granted to local governors or other officials to rent out in lieu of salary.[40] In some respects, these lots offered better commercial prospects than the Great Lake: they could be completely blocked with fish traps before the water drained and everything within quickly harvested by a few workers; and certain valuable species inhabited them. They were also the main locations for fish oil production and later for extracting valuable fish bladders, although this activity became commercially important only from the 1880s (see table 1).[41] Nevertheless, during this period, local villages with age-old customary rights to particular areas vastly outnumbered such leases, while less productive areas were not fished at all.

Apart from these rents, and a small kingdom-wide customary tax levied by local officials on fishing gear, the only fiscal impost on fishing was the traditional royal customs duty on all commodities, payable at Phnom Penh. In 1862, Andrew Spooner reported these duties were collected only haphazardly, and mostly to the exporters' advantage.[42] From the early 1870s, however, matters changed dramatically, after King Norodom transformed his customs receipts into a revenue farm and auctioned the right to collect them.[43] Successful bidders in the 1870s included local Chinese businessmen and some Cambodian courtiers, whose sub-farmers or agents, appointed as royal officials to mask their activities from the disapproving French representative in Phnom Penh, swiftly began to levy the full royal 10 percent, plus an extra 1 percent for their own expenses. It was a harbinger of things to come.

The Fishing Industry under the General Revenue Farm, 1879–1908

In the three decades during which revenue farming interests came to dominate the Cambodian fishing industry, the export value of its products boomed, thanks in part to the pursuit of new markets by downriver Chinese exporters. The pressing need to return a profit on increasingly expensive revenue farm investments and fishing leases also drove diversification into profitable secondary activities. One such valuable activity was the export of dried fish bladders to China, where they were processed and either used industrially, as a water-soluble glue added to liqueurs, wines, beers, and woven silk, or widely consumed in thickened soups.[44] These secondary products became increasingly important over time. By 1910, Cambodia exported about 15,000 piculs (or 900 tons) of fish oil and fats, and 12,500 piculs (or 750 tons) of fish bladders, more than 15 times the derisory 1873 quantities reported in table 1, while by the mid-1920s, the combined export of fish oils and bladders had soared to over 4,000 tons.[45] By 1910, too, the worth of the entire export industry had almost trebled. In 1873, Étienne Aymonier had valued processed fish and fish product exports—overwhelmingly from the Tonle Sap Great Lake and River—at 2,651,345 francs.[46] Although dried and salted fish had not even doubled in quantity by 1910 (from 128,000 to 220,000 piculs), the value of fish-related exports had soared to 7,225,000 francs.[47] Indeed, the total quantity of processed fish exports for 1910 was only about 30 percent higher than those in 1882 (see table 1), but while the latter had fetched 593,479 piasters, those of 1910 were worth 1.5 million piasters.[48]

Large-scale operators were particularly well placed to benefit from the

export boom. They could negotiate equitable contracts with the mainly Chinese companies whose steam launches began plying Cambodian waters in the 1880s, and thus transport their products more efficiently to market, a change that occurred just as Chinese export networks downriver were also developing new markets and while the demand for cheap Cambodian dried fish in colonial Asia was increasing. In 1900, Cambodia and Cochinchina together exported nearly nine million francs worth of fish products to Singapore (6,357,930) and Hong Kong (2,296,577), about two-thirds of which probably originated in Tonle Sap waters.[49] Lê Thượng Tiếng demonstrated the vast fortunes generated by this expanding commodity trade when he compared his costs and profits to those of his father fifty years before. In 1901, capital costs were five times higher. The price of salt had doubled, to 3,800 piasters for 2,000 piculs, as had the wage bill for 120 employees (80 men and 40 women), who now cost up to 6,000 piasters annually, and the price of other necessary inputs had risen even further. Lê Thượng Tiếng's annual catch was also five times more than his father's, on average 300 tons. His profits, however, were seven or eight times higher, thanks to new markets in Hong Kong, Singapore, and China, to the dramatic increase in the price of premium fish, and to his move into processing fish oil, fats, and bladders.[50]

Perhaps just as important, well-capitalized fishery operators like Lê Thượng Tiếng could now also take advantage of the new opportunities opened up by King Norodom's creation of a general revenue farm on fishing leases and equipment taxes. The old Vietnamese fisheries entrepreneur was also exemplary in this respect, for at one stage he was also the general revenue farmer for Cambodian fisheries and thus the monopolist entitled to dispose of the largest area of fishing leases in the country.[51] The benefits of such a situation for a fishing entrepreneur are self-evident. But in another respect Lê Thượng Tiếng was quite unusual, for the position of general revenue farmer very quickly came to be dominated by big Chinese businessmen who were mostly speculative capitalists with few direct links to fisheries production. As investors anxious to recoup their outlays and make profits, they all quickly moved to share their risks with numerous layers of sub-farmers to whom general farmers sold shares in their monopolies. In fewer than two decades, the operational demands of this typical revenue farming financial structure would catalyze the Cambodian export-fishing industry into its long-standing twentieth-century form, in which Chinese financiers employing Vietnamese fishing masters would dominate export-oriented production on Tonle Sap waters and elsewhere.

In 1862, only two revenue farms existed in Cambodia, on opium and gambling.[52] By late 1891, when Resident Superior Huynh de Vernéville persuaded Norodom to exchange the royal revenue farming system for an annual civil list, the king had converted almost every fiscal obligation in the kingdom, including ones not customarily paid to the crown, into revenue farm monopolies that he rented out to the highest bidders. Despite signing a convention in 1877 that forbade the creation of any new taxes and which only allowed revenue farms on opium, alcohol, and gambling, Norodom had managed to outmaneuver a series of French officials and establish a voraciously expanding revenue farming system that, by 1892, had taken major steps towards rationalizing and modernizing the traditional Cambodian fiscal system. However, unlike the revenue farms discussed elsewhere in this volume, Norodom devoted almost none of the millions the system generated to the modernization of the Cambodian state.[53] Instead, its profits went to him personally and to those favored businessmen, mainly but not exclusively Chinese, who secured monopoly rights to collect the various taxes, charges, and rents.[54]

Two specific revenue farms affected the fisheries. The first was the general fisheries farm that came into effect in 1880; the second was a separate revenue farm on processed fish customs duties established in 1882. In operation, they significantly increased business costs in the industry. The general fisheries farm began in 1879, when the king secretly resumed the customary tax levied by Khmer officials on fishing gear, standardized it for all fishing equipment, and then farmed it out, initially for about 300 silver taels.[55] In 1880, after the French failed to respond, Norodom combined the new farm with all preexisting royal fisheries leases into a single monopoly that immediately yielded him 2,000 silver taels (roughly 30,000 piasters).[56] Disgruntled Cambodian officials reacted locally to the loss of their ancient rights by making demands on waterways traditionally reserved for Khmer villagers, beginning the countrywide systemic encroachment on previously free waterways that would pose a major problem for fish conservation by the early twentieth century.[57] By 1884, after two other Chinese businesses had bought the general monopoly—the second for 4,000 silver taels (or 48,000 piasters)—Norodom had doubled his profits.[58] Thereafter, the bidding war for the general fisheries farm continued relentlessly. In 1890, the successful tenderer was the royal crony and Cantonese businessman Lư'u Chap, who offered 90,000 piasters per year, plus several valuable secret secondary payments.[59] In the final years of its operation, the annual rent soared even further, to 240,000 piasters.[60]

Ever-spiraling costs urgently pressured general fisheries monopolists

to insure their huge investment by on-selling substantial shares to sub-farmers, who also usually followed suit by selling off parts of their shares. By the early twentieth century, one French official described the resulting pyramid of speculators as holding "five, six or seven levels of exploiters between the State disposing of the concession and the fisherman who was actually doing the work."[61] While it was in the interest of every one of those many sub-farmers to pressure those below for timely payments, in order to cover their own commitments to those higher in the pyramid, the temptation for low-paid men at the base, who dealt directly with producers, to extract something extra must have been enormous. Reports of such behavior appeared right from the start of the new system. Late in the 1880 season, Aymonier met numerous angry Vietnamese fishermen who complained of being charged double, triple, or even quadruple the customary rate on their gear.[62] In 1881, St. Sernin heard similar stories on the lake, where even small 300 meter nets had been assessed at twice the usual amount for the largest nets, even though it was a catastrophic season when an average operation that normally produced 200–250 piculs of processed fish could only manage 70.[63] Instead of a 250 piaster profit on a 1,000 piastre outlay, these operations had little return on their fixed costs of 650 piasters, forcing many to borrow to survive.[64] Then, in 1882, when the separate monopoly on customs duties on processed fish came into effect, producers and merchants alike discovered that Chinese sub-farmers, appointed as temporary royal officials, simply refused to allow their boats to pass until the amounts unilaterally levied in tax were paid in full.[65]

By 1884, a number of local fisheries operators had recognized the importance of controlling the general farm and combined to bid for it. However, not only was their offer too low, but several also fell foul of the new requirement to lodge bids personally in Phnom Penh.[66] This early failure typified the difficulties producers experienced in bidding for the general farm, with Lê Thượng Tiếng being the only one to succeed, to my current knowledge. Later that year, the French tried to take greater control of the kingdom's finances and administration, but the ensuing countrywide anticolonial uprising forced them to tacitly accept Norodom's revenue farming system for several more years. Protectorate officials did, however, manage to insist that its tender processes conform more closely to existing norms in Cochinchina. Ironically, the elaborate terms and conditions documents that ensued, with clauses stipulating tenderers had to be creditworthy and to provide contractual guarantors against failure, largely ensured that only Chinese business

interests would qualify. Ordinary producers were automatically disbarred from competing with speculative capitalists by the need for two solvent guarantors who agreed to cover any defaulting payments. The only such eligible individuals in Norodom's Cambodia were a few favored courtiers, Chinese among them, and Chinese businessmen who appeared wealthy enough to guarantee repayments. Under Norodom it was also genuinely a matter of appearance: if a monopoly did fail, it was never in his interest to enforce his rights over the important Chinese guarantors, for fear of lowering future revenue farm bids. In fact, so secure were these personages that when the widow of the former Cantonese general fisheries farmer, Lưu Chap, sought to extend her husband's rights to certain fisheries leases with the Queen Mother in 1894, leaders of the Teochiu, Cantonese, and Fujianese communities willingly acted as guarantors.[67]

This highly extractive revenue farming system, operating in an environment of perennial capital scarcity, increasingly squeezed out the small to medium independent fishing operations that St. Sernin and others had described on Tonle Sap waters in the early 1880s. By the end of the 1890s, they were largely replaced with bigger fisheries owned by Chinese, Sino-Khmer, or Vietnamese capitalists who employed specialist Vietnamese fishing masters to organize and superintend operations. By the early twentieth century, all but the largest operations were completely dependent on loans from Chinese financiers, whether revenue farmers or itinerant salt sellers, to even begin their annual operations.[68]

The nature of the workforce on the lake also changed in these years. Difficulties in attracting enough laborers into the expanding 1890s industry had led to the pernicious practice of providing advances that exceeded their total contracted salary, in order to bind workers through indebtedness. Some workers responded, however, by signing the following year for a higher advance with another employer and using this cash to repay the earlier boss. Several rounds of such juggling left workers hopelessly enmeshed in debt and prompted a substantial minority to abscond at the last minute with the final employer's total advance. In such cases, local Cambodian administrators might refuse to act against the absconders; but if fishing bosses exercised their former age-old right to arrest and punish fleeing coolies, French magistrates now held them, rather than their workers, culpable. As a result, fishing masters who worked the Great Lake, where labor was at a premium, found it increasingly difficult to maintain their earlier authority over their workforce. Most were obliged to sacrifice several days of the fishing season

while their employees enjoyed the disreputable pleasures of Snok Trou, the only sizeable settlement between Kampong Chhnang and the vastness of the inhospitable lake.[69] If, as Lê Thượng Tiếng complained in 1901, it now required three times as much effort as in his father's day for the same result, we might perhaps detect in this the impact of a sullen and demoralized work force on the industry's productivity.

The general fisheries farm was abolished in mid-1908 and replaced by direct taxation on fishing gear and a system of fixed-term leases on fisheries lots. Published colonial documents claimed the general farm was scrapped because certain Chinese businessmen, who had conspired in 1906 to offer 100,000 piasters less than the administration wanted, had tried the same thing in 1908, as a deliberate attempt to undermine the French administration's budget.[70] Given the accumulating economic problems at the time, however, this seems unlikely. The low 1906 bid had followed two bad years that had visited severe losses on many fisheries outside the Great Lake. Unable to attract a higher Chinese bid, the protectorate had finally negotiated a contract with a Cambodian named Pean, but by then the fishing season was already six weeks old, and by late January 1907 Pean had still not finished organizing his sub-farmers.[71] The large losses incurred by the initial delay were compounded by slow payments from Chinese and Vietnamese sub-farmers, all of which doomed the endeavor, forcing Pean to seek several delays on his scheduled payments.[72] By November 1907, the frustrated resident superior, Paul Luce, was consulting residents about the future of the fisheries system, with a countrywide revenue farm covering all fisheries being one possibility canvassed.[73]

Low Chinese tenders in 1908 probably decided matters in favor of a system of defined fishing lots and direct taxation on fishing gear. The reform brought immediate productivity benefits, with the jump in exports suggesting the revenue farming system had ended by depressing fisheries' productivity (see table 2). The new system was also profitable, with the protectorate treasury collecting 337,816 piasters in 1908, or nearly 100,000 piasters more than the general fisheries farm for 1907.[74] While the premium Chinese speculators reaped during the life of the revenue farm is unknowable, this statistic suggests it was quite substantial.

However, if the abolition of the general fisheries farm instantly boosted export figures and protectorate tax yields, over the next decade it would have serious unintended consequences for the health of the Cambodian fish stocks on which both relied.

Table 2 Cambodian Processed-Fish Exports, 1909–1910

Commodity	1909	1910
Processed fish	11,500 tons	16,000 tons
Fish oil or fats	1,600 tons	1,828 tons
Fish pastes, sauces	220 tons	295 tons

Source: Loÿs Petillot, *Une richesse du Cambodge: La pêche et les poissons* (Paris: Challamel, 1911), 131.

A Crisis of Fish Conservation, c. 1900–1920

From the 1890s, the French had repeatedly subdivided fisheries leases not included in the general farm, causing a huge proliferation in lessee numbers locally.[75] After 1908, the abolition of the general fisheries farm, combined with the creation of contracted fishery lots for Tonle Sap Great Lake after the retrocession of Battambang and Angkor Provinces by Siam in 1907, saw leases multiply enormously. Under the former system, the general fisheries farmer, however ineffectually at times, had been legally responsible for the activities of the sub-farmers who leased waterways from him. Between 1908 and 1920, however, no effective regulation of fishing existed, and the impact on fish numbers was potentially catastrophic. If fisheries leases all contained start and end dates for fishing, and described the general locations of fisheries lots, no sanctions punished those who broke the rules.[76] A solitary 1911 circular from the Residence Superior which stipulated that fishing must end no later than 15 June rapidly became "quite ineffectual," in part because local Khmer often rebuilt leaseholders' barrages as soon as they were dismantled, claiming a "traditional right" to fish out of season.[77] Leaseholders also commonly pushed the geographical limits of their allotments without administrative penalty, while everyone shortened the off season, progressively reducing the number of spawning females that could lay their eggs before being caught.[78] Within a few years, millions of fish disappeared.

Large-scale fisheries on the Great Lake were just as destructive on fish stocks as smaller fisheries on leased waterways. Spurred on by the booming export market, professional operations began to work year-round on the lake. In the nineteenth century, fishing with large nets had begun only in December or January, but by the 1910s fishing bosses were dragging the submerged forest with huge nets, joined end to end and six to seven meters deep, from September through to December, and again in June and July,

when spawning females were often caught in large numbers. For the rest of the year, they used a variety of barrages and traps. In particular, they favored the destructive *samras* that lured fish to spawn within its confines but was nevertheless lightly taxed compared to other devices.[79]

In less than a decade of intensive, unregulated fishing, the number and size of fish caught in the Great Lake and in Cambodia had visibly dwindled. Buoyant export statistics and rising treasury receipts saw initial reports of the situation dismissed. As late as 1916 one French provincial official claimed that "fish formed a resource . . . in no way about to disappear."[80] But after the Council of Ministers officially requested an inquiry into fish stocks in 1917, French officials discovered that changes in fishing activities at all levels of the industry over the previous decade, from the use of dynamite through to the increasing height and narrowness of barrages, were indeed placing unsustainable pressure on fish numbers.[81] After considerable internal debate, a reformed system combining detailed maps of local fishing boundaries with a properly policed non-fishing season came into effect in 1920, when all existing contracts were due for renewal. Although modified slightly in 1938, this system basically organized the Cambodian fishing industry for the rest of the colonial era and beyond, until the Khmer Rouge (1975–1979) abolished fishing lots and attempted to turn swaths of the submerged forest, so essential to fish reproduction in the Tonle Sap Great Lake, into rice fields.[82]

Conclusion

From small beginnings, a processed fish industry developed in Tonle Sap waters and became a major colonial commodity exporter in the late nineteenth and twentieth centuries. Chinese played crucial roles in every phase of this development, whether as itinerant merchants who made large-scale fishing possible by supplying the everyday needs of tens of thousands of people along the inhospitable shoreline, as the owners or crew of the many vessels that shipped the fish or fish derivatives to markets downriver, or as the exporters whose networks opened new markets for Cambodian processed fish throughout colonial Asia. Chinese and Sino-Khmer also worked at every level of the industry, from fishing lot concession-holders down to coolies. However, it was as speculative financiers able to take advantage of the new opportunities created by the general fisheries farm that Chinese capitalists came to greatest prominence in the industry. By the twentieth century, revenue farming had enabled cashed-up Chinese financiers to squeeze out many small to medium operators on the lake and to monopolize the most productive fishing lots elsewhere. Overwhelmingly, they employed Vietnamese spe-

cialist fishing masters who preferred to hire non-Khmer labor. Unregulated overexploitation of fish stocks threatened the industry's viability after the general farm was abolished in 1908, but after sensible conservation rules were finally imposed in 1920 the commodity export industry flourished for the rest of the colonial era. Within a few decades, Chinese capital and commercial networks had helped Vietnamese fishing bosses and their crews transform an age-old Khmer subsistence sideline occupation into an important bulk-commodity industry whose consumable products were available throughout colonial Southeast Asia, and beyond.

Notes

My thanks to the Australian Research Council for the funding that made this research possible, and to the staff of the Centre des Archives d'Outre-Mer, Aix-en-Provence, France, and the National Archives of Cambodia, Phnom Penh, for their assistance.

1. Renaud Bailleux, *The Tonle Sap Great Lake: A Pulse of Life* (Bangkok: Asia Horizon, 2003), 1–12, 38, 82–87; K. G. Hortle, S. Lieng, and J. Valko-Jorgensen, *An Introduction to Cambodia's Inland Fisheries*, Mekong Development Series No. 4 (Phnom Penh: Mekong River Commission, 2004), 10–20.

2. Hortle, Lieng, and Valko-Jorgensen, *Cambodia's Inland Fisheries*, 22–23.

3. Bailleux, *The Tonle Sap Great Lake*, 72.

4. In 2001 official figures recorded 24,000 tons of inland fish exported to Thailand. Hortle, Lieng, and Valko-Jorgensen, *Cambodia's Inland Fisheries*, 24.

5. Both quotes from *Annuaire générale de l'Indochine* (Hanoi: Schneider, 1906), 786.

6. Figures in a letter of 15 May 1936 from the President of the Cambodian Mixed Chamber of Commerce to the Resident Superior of Cambodia [RSC], National Archives of Cambodia [NAC], 13129.

7. Ian Mabbett and David Chandler, *The Khmers* (Oxford: Blackwell, 1995), 37.

8. David P. Chandler, *A History of Cambodia*, 2d ed. (Sydney: Allen and Unwin, 1993), 100.

9. Andrew Spooner, "Rapport sur le Cambodge: Voyage de Sai-gon au Bat-tam-bang," 30 December 1862. Typescript copy, Centre des Archives d'Outre-Provence, Gouvernement-générale de l'Indochine, [CAOM GGI], Fonds amiraux [FA], dossier 12705, 21–22 for the early 1860s. For an English language translation, see Nola Cooke, "Rapport sur le Cambodge: Voyage de Sai-gon au Bat-tam-bang," *Chinese Southern Diaspora Studies* 1 (2007): 154–69, available on the *Chinese Southern Diaspora Studies* website, http://csds.anu.edu.au/.

10. Jean Moura, "Notes sur la pêche du Tonli-Sap (Lac du Cambodge)," *Revue maritime et coloniale* (June 1880): 536.

11. "Trấn Tây phong thổ ký" [The customs of eastern Cambodia], trans. Li Tana, *Chinese Southern Diaspora Studies* 1 (2007): 148–53, available on the *Chinese Southern Diaspora* Studies website, http://csds.anu.edu.au/. The Nguyễn called Cambodia Trấn Tây, meaning the western protectorate, during the disastrous Vietnamese attempted annexation,

from the mid-1830s to 1847. For the tax system, see Étienne Aymonier, *Le Cambodge: Le royaume actuel* (Paris: Ernest Leroux, 1900), 77.

12. "Trấn Tây phong thổ ký," 150.

13. Adhémar Leclère, "La pêche dans le Grand Lac du Cambodge," *Bulletin économique de l'Indochine* 38 (1901): 675. The quantity in the text was 1,000 piculs, or 60,000 kilos. For the longer, original version, see A. Leclère, report to RSC, 14 June 1900, NAC 11591.

14. Spooner saw smoked fish going to Cochinchina, but it was probably eaten there. Spooner, "Rapport sur le Cambodge," 21; Loÿs Petillot, *Une richesse du Cambodge: La pêche et les poissons* (Paris: Challamel, 1911), 98–99.

15. For the first, see Leclère, "La pêche dans le Grand Lac du Cambodge," 676. For the others, see Moura, "Notes sur la pêche du Tonli-Sap," 552; and H. Buchard, "Rapport à M. le Gouverneur sur la mission du Grand-Lac," *Cochinchine française: Excursions et Reconnaissances* 4 (1880): 276. It probably reflected the different quantities required for lightly drying and heavily salting.

16. Cambodia's "province de sel." Bertrand d'Azéma to Apostolic Vicar, 25 December 1755. Archives des Missions-Étrangères de Paris, vol. 744, fol. 277.

17. Trịnh Hoài Đức, *Gia Định Thành thông chí* [Gia Dinh gazetteer], trans. Nguyễn Tạo (Saigon: Nhà Văn Hòa, 1972), 3: 40.

18. For 1836, see Nguyễn Đình Đầu, *Nghiên cứu địa bạ triều Nguyễn, Biên Hòa* [Research into the Nguyen dynasty cadastral registers for Bien Hoa] (Ho Chi Minh City: NXB Thành Phố HCM, 1994), 263. For 1863, see Philippe Langlet and Quach Thanh Tâm, *Atlas historique des six provinces du sud du Vietnam du milieu du XIXe au début du XXe siècle* (Paris: Les Indes Savantes, 2001), 214, 242.

19. It had been a major producer of cheap salt earlier in the century and had restricted Bà Rịa's growth [*Gia Định Thành thông chí* 3: 40]. In 1865, 1,200 junks traded from here to Saigon, with a carrying capacity of 33,300 piculs, second only to the Bà Rịa junks' capacity of 46,085 piculs. These two ports represented 65 percent of Saigon's 1865 cabotage trade. Most of their cargo was probably salt.

20. The article says 508,798 piculs of salt, or more than 30,500 tons, were imported in 1865. This figure may be a misprint but the increase over 1864 was underlined in the text, as were the 100,000 piculs from Vietnamese ports. "Commerce et navigation de la Cochinchine en 1865," *Revue maritime et coloniale* 17.1 (1866): 190, 192.

21. The first figure is from Lê Thượng Tiếng (Leclère, "La Pêche dans le Grand Lac du Cambodge," 676) and the second from Spooner's enquiries in 1862 ("Rapport sur le Cambodge," 21). For more information, see Nola Cooke, "Water World: Chinese and Vietnamese on the Riverine Water Frontier, from Ca Mau to Tonle Sap (c. 1850–1884)," *Water Frontier: Commerce and the Chinese in the Lower Mekong Region*, ed. Nola Cooke and Li Tana (Lanham, Md.: Rowman and Littlefield / Singapore University Press, 2004), 144–45.

22. Rieunier, "Le Commerce de Saïgon pendant l'année 1862," *Revue maritime et coloniale* 12.2 (1864): 224. In 1862, the quantity of dried fish exported from Saigon was topped only by rice.

23. For 1862 data throughout, see Rieunier, "Le Commerce de Saïgon pendant l'année 1862," 220, 224. For 1865 figures, my calculations are from data in "Commerce et navigation de la Cochinchine en 1865," *Revue maritime et coloniale* 17.1 (1866): 189.

24. Spooner named these places ("Rapport sur le Cambodge," 21).

25. Rieunier, "Le Commerce de Saïgon pendant l'année 1862," 220.

26. Buchard, "Rapport à M. le Gouverneur sur la mission du Grand-Lac," 252.

27. Louis de Carné, *Travels on the Mekong: Cambodia, Laos and Yunnan* (Bangkok: White Lotus, 1995), 38–39.

28. De Carné reported loans could be as high as 100 percent (ibid., 39).

29. Moura to Governor of French Cochinchina [GOVCC], 1 April 1869, CAOM GGI, FA 10127; and Moura, "Notes sur la pêche du Tonli-Sap," 548.

30. Moura, "Notes sur la pêche du Tonli-Sap," 548.

31. Salt loans heavily discounted the value of the fish, so itinerant salt merchants doubled their outlays downriver. Petillot, *Une richesse du Cambodge*, 108.

32. Buchard, "Rapport à M. le Gouverneur sur la mission du Grand-Lac," 279.

33. Buchard described a fishery of this size as large in "Rapport à M. le Gouverneur sur la mission du Grand-Lac," 252. The nets were often extended to two kilometers, according to Moura, "Notes sur la pêche du Tonli-Sap," 537.

34. Petillot, *Une richesse du Cambodge*, 92–93; Leclère, "La pêche dans le Grand Lac du Cambodge," 676.

35. Henri Mouhot, *Travels in Siam, Cambodia and Laos, 1858–1860* (Singapore: Oxford University Press, 1992), 262.

36. Leclère, "La pêche dans le Grand Lac du Cambodge," 675. In 1848 15,000 to 20,000 francs (2,700 to 3,500 piasters) was regarded as a "colossal" fortune in southern Vietnam. Charles-Émile Bouillevaux, *Voyage dans l'Indo-Chine, 1848–1856* (Paris: Victor Palmé, 1858), 45.

37. Moura, "Notes sur la pêche du Tonli-Sap," 549–51.

38. Moura to GOVCC, report of 1 April 1869, CAOM GGI, FA 10127. A *quan* was a Vietnamese string of cash, called a *ligature* in French sources. It was worth about 90 French centimes at the time.

39. Spooner, "Rapport sur le Cambodge," 14; Buchard, "Rapport à M. le Gouverneur sur la mission du Grand-Lac," 277; Moura, "Notes sur la pêche du Tonli-Sap," 544, 547; Petillot, *Une richesse du Cambodge*, 98–100; St Sernin, "Voyage au lacs du Cambodge," *Revue maritime et coloniale* 98.12 (1888): 395, referring to a trip in 1881.

40. Aymonier, *Le Cambodge*, p. 77.

41. Spooner, "Rapport sur le Cambodge," 21–22.

42. Ibid., 2.

43. Moura, letter of 5 March 1871 to GOVCC, CAOM GGI, FA 10033.

44. The fish bladder trade began in the 1870s. See Moura, "Notes sur la pêche du Tonli-Sap," 544–46; and Petillot, *Une richesse du Cambodge*, 102–3.

45. Under-Director of Customs, letter of 10 October 1929 to RSC, NAC 3081. The average for the rest of the decade was only about 3,000 tons.

46. In 1901, Lê Thượng Tiếng even estimated the Mekong contributed only 1 percent to the fish catch, with the rest from Tonle Sap waters. Leclère, "La pêche dans le Grand Lac du Cambodge," 676.

47. All figures from Petillot, *Une richesse du Cambodge*, 138–40.

48. For the 1910 figures, and the value of the 1873 processed fish, see ibid.

49. For the export figures, see Leclère, "La pêche dans le Grand Lac du Cambodge," 675. At the time, there were no separate customs figures collected for Cambodia, following the 1893 customs union with Cochinchina.

50. Leclère, "La pêche dans le Grand Lac du Cambodge," 675–76.

51. Petillot does not give a precise date, but it was likely to be after 1901 since Leclère never mentioned it (*Une richesse du Cambodge*, 92–93).

52. Spooner, "Rapport sur le Cambodge," 2. Both in Chinese hands, they returned 150,000 piasters.

53. See essays by Carl A. Trocki and Wu Xiao An in this volume.

54. For a detailed discussion, see Nola Cooke, "King Norodom's Revenue Farming System in Later Nineteenth-Century Cambodia and His Chinese Revenue Farmers (1860–1891)," *Chinese Southern Diaspora Studies* 1 (2007): 30–55, available on the Chinese Southern Diaspora Studies website, http://csds.anu.edu.au/.

55. Aymonier to GovCC, 18 June 1881, CAOM GGI, FA 12694.

56. Aymonier, "Rapport sur le Cambodge," 18 November 1880, CAOM GGI, FA 10289.

57. Ibid.

58. Fourès to GovCC, 1 July 1884, CAOM GGI, FA 13469.

59. A certified copy of the contract with the resident superior is at CAOM GGI, FA 9430. Other documents show he had acquired a partner in 1891, about whom no details were given.

60. Negotiated agreement between RSC and A. Pean, 1906–08, 19 October 1906, CAN 1343.

61. Petillot, *Une richesse du Cambodge*, 112.

62. Aymonier to GovCC, 14 June 1880, CAOM GGI, FA 12603.

63. In 1880 Moura reported the tax rate was 150 Viet quan, or about 1.5 silver bars, but without mentioning net size ("Notes sur la pêche du Tonli-Sap," 552). St. Sernin, "Voyage au lacs du Cambodge," 387.

64. St. Sernin, "Voyage au lacs du Cambodge," 387.

65. Fourès to GovCC, letter of 7 July 1885, CAOM GGI, FA 10007; and also his letter of 26 April 1884, CAOM GGI, FA 10027.

66. Fourès to GovCC, letter of 2 September 1884, CAOM GGI, FA 12694.

67. Document 57 in CAOM GGI, FA 9430.

68. This widespread dependence on loans from itinerant Chinese salt traders even caused the French to close the official Kompong Cham salt depot, for lack of patronage. Letter from the Under-Receiver of Customs, Kompong Cham, to RSC, 1 December 1908, NAC 8926.

69. All details from Leclère, report of 14 June 1900, NAC 11591.

70. For the official documentation, see Petillot, *Une richesse du Cambodge*, 118–27.

71. See the letters of 21 January 1907 from the Kratié Resident to RSC and to A. Pean, about the latter's erroneous claim to rights in Kanhchor and Chhlong, NAC 1343.

72. See the various documents on this subject dated 9 May, 13 May, 30 May, 13 June, 1 July, 24 December, and 28 December 1907, in NAC 1343.

73. Resident Jeannerat of Kandal to RSC, letter of 29 November 1907, NAC 1343.

74. Petillot, *Une richesse du Cambodge*, 129–30. This represented one-ninth of the protectorate budget, with rice only responsible for a little more (one-eighth).

75. Alain Forest, *Le Cambodge et la colonisation française* (Paris: L'Harmattan, 1980), 207.

76. Extract from Report No. 802, 29 July 1920, NAC 25719.

77. Both quotes from ibid. The circular of 12 August 1911 is also at NAC 25719.

78. Several documents address this matter in NAC 25719. For example, a request from the Cambodian naval minister, dated 23 February 1917, for RSC to inquire into fish stocks, or a report by the Resident of Kampong Chhnang dated 30 May 1918.

79. Pursat Resident's report, 17 November 1917, NAC 37158. These devices are now prohibited in Cambodia.

80. Kampong Chhnang Resident's report, 30 May 1918, in NAC 25719.

81. For instance, barrages that had previously been 2–2.2 meters high had reached 3.5 meters by 1917, allowing fishing to continue during periods of much higher water than had traditionally occurred, while the gaps between the bamboo poles from which the barrages were woven had reduced from 3 centimeters to almost half that width. In addition, these barrages were set up in December rather than late January. Pursat Resident's report, 12 November 1917, NAC 37158. Fishing by use of dynamite or drugging the fish was officially banned in 1908. See NAC 34495 for the ban.

82. Bailleux, *The Tonle Sap Great Lake*, 123–29.

MOSES'S ROD

The Bible as a Commodity in Southeast Asia and China

〜〜〜 Jean DeBernardi

[The Bible] is to us what Moses' rod was to him, the instrument we employ in accomplishing the purposes of God; the instrument, too, with which every one of our own hearts must be struck, before there can gush from them the waters of life.
—James Legge, addressing the 42nd Annual Meeting of the British and Foreign Bible Society (May 30, 1846)

Compelled by the challenge posed by its enormous population, evangelical Protestant Christians have long aspired to distribute the Bible to every person in China. In 1815, the London Missionary Society (LMS) launched an important program of Chinese translation and printing in its Ultra-Ganges Mission (Singapore, Penang, Malacca, and Batavia) under the umbrella of colonial rule. The LMS directors relocated this translation and publication work to China after the 1842 Treaty of Nanjing opened five cities to residence by British subjects and awarded Hong Kong to Britain. By midcentury, progress in translation projects, technological improvements (including the use of the cylinder press), and the promise of political change prompted leaders of the British and Foreign Bible Society (BFBS) to decide that the goal of placing a Bible in every Chinese household was finally within reach. Consequently, in conjunction with its 1854 Jubilee celebrations, the BFBS launched a Million Testament Fund for China. Although funds flowed in from throughout the British Empire, the campaign foundered when the missionaries and their Chinese assistants met with insurmountable obstacles in distributing the books.

The printing and distribution of cheap Bibles was the particular aim of the BFBS, which had been established in 1804 to promote a Christian moral-

political economy through the wide circulation of the Bible. The society's 1854 Jubilee coincided with a fifty-year history of Chinese Bible translation and publication in Canton and Southeast Asia for which the BFBS had provided considerable funding, printing equipment, and technical support. After the LMS missionaries moved from Southeast Asia to China in 1843, the diverse Protestant denominations collaborated on a new translation of the New Testament as a sign of their union. Although the attempt at collaboration foundered when the missionaries failed to agree on the translation of key terms, the BFBS supported the British missionaries' translation, raising enough funds to print and distribute more than two million copies of the Delegates Version New Testament in China (although in the end, not even a million were printed).

Although the Bible has obvious significance for all Christians, there were many complex reasons why the universal distribution of the Bible was so important to mid-nineteenth-century British Protestants: the Bible was both an instrument of personal transformation and an expression of British national character; its distribution addressed issues of national guilt and served as a form of atonement; the New Testament prescribed a moral economy based on humility and benevolence that (British elites argued) had a good influence on political communities; and finally, the Bible was a sign of Protestant unity in opposition to Catholicism. When British Christians raised funds to donate a million New Testaments to China, they mobilized all of these meanings.

James Legge's allusion to Moses's rod in the epigraph suggests further that British Christians regarded the Bible as having extraordinary and transcendent powers to rescue people from their adversaries, including despotic rulers. The Old Testament Book of Exodus described how God instructed both Moses and Aaron to use the rod (by some accounts a branch from the tree of knowledge in the Garden of Eden) as the instrument by which the Israelites were to be rescued from Egypt. Aaron used the rod to afflict the Egyptians with seven plagues. When thrown down, it transformed into a serpent and swallowed up the rods-turned-serpents of the Egyptian priests. Later, Moses used the rod to produce water from the rock, and also to part the Red Sea. Thus, the rod symbolized true miracles caused by God through his chosen leaders in contrast with the false magic employed by the Pharaoh's magicians and priests. The magical rod was the instrument of their rescue, thus the credit for the redemption of the Israelis belonged not to Moses but rather to the God who had worked these miracles. To this anthro-

pologist, the rod further suggests the tree of life—the world axis connecting heaven and earth—and hints at divinely ordained rule and its associated sacred centers.

Victorian Christians believed that the Bible performed real "magic" on a person's heart as an instrument of personal transformation. However, not all persons were alike. Starting in the period after the French Revolution, influential members of the British elite regarded Christianity as a means to promote vertical integration in a society whose moral economy had significantly broken down. Although many opposed state intervention in relief for the poor, they supported Christian social activism of varying sorts, including education through Sunday schools, protection for vulnerable populations such as child workers and prostitutes, the abolition of slavery, and later on, the anti-opium movement.

The founders of the BFBS included a number of influential figures who were active in the antislavery movement, and cofounder William Wilberforce's writings on slavery demonstrate his skepticism concerning the utilitarian perspective that the pursuit of pleasure and avoidance of pain would naturally result in the greatest good for all. Wilberforce was especially well-known for his 1818 work, *A Practical View of the Prevailing Religious System of Professed Christians in the Higher and Middle Classes in this Country, Contrasted with Real Christianity*, which is often simply called *Practical Christianity*. In chapter 6, he comments on the way that religion promotes "the temporal welfare of political communities," a fact that he observes has been maintained by "the most celebrated philosophers and moralists and politicians of every age." Consequently, he concludes, the state of religion in a country in any given period is a "question of great political importance."[1]

In *Practical Christianity*, Wilberforce characterized English Protestantism as complacent, "embodied in an Establishment" and lacking in passion. In the midst of growing affluence, religion had sunk low in life, and the relaxed morals and dissipated manners of the upper classes had diffused downward to the newly wealthy members of the middle class. If nominal Christianity were replaced by true religion, he suggested, this would promote greater happiness and peace for all. In particular, Wilberforce argued that Jesus prescribed universal love, and he recommended Christian benevolence as essential to the well-being of political communities, and indeed as "the most exalted patriotism." He took the river as a metaphor for the fertilizing power of benevolent action, which might start out locally, but which has the potential for global reach.[2]

Wilberforce proposed that even a so-called false religion that prescribed

good morals would produce good effects on political societies. Nonetheless, he promoted Christianity as being the religion most "powerfully adapted to promote the preservation and healthfulness of political communities." By contrast with individual selfishness, he concluded, public spirit and "enlarged vigorous operative benevolence" was Christianity's master principle.[3]

Evangelical Christians often propose that Christians win salvation through faith, not deeds. However, the British Christian elites who supported the foundation of the Bible Society regarded Christianity as prescribing a moral economy that accepted social inequality but urged elites to demonstrate benevolent concern for nonelite members of society. In a period of social change, urban migration, and industrialization, the elites who promoted publication and distribution of the Bible sought to persuade non-elite members of society that they were part of the social body, attached and interdependent.

Christian concern with the health and integrity of the social body extended to the conduct of global mercantile activities, and evangelical Christians used their programs of charitable outreach to promote moral accountability in the European diaspora, from soldiers and sailors to mercantile and administrative elites. Rather than use Christianity unreflectively to justify and support the imposition of colonial power, nineteenth-century Christians publicly addressed issues of national accountability and guilt. Many held that God would punish nations for their sins and that all citizens were responsible for moral behavior to win blessings. They engaged in acts of charity and sought to shape social policy in light of notions of "expiation and regeneration," hoping that the far-flung distribution of the Bible would "make up for the sins of England's past," including the slave trade.[4]

By 1854, the year of the Million Testament Fund drive, many British Christians were deeply ashamed of Britain's role in the opium trade and critical of the military means by which they had won access to China's treaty ports. However, they also considered the Chinese political system to be despotic and its religious practices to be dark and superstitious. They viewed the translation and distribution of the Bible throughout China as a vehicle through which they could convince the Chinese of the superiority of the Christian moral economy and aspired to transform China into a Christian nation.

Translating and Distributing the Bible: From Southeast Asia to China

BFBS funds supported the translation, printing, and distribution of tracts and Bibles. Missionaries who had specialized linguistic competence some-

times were seconded for long periods to the BFBS to engage in the work of Bible translation. The society's directors also sometimes sent (or assisted missionary agencies in sending) modern printing equipment to missionaries so that they could print and distribute Christian literature locally.

Just as the Bible Society employed colporteurs (as those distributing religious books are known) in Britain, the BFBS supported individuals who traveled widely in Asia to distribute Bibles and tracts. With support from the BFBS, and sometime accompanied by BFBS agents, the missionaries and local evangelists often took long tours by sea, which allowed them access to coastal cities, or followed rivers and canals inland by boat (at least until an extensive network of railways was built) to distribute the Bible, Testaments, and religious tracts that had been translated into many languages.

In a study that focuses on the BFBS's position in the history of nineteenth-century publishing and printing in Britain, Leslie Howsam sums up the society's approach to publishing and distributing the Bible.

> The dynamic nature of the BFBS can best be described as a "Bible transaction," a complex set of relations that were commercial, personal, philanthropic and cultural. The transaction was inescapably commercial, based upon the purchase and resale of printed books. But its importance was characterized by contemporaries in terms that transcended the cash nexus. The Bible transaction was conceived as a personal relation, too, involving face-to-face encounters between people. Despite this commercial aspect, it was also philanthropic, because charitable funds underwrote the low retail prices that were charged to the Society's customers. Finally it was a cultural transaction, a medium through which the virtues of Protestant Christianity, as interpreted among the more prosperous classes of the British Isles, could be conveyed to less fortunate individuals, whether they lived at home in poverty or infidelity, or abroad in heathenism, or under the "yoke of Rome." This notion became identified as a mark of the British national character.[5]

In China and Southeast Asia, as in Britain, all four of these dimensions came into play in the translation and distribution of the Bible.

The project of translating the Bible into Chinese was one of the earliest on the BFBS agenda. The founders knew that a Chinese translation of most of the New Testament had been deposited in the British Museum and recommended its publication. However, due to the high estimated cost of the project, the committee declined to pursue it. Nevertheless, Baptist missionaries at Serampore, India, were independently at work on a new translation

of the New Testament at Fort William, which they completed in 1810 with a £500 grant from the BFBS. They printed this edition with movable metal type—an innovation introduced and refined by agents of the BFBS—but also used the more traditional wooden block printing.[6]

Robert Morrison (1782–1834) joined the London Missionary Society in 1804—the same year in which the BFBS was established—and after language training in Britain, went to China in 1807. He studied Chinese well enough to translate the Bible into Chinese, using the translation of the New Testament in the British Library as a basis for his work. In 1812, the BFBS committee voted to grant him £500 and forwarded further grants as his work progressed. He and William Milne (1785–1822) collaborated on another translation of the New Testament, which was printed in Canton in 1814. In 1823, the son of Joshua Marshman (1768–1837), the Serampore Baptist missionary translator, presented the BFBS with a complete copy of the Bible in Chinese; in 1824, Morrison visited the society and presented the translation he had completed in Canton; a copy was also "graciously received" by His Majesty George IV.

Southeast Asia was a particular focus for distribution of the Chinese Bible, since an estimated 200,000 Chinese settlers lived there. Milne reported that they found many opportunities to circulate the scriptures among Chinese immigrants throughout Southeast Asia, "from Penang, through the Malay Archipelago, to the Molluccas and Celebes, on the one hand; and from Kiddah, round the Peninsula, through the Gulf of Siam, and along the coast of Cochin-China, on the other."[7] Morrison reported that the Chinese in the Malayan Archipelago could receive the scriptures without any impediment; and that "it was hoped, that through these individuals the Scriptures might, and would find their way into China itself."[8]

Because Southeast Asia afforded such ready access to the migrant Chinese population, with support from the London Missionary Society (LMS), Morrison and Milne established the Ultra-Ganges Mission there, including the Anglo-Chinese College in Malacca, and mission stations in Penang, Singapore, and Batavia (Java). The work of translation was conducted both in Canton and Malacca, where it was carried out under the auspices of the Anglo-Chinese College (est. 1818), which took the printing and publishing of religious literature as a primary concern.[9] By 1820, a translation of the Chinese Bible, supervised by Morrison and Milne, was complete and ready for printing. In 1822, Morrison sent 1,000 copies of the Chinese New Testament to Singapore, which "became, after a few years, the seat and centre of considerable Scripture distribution."[10]

When a committee to promote Christianity was formed in Singapore in 1827, one of its members wrote to the BFBS to offer their services in the task of Bible distribution, noting Singapore's enormous potential as a Bible depot and distribution center. As this unknown member described it, Singapore was a multiethnic city whose population comprised Chinese, Malay, Bugis, Malabar, Bengali, Portuguese, Armenian, and British residents. Moreover, Singapore's harbor was visited daily by boats from China, Siam, Cochinchina, Java, Europe, and South America, which offered further opportunities for Bible distribution. The committee anticipated that the extra Bible copies that they gave to the Chinese to carry with them on their return to China would be passed on to those at home.[11]

Some have observed that Christian missionaries followed the flag of colonial rule, but the distribution of the Chinese Bible and tracts also followed circuits of commerce and migration. After 1815, European missionaries and Chinese evangelists based in Singapore, Malacca, Penang, and Batavia rode the expansive sea highway of the Asian Mediterranean, seeking immigrant Chinese who might be receptive to their message, including the Chinese miners of Bangka and Phuket (Junk Ceylon).[12]

Although details are scant on the work of Chinese Christians who returned from Southeast Asia to China to proselytize, there is one well-documented case. Morrison's and Milne's first convert was the Cantonese printer Liang Ah Fa (1789–1855), who together with his assistant, Kew Ah Gung (1818–1843), joined the Ultra-Ganges Mission in Malacca in 1815. Liang Ah Fa returned to China in 1819, where Morrison ordained him, but then fled back to Southeast Asia in 1821 after the Qing government restricted his evangelical work. Although Liang Ah Fa and Kew Ah Gung returned to Hong Kong on a permanent basis with Legge only in 1843, in 1830 they visited China and traveled 250 miles inland from Canton to distribute Chinese tracts. Among those whom they approached with their Christian message were candidates for positions in the imperial bureaucracy.[13]

In 1833 or 1834, Hong Xiuquan—the future leader of the Taiping Rebellion—received one of Liang Ah Fa's tracts, "Good Words to Admonish the Age," when he sat the imperial examinations in Canton.[14] The tract deeply impressed him, serving as one important inspiration for the Christian-syncretic ideology of the Taiping Heavenly Kingdom. However, before 1843, China remained largely inaccessible to Christian evangelists, European and Chinese alike.

When the five treaty ports were opened to missionaries, the LMS decided to close the Ultra-Ganges Mission, including their mission stations in

Penang, Malacca, and Batavia. The LMS continued to support a Malay mission in Singapore for a time and left behind a printing press, but the society moved their China mission entirely to China, leaving the work of proselytizing Chinese immigrants in Southeast Asia to others. Although most of the graduates of the Anglo-Chinese College took jobs in Singapore, a few joined Legge in Hong Kong when the LMS mission relocated from Southeast Asia to China in 1843, including the printers Liang Ah Fa and Kew Ah Gung.[15] Shanghai soon joined Singapore and Hong Kong as a major hub for the printing and distribution of religious literature, including the Bible.

After the Ultra-Ganges mission ended, first independent, then Plymouth Brethren missionaries took over the work of evangelical Christianity in Singapore and Penang.[16] One of the missionaries who continued the work in Penang was an independent German missionary named Johann Georg [John George] Bausum (1812–1855), who received support from the Chinese Evangelization Society and the Bible Society, not only for himself but also for Chinese evangelists whom he trained. The eventual goal was to prepare them to return to China and work as colporteurs, following the model set by the Chinese Union, an evangelistic society that Gützlaff and seven Chinese had formed in 1844.

Karl Friedrich August Gützlaff (1803–1851) was an independent missionary who resigned from the Netherlands Missionary Society and lived and worked in Thailand from 1829 to 1831. After his wife's death in 1831, he traveled along the coast of China, as far north as Tianjin, before settling in Macau. For the next few years, Gützlaff acted as an interpreter for foreign traders (including opium smugglers) on various ships, taking advantage of the opportunity afforded him by travel to distribute tracts, proselytize, and offer basic medical assistance. In 1834, he published a widely popular account of his adventures in Thailand and China.[17]

As Jessie Lutz explains, Gützlaff proposed to sinify the work of evangelism by having Chinese present the essence of Christianity in local dialects, compose tracts that were Chinese in tone and style, and supervise the proselytizing, so that in the end "Chinese would win China for Christ."[18] The Chinese Union raised funds to train Chinese colporteurs to carry tracts and New Testaments to the interior of China, and the Chinese workers reported spectacular successes. Inspired by Gützlaff, in 1850, British evangelical Christians formed the Chinese Society for Furthering the Promulgation of the Gospel in China, and Adjacent Countries, by Means of Native Evangelists, which they soon renamed the Chinese Evangelization Society (CES). Although they later broke their connection with the Chinese Union, British

evangelicals printed, as one of their first projects, 10,000 copies of a corrected edition of Gützlaff's Chinese translation of the New Testament.[19]

Among the first applicants to the CES was Bausum, who applied to them for assistance in the training of four native evangelists (three Chinese boys in his Penang school and a young Malay), whom the CES directors hoped would some day "enter their native land as heralds of the gospel, and aid in the glorious work of putting down the strongholds of Satan."[20] The Million Testament Fund provided an incredible level of financial support for colportage starting in 1854, including independent missionaries like the newly arrived James Hudson Taylor and a number of Chinese agents. Chinese Christians commonly traveled between Penang and Singapore and China, and it seems likely that some of those trained at mission stations in Southeast Asia returned to engage in colportage and evangelism in China just as their supporters hoped. However, as with the Chinese who assisted the missionaries in Bible translation projects, their names usually were not publicized, so the records are regrettably silent on this point.[21]

Bible Translation in China: The Delegates Version New Testament

One of the first projects that Protestant missionaries in China pursued was a new translation of the Bible, a project that they resolved to undertake cooperatively at a conference in 1843, and for which they received pledges of support from the BFBS and the American Bible Society.[22] For the Protestant missionaries in China, Bible-centered outreach distinguished them from the Catholic missionaries, whom they viewed as their chief competitors.[23] For example, in 1846, Walter Medhurst and Dr. Lockhart wrote to the LMS foreign secretary that their translation work was urgent since "the agents of a corrupt Christianity are at our elbow diffusing the Popist agenda and monkish fables, the only antidote to which is the tree of life intended for the healing of nations," by which they meant the Bible. At the same time, the BFBS committee learned that the missionaries had new opportunities to proselytize since the Chinese authorities had announced that missionaries were at "liberty to teach, receive, and profess the Christian religion." In response, the BFBS granted the LMS £1000 to send a cylinder printing press, additional metal type, and assistants to Shanghai to help the missionaries produce the Chinese scriptures.[24]

While the Bible distinguished them from Catholics, it was, at the same time, intended to be a sign of Protestant Christian unity. For example, an LMS missionary notes that when a Parsee, whom he met in China, asked him why Christians were so divided, he responded by explaining the "origin, rise

and progress of the Bible Society" and gave him an English Bible, "not only as a memorial of [his] own individual interest in his eternal welfare, but also as a monument of the unity of Christians."[25] Nonetheless, unity was an issue among Protestant missionaries, and the project of translating the Bible revealed its points of fracture. Indeed, this translation of the New Testament, which came to be known as the Delegates Version New Testament, is a more apt symbol of disunity than of unity.

The project had been launched in 1843 at a conference in Hong Kong attended by members of several mission societies, including the LMS, the American Board of Commissioners for Foreign Missions, and representatives of the American Baptists and Presbyterians.[26] Their resources included not only financial support but also human capital that an earlier generation of missionaries had not had. Most important to their effort were Chinese converts, who assisted them in the work of translation, tract composition, printing, and colportage. By 1843, a new generation of European Christians who had been born in Asia and who had grown up speaking Chinese languages also contributed to the China mission effort, including the work of translation and printing. Among these European Christians were the sons and daughters of Robert Morrison, William Milne, and Samuel Dyer.[27]

The translation work started in 1847, but the delegates almost immediately began arguing over how best to translate the term for God into Chinese. Morrison and Milne had used *shen* (spirit) in their earlier translations, but Medhurst, Gützlaff, and Bridgman had chosen to use the term *shangdi* (supreme ruler). The LMS missionaries preferred *shangdi*, and further amplified the discord by proposing to use the disputed term *shen* (spirit) to translate Holy Spirit, whereas the missionaries who advocated using the term *shen* to refer to God promoted *ling* (numinous power) as the best translation for Holy Spirit.[28]

The LMS missionaries justified their preference for *shangdi* with a historical argument, claiming that God had revealed himself to the Chinese in the Zhou dynasty (c. 1122–235 B.C.) as *shangdi*—the highest deity and the creator of all things. This allowed them a certain rhetorical purchase, since they could claim that the Chinese who converted were returning to an earlier golden age, rather than turning their backs on Chinese culture (and missionaries still use this term and argument to good effect). Because the translation committee could not agree on a compromise, they continued their debate in writing, producing about 600 handwritten pages, many of which were published in the *Chinese Repository* and *Chinese Recorder*.[29]

Because the group of delegates had no final authority to whom they could

appeal for a decision, each group made arguments to their respective Bible societies. The BFBS's editorial subcommittee found that they could only express an opinion on the alternatives proposed, but gave grants to both the LMS missionaries and the Church Missionary Society (CMS) missionaries. The CMS missionaries preferred *shen*, and when an agreement could not be reached with the LMS and the BFBS for a "united plan of action," they chose to decline the grant.[30]

In 1850, the American Bible Society also came down in favor of *shen*. The missionaries could have resolved the dispute by publishing different versions of the translation, leaving blanks in the text where the disputed terms appeared, but finally the committee split, and the BFBS edition of the Delegates Version New Testament was the only one published. Due to the split, funds that had been pledged by the American Bible Society were not forthcoming, and the BFBS financed the project almost entirely on its own.[31] In 1852, the LMS missionaries printed 5,500 copies of the new translation. Copies were not only distributed in China, but also sent to Batavia, Penang, Calcutta, California, London, and Australia.[32]

The Delegates Version NT was small, lightweight, and inexpensive to produce, and was praised for its elegant literary style (a style that, while praised, was nonetheless superseded when the missionaries discovered Mandarin and a more widely accessible lower classical style).[33] The timing of the Delegates Version NT was fortuitous, falling in the year before the BFBS started to plan its Jubilee Year, and just as the Taiping rebels were becoming well known to the British public.[34]

The Jubilee Year

1854 was the British and Foreign Bible Society's fiftieth year, and the society marked its Jubilee with a variety of activities, including special initiatives to distribute the Bible throughout Great Britain, to supply emigrants with Bibles, and to distribute Bibles and Testaments in schools, prisons, missions, and other institutions; they also made special efforts in India, Australia, and other British colonies. Finally, they launched an ambitious appeal—the Million Testament Fund for China.

The Taiping Rebellion raised Christian hopes that a new government whose leaders were Christian-influenced, if not Protestant like themselves, might overthrow the Qing dynasty. On 19 March 1853, the Taiping rebels entered Nanjing, and on 29 March, their leader, Hong Xiuquan, was carried into the city on a golden palanquin, wearing a yellow robe and yellow shoes—signs of his claims to imperial sovereignty.[35] The Taiping leader

had read a tract written by Liang Ah Fa and became convinced of the truth of Christian revelations. Among the Taiping leaders' first acts was the printing of the Books of Genesis and Exodus, and by the end of 1853, they had also printed Leviticus and Numbers, all based on an early translation of the Old Testament completed by Gützlaff.[36]

Between 1853 and 1854, representatives of the British, French, and American communities in China met with the Taiping leaders and as a result, received and examined copies of their publications. Although the missionaries found much encouragement in Taiping assurances that "as children and worshippers of one God we were all brethren," others were more skeptical, finding Taiping decrees and messages—some of which included claims to universal sovereignty—to be unreasonable and bizarre.[37] Nonetheless, reports of these extraordinary events were widely reported in British newspapers and were a topic of intense interest to evangelical Christians. Many saw in these events the workings of providence, and the coincidence of the rebellion with the BFBS's fiftieth anniversary events suggested that five decades of support for Bible translation, publication, and distribution was about to pay off handsomely with the creation of a new Christian dynasty in China.

Reverend J. A. James proposed the Million Testament Fund in an address entitled "China: Something Must Be Done, and Done Immediately, for China—What?," which was subsequently published in *The British Banner*, in September 1853.[38] James had learned about the Taiping Rebellion from published letters written by Legge and Hobson that had appeared in British newspapers, and he declared the Chinese movement to be "the wonder of wonders."

James cited a letter from one of the insurgent chiefs to Dr. Charles Taylor, which had been translated into English and published. In that letter, the leader declared that the Taiping celestial dynasty had received the command of heaven to rule the empire. The leader also mentioned that Taylor had brought him books, and because Taylor also worshipped God (the author pointedly added *Shang-te* [*shangdi*] in brackets), they acknowledged him as a brother. James concluded that this new faith was Christian and that the insurrection was "essentially a Protestant and not a Popish movement." Most important, he celebrated the fact that the Taiping rebels were willing to enter into fellowship with them. The door that had been closed for so many decades was now opened, and he concluded that the duty of the church was to multiply missionaries. James had received a letter from Thomas Thompson proposing that they launch a fund for printing and circulating in China "A

Million Copies of the Chinese New Testament," asking for his help in putting the proposal before the public through the press, and calling all Sunday-school teachers and scholars to do the work of fund-raising. James proposed that it become a basis for "Christian union for action," and suggested that the BFBS would be the organization best suited to carry out the project.

James further proposed that donations be taken down not in dollar amounts, but in the number of testaments, since "giving sixty copies of scripture to sixty chinamen sounds more pleasant than giving a pound to a fund for purchasing a million copies. *It brings out more forcibly the value and importance of individual effort*" (emphasis in original). He proposed that the distribution be entrusted to missionaries and that Protestants of all denominations ally against their competitor, Rome. He acknowledged that "errors" were mixed into the religious views of the movement, but proposed that circulating the Bible would help to correct these. An editorial in *The Watchman* further noted that the rebels had published Old Testament books, but lacked the New Testament, which the author predicted would "temper their polygamy and fanaticism." Meanwhile, news had reached England that William Chalmers Burns had completed a Chinese translation of *Pilgrim's Progress* and that this would be printed at a mere four cents a copy.

Among the earliest responses to his appeal was a letter from the Earl of Gainsborough, who sent a check to James for £20. A person identifying himself only as a Father also wrote to the editor of *The British Banner* to report that he and his wife and six children had all agreed that each would give a Bible to a Chinese family, so that eight families would be supplied with the Word of God. Two individuals were so moved by the proposal that they wrote poems extolling the wondrous doings in China, and calling on British Christians to "give them the Bible" so that they could uproot "heathenish notions" and assert themselves against despots.[39] A number of British newspapers—including the *Nonconformist*, the *Record* (Evangelical Church Party), the *Watchman* (Methodist Conference), the *Wesleyan Times* (Wesleyan Reformers), the *Patriot*, *British Banner*, and *Christian Times*—rallied support for the interdenominational project.

The secretary of the Bible Society agreed to take on the responsibility for the Million Testament Fund, noting that "China is ready for the Bible Society, and, thank God, the Bible Society is ready for China." A torrent of donations followed, some accompanied with touching letters published in the society's *Monthly Extracts From the Correspondence of the British and Foreign Bible Society*. Most of the donors were British, but donations also came from South Africa, Canada, the United States, Barbados, Antigua, and even Syria and the

Holy Land, where students in a mission school donated funds and "a gift of the Bible from the Bible's birth-place to Eastern Asia."[40]

In his second appeal, James also noted with approval that the insurgents had prohibited opium, adding that the use of the drug had become common and was "a still more formidable obstacle in the way of moral reformation than even drunkenness is in these Kingdoms."[41] His comment raises a significant issue: British evangelicals might have won the battle against slavery with the 1807 Slave Trade Act and the 1833 Slavery Abolition Act, but they faced further issues of national guilt over the opium trade.

Christians felt great joy at gaining access to China, but also expressed enormous ambivalence about the military means by which that access had been obtained, and about the motives for war, which included forcing the Chinese authorities to accept the opium trade. The Christian stance on temperance conflicted with the European merchants' promotion of this highly addictive drug, whose sale also provided significant funding for the colonial enterprise in the Straits Settlements.[42] Even before the opium wars, missionaries in Southeast Asia regarded opium as a vice, visiting opium dens in Singapore and Penang to exhort against its use and offering treatment to addicts. However, when they addressed Chinese on street corners and in public settings like temple festivals, their listeners sometimes retorted that even as European missionaries encouraged them to give up opium, it was Europeans who sold it to them. The missionaries confessed in their letters the sense of shame they felt.

Meanwhile, William Milne's son, William Charles Milne (1815–1865), reported that the insurgents had "broken loose from all the bands of superstition; they were determined to put down idolatry; they went from one place to another, upsetting their idols, ransacking their temples, emptying their monasteries, discarding their priests." However, the insurgents went further, notifying the public that "the living and true God was the only God to be worshipped by the people; and moreover they prescribed a sacred ritual for His service, and set apart one day in seven as a holy day."[43] Milne was uncertain as to the outcome of the rebellion, but was encouraged by the prospect that China might one day have an emperor who printed the scriptures, and displayed to the BFBS committee a copy of the Book of Genesis that Hong Xiuquan had printed, on which he had placed his "sign and stamp, the insignia of government, like the arms of our beloved Queen on the Scriptures in our own honoured country."[44] The British Christians found encouragement in Hong Xiuquan's opposition to both idol worship and opium use.[45]

As a result of the scale of this project, the BFBS set up a separate account for contributions, suggesting that donors might either send a sum of any amount, or the exact value of a specific number of copies, estimated at 4d. (four cents) a copy. The fund-raising program was an extraordinary success.

> The intensity, activity, and rapid result of this new effort of Christian zeal, were perhaps never surpassed; contributions flowed in from all quarters, and from all classes, in almost endless variety of amount. In this, as in the general Jubilee Fund, the poor man vied with the rich, the child with the aged sire, the Colonies with the mother country, and even foreigners, in climes far distant from each other, pressed to take, though it were but a humble part in this magnificent act of charity.[46]

Many members of the society were optimistic that China was soon to become a Christian nation, and indeed anticipated that China would become "the largest ruby that is to blaze, the most precious diamond that is to sparkle, in the diadem of Immanuel [Jesus]."[47]

The BFBS raised enough money to print a million New Testaments by February 1854, but continued until they had amassed a total of £52,368.[48] Meanwhile, the missionaries commenced the project by printing 250,000 copies of the New Testament (115,000 at Shanghai, 50,000 in Hong Kong, and 85,000 at other mission stations). However, the Bishop of Victoria and the missionaries soon cautioned the BFBS that it would be unwise to print a large number of scriptures that the country was not yet open to receive, and which they did not have adequate means to distribute. In response, the committee voted to give the missionaries an additional £1000 to pay for colportage.[49]

Starting in 1855, the BFBS published numerous letters from China reporting extensive travel by the missionaries and their colporteurs, and the distribution of tens of thousands of New Testaments. However, by 1856, the BFBS committee members were discouraged. Although they had expected to be able to accomplish "a great work" in a very short period of time, their hopes were not realized, since "the facilities anticipated for diffusing, far and wide, the Scriptures, have not been presented."[50]

Among those involved in Bible colportage were the missionaries William Chalmers Burns (1815–1868), who worked for the English Presbyterian mission, and James Hudson Taylor (1832–1905), who came to China with support from the Chinese Evangelization Society and who later founded the China Inland Mission. As his brother described it in his memoir, in 1854 Burns itinerated in Fujian, traveling to Britain briefly before returning in

1855. Between 1855 and 1858, Burns was based in Shanghai, but made frequent trips around the region, living on his boat and following in his leisurely travels the network of canals and rivers that "spread over the whole face of the country"—in China, as in the Cambodian water world, "economic activities followed the movement of water."[51]

The British evangelists typically traveled with local Christians, and Burns's memoir offers the conversion stories of three Chinese with whom he itinerated in Fujian in the mid-1850s. The first was a glib fortune-teller who used his talents to provide the "fit word at the fitting time," the second a soldier who viewed evangelism as offering him the opportunity to learn the craft of professional storytelling.[52] Finally, the memoir describes Tan See Boo, a young man who, before his conversion, had carved small idols for family altars.[53] Tan relinquished his trade and "cast himself on the providence of God," carving beads and ornaments instead of god images.[54]

In late 1855, Burns traveled with an unnamed Chinese Christian who was employed "in connection with the Million Testament Scheme," and in 1856, Taylor joined him in this work. The BFBS not only offered Taylor as many copies of the New Testament as he could distribute, but also paid most of his travel expenses, and he and Burns traveled together to distribute tracts and Testaments in areas of Jiangsu, Zhejiang, and Guangdong.[55] When they worked in nearby Shantou (Swatow), an American missionary based in Hong Kong dispatched two additional Chinese Christians to assist them.

Taylor returned to Shanghai, but when Burns and the Chinese colporteurs stopped in Chaozhou, the authorities arrested them on the boat. Commissioner Yeh dispatched Burns and his books to Shanghai with an escort and an official statement addressed to the British consul in which he charged that Burns's penetration into the inland riverine region wearing Chinese dress was highly improper. The local authorities detained the Chinese Christians, whom they beat and imprisoned for four months.[56]

Although the Christians had celebrated when the Taiping rebels had printed the scriptures, they now found that this put them in considerable danger. The following year, the LMS missionary William Muirhead wrote to the BFBS after two colporteurs and their boatmen were arrested and imprisoned, reporting that the mandarins associated books with the name Jesus in the title with the rebels, who were widely known to have adopted the "religion of the Heavenly Father and Jesus." The colporteurs were imprisoned for a month and only freed after the British consul intervened.[57]

Meanwhile, the outbreak of the Second Opium War (1856–1860) further hampered their efforts. In 1857, Legge announced that colportage would

have to be suspended since the Chinese colporteurs did not dare to go into the interior, to let it be known that they associated with foreigners, or to circulate books printed by foreigners.[58] Nonetheless, in 1857, the BFBS shipped out an additional cylinder printing press for the use of the corresponding committee at Shanghai; it also decided to print 50,000 copies of the entire Bible in Chinese as soon as possible, determined to use the surplus funds.

Blocked from distributing New Testaments in China, the missionaries briefly refocused their efforts on the Chinese populations in the Straits Settlements. In 1857, B. P. Keasberry, the LMS missionary to the Malays, formed the Bible and Tract Society in Singapore (which had been without a Chinese mission since 1843) and Medhurst sent him 3,000 Chinese New Testaments for distribution.[59] The next year, the British Methodist missionary Josiah Cox, whose hopes of establishing a mission in the rebel capital Nanjing had been disappointed, itinerated in the Straits Settlements and distributed over 3,000 New Testaments.[60] However, he returned to China, where he eventually established a mission in Hankow.

The BFBS had raised enough funds to print 2,334,000 copies of the scripture at fourpence each, but disbursement of the sum proved more difficult than the collection. By 1859, the BFBS reported that only 313,000 copies of the New Testament had been printed in Shanghai, Hong Kong, Canton, Fuzhou, and other places, and that many still sat in storage (especially in Shanghai) since the means to distribute them was lacking. They found innovative uses for the fund (for example, to produce a Chinese version of the Bible with raised characters for the blind), but could not expend the money as they had planned. The committee expressed their hope that they might still see "enlarged opportunities" in the future on which they might expend the funds remaining. Meanwhile, they reported their satisfaction that "China had received from the hands of England that rich supply of Scriptural truth 'the merchandise of which is better than the merchandise of silver and the gain thereof than fine gold.'"[61]

Conclusion

As C. Patterson Giersch has observed in this volume, circulation implies both the movement of people and goods, and the movement of technology, ideas, and forms of cultural production. The Million Testament Fund not only supported the widespread distribution of the Chinese New Testament to Chinese communities in China, Southeast Asia, Australia, and North America, but also paid for the introduction of the most up-to-date printing technology to China: the cylinder press and the use of metal type. The

Testaments themselves were not just utilitarian goods but the vehicles with which Christians hoped to convey their religious ideas, which the founders of the British and Foreign Bible Society regarded as the foundation of a just political economy.

The Christian founders and leaders of the BFBS sought to widely circulate the Bible (and an associated set of ideas and practices) in a competitive marketplace of ideologies and agendas. In the early nineteenth century, Christian texts competed with Thomas Paine's revolutionary pamphlets (and also pornography) in Britain, whereas in China, missionaries viewed the Bible as competing both with Catholic translations of the stories of the saints (which they abhorred as a form of idol worship) and the Confucian classics (which they disliked, since Confucius taught that humans were essentially good, rather than innately sinful). When British Christians donated money to the Million Testament Fund, they sought to promote through their gift a utopian view of a just global ecumene that offered an alternative not only to Chinese political and social practices, but also to economic utilitarianism and unbridled capitalism.

In raising funds for collective projects, Christians translated passionate convictions (including the abhorrence of slavery and compassion for opium addicts) into campaigns whose tone and momentum were measured by the level of participation and the degree of financial success. Donations created a social body of like-minded Christians, announced through a published donation list (figure 1). These lists gave equal weight to the donations of the child and the wealthy man, and often were printed together with stories of personal sacrifices, or of unexpected windfall gains that the recipients viewed as providential.

Fund-raising was an index of moral opinion, and donation a form of moral participation—a kind of plebiscite, if you will. Indeed, Milne observed that the "Bible Christians" of Britain had come forward to "vote One Mission Testaments to the people of China."[62] When Christians donated to charity, they made their virtue visible and quantified their values.

Donors were aware that contributions, however small, made them participants in a project of unimaginable scope and ambition, and they reveled in it. Take, for example, this letter published in the Bible Society's *Monthly Extracts*:

DEAR SIR—I've been thinking about the Million Testaments for China, and I thought they never could be gathered together. What a heap! It is impossible it can be done. Whilst I was musing one day, it came into my

mind what a Minister once said—"The ocean is made up of drops; the shore is only a multitude of little grains of sand."—Then I thought, If everybody would only put down one Testament as one little grain of sand, we should have the heap out of hand. So I made up my mind to give my little savings this year to China. Please to put it down from Elizabeth.[63]

This donor was dazzled by the enormity of the project, which she found unthinkable until she imagined the million testaments metaphorically as grains of sand or drops of water, joining together to create a vast ocean or seashore. But the New Testaments also symbolized the collective action of British Christians who translated their financial means into signs of Christian benevolence towards China. They imagined their donations as buying Bibles that were gifts from British families to Chinese families, from British children to Chinese children.

Although the Million Testament Fund of 1854 fell far short of the goal of distributing a million Chinese testaments in China, and in Chinese communities in the Nanyang and elsewhere, the Christian quest to distribute the Bible to every Chinese household continues. In a development that the leaders of the Bible Society of Singapore hail as a "modern miracle," the United Bible Societies (a global network of 141 Bible societies) recently collaborated with the China Christian Council to establish the Amity Printing Company in Nanjing.

Foreign evangelists still sometimes smuggle Bibles into China, but since 1988 Amity Printing has engaged in legal Bible printing and distribution. The company has now printed over 50 million Chinese Bibles and Testaments at a subsidized cost for sale through Chinese churches and distribution centers. The effort is a global collaboration, but the Nanyang Chinese continue to play a key role in this effort through organizations like the Bible Society of Singapore.

Scholars and sectarians may argue over the authenticity and correctness of different versions and translations of the Bible, but Christians worldwide regard the Bible as a single text whose global distribution in many languages symbolizes Christian unity-in-diversity. Today, as in 1854, they have pooled global financial resources to underwrite the production and distribution of Bibles in China, which allows Amity Printing to sell the Bibles that it prints very cheaply.

Christians still measure the success of their undertaking in the number of Bibles produced and distributed. However, rather than experiencing results that fall short of their ambitions, the United Bible Societies reports nearly

CONTRIBUTIONS TO THE CHINESE NEW TESTAMENT FUND,

RECEIVED UP TO MARCH 31, 1854.

	Copies.	£	s.	d.
Previouslyackowl.	1,102,925½	18,382	1	10
Bow Baptist Chapel.....	540..	9	0	0
Hanwell Indep. Chap....	309..	5	3	0
Coll. by Mr. Stanbridge..	90..	1	10	0
Moorfields and Finsbury Ladies' Society:				
Coll. by Mrs. Ingoldby's Children...........	46¾..	0	15	7
Coll. by Miss Shelton..	60..	1	0	0
Small Sums...........	74½..	1	4	10
Major Fenning	63..	1	1	0
BrixtonTrinityChap.(add.)	111..	1	17	0
Major Marsh Hughes....	63..	1	1	0
Enfield: Bapt. Sun. Sch.	10½..	0	3	6
Aberdeen.perMissRussell:				
Rev. J. D. Miller......	106..	1	15	4
Sir W. Dunbar	31½..	0	10	6
Mr.D.Simpson,Guernsey,	30..	0	10	0
Per Rev.J.Hands, Dublin:				
Rev. J. Heard.........	60..	1	0	0
Miss Foster, Derry....	51¾..	0	17	3
Small Sum............	5¼..	0	1	9
A. B. A.................	7200..	120	0	0
Sheffield Society:				
Coll. at St. Mary's Adult Schools..............	135..	2	5	0
J. W. Pye Smith, Esq..	60..	1	0	0
Children of ditto......	60..	1	0	0
Miss Denkin..	60..	1	0	0
Miss Whitridge.......	30..	0	10	0

	Copies.	£	s.	d
Miss Shearman.......	39..	0	13	0
A Friend.............	30..	0	10	0
AFriend.perMissWalker,	120..	2	0	0
Mrs.Rawson & Friends,	300..	5	0	0
Misses Shatwill	60..	1	0	0
Mrs. Burnclough......	120..	2	0	0
Birmingham: Rev. J. A. James's Cong., per Mr. Phipson....... (add.)	657½..	10	19	2
Mr. Peters, Caergwrley..	60..	1	0	0
Blandford Soc.:				
Rev. J. Penny	90..	1	10	0
MeltonAbbasGram.Sch.	90..	1	10	0
Merthyr:				
Coll. byMrs. Rowlands,	445½..	7	8	6
Lampeter:				
Coll.at Calv.Meth.Chap.	213..	3	11	0
St. Helen's:				
Coll. by Miss Moore...	57..	0	19	[illegible]
Coll. by Miss Marsh...	22½..	0	7	6
Mochdre.....	410¾..	6	16	11
Llandrillo Sund. School..	188¾..	3	2	9
Newton-le-Willows......	118..	1	19	4
Bala:				
Coll.byMissE.A.Sanderson...............	121..	2	0	4
Coll.byMissesWilliams,	135..	2	5	0
Chepstow:				
Coll. by Miss Jones...	131..	2	3	8
Brierly Hill Ind. Sun. Sch.	60..	1	0	0

	Copies.	£	s.	d.
Per Rev. J. A. James:				
TheMisses Rogers, Birmingham	120..	2	0	0
Anonymous, Lisburn..	120..	2	0	0
J. L. B., London......	300..	5	0	0
Cong. Church, Harray, Orkney.............	60..	1	0	0
Rev E Russell&Friends, Dawley, Salop......	81..	1	7	0
Indep. Ch., Jedburgh..	163¼..	2	14	7
Three LittleBoys,Rathfrisland,CountyDown	302¾..	5	0	11
Small Sums...........	30..	0	10	0
Louth:				
Coll. by Mrs. Chapman,	292½..	4	17	6
Bilston: Coll. byRev.R.J. Heafield:				
C. Snewing, Esq......	90..	1	10	0
Rev. R. J. Heafield....	100..	1	13	4
Mr. R. Thompson.....	60..	1	0	0
Mrs. Snewing.........	30..	0	10	0
St.Luke's Congregation,	76½..	1	5	6
Plymouth Society:				
Mr. J. B. Rowe.......	30..	0	10	0
Miss Prance,Hampstead,	60..	1	0	0
Coll. by Mrs. Mead....	36..	0	12	0
Coll.byMissA.M.White,	135..	2	5	0
Small Sums...........	30..	0	10	0
Carne Society.........	30..	0	10	
Brixton, &c., Society...	67..	1	2	4

Figure 1 Extract from a fifteen-page list of contributions to the Chinese New Testament Fund published in the *Monthly Extracts from the Correspondence of the British and Foreign Bible Society*, no. 36 (29 April 1854): 382. The British and Foreign Bible Society listed contributions by the names of individuals and societies, and included both the amount of the contribution and the number of New Testaments that would be produced with that contribution at fourpence a copy. Reprinted by permission of the Bible Society Library, Cambridge University Library.

unqualified success. During the Cultural Revolution, the Bible was banned and copies destroyed. Nonetheless, by 2007, the United Bible Societies' China Partnership Coordinator, Kua Wee Seng, could claim that there were more Bibles than any other book in China. Although Buddhists and Daoists now widely distribute free copies of their own sacred texts, and although the government now celebrates the contribution that these two official religions have made to social harmony, this claim may well be true.[64]

Due to low production costs in China, Amity Printing can further realize a profit by producing Bibles for export to Asia and Africa. Chinese Christians see God's hand in China's recent transformation: a country whose ideologues once destroyed Bibles now allows their production and export. Indeed, an article in the United Bible Societies' newsletter shows a photograph of a pile of Bibles next to a photograph of a pile of shoes, with the caption "Bibles (left) and shoes (middle) are among the many products that China is now exporting across the world."[65] However, unlike a pile of shoes, a pile of Bibles carries a heavy freight of meaning.

When Christians sell the Bible, one might say that they are not selling a

book so much as an entire worldview. Christians recognize that this world-view competes with other ideologies, including Marxism and materialism. In a contemporary Chinese textbook used to prepare evangelists for work in China, for example, the authors pay special attention to explicating Marxist ideology, offering the interesting observation that communist and Christian ideals are very similar, and that some even regard Marxism as an atheist sect of Christianity. They conclude, however, that Christianity and Marx's theory are opposed: "God's way of changing society is to change individual hearts (from the grassroots), Marx's way is to change the economic and political system (from the top)." [66]

Christians hope that the distribution of the Bible in China and in overseas Chinese communities will stimulate non-Christians to seek them out, so that they can teach them their cosmology (which explains human history from eternity to eternity), their salvation message, and their moral framework. In a world that many believe to have lost its moral compass, Christians seek to transform others, one person at a time, and view the Bible—Moses's rod—as a near-magical instrument of that transformation.

Notes

James Legge, address at the 42nd Annual Meeting of the British and Foreign Bible Society [BFBS] in Monthly Extracts of Correspondence of the British and Foreign Bible Society 13 (30 May 1846): 141. All Bible Society sources were consulted at the Bible Society Library at Cambridge University Library.

This essay is part of an ongoing program of research on evangelical Christianity and the Brethren movement in Singapore and Penang, Malaysia, but is primarily based on archival research conducted in the Bible Society Library, Cambridge University Library, in May 2006, with support from the University of Alberta Humanities, Fine Arts and Social Science Research committee. Special thanks are due to the Bible Society librarians Peter Meadows, who extended permission to use Bible Society materials in this paper, and Rosemary Mathew, who was extraordinarily helpful in introducing me to the archive and assisting me in locating relevant materials. I also thank Eric Tagliacozzo and Wen-Chin Chang for their timely invitation, which came just as I had discovered the Million Testament Fund and which sent me back to the Bible Society archive to see what more I could learn about it.

1. William Wilberforce, A Practical View of the Prevailing Religious System of Professed Christians in the Higher and Middle Classes in this Country, Contrasted with Real Christianity (London: T. Cadell and W. Davies, 1818), 307.

2. Ibid., 335.

3. Ibid., 337.

4. Leslie Howsam, Cheap Bibles: Nineteenth-Century Publishing and the British and Foreign Bible

Society (Cambridge: Cambridge University Press, 1991), 4; see also Boyd Hilton, *The Age of Atonement: The Influence of Evangelicalism on Social and Economic Thought, 1795–1865* (Oxford: Clarendon, 1988).

5. Ibid., 2–3.

6. On the history of early translations of the Bible into Chinese, see George Browne, *The History of the British and Foreign Bible Society, From Its Institution in 1804, to the Close of Its Jubilee in 1854* (London: Society's House, 1859), 2: chapter 11.

7. Ibid., 2:197.

8. Ibid., 2:202–3.

9. Brian Harrison, *Waiting for China: The Anglo-Chinese College at Malacca, 1818–1843, and Early Nineteenth Century Missions* (Hong Kong: Hong Kong University Press, 1979).

10. Browne, *History of the British and Foreign Bible Society*, 2:202.

11. Ibid., 2:205.

12. See Anthony Reid's essay in this volume.

13. Harrison, *Waiting for China*, 94, 117.

14. *Quan Shi Liang Yan* (Canton: n.p., 1832).

15. Harrison, *Waiting for China*, 130–31.

16. Jean DeBernardi, "'If the Lord Be Not Come': Evangelical Christianity and the Brethren Movement in Singapore and Penang, Malaysia," unpublished manuscript.

17. Karl Friedrich August Gützlaff, *Journal of Three Voyages along the Coast of China in 1831, 1832 and 1833, with Notices of Siam, Corea, and the Loo-Choo Islands* (London: Frederick Westley and A. H. Davis, 1834), available at the National University of Singapore website, http://www.lib.nus.edu.sg/digital/3voyage.html (accessed 5 July 2007). For details of Gützlaff's life, I draw on Gary Tiedemann's biography, "Gützlaff, Karl Friedrich August 郭實獵 (1803–1851)," available on the Ricci Roundtable website, http://ricci.rt.usfca.edu/biography/view.aspx?biographyID=86 (accessed 5 July 2007).

18. Jessie Lutz, "Karl F. A. Gützlaff: Missionary Entrepreneur," *Christianity in China: Early Protestant Missionary Writings*, ed. Suzanne Wilson Barnett and John King Fairbank (Cambridge: Harvard University Press, 1985), 67. See also Jessie G. Lutz and R. Ray Lutz, "Karl Gützlaff's Approach to Indigenization: The Chinese Union," *Christianity in China: From the Eighteenth Century to the Present*, ed. Daniel H. Bays (Stanford: Stanford University Press, 1996), 269–91.

19. "Chinese Evangelization Society (CES)," *Report of the Chinese Evangelization Society* (London: Nisbet, 1853), 2.

20. Ibid., 5.

21. Thor Strandenaes, "Anonymous Bible Translators: Native Literati and the Translation of the Bible into Chinese, 1804–1904," in *Sowing the Word: The Cultural Impact of the British and Foreign Bible Society 1804–2004*, ed. Stephen Batalden, Kathleen Cann, and John Dean (Sheffield: Sheffield Phoenix Press, 2004), 121–48.

22. Browne, *History of the British and Foreign Bible Society*, 2:218.

23. In her essay in this volume, Lucille Chia comments on the fact that Catholic missionaries in the early Spanish Philippines were reluctant to publish in Chinese. Al-

though the technology and skilled labor were available to them, she notes, there are no known Chinese books printed in the Philippines by missionaries or commercial publishers after the beginning of the seventeenth century, a situation that persisted for three centuries.

24. *Monthly Extracts* (November 1846): 190–91; Browne, *History of the British and Foreign Bible Society*, 2:221–22.

25. *Monthly Extracts* (May 1847): 254–55.

26. Jost Oliver Zetzsche, *The Bible in China: The History of the Union Version, or The Culmination of Protestant Missionary Bible Translation in China* (Sankt Augustin, Germany: Monumenta Serica Monograph Series 45, 1999), 77–78.

27. The children of these missionaries often returned to England for their education, but many came back to China as adults. The LMS missionaries Samuel and Maria Dyer, for example, had three children while they worked in the Ultra-Ganges Mission in Penang and Malacca. Their two daughters, Burella and Maria, were sent to England after their parents' deaths, but were soon recruited to teach in a Christian girls' school in Ningbo, where one met and married James Hudson Taylor. Samuel Dyer Jr. also returned to Asia, acting as the BFBS's agent in China in the 1870s.

28. Zetzsche, *The Bible in China*, 82–84.

29. Ibid., 82–83.

30. *Forty-Seventh Annual Report of the BFBS* (1851): 90–91.

31. Zetzsche, *The Bible in China*, 96–97.

32. *Fiftieth Annual Report of the BFBS* (1854): 111–12.

33. Zetzsche, *The Bible in China*, 364. Although I was allowed to look at the Delegates Version New Testament at the Bible Society archive, I was not allowed to photograph or photocopy the cover since the thin paper is exceptionally fragile.

34. The LMS missionaries decided to work separately on a translation of the Old Testament, which they published in 1854, and which was published together with the New Testament in 1858.

35. Jonathan D. Spence, *God's Chinese Son: The Taiping Heavenly Kingdom of Hong Xiuquan* (New York: W. W. Norton, 1996), 171.

36. Ibid., 177–79.

37. Ibid., 192–209.

38. J. A. James, "Something Must Be Done, and Done Immediately, for China—What? An Appeal to the Protestants of the United Kingdoms of Great Britain and Ireland," *British Banner* (14 September 1853), reprinted in the *Patriot* (26 September 1853). The 1853 news articles cited in this essay were compiled in a newspaper-clipping file entitled "One Million New Testaments for China 1853" at the Bible Society Archive.

39. J. B., "Light for the Millions of China," *British Banner* (28 September 1853).

40. *Monthly Extracts* (June 1854): 431.

41. Reverend James, "Letter to the Editor," *Patriot* (1853).

42. Carl A. Trocki, *Opium and Empire: Chinese Society in Colonial Singapore, 1800–1910* (Ithaca: Cornell University Press, 1990). See also Trocki's essay in this volume.

43. Fiftieth Anniversary Meeting of the BFBS in *Monthly Extracts* (May 1854): 409.

44. Ibid.: 412.

45. William Canton, *History of the British and Foreign Bible Society* (London: John Murray, 1904), 2:405. William Canton notes that the Bible Society in London displayed a rubbing from a stone that had stood at the entrance to the palace of the Shield King in Nanjing, and which was destroyed by imperial troops in 1864. A prominent symbol for "Happiness" (probably *fu*) was prominently displayed, and over it in smaller characters, the eight Christian beatitudes.

46. Browne, *History of the British and Foreign Bible Society*, 2:265–66.

47. J. A. James, speaking at the Fiftieth Anniversary Meeting of the BFBS in *Monthly Extracts* 37 (May 1854): 404.

48. Howsam, *Cheap Bibles*, 185–87.

49. *Fifty-First Annual Report of the* BFBS (1855): 105–6.

50. *Fifty-Second Annual Report of the* BFBS (1856): 140.

51. Islay Burns, *Memoir of the Rev. William C. Burns, M.A.: Missionary to China from the English Presbyterian Church* (London: James Nisbet, 1870; repr., San Francisco: Chinese Materials Center, 1975), 441. He observed that the Great Canal's Chinese name literally meant "Transport-provision-River" (ibid., 430). See Nola Cooke's chapter in this volume for a detailed analysis of the Cambodian "water world," a phrase that I have borrowed from her.

52. Burns, *Memoir of the Rev. William C. Burns*, 402.

53. See DeBernardi, " 'If the Lord Be Not Come.' "

54. Since Tan was self-supporting, he expected no pay when he itinerated with Burns on the "Good News [Gospel] Boat." In 1857, the Presbyterian mission in Amoy dispatched Tan to Singapore as a paid catechist working with Chinese immigrants from Fujian. A decade later, Tan separated from the Presbyterian Church and joined his semiautonomous Chinese Church with the Brethren Gospel Hall. He adopted the Brethren practice of living by faith (rather than expecting a salary) and supported the new church in part with income from successful business ventures.

55. Dr. and Mrs. Howard Taylor, *Hudson Taylor in Early Years: The Growth of a Soul*, vol. 1, 1776–1860 (Singapore: OMF International, 1998), 293.

56. Burns, *Memoir of the Rev. William C. Burns*, 454–64.

57. *Monthly Extracts* (December 1857): 84–85.

58. *Fifty-Third Annual Report of the* BFBS (1857): 189.

59. *Monthly Extracts* (March 1858): 107–8.

60. *Fifty-Fourth Annual Report of the* BFBS (1858): 115.

61. *Fifty-Fifth Annual Report of the* BFBS (1859): 225–26.

62. Milne, speaking at the Fiftieth Anniversary Meeting of the BFBS in *Monthly Extracts* 37 (May 1854): 409; emphasis mine.

63. *Monthly Extracts* (December 1853): 318.

64. Jean DeBernardi, "On the Modernization of Daoism: A Preliminary Analysis of the 2007 International Forum on the Daodejing in Xi'an and Hong Kong," unpublished manuscript.

65. Kjell Hagen, "From Banned to Best-seller," World Report Number 410, 1 (April 2007), consulted at the United Bible Societies website, http://www.biblesociety.org/we_410/410_1.htm (accessed 2 November 2007), now available at http://www.ubscp.org/wordpress/wp-content/doc/2007wr.pdf (accessed 5 August 2010).

66. *Good News Reader* [Xinyang Duben] (no date or place of publication given), 134.

PART V ~~~~ Postcolonial

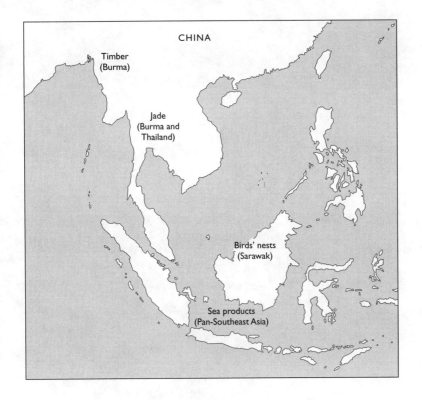

MARKET PRICE, LABOR INPUT, AND RELATION OF PRODUCTION IN SARAWAK'S EDIBLE BIRDS' NEST TRADE

~~~~~ Bien Chiang

Edible birds' nest, or *yen-wo* 燕窩, ranks among the top of the long list of Chinese delicacies-cum-tonics.[1] A large majority of Chinese people have likely never seen nor consumed any edible birds' nests before, but almost all have heard about them and can claim to know a few things about them. To most Chinese, edible birds' nest carries the aura of royalty, extravagance, luxury, and exoticism. People usually have only a vague idea about the origin and the zoological and medical details of birds' nests, but all are aware of the legendary amount of labor and money involved in their procurement.

Birds' nest is well known to scholars of Southeast Asian studies as an exotic commodity that caters to the Chinese market. According to an estimation done by the Singapore-based ASEAN Birds' Nest Traders Association, the annual export of edible birds' nest from Indonesia alone, which contributes 70 percent of global production, is worth between US$200 and US$250 million. In 1997, Indonesian exports of edible birds' nest weighed 170 tons, with a projected 10 percent growth for 1998. Other major birds' nest–producing countries include Vietnam, Malaysia, and Thailand.[2] Environmentalist and international wildlife conservation agents keep a close watch on this trade, fearing endangerment of the two species of swiftlets that are credited with building these nests.

Nowadays it is common knowledge to scientists and general consumers alike that the edible ingredient of these nests comes from the saliva of the birds. One does not need exceptional curiosity to be intrigued by the source of "value" of this saliva-based commodity. What sociocultural values and political economic realities have been joining forces to keep this transnational trade in birds' nest going? Some angles for investigation are evidently in order. On the one hand, on the consumer side, the body of Chinese medici-

nal knowledge has apparently sanctioned the "subjective value" of birds' nest. On the other hand, the well-known difficulty in procuring birds' nest no doubt warrants an examination along the line of "labor theory of value." However, it is not my goal in this essay to defend one value theory against the other. Rather, based on textual as well as ethnographic data, I present an—admittedly not yet complete—picture of how value is constructed respectively on the production and the consumer ends of the birds' nest trade. I also show how the value of birds' nest on both ends is related to social production and reproduction.

Scholarly, business, and public attention notwithstanding, systematic studies of the modes of production and trading of edible birds' nest are relatively few. The few noteworthy articles are either solely descriptive or policy oriented.[3] In contrast to these works, Leonard Blussé's article "In Praise of Commodities: An Essay on the Cross-cultural Trade in Edible Bird's Nests" is written with a much clearer scholarly goal.[4] In the article, Blussé hopes to shed light on "the true nature of Oriental Trade" through an examination of trade in birds' nest. Relying on various historical documents, Blussé examines the patterns of collecting and trading birds' nest in four places— Eastern Kalimantan, Java's South Coast, Batavia's countryside, and the Champa Islets—from the mid-eighteenth century to the early nineteenth. The organization of production differed from one case to another. In eastern Kalimantan, native Bornean "slaves" worked the caves owned by Sulu grandees. In Java's South Coast and the countryside of Batavia, birds' nest–producing caves were owned, variously, by local rulers, the Dutch East India Company (VOC), the colonial government, and private Dutch landowners, but the mode of production at the base remained the same: the caves were worked by the local population as a kind of corvée duty. In the Champa Islets, the Nguyen regime set up brigades, "which were allowed to exploit the resources under payment of heavy annual taxes."[5] The brigades, in turn, taxed the nest-collecting fishermen either by ship or by head.

Significantly, these various arrangements in birds' nest production gradually gave way to a Chinese monopoly in the trade by the mid-nineteenth century. According to Blussé, this was due to Chinese tax farmers moving inland, as close as possible to the production region, and providing the natives with the much sought-after Chinese industrial products at a highly competitive price. The Chinese also sent home birds' nest as a substitute for silver to fulfill their familial obligations. In Blussé's words, "A once cross-cultural trade network had now effectively become a mono-cultural one."[6] Further-

more, if we "focus on the power struggle surrounding the mode of production and the production areas of a specific commodity," we notice that the "Western expansion of power meant paving the way for Chinese expansion of trade."[7]

This "Sinification" of trade in specific commodities is echoed in Heather Sutherland's study of Indonesian tortoiseshell trade in the late seventeenth century and the eighteenth.[8] The picture presented by Sutherland is a more complex one: the Chinese monopolization of trepang trade, in which only the Chinese own the cultural knowledge of its use-value, results in the penetration of the Chinese into the "upstream levels of the trade, once dominated by Sulawesians,"[9] such as the trading of tortoiseshell, which was used more widely in local handicrafts before the coming of Chinese traders. Sutherland's conclusion is applicable to a broader range of phenomena: "Ethnic differentiation was important in that it related directly to relevant knowledge about production and consumption, and to social capital embodied in networks of trust."[10]

In a similar vein, I explore further the knowledge that the Chinese traders command regarding the production and consumption of edible birds' nest—how their knowledge of the commodity's use-value allows them to manipulate its exchange value. Also, I demonstrate that the local communities responsible for the actual collecting of birds' nest are not without agency in the trade. Their agency is shown in the more or less successful conversion of the profit from their involvement in the birds' nest trade into means of social production and reproduction.

Birds' Nest in Chinese Medicinal Tradition

NOT SO ANCIENT A TRADITION

The prominent position of edible birds' nest in Chinese medicine and cuisine notwithstanding, documentation about its origins and attributes is surprisingly scanty. Contrary to some literature that conceives of birds' nest consumption as an "ancient Chinese custom," the mention of birds' nest in historical documents appears no earlier than the fourteenth century.[11] Blussé accepts the opinion of the Japanese historian Shinoda Osamu that "the first reference to edible birds' nest is the entry in Chia Ming's Yin-shih hsü-chih ('What we need to know about food and drink'), a book that appeared in the early years of the Ming dynasty."[12] In this book, the author simply noted, "Yen-wo tastes sweet and has a mild quality; the yellowish, blackish, and rotten ones are poisonous and should not be eaten."[13]

Throughout the Ming dynasty (1368–1644), however, references to birds' nest are rather sporadic. As Blussé notes, "Neither Wang Ta-yüan in his TICL (1350) nor Ma Huan, who in the YYSL described the famous travels of the eunuch Chen Ho to Southeast and South Asia in the early decades of the fifteenth century, mention edible bird's nests as an import-commodity from the Nanyang."[14] Chang Hsieh in his *Dung Xi Yang Kau* [Investigation of the east and the west oceans] (1618) did record edible birds' nest among the local products of Jiau-zhe, Champa (Vietnam), Pahang, Melaka, Kelantan, Johor (Malaysia), Aceh (Sumatra), and Cambodia. Under the entry for the kingdom of Jiau-zhe, Chang noted, "The swiftlets feed on seaweed and then spit it out to make nest. The nests are attached to the walls of grottoes. In the nests, the swiftlets lay eggs and rear broods. It is therefore full of feather. The natives climb ladders to collect them."[15] For Champa, he said, "The swiftlet is about the size of pigeon. They come back to grottoes or cliff to make nests every spring. . . . The island natives wait for them to leave in the autumn, fixing spade to pole, collecting the nests and eating them. The nest is referred to as *yen-wo*, a delicacy in feast."[16] Except for the size of the bird and the building material of the nest, Chang's description is not very far from the facts. What is worth noting is that he seems to be indicating the habit of eating birds' nest among the natives and at the same time the existence of a market for it in China. Other than mentioning edible birds' nest as a local product, *Dung Xi Yang Kau* provides no detail of its use as medicine or a tonic.

Nor does the famous encyclopedia of Chinese herb medicine written by Li Shih-chen (1518–1593), *Pen-ts'ao kang-mu* [Compendium of materia medica], list birds' nest. Only in the supplement to this work, *Pen-ts'ao kang-mu shih-i* [Supplement to Compendium of materia medica], which appeared almost two hundred years later, in 1765, did birds' nest receive extensive coverage. The author of the supplement, Chao Hsüe-ming, compiled a substantial amount of firsthand as well as secondhand information about the healing effects of birds' nest and remarked, "The pity is that it is not listed in *Pen-ts'ao* and rarely used in prescription."[17] Among the literatures that Chao Hsüe-ming cited, the earliest is *Cüan-nan Tsa-zhe* [Miscellaneous notes on southern Fujian], written by a Ming officer, Chen Mau-ren.[18] According to Chen,

> Far offshore of Fujian and closer to the aborigines' territory, there is a kind of swiftlet called *chin-si* [golden thread]. Its head and tail look like that of the swallow, but it is much smaller in size; the feathers are like golden threads. Before laying eggs and rearing broods, the whole flock would descend on a beach that is sandy with scattered rocks and feed on

the "silkworm conch." The seafaring trader I interviewed claims that, according to the aborigines, inside the flesh of the silkworm conch there are two "ribs," white and sturdy like the silk of the "maple silkworm." Taken internally, the "rib" is replenishing to asthenia and can stop diarrhea. The swiftlet eats the conch, digests the flesh but not the "ribs," spits out the "ribs" along with saliva and uses them to build nests on grotto walls. As time passes, the swiftlets fly away with the new fledglings, and the coastal peoples collect the nests in season. This is called *yen-wo*.[19]

The edible birds' nest was not mentioned in earlier Chinese medicinal literatures. Both *Dung Xi Yang Kau* and *Cüan-nan Tsa-zhe*, on the other hand, suggest the possibility of it being consumed originally by the native peoples of Southeast Asia. It is still uncertain as to the dates of its initial introduction into China. It seemed to be quite rare in the Ming dynasty. What is certain is that starting from the early Qing dynasty, the number of times yen-wo is mentioned increased dramatically. It is listed among the royal tributes from Southeast Asian polities, mentioned as a taxable commodity, referred to in popular novels, and served on the imperial table. It was also during the Qing dynasty that more systematic knowledge about yen-wo's healing effects began to accumulate.

HEALING AND THERAPEUTIC EFFECTS

The entry on yen-wo in the "Grand Dictionary of Chinese Medicine," compiled and published by the Jiang-su New Medical College in 1986, lists its healing effect as "nourishing the yin element, moisten the malign dryness inside the body, strengthening the chi and replenishing the middle warmer. It provides remedy to asthenia, impairment, pulmonary overstrain, coughing, respiration with phlegm, bloody sputum and hematamesis, chronic diarrhea, chronic intermittent fevers, frequent dysphagia and regurgitation."[20] This is basically the same range of effects listed in *Pen-ts'ao kang-mu shih-i*. Birds' nest is considered beneficial to the pulmonary and digestive systems. It can be boiled into "juice" either by itself or in combination with other herb medicines. In addition to naming these principal healing effects, *Pen-ts'ao kang-mu shih-i* mentions that birds' nest can cure micturition; that it is capable of strengthening the yang element, supplementing the chi, regulating the middle warmer, improving appetite, adding the essence of life, and replenishing the marrow; and that the red ones can cure dysentery with bloody stools.[21]

In some of the literature cited by *Pen-ts'ao kang-mu shih-i* are explanations

as to the healing effects of birds' nest. A common opinion is that it has something to do with the food of the swiftlets. In addition to "silkworm conch" and seaweed, small fish are also considered to be part of the swiftlet diet. The most significant remarks, however, are the following.

> On the surface of the rocks by the seashore, "sea powder" gathered like moss. The swiftlets feed on this powder and spit it out to make nest. . . . The sea powder is cold in nature; being taken in and spat out by the swiftlets makes it warm. The sea powder tastes salty; being taken in and spat out by the swiftlets makes it sweet. Its appearance and quality are totally transformed; therefore, it has the effects of resolving sputum and improving appetite. The nests come in either black or white; the red ones are hard to come by. Since the swiftlet belongs to the category of fire, the red nest is especially the essence.

> The swiftlet carries sea powder in its mouth for nest building. With the help of the mild chi from the sun and the wind, the saltiness and the coldness are transformed into sweetness and neutrality. This will cause the mutual generation between the metal and the water elements, elevate the chi of the kidney to nourish the pulmonary system and also to calm the chi in the stomach.[22]

The "Grand Dictionary of Chinese Medicine" states, "The sea powder is salty and cold. After the swiftlet carries it in the mouth and into the high wind, it becomes sweet and neutral. . . . The birds' nest replenishes without causing malign dryness, moistens without causing sluggishness; it is the mildest and fairest of all medicines."[23]

It is now well established that the edible component of the nest is actually the swiftlet's saliva, rather than transformed foodstuffs.[24] In the systematic knowledge of Chinese medicine, however, the transformative capacity of the swiftlet is considered the key factor in the therapeutic effects of birds' nest. Being classified as "fire," the swiftlet transforms things from the sea, which are "salty and cold" by nature, into something mildly cool and having calming, cooling, and cleansing effects on the pulmonary and digestive systems.

On the other hand, among Chinese consumers, there is always an aura of mysticism surrounding the therapeutic effects of birds' nest. In the 31 October 1964 issue of the *Sarawak Gazette*, an author named Chu Chin Onn contributed a short essay entitled "Birds' Nests: Sarawak All-Cure." Chu was a Chinese Sarawakian with a background in traditional medicine and was working with the Sarawak Museum at the time.[25] In this essay, Chu offered his own rather unique interpretation of birds' nest's therapeutic effects.

It is logical that the person who wishes to take birds' nests, he himself should not do the work—cleaning, picking, etc., for this is a tedious job, which requires time, concentration and energy; and also this work is liable to exhaust health, breath and energy which may be absorbed and *radiate to the birds' nests*, so that he takes away his own energetic health instead!

In olden days persons were exceptional and cunning. They used to engage healthy young and *unmarried* person to do the job and to prepare the steaming at a quicker pace, as special preparation for health sake. Quicker pace saves a lot of time, avoids the birds' nests remaining (dipped) in water to soak away the good properties. Healthy young persons possess stronger health, energetic heat and breath. These can warm the birds' nests through contact of body heat, circulating around the working area at the time of concentration, when the young clean and pick the nests, which can then absorb the healthy heat and energetic process from them, the young.[26]

Chu's opinion is not in line with those of the Chinese medicinal classics; and presently it is difficult to decide how much it can be considered as representing the popular folk notion. His idea of radiating breath and energy is more like a crude imitation of the chi theory. However, the *Sarawak Gazette*, though not a scholarly journal, is a well-respected magazine that has been in press for over a hundred years. Chu's English writing leaves plenty of room for improvement but carries the flavor of colonial "Chinglish." In the same issue, next to Chu's essay, the editor of the *Sarawak Gazette* published another article entitled "Cave Swiftlets and Birds' Nest." The author, Michael Fogden, wrote in a naturalist's manner about the varieties of the swiftlets, the components of the nest, the birds' ecology and breeding patterns as well as some sociocultural background to the collection of birds' nest. The juxtaposition of the two essays revealed the editor's intention of providing a balanced report that included both the point of view of a naturalist and that of the major consumers. Once published, Chu's explanation became public knowledge and could not be casually brushed aside.

In a sense, Chu's point can also be viewed as a parable—it tells the truth about the huge labor input in birds' nest production. It is well known that the collecting and processing of birds' nest is extremely labor-intensive and time-consuming. Birds' nest collectors need to ascend high into the chimneys of caves or descend down formidable cliffs with very simple gear, and accidents are often fatal. The cleaning and feather removing works are,

furthermore, both tedious and taxing on workers' eyesight; these processes are usually handled by Chinese traders, rather than the collectors, while the real work is always done by hired young female laborers. These women come from all ethnic groups and are usually not very well paid. In a home video on the processing of house-farmed birds' nest in Indonesia, one sees rows of female workers in uniform sitting in a room about the size of a classroom. In front of each worker is a bowl of water containing unprocessed birds' nests and another small dish of water in which to rinse feathers off the tweezers. The room is filled with clinks as the women rap the tweezers against the ceramic dish to rinse off the feathers. When the male boss, hands behind his back, walks down the aisle to inspect the jobs of the workers, the scene becomes rather oppressive.[27] In other words, the preparation of birds' nest requires a huge amount of labor input, a fact of which consumers are aware. Both objectively and subjectively speaking, therefore, consuming birds' nest is essentially consuming behind-the-scenes labor.

Now we should turn to another aspect of the value of birds' nest that is also based on, and sanctioned by, Chinese medicinal knowledge. Retail stores carry a kind of dark-reddish birds' nest that commands the highest price; this is the so-called blood nest. We have already seen that, according to Pen-ts'ao kang-mu shih-i, the red ones can cure dysentery with bloody stools. The traditional explanation holds that the swiftlet, having built two nests continuously and having had both removed by a collector, is so exhausted when building the third nest that it spits blood. These reddish nests are considered the most nourishing and the most exquisite, and are therefore the most expensive among all the types of birds' nest. Although we now know that the tints in birds' nest, be they reddish, brownish, or yellowish, result from the different minerals in the rock on which the swiftlets choose to build their nest, the legend of the "blood nest" remains prevalent.[28]

For scientists and birds' nest collectors, the blood nest category does not exist. In Sarawak, only two kinds of birds' nest have commercial value. Those built by Aerodramus maximus are called the "black nest." The "black" refers to the large number of feathers that cover and intermix with the "substance" that is the saliva. Before being cleaned, the whole nest looks blackish. After the feathers and other particles are cleared away, the birds' nest substance looks white, yellowish, or reddish. The price of black nest on the production site—between middleman and collectors—is determined by the portion of the nest substance that each piece contains. The more feathers and less substance, the lower the price.[29] The price here actually reflects the ratio between the labor that would be needed in the cleaning process and

Table 1 Retailer Price of Birds' Nests in Kuching

	Retailer #1	Retailer #2	Retailer #3
Blood nest cup[i]	n/a	n/a	500[ii]
Blood nest cake[iii]	200	180	250
Light reddish and yellowish cake	n/a	n/a	220
White nest cake	180	200	190

i. "Cup" refers to the original shape of the nest.
ii. Prices are in Malaysian ringgit (1 US$= 3.8 ringgit, as of September 1999). All items come in 37.5g packs.
iii. "Cake" refers to the way in which the nest breaks up into strips of jelly-like substance after cleaning, which are then dried and molded into oval-shaped pieces.

Source: Field data.

the amount of substance that can be recovered. In fact, according to Charles Leh, a zoologist and curator of Sarawak Museum, the reddish ones command a lower price.[30]

The other kind of nest is built by *Aerodramus fuciphagus* and is called the "white nest." It contains very few feathers and needs less cleaning. The bare birds' nest substance generally looks whitish, but is also susceptible to the tints from rock. White nest commands a higher price at the production site.

In retailer's shops, however, the price ranks among different categories of birds' nest are almost totally reversed. Three retail stores in Kuching City, the capital of Sarawak, price birds' nest categories as listed in table 1. We can compare these with the price list of an Internet retailer as listed in table 2.

In both cases, blood nest fetches the highest price; the yellow nest comes in second, and the white nest the lowest. Nowadays, the yellow nests on the retail market are mostly house-farmed birds' nests from Indonesia. They are generally better in shape and are consider by some consumers to be cleaner. As for the blood nest, the Internet retailer claims that it is "the most nutritious of all swiftlet nest. Best for pregnant women, patients after surgery. Healthy Nest Bloody is a house type nest. Hence, Healthy Nest Bloody is much more delicate and tasty than the Cave type Bloody."[31] It is not at all clear how house-farmed birds' nest can be reddish, since such nests are built either on cement or wooden walls. But during a conversation, the third-largest shopkeeper in Kuching City assured me that "our blood nest is one hundred per cent *natural color*. The redness is *original*. Unlike some other shops who use *artificial color* to turn the nest dark red." However, he avoids

Table 2 Retail Price of Birds' Nests from an Internet Advertisement

Merchandise	Price per tael (US$)
Blood Nest Whole Nest Grade 1	220
Blood Nest Whole Nest Grade 2	170
Blood Nest Ungrouped Small Piece	118
Yellow Nest Whole Nest	188
Yellow Nest Regrouped Large Piece Grade 1	156
Yellow Nest Regrouped Large Piece Grade 2	145
White Nest Regrouped Large Piece Grade 1	139
White Nest Regrouped Large Piece Grade 2	128
White Nest Regrouped Large Piece Grade 3	118

Source: Healthy Nest website, http://healthynest.com (accessed January 1999).

confirming that the "original redness" is from blood. "We Chinese have this old belief that it is from the blood spat by the swiftlets, but I am not sure. I think it has something to do with the food of the birds." According to one middleman at Long Lama, near the cave sites along the middle Baram area, artificial colors are widely used during the processing, either to turn the white one whiter or the brownish and reddish ones redder.

In short, at the production end, the price is decided more by the estimated labor that is needed to process the raw nests. At the consumption end, the price is decided by a long-established conceptual framework that, based on its own understanding of bird ecology, connects a color classification with a system of nutrition evaluation (red signifies blood). In the present time, helped by much more effective communication technology and wrapped in a new set of technical jargon and biochemical terminologies, birds' nest remains at the top of popular health and food therapeutic discourse for many Chinese. "Scientific" revelation of the "true nature" of coloring (or discoloring) of the nests has not been very successful in discrediting the conventional framework of evaluation.

Early History and Folklore of the Birds' Nest Trade in Sarawak

Sarawak is presently a state of the federation of Malaysia, and is located in northwestern Borneo. The name Borneo derives from the name of the sultanate of Brunei. Since the thirteenth century, Brunei has been documented in various sources as a major player in maritime trade; its influence covered the entire coastal area of Borneo and extended to the Philippines and the Sulu Sea. Its power began to wane after the Spanish took over Manila, in

1571, and invaded Brunei Bay, in 1578.[32] After 1777, the Taosug from the Sulu started attacking Bruneian ships and settlements on the northeastern coast of Borneo, and by 1820 had formally driven the sultan's influence out of the area.[33] Their losses on the eastern front notwithstanding, before 1842, Brunei still nominally controlled the area that was to become Sarawak. In 1842, Sultan Omar Ali asked for the help of the Englishman James Brooke to put down a rebellion along the Sarawak River and granted him the title "Raja of Sarawak." For the following half century, the Brooke regime managed to annex all the regions of Sarawak at the expense of the sultan of Brunei. Even Brunei itself would have been annihilated had it not been for intervention by the British government in 1906.

Major power in maritime trade as Brunei was, neither Chinese sources, such as *Dung Xi Yang Kau* (1618), nor the observation of the Dutch admiral Olivier van Noort, who visited Brunei around 1600, mentioned birds' nest as among the trade or tribute items.[34] The documentation that Blussé cites regarding birds' nest production in the Sandakan area of northeast Borneo dates back to 1849.[35] The earliest documentation of birds' nest production in Sarawak points roughly to the same period of time. There were, and still are, three major birds' nest production sites in Sarawak: the Bau area in Western Sarawak, the Niah Caves, and the Middle Baram area in northeast Sarawak.[36]

The caves at Niah produce black and yellow nests. According to local folklore, the original inhabitants at Niah were the Preban. After floods destroyed the Preban settlement at Niah, the Penans from Beluru, Bakong, and upper Bintulu migrated into the area.[37] On hearing of the arrival of the Penans, some of the Preban returned to Niah and formed a large village called Manong, where people of different ethnic groups lived together, including the Segans, Bakongs, Bruneis, and the Chinese. The first Chinese trader was a certain *towkay*, Moh Khim, from Brunei.[38] According to Benedict Sandin, "It was really a Penan named Nyerulang who first discovered the Subis cave. This discovery was made by him while shooting with his blowpipe along the Subis stream. When Nyerulang first brought the edible birds' nest home, Moh Khim told him that the stuff was eatable and exportable. It was from this time that many traders from Brunei and Bintulu started to come to Niah to buy bird's nest."[39]

Another story started with the people who lived in Suai, whose leader was Dudop. After having lived there for some time, the people were forced, due to sanitary problems, to desert the village and stay separately in small huts in the jungle. Stricken by epidemic in the jungle, they moved back to Suai, only to be afflicted again by diarrhea. This time, some people moved back

to the jungle, while others went to live in the caves at Niah. Many, including Dudop, died at the Niah Caves.

> After this epidemic ceased, Dudop's son, Murai, afterwards moved downriver and lived at Pelalid, below the present site of the Niah Fort.
>
> Some years after Murai had lived at Pelalid, a Brunei official came to enquire whether the people of Niah agreed to purchase from Brunei Government foodstuffs which the latter would sell to them. Murai and his people agreed to buy them if they were brought to Niah.
>
> After this had been agreed, the official returned to explain to the Sultan his successful mission. In due course the foodstuffs were brought to Niah. As there was no money in those days, the natives bartered these foods with rattan, bezoars-stones and *kulat dalam batu* (edible birds' nest). To regulate the trading in these foods, a special agent was appointed in Niah. About fifteen years afterwards the people of Niah became more civilized. Twenty years later, the trade became more flourishing, and Niah was ceded to Sarawak with Baram.[40]

In both accounts, the origin of the collection and sale of birds' nest is preceded by disasters and diasporas. It is not clear at the moment whether, in a demographic sense, birds' nest production and exportation actually contributes to the formation of a more or less sedentary lifestyle among the local populations. The Punan (Penan) of the Niah are now dispersed again throughout the area for different reasons. Nevertheless, in both cases, the collection and sale of birds' nest is recounted as a major event in economic development. In the first case, it attracted traders from different places to come to Niah, where the birds' nest operation today is still a significant part of local life. In the second case, birds' nest was remembered as a factor that brought "civilization" to Niah through trading connections with Brunei.

Birds' Nest Production at Niah

THE NIAH CAVES AND THE PRACTICE OF BIRDS' NEST COLLECTION

The Niah Caves are located in the Subis limestone massif, on the north coast of Sarawak. The total area is 10.5 hectares and divided into many branches and sections. Among the many entrances and openings, the West Mouth is the biggest one, with an opening 250 meters wide and 60 meters high. The archeological evidence of human activities at the West Mouth covers a time span from 40,000 to 2,000 years before the present. Presently, the archeological sites are under the administration of the Sarawak Museum, the birds' nest

operations are controlled by the forest department, while the caves themselves are managed by the national park agency. Niah is 109 kilometers from the city of Miri. A bus ride of a little more than two hours takes one from Miri to Batu Niah; from there, it is a fifteen-minute boat ride to the park entrance, followed by a forty-five-minute walk to the West Mouth of the Main Cave. The place is easily accessible and located near a fairly populated area. The settlement closest to the West Mouth is an Iban longhouse, Rumah Chang.

Boardwalks are constructed along the main tourist path that cuts across the national park area. Before arriving at the West Mouth, one comes to a rock shelf about 200 meters wide, 50 meters deep, and 7–10 meters high. This is the Traders' Cave, which used to shelter tens of roofless housing units—some connected in rows, some detached—on piles. According to local records, until 1985 a bustling community would fill the place for a period of two months during the collection season. Chinese and Malay traders, from either nearby towns or as far as Brunei, would come and stay in their own quarters, wait for the nest collectors on their way back from the caves, and purchase the nests directly from them. There was a common water spring, a big earthen stove for communal use, and even a coffee stall in this cave. According to Cranbrook,

> The pattern of ownership of cave rights and the nature of the harvesting contract thus lends itself to corporate (if not cooperative) enterprise. Traditionally, the nest harvest at Niah occurred twice annually, for two 60-day periods, during which all interested parties assembled at the lower cave (Traders' Cave), in the famous roofless village, to participate and no doubt to monitor all aspects of the proceedings. Under such arrangements, collective decisions must be made and the community itself can check infringement of the accepted conventions.[41]

Lord Medway also noted that "the biggest crowd came at the pupol tahun, the New Year season (January and February), when the collection was mostly better than the August pupol merai, the Moult season."[42] Today, the Traders' Cave is totally desolate; only the belian hardwood skeletons of those housing units remain.

Another few minutes' walk from the Traders' Cave brings one to the West Mouth. In addition to the sheer size of the opening and the stalactite pillars, the most stunning scene in the West Mouth is no doubt the many bamboo and belian masts for birds' nest collection. At the same time, one is also struck by the strong smell of guano. According to Medway's estimation, at

that time, there were one and a half million swiftlets in Niah Caves.[43] Like birds' nest, guano was also a source of income for the local people, but with a much lower value.

Inside the main caves, the clefts and many of the chimneys, where the swiftlets build their nests, are often more than sixty meters above the ground. The collectors usually work in teams of two, a *tukang julok*, who climbs the mast and scrapes down the nest, and a *tukang pungut*, who stays on the ground to pick up the fallen nests. Medway provides this vivid description of the scene.

> The most striking sights in the big cave at Niah are the tall *tiang* (masts) of bamboo or *belian* that reach up to or hang from, respectively, the roof two hundred feet above. They lead to thick clutters of spiders' web scaffolding, again *belian* or bamboo, wedged in the clefts and chimneys where the swifts nest. When climbing a tall *tiang*, the collector first knots a cloth over his insteps, to tie his feet together in such a way that if he opens his knees, the downward pressure of his weight will increase the grip of his soles on the pole,
>
> The rising bamboos are built before the hanging *belian*. Lengths of a conveniently strung local bamboo, *buloh betong*, that grows in single stems about forty feet high, topped by a palm like tuft of fronds, are cut and brought to the cave. A stem is stood upright and guyed with rotans; another may be hauled up, and joined to it, male and female-wise, and again stayed with rotans. Ultimately the roof is reached. A prepared beam of *belian* is wedged again among the rock, and from it is hung, on *belian* pegs, the *tiang* of the square cut lengths of *belian* joined by *belian* pegs, not lashed. The *belian* structures are permanent; there are about 50 of them in the 26 acres of cave. Some have fallen, some are no longer safe, but others are still in regular use, although they may have been first erected 50 years ago. . . . Bamboo *tiang* do not have a life of more than two years, in the damp cave air, and are stood up whenever needed, and left standing after use. A crowd of them on Bukit Bungkok, between the main East and the main West mouths, look like Trafalgar relics, sinking in the sea of guano.[44]

On top of these masts and the crisscross beams, the tukang julok uses a *penyulok* to scrape loose the nests: "The *penyulok* is made of light, dry bamboo, bound at the joints with patterned whippings of split rotan. It is in four long sections, which can be joined end to end; the head is a hoe-like, but straight, steel blade, also rotan bound, and just below the head is a loop, of

rotan again, to take the long beeswax candle that lights the wavering rod."[45] Except that the beeswax candle is nowadays replaced by an electric flashlight, the tools of today's birds' nest collectors are basically the same as those described by Medway some fifty years ago. On the ground, the tukang pungut is responsible for the gathering of the fallen nests. At places where the nests might tumble irrecoverably to the bottom of a crevasse, a light net (selambau) is installed on the ground to catch the nests.

From the West Mouth, walking deeper into the caves, one sees the tiang standing here and there, some on the side of the boardwalk, some farther away. A few of them have people working on the tops, and invariably there is someone waiting underneath. Further away from the boardwalk and in the total darkness of the caves, here and there one sees dim camp lights accompanied by music that comes from either a guitar or a cassette player. These are the guardsmen who are hired to watch each designated area against thefts. Theft is a serious problem at Niah. This is only partly due to the accessibility of the location; the more important reason lies in the social relations of birds' nest production here.

OWNERSHIP, LEASE, AND HIRED LABOR

The Punan are officially recognized as the earliest inhabitants of Niah. After settling down at Kuala Tangap, however, these Punan gradually converted to Islam. They changed their residential pattern into independent houses and claimed to be Malay. Many of them moved out of the area, some to Miri or Bintulu. After the Second World War, when the Sarawak government launched the registration of birds' nest collection rights, they were first turned down by the then curator of Sarawak Museum, Tom Harrisson, on the ground that they were not Punan, but Malay. Only after they had managed to produce genealogies to demonstrate their Punan heritage were their rights officially recognized. Currently, every birds' nest producing section of the Niah Caves is registered under individual Punan-Malay families.

The actual operation rights of birds' nest collection at Niah, however, have almost entirely been leased by the Punan-Malay owners to different Chinese traders, at prices ranging from 10,000 to 20,000 ringgit per year, depending on the production of the specific section concerned, and for the duration of ten to fifteen years. The Chinese traders, however, do not work the caves themselves either; they hire the local Iban, Malay, and Bugis to do the guarding and collecting jobs. It is said that many Chinese traders like to hire Bugis as guardsmen because of their reputed fierceness.

The Iban in both Niah and the Lower Baram migrated into these areas

from southeastern Sarawak during the latter half of the nineteenth century. The Iban longhouse Rumah Chang, which is the nearest to the West Mouth, moved here from Bintulu about fifty years ago. When the settlers first arrived here, there were only twelve doors (bilek). Now Rumah Chang has seventy doors, which form two parallel blocks. Except for the very old and the very young, almost every male at Rumah Chang works the caves at one point or another, either as guardsmen or collectors, or both.[46] The households in Rumah Chang are divided into several working units; each unit is contracted by a Chinese towkay to work in one or several sections in the caves that the Chinese towkay leases from respective Punan-Malay owners. The biggest working unit in Rumah Chang consists of forty-two households. All the able-bodied males of the forty-two households are grouped into teams of three. Each team works a half-day shift, guarding as well as collecting the nests. Although the government regulations stipulate that there should be only two harvest seasons per year at Niah, workers at Rumah Chang say that the Chinese towkay would push for more frequent, even monthly, harvesting, each time from a different part of the sections that he leased.

The Iban workers are not paid by fixed wages. After each harvest, the working unit is entitled to half of the sale. According to my informants at Rumah Chang, between 1988 and 1990, when the price of birds' nest was at its highest, one kilogram could fetch 1,000 ringgit, and each harvest could amount to 40 kilograms. During that period of time, each household could earn 400 to 500 ringgit, sometimes even 1,000 ringgit a month. In 1999, however, both the harvest and the unit price declined. Nowadays each harvest of birds' nest amounts to only 15 kilograms, and the price is 600 ringgit per kilogram. The monthly household income from birds' nest sales are therefore down to 80 to 200 ringgit. The Iban of Rumah Chang have never given up rice cultivation; there are both hill and swamp paddies in their territory. When birds' nest operation was at its peak, women were almost entirely in charge of the agricultural works. When the price of birds' nest was good, it was the sole source of cash income for the household. Now the major sources of cash income are pepper planting and working oil palm operations.

"Working in the caves" actually includes three kinds of work. The climber-cum-scraper is called tukang julok. This is the most difficult and dangerous work in birds' nest collection. The one who stays on the ground and collects the fallen nests is called tukang pungut. The third kind of work, which is seldom mentioned in birds' nest literature, is the guardsman (jaga). If one walks deep into the darkness of the Great Cave, one will see the entire area

is dotted with dim lights of candles or oil lamps. Each titled section in the cave is guarded by a hired jaga, who wards off trespassers. While the role of jaga is a year-round job, climbers and collectors work, in theory, only during the harvest season that is stipulated by the authority and agreed on by the cave leaseholders. Therefore, the jaga can also work as tukang julok or tukang pungut during the collecting season, and vice versa. The cave needs to be guarded due to an extremely high rate of trespassing and illicit collecting. Because of the size, openness, and accessibility of the caves, the birds' nests in Niah Cave are highly susceptible to theft. According to some Chinese traders in Batu Niah and veteran tukang julok from other villages in the region, theft started to become a serious problem only after 1975, and the people of Rumah Chang were in fact the original perpetrators. They recalled that, in the years after the Second World War, the birds' nest trade, although it enjoyed a stable regional market, was not highly lucrative. Everybody honored regulation of the harvest season and the individual rights of owners and leaseholders over particular sections of the caves. Starting around 1975, the people of Rumah Chang were granted permits to collect guano in the caves. After becoming familiar with the caves and learning the technique by observing veteran tukang julok at work, they started to collect birds' nest illegally and recklessly. The birds' nests thus collected were continuously brought down to the bazaar in small amounts and sold to "crooked" Chinese towkay. By 1985, as the situation was getting out of hand, Chinese leaseholders asked the police force to intervene and track down the perpetrators. The police operation was met with armed resistance staged by the people of Rumah Chang. In the late 1980s, the leaseholders were forced to seek reconciliation with the Rumah Chang people and start hiring year-round guards to protect their interests. Rumah Chang has since become the main supplier of jaga, tukang julok, and tukang pungut to the birds' nest industry at Niah.

The people of Rumah Chang have a different point of view regarding this episode. One informant says, "Last time when the Malay were the owners of the caves, we Iban were free to collect whatever [was] useful in the caves. After they leased the caves to the Chinese, we could not do that anymore. Nowadays we have to work as julok or jaga to earn wages. We are becoming coolies to the Chinese. We Iban were definitely not coolies to the Malay."

This might be the case in the eyes of Iban Rumah Chang, but one can also see the people of Rumah Chang, with their agency, as having created an unprecedented job opportunity for themselves through their energetic and aggressive exploitation of the caves. The regional commodity market might be beyond the control of local communities, and its encroachment unavoid-

able. At the juncture when the regional or global system needs to be articulated with the local, however, the chaos created by the people of Rumah Chang has successfully forced the birds' nest trade to come to terms with them. They earn their share (though not the biggest one) in the profit that is generated from this regional trade and use it to embellish their community life.

FROM BIRDS' NEST COLLECTION TO LONGHOUSE AND REGIONAL SOCIAL PRODUCTION

The Iban of Rumah Chang did not spoil their once brilliant financial opportunity. They put their money effectively in the renovation of the longhouse and they did this in a collective way. The present longhouse, beautifully renovated in the mid-1990s, has a uniform appearance for each bilek (family apartment), spacious open walkways with sitting areas, and verandas. The outside of the entire longhouse is painted light blue. Electric wiring is professionally done throughout the house. Many households have ceiling fans, and one bilek even has an air conditioner. My informant, showing me around and pointing at all the things in sight—including the air conditioner—said unhesitatingly: "Birds' nest money."

The longhouse of Rumah Chang won the third prize in a 1998 subdistrict longhouse contest. People of Rumah Chang often comment about their longhouse—always with traces of pride and contentment detectable underneath their cultivated modesty—that although it is not the most beautiful and modern longhouse in the subdistrict, all the bilek were finished around the same time: "Unlike most other longhouses, where some of the bilek are finished while others are still skeleton." This indicates both the financial might of most of the households and the spirit of community solidarity. The rebuilding was proposed by the tuai rumah (longhouse head) in 1990, after he visited some modern longhouses near Bintulu. The old building was already fifty years old at the time and deteriorating. Tuai rumah Chang brought the idea to the people and, after a thorough discussion, won the support of the entire village. Two Iban architects from Bintulu were commissioned to prepare the blueprint. It was agreed that all the units of the two blocks of the longhouse would follow basically the same design. Minor variations in terms of the quality and style of wooden planks, doors, and windows were allowed, but there were only a few designated varieties to choose from. According to some villagers, after the decision to rebuild the longhouse was made, there was a preparation period that lasted about three years. Even though Rumah Chang was already a well-off community, not every family could immedi-

ately come up with enough cash for the completion of the project. During the following three years, almost all the households had someone working somewhere for money. Some villagers went to work in the oil industry in Miri or Brunei, some in commercial construction. The most available source of cash income close to home, however, was the birds' nest industry in the Niah Caves. When the rebuilding was completed, each household had spent from 20,000 to 60,000 ringgit.

The two blocks of the longhouse of Rumah Chang now look absolutely polished and neat, with sturdy common staircases on both ends, wide and bright *ruai* areas, and similar-looking ceiling fans in front of almost all the bilek. Beside the one bilek with air-conditioning, most bilek are equipped with a television, a VCR or VCD player, a stereo, a gas stove, and a refrigerator. Nowadays, sitting on the ruai for late afternoon or evening chatting, people still occasionally compare and comment on the different quality and price of the building materials that each bilek uses. Out on the ruai of Rumah Chang, one experiences and witnesses the realization and perpetuation of the core Iban value that emphasizes both the spirit of community solidarity and individualistic competition.

A ritual called *semah* used to be performed annually to appease the spirits of the caves and to ask them to protect the birds' nest and guano collectors working in the caves. It is considered a Punan ritual, to be performed every year before the opening of the first formal harvest season, in April. A spiritual medium (*dayung*), who has exclusive knowledge of the names of the spirits and can perform the chanting, conducts the ritual. After the dayung communicates with the spirits, a chicken is sacrificed and various kinds of rice cake are offered to the spirits. After the performance of the ritual, no one is to enter the caves for three days, so the spirits can enjoy the offerings in peace; there are stories relating the breaches of the taboo and their fatal outcomes. By the early 1990s, the ritual had already been discontinued for a long time due to the dispersal of the Punan and the unavailability of dayung. In 1998, the Punan community managed to have an aging dayung, Pa' Udek Seman, conduct the ritual. Several hundred people, including Punan Muslims, Malays, Iban, and Chinese, attended the ceremony. The Chinese traders community is said to have contributed a significant amount of money to cover the expense of the ceremony, but there is talk of disputes inside the Punan community regarding their share of financing the ritual. Unfortunately, Pa' Udek Seman passed away in late 1998. Under the current worldwide trend of nativistic movements, the desire to "revive" the ritual is rather strong both in the government and among the various parties concerned, but it is not

certain whether or not the Punan community can produce another dayung to continue the ritual in the future.

There is unavoidably a dark side of the birds' nest enterprise at Niah. The decline both in the swiftlet population and in birds' nest (and guano) production is evident. Evasion of the stipulated harvesting schedule by the Chinese towkay is compounded by the problem of theft. Hiring full-time guardsmen does not solve the problem, since many of the "thieves" are either the guardsmen themselves or their friends and relatives. Presently almost all the locals coming out of the caves—off-duty guards, designated collectors, and people just "visiting"—have some birds' nest in their pocket. Each one would have 20 to 30 ringgit worth of "pocket money birds' nest." In the short run, this appears to be a swindling of the Chinese towkay. In the long run, however, everybody loses.

In addition to the accessibility of the place, Niah's plight also has something to do with the once huge population of the swiftlets and the low price of the black nests. Large amounts of harvested nests were needed to make the sale profitable, and very few parties really work to protect the diminishing swiftlet population. It is also closely related to the social relation of production. The real owners of the cave rights, the Punan, are by now mostly absentee landlords. The Chinese towkays have the capital and business connections to process and market the nests, but they do not have the skill or the will to work the caves themselves. The onsite workers do not have much of a personal interest in following conservation guidelines or in safeguarding the interest of the Chinese towkay. The manifold administrative arrangement at Niah results in a virtual vacancy of authority to enforce the policy stipulated by laws. The problems foreseen by Sarawak lawmakers in the first half of this century are now emerging.

Amid this highly commoditized and rather alienated productive relation, traces of sociality survive. Some may lament the disappearance of the once lively seasonal multiethnic community in the Traders' Cave. But the material well-being of the Iban worker at Rumah Chang is certainly a demonstration of the underlying sense of community and cooperation. Most significant of all, despite the predominance of Chinese capital and Iban (and others') labor, the Punan still retain the authority of ritual sanction over birds' nest production. The semah ritual contains the potential for sustainable multiethnic social production. This is especially so in face of mounting international pressure on the birds' nest trade. While more effort and enforcement

in conservation is definitely crucial and beneficial to all the parties involved, including the swiftlets, the continuation or revival of a traditional ritual that unites different peoples to establish a harmonious and productive relationship with the spiritual beings in the cave is probably no less effective as a means to neutralize or disarm the stiff gaze of international wildlife agencies, at least to a certain extent. Some of the Sarawak government agents, such as the Sarawak Museum, are certainly aware of this prospect and are taking an encouraging attitude toward its continuation. Now it is largely up to the Punan to maintain the transmission of their ritual knowledge.

Conclusion

It has been demonstrated that the value of birds' nest is constructed and sanctioned by Chinese medicinal tradition. This includes both the general therapeutic effects of all kinds of birds' nest as well as the especially fabulous effects of the "blood nest." Judging from the expanding scope of the Southeast Asian transnational birds' nest trade, one may say that neither the demythification of the true quality of birds' nest nor the disapproving gaze of the environmentalists is deterring the consumer's enthusiasm for the yen-wo. The use-value (subjective value) of birds' nest thus determined is further differentiated into several grades, with "blood nest" on the top and white nest regrouped at the bottom. This value categorization is conspicuously different from the categorization at or near the locations of production, where whole white nest fetches a much better price than do the colored ones. There is ample room for the middlemen, almost exclusively ethnic Chinese, to manipulate this discrepancy to their benefit. This is because they have a much better comprehension of what Sutherland calls "relevant knowledge about production and consumption." The situation is also a vivid illustration of what Arjun Appadurai says about transactions in the precapitalist context.

> In precapitalist contexts . . . the translation of external demands to local producers is the province of the trader and his agents, who provide logistical and price bridges between worlds of knowledge that may have minimal direct contact. Thus it is reasonably certain that traditional Borneo forest dwellers had relatively little idea of the uses to which the birds' nests they sold to intermediaries have played in Chinese medical and culinary practice. This paradigm of merchant bridges across large gaps in knowledge between producer and consumer characterizes the movement of most commodities throughout history, up to the present.

Problems involving knowledge, information, and ignorance are not

restricted to the production and consumption poles of the careers of commodities, but characterize the process of circulation and exchange itself. In a powerful cultural account of the Moroccan bazaar, Clifford Geertz has placed the search for reliable information at the heart of this institution. . . . Much of the institutional structure and cultural form of the bazaar is double-edged, making reliable knowledge hard to get and also facilitating the search for it. . . . [To put it] in a more general form: bazaar-style information searches are likely to characterize any exchange setting where the quality and the appropriate valuation of goods are not standardized, though the reasons for the lack of standardization, for the volatility of prices, and for the unreliable quality of specific things of a certain type may vary enormously.[47]

While the birds' nest example might serve as a strong case in favor of the subjective value theory, it also represents an interesting cultural twist to the labor theory of value. The use-value recognized by the Chinese consumers in birds' nest is actually based on the recognition of huge labor input behind the procurement of the commodity. Derived from a reputed holistic cosmology, both professional and folk ideas in Chinese medicinal tradition regard the therapeutic effects of birds' nest as substantiated by the life essence of other living things, in this case including both working human beings and the nest-constructing birds themselves. In other words, in the case of this commodity, birds' nest, the subjective and the labor theories of value actually merge.

On the other hand, the communities that occupy the laborer position in this commodity chain are not entirely exploited passive players. Their agency is not negligible in the processes. At Niah, in appearance, each group involved in the production is alienated in different ways: the cave-owning Punan-Malay do not manage the operation; the Iban that work the caves are only wage earners; and the Chinese traders do not have the legal status to own the cave or the physical capacity to work the cave, but can only lease it from the Punan-Malay and hire the Iban as laborers. However, a trace of sociality or communalism is produced, or at least shows the potential of social production at a different level. This is demonstrated in the multiethnic celebration of the semah ritual. The Iban of Rumah Chang, on the other hand, have successfully converted the cash income generated from their participation in the birds' nest trade into capital for their social production, as represented in the building of their prize-winning longhouse.

Notes

I thank Daniel Chew of Sarawak Development Institute, Lim Khay-thiong of National Chi Nan University, and Anyi Won of Sarawak Museum for their invaluable assistance, which made my research possible. Funding for my fieldwork was provided by the project Upland and Lowland Cultures and Societies of Monsoon Asia, Academia Sinica.

1. Literally meaning "swiftlets' nest."

2. Margot Cohen and Tanjung Redeb, "Million-dollar Saliva," *Far Eastern Economic Review* 162.3 (1999): 48–50.

3. See, for example, Earl of Cranbrook, "Report on the Birds' Nest Industry in the Baram District and at Niah, Sarawak," *Sarawak Museum Journal* 32.54 (1984): 146–70; Charles M. U. Leh, *A Guide to Birds' Nest Caves and Birds' Nests of Sarawak* (Kuching: Sarawak Museum, 1993); Lord Medway, "Birds' Nest Collecting," *Sarawak Museum Journal* 7.10 (1957): 252–60.

4. Leonard Blussé, "In Praise of Commodities: An Essay on the Cross-cultural Trade in Edible Bird's Nests," *Emporia, Commodities and Entrepreneurs in Asian Maritime Trade c. 1400–1750*, ed. Roderich Ptak and Dietmar Rothermund (Stuttgart: Franz Steiner Verlag, 1991), 317–35.

5. Blussé, "In Praise of Commodities," 331.

6. Ibid., 332.

7. Ibid., 334.

8. See Heather Sutherland's essay in this volume.

9. Ibid, 191.

10. Ibid, 191.

11. See, for example, the Trade and Environment Database (TED); and Barbara Harrisson, "Niah's Lobang Tulang: 'Cave of Bones,'" *Sarawak Museum Journal* 7.12 (1958): 596–619.

12. Blussé, "In Praise of Commodities," 321.

13. Chia Ming, *Yin-shih hsü-chih* [What we need to know about food and drink] (Beijing: Renmin weisheng chubanshe, 1988). The Ming dynasty lasted from 1368 to 1644, while Chia Ming lived between 1268 and 1370.

14. Blussé, "In Praise of Commodities," 321.

15. Chang Hsieh, *Dung Xi Yang Kau* [Investigation of the east and the west oceans] (Taipei: Zheng-zhong, 1962), 31.

16. Ibid., 57.

17. Chao Hsüe-ming, *Pen-ts'ao kang-mu shih-i* [Supplement to Compendium of materia medica] (Hong Kong: Commercial, 1971), 429.

18. Chen Mau-ren's biodata is not clear. In this work, however, he listed a number of his colleagues who all started their service during the third decade of the Wan-li reign (1573–1620). Fujian is one of the southeastern coastal provinces of China.

19. Chao Hsüe-ming, *Pen-ts'ao kang-mu shih-i*, 428.

20. Jiang-su New Medical College, *Chung-yao ta tz'u-tien* [Grand dictionary of Chinese medicine] (Shanghai: Shanghai kexue chishu chubanshe, 1986), 2, 654. *Chi* is one of

the focal concepts in Chinese medicine and can be roughly translated as "vital force or vital energy."

21. Chao Hsüe-ming, *Pen-ts'ao kang-mu shih-i*, 429. Essence of life, *jing*, could also refer to semen.

22. Ibid., 428–29, emphasis added.

23. Jiang-su New Medical College, *Chung-yao ta tz'u-tien*, 2, 654.

24. For example, Cranbrook, "Report on the Birds' Nest Industry in the Baram District and at Niah, Sarawak," 146. Bernard E. Read, however, still regarded the edible part of birds' nest as being "made out of certain species of Gelidium and other seaweeds" (*Chinese Materia Medica: Avian Drugs* [1932; repr., Taipei: Southern Material, 1982], 54).

25. This is based on personal correspondence with a veteran Museum worker.

26. Chu Chin Onn, "Birds' Nests: Sarawak All-Cure," *Sarawak Gazette*, no. 1280 (1964): 259.

27. This home video was taken by one of my Middle Baram informants, who had recently visited this house-farmed birds' nest operation in Indonesia. I viewed the video with my informant in his house.

28. One of my colleagues, a senior scholar of Chinese history and a regular birds' nest consumer, asked me to bring him some top-quality birds' nests on my next trip to Sarawak. "Bring me some of the best ones, the blood nests," he said.

29. The Earl of Cranbrook reports, "One feature of note, here [the Baram] as at Niah, is the occasional presence of rusty red stain in the nest-cement forming the base (i.e. attachment) of the nest. At both locations this discoloration (termed *salai* in the Baram) is attributed by nest collectors to a character of the parent rock of the cave. Its effect on quality (judged from expected sale value) may be either neutral or, if the stain is invasive, detrimental" ("Report on the Birds' Nest Industry in the Baram District and at Niah, Sarawak," 155).

30. Leh, *Guide to Birds' Nest Caves and Birds' Nests of Sarawak*, 5.

31. Healthy Nest website, http://www.healthynest.com.

32. Graham Saunders, *A History of Brunei* (Kuala Lumpur: Oxford University Press, 1994), 21–61.

33. James F. Warren, *The Zulu Zone 1768–1898: The Dynamics of External Trade, Slavery, and Ethnicity in the Transformation of a Southeast Asian Maritime State* (Singapore: Singapore University Press, 1981), 77–78.

34. Robert Nicholl, ed., *European Sources for the History of the Sultanate of Brunei in the Sixteenth Century* (Bandar Seri Begawan: Brunei Museum, 1990), 95. In contrast to the absence of birds' nest, officers following Olivier van Noort on his visit did record large amounts of bezoar stones for trade, as well as an active Chinese merchant community.

35. Blussé, "In Praise of Commodities," 326.

36. Hugh Low, *Sarawak* (1848; repr., Singapore: Oxford University Press, 1988), 316–17. Low documented the activity of birds' nest collection at Bau by the local Bidayuh people. The birds' nests from Bau area are of the black type.

37. In most of the later literature, the Penan in this area are renamed Punan.

38. *Towkay* is Southern Fujian dialect for "boss." The term is commonly used by native Sarawakians to address or refer to Chinese, shopowner or not.

39. Benedict Sandin, "Some Niah Folklore and Origins," *Sarawak Museum Journal* 8.12 (1958): 646–62.

40. Ibid., 662.

41. Cranbrook, "Report on the Birds' Nest Industry in the Baram District and at Niah, Sarawak," 157.

42. Medway, "Birds' Nest Collecting," 254.

43. Ibid., 260.

44. Ibid., 256–57.

45. Ibid., 252.

46. Women do not work in the caves, not even as tukang pungut. The reason given for this is that the work is too filthy and no woman would want to go. In the semah ceremony held in 1998 at the West Mouth to appease the cave spirits, however, both men and women, the elderly as well as children participated.

47. Arjun Appadurai, "Introduction: Commodities and the Politics of Value," *The Social Life of Things: Commodities in Cultural Perspective*, ed. Arjun Appadurai (Cambridge: Cambridge University Press, 1986), 42.

A SINO-SOUTHEAST ASIAN CIRCUIT

Ethnohistories of the Marine Goods Trade

〜〜〜 Eric Tagliacozzo

The renowned sociologist Georg Simmel has famously written of the paradoxical nature of "the stranger"—at once alien and uncomfortable in any given local society, but also able to use this status to further economic and even occasionally political ends, often associated with trade.[1] Simmel was building on the work of others who had thought about these processes, most notably Max Weber and his interrogations of the so-called Protestant ethic, with all that this historical "ethic" supposedly signified.[2] Many contemporary scholars have seized on these ideas to study the mechanics of "stranger communities" in their own academic bailiwicks, encompassing Indians in East Africa, Jews in Europe, and even Armenians spread out across the Middle East. Scholars of overseas Chinese communities have been no exception: some of the most important analytic writing about diasporic communities and their linkages with trade and long-distance commercial enterprises has focused on these populations. The reasons for this have been disparate, but one of the most important among them is that the Chinese—and those who conducted business with them—have often left very good records, though accessing these records across the bandwidth of societies and languages that Chinese traders visited has not always been the easiest of tasks.[3]

In this essay I look at overseas Chinese networks through one window: the historical and contemporary trade in marine produce, which linked China and the many countries of Southeast Asia in an economic embrace for hundreds of years. In the first third of this essay, I note some of the theoretical, historiographical, and historical outlines for examining these communities and processes across historical time. This is done in fairly shorthand form, as I have written about these connections in more detail in other places.[4] The second two-thirds of the essay link these historical peregrinations with

how the marine-goods trade works now between China and Southeast Asia. This portion of the essay is based on published academic literature, but also significantly comprises my own oral-history interviews with these traders throughout East and Southeast Asian ports, as well as visits to collecting and transshipment sites of these commodities too. I hope to show the broad dimensions of this commerce in both historical and contemporary terms, as a crucial connective link between China and Southeast Asia over the past several centuries. Far from being an antiquated trade in strange and often exoticized objects culled from the sea, the traffic in marine goods can be seen as an important vestige of historical transoceanic connections. This commerce echoes the past in nostalgic and interesting ways, but it also continually evolves into the future, as the statements of these traders reveal when they speak into the record on their own terms.

Marine Goods in the Past: Woven Threads

SINO–SOUTHEAST ASIA: CONNECTIVE HISTORIES

Scholarship on the historical dimensions of the Chinese economy has come a long way in the past several decades in attempting to explain how and why Chinese commerce expanded in the last three to four centuries. Some of these studies have focused on guild and clan associations, the famous *gongsi* that G. William Skinner and others researched in such fine detail in the 1970s and earlier.[5] Other studies have combed the *Ming Shi-lu* (or Ming Veritable Records), as well as the archives of particular provinces, such as Fujian, for clues as to how commercial activities expanded in the early modern period before exploding in number, importance, and volume in the nineteenth century.[6] Most of these earlier studies looked at the oceans when the tendrils of commerce were scrutinized as moving away from the Chinese polity, but now such research also deals with overland connections in detailed and sophisticated ways as well.[7] There has even been an effort more recently to highlight particular commodities and to follow them as "tracers" in unraveling these processes, with goods such as opium proving to be particularly useful in this regard.[8] If analyses of the Chinese historical economy used to be the realm of dry number-crunchers and arcane local archives, more recently these inquiries have sprouted off in new and different directions, to the profit of Chinese historiography as a whole.

One of the most pressing contemporary research agendas on the nature of Chinese social and economic history has been the role of Chinese merchants in trans-Asian networks. This research has built on some of the foundational work of Skinner, R. Bin Wong, Peter Purdue, and William Rowe, and

now asks a range of questions on how commerce has worked in China, but particularly as one of several strands of commodity movement that became important during the last two centuries. The connections with Western firms have been queried in this regard, as well as links and commercial piggy-backing with Japanese business concerns as well.[9] Some of the research has looked at particular dialect subgroups as windows into these processes on both a micro and a macro scale, while other studies have examined how the efforts of many different actors—Chinese, French, Dutch, British, Spanish, and even Persian—have combined to push and pull certain items through Asian geographies on an unprecedented scale.[10] It is clear that the old story of a more or less "sealed Chinese economy" via dictate of the Ch'ing state is no longer tenable, as more and more research is brought to bear on the way networks have expanded outward from China proper to other places, some as far away as Chicago and Peru.[11]

Though Chinese did indeed end up in places as far afield as this, it is clear that the locus classicus for both Chinese emigration and Chinese commercial expansion during this period was the Nanyang, or "South Seas" (Southeast Asia). This is particularly true for the history of marine-goods procurement, but it is also true on the whole for most fields of business and endeavor, as the numbers of Chinese who eventually left for these places attest to over many years. French scholars (writing in French) have been particularly good at theorizing these connections, showing how the South China Sea acted as a fulcrum for movement and radials of contact and dispersion, even as far away as the distant island of Java.[12] English-language scholarship has also worked on these connections, either via longue durée histories or through the vantages of particular institutions, such as Chinese revenue farming as a connective strand between China and Southeast Asia.[13] Japanese writers (translated into English) and Chinese scholars have also become involved, ensuring that not all attempts at explanation of these phenomena are grounded solely in Western social-science paradigms.[14] Taken as a whole, the collective has set up very useful parameters in helping us understand the template of historical travel, whether this was for commercial reasons, such as the trade in marine goods, or for any other rationale.

IN SOUTHERN WATERS

One of the most important destinations in the Nanyang for Chinese traders and immigrants was Java. Java had long had contact with China, but the establishment of a Dutch presence in Batavia around the turn of the seventeenth century increased the demand for Chinese merchants, artisans, and

workers in far greater numbers than had previously arrived. The autocratic Jan Coen was the despot of the town, but Dutch-language scholarship shows us that Chinese *kapitans* were quickly established to look after the Chinese population, especially with regard to regulating commerce along lines of which the Dutch approved.[15] Things went fairly smoothly at first, but by the eighteenth century there were significant troubles, including massacres of these same Chinese populations.[16] When the Chinese inhabitants were not being periodically culled in such ruthless ways by the colonial overlords of the island, they were used to expand Dutch commerce in many sectors of the economy, such as petty trade, agriculture, and increasingly, the sale of *chandu*, or retail opium.[17] Intermarriage with local women took place on a fairly large scale, and the Chinese on Java gradually phased into both a separate community as well as a mestizo society that was mixed with the indigenes themselves.[18] Many Chinese were, in fact, scattered in the port towns and on other parts of Java's coasts, and they played a large part in the buying, selling, and transport of marine products to these larger towns, where such commodities were consumed or packaged for export to other places.

Dutch-language scholarship shows us how quickly the Chinese, and Chinese marine-goods traders in particular, spread into the rest of the burgeoning Dutch Indies as well, away from the center of Dutch authority on Java.[19] Economically, this community began to serve a crucial feeder role for the Dutch via all things that the latter needed to make their colony profitable — dried fish, pearls, and fish maws among them. The most famous Chinese fishing station in the archipelago was located at Bagan Si Api-api, off the coast of north-central Sumatra, and the amounts of sea produce collected, dried, and packaged for sale here reached huge quantities by the late nineteenth century and early twentieth. Proximity to British-controlled Singapore, with that island's huge port and transregional shipping connections, was at least as important as Bagan Si Api-api's connections to the Dutch primate port city of Batavia, further south and away from the mouth of the Straits of Melaka (see fig. 1).[20] Yet Chinese appeared elsewhere as well, on the long outstretched coasts of Borneo, for example, in Sulawesi, in Eastern Indonesia, and especially in Riau, as fishers, driers, collectors, and packagers of marine goods.[21] Ethnic business connections with other Chinese merchants and with Dutch colonial officials ensured that much of this produce reached Dutch and foreign markets quickly and fairly efficiently. Chinese communities were so important in this respect that the Dutch undertook extensive surveillance on these populations to ensure that Batavia would always get its cut of moving merchandise.[22]

Figure 1 Fishing and other local ships in Singapore, c. 1900. KITLV: Image Code 50215; Haven in Singapore, c. 1900; Oost Java Album no. 70, Lambert and Company, photo, 14 x 21 cm.

Further north in the waters of the British dominions of Malaya and Borneo, a similar state of affairs existed with respect to Chinese communities and the collection of ocean produce. On Borneo, both in today's modern Malaysian states of Sarawak and Sabah, as well as in the sultanate of Brunei, Chinese took on busy roles as the organizers and collectors of ocean produce in a variety of places.[23] The coasts of Borneo were found to be underexploited compared to many other places, so Chinese merchants and occasionally small business concerns often had their pick as to where to set up shops, drying facilities, purchase points, and other institutions to make these businesses run.[24] Revenue-farming syndicates with primary interests in other products, such as opium or alcohol, sometimes helped in smoothing out some of these arrangements.[25] On the Malay Peninsula in places such as Penang, where Chinese syndicates such as the well-studied Khaw Group held economic sway, the connections between marine produce and efficient forms of Chinese business organization were even more in evidence, especially with large populations of Chinese and other ethnic laborers nearby needing to be fed.[26] The buying, sorting, packaging, and eventual shipping of marine products were a crucial part of the local economy in places such as Penang, connecting the British port to Sumatra, the Malay Peninsula, Siam, and even Burma in one large, maritime economic arena.

Finally, in the Philippines, first run by the Spanish and eventually run for

half a century by the United States, we see a similar story, though with different local permutations. Chinese had been coming to the Philippines for many centuries and often in larger numbers than in other parts of Southeast Asia, as the archipelago was closer and easier to reach using prevailing wind and current patterns of the monsoons. With more than 7,000 islands, Chinese became heavily involved in the marine-produce trades of the colonial Philippines very easily, often using ships that they had originally piloted to the Philippines, first as vessels of transport and eventually as carriage containers for marine produce heading back to Fujian.[27] The ocean produce trade from the Philippines was extremely important, first for supplying cities with food (such as Manila and Cebu), but also in mining the exceedingly plentiful waters of Sulu in the southern parts of the archipelago, where pearls, mother-of-pearl, shark fins, and fish stomachs could be procured in very large quantities. Chinese crews sailed from South China to take advantage of these riches, but they eventually also came from Singapore and other Southeast Asian ports, all in an effort to make a living off these fecund seas.[28] Though the Spanish, in particular, periodically legislated against Chinese over-involvement in regional trades outside of the cities, the rules often went unenforced because of Spanish weakness, and because of the outstretched geography of the islands.[29] Even into the early twentieth century and after the arrival of the Americans, Chinese involvement in these trades was maintained, though other agricultural staples—often fetching very high prices on world markets, at least until the Great Depression—later drowned marine goods as one of the most important items of commerce in maintaining long-distance commercial connections.[30]

Marine-Goods Connections in the Contemporary Period
THEORIES, CONTEXTS, AND THE CHINESE "HEARTLAND"

Fast-forwarding to the last two decades of the twentieth century and the first few years of the twenty-first century, a remarkable picture of change and continuity appears in the transit of ocean commerce between China and Southeast Asia. If the period between roughly 1780 and 1860 was a high point of this commerce, followed by a lessening in importance of this trade as it was swamped by the much larger movement of goods in the so-called high colonial era, then the last two to three decades have seen a resurgence in these items, as the record-growth economies of both China and many Southeast Asian states have spun off the charts. If the worldwide depression of the 1930s, the Second World War, and the early years of Southeast Asian nation-states after decolonization continued the pattern of marine goods

living in the shadow of other, more important lines of commerce since the late nineteenth century, then the explosive growth of economies in East and Southeast Asia since the 1980s has revitalized this traditional conduit of trade between the two regions in new and interesting ways. Much of this growth has been attributed to the overall dynamism of regional economies, which has encouraged a brisk flow of goods between subregions that have traditionally traded with one another for many hundreds of years. Yet it is noticeable that the passage of marine goods has become an important sub-rubric of this larger economic success story, begging the question as to why and how this trade fits into a larger story of growth. I address this question both through social-science literature on the topic, and through my own interviews with Chinese marine-goods merchants in various parts of China, Taiwan, and Southeast Asia itself. Both avenues of inquiry are supplemented as well by my observations from field trips to marine-collecting sites scattered throughout the region (see map 1).

Certainly the success of Chinese business in reasserting itself throughout Southeast Asia since the fall of the colonial powers at midcentury has drawn no lack of interest from social theorists seeking to explain this success. The reasons put forward for this dynamism have been various in nature, from the importance of clan associations and language-dialect groups, to notions of *guanxi* and transnational networks, to an interesting thread reflecting on the nature of "Chinese capitalism" itself as a modus operandi for a range of ethnic Chinese merchants scattered throughout Southeast Asia.[31] Some of these explanations have been more sophisticated than others, but all of them point to an opinion and a worldview that Chinese business has been in a growth mode not only in "Greater China" (the People's Republic of China (PRC), Hong Kong, and Taiwan, over the last twenty-five years or so), but also in Southeast Asia, a traditional field for Chinese merchant activity over the centuries (known collectively as the Nanyang).[32] Several important scholars have looked specifically at the dynamics of these interactions from China down to Southeast Asia itself, both historically and in the years leading up to our own time.[33] Others have concentrated more on the Southeast Asian side of things, analyzing patterns in the receiving countries of these flows, rather than from the source areas of migration and merchant movement in East Asia as a whole.[34] Regardless of the approach chosen, it is clear that marine-goods movements between the two spheres connect these literatures very well, and help show some of the mechanics of commerce and ethnicity in action. The business radials operate over a very large field and are

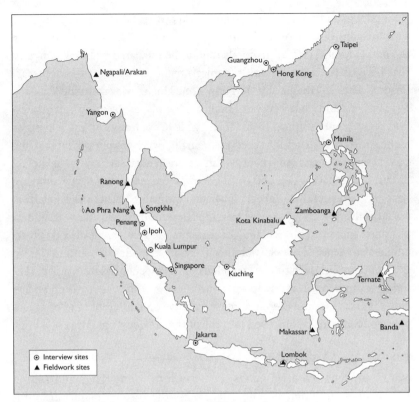

Map 1 Fieldwork sites for oral history interviews and field research.

therefore instructive in showing how an old trade such as the one in marine goods survives and changes over time.

China, Hong Kong, and Taiwan are mostly end-destinations for the flow of goods, as the majority of items come from Southeast Asia, but sometimes also from further afield than this. Interviews done in these places with shop owners show how truly transnational their contacts can be: owners signaled their entrenchment in much larger geographic systems in interesting ways. Some shops, such as the Kin Sang Dispensary in Kowloon, Hong Kong, are very low on the chain—they are merely bottom-rung outlets for these goods, and sell such products only in very small quantities per package, and only to local consumers.[35] These stores are common in Hong Kong, but also in China proper, where comparatively small numbers of large-sized concerns deal with the outside world. This was certainly true in Xiamen, Fujian (one of the most "networked" places in China), but it was also true in Guangzhou,

Guangdong, and even in Ching-ping Market, where dried sea products are sold by many dozens of merchants side by side.[36] Their connections with the outside world of marine goods tend to be mediated by larger concerns that have better contacts with the government and can get the necessary licenses. Back in Hong Kong, and only a few blocks away from the Kin Sang Dispensary, Citiherb is a very different kind of place: gleaming and impressive, its wares are shipped from far and wide in the Nanyang. The fish maws alone (dried fish stomachs, used medicinally) were among the largest and best-preserved specimens that I saw anywhere in my interviews in Asia.[37] Yet even this apothecary paled in comparison to the Ho Sheng Tang Company, headquartered in Taipei, Taiwan. Ho Sheng Tang obtained its shark fins from the large fleets of Taiwanese fishing ships that comb the world's seas, and its abalone came from Mexico and California, across the vast Pacific itself. Its edible-sea-cucumber stocks not only had various grades of Southeast Asian holothurians, but even tiny, extremely expensive specimens from Japan, selling at NT$9,800 (or at US$300 per specimen).[38] This was the high end of end-destinations, and therefore representative of a different kind of access to the outside world compared to some of the previously mentioned shops.

THE COASTS OF THE SOUTHEAST ASIAN MAINLAND

Marine produce and dried goods come to China, Hong Kong, and Taiwan from many parts of the Nanyang, but certainly the coasts of mainland Southeast Asia have a very long history of shipping such products north. Vietnam is China's closest neighbor in Southeast Asia, and because of its long, extended coastline, fish has very often been transported to South China, frequently by ethnically Sino-Vietnamese merchants. Even fishermen themselves do this on occasion, evading customs patrols, as they know where they can land their boats to quietly unload large holds of precious fish. Observers of Vietnamese economic life have often commented on the importance of the Sino-Vietnamese community, centered on Cholon in Ho Chi Minh City, but present in large stretches of the rest of the country too, in connecting the Chinese and Vietnamese economies.[39] It is clear that, in the realm of marine goods and dried natural products, these binding commercial sinews have been very important. In Cambodia, too, the marine industry has been vital both in feeding Cambodia's own population and as an export industry for profit, often to China. Nola Cooke has studied some of these patterns over the course of the nineteenth and twentieth centuries, particularly as they related to fish and marine life coming from the Tonle Sap, Cambodia's great lake.[40] This lake is said by scientists to have the greatest density

of fish in the world, and some of that density is shipped off to China every year in dried form, both by Sino-Khmer merchants and by Chinese traders who know to come to Cambodia's markets on a seasonal basis to pick up their supplies.

In Thailand, the picture is little different. Ethnically Sino-Thai merchants are also important in this country, and help to form an economic conduit between the kingdom, which also boasts a large, extended coastline, and China, which is often a market-destination for sea produce caught both in the Gulf of Thailand and in the Andaman Sea. From fieldwork done on the docks of Songkhla, on the gulf coast in the south, it is clear that very large specimens of fish—including shovel-nosed sharks and various species of rays—are being sold to China for the feeding of both humans and animals alike (for the latter, some of these fish species are ground up to make animal feed).[41]

On the Indian Ocean coast of southern Thailand, astride the Andaman Sea, slightly different dynamics rule the market in these goods. In places like Ao Phra Nang, a Muslim fishing village just north of Krabi, a small resort town catering to Western travelers (as opposed to tourists, who tend to flock to Phuket and other offshore islands), much of the fishing economy is also geared toward export. Here, shellfish are collected seasonally and with the tides, mostly by women in the mud-flat shallows, and then boxed and transported to collection depots for eventual resale to the Chinese market.[42] Further north along this same coast, and at the bottom terminus of Burma, the border town of Ranong is also an important fishing and collecting center for marine exports from Thailand. Here, as opposed to Ao Nang, the industry is just that—industrial—with large, oceangoing fishing trawlers setting out each day from Ranong's docks, the boats fishing for catch in Thai waters, international waters, and sometimes (illegally) in Burmese or Malaysian waters too (see fig. 2). Here too, I have been told in interviews on the docks, a large portion of the eventual catch is dried and shipped to Hong Kong and China to meet demand.[43]

Finally, in Burma, too—one of the world's most isolated countries, because of the coup that brought the Burmese military to power, in 1962—traditionally sought marine goods are shuttling en masse to China, and only sometimes in officially recorded fashion. Here, as in the shops and dispensaries of Hong Kong, there are different kinds of concerns with different kinds of reach into the marine-goods trade. Small shops, such as the one in Yangon (Rangoon) owned by U Myint Thein, have traditional roots in the trade and have been passed on from generation to generation. One of

Figure 2 Burmese and Thai fishing boats: Ranong and Songkhla (Andaman Sea and Gulf of Thailand). Photos by author.

U Myint Thein's parents was ethnically Burmese, but one was also Yunnanese Chinese, and it was from this generation that he learned how to conduct his business in the buying and selling of items inside this pharmacopeia.[44] A nearby shop, also in Yangon, had firmer roots in this commerce, and because Burma is still relatively isolated, many of the wares on view in this store were new to me, and I had not seen them in markets outside of Burma. These included items such as several species of dried fish (some black in color, others white), though there were also very expensive species of holothurians on offer, which was surprising for a country as economically poor as Burma.[45] Fieldwork done on the Arakan coast, not too far from the Bangladesh border, also confirmed that the fishing was on a small-scale, community basis, and not just by large fishing boats owned by industrial concerns. In one village alone, I saw huge drying mats set out with fish of several different species (Commerson's anchovy [*Stolephorus commersonii*]; Silver Pomfret [*Pampus argenteus*]; and Lonfin Mojarra [*Pentaprion longimanus*]), all baking in the sun.[46] When I asked a Chinese merchant in town where these small species of dried fish were heading, he told me that some were used for local consumption, some were eaten in Yangon and in other big cities of Burma, and that others were on their way to China, though that was certainly very far away.

SOUTHEAST ASIA'S ISLAND WORLD

If these patterns are discernible on the coasts of the mainland world of Southeast Asia, then they are nearly omnipresent in insular Southeast Asia, where the sea is literally everywhere, and its bounty is readily available for transport. A large literature has sprung up to study the tendril of Chinese commerce in the contemporary Philippines, for example, where Chinese families have mixed into mestizo communities with local Filipinos for hundreds of years.[47] Some of these networks are centered on Manila, the "primate city" of the Philippines and by far its most important economic engine, but there are also important Chinese merchant interests in the provinces as well, especially in places such as Ilo-ilo in the Visayas.[48] Chinese marine-goods sellers in the warehouse districts of northern Manila (Binondo and Divisorio) told me of huge orders that they received for ocean produce from China, from both Hong Kong and the PRC proper. Most of these merchants are Hokkien speakers whose ancestors came to the Philippines from Fujian, and many of them still have good contacts and family scattered throughout southern China, as well as more formal business associates in Hong Kong.[49] It is a noticeable attribute of these Filipino-Chinese families that sons and

daughters help with the business, especially because so many of them can speak good English, and this connects them to wider radials of procurement than merely the Chinese-speaking contacts allow. Because the Philippines is one of the world's largest archipelagos (with some 7,000 islands), there is no lack of maritime environment from which to find supplies for this outstretched commerce, either. Contacts of these families stretch all the way south to Zamboanga and the Sulu Sea, one of the richest historical marine grounds for maritime-goods procurement, going back to at least the fifteenth century.[50]

If this state of affairs holds true for the Philippines, then it is even truer for Indonesia, the world's largest archipelago bar none. Scattered among Indonesia's 13,000-plus islands is also a large ethnic Chinese merchant community, some of whom have been there for centuries, and others who are more recent arrivals from elsewhere in East or Southeast Asia (China, Singapore, Malaysia, etc.). Chinese merchants have been involved in the sea-products trade of this region for a very long time, and their tendrils of business and association extend far and wide.[51] It is not only Western social scientists who are interested in this phenomenon, but Indonesian scholars too—many, but not all, of them of Chinese ancestry—and the latter have also written about this phenomenon, sometimes in English, but also in Bahasa Indonesia.[52] Fieldwork done in harvesting areas such as Lombok in Nusa Tenggara, Makassar in Sulawesi, and Ternate and Banda in Maluku, Eastern Indonesia, shows that Chinese capital finances sea-products collecting on a grand scale, across large parts of this scattered archipelago.[53] Jakarta is often the national collecting depot for such products, but the items can also be sent directly to Singapore, or occasionally to Hong Kong to bypass layers of middlemen.[54] The commodities are almost always harvested from the sea by local indigenes, but as soon as they get to market, they go through various rungs of sorting and sale through ethnic Chinese merchants, often locally born, but based progressively further and further away from acquisition sites. This is, in fact, a broad pattern throughout Southeast Asia, whether it is mother-of-pearl, sea cucumbers, fish maws, or other items that are being collected.

In Malaysia, having conversations with Chinese marine-goods merchants is easy: there is little of the occasional discomfort (or even downright fear) that pervades Chinese Indonesians during interviews, and there is plenty of commercial activity in the sea-products arena here, too. Speaking to these traders throughout Malaysia's major cities is an exercise in tracking the Chinese diaspora over time, and seeing the fullest expression of its breadth,

all in dealing with one product line. In Kuala Lumpur the majority of these traders are Cantonese, in keeping with historical migration patterns to the city, while in Penang and Ipoh they are Hokkien for the most part.[55] In Malaysian Borneo, where Chinese migrants came from different parts of China, and for different reasons, the majority are Hakka.[56] Yet despite these varying sub-ethnicities among the merchants, many of them seem to be buying and selling the same goods, though often along dialect lines when they can. In other cases these traders use Mandarin as a lingua franca among other ocean-products businessmen scattered throughout Malaysia, in Southeast Asia, and back to East Asia itself. Quite a number of these Malaysian Chinese merchants spoke of doing their business along "traditional lines"; they do indeed use computers, faxes, and telexes in their daily transactions, but they also make use of abacuses and good tea when doing business, as their fathers before them would have done, and perhaps their fathers' fathers before that. These links to the past are interesting and widespread, and they also seem to be of both sentimental and utilitarian value to many traders who are still concerned with this highly traditional line of Chinese commerce. This may be not only the case in the marine-products trade, but may also be true among other product lines, according to studies on Chinese business in that country.[57]

Singapore Redux: Back to the Center

Yet perhaps the best place to study the warp and weft of the traditional (and modern) Chinese marine-products trade, as well as its connections and dissonances with its own long past, is probably Singapore, then—as now—the central organizational axis for this commerce in Southeast Asian waters. Singapore has been a favored place to study the ins and outs of Chinese commerce for several reasons, not least of these being that China was closed to such study for a very long time, and Singaporean merchants' facility with the English language meant that research could be conducted in both Chinese and English, side by side. As a result of this, the literature on Chinese commerce in Singapore is particularly rich, including several somewhat recent dissertations that achieve a level of detail that would previously have been very difficult to achieve in a mainland Chinese context.[58] Sophisticated theories of Chinese merchant behavior have sprung from Singaporean field examples, and often have been put forward as being representative in some ways of Chinese business practices as a whole across wider regional geographies.[59] There has been some truth to these assertions, but also—perhaps—some overreach, in figuring out how emblematic Chinese business in this

one small place may be of the larger dynamics and mechanics of Chinese commerce generally, in East and Southeast Asian waters.

For marine- and dry-produce sellers, these patterns are very much in evidence, though they are only infrequently mentioned in the actual literature on trade and ethnicity among Chinese communities. In Singapore, the main area for these trades is scattered around South Bridge Road and its cross streets, near Singapore's traditional Chinatown area, and north of the modern-day financial complex centered around Shenton Way.[60] Walking into these shops, in some senses, is like walking into a different time. Big burlap sacks of samples sit scattered on the floor, and on the burlap of the sacks one can see stenciled the ports of many countries: Dobo (in Aru, Eastern Indonesia); Davao (in Mindanao, the Southern Philippines); even Australia (some sea cucumbers make it all the way north from Darwin, which has a monsoon climate and is more connected to Southeast Asia's maritime rhythms than to those of Australia). You can touch and taste specimens of the produce, even though these are company headquarters with modern communications equipment and orders are coming in (or going out) to the four corners of the world. The fact that many Chinese marine-goods sellers have kept their shops in this area is important in and of itself—it is a continuity with tradition, a conscious choice, though other real estate (for all intents and purposes) would now be just as good. Dialect-group preferences still manifest themselves in this community, though Singapore's Chinese population is more diverse (sub-ethnically) than most other places in Southeast Asia, simply because it is so large.

Yet the changes are just as noticeable. Fifty or one hundred years ago, it was a good bet that many of these shops would have had sons involved with the business, learning the trade and helping out with day-to-day operations—this is no longer the case in most of these concerns. Most shop owners with whom I spoke lamented the fact that their sons would not follow them into their line of work, though some were glad of this, citing it as too competitive a way to make a living. Others were more philosophical: they wanted their children to receive better educations than they had, so that their lives would not be taken up with pushing odoriferous, salt-caked merchandise around Asia as a means of making ends meet.[61] Singapore is still the center of these trades in Southeast Asia; it is still a collection and transshipment point for large quantities of these goods, which are collected elsewhere in Southeast Asia and eventually transited up to China, Hong Kong, and Taiwan. Yet even this competitive advantage—and link to the past—is disappearing, as ethnic Chinese concerns in various other Nanyang coun-

tries are now making their own deals with East Asia, to obtain products to market quicker and without the rising costs of Singaporean middlemen. The trade has a remorseless logic to it—the passage of marine goods must compete (like all other lines of trade) in the ferocity of today's global market.[62] Though sea cucumbers, seahorses, fish maws, pearl products, dried-fish varieties, abalone, and many other commodities of the traditional trade still pass through Singapore, the days of the port city acting as the arbiter of this trade may now be numbered. Singapore has competed too well, in a sense, in the global economy; it has bypassed these trades in its own economic lifecycle. The men I spoke with over the last eighteen years may in fact be the last generation to control this trade, as it passes from Singapore into the periphery, and is guided by other Chinese hands.

Conclusion

It seems a truism that the development of the global political economy in the last two to three centuries had much to do with the spread of capitalism, as new ways of conducting commerce filtered to nearly every corner of the known world. These processes have been discussed within the larger structures of colonialism and existing patterns of trade, with scholars such as Philip Curtin and others showing how this happened in a variety of places, and at a variety of times, over the past several hundred years.[63] Critical to this discussion has been the role of ethnic middlemen, those who competed and later collaborated with the advancing imperial projects of the West, but who also carved out their own niches within the new parameters of commerce that came into being. These racialized networks have been visible across a number of empires and creeping colonial projects, showing that there were indeed interstitial spaces within the larger economic structures where such communities could carve their own niches of importance.[64] Chinese marine-goods sellers were one among these many groups, moving from a position of early significance in the centuries before imperial rule to compradors in the nineteenth century and early twentieth, before being reborn yet again into new post-independence roles after the end of the Second World War.

Many of these networks still have salience in the economic world of East and Southeast Asia today. Though marine-goods traders possess only an echo of the importance they once had in helping to prop up intraregional systems of exchange, in numerical and value terms these trades are actually larger and richer than they have ever been. This is in keeping with the growth of Asian and global markets, and it is also in keeping with the rising abilities of human beings to elicit the varied riches of the sea in ever-larger

numbers. It is clear that some of the centuries-old ways of "doing business" in this arena are still with the Chinese marine-goods sellers of East and Southeast Asia, and that some of their own specific traits and traditions as a community have been lost, or are quickly being lost right now. This has to do with the passage of time, but it also has much to do with shifting perceptions of what is important, profitable, and desirable for Chinese families and Chinese family firms, whose interests used to overlap, possibly more so than they often do today.[65] The outstretched community of Chinese marine-goods traders is a very useful population to question and map some of these changes in commercial history, as this trade—like many others—tries to fit itself into the dictates of the modern commercial world.[66] Using a combined approach of historical and ethnographic methods makes visible these changes over time and space, and allows us to watch as the members of these families and diasporic commercial concerns continue an avenue of commerce that has been important for a very long time.

Notes

1. D. N. Levine, "Simmel at a Distance: On the History and Systematics of the Sociology of the Stranger," *Georg Simmel: Critical Assessments*, ed. D. Frisby (London: Routledge, 1994), 3:174–89; A. Schuetz, "The Stranger: An Essay in Social Psychology," *American Journal of Psychology* 49 (1944): 499–507; Georg Simmel, "The Stranger," *The Sociology of Georg Simmel*, ed. K. H. Wolff (New York: Free Press, 1950), 402–8.

2. Max Weber, *The Protestant Ethic and the Spirit of Capitalism*, 2nd ed. (London: George Allen and Unwin, 1976). For an early attempt to marry Weber to the study of Asian trade communities, see R. E. Kennedy, "The Protestant Ethic and the Parsis," *American Journal of Sociology* 68 (1962–1963): 11–20.

3. The list is long here; for just a few of the possibilities, some of them critical and useful, others far less so, see Edgar Wickberg, "Overseas Adaptive Organizations, Past and Present," *Reluctant Exiles? Migration from the Hong Kong and the New Overseas Chinese*, ed. Ronald Skeltond (Armonk, N.Y.: M. E. Sharpe, 1994); Wu Wei-Peng, "Transaction Cost, Cultural Values and Chinese Business Networks: An Integrated Approach," *Chinese Business Networks*, ed. Chan Kwok Bun (Singapore: Prentice Hall, 2000), 35–56; I-Chuan Wu-Beyens, "Hui: Chinese Business in Action," *Chinese Business Networks*, ed. Chan Kwok Bun (Singapore: Prentice Hall, 2000), 129–51; Jamie Mackie, "The Economic Roles of Southeast Asian Chinese: Information Gaps and Research Needs," *Chinese Business Networks*, ed. Chan Kwok Bun (Singapore: Prentice Hall, 2000), 234–60; Peter S. Li, "Overseas Chinese Networks: A Reassessment," *Chinese Business Networks*, ed. Chan Kwok Bun (Singapore: Prentice Hall, 2000), 261–84; Sterling Seagrave, *Lords of the Rim: The Invisible Empire of the Overseas Chinese* (New York: Putnam, 1995).

4. Eric Tagliacozzo, "A Necklace of Fins: Marine Goods Trading in Maritime Southeast Asia, 1780–1860," *International Journal of Asian Studies* 1.1 (2004): 23–48.

5. For a good overview, see, for example, P. J. Golas, "Early Chíng Guilds," *The City in Late Imperial China*, ed. G. W. Skinner (Stanford: Stanford University Press, 1977), 555–80.

6. Geoffrey Wade, *The Ming Shi-lu (Veritable Records of the Ming Dynasty) as a Source for Southeast Asian History, Fourteenth to Seventeenth Centuries*, 8 vols. (Hong Kong: Hong Kong University Library Microfilms, 1996); Ng Chin-Keong, *Trade and Society: The Amoy Network on the China Coast, 1683–1735* (Singapore: Singapore University Press, 1983); Hao Yen-p'ing, *The Commercial Revolution in Nineteenth-Century China: The Rise of Sino-Western Mercantile Capital* (Berkeley: University of California Press, 1986).

7. Michael R. Godley, *The Mandarin-Capitalists from Nanyang: Overseas Chinese Enterprise in the Modernization of China, 1893–1911* (Cambridge: Cambridge University Press, 1981); Wen-Chin Chang, "Guanxi and Regulation in Networks: The Yunnanese Jade Trade Between Burma and Thailand," *Journal of Southeast Asian Studies* 35.3 (2004): 479–501.

8. Zheng Yangwen, *The Social Life of Opium in China* (Cambridge: Cambridge University Press, 2005).

9. Sherman Cochran, *Encountering Chinese Networks: Western, Japanese, and Chinese Corporations in China, 1880–1937* (Berkeley: University of California Press, 2000); Peter Post, "Chinese Business Networks and Japanese Capital in Southeast Asia, 1880–1940: Some Preliminary Observations," *Chinese Business Enterprise in Asia*, ed. Rajeswary A. Brown (London: Routledge, 1995), 154–76.

10. Wang Gungwu, "Merchants without Empire: The Hokkien Sojourning Communities," *The Rise of Merchant Empires: Long-Distance Trade in the Early Modern World, 1350–1750*, ed. J. D. Tracy (Cambridge: Cambridge University Press, 1990), 400–21; Tagliacozzo, "A Necklace of Fins," 23–48.

11. Adam McKeown, *Chinese Migrant Networks and Cultural Change: Peru, Chicago, Hawaii, 1900–1936* (Chicago: University of Chicago Press, 2001).

12. C. Salmon, "Les Marchands chinois en Asie du Sud-est," *Marchands et hommes d'affaires asiatiques dans l'Ocean Indien et la Mer de Chine 13e–20e siècles*, ed. D. Lombard and J. Aubin (Paris: Éditions de l'École des Hautes Études, 1988), 330–51; D. Lombard, *Le Carrefour Javanais: Essai d'histoire globale*, 2 Les réseaux asiatiques (Paris: Éditions de l'École des Hautes Études en Sciences Sociales, 1990).

13. Anthony Reid, ed., *Sojourners and Settlers: Histories of Southeast Asia and the Chinese* (Sydney: Allen and Unwin, 1996); John Butcher and Howard Dick, eds., *The Rise and Fall of Revenue Farming: Business Elites and the Emergence of the Modern State in Southeast Asia* (Basingstoke: Macmillan / New York: St. Martin's Press, 1993).

14. Shozo Fukuda, *With Sweat and Abacus: Economic Roles of the Southeast Asian Chinese on the Eve of World War 2*, ed. George Hicks, trans. Les Oates (Singapore: Select Books, 1995); Qiu Liben, "The Chinese Networks in Southeast Asia: Past, Present and Future," *Chinese Business Networks*, ed. Chan Kwok Bun (Singapore: Prentice Hall, 2000), 193–206.

15. H. T. Colbrander, ed., *Jan Pietersz. Coen: Bescheiden Omtremt Zijn Bedrif in Indië*, 4 vols. (The Hague: Martinus Nijhoff, 1919–22); B. Hoetink, "Chineesche Officiern te Batavia Onder de Compagnie," *Bijdragen tot de Taal-, land- en Volkenkunde van Nederlandsch In-*

dië 78 (1922): 1–136; B. Hoetink, "Ni Hoekong: Kapitein der Chineezen te Batavia in 1740," *Bijdragen tot de Taal-, land- en Volkenkunde van Nederlandsch Indië* 74 (1918): 447–518; B. Hoetink, "So Bing Kong: Het Eerste Hoofd der Chineezen te Batavia (1629–1636)," *Bijdragen tot de Taal-,land- en Volkenkunde van Nederlandsch Indië* 74 (1917): 344–85.

16. J. T. Vermeulen, *De Chineezen te Batavia en de Troebelen van 1740* (Leiden: Eduard Ijdo, 1938); J. F. van Nes, "De Chinezen op Java," *Tijdshcrift loor Nederlandesh Indië* 13.1 (1851): 239–54, 292–314.

17. M. van Alphen, "Iets over den Orsprong en der Eerste Uibreiding der Chinesche Volk-planting te Batavia," *Tiderschrift voor Nederlandesch Indië* 4.1 (1842): 70–100; V. B. van Gutem, "Tina Mindering: Eeninge Aanteekenigen over het Chineeshe Geldshieterswesen op Java," *Koloniale Studiën* 3.1 (1919): 106–50.

18. See Leonard Blussé, *Strange Company: Chinese Settlers, Mestizo Women and the Dutch in VOC Batavia* (Dordrecht: Foris, 1986); P. Carey, "Changing Javanese Perceptions of the Chinese Communities in Central Java, 1755–1825," *Indonesia* 37 (1984): 1–47.

19. Among many other sources, see Phoa Liong Gie, "De Economische Positie der Chineezen in Nederlandesch Indië," *Koloniale Studiën* 20.5 (1936): 97–119; J. L. Vleming, *Het Chineesche Zakenleven in Nederlandesch-Indië* (Weltevreden: Landsdrikkerij, 1926); Siem Bing Hoat, "Het Chineesch Kapitaal in Indonisië," *Chung Hwa Hui Tsa Chih* 8.1 (1930): 7–17; Ong Eng Die, *Chinezen in Nederlansch-Indië: Sociographie van een Indonesische Bevolkingsgroep* (Assen: Van Gorcum, 1943).

20. Siauw Giap, "Socio-Economic Role of the Chinese in Indonesia, 1820–1940," *Economic Growth in Indonesia, 1820–1940*, ed. A. Maddison and G. Prince (Dordrecht: Foris, 1989), 159–83; W. J. Cator, *The Economic Position of the Chinese in the Netherlands Indies* (Oxford: Basil Blackwell, 1936).

21. M. R. Fernando and D. Bulbeck, *Chinese Economic Activity in Netherlands India: Selected Translations from the Dutch* (Singapore: Institute of Southeast Asian Studies, 1992).

22. See the arguments presented in Eric Tagliacozzo, *Secret Trades, Porous Borders: Smuggling and States along a Southeast Asian Frontier, 1865–1915* (New Haven: Yale University Press, 2005).

23. Eric Tagliacozzo, "Onto the Coast and Into the Forest: Ramifications of the China Trade on the History of Northwest Borneo, 900–1900," *Histories of the Borneo Environment*, ed. Reed Wadley (Leiden: KITLV Press, 2005), 25–60.

24. Eric Tagliacozzo, "Border-Line Legal: Chinese Communities and 'Illicit' Activity in Insular Southeast Asia," *Maritime China and the Overseas Chinese in Transition, 1750–1850*, ed. Ng Chin Keong (Wiesbaden: Harrassowitz Verlag, 2004), 61–76.

25. Michael R. Godley, "Chinese Revenue Farm Network: The Penang Connection," *The Rise and Fall of Revenue Farming: Business Elites and the Emergence of the Modern State in Southeast Asia*, ed. John Butcher and Howard Dick (Basingstoke: Macmillan / New York: St. Martin's, 1993), 89–99.

26. J.W. Cushman, "The Khaw Group: Chinese Business in the Early Twentieth-Century Penang," *Journal of Southeast Asian Studies* 17.1 (1986): 58–79.

27. See the contributions by R. Bernal, L. Diaz Trechuelo, M. C. Guerrero, and S. D.

Quiason in *The Chinese in the Philippines 1570–1770*, ed. A. Felix Jr., vol. 1 (Manila: Solidaridad, 1966).

28. E. Wickberg, *The Chinese in Philippine Life, 1850–1898* (New Haven: Yale University Press, 1965).

29. Benito Legarda, *After the Galleons: Foreign Trade, Economic Change and Entrepreneurship in the Nineteenth Century Philippines* (Madison: University of Wisconsin Southeast Asia Program, 1999).

30. Wong Kwok-Chu, *The Chinese in the Philippine Economy, 1898–1941* (Manila: Ateneo de Manila Press, 1999).

31. See, among many other contributions, Cheng Lim Keak, "Reflections on Changing Roles of Chinese Clan Associations in Singapore," *Asian Culture* (Singapore) 14 (1990): 57–71; S. Gordon Redding, "Weak Organizations and Strong Linkages: Managerial Ideology and Chinese Family Business Networks," *Business Networks and Economic Development in East and Southeast Asia*, ed. Gary Hamilton (Hong Kong: Center of Asian Studies, University of Hong Kong, 1991), 30–47; Edmund Terence Gomez and Michael Hsiao, eds., *Chinese Enterprise, Trans-nationalism, and Identity* (London: Routledge, 2004); S. Gordon Redding, *The Spirit of Chinese Capitalism* (Berlin: de Grutyer, 1990); Kunio Yoshihara, "The Ethnic Chinese and Ersatz Capitalism in Southeast Asia," *Southeast Asian Chinese and China: The Politico-Economic Dimension*, ed. Leo Suryadinata (Singapore: Times Academic, 1995); Arif Dirlik, "Critical Reflections on 'Chinese Capitalism' as Paradigm," *Identities* 3.3 (1997): 303–30.

32. Rupert Hodder, *Merchant Princes of the East: Cultural Delusions, Economic Success and the Overseas Chinese in Southeast Asia* (Chichester: Wiley, 1996). Better studies include Edmund Terence Gomez and Michael Hsiao, *Chinese Business in Southeast Asia: Contesting Cultural Explanations, Researching Entrepreneurship* (Richmond, Surrey: Curzon, 2001); and J. A. C. Mackie, "Changing Patterns of Chinese Big Business in Southeast Asia," *Southeast Asian Capitalists*, ed. Ruth McVey (Ithaca: Cornell University Southeast Asia Program, 1992), 161–90.

33. Michael Godley, *The Mandarin-Capitalists from Nanyang*; M. Freedman, *Chinese Lineage and Society: Fukien and Kwangtung*, 2d ed. (London: Althone, 1971); J. A. C. Mackie, "Changing Patterns of Chinese Big Business in Southeast Asia," 161–90; Rajeswary A. Brown, ed., *Chinese Business Enterprise in Asia* (London: Routledge, 1995); Yen Chinghwang, ed., *The Ethnic Chinese in East and Southeast Asia: Business, Culture, and Politics* (Singapore: Times Academic, 2002).

34. Linda Y. C. Lim, "Chinese Economic Activity in Southeast Asia: An Introductory Review," *Ethnicity and Economic Activity*, vol. 1 of *The Chinese in Southeast Asia*, ed. Linda Y. C. Lim and L. A. Peter Gosling (Singapore: Maruzen Asia, 1983), 1–29; Leo Suryadinata, ed., *Southeast Asian Chinese: The Socio-Cultural Dimension* (Singapore: Times Academic, 1995); J. A. C. Mackie, "Overseas Chinese Entrepreneurship," *Asian Pacific Economic Literature* 6.1 (1992): 41–46; Victor Simpao Limlingan, *The Overseas Chinese in ASEAN: Business Strategies and Management Practices* (Manila: Vita Development Corporation, 1986).

35. Interview, Kin Sang Dispensary, Hong Kong, 4 April 2005.

36. Interviews were done in Xiamen, Fujian (PRC) in the spring of 2005. Fieldwork in Ching-ping Market, Guangzhou, took place in January 1990. The range of goods available in this market, in particular, was truly astounding: marine produce from the four corners of the globe could be found here, though usually from Southeast Asia (via ethnic Chinese networks).

37. Interview, Citiherb Chinese Medicine Clinic, Hong Kong, 4 April 2005.

38. Interview, Ho Sheng Tang Company, Taipei, Taiwan, 7 January 2005.

39. Tsai Mauw-Kuey, *Les Chinois au Sud-Vietnam* (Paris: Bibliothéque Nationale, 1986); Tranh Khanh, *The Ethnic Chinese and Economic Development in Vietnam* (Singapore: Institute of Southeast Asian Studies, 1993). Also my interviews done with ethnic Chinese marine-goods merchants in October 2009, in Hanoi (Cua Hang 49 Marine Goods Shop) and in Ho Chi Minh City (Huong Xian Marine Goods Shop in Ben Thanh Market, and Lien Saigon Marine Goods Shop).

40. See Nola Cooke, "Chinese Commodity Production and Trade in Nineteenth-Century Cambodia: The Fishing Industry," paper presented to the Workshop on Chinese Traders in the Nanyang: Capital, Commodities and Networks, Academica Sinica, Taipei, Taiwan, 19 January 2007.

41. Fieldwork notes, Songkhla docks, Songkhla, South Thailand (Gulf of Thailand coast), December 1989.

42. Fieldwork notes, Ao Phra Nang village, South Thailand (Andaman Sea coast), December 1989.

43. Fieldwork notes, Ranong docks, Ranong, South Thailand (Andaman Sea coast), December 1989.

44. Interview with U Myint Thein, Yangon, Burma, 4 January 2007.

45. Interview at unnamed spice and marine-goods shop, also in Yangon, Burma, four streets over from U Myint Thein's apothecary–marine goods–spice store, 4 January 2007.

46. Fieldnotes, fishing villages just north of Ngapali, Arakan State, Burma, January 2007.

47. John T. Omohondro, "Social Networks and Business Success for the Philippine Chinese," *Ethnicity and Economic Activity*, vol. 1 of *The Chinese in Southeast Asia*, ed. Linda Y. C. Lim and L. A. Peter Gosling (Singapore: Maruzen Asia, 1983), 65–85; Arturo Pacho, "The Chinese Community in the Philippines: Status and Conditions," *Sojourn* (Singapore) (February 1986): 80–83; Ellen H. Palanca, "The Economic Position of the Chinese in the Philippines," *Philippine Studies* 25 (1977): 82–88; Liao Shaolian, "Ethnic Chinese Business People and the Local Society: The Case of the Philippines," *Chinese Business Networks*, ed. Chan Kwok Bun (Singapore: Prentice Hall, 2000), 224–33.

48. J. Amyot, *The Manila Chinese: Familism in the Philippine Environment* (Quezon City: Institute of Philippine Culture, 1973); J. T. Omohundro, *Chinese Merchant Families in Iloilo: Commerce and Kin in a Central Philippine City* (Quezon City: Ateneo de Manila University Press / Athens: Ohio University Press, 1981).

49. Interview, Inter-Asian Pacific Company, Manila, the Philippines, January 1990. The

general manager of this dry-goods concern, Vicente Co Tiong Keng, gave me this information during a long interview on the premises of his shop in the warehouse district of northern Manila.

50. Fieldwork, Zamboanga and environs, Zamboanga, Mindanao, Southern Philippines, July 2004.

51. Liem Twan Djie, *De Distribueerende Tusschenhandel der Chineezen op Java*, 2d ed. (The Hague: Martinus Nijhoff, 1952); J. Panglaykim and I. Palmer, "The Study of Entrepreneurship in Developing Countries: The Development of One Chinese Concern in Indonesia," *Journal of Southeast Asian Studies* 1.1 (1970): 85–95; L. E. Williams, "Chinese Entrepreneurs in Indonesia," *Explorations in Entrepreneurial History* 5.1 (1952): 34–60; Robert Cribb, "Political Structures and Chinese Business Connections in the Malay World: A Historical Perspective," *Chinese Business Networks*, ed. Chan Kwok Bun (Singapore: Prentice Hall, 2000), 176–192.

52. Zhou Nanjing, "Masalah Asimilasi Keturunan Tionghoa di Indonesia," *Review of Indonesian and Malaysian Affairs* 21.2 (summer 1987): 44–66; Thung Ju Lan, "Posisi dan Pola Komunikasi Antar Budaya Antara Etnis Cina dan Masyarakat Indonesia Lainnya Pada Masa Kini: Suatu Studi Pendahuluan," *Berita Ilmu Pengetahuan dan Teknologi* 29.2 (1985): 15–29; Mely Tan, *Golongan Ethnis Tinghoa di Indonesia: Suatau Masalah Pembinan Kesatuan Bangsa* (Jakarta: Gramedia, 1979).

53. The fieldwork to support this observation was done in scattered parts of Indonesia over several years, always in coastal communities: in Lombok, Nusa Tenggara, summer 2005; in Makassar, South Sulawesi, summer 2005; in Ternate, North Maluku, spring 1990; and in Banda, Central Maluku, spring 1990.

54. Fieldwork and interviews with sailors, Jakarta docks (Sunda Kelapa), spring 2000.

55. For Kuala Lumpur, see interviews with Fook Hup Hsing Sdn Bhd, Tek Choon Trading Sdn Bhd, and Tai Yik Hang Medical Hall, all completed in November 1989; in Penang, see interviews with Kwong Seng Hung Pte Ltd, and Soo Hup Seng Trading Company Sdn Bhd, completed in November 1989; and in Ipoh, see interview with Wing Sang Hong Sdn Bhd, also completed in November 1989.

56. For Kuching, see interviews with Syn Min Kong Sdn Bhd and Voon Ming Seng Sdn Bhd, both completed in March 1990; fieldwork done in coastal areas of Sabah, in and near Kota Kinabalu, was also useful for uncovering these patterns in 2004.

57. Edmund Terence Gomez, *Chinese Business in Malaysia: Accumulation, Accommodation and Ascendance* (Richmond, U.K.: Curzon, 1999); Edmund Terence Gomez, "In Search of Patrons: Chinese Business Networking and Malay Political Patronage in Malaysia," *Chinese Business Networks*, ed. Chan Kwok Bun (Singapore: Prentice Hall, 2000), 207–23.

58. Wolfgang Jamann, "Business Practices and Organizational Dynamics of Chinese Family-Based Trading Firms in Singapore," Ph.D. diss., department of sociology, University of Bielefield, 1990; Thomas Menkhoff, "Trade Routes, Trust and Trading Networks: Chinese Family-Based Firms in Singapore and Their External Economic Dealings," Ph.D. diss., department of sociology, University of Bielefield, 1990.

59. Yao Souchou, "The Fetish of Relationships: Chinese Business Transactions in Sin-

gapore," *Sojourn* 2 (1987): 89–111; Cheng Lim Keak, "Chinese Clan Associations in Singapore: Social Change and Continuity," *Southeast Asian Chinese: The Socio-Cultural Dimension*, ed. Leo Suryadinata (Singapore: Times Academic, 1995); Wong Siu-Lun, "Business Networks, Cultural Values and the State in Hong Kong and Singapore," *Chinese Business Enterprise in Asia*, ed. Rajeswary A. Brown (London: Routledge, 1995).

60. See interviews completed in Singapore with Fei Fah Drug Company and Ming Tai Company Pte Ltd, both in October 1989.

61. Interview with Ban Tai Loy Medical Company, Singapore, November 1989.

62. Interviews with Guan Tian Kee Spices and Dry Goods Company, and Nam Yong Marine Products, both in Singapore, October 1989.

63. P. D. Curtin, *Cross-Cultural Trade in World History* (Cambridge: Cambridge University Press, 1984); A. Cohen, "Cultural Strategies in the Organization of Trading Diasporas," *The Development of Indigenous Trade and Markets in West Africa*, ed. C. Meillassoux (London: Oxford University Press, 1971), 266–80; E. Bonadich, "A Theory of Middleman Minorities," *Majority and Minority: The Dynamics of Racial and Ethnic Relations*, 2d ed., ed. N. R. Yetman and C. H. Steele (Boston: Allyn and Bacon, 1975), 77–89.

64. Z. Bader, "The Contradictions of Merchant Capital 1840–1939," *Zanzibar under Colonial Rule*, ed. A. Sheriff and E. Ferguson (London: James Curry, 1991), 163–87; R. Robinson, "Non-European Foundations of European Imperialism: Sketch for a Theory of Collaboration," *Studies in the Theory of Imperialism*, ed. R. Owen and B. Sutcliffe (London: Longman, 1972), 117–41; Ruth McVey, "The Materialization of the Southeast Asian Entrepreneur," *Southeast Asian Capitalists*, ed. Ruth McVey (Ithaca: Cornell University Southeast Asia Program, 1992), 7–34.

65. B. Benedict, "Family Firms and Economic Development," *Southwestern Journal of Anthropology* 24.1 (1968): 1–19; A. Sen, "Economics and the Family," *Asian Development Review* 1.2 (1983): 14–26.

66. Aihwa Ong, *Flexible Citizenship: The Cultural Logics of Transnationality* (Durham: Duke University Press, 1999); William G. Ouchi, "Markets, Bureaucracies and Clans," *Administrative Science Quarterly* 25 (1980): 129–41.

FROM A *SHIJI* EPISODE TO THE FORBIDDEN
JADE TRADE DURING THE SOCIALIST REGIME IN BURMA

────── Wen-Chin Chang

Shiji is the first book that contains records of the communication between present southwestern China and its neighboring countries. The following passage from *Shiji* has been frequently quoted and studied by scholars working on this region.

In the first year of *Yuanshou* (122 B.C.), Zhang Qian, the Bowang marquis, returned from his mission to the land of Daxia (Bactria) and reported that while he was there he had seen cloth produced in Shu and bamboo canes from Qiong. On inquiring how they had arrived in Daxia, he was told, "They came from the land of Shendu (India), which lies some several thousand li west of here. We buy them in the shops of the Shu merchants there." He was also told that Shendu was situated some 2,000 li west of Qiong. "Daxia, which is situated southwest of our country," Zhang Qian reported to the emperor with enthusiasm, "is eager to open relations with China and is much distressed that the Xiongnu are blocking the road in between. If we could find a new route from Shu via the land of Shendu, however, we would have a short and convenient way to reach Daxia which would avoid the danger of the northern route."

The emperor therefore ordered Wang Ranyu, Bo Shichang, Lü Yuerren, and others to go on a secret expedition through the region of the southwestern barbarians and on to the west to search for the land of Shendu. When they got as far as Dian, Changqiang, the king of Dian, detained them and sent a party of ten or twelve men to the west to find out the way to Shendu for them. The Chinese party waited over a year, but all the roads to the west had been closed off by the inhabitants of Kunming, so that none of the men who had been sent ahead were able to reach Shendu.[1]

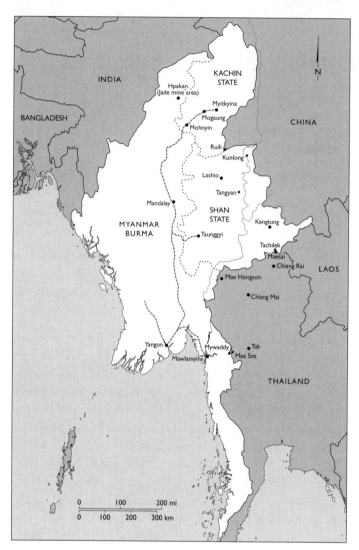

Map 1
Jade trade
between
Burma and
Thailand.

This passage underlines a few points of significance. First, transnational economic activities had been going on between southwestern China, Daxia, and Shendu, prior to the knowledge of the powerful Han court. Second, the economic activities were possibly undertaken via a convenient trading route connecting today's Sichuan, Yunnan, Burma, and India that led to Bactria (in present Afghanistan). Third, on hearing Zhang Qian's report, the Han emperor Wu gave orders to uncover this trading route in order to secure the expansion of cultural, economic, and political influence. However, the mission

was impeded by local powers and did not succeed. Regional kingdoms remained as uncertain forces in relation to China proper, sometimes serving as subjugated tribute states, at other times as rebellious polities. Turning over this underlined state-centric perspective that is characterized by the rhetoric of Sinocentrism in Shiji, one nevertheless finds the operation of the unofficial connections among regional traders across different political entities.

While conducting fieldwork among the migrant Yunnanese Chinese dispersed in upper Burma and northern Thailand, my mind often moves between different layers of time, connected to people's migration history and their memories about their ancestors' movement into Yunnan and their subsequent economic and military explorations.[2] Relevant passages from Shiji have frequently echoed in my mind. They are the earliest written sources for tracing Chinese influence to this ethnically diverse borderland. While Shiji and other historical materials remind me to view my ethnographic findings of Yunnanese transborder engagement from the perspective of the longue durée, the mobility and economic dynamism of migrant Yunnanese suggest the limitations of the state-oriented viewpoint embedded in Chinese imperial historiography, and spur me to go beyond written texts with such a viewpoint.

Using the Shiji passage extracted above as a starting point, I am intrigued by several underlying questions related to the issue of the underground jade trade in Burma during the socialist period (1962–1998). How did the Shu merchants engage in the long-distance trade to Shendu without the involvement of the state regulations issued by the Chinese court? How did they manage to pass through all the countries en route that even the Han empire was unable to gain access to? In other words, how did they interact with the hierarchy of different regional powers? Furthermore, how did they handle capital transference and currency conversion? While the era's remoteness in time and a lack of sources make it difficult to find answers, I think of the transnational Shu merchants over two thousand years ago and of the Yunnanese jade traders in question, who were confronted with parallel circumstances, and regard the questions raised above as inspiration for the present study.

The concerned jade trade was dominated by migrant Yunnanese traders based in Burma and Thailand.[3] It was a transnational business from Burma to northern Thailand and then to other Chinese societies, mainly Hong Kong and Taiwan, from the 1960s to the mid-1990s, largely during the Burmese socialist period. Such a trade required flexible flows of capital, information, goods, and people. However, to the private sector inside Burma, it was a for-

bidden trade. Not only were there no state regulations to back up the trade, but the official ban entailed forceful restrictions, as well as risks and dangers for participating traders. In response to the external situation, the Yunnanese merchants had to interact with complex power structures consisting of local ethnic militias and Burmese troops and officials. In light of the case of the Shiji and that of the Yunnanese jade trade, the traders then and now all demonstrated marvelous economic agency in the face of similar constraints. The Shiji episode accordingly provides meaningful threads for reflection and comparison.

In addition, the antiquity of the Shiji episode suggests another significant point of reference that draws attention to the double aspects of historical continuity and contingency. The participation of Chinese merchants in commerce in this historical activity space has been persistent in the form of long-distance caravan trade.[4] Especially with the incorporation of the Yunnan province into the territory of the Yuan dynasty (1271–1368 C.E.), and subsequent massive Chinese resettlement to the province throughout the Ming (1368–1644 C.E.) and Qing (1644–1911 C.E.) dynasties, the Chinese (now called Yunnanese Chinese or simply Yunnanese) merchants have played a predominant role in the transboundary trade of the region.[5] On the other hand, they have been constantly shaped and reshaped by changing sociopolitical contexts. Their economic acumen and risk-taking spirit have interacted with varied challenges emanating from the complex trading environment in terms of its physiography, ethnic structure, and political systems. Their trading history is composed of numerous life and death experiences in the face of the external changes of each period and the severe conditions posed by nature.[6] While focusing on the period of the Burmese socialist regime, one must consider the persistence of the Yunnanese cross-border movement and economic activities.

Bearing in mind the inquiries derived from the Shiji episode on non-state regulations, merchants' interaction with different political entities en route, and the means of capital flows, the present study looks into Yunnanese migration and resettlement in Burma, Yunnanese interaction with state agents and other ethnic communities, the mining and trading regulations involved, the internal transaction, and the operation of capital flows. Although the focus is on the Burmese socialist period, comparisons are made with relevant economic practices by the Yunnanese in previous times. While my earlier work on the jade trade has centered primarily on Thailand,[7] I turn in this present study to an examination of Burma, with the attempt to shed

light on a significant part of the politico-economy of contemporary Burma which has been much neglected.

In 1962, Burma entered a period of isolation with the authoritarian Ne Win regime. This junta, set up by a military coup, was preceded by a short-lived parliamentary government that had come into power in 1948, after the end of British colonial rule. The Ne Win regime steered the country with the guiding ideology of the "Burmese Way to Socialism." Its operation was carried out with a series of economic measures to nationalize trade and industry, and was, unfortunately, characterized by gross mismanagement, lack of infrastructure, and policy mistakes. The country quickly fell into a mire of economic recession and suffered from drastic shortages of essential everyday goods.

As a result, the demand for consumer goods by the Burmese people was satisfied by the black market (hmaung-kho) economy with links to the underground border trade. Cattle and products like rice, teak, antiques, hides, ivory, opium, and jade stones were illegally taken to neighboring countries, exiting Burma from areas under the control of rebel groups. In exchange, consumer goods and weapons were smuggled into Burma by mule-driven caravans.[8] Ethnic militias financed their expenses by levying taxes on these goods. Most of the goods came from market-oriented Thailand, which emerged as Burma's main partner in this illegal trade.[9]

The socialist rule impoverished Burma and aggravated ethnic divisions. The junta was finally toppled in 1988, following a series of nationwide revolts by the people. However, democracy did not ensue; the country is still controlled by a military regime named the State Law and Order Restoration Council (SLORC), which was later renamed the State Peace and Development Council (SPDC), in 1997. Certain changes have been made, including, significantly, the launch of a market economy, although it is one based on capricious policies and inefficient socioeconomic infrastructure. Many former underground businesses and enterprises have turned legal, and the jade trade is among them.

To obtain an insight into the migrant Yunnanese traders' economic dynamism beyond the restrictions imposed by the state, and also to suspend unnecessary moral judgments on the question of legality, it is necessary to avoid taking a state-dominated perspective. As Kyaw Yin Hlaing has pointed out, a state-centric perspective tends to present Burma as a unitary society and the government as the highest legitimate power.[10] According to such a view, traders' agency exercised in underground trafficking is easily dis-

missed. In addition, it gives the "illegal" transnational trade a criminal image and prevents reflection on a parallel system that operates according to its own set of unofficial rules and links with the daily life of the people.[11]

What I intend to develop here could be called the *minjian* (popular realm 民間) perspective, which highlights the unofficial connections interacting with and reacting against the state bureaucracy.[12] The composition of these connections is often diversified; some are founded on personal bases, others on institutional formation. In Burma during the time in question, there existed ethnic forces and a large dissatisfied public. Alliances and struggles coexisted among these unofficial nexuses; their power structures were complex and alternating. It is thus important to discern the intricate relations from the viewpoint of the unofficial order. Seen from this viewpoint, it is also possible to perceive how state agencies were incorporated to a certain degree into the operation of the popular realm, since the government was only one of the power regimes. Therefore, I will explore the Yunnanese jade business in Burma from the people's perspective rather than that of the state, by delving into the historical contingency that they faced during this particular period, and the historical continuity in Yunnanese commercial skills and spirit in transboundary endeavors.

Yunnanese Migrants in Transborder Trade

Cross-border economic ventures have always figured prominently in the lives of the Yunnanese.[13] Continuity in this engagement is especially notable in Yunnanese border towns. The common Yunnanese proverb *qiong zou yifang ji zou chang* 窮走夷方急走廠 best describes the situation: when one needed money, one joined the caravan trade and went to areas occupied by "barbarians" (other ethnic groups), or alternatively tried one's luck in jade or other mineral mines in Burma. Those who were hesitant to take up such ventures were considered timid and often teased by fellow Yunnanese.[14] According to the interpretation of the culture of migration attributed to Douglas S. Massey et al., transborder movement can be seen as "deeply ingrained into the repertoire of people's behaviors" in areas bordering Yunnan.[15] It has even developed as a "rite of passage" to indicate the transition to adulthood among males. From a historical point of view, the continuous flow of Han Chinese to Yunnan and their involvement in long-distance trade constitute a vital part of the long history of the movement of Yunnanese overland.

Among its neighbors, Burma in particular has been the major country that the Yunnanese look to for economic adventures, as well as for political asylum when unrest occurs, due to its physiographical connection with Yun-

nan. Some Yunnanese even established home bases in both places.[16] The year 1949 witnessed a Yunnanese exodus to Burma on a hitherto unseen scale due to the communist takeover in China. Large immigration flows continued into the 1970s owing to a series of political movements launched in China. Some informants estimated that the Yunnanese refugees who arrived after 1949 together with their descendants account for 80 to 90 percent of all Yunnanese immigrants in Burma today. Without legal permission to stay in the country, most of the Yunnanese refugees settled in the mountain areas of Shan and Kachin states in the early stage.

Among these refugees, a group of stragglers from the Chinese Nationalist (Kuomintang or KMT) armies and local self-defense guards from Yunnan organized themselves into guerrilla forces in early 1950. They established connection with the Chinese Nationalist government, which had retreated to Taiwan in 1949. Many civilian refugees stayed around the KMT troops, seeking protection against the harassment of the Burmese army or ethnic militias. During the 1950s, the KMT forces repeatedly launched guerrilla battles in Yunnan and had military confrontations with the Burmese army, too. These actions, however, compounded the political tension in the region and provoked debates in the United Nations on the legitimacy of the KMT forces.[17] They were then compelled to disband first between 1953 and 1954, and again in 1961; but two armies, code-named the Third and Fifth Armies under the respective leadership of Generals Li and Duan, survived the disbandment, and later entered northern Thailand.[18] Due to subsequent socioeconomic instability caused by the Ne Win regime, many civilian Yunnanese followed Li's and Duan's armies and escaped to Thailand. (Nevertheless, a much larger number of Yunnanese stayed behind.) These KMT troops helped their fellow refugees establish villages along the border, which functioned as havens for later Yunnanese migrants throughout the 1970s and 1980s.

Informants pointed out that prior to the flight from Yunnan, many KMT soldiers, as well as fellow civilians, had been caravan traders traversing annually to upper Burma. During the guerrilla period, many troops were involved in the drug trade. "The troops were caravan traders and the caravan traders were troops. Both were combined as a unit," a former KMT official wrote.[19] After entrenching themselves along the border of northern Thailand, the armies of Li and Duan continued to grow in strength, essentially by engaging in transborder trade between Thailand and Burma. They developed spheres of influence in the region by forming alliances with or struggling against other ethnic rebels. Moreover, their commercial acumen, familiarity with Shan State, and the demands of the black-market economy in Burma

resulted in their predominance in handling the trade throughout the 1960s and 1970s.[20] The armies controlled several major trading routes and played a primary role in the underground circulation of merchandise, people, capital, news, and intelligence. A great number of Yunnanese migrants in northern Thailand and upper Burma were dependent on the KMT forces for movement, resettlement, and armed escort of their trade.

The status of these KMT armies was ambivalent. Seen by the Thai government as buffer forces along the border for the prevention of communist penetration, they took part in quelling the Thai communists, following a request by the government. They were, however, definitely regarded as insurgent groups by the Burmese junta. By the end of the 1970s, due to aging among the troops, the KMT's power began to decline and was gradually surpassed by another militia, called the Shan United Army, led by the notorious warlord Khun Sa. Most of Khun Sa's key officers were also Yunnanese, with connections to the KMT armies. Despite the shift in the power structure among the ethnic militias, Thai-Burmese trafficking was basically unaffected; the Yunnanese persisted in their foremost engagement.

Informants often attributed their predominance in the trade to factors related to time, geography, and human reciprocity, and described such conditions with the Chinese expression *tianshi dili renhe* 天時地利人和. The Yunnanese migrants were compelled to flee, owing to a series of historical contingencies as mentioned above. Their economic activities in Burma and transnational networks that connected to the KMT troops greatly facilitated their movement. In addition to transnational migration, Yunnanese migrants in Burma also experienced repeated internal movement. An important event was related to the Burmese government's suppression of the Ka Kwe Ye (KKY) forces that were entrenched in the mountainous areas. The KKY had been officially accepted as auxiliary local defense troops based on a policy promulgated in 1963, but the government decided to wipe out these forces in 1973. The military action simultaneously forced local civilians to leave. An elderly female informant related: "[At that time] mountain areas were not quiet. Government troops came to fight against the rebels. They recruited civilians by force and often burned down villages. We had to run." Many Yunnanese gradually moved to the cities. Corruption among state officials was rampant at that time because their salaries were meager. By bribing the officials, most Yunnanese obtained the legal status to stay. Their economic power thus expanded to urban areas in upper Burma.[21] This urban expansion when integrated with their knowledge of rural trading routes enabled them to take control of both import-export trafficking

and the redistribution of smuggled goods in upper Burma. Whether internal or transnational, Yunnanese mobility brought about the formation of widespread networks that greatly enhanced their participation in the Burmese black-market economy.

Embedded Regulatory Practices

To ensure the operation of network flows in an environment with diversified ethnic communities and political entities, it has been essential to initiate and implement trading regulations. Andrew Walker, in his research on the recent Economic Quadrangle cooperation of the Upper Mekong area, argues against the popular perception of the borderlands as lawless. His findings lead to the conclusion that the quadrangle is the latest stage in a series of regimes of Upper Mekong regulation, and that "state (and non-state) regulation is intrinsically involved in the creation of the contexts in which markets flourish."[22] The jade trade in question, too, was predicated on a series of regulatory practices that had been developed for several centuries.

Although informative records concerning the Burmese jade business only appeared in the late nineteenth century, when the British colonial government tried to take control of the trade, piecemeal sources point to the popularity of Burmese jade stones among the Chinese several centuries earlier. Historical records indicate that the Ming eunuchs were assigned to Yunnan from the fifteenth century to purchase gemstones, including jadeite, from Burma.[23] By the end of this dynasty, the imported volume of Burmese jade was notable. Reflecting the Qing court's growing passion for this precious stone, demand continued to increase, and the appreciation of Burmese jade gradually spread to the general public.[24] In the eighteenth century, great numbers of Yunnanese miners and jade traders flowed into the mining region in upper Burma to seek their fortune.[25]

The mining and trading of the Burmese jade stones involved a complex power hierarchy that included the indigenous chiefs, the Burmese king, the Chinese officials, the imperial court, and, later, the British colonial government. To ensure its operation in response to the different political parties, the mining and trading of jade was predicated on a series of regulatory practices developed over several centuries. A description of relevant tax regulations appeared in the *Burma Gazetteer: Myitkyina District* in the early nineteenth century.

The Burmese Collector imposed no tax upon the stone until it was ready to leave Mogaung, when he levied an *ad valorem* duty of 33 per cent, and

issued a permit. . . . After this the stone passed freely anywhere in Burma without further charge or inspection. The value of jade was determined for purposes of taxation by an official appraiser. . . . The actual duty paid was therefore small and business proceeded smoothly, cases of friction between the traders and the customs officers being of very rare occurrence. All payments were made in bar silver. The metal used was at first fairly pure. . . . Rupees did not come into general use until 1874.

Besides the duty leviable at Mogaung, the stone had to bear certain charges, authorized and unauthorized, at the mines and Namiakyaukseik (Nanyaseik), one day's journey from the mines: (1) The Burmese officer at the mines imposed a monthly tax of 1 tael (about 4 annas) on everybody who came to trade; from this charge Burmans and actual workers in the mines were exempt; (2) a further sum of 2.5 taels (about 10 annas) was charged for a pass which was issued for each load of jade leaving the mines for Namiakyaukseik; (3) at Namiakyaukseik, 4 taels (about a rupee) was paid on the arrival of every load to an agent of the Mogaung Collector, permanently stationed there.[26]

Be it under Burmese or British rule, the ownership of the jade mines by the local Kachin chiefs (*duwas*) was respected and officially recognized. The *Burma Gazetteer* recorded: "[The rights of the Kachins] appear to have been well under[s]tood and respected. They were regarded as the absolute owners of all the stones produced in their country. This ownership was never directly called in question by the King of Burma."[27] In addition to listing the tax categories, the *Burma Gazetteer* detailed the duties on excavation, transaction, and gambling, and the tolls on imported food and house tax. Parallel information was also documented by a Chinese officer, Yin Deming, on his expedition to the Kachin mining region in 1929–1930.[28] Yin vividly described the mining conditions and methods, and various regulatory practices that he observed. He recorded that most miners he encountered were Yunnanese Han. During each dry season from the tenth month of the lunar calendar to the fourth month of the following year, nearly twenty to thirty thousand Yunnanese worked at the mines. On choosing a spot to work, the mine boss had to pay an amount of money to the local chief to purchase the excavation right; he then marked his right to the place by sticking a piece of bamboo or plant into the land. Between the second and the third months each year, the region received another ten thousand jade dealers from Yunnan.

These regulatory practices ensured the rights of the different parties, and served to maintain order in the region. Even the rights of the mine workers

were protected. Aside from receiving food and board, the miner, on excavating a piece of jade stone, was entitled to half the share of its estimated value. Despite the change in regional politics, these regulations were largely preserved. With the establishment of the parliamentary government, the jade enterprise proceeded without interruption. In 1959, Ne Win forced the local chiefs to resign. However, in the 1960s, local auxiliaries arose and resisted the junta; subsequently, they replaced the traditional authority of original chiefs and supervised the implementation of the mining and trading regulations. Most jade mines were under the control of the Kachin Independence Army (KIA).

The mining methods and living conditions during the socialist period remained as rudimentary as they had been during the colonial period. Yet, in the face of social instability, this venture provided an opportunity and a grand get-rich dream predicated on the possibility of discovering good jade stones. In his autobiography, Yushi tianming 玉石天命 (Destiny of jade stone), Zhou Jinglun relates his own life story: having become a Yunnanese refugee in upper Burma from 1969, he eventually became a jade miner, a foreman, and then a jade trader.[29] His story combines his understanding of the philosophy underlying Chinese jade culture with the sociopolitical conditions encountered in the mining areas during the socialist regime. The regulatory practices were inclusive and, in general, corresponded to the earlier ones. As Zhou describes,

> Anyone who would like to go to the mines had to register first and pay registration fees and passage toll [to the Kachin troops]. The petty traders who imported consumption goods paid business tax. Those who purchased zhuangtou (庄頭 [large-sized jade stone with mediocre quality]) paid a [smaller amount] of tax. Those who purchased feicui (翡翠 [valuable jade with clear green color]) paid a [higher amount] of tax. The miners paid labor tax; and the mine bosses the mining tax. Excavated jade was taxed ad valorem dues of 10 percent. On payment of each tax, a receipt was given, which also served as a kind of license. Cattle carts, elephants, and motorcars were also taxed. The Kachin rebels thus earned great profits from taxes.[30]

In an interview, Zhou told me that the interaction between the Kachin troops and civilians was generally satisfactory. Though the tax categories were encompassing, the dues were bearable and also negotiable. Moreover, their implementation contributed to the maintenance of law and order in the region. When disputes occurred between mine owners, they would go to the

Kachin officers for arbitration. Nevertheless, on discovering high-quality jade stones, they tried to hide them from the Kachin rebels for fear that they would be confiscated. With regard to the Burmese authority, people deemed it alien. Zhou mentions that the Burmese police and army carried out two routine arrests every year, in which a few hundred people were put in jail. However, the payment of probation money was enough to ensure their freedom. Zhou writes,

> A [Burmese] soldier's monthly salary was about 100 kyat; a [Burmese] policeman's salary was about 200 kyat. But a jade miner's board and food amounted to 400 kyat. How could the [Burmese soldiers] and policemen support their family with their meager pay? When catching miners, the Burmese authority was willing to let them go when [their bosses or families] could put up a bail to secure their release. It was also an opportunity for the Burmese officers to be friends with local people.[31]

Accordingly, the local Burmese authority was integrated into the operation of this underground enterprise. The bribes they received amounted, in fact, to much more than their state salaries. The world of the jade mines reflected complex interactions between the different groups, intertwined with symbiotic and conflicting relations, and this world's sustenance was predicated on the continuity of regulatory enforcement and observance despite political changes at different times.

Internal Transaction

Regardless of great hardships and dangers, the jade mines continued to attract fortune-seekers annually. Before 1980, the number of Yunnanese jade traders and mine bosses in the mining areas was still small due to the restriction implemented by the local rebel group, the KIA. The Yunnanese had to disguise themselves as Kachin or Shan in order to obtain permission to enter the areas. Nevertheless, after 1980, the KIA relaxed its control, and increasing numbers of Yunnanese arrived to venture into the business. They gradually became the majority. However, whether it was before or after 1980, informants claim that outside the mining areas, the jade trade was dominated by male Yunnanese operators with their well-organized networks and knowledge of the trade that enabled them to get around the state laws of Burma and Thailand, and to compete among themselves, and also against other ethnic traders. The extension of the trade to Thailand was nearly monopolized by Yunnanese traders, and made it primarily a Yunnanese ethnic enterprise. Nevertheless, the Yunnanese had to rely on the assistance of local

people in transactions that took place in Burma. Unlike the situation in Thailand, where there were jade companies that helped to store sellers' stones and arrange deals between sellers and buyers, all transactions in Burma were dependent on personal arrangement—local people primarily took up this job. Mr Hong, who was in the jade trade for more than twenty years, said, "When a Yunnanese trader obtained some jade stones, he first placed the stones in a Burman's house. If cutting stones were required [mostly for the very big sized ones], they were done in Burmans' places too. The Burmese authorities usually did not catch their own people; even if they knew which house stored jade stones. Most Burmans had kith and kin working at government offices and had their connections. Most of them had family members in the army too."

Local brokers (*jieshouren* 介紹人), comprising mostly Burmans, Indians, Kachins and Shans, helped to introduce buyers. The service had been part of the trading tradition. The *Burma Gazetteer* records, "The stone is purchased at the mines by Chinese traders. All payments are made in rupees. An expert, or middleman, is nearly always employed to settle the price. These middlemen, who are without exception Burmans or Burmese-Shans, have from early times been indispensable to the transaction of business at the mines; they charge the purchaser 5 percent on the purchase money."[32] During the socialist period, it was said, the movement of local people was safer than for the Chinese. Unlike the sophisticated jobs involved in the brokerage that were handled by the jade companies in Thailand, the practice of brokerage in Burma did not require money for investment or tax arrangements, or the transport of traded stones abroad. Yunnanese traders only needed to pay petty commission for the brokerage. The Yunnanese did not consider the involvement of local people in brokering to be competition, but more as mutual reciprocity.

In addition to the Yunnanese traders based in Burma, some Yunnanese buyers came from Thailand. The purchase of jade stones was preceded by shopping around and price negotiations between buyers and sellers. In areas where the jade mines were located, buyers would wander the excavation spots seeking interesting stones. The shopping was called *guang dongzi* (逛洞子), or "roaming the holes." Mine bosses also purchased stones from one another. Before leaving the mines, the traded stones would have "passed a few hands" (*zhuanle jishou* 轉了幾手). They were carried by porters or mules, cattle, or elephants to the nearest train stations, for instance Mogaung, Hopin, and Mohnyin, and then by train to Mandalay. These places were all underground trading centers, and Mandalay was especially important. In these places,

buyers were taken to private houses where the stones were stored; if they were interested in buying a piece, they would check the price and then try to bring it down through long negotiations with the seller. Mr Hong described the process vividly.

> When the buyer is interested in a piece of stone, he would first ask the broker about the price. He normally did not ask the seller directly. After he thought that the price was O.K., he would then start to bargain with the seller for a lower price. When the seller asked for a certain price, for example one million [kyat], the buyer would then offer a much lower price, for example five hundred thousand. The seller would say no way. The buyer would then increase his offer. Price negotiation often took the whole day when both parties were interested in making a deal. After the buyer had raised the price several times, for example up to seven hundred thousand, but the seller was still not willing to sell, the buyer would call this his last offer. Though the deal was not settled, the seller may agree to have the stone packed with a piece of cloth and have the potential buyer sign his name on the cloth. On doing this, other buyers were not allowed to open it. That was the rule. A meal often followed afterwards. Negotiations could continue the next day. . . . If afterwards the seller was willing to sell the stone with the last price offered by the buyer, then the buyer must purchase the stone, because he had proposed that price and signed his name on the packed stone. . . . [But] if the buyer discovered that the packed stones had been opened, he could refuse to buy it.

Price negotiation was like a game, predicated on many unwritten rules. It required patience, negotiation skills, and the ability to read the mind of one's counterpart. Informants commonly referred to the process as a kind of psychological battle (xinlizhan 心理戰). Most traders were Yunnanese, but some Burmans, Indians, Kachins, and Shans also engaged in the jade trade. The amount of capital involved was said to be comparatively much smaller, and the participation of these traders took place primarily within Burma, as very few of them had access to transnational networks that could extend their business abroad.[33]

After having purchased jade stones, Yunnanese merchants often entrusted them to caravan companies for conveyance to Thailand. Most caravan companies were also run by the Yunnanese. Transportation was accomplished by bribing officials of the customs house, police stations, immigration office, intelligence department, and the military. The bribes resembled the regulated taxes levied on different ethnic insurgent groups located on the way.

When the stones arrived at Thai border points, representatives of the jade companies, who had been contacted in advance, would show up to receive the stones. The import of jade stones operated with tacit permission from the Thai government. The jade companies helped pay tax to the Thai customs house and thus transform the illegally smuggled stones into legal commodities. Meanwhile, the caravan traders would buy Thai goods and sell them on the black market in Burma. In short, the Yunnanese jade trade networks from Burma to Thailand were essentially composed of three nodes: the traders (based in both Burma and Thailand), the caravan companies (mostly based in Burma), and the jade companies (based in Thailand).

Capital Flow

Apart from the widespread network formation, the flexibility of the Yunnanese in handling capital flow was another key factor that facilitated their transnational economic operation. "No matter legal or illegal, we Chinese merchants know how to launch business," commented Mr Chuan, who used to travel from Mae Sot (a Thai border town in Tak Province, Thailand) westward to Mawlamyaing, then north to Mandalay (in Burma) for the purchase of jade stones in the 1980s and early 1990s. The transnational jade trade in question required capital flow between various nodes. In the mining areas, there were different means of capital transference to meet demand during the excavation period, which lasted for about half a year. The period coincided with the dry season; it started in the ninth or tenth month of the lunar calendar and ended in the third or fourth month the following year. When the rainy season began, the miners had to leave for fear of catching malaria and other diseases. People with little capital took the money they had to the mines and tried their luck in excavation until they had used up the money. If they discovered any marketable stones, they could sell them in the mines or in the nearby marketplace, acquire more capital, and extend their stay in the mines. However, if no valuable stones were found, they would have to leave or work for other mine owners.

Those with more capital could hire more people to work for them. Three to five miners worked at a "jade hole." The mine boss had to take care of the miners' food and board and provide pocket money for smoking. The half-year stay required a large amount of money, and it was both inconvenient and dangerous to carry all one's money at one time to the mining area. Big grocery stores at nearby marketplaces therefore also functioned as underground stations for money transference. Those stores had urban bases for business connections. A mine boss could send his foreman to a certain shop

to purchase the consumption goods his work team needed, and have his family or partner pay the money at one of the shop's urban bases. The urban base of the shop used the money to replenish and transport the merchandise to the mining area. The mine boss could also borrow money from the shop for buying stones from other jade holes. In addition to the underground transference stations, there were individuals who also participated in this process. They packed money in sacks or cartons and took them to the mines by train or car. They lent the money to the familiar mine bosses and jade traders, and afterward collected debts from the debtors' families in the cities with a certain percentage of interest added. However, there was always the chance of not being able to retrieve debts, especially when traders or mine bosses went bankrupt.

The transaction of jade stones also illustrates the Yunnanese penchant for finance management. Merchants often traded in uncut stones. High-quality jade stones were mostly small in size, and their value was not revealed until they were cut. Traders could only evaluate stones by observing features indicated on the surface. While price bargaining took place, both the buyer and seller appropriated their jade knowledge with reference to the marked features on the stone. The former would point out as many defects as possible, in order to bring down the price, while the seller would boast about the quality of his stone. The manipulation of jade knowledge became a tactic in the trade, and the transaction thus came to resemble gambling. In general, traded stones, except for large pieces weighing hundreds of kilos, remained uncut in Burma, and the price fluctuations were not too extreme. However, once the stones were safely transported to Thailand and traded at the jade companies, the process of price bargaining would intensify.

Most buyers at the jade companies were dealers from Hong Kong or Taiwan, the major jade trade centers among Chinese societies. After a transaction, the Hong Kong and Taiwan dealers would either have the stones cut immediately in Thailand or after they were transported back to their countries. To reduce economic risk, both sellers and buyers were usually composed of a group of three to five partners. The selling partners often came from Burma and Thailand, which aided in the allocation of tasks according to each one's special abilities. Those in Burma handled the purchase of stones from jade mines and arranged to have them trafficked to Thailand; those in Thailand participated in the sale through the brokerage of a jade company. Moreover, the formation of a trading group helped in the accumulation of capital, which enhanced the possibilities of buying good jade stones.

In addition to their brokerage services, the jade companies provided money transference and loan services too. Like the grocery stores of the mining places, they functioned as informal finance stations. Prior to selling their stones, jade merchants from Burma in Thailand could borrow money from the companies to finance their living expenses. After selling their stones, they would ask the companies to help transfer their remaining money back to Burma. This money was usually converted to Burmese kyat. On establishing a good relationship with the jade companies, traders could also borrow money from those companies for purchasing jade stones in Burma. These traders were said to be experienced and good at procuring high-quality stones. In this way, the traders could acquire capital for investment, and the jade companies were guaranteed a sufficient supply of good commodities, with which they could attract dealers from Hong Kong and Taiwan.

Looking closer into this underground finance system, one finds that in addition to the danger of being arrested, traders faced the threat that the Burmese government might implement demonetization without warning or guarantee of reasonable compensation. Despite the involvement of foreign currencies and gold bars in the transnational trafficking of different commodities, monetary circulation in the black markets inside Burma was still based on kyat.[34] Each demonetization caused tremendous loss to local traders. To combat this uncertainty, well-off Yunnanese merchants reinvested part of their profit in Thailand in cash cropping, restaurants, or hotels.

The uncertainty of the Burmese situation paralleled the indeterminacy of the quality of jade stones that compounded the risk of the trade. Many traders whom I interviewed confessed to multiple bankruptcies, which were due either to economic loss through price gambling or to the demonetization of the Burmese currency. Moreover, several of them had been arrested and jailed in Burma. The wonder was that they continued to try their luck at all with the help of partnerships or capital loaned from various underground finance stations. Informants explained that involvement in the jade trade is like a drug addiction—the temptation of obtaining an invaluable piece of jade stone overcomes any fears. A popular saying among traders is that one should never look down on anyone in the trade, for even miners may suddenly become millionaires when luck knocks on their doors. Even though the number of people who have encountered such good luck is very small in reality, the possibility is tempting enough to lure Yunnanese traders, who are said to be gamblers by nature, to stick to the trade.

The Yunnanese traders created a system of flexible capital flow in connection with different parties for constant reinvestment and maximization of their profit. Even the Burmese official apparatuses, local insurgent groups, and the Thai authority were incorporated into the trade. Facing the difficulties presented by the Burmese socialist economy, the migrant Yunnanese dispersed throughout Burma and Thailand, and opened up an underground market economy that connected to the capitalism of the outside world. Their uncertain status did not confine them geographically; instead, it resulted in their mobility, building of networks, and engagement in transborder economic activities.

Seen from a long historical perspective, the traders' adventurous commercial endeavors were not simply contemporary practices but an extension of the *longue durée* of Yunnanese overland activities. In terms of economic undertaking, the Yunnanese have, throughout history, oriented themselves more toward Southeast Asia and South Asia than toward China. The *Shiji* episode has pointed this out, and the persistence of long-distance caravan trade affirms its development. Furthermore, Yunnanese adoption of the regional monetary system by using cowries best illustrates this economic orientation. Archeological excavations have shown that Yunnan had been importing cowries from South Asia and Southeast Asia since ancient times. Cowries were traded both as commodities and as a primary medium of exchange for the regional monetary system; in other words, they were the major commodity currency.[35] Traces of their use in Yunnan have been found particularly along the trading routes connecting these neighboring countries. Other currencies used in Yunnan included silver, gold, copper, cloth, and salt. These multiple currencies illustrated the diversified conditions of Yunnanese commerce and the traders' flexibility in their mutual conversion.[36] The Chinese court was not successful in integrating Yunnan into its national monetary system until the seventeenth century.

Following the penetration of Western powers in the nineteenth century, various currencies issued by respective colonial governments flowed from India, Burma, Vietnam, and Laos. Even so, Western powers did not take economic opportunities away from the native population. Indigenous traders reacted positively to the new situation. With the help of existing trading networks, Yunnanese merchants set up many trading firms (*shanghao* 商號), with branch offices in the major cities of Yunnan and neighboring countries. They were linked to foreign firms and engaged in import-export trade, and thereby responsible for a large flow of goods to widespread local mar-

kets. They also bought and sold foreign currencies and made remittances for their clients across countries.[37] Accordingly, Yunnanese traders have been dynamic in the area of capital flow since ancient times. Their management has been in response to the external circumstances of each period, and has been transnational rather than national, and unofficial rather than official. The underground finance system of the jade trade serves as another contemporary example.

Concluding Remarks

The jade trade effectively highlights the economic agency of Yunnanese migrants during the Burmese socialist period. It was a time of darkness, but these people created different means by which to survive. Informants often referred to the paradoxical belief in Burma that "many things were not possible, but everything was possible." Departing from the *Shiji* episode, I have pointed out the embedded significance of historical continuity and contingency, using them as the foundation of the analytical framework to bring out the insights of the trade. On the one hand, throughout history the Yunnanese adoption of practical tactics in dealing with local powers and state agencies and integration of regulatory practices, and the system of brokerage and flexible capital flow have both carried forward the persistence of a regional politico-economy. On the other hand, in response to different external contingencies they face, the strategies applied have varied in different periods. Informants themselves are also aware of the interaction of these two aspects in the formation of their trading spirit. They refer repeatedly to their risky endeavors as being the result of external circumstances on the one hand, and of the persistent Yunnanese tradition of long-distance trade in the region, on the other. The former points to environmental influences and a series of sociopolitical contingencies, and the latter, to a Yunnanese commercial ethos developed throughout history. Mr. Huang, who participated in the jade trade for over thirty years, said,

> We Yunnanese have a kind of daring spirit [*maoxian fannan de jingshen* 冒險犯難的精神] and tough personality. This is mainly due to the mountainous environment. The land is not fertile for agriculture. Yunnanese simply have to leave their homeland to make a living. Our ancestors had been engaged in the caravan trade for hundreds of years. . . . On account of not having legal status when we arrived [in Burma], we had to stay in mountains . . . and engaged in illicit trade. Yunnanese are the best group among the ethnic Chinese abroad who are capable of enduring hardship.

Similar remarks were made by other informants. They commonly stress their risk-taking behavior and audacity as the distinctive "overland" temperament in this ethnically diverse land, and often apply it to distinguish themselves from the more conservative overseas Chinese from the Fujian and Guangdong Provinces. Ah Song, a second generation Yunnanese businessman in Chiang Mai, vividly describes their differentiation: "We Yunnanese love gambling on big trade. . . . [We] have a sort of wild temper [shanba piqi 山巴脾氣]. . . . Those Teochiu are good at business.[38] They are willing to earn one baht, two bahts [yikuai laingkuai douzhuan 塊兩塊都賺, meaning making small profits]. We Yunnanese aim only at big profits [douzhi zuo dade 都只做大的]."

Nonetheless, when asked to explain their economic predominance in comparison with non-Chinese ethnic groups, Yunnanese Chinese informants replace the statement of the overland disposition with an ethnocentric response tied to their Han Chinese origin. Mr. Huang says: "I think it is the question of cultural standard. Those Kachins do not have the brain of we Han Chinese. They mostly take up manual work, such as mining. The Shans, too, generally work as laborers." Even the majority of Burmans and Thais are said to lack the talent and guts needed in the jade trade.[39] The mercantile ethos of the Yunnanese is thus illustrated with a double nature, grounded both on local Yunnanese tradition and on Han Chinese ethnicity. The Yunnanese switch to either emphasis depending on which group they are related to. Vis-à-vis the ethnic others, they naturally emphasize the dimension of civilized Chineseness, which they use to highlight their ethnic superiority.[40] This cultural superiority also embraces their shrewdness in trade. Stories of how some Burmese and minority traders are compelled to sell high-value jade stones with low prices were repeated by informants.[41]

However, regardless of their overland toughness and ethnic superiority, the Yunnanese traders had to rely on assistance from local people. In reality, they were sometimes betrayed by indigenous collaborators. Informants reported having lost stones that were stored at local people's houses or while being transported from one location to another. They accused the homeowners of releasing information to the Burmese authority in order to make large profits. Once such an incident took place, the traders would end the business relationship with the collaborators, and the latter would be barred by other traders, too. According to informants, this strategy was useful to a certain degree, but the danger of being sold out still existed, and they had to be constantly alert. Moreover, bribes to the Burmese officials did not guarantee absolute safety. Sometimes, checks became more stringent or would occur unexpectedly. At other times, military conflicts between the Burmese

army and ethnic rebels flared up. Such situations obstructed the operation of the trade, and merchants had to wait until things calmed down.

By adopting a minjian perspective, I have illustrated the complex trading environment and relations involved in the jade trade. I have moved beyond a state-centric stance that would simply label the jade trade illegal, depriving the government of a huge amount of tax income and foreign exchange, and posing serious threats to national security. I have instead followed the mobility of the migrant Yunnanese and tried to illuminate their strength and resilience, as well as the limitations in their interaction with multiple regimes of power. The Burmese socialist junta was only one of the involved parties. Moreover, it was not a unified one. Likewise, the community of Yunnanese traders was fragmented. Deception among Yunnanese trading partners occurred more often than betrayals by local collaborators.[42] Partnerships based on ties of kith and kin were not everlasting, given the temptation of massive economic margins. Almost all informants confided that they had been cheated by their partners or fellow traders. Despite all the internal and external complexities, based on the double nature of their trading ethos, the contemporary migrant Yunnanese have maintained the rationale of maximizing economic gain and assuring a continuity that underlies their transnational trading activity.

Notes

I conducted fieldwork for this paper in Burma (Mandalay, Yangon, Taunggyi, Lashio, Maymeo, and Myitkyina), Thailand (Chiang Mai Province, Chiang Rai Province, and Bangkok), Taiwan, Hong Kong, and Guangzhou in 2000, 2002, 2004–2005, and 2006, totaling nine-and-a-half months. During my field research, I conducted in-depth interviews, in addition to participant observation. I would like to thank C. Scott Walker, digital cartography specialist at Harvard Map Collection, for his help with producing the map.

1. Sima Qian, *Records of the Grand Historian, Han Dynasty 2* [Shiji], vol. *Southwestern Barbarians*, trans. Burton Watson (Hong Kong: Columbia University Press Book, 1993), 256–57. Shu was a prefecture of Han; Qiong, Dian, and Kunming were small tribal kingdoms. They were all located in present southwestern China. Shu and Qiong were situated inside present Sichuan province, and Dian and Kunming in Yunnan province. The Xiongnu was a powerful tribe to the north of the Han. A similar passage was documented in volume *Dawan* (*Dayuan* in Watson's translation) of the same book.

2. See Wen-Chin Chang, "Home Away from Home: Migrant Yunnanese Chinese in Northern Thailand," *International Journal of Asian Studies* 3.1 (2006): 49–76.

3. According to informants based in Burma and Thailand, the Han Chinese comprised 90 to 95 percent of the Yunnanese jade traders, and the rest were Yunnanese Muslims.

4. Chiranan Prasertkul, "Yunnan Trade in the Nineteenth Century: Southwest China's Cross-Boundaries Functional System" (Bangkok: Institute of Asian Studies, Chulalongkorn University, 1990); Wang Mingda and Zhang Xilu, *Mabang wenhua* [Culture of caravan trade] (Kunming: Yunnan renmin chubanshe, 1993); Shen Xu, *Zhongguo xinan duiwai guanxishi yanjiu: Yixinan sichou zhilu wei zhongxin* [A historical study of the cross-boundary interrelationship between southwest China and its neighboring countries] (Kunming: Yunnan meishu chubanshe, 1994); Andrew Forbes and David Henley, *The Haw: Traders of the Golden Triangle* (Chiang Mai: Teak House, 1997); Sun Laichen, "Ming-Southeast Asian Overland Interactions, 1368–1644," Ph.D. diss., University of Michigan, 2000; C. Patterson Giersch, in this volume.

5. Ann Maxwell Hill, *Merchants and Migrants: Ethnicity and Trade among Yunnanese Chinese in Southeast Asia* (New Haven: Yale Southeast Asia Studies, 1998).

6. Fan C., *The Man Shu* (Book of the Southern Barbarians), translated by Gordon H. Luce, ed. G. P. Oey (Ithaca: Southeast Asia Program, Cornell University, 1961); Wang and Zhang, *Mabang wenhua*.

7. Wen-Chin Chang, "Three Jade Traders from Tengchong," *Kolor: Journal on Moving Communities* 3.1 (2003): 15–34; Wen-Chin Chang, "Guanxi and Regulation in Networks: The Yunnanese Jade Trade between Burma and Thailand, 1962–88," *Journal of Southeast Asian Studies* 35.3 (2004): 479–501; Wen-Chin Chang, "The Trading Culture of Jade Stones among the Yunnanese in Burma and Thailand, 1962–88," *Journal of Chinese Overseas* 2.2 (2006): 269–93.

8. Martin J. Smith, *Burma: Insurgency and the Politics of Ethnicity* (1991; repr., London: Zed, 1993), 25; Chen Wen, *Kunsa jinsanjiao chuanqi* [Khun sa: Stories of the Golden Triangle] (Taipei: Yunchen wenhua, 1996), 144.

9. Mya Than, *Myanmar's External Trade: An Overview in the Southeast Asian Context* (1992; repr., Singapore: ASEAN Economic Research Unit, Institute of Southeast Asian Studies, 1996), 57.

10. Kyaw Yin Hlaing, "The Politics of State-Business Relations in Post-Colonial Burma," Ph.D. diss., Cornell University, 2001, 8–9.

11. Chang, "Guanxi and Regulation in Networks," 487.

12. The use of the term is drawn from Mayfair Yang's work, *Gifts, Favors, and Banquets: The Art of Social Relationships in China* (Ithaca: Cornell University Press, 1994). She uses the term to refer to the unofficial order, the popular realm, that is generated through the infinite weaving and spreading of personal connections and group formations.

13. Wang and Zhang, *Mabang wenhua*; Hill, *Merchants and Migrants*; Sun, "Ming-Southeast Asian Overland Interactions, 1368–1644"; Yang Bin, *Between Winds and Clouds: The Making of Yunnan (Second Century BCE–Twentieth Century CE)* (New York: Columbia University Press, 2008).

14. Heshun (和順) is a prominent example of a famous township with a distinctive migration culture. See Yin Wenhe, "Yunnan han heshun qiaoxiangshi gaishu" [A general migration history of Heshun], *Yunnansheng lishi yanjiusuo jikan* 2 (1984): 273–301; Chang, "Three Jade Traders from Tengchong"; Fang Yijie, "Dijing fengshui yu rushang wenhua: Yunnan Heshun qiaoxiang de minjian wenhua yu guojia xiangzheng shijian" [Land-

scape geometry and the culture of gentry businessmen: The folk culture and practices of state symbolism in Heshun Township of Yunnan], master's thesis, Qinghua University, Xinzhu, Taiwan, 2003.

15. Douglas S. Massey et al., "Theories of International Migration: A Review and Appraisal," *Population and Development Review* 19 (1993): 453.

16. Dong Ping, *Heshun fengyu liubainian* [The six-hundred-year history of Heshun] (Kunming: Yunnan renmin chubanshe, 2000).

17. Union of Burma Ministry of Information, *The Kuomintang Aggression against Burma* (Rangoon: Ministry of Information, 1953); Republic of China Ministry of Defense, *Dianmian bianqu youji zhanshi* [History of guerrilla wars in the Sino-Burmese border areas], 2 vols. (Taipei: Guofangbu shizheng bianyinju, 1964); Kenneth Ray Young, "Nationalist Chinese Troops in Burma: Obstacle in Burma's Foreign Relations, 1949–1961," Ph.D. diss., New York University, 1970; Robert H. Taylor, "Foreign and Domestic Consequences of the KMT Intervention in Burma," Data paper no. 93, Southeast Asia Program, Department of Asian Studies, Cornell University, Ithaca, New York, 1973.

18. The number of KMT guerrillas in the 1950s was around ten thousand; and the numbers of troops in the Third and Fifth Armies was about 3,200.

19. Hu Qingrong [Ding Zuoshao], *Dianbian youji shihua* [History of Yunnanese guerrillas] (Tainan: Zhongguo shiji zazhishe, 1974), 195.

20. See Chao Tzang Yawnghwe, *The Shan of Burma: Memories of a Shan Exile* (1987; repr., Singapore: Institute of Southeast Asian Studies, 1990); Bertil Lintner, *Burma in Revolt: Opium and Insurgency since 1948* (Bangkok: White Lotus, 1994); Wen-Chin Chang, "Identification of Leadership among the KMT Yunnanese Chinese in Northern Thailand," *Journal of Southeast Asian Studies* 33.1 (2002): 123–45.

21. Today, all major cities in upper Burma, such as Myitkyina, Mogaung, Lahio, Maymeo, Mandalay, Taunggyi, Kengtung, and Tangyan, are full of Yunnanese.

22. Andrew Walker, *The Legend of the Golden Boat: Regulation, Trade and Traders in the Borderlands of Laos, Thailand, China and Burma* (Honolulu: University of Hawaii Press, 1999), 14.

23. Xia Guangnan, *Zhong yin mian dao jiaotong shi* [History of traffic between China, India and Burma] (Shanghai: Zhonghua shuju, 1948), 77–78; Chen Yi-Sein, "The Chinese in Upper Burma before A.D. 1700," *Journal of Southeast Asian Researches* 2 (1966): 81–89; Qiu Fuhai, *Guyu jianshi, vol. 4, ming qing ji feicui pian* [History of ancient jade, the periods of Ming and Qing] (Taipei: Shuxing chubanshe, 1997), 206–11; Sun, "Ming-Southeast Asian Overland Interactions, 1368–1644." The jade mines in Burma are located in Kachin State, especially where the alluvial deposits of the Uru river conglomerate are found.

24. See Sun Laichen's essay in this volume.

25. Khin Maung Nyunt, "History of Myanmar Jade Trade till 1938," *Traditions in Current Perspective: Proceedings of the Conference on Myanmar and Southeast Asian Studies* (Yangon: Universities Historical Research Centre, 15–17 November 1995), 258.

26. The extract originates from a report written by an Englishman, W. Warry, who accompanied a British military expedition to the Kachin jade mines in 1888; it was later included in W. A. Hertz, *Burma Gazetteer: Myitkyina District, Volume A* (1912; repr., Rangoon: Superintendent, Government Printing and Stationery, Union of Burma, 1960), 119–20.

27. Ibid., 120. See also Thanyarat Apiwong, "Jade and Myanmar Economy in the Colonial Period (1885–1948)," paper presented at SEASREP Tenth Anniversary Conference, 8–9 December 2005, Chiang Mai, Thailand. In addition to the Kachin chiefs, Shan chiefs had ruled the mining region in earlier periods (Sun Laichen, "Shan Gems, Chinese Silver, and the Rise of Shan Principalities in Northern Burma, c. 1450–1527," *Southeast Asia in the Fifteenth Century: The Ming Factor*, ed. Geoff Wade and Sun Laichen [Singapore: Singapore University Press, 2009]).

28. Yin Deming, *Yunnan beijie kanchaji* [Investigation of Yunnan Frontiers] (Huawen shuju, 1933), vols. 1 and 5; Yin Deming, *Nan tian pian yu* (N.p., 1934). See also H. L. Chhibber, *The Mineral Resources of Burma* (London: Macmillan, 1934).

29. Zhou Jinglun, *Yushi tianming* [The destiny of jade stone] (Taipei: Haojiao chubanshe, 1989).

30. Ibid., 266.

31. Ibid., 281.

32. Hertz, *Burma Gazetteer: Myitkyina district, Volume A*, 131.

33. In contrast to the Yunnanese, local traders liked to discuss their trade in teahouses. Burmese informants pointed out that two teahouses located on 34th Street in Mandalay were especially frequented by local traders.

34. Informants pointed out that gold bars were used in the drug trade, and the Thai baht or Hong Kong dollar was used in the jade trade in Thailand.

35. Cowries had been the major currency in Yunnan between the ninth and seventeenth centuries, but some scholars argue that their use in Yunnan can be traced back 2,500 years. See Fang Guoyu, *Dianshi lunchong* [Research on Yunnanese history] (Shanghai: Shanghai renmin chubanshe, 1982), 246–80; Tang Guoyen et al., eds., *Yunnan lishi huobi* [The historical currencies of Yunnan] (Kunming: Yunnan renmin chubanshe, 1989); Hans Ulrich Vogel, "Cowry Trade and Its Role in the Economy of Yünnan, the Ninth to the Middle of the Seventeenth Century," *Emporia, Commodities and Entrepreneurs in Asian Maritime Trade, c. 1400–1750*, ed. Roderich Ptak and Dietmar Rothermund (Stuttgart: Franz Steiner Verlag, 1991), 231–62; Lin Wenxun, "Yunnan gudai huobi wenhua fazhan de tedian" [The distinctive characteristics of the development of Yunnanese ancient currencies], *Xixiangzhansian* 6 (1998): 63; Yunnansheng qianbi xuehui, ed., *Yunnan huobi jianshi* [A short history of currencies in Yunnan] (Kunmin: Yunnan minzu chubanshe, 2002).

36. Historical materials recorded the rates of their mutual conversion. See Yunnansheng qianbi xuehui, *Yunnan huobi jianshi*, 65, 82.

37. Issue no. 42 of *Yunnan wenshi ziliao xuanji* contains several articles that discuss the organization and management of several Yunnanese trading firms that existed prior to the Communist regime; Yunnan zhengxie wenshi ziliao yanjiu weiyuanhui, ed., *Yunnan wenshi ziliao xuanji* [Anthology of Yunnan history], no. 42 (1993). The Yunnanese economic orientation toward Southeast Asia and the significance of Yunnanese networking ability are also examined by C. Patterson Giersch in this volume.

38. The Teochiu are the most prominent group in terms of number and economic de-

velopment among the ethnic Chinese in Thailand. The Yunnanese often refer to them to represent all the ethnic Chinese in the country who came by sea.

39. Even Yunnanese Muslim traders appropriate the integrating category of the Chinese identity to explain their superior trading capacity in relation to other ethnic groups.

40. For elaboration on the subject of the different dispositions embedded in the subjectivity of the migrant Yunnanese, see Wen-Chin Chang, "The Interstitial Subjectivities of the Yunnanese Chinese in Thailand," *Asia-Pacific Journal of Anthropology* 9.2 (2008): 97–122.

41. See Chang, "The Trading Culture of Jade Stones Among the Yunnanese in Burma and Thailand, 1962–88," 279–80.

42. See Chang, "*Guanxi* and Regulation in Networks" and "The Trading Culture of Jade Stones Among the Yunnanese in Burma and Thailand, 1962–88."

CONFLICT TIMBER ALONG THE CHINA-BURMA BORDER

Connecting the Global Timber Consumer with Violent Extraction Sites

───── Kevin Woods

As China continues to surge ahead with the world's fastest-growing economy, the Chinese government and businessmen are increasingly looking toward Southeast Asia as a cheap source of natural resources to feed their expanding markets. The resulting economic-social-environmental cost is currently redefining China's relationship with Southeast Asia. China's economic miracle, massive rural migration to urban centers, market neo-liberalization, and logging bans all contribute to China's extended reach into Southeast Asia's tropical forests. Chinese businessmen and the markets they serve increasingly covet unprocessed tropical timber from other countries in order to rebuild China and reap huge profits from processing wood for the the international tropical-timber market. Sources of tropical timber, however, are becoming scarce in industrialized and politically stable countries and, as a result, are protected with strict national conservation laws. Valuable global commodities, such as tropical timber, will therefore increasingly originate from areas such as conflict areas in Burma, which are not as yet well integrated into global natural-resource-extraction/conservation networks. It is, however, exactly these conflict zones where natural resource concessions can be most prone to compounding violence.

In this essay I trace "conflict timber" originating in northern Burma (Myanmar), traveling overland to Yunnan Province, China, and on to Chinese domestic and global tropical-timber markets.[1] Burma has the world's longest-running civil war, with ongoing conflicts situated in the mountainous ethnic border regions. Kachin State, in northern Burma, bordering Yunnan, China, remains extremely rich in natural resources and has been intimately involved with the arms struggle against the Burmese junta since the fight for autonomy began more than sixty years ago (see map 1). My analysis

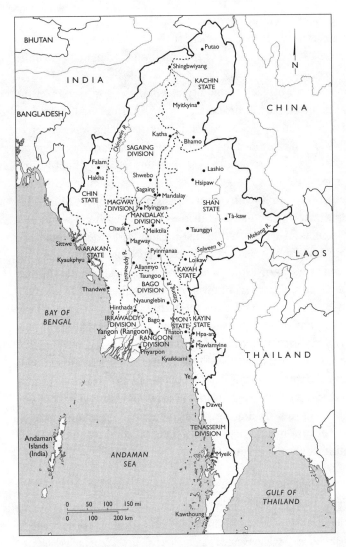

Map 1 Burma.

of the Sino-Burmese conflict timber trade will exclusively examine Kachin State since the cease-fires.[2] Although cease-fires were signed by the different Kachin insurgent groups in the early 1990s, ostensible peace optimistically describes this war-torn sub-Himalayan mountainous region, where the Kachin political resistance groups still possess armies and territories. Chinese logging companies cutting down forests in this hostile ethnic border region incites further violence among the Burmese government (the State Peace and Development Council, or SPDC), the various ethnic political resistance groups, and Kachin villagers. However, it is exactly this manifesta-

tion of violence that becomes deleted while the timber travels from extraction sites to consumption nodes. As such, there is a complete erasure and subsequent re-creation of the image of the commodity to match consumer desires.

In a wider context, I utilize commodity-chain analysis to reconnect the slippage between international consumers buying furniture made from Burmese tropical timber and the place and conditions in which it was extracted. More specifically, I will examine the political ecology of war that underpins the overland timber trade between these two countries. The China-Burma border fuses global tropical timber-market networks—facilitated by the SPDC, the cease-fires with Kachin political resistance groups, Chinese domestic corporations, and transnational investment—with a Kachin war economy. The result is an overhaul of the historical cross-border timber trade between Kachin and Yunnanese traders, into the control of SPDC and Chinese officials and overseas investors, at the expense of the Kachins. This has led to a process of consolidation of power over the timber trade by the Burmese regime as a means to obtain more funds and subsequently cut off the access of Kachin political resistance groups (notably the Kachin Independence Organization, or KIO) to capital that primarily funds their fight. This situation thus provides insight into the loose relationships between national versus insurgent economies, legal versus illegal resource extraction, (trans) national versus local resource control, and trade versus trafficking. Zones of conflict experiencing the "natural resource curse" help unbundle some of these binaries, because insurgency uproots political stability and national government authority and legitimacy.

Global-Commodity-Chain Analysis:
Connecting Conflict Timber to the Consumer

"Distancing": the severing of ecological and social feedback along the commodity chain as points are increasingly separated along dimensions of geography, culture, agency, and power.
—Michael S. Carolan, "Unmasking the Commodity Chain"

The global commodity chain (GCC) has been defined by Emily Hartwick: "[The] radiating effects of the commodity at the consumption node, the social and natural conditions at the production node, and the complex intersections of commodity chains at various intermediating and terminal points are added to a simple model of commodity movement to complete integration of the vertical and horizontal dimensions."[3] In this way, the commodity

links extraction sites, people, enterprises, and states through sets of inter-organizational networks. Formerly placeless commodities suddenly become grounded at different nodes along the commodity chain, giving light to social relations and political realities. The global-commodity-chain framework exposes the well-hidden timber trade by connecting places of production and consumption, and highlighting the cultural, social, and environmental conditions of global timber commodities originating from northern Burma.

Focusing on the different actors at each commodity-chain node reveals the political relations tied to resources, thus highlighting the politics of natural-resource extraction. The players collude and collide to access the timber, to control its trade routes, and to finance its processing in order to put it onto the global tropical-timber market. The China-Burma timber trade is a complex mix of involved parties: Chinese provincial and national government authorities, Chinese logging and processing companies, Asian finance corporations, on-the-ground middlemen connecting the Chinese logging companies to inside Burma, Burmese government officials, ethnic Kachin and Burmese elite businessmen and political leaders, Kachin headmen, and international consumers, among others. Cashing in on timber has enabled insurgent business elites to supersede enemies in order to profit from the chaos and absence of the rule of law in the cross-border region. In such confusion and political instability, the multinational, state, and local elites have brought their business into the border black-market economy. Friction exists between historical cross-border local trading schemes and forming a centralized, regulated national economy. The result: a fusion of global capital with ethnic political resistance groups.

A Briefing on the Cross-Border Timber Trade

China is the world's only developing country that is a major net timber importer and is the world's fastest-growing market for tropical-timber products. China went from seventh to second place in the world in just ten years for the total value of imported forest products, and it is now the leading importer of industrial round wood.[4]

China's trade in timber products with Burma grew substantially from 1997 to 2002, from 295,474 m³ (round wood equivalent, RWE) in 1997 to 947,765 m³ (RWE) in 2002.[5] In 2005, cross-border exports from Burma to China totalled more than 1.5 million m³ with an estimated value of US$350 million.[6] China's timber sales officially accounted for 20 percent of Burma's foreign-exchange earnings from 1990 to 2000.[7] In 2004–2005, timber was the Burmese government's second most important source of legal foreign

exchange, generating about US$427 million.[8] In 2003 98 percent of Burma's timber exports to China were considered "illegal" (i.e., overland).[9]

Despite Burmese restrictions mandating that all processed-timber exports must either pass through Yangon and be shipped by sea, or through the Muse (Burma)-Ruili (China) border (the only government-sanctioned legal checkpoint along the China-Burma border), 96 percent of China's imports of logs and sawnwood from Burma arrived in Kunming overland in 2003.[10] This statistic reveals that the vast majority of timber leaving Burma is done through nongovernment channels, namely ethnic political resistance groups. Most of China's increase in timber-product imports from Burma occurred between 1998–1999 and 1999–2000, due to a host of factors: the implementation of China's national logging ban (Natural Forest Protection Program) in 1998; cuts in China's forest-product tariffs in 1999; the opening up of new tracts of virgin forest in Kachin State to Chinese companies in the late 1990s due to the cease-fire agreements; China's increasing consumption of forest products due to exceptional economic growth; increasing international demand for low-cost forest products manufactured in China; and China's tree plantations being unable to meet domestic demand.[11] It is thus a combination of factors working in concert to get logs from Burma into China and beyond, but just two aspects co-drive the clear-cutting machine: partial liberalization of China's economy (supported by transnational financial capital), and tropical-timber consumer demand (encouraging the former).

Patron-Client Networks: Local and National

MILITARY ECONOMIES MERGE THROUGH TIMBER TRADING

The Chinese were putting heavy pressure on the Kachins to strike a deal with Rangoon: private merchants and state corporations in Yunnan were eagerly waiting to exploit the vast resources of timber and jade in Kachin State.
—Bertil Lintner, *The Kachin: Lords of Burma's Northern Frontier*

The entrenched economy within state military control in cease-fire areas creates avenues for furthering informal channels of personal patronage among military personnel, bringing the military-command economy into the local, insurgent economy. Mya Maung comments that "all foreign trade and investment transactions are conducted through personal contact and connection with the ruling military elite and their families, cabinet ministers, and directors of various government ministries and departments."[12] The Burmese government operates under the *hmaung kho* sector, an informal

business based on patron-client relationships, and in the military regime's case, through military connections.[13] The forests provide the SPDC a sink of potential revenue, a source to be used as brokerage for leveraging power, making new clients, and redistributing power through granting logging concessions.

Putting down weapons in favor of cooperative plundering broke up the unified Kachin political-resistance group, the KIO, into two other Kachin cease-fire political factions: the New Democratic Army-Kachin (NDA-K) and the Kachin Defense Army (KDA). Soon thereafter, in 1994, the KIO and their army, the Kachin Independence Army (KIA), also signed a cease-fire, which acted only as a temporary halt to open fighting; the KIO still retains their arms, soldiers, and limited political territory. In this way, the cease-fires have shifted political alliances such that "it is the businessmen, not the politicians, who are controlling everything."[14]

For example, in return for ending all military activity, the NDA-K, with direct links to Yunnan through their political leadership, focused exclusively on operating logging and mining concessions with consent from the SPDC. Ethnic political leaders-cum-businessmen aligned themselves with the Burmese and Chinese businessmen and government officials to gain greater access to profits through access to transnational military and business-client networks than informal, local networks would originally allow. Several Kachin informants told me that they did not have the trading knowledge necessary to accelerate the timber trade further into global timber markets, which reflects how in the jade trade "very few [Burmans, Kachins, and Shans] had access to transnational networks that could extend their [jade] business abroad."[15] Furthermore, the Burmese military and their companies simultaneously strengthened and gained cross-border business partners with control over access to lucrative resources in Kachin State.

CHINESE CONNECTED TO CONFLICT TIMBER IN NORTHERN BURMA

We don't have enough investment so we need to cooperate with the Chinese. We have to pay 50,000 kyat [US$60] for each truck carrying logs at every SPDC checkpoint. That is why we do not have enough money ourselves to invest. That is why we are sharing with the Chinese.

—Interview with Kachin logging businessman by Kachin field staff for Images Asia Environment Desk, Chiang Mai, Thailand, 2001

Two interrelated alliances enable this complex web of timber trading from northern Burma to China and beyond: domestic (SPDC and ethnic political

groups in Burma, and private firms and state authorities in China) and transnational Asian finance centers linking the two nations to the international tropical-timber markets. Along the China-Burma border, many actors work together to make the logging business profitable in an increasingly competitive and liberalized market. The main border timber industry actors include local villagers, migrant workers, and national nonlocal logging companies, all of whom are looking for quick profits. China's tropical-timber-industry boom involves three main nodes: the Chinese logging and small wood-processing companies based along the China-Burma border; the Chinese wood-processing and manufacturing companies based in Shanghai and Guangdong Province, who purchase the timber, process it, and sell it either domestically or abroad; and the international finance corporations who provide enough capital to make it all happen.[16] The desire for profits connects the different players, while the timber commodity is physically connected to them through transportation systems that deliver the wood further down the commodity chain.

CONFLICT TIMBER LINKING GOVERNMENTS AND
BUSINESSMEN ON BOTH SIDES OF THE BORDER

Before there were no relations between the Chinese government and the Burmese government to deal with the border "*min jian mao yi*" [unofficial small-time trade]; but the more the central governments on both sides increased power, the closer they got to the border.
— Interview with Chinese academic in Kunming, 2004.

Perhaps one of the most contested, and therefore most interesting, aspects of the conflict-timber trade is the degree to which Chinese government authorities and national and local policies promote its continuation. National and provincial Chinese policies have been established to aggressively develop the Yunnan border. China's grandest national campaign, the "Great Opening of the West," or *Great Western Development Program* (GWDP), strives to "not only equalise living standards between the interior and coastal regions of the country, but also to integrate more tightly with the rest of the country's politically troublesome regions."[17]

Local government officials backed by national Chinese policy are aggressively promoting cross-border trade and infrastructure linking the borders. Since August 1988, just days before the 8-8-88 bloody massacre in Rangoon against Burmese calling for democracy in their military-ruled nation, Beijing, as well as Yunnan provincial and prefecture government officials, have

been rapidly signing numerous trade agreements with the SPDC. Furthermore, Chinese fiscal incentives, encoded in various laws aimed at attracting investment, have been supported by the development of infrastructure to facilitate border trade. These roads and bridges, however, have done little more than pave the way for large-scale natural-resource extraction and the dumping of cheap Chinese goods. One Kachin activist laments, "The only thing the Kachin people get is roads to get the trees out."[18] This has outraged one Kachin religious leader, who shouts, "The roads are only for taking trees! They are not for the people!"[19] These roads not only enable resource extraction, but also act as a conduit for other commodities, such as drugs, as well as migrants and related social and public-health problems.

In 1991, when the provincial Kunming government designated Pianma Township—a provincial-level checkpoint in Lushui County, Nujiang Prefecture—as one of twelve Special Economic Zones, it became a "provincial level open port" for trade, and is now one of the busiest border-crossing points.[20] This merging of Chinese national and provincial policy with private business interests provided a crucial state-sponsored incentive for the logging boom, while at the same time, like many resource-extraction frontiers in the world, created a space of scant government regulation. For example, in Pianma Township there were only four legally registered logging companies in 2003, despite all of the smaller-scale companies operating along the border.[21] To encourage more logging companies along the border in other towns, local government authorities have opened "International Border Ports," but according to Global Witness, "these ports are simply logging roads."[22] Forest Trends estimates that between 800 and 950 sawmills that process Burmese timber are located along the China-Burma border.[23]

In Gongshan County, six Chinese logging companies paid the county government 1 million yuan (US$120,000) for the 2002–2003 period to extract timber from Burma via the Danzhu path, with a road recently built to help increase the timber flow.[24] In the early 1990s, the KIO and the Yunnan Forest Department in Kunming met to discuss the N'Mai Hku project, located within an area known as the "Triangle," a large territory mostly controlled by the KIO and situated between two major rivers (the N'Mai Hku and Mali Hka). Global Witness believes that "given the size of the project, its strategic importance and the level of investment, it is highly likely that the authorities in Beijing were also involved."[25] The Huaxin Group, based in Kunming, is an alliance of six companies from Kunming, Beijing, Shanghai, two from Guandong, and the Ministry of Railways, and has a contract to extract all timber resources from the lower Triangle area for fifteen years. According to

Huaxin, the cooperation of the Nujiang Prefecture authorities in Yunnan is crucial to the success of the project, as the county is a major partner through its control of land along the border.[26]

Burmese businessmen, backed by high-level SPDC officials and their military support, control more cease-fire logging concessions as they penetrate further into Kachin State. Control over logging operations has been devolved to key figures in the military, who in turn grant logging permits in SPDC-controlled areas to influential Burmese businessmen and companies for their support. In this way, the logging concessions act as a medium of exchange used to mutually support allies. The Burmese business partners then contract Chinese companies to do the actual logging as a joint venture to share the profits, with generous kickbacks to the SPDC top officials and the likelihood of more future collaboration. For example, Awng Mai Company, presumably a Chinese company with a Kachin-sounding name, received a teak-logging contract from SPDC's former northern military commander, General Ohn Myint, to log large tracts of forest along the Kachin State border from 2005 to 2009. In addition, the Htoo Trading Company obtained a logging concession in the beginning of 2006 in Bhamo district on the Chinese border in Kachin State. Htoo is owned by Tay Za, a Burmese millionaire who has very close relations with the SPDC's senior general, Than Shwe, including his recent marriage to the general's daughter.

Much of the logging in Kachin State involves the SPDC, so that Chinese companies, even if at times indirectly, are aiding the military regime to gain more control, territory, and income from granting logging concessions and taxing the trade. "As the Burmese government encroaches into [northern] Burma [due to the cease-fire agreements], the Chinese companies will have to cooperate with them."[27] As more territory comes under the control of the SPDC (about 60 percent of Kachin State) and ethnic elites submerge themselves into patron-client relationships with the central SPDC authorities at the capital, the regional SPDC authorities (northern military commander and his military associates), and local SPDC troops, the more the SPDC acts as a proxy for the conflict-timber trading. According to Global Witness, "The Northern Command and front-line Tatmadaw [military branch of SPDC] perform essential organising or facilitating roles and scant commercial resource extraction occurs in Kachin State without the SPDC, at different levels, being paid off."[28]

The following case study illustrates how the SPDC takes political and economic advantage of the increasingly globalized timber trade originating

in northern Burma by expanding their control over the cross-border timber trade, in cooperation with Chinese officials, thus pushing the Kachin out. While the timber trade has become more internationalized, it simultaneously becomes nationalized as both the Burmese regime and Chinese government steer the trade through their channels en route to international markets. The Burmese forest minister Brigadier-General Thein Aung finally publicly admitted, in January 2006, that timber was crossing the border into China without official SPDC permission. High-level SPDC officials and their business partners in Rangoon (Yangon) realized how much cash was bypassing their channels and was instead filling the pockets of Kachin businessmen and resistance groups as well as of local government officials along the border. The regime wants logging revenue to go exclusively through the state-owned Myanmar Timber Enterprise (MTE), the commercial arm of the forestry department, and their associates' timber-export businesses, which would not only make them wealthy, but also squeeze the KIO out of the timber business and thus weaken their political position against the regime. According to the SPDC, "legal" timber is that which is cut by the MTE and transported by the SPDC to either Rangoon and then shipped overseas or to cross into China at Muse (Burma-side)/Ruili (China-side), the only legal overland checkpoint with China. Thus "legal" timber translates into a *national* natural resource; that is, a resource owned by the military state.

The Chinese government decided they would respect Thein Aung's request to only support logging in Burma that is done by the SPDC. At the end of March 2006, the Yunnan provincial government, in cooperation with the Chinese People's Armed Police Force for Border Affairs, declared it illegal for Chinese to enter Burma for mining and logging purposes. "Every border checkpoint and workstation will stop transacting the approval for Chinese labour and transportation to Burma on the purpose of logging and mining. The timber and minerals being transported from Burma to China and the illegal action of leaving the country will be stopped as well."[29] Subsequently, the Chinese provincial government authorities began to clamp down on a few of the major border crossings.

The Chinese national government and provincial officials in Yunnan controlling the Ruili border trade will profit from collecting timber taxes since enforcement measures will try to cut off all timber coming over the border controlled by nongovernment parties. There is apparently only one Chinese company that has a legal contract with the SPDC to import logs along the Burmese border; and supposedly one company that can legally export across

the border (Awng Mai Co., allegedly owned by former northern military commander Ohn Myint). The "legalization" of logging in northern Burma equates to a national "militarization" of local Kachin forests.

CONFLICT TIMBER LINKING KACHIN TO THE
CHINESE GOVERNMENT AND BUSINESSMEN

Despite the recent effort by the SPDC and Chinese government to direct logging and its generated revenue into government channels, the Kachin businessmen and ethnic political leaders remain intimately involved in the logging trade. However, since the 2006 bilateral cross-border timber trade clamp down, their involvement continually decreases in competition with national government and businessmen. Those ethnic elite who maintain close relationships with those people who increasingly control the timber trade (for example, Burmese and Chinese officials or businessmen) will subsequently merge into the "legal" timber trade network. Many ethnic leaders in northern Burma have close connections to Chinese authorities and businessmen at the prefecture and district levels in Yunnan Province. Yunnan's Gongshan government has close relations with the Kachin political resistance group NDA-K, which controls the area across from Pianma on the Burmese side of the border. Ting Ying, the most senior NDA-K general, is ethnic Chinese but a Burmese citizen with a Kachin identity, and was born in Baoshan prefecture, Yunnan. Gao Liang is the director of the finance division for the NDA-K, with a representative office in Yunnan; he has reputedly made contracts with Chinese logging companies. Ting Ying and Gao Liang have made a lot of money and then invested it in their birthplace of Baoshan.[30] Their success is built on their relationships expanding beyond this locality into both the Burmese and Chinese governments and companies. According to one informant, the Chinese company needs to foster a relationship with someone who has control over the border, such as Ting Ying, in order to access the forest across the border; the best people to connect with are ethnic political leaders and powerful Burmese government officials. In order to meet these high-demand, high-level people, however, the Chinese must first meet a middleman in order to be brought to the person who administers concessions. Further research needs to be undertaken to examine the role of local Kachin and Shan brokers, or *jieshouren*, in introducing Chinese middlemen to Burmese concession-holders.[31] It is suspected that Chinese middlemen from previously out-competed smaller logging companies connect with local Kachin brokers, who in turn put them in contact with both Kachin headmen, to find a concession site, and regional elites, such as the

Kachin administrative unit or SPDC officials controlling that area, to get permission to log the concession.

Several interviews conducted in Kachin State in 2001 by Kachin field staff of Images Asia Environment Desk in Chiang Mai, Thailand, outline the process of Chinese companies connecting with Kachins. Buyers from China's east coast go to the Yunnan-Burma border to meet agents who then connect them with local Kachin logging-permit holders inside Kachin State, who were either granted permits from the political groups controlling that area, the SPDC, or at times, both. For example, local Kachin people request logging permits from the KIO administration office, which justifies giving out the permits as the method to bring development to their Kachin people.[32] According to 2001 data, each permit, issued by the KIO Trade Department, cost about 3,000 yuan (US$360), and after the trees are cut, another tax needs to be paid to the KIO, according to the volume of timber cut.[33] The complex logging concession process unfolds as follows.

> They [the KIO granting the concessions] divide the logging area by blocks. The local concessionaire pays the Chinese to cut the logs as workers, and the Chinese also build roads and transport the logs for the local concessionaire. Then the concessionaire sells the logs to the Chinese. After the concessionaire gets the money from selling the timber, he pays the [Chinese] people who cut the trees; he also has to pay for the road construction [done by the Chinese] to his logging area, and for the transport of the logs [also provided by the Chinese]. After cutting the trees, they weigh the logs at the KIO office. This station will check the logs and their prices and also determine the taxes to be levied. The Chinese come to this station to buy logs, and the local concessionaires also sell their logs there. The KIO collects a type of tax. They also collect taxes to undertake local development, such as building schools. In addition, the KIO collects another tax to support their army, the KIA.[34]

This does not equate, however, to any sort of stable condition wherein the "tickets" are always honored. The ethnic insurgencies in northern Burma have created a very unpredictable political situation with constantly shifting alliances within and among insurgent groups.

Territories in northern Burma are loosely controlled by various ethnic political groups, all of whom in Kachin State have already entered into a ceasefire agreement with the SPDC. Nevertheless, their control of territory often overlaps, and in some places is co-controlled with the SPDC. Therefore, in order to obtain a logging concession, a Chinese company must appease all

of those in loose control of the area and the transportation route to the border. It is, therefore, nearly impossible to separate ethnic involvement with SPDC control in natural-resource extraction. For instance, in the Triangle, in Kachin State, although the KIO controls most of the region, logs leaving this area going to the China border pass through NDA-K areas, where the logs and a number of trucks are subsequently taxed. The SPDC also taxes the logs passing through this area and has a checkpoint near the Jubilee Bridge at Magramyang Village.[35] The control of logging areas versus checkpoints can be reversed as well. Ethnic cease-fire groups controlling border checkpoints tax timber as it goes to Yunnan, but this timber sometimes does not even come from territories under the control of those ethnic political groups, as it is often cut in SPDC-controlled areas.

Timber Travels: From the Border to Beyond

They [Kachin] do not know how or where to sell the wood abroad, and that is why they sell the wood for a low price in the local area. . . . [S]o they have to sell to the Chinese companies, and the companies don't give them a good price for the wood—that is why they are suffering.

—Interview with retired KIO official in Kachin State by Kachin field staff for Images Asia Environment Desk, Chiang Mai, Thailand, 2001

FROM THE YUNNAN BORDER TO CHINA'S EASTERN SEABOARD

As China commits itself to unfettered economic growth, the timber industry has shifted toward concentrating on importing unprocessed forest products to match its mushrooming wood-manufacturing capacity. After the timber is transported across the border into Yunnan, another node of the commodity chain thus unfolds. Timber first travels from the border to Dali, and then to Kunming, the provincial capital of Yunnan, where it either undergoes further processing or simply awaits further transportation to China's eastern seaboard, mainly Guangdong Province or Shanghai. As the timber travels from rural Kachin villages to the eastern seaboard, there is a corresponding increase in organizational structure of the timber industry: from Kachin villages to small logging companies in Kachin State, to small-scale border-processing companies, to buyers and medium-sized companies for partial processing in Kunming, to wholesalers and large-scale processing companies along the eastern seaboard.[36] This new commodity-chain configuration for the Chinese tropical-timber trade is partly a response to greater timber industry liberalization, with the partial elimination of import and export licenses in 1999 and growing manufacturing specialization on the east coast.

The border and Kunming are connected to the eastern seaboard mostly through private family-run timber businesses propped up by relatives.[37] In most cases, buyers working for large-scale timber-processing companies come from outside of Yunnan, mostly from Guangdong Province, to strike deals with logging and processing companies and small- and large-scale sawmills along the border. The border company then arranges either for the timber to first undergo crude processing or for timber to be shipped directly to the company's own sawmills for value-added processing. Alternatively, processing companies or wholesalers make arrangements with larger sawmills to purchase high-quality sawnwood or finished products.[38] The Chinese business diaspora continues to fuel the timber trade and keep out Western competition by increasingly connecting the different production nodes through linkages that combine production, processing, and marketing networks.

The mixture of Burmese and domestic Chinese timber, as well as timber from other countries, in China's timber markets signals a major "place-erasure" step in the commodity chain. For example, the majority of "domestically produced timber" (*guochan cai*) from Yunnan is actually cross-border timber (*bianmao cai*) from Burma. Timber products produced in China but with Burmese timber are then labeled as *guochan* or *yunnan cai* (Yunnan timber). In fact, wood products using Burmese timber constitute about 30–40 percent of wholesale products in Chinese timber markets.[39] Thus, Burmese timber becomes, in the eyes of the consumer, Chinese timber during the shift from one node—extracting—to another node further down the commodity chain. It is this blinding of the true timber source that erases the conflict aspect of the timber, and thus makes the purchase by the distant consumer possible and indeed acceptable.

FROM CHINA'S EASTERN SEABOARD TO THE INTERNATIONAL TROPICAL-TIMBER MARKET

After the timber has been processed on China's eastern seaboard, the timber enters the international tropical-timber market, yet another node of the commodity chain. For this to happen, however, international firms and domestic Chinese companies must cooperate, or at times merge, as part of a joint investment. This "transnational alliance capitalism" is exactly what makes the cross-border timber trade financially viable.[40] The mounting demand for cheap wood-based products, especially furniture, in the developed world has prompted a reconfiguration in China's export-oriented forest industry. The result is a hybrid of domestic Chinese and international finance

corporations, often managed by overseas Chinese, who invest in Burmese timber logging, processing, and marketing all along the commodity chain. Taiwanese (perhaps the largest investor), Hong Kong, and Singaporean companies provide the majority of finance and corporate structure for the Yunnan-Burma border timber trade.[41] For example, of the forty furniture-production lines in Guangdong, about 80 percent are Taiwanese invested.[42] De Long Forest Resource Development, based in Xingjiang Province in northwest China, is a joint venture between Taiwanese and Japanese companies, worth 20 million yuan (US$2.5 million).[43] Another example is the largest sawmill in Liuku, the Nu Jian Hong Ta Chang Quing wood factory, which is the largest single investment along the border and a joint venture between a Malaysian company (60 percent) and the Chinese state-owned Hong Ta Group (40 percent). The company purchases most of its timber from the De Long company in Pianma and exports over 1,000 m³ of processed timber each month, of which much goes to Korea in the form of doors and window frames.[44]

China has become a re-exporter of finished wood-based products (mostly imported from Hong Kong) due to a host of events, such as forest-product tariff reductions in 1999 (to ensure a constant supply of timber after the Chinese logging ban in 1998), great improvements in domestic-manufacturing capacities, and the agglomeration of wood-based industries in key manufacturing hubs along the eastern seaboard. For instance, a substantial portion of timber products from Hong Kong imported into China have in fact been transshipped or processed and then re-exported.[45] China's re-exported timber products serve international tropical-timber demand, rather than domestic Chinese consumers.[46]

However, there is Chinese domestic consumption of Burmese timber. Domestic products made from high-value Burmese timber are mostly processed into veneers that overlay composite boards, since the former is expensive. Low-value timber is instead processed into solid wood products for domestic consumption.[47] China's population and increasing consumption patterns, especially for timber, give reason for concern. Burmese timber follows China's domestic demand by becoming a popular substitute for more expensive hardwoods because of its cheaper cross-border price. With China's aspiration to be rich, the tropical-timber market will become less directed by international markets, and instead follow domestic Chinese tropical-timber demand.

It would be easy to blame only China for the conflict-timber trade on the Yunnan border, but it must be stated clearly that the international tim-

ber and timber-product markets significantly influence Chinese logging in Burma. The largest Asian destinations for China's secondary processed wood products manufactured from Burmese timber are Taiwan, South Korea, and Japan, with the first being the largest importer, and lesser amounts exported to Malaysia and Thailand.[48] Hong Kong is the largest Asian importer of Chinese furniture (followed by Japan and South Korea), but this is misleading since 99 percent of Hong Kong's furniture exports were in effect re-exports from mainland China, and 70 percent of these exports were shipped to the United States.[49] If this is taken into account, then the United States would be the largest importer of Chinese wooden furniture. The United States is the largest importer of Chinese manufactured timber products in 2007, followed closely by the European Union, of which the United Kingdom is the top importer, capturing about one-third of all E.U. timber products imported from China. The other countries distantly trailing include Japan, Hong Kong, South Korea, and Taiwan, in that order.[50] According to the general manager of the American Forest and Paper Association's China office, the United States is certainly responsible for China's high timber imports, due to China-U.S. bilateral trade.[51]

Timber and wood-product imports into the G8 countries account for nearly two-thirds of the global timber trade, and about 50 percent of tropical-timber imports into the European Union are in fact illegal.[52] One reason for this is that it is still legal to import timber, even if it is illegal to import timber from the country of origin, into timber-consuming countries (including the G8 nations and China). This is because once the timber has been "substantially transformed" (for example, processed into wooden furniture), its designated country of origin becomes the country where the timber was processed, not where it was logged. As such, timber illegally logged in Burma and then processed into furniture in China is legally exported to Western countries despite existing embargoes against Burma. In this sense, the timber-extraction sites become hidden both by marketing gimmicks and by timber-import policies.

Frontier War Economies: Connecting Timber to Violence

Violence stems from existing power relations . . . the underlying causes of conflict lie in these unequal power relations and the resulting violence reinforces them.
—Catherine Brown, "The Political Economy of Violence"

Violence has been transformed, rather than terminated, following the cease-fires between the Kachin insurgent groups and the Burmese regime. The

cease-fires transformed conflict from brute force (i.e., "war violence") into both "structural violence" (i.e., violence embedded within economic, political, and religious structures) and "internal violence" (i.e., violence manifested within Kachin society and their representative political leadership).[53] Such structuralized violence has been channeled through "extractive development" (that is, development stemming from extracting natural resources) in Burma, which does not bring peace as purported by the Burmese regime and the Kachin elite who helped administer the cease-fires. Most Kachin believe that "the Burmese government is exploiting natural resources for their personal use and benefit—they put the money into banks; this is clear abuse."[54] Logging concessions coerce Kachin elites into cease-fires with the Burmese military regime, which results in the physical displacement of the Kachin from their land, widening economic inequalities, heightening ethnic disparity, and the carving out of denuded land—and in so doing, linking violence to environment. These concessions offer a valuable vantage point from which to analyze violent military territorialization.[55] Cease-fires cease to be about bringing peace and development to Kachin State, and operate instead as loss of resources for the majority and increasing wealth and corruption of the elite minority, which has already led to increased social and political unrest in Kachin State. "They [the SPDC] are not coming for the peace; I am afraid of a situation worse than before the cease-fire agreement."[56]

Conflict can be profitable by providing an alternative system of profit and clientism, for example, "war economies." Economic coercion transformed Burma's "frontiers" into sources of military revenue enacted through cease-fires, which dissolved the political boundary, but left behind a fermenting ethnic divide and growing resentment about the degraded environment. As such, Burma's political war economy operates such that warfare acts as an "instrument of enterprise and violence as a mode of accumulation."[57] The privatization and institutionalization of violence act as an exercise of power that allows elites to access resources through relations. Thus, "economic violence" is violence which accrues profit, a system in which "elites try to privatize conflict by exploiting the civilian economy."[58] This act of privatizing violence becomes especially prevalent in states without a strong state capacity for preventing elites from using violence for personal profit. In short, the economic benefits of violence may outweigh those of peace.

The SPDC incites conflict between the ethnic political groups as another way to weaken them—because if they are fighting each other, then they cannot organize against the government as effectively. For example, the NDA-K is currently expanding its logging activities into the southern Triangle since

most territory under their control has already been deforested of valuable species.[59] This is being done with the permission and possible encouragement of the SPDC, and with the cooperation of Yunnan's Tengchong County government, despite the fact that these areas were granted to the KIO as part of their cease-fire agreement. The result of this intrusion is greater animosity between the KIO and the NDA-K, which perhaps was SPDC's intended result.

Violence not only escalates among the ethnic political groups and the SPDC, but as well within ethnic political groups. According to a report investigating environmental-rights abuses in Burma, the conflict-timber trade has "played a key role in further dividing political opposition to the regime by financially rewarding certain groups at the expense of others."[60] Pillaging of natural resources in cease-fire areas by the respective ethnic political groups has led to increased corruption from rent-seeking activities and has thus subverted the functional and political capacity of the ethnic groups. The ethnic political groups, especially the KIO, have lost political direction, unity, strong leadership, and committed followers since the rampant wholesale of their natural resources that has taken place since they signed the cease-fire agreement.

The denuded landscapes and political disunity act as potential sources of renewed social and political turmoil for the Kachin. Many Kachin people have blamed their political leaders for forcing their society into their current cease-fire situation and its resulting economic and social marginalization and environmental destruction, despite the obvious benefits of ending open warfare. "It is difficult to consider the KIO as good leaders for us, because they made an agreement with the SPDC; but no benefits from the agreement have come to our community."[61]

Several coups within the KIO and NDA-K have occurred since 2001, spurred by jealousy resulting from ethnic political leaders sealing close ties to Chinese businessmen from Yunnan and offering plentiful logging concessions to them. Disputes between and within the KIO and NDA-K have in part been triggered by the desire for control over logging revenue and territorial control of the remaining areas with valuable timber, especially in the Triangle. The attempted internal coups and external attacks on Kachin political leaders and cease-fire groups signal a recurrence of Kachin political conflict. Logging business interests have led to strife both among and within ethnic political groups, which in turn has aggravated political and social instability in Kachin State.

The Forgotten Landscape: Local Kachin Livelihoods

After the cease-fire agreement, many companies came [into Kachin State]; the SPDC created private property and kicked the Kachin people out.
—Interview with Kachin youth in Kachin State, 2003

A new power struggle has emerged, further marginalizing local Kachin villagers at the expense of patron-client networks involving the SPDC, Kachin leaders, and Chinese businessmen. The civil-war situation in Kachin State created conditions in which more marginalized sections of Kachin society were able to access resources and integrate themselves into a peripheral insurgent economy. As the Burmese junta gains further control over previously hostile areas, the Kachin villagers are pushed out of their local resource-extraction networks to make way for the SPDC and their business partners. Philippe Le Billon outlines a similar process in Cambodia, where the marginalized lose economic maneuverability during the "political ecology of transition." "The illegal character of logging shaped this ordering and reduced the share of profits for many of the less powerful groups, as people in positions of power—high-ranking officials and military commanders—were able to extract large benefits for turning a blind eye, protecting, or even organizing these activities." [62] For Kachin State, the political ecology of cease-fires illustrates this transition from war to cease-fire peace, and how this relates to a corresponding shift from marginal villager participation to exclusion from natural-resource access and extraction.

Village headmen have lost autonomy but have expanded their own patron-client networks since the cease-fires, being now under the administrative control of local KIO offices that were established in post-cease-fire Kachin State. The head of the village committee, who is often appointed by the KIO, not the villagers, asks the KIO for permission to sell off their land for logging by Chinese companies in order to generate money for schools, electricity, and water pipes. "The village committee doesn't say no to logging, they don't know about the forest, they only know money," while "the villagers can't say anything because the committee has the authority." [63] Thus, while it remains unclear how much influence the local villagers have in protecting their own land from outside loggers, the village headmen seem to be very willing to exchange their land for expensive electricity and water pipes, and of course, a large private commission for administering the deal.

Chinese companies, through their logging contracts with local Kachin leaders, have gained more power and authority in Kachin State, such that

the companies, supported by Kachin political leadership, often kick out villagers in the area so that they can extract the timber. "The area is controlled by the KIO. It is a very new logging area and the KIO issued an announcement that people are not allowed in the area."[64] Local inhabitants are also frequently removed from logging areas by the military. As another person explained, "Whenever they do logging, a lot of soldiers come around our village and they go everywhere. They go deeply into the jungle, they force the local villagers to move to town and then destroy their houses."[65] Keeping the forests off-limits to local Kachin takes away their livelihoods by denying them access to forest products and non-timber-forest products, which they rely on for supplemental income and food. The Chinese workers bring in most of their own food and hunt in the forests for meat, thus limiting any trading with the local Kachin while also killing off wildlife. Very little timber processing, other than some crude sawmilling, occurs in Kachin State along the Burma side of the border, thus offering only marginal employment opportunities for Kachin people.

The KIO sometimes sells traditional village forests, or permits villagers to sell it themselves, to pay for basic services such as electricity from China and piped water. "Because of the prices of road construction and electricity are high (1.2 yuan/kilowatt) the villagers have to sell off their forests; for electricity for one village they have to pay 30,000 yuan (US$3,615). So the Chinese got concessions from the villagers, but the land given away by the villagers is just enough to exchange for the electricity."[66]

Logging roads are built, with a trail of tree stumps and muddy rivers, prostitution, HIV/AIDS, drug abuse, and gambling brought by migrants left in their wake.[67] United Nations Office on Drug Control (UNODC) regional director Akira Fujino attributed the increase in [opium] production in Kachin State in part to rampant deforestation and the corresponding influx of more sophisticated opium farmers and techniques.[68] Just one environmental catastrophe thought to be linked to rampant logging occurred in July 2004, when the Irrawaddy River flooded—reportedly the worst flooding in thirty years. The environmental destruction in Kachin State will have a direct negative impact on the people of Kachin State, since those living in the few nonurban areas rely on the health of forest ecosystems for their day-to-day survival.

> Even in summer the Mung Lai River in Laiza [KIO headquarters] used to be very deep and to cross the river was difficult. But now the river only comes up to the knee. The Laiza stream [another stream] is also the same.

In the past, we can drink the water from Laiza stream, it was very clean and clear, but now on the upstream part of the stream logging is being done as well as road construction through the forest, so the stream has become muddy. It is not good for the next generation.[69]

These ecological concerns are also reflected in the following observation, made by a pastor: "Villagers are very worried now, even the small logs are going, so that in ten years there will be no wood for them to build houses, barns and hoes, and the water will slowly dry up."[70]

Local Kachin people lose land to the cease-fire logging-concession areas, and have no legal recourse to voice concerns. Local SPDC and cease-fire groups, for example, frequently require local people to purchase a "permit" to farm their own fields, harvest timber and non-timber forest products, and undertake informal trading. When the land has coveted natural resources, such as valuable hardwoods, different "permits" are sold to businesses. In exchange, the military units and cease-fire groups impose a tax. Villagers do not possess official papers proving their ownership of the land, and they do not have the funds to purchase any permits. Neither do they have the political leverage to make deals with the local elite, and thus they are forced off their land.[71] Local Kachin are also further marginalized from their own land by being physically moved down from the mountains to the roads to be re-settled into larger, controlled villages, the reason ostensibly being to protect the forest from shifting cultivation. This is despite the fact that these areas often soon become logging concessions.[72]

Even for the few Kachin who participate in the logging industry, life can be very difficult. Having lost their financial security, they are now dependent on the unstable cash economy. A Kachin youth who has experienced this firsthand explains this difficult transition.

I didn't know that after they cut the trees, everything is quite expensive. Before, we can survive on my mother's salary. After that we can't survive on her salary. We can see the situation changing day by day . . . hard to survive for even one day. Now it is difficult—my father is a buyer/trader before—now he can't survive with that and he is now in the forest doing the logging for the last 2 years. Logging can't get much money—because you have to pay to the Burmese, the workers, machines and the gates [checkpoints].[73]

For all of the reasons outlined in this essay, one Kachin elder Baptist leader agrees "the environment is the most important issue in Kachin State right

now."[74] One Kachin environmentalist pushes this view further in believing that "environmental damage is furthering [Kachin] nationalism in Kachin State."[75] The increasing ecological destruction in Kachin State, intricately tied to the ethnic political crisis in Kachin State, thus provides an environmental platform for an "ethno-ecological" resistance.

Conclusion

The global commodity-chain approach, from the logging sites in Kachin State to the tropical-timber consumers, helps to highlight the underlying conditions of the trade. The GCC analysis helped reveal some of the socio-cultural and political elements embedded within the China-Burma timber trade: the Chinese trade-relation networks stretching from Asian financial centers to China's eastern seaboard to the border; the political ecology of war embedded along the Kachin State-Yunnan border; the Burmese regime attempting to gain greater control of the increasingly globalized overland timber trade; and the structural violence inflicted on Kachin villagers as a result of the burgeoning trade. Examining the different nodal points along the commodity chain enables one to travel beyond the border, to situate outside a statist, "legal" analysis, and into a more locally nuanced, globalized perspective. Chinese domestic businessmen in search of logs, supported by regional financial centers with investment capital, pried open a broader transnational cease-fire space to enable them to integrate more with northern Burma's timber-extraction networks for the purpose of securing logging concessions. In this essay I have revealed the elements that support this transnational logging trade, with transborder patron-client relationships, transnational alliance capital, and international consumer desires radiating from and penetrating the border—all in all, a truly awesome global game.

Before the cease-fire agreements in Kachin State, the small-scale timber trade remained more within local and traditional Kachin networks. This is not to say that historical pre-cease-fire trading did not spread beyond the Kachin communities; Eric Tagliacozzo describes how local villagers in Northwest Borneo, despite living within geopolitical margins, became firmly grounded within global networks through trading high-demand forest products.[76] The cease-fires, however, expanded the scale on which cross-border trading operated, both in terms of volume extracted and destinations reached, further marginalizing local Kachin traders in the process. The cease-fires in Kachin State forged new political space, offered financial incentives, and shifted minjian, which enabled the SPDC, Chinese business-

men from the eastern seaboard, the Chinese government, and international finance corporations to reach deeper into Kachin State to accelerate timber extraction by linking it to the global timber trade. Several Chinese factors have overhauled the local war economy into a more globalized form. These are China's partially liberalizing economy (including forest-product tariff reductions), improved manufacturing specialization capacity on China's eastern seaboard, China's partial ban on domestic logging, cheap Chinese migrant labor, a lack of Chinese government regulation, and a transportation infrastructure stretching from China's coast.

These circumstances in effect reshape local Kachin natural resources into transnational resources. However, Chinese local and national governments and the Burmese regime have recently been clamping down on the cross-border timber trade to ensure national control of logging and its generated revenue. Underneath the mounting national control of the transnational timber trade, however, Kachin political resistance groups contest their loosening grip on the extraction networks as they continue to fight for their autonomy and fund their armies. Tension thus exists among Kachin villagers, Kachin political leaders, national and local government authorities on both sides of the China-Burma border, and Chinese and international businessmen, but this tension to some extent eases through profit-sharing. All of these different players collude and collide over quick profits from selling and buying tracts of forests in Kachin State, at the expense of Kachin villagers.

"Transnational alliance capital" carries the capital necessary to ignite the commodity chain, enabling large multinational corporations based in East and Southeast Asian finance centers to connect North American and European tropical-timber consumers with tropical trees from northern Burma. Transportation and digital infrastructure glue these unlikely allies together. The inherent violence in this conflict zone becomes erased as the commodity becomes globalized as a product to be consumed. Regardless, those involved in the trade, including the consumers, leave their large and heavy footprint along the Kachin State-Yunnan border. Although much of the Burmese timber is destined for international markets, the Chinese businessmen, supported by their nation's policies and liberalizing economy, help to make this a "China problem" as well. And as Chinese strive to be modern capitalists in industrial cities, the conflict border timber trade will increasingly serve domestic Chinese demands, rather than just those of their international consumer companions.

Notes

1. The current regime in power, the SPDC, changed the country's official name to Myanmar in June 1989. Although this name is recognized by the United Nations, ethnic minority groups and Burma activists refuse to accept this name; for this essay I will refer to the country as Burma. However, I retain the name that authors use in the quotes that I cite.

2. Focusing only on Kachin State excludes data from Shan State border regions, as well as government timber traveling through Yangon en route to global destinations. Although limiting the scope of analysis to begin only after the cease-fires of the 1990s does not provide much pre-cease-fire historical context of the trade, it makes the essay more manageable and allows for an understanding of where the current timber trade is headed.

3. Elaine Hartwick, "Geographies of Consumption: A Commodity-Chain Approach," *Environment and Planning D: Society and Space* 16 (1998): 425. For literature examining the commodity-chain approach, see Gary Gereffi and Miguel Korzeniewicz, eds., *Commodity Chains and Global Capitalism* (Westport, Conn.: Greenwood, 1994); and for how this analysis may relate to natural resources, refer to Paul Gellert, "Renegotiating a Timber Commodity Chain: Lessons from Indonesia on the Political Construction of Global Commodity Chains," *Sociological Forum* 18.1 (2003): 53–84.

4. Andy White et al., "China and the Global Market for Forest Products; Transforming Trade to Benefit Forests and Livelihoods," *Forest Trends* (March 2006): 4.

5. Fredrich Kahrl, Horst Weyerhaeuser, and Su Yufang, "Navigating the Border: An Analysis of the China-Myanmar Timber Trade," World Agroforestry Center, *Forest Trends* (2004): 1.

6. Global Witness, "China Must Act on Pledge to End Illegal Burmese Timber Imports," press release, 8 March 2006.

7. Fredrich Kahrl, Horst Weyerhaeuser, and Su Yufang, "Navigating the Border," 7.

8. Global Witness, *A Choice for China: Ending the Destruction of Burma's Northern Frontier Forests* (London: 2005), 9.

9. Ibid., 9. According to this report, with timber costing an average of US$250 per cubic meter, illegal exports in recent years would be worth over US$200 million annually. However, "illegal" timber may be misleading in the context of Burma which has no rule of law, with "legal" being defined as that timber which is under the complete control of the military regime.

10. Ibid, 9.

11. See analysis in Fredrich Kahrl, Horst Weyerhaeuser, and Su Yufang, "Navigating the Border"; and White et al., "China and the Global Market for Forest Products; Transforming Trade to Benefit Forests and Livelihoods."

12. Mya Maung, *The Burma Road to Capitalism: Economic Growth versus Democracy* (Westport: Praeger, 1998), 209.

13. Wen-Chin Chang uses an equivalent Chinese term, *minjian*, to mean the "unofficial

connections interacting with and reacting against the state bureaucracy" (see Chang's essay in this volume, 460).

14. Interview with Kachin school headmaster along the China-Burma border, 2004.

15. See Wen-Chin Chang's essay in this volume, 455–79. According to her analysis, the jade trade appears to remain more embedded with Kachin-Yunnan networks than the timber trade due to the lack of demand for jade outside of Asia, whereas the timber from Burma mostly serves the demand of Western consumers.

16. Wood processed along China's eastern seaboard is often shipped to Hong Kong to undergo further processing and manufacturing.

17. Elizabeth Economy, "China's Go West Campaign: Ecological Construction or Ecological Exploitation," *China Environment Series* 5 (2002): 1–12.

18. Interview with Kachin youth social activist in Kachin State, 2003.

19. Interview, 2003.

20. Across the border from China's Pianma lies Burma's Datainba in Kachin Special Region 1, which is nominally controlled by the NDA-K as part of their cease-fire deal, with various cease-fire logging concessions administered in the region.

21. Fredrich Kahrl, Horst Weyerhaeuser, and Su Yufang, "Navigating the Border," 33.

22. Global Witness, *A Conflict of Interests: The Uncertain Future of Burma's Forests* (London: 2003), 85.

23. Fredrich Kahrl, Horst Weyerhaeuser, and Su Yufang, "An Overview of the Market Chain for China's Timber Product Imports from Myanmar," *Forest Trends* (2005): 4.

24. Global Witness, *A Choice for China*, 42.

25. Ibid, 66.

26. Ibid, 66–67.

27. Interview with Chinese academic in Kunming, 2004.

28. Global Witness, *A Choice for China*, 56.

29. Xinhua News Agency, "Yunnan Frontier Defense Brigade Takes Actions to Ensure the Yunnan-Burma Timber and Mineral Trading Cooperation," 28 March 2006.

30. Interview with Chinese academic in Kunming, 2004.

31. See Wen-Chin Chang's essay in this volume for an examination of how *jieshouren* relates to the jade trade originating from Burma.

32. Interview with KIO development officer along the China-Burma border, 2004.

33. Interview with retired KIO official in Kachin State, 2001, by Kachin field staff for Images Asia Environment Desk, Chiang Mai, Thailand.

34. Ibid.

35. Global Witness, *A Choice for China*, 61.

36. Fredrich Kahrl, Horst Weyerhaeuser, and Su Yufang, "An Overview of the Market Chain for China's Timber Product Imports from Myanmar," 1–2.

37. Ibid, 4.

38. Fredrich Kahrl, Horst Weyerhaeuser, and Su Yufang, "Navigating the Border," 25.

39. Fredrich Kahrl, Horst Weyerhaeuser, and Su Yufang, "An Overview of the Market Chain for China's Timber Product Imports from Myanmar," 15.

40. I borrow the phrase "transnational alliance capital" from Gellert, "Renegotiating a Timber Commodity Chain," 56.

41. Fredrich Kahrl, Horst Weyerhaeuser, and Su Yufang, "Navigating the Border," 24.

42. Fredrich Kahrl, Horst Weyerhaeuser, and Su Yufang, "An Overview of the Market Chain for China's Timber Product Imports from Myanmar," 16.

43. Global Witness, A Conflict of Interests, 86.

44. Ibid, 49.

45. T. Castren, "Timber Trade and Wood Flow Study: Myanmar," technical paper commissioned for the Asian Development Bank's Regional Environmental Technical Assistance 5771 Poverty Reduction and Environmental Management in Remote Greater Mekong Subregion (GMS) Watersheds Project (Phase I) (Helsinki: Regional Environmental Technical Assistance 5771, 1999), http://www.mekonginfo.org/.

46. Despite China's high demand for timber, its average timber consumption is only 0.12 m³/person/year, less than one-fifth the global average. Consumption in the United States is almost twenty times this figure, making Americans the world's largest consumers of wood products per capita.

47. Fredrich Kahrl, Horst Weyerhaeuser, and Su Yufang, "An Overview of the Market Chain for China's Timber Product Imports from Myanmar," 18.

48. This analysis is based on Fredrich Kahrl, Horst Weyerhaeuser, and Su Yufang, "Navigating the Border"; and Fredrich Kahrl, Horst Weyerhaeuser, and Su Yufang, "An Overview of the Market Chain for China's Timber Product Imports from Myanmar."

49. Fredrich Kahrl, Horst Weyerhaeuser, and Su Yufang, "An Overview of the Market Chain for China's Timber Product Imports from Myanmar," 19.

50. White et al., "China and the Global Market for Forest Products; Transforming Trade to Benefit Forests and Livelihoods," 10.

51. Peter Kammerer, "Timber Trade's Unkindest Cut," South China Morning Post, 11 November 2003.

52. This analysis is based on Global Witness, A Conflict of Interests; and Global Witness, A Choice for China.

53. Before the cease-fires, the SPDC used a military tactic known as the "Four Cuts Policy," which involved the explicit intention of depriving opposition groups of food, funds, recruits, and intelligence.

54. Interview with Kachin Baptist leader in Kachin State, 2003.

55. Logging concessions alter the geopolitical space through "territorialization," or an "attempt by an individual or group to affect, influence, or control people, phenomena, and relationships by delimiting and asserting control over a geographic area" (see Peter Vandergeest and Nancy Peluso, "Territorialization and State Power in Thailand," Theory and Society 24 [1995]: 385–426).

56. Interview with Kachin school headmaster along the China-Burma border, 2004.

57. William Reno, "Shadow States and the Political Economy of Civil Wars," Greed and Grievance: Economic Agendas in Civil Wars, ed. Mats Berdal and David Malone (Ottawa: International Development Research Centre, 2000), 57.

58. David Keen, "The Economic Functions of Violence in Civil Wars," *Adelphi Paper* 320 (Oxford: Oxford University Press, 1998), 24–25.

59. Interview with a retired KIO official in Kachin State, 2002, by Kachin field staff for Images Asia Environment Desk, Chiang Mai, Thailand.

60. Ken MacLean, *Capitalizing on Conflict: How Logging and Mining Contribute to Environmental Destruction in Burma* (Chang Mai, Thailand: Earth Rights International and Karen Environmental and Social Action Network, 2003).

61. Interview with Kachin Baptist elder leader in Kachin State, 2003.

62. Philippe Le Billon, "The Political Ecology of Transition in Cambodia 1989–1999: War, Peace and Forest Exploitation," *Development and Change* 31 (2000): 791–92.

63. Interview with Kachin villager in Kachin State, 2002 by Kachin field staff for Images Asia Environment Desk, Chiang Mai, Thailand.

64. Pan Kachin Development Society and Karen Environmental and Social Action Network, *Destruction and Degradation of the Burmese Frontier Forests: Listening to the People's Voices,* ed. Searchweb (Amsterdam: Kaboem, 2004).

65. Global Witness, *A Conflict of Interests,* 55.

66. Interview with Kachin Baptist pastor along the China-Burma border, 2002, by Kachin field staff for Images Asia Environment Desk, Chiang Mai, Thailand.

67. For instance, Kachin State has the highest rate of HIV/AIDS infections in Burma; in Myitkyina Township 90 percent of male intravenous drug users have HIV/AIDS (Global Witness, *A Choice for China,* 17).

68. Deutsche Presse-Agentur, "Deforestation in Myanmar Facilitates Opium Cultivation," 1 November 2005.

69. Interview with an elder KIO officer in Kachin State, 2001, by Kachin field staff for Images Asia Environment Desk, Chiang Mai, Thailand.

70. Interview with an elder Kachin Baptist pastor in Kachin State, 2002, by Kachin field staff for Images Asia Environment Desk, Chiang Mai, Thailand.

71. MacLean, *Capitalizing on Conflict,* 12.

72. Global Witness, *A Choice for China,* 60.

73. Interview with a young Kachin villager in Kachin State, 2002, by Kachin field staff for Images Asia Environment Desk, Chiang Mai, Thailand.

74. Interview with Kachin elder Baptist leader in Kachin State, 2003, by Kachin field staff for Images Asia Environment Desk, Chiang Mai, Thailand.

75. Interview with Kachin environmentalist in Kachin State, 2003, by Kachin field staff for Images Asia Environment Desk, Chiang Mai, Thailand.

76. See Eric Tagliacozzo's essay in this volume.

CONTRIBUTORS

Leonard **Blussé** is a professor of history at Leiden University, The Netherlands.

Wen-Chin **Chang** is an associate research fellow at the Center for Asia-Pacific Area Studies, RCHSS, Academia Sinica, Taiwan.

Lucille **Chia** is an associate professor of history at the University of California, Riverside.

Bien **Chiang** is an associate research fellow at the Institute of Ethnology, Academia Sinica, Taiwan.

Nola **Cooke** is a visiting fellow at the College of Asia and the Pacific, The Australian National University.

Jean **DeBernardi** is a professor of anthropology at the University of Alberta, Canada.

C. Patterson **Giersch** is an associate professor of history at Wellesley College.

Takeshi **Hamashita** is a professor emeritus at Tokyo University.

Kwee Hui Kian is an assistant professor of history at the University of Toronto.

Li Tana is a senior fellow at the School of Culture, History, and Languages, The Australian National University.

Man-houng **Lin** is president of the Academia Historica, Taiwan.

Masuda Erika is a postdoctoral researcher at the Center for Asia-Pacific Area Studies, Academia Sinica, Taiwan.

Adam **McKeown** is an associate professor of history at Columbia University.

Anthony **Reid** is a professor emeritus of the Department of Political and Social Change at the College of Asia and the Pacific, The Australian National University.

Sun Laichen is an associate professor of history at California State University, Fullerton.

Heather **Sutherland** is a professor emeritus of the departments of anthropology history at Vrije University, The Netherlands.

Eric **Tagliacozzo** is an associate professor of history at Cornell University.

Carl A. **Trocki** is a professor of Asian studies in the Humanities Program, Queensland University of Technology, Australia.

Wang Gungwu is University Professor at National University of Singapore, and professor emeritus at The Australian National University.

Kevin **Woods** is a doctoral student in environmental science, policy, and management at the University of California, Berkeley.

Wu Xiao An is a professor of history at Peking University.

Note: *Italicized page numbers indicate figures, maps, and tables.*

Bajo (*continued*)

status of, 197n61; routes of, 175; turtle-catching of, 179–80, 187

Bali: coin circulation in, 138, 139, 147n58; cotton trade of, 286

bamboo network, 173

Bangka islands: Bible distribution and, 386; location of, 87; opium trade and, 86, 88, 90, 93; tin mining of, 28–30, 32, 93; tin of, in junk cargoes, 248–54

Banjarmasin: junk visits and fairs at, 234–36; tin mining of, 93; tortoise-shell trade of, 183, 185, 190; VOC post at, 189

baoshi (rubies, sapphires, tourmaline): factors in popularity of, 204–6, 215; *feicui* overtaking sales of, 212–14; list of, 208–9; terminology and classifications of, 8, 207. *See also* gem trade

Batavia: attempts to control junk trade in, 223–24, 235–37; birds' nests collection near, 408; coin circulation of, 138–39; cotton trade and, 287, 289; customs, safe-conduct fees, and poll taxes collected in, 229; decline of trade influence, 236, 247; junk cargoes for, 136–37, 230; junk cargoes in, 1750–1759 (statistics), 237, 238–44, 244–45; junk cargoes' arrival at, 225–26, 234; junk trade data from, 226; marine-products trade of, 178, 181, 434–35; massacre at (1741), 234; missionaries and Bible distribution in, 385–87; opium trade and, 84–85, 101; redemption fees on junk cargoes at, 227–28, 227; tin trade and, 28; trade routes including, 8, 87, 93. *See also* Verenigde Oostindische Compagnie (VOC)

batiks and batikking, 284–96

Bausum, Johann Georg, 387–88

Begbie, P. J., 30

Bello, David A., 85, 101

Benavides, Miguel de, 280n27

bencharong (royal Thai porcelain), 157, 168n32

benevolent neutrality, 68

BFBS. *See* British and Foreign Bible Society

Bible distribution: area discussed, 303; beliefs underlying, 381–83, 399–400; British fund-raising for, 380, 383, 388, 390–92, 395–98, 399; context of, 380–81; Delegates Version New Testament in, 381, 388–90; summary of, 11, 396–400; Taiping Rebellion and BFBS Jubilee Year appeal in, 380–81, 390–95; translation, printing, and distribution in, 383–88. *See also* books and printing trade; printing technologies

Billon, Philippe Le, 498

birds' nests. *See* edible birds' nests (*yen-wo*) trade

Blancas de San José, 265–67, 279n18

Blue, Gregory, 3

Blussé, Leonard: on birds' nest trade, 408–10, 417

Bonham, George, 72

books and printing trade (Chinese in Philippines): area discussed, 201; audience for, 262; Chinese books sought by Spanish, 271–74; context of, 259–60; description of, 260–63, 265–74; examples of, 261, 264, 270, 272–73; missionary's translations and works, 260–63, 261, 264, 265–68; movable-type printing preferred and used, 265–67; papers used, 278n10; price of books, 262, 265, 278n10; printer's colophon and name, 270–71, 271, 281n39; Siamese translation of Chinese literature, 159–60, 169n41; song collections in chapbook form, 270–71, 270–73, 282n42; summary of, 9, 274–76; theatrical performances and

written plays, 269, 273; title page and authorship, 263, 264, 265; typical page of, 261, 277n8; Western innovations in, 261–62. See also Bible distribution; printing technologies

Boomgaard, Peter, 283, 295–96

Borneo: cotton trade of, 289–90; goldfields of, 25–26; marine-products trade of, 436, 445; mining frontier of, 22–25; name and history of, 416–17. See also Banjarmasin; Sarawak State

Bowring, John, 70–71, 169n40

Bradley, Dan Beach, 31–32

Braudel, Fernand, 1

Brethren missionaries, 387

British and Foreign Bible Society (BFBS): Delegates Version New Testament and, 388–90; founders of, 382–83; goals of, 380–81, 383–84, 397; Million Testament Fund drive of, 380, 383, 388, 390–92, 395–98, 399; Taiping Rebellion and Jubilee Year appeal of, 380–81, 390–95; translation, printing, and distribution under, 383–87

British Malaya: government policy on paddy cultivation in, 344–46; imports of, 338–39; opium-rice-labor nexus in, 336–38; rice combine (hierarchy) in, 341–44, 342–45; rice export duty in, 349–52, 351; rice millers and government in, 346–47, 347; rice millers and peasantry of, 338, 352–54; rice milling in, 340–41, 354–55; rice price in, 347–49. See also Singapore; Straits Settlements

British merchants: Dutch challenged by, 223; opium trade of, 85–86, 89–90; Singapore trading center of, 92–95; tin trade of, 28; tortoiseshell trade of, 180–81. See also British Malaya; Great Britain; Hong Kong; Singapore

bronze age, 21–22, 140

Brook, Timothy, 3

Brown, Catherine, 495

Bugis merchants: Chinese junk trade linked to, 236; junk trade, generally, 228; marine-products trade of, 190; Singapore central to, 94; tin trade of, 28; tortoiseshell trade of, 181, 183–86, 188–89; trade routes of, 178

building material imports (Siam), 156–57. See also conflict timber trade

Burma (Myanmar): British seizure of (Upper), 55; cease fires signed in, 480–82; Chinese campaign against, 165n6; circulation patterns in, 39–41; cotton (and silk) circulation of, 48–55; democracy movement in, 486–87; gem trade of, 203–7, 208–9, 210–16; informal business sector in, 484; jade miners and mine ownership in, 464–66; king's title in, 215–16; local livelihoods and political power in, 498–501; maps of, 201, 405, 456, 481; marine-products trade of, 436, 441, 442, 443; mining frontier of, 24; name of, 503n1; personalized and reciprocal transactions in, 466–69; rice exports of, 336, 339–40; socialist period in, summarized (1962–1998), 459; timber, violence, and economics linked in, 495–97; timber exports to China (overview), 483–84; tin production of, 28; Yunnanese migrants in jade trade of, 457–63, 466–75, 475n3, 477n21. See also conflict timber trade; jade trade; Kachin State; State Peace and Development Council

Burns, Islay, 304–95, 403n51

Burns, William Chalmers, 392, 394–95

Buton (sultanate): ignored by traders, 183; location of, 175; tortoiseshell trade of, 185–86; trepang trade of, 198n78

conflict timber trade (*continued*)
  ing from Yunnan border to China's
  eastern seaboard, 492–93; national
  and local promotion of, 486–90;
  parties to, 483; patron-client networks
  in, 484–92; political context of, 480–
  82; summary of, 12–13, 501–2; violence
  linked to, 495–97
Confucian classics: Protestant attitudes
  toward, 397; translation of, 262–63,
  276–77n5
consumer goods: global commodity-
  chain approach to, 12–13, 482–83;
  opium as prime, 100–101; timber demanded as, 484, 493–95. *See also* commodities; commodity trade; *specific
  commodities*
contract service, labor as: labor as commodity and, 63–64; vocabulary about,
  66–70. *See also* Chinese migrant labor;
  indentures; labor as commodity
coolie trade: approach to, 5; assumptions
  about, 66–67; migrant labor distinguished from, 74–75. *See also* Chinese
  migrant labor; indentures; labor as
  commodity
copper: amount (by tons), 43; coins of,
  131, 140; cost in Cochinchina, 144n14;
  purchases and shipments of, 43–45;
  shortages of, 42
copper mining: charcoal for smelting,
  45–46; Chinese merchants' control
  and, 47; coin casting and control of,
  131; frontier of, 24–25; merchant associations' role in, 50; money supply
  and, 41–44; population growth and,
  47–48; production levels of, 43; state
  policies on, 42–43, 48; urbanization
  and infrastructure development due
  to, 46
copper to zinc ratio, 144n13
copper trade: area discussed, 19; descrip-

tion of, 41–48; geographic, demographic, and economic contexts of,
  37–41; post-1870s changes in, 53–55;
  provincial mints in, 43–45; summary
  of, 4, 55–57; tax regulation on, 143n8.
  See also coin business
core-periphery model: commodity-chain
  analysis in, 173–74; Ryukyu tribute
  system in, 125–27; Yunnan Province in,
  37, 38, 47, 47–48
cotton trade: description of, 48–52; development and organization of Javanese, 284–89, 291–95; Dutch intervention in, 289–91; geographic,
  demographic, and economic contexts
  of, 37–41; industrialization and questions about, 283–84; merchant associations' role in, 49–50; post-1870s
  changes in, 53–55; prices of Javanese
  goods, 289–90; summary of, 4, 55–57,
  295–96
Crawfurd, John: on coin casting, 139,
  147n58; on Siamese and trade, 164n1;
  on Siamese ceremonies, 160–61; on
  Singapore trade, 94; on textile trade, 49
cultural ties in economic relations: area
  discussed, *303*; concept of, 305; essentializations of, 3; immigration and,
  306–7, *307–9*, 309–12; investment
  and, 312–14; Manchukuo investment
  and, 317; passport system and, 309,
  318–22, 321; politics and economics as
  trumping, 322–25; public works investment and, 314–16; summary of, 10,
  325–28; trade and networks based on,
  317–18. *See also* capital and investment
Curtin, Philip D., 1, 2, 447
Cushman, Jennifer Wayne, 98–99, 153

Dampier, William, 25
Dang Ngoai. *See* Tonkin
Dang Trong. *See* Cochinchina

Daxia (Bactria), Han communication records on, 455–57, 475n1
deforestation, 45–46, 497, 499
Dhiravat na Pombejra, 153, 167n47
diasporas: analytical approach to, 1–2, 172; culture accompanying, 259–60; current preoccupations with, 173; language issues in studying, 13–14. *See also* Chinese merchants; Chinese migrants, generally; migration
diseases: Chinese miners killed by, 24, 33; efficacy of birds' nests as cures, 411–16; HIV/AIDS rates, 506n67; opium as hiding symptoms of, 89
Dobbin, Christine E., 2
doctrinas christiana (books): blockprinted edition of, 263, 264, 265, 268; colloquial version of, 279n16; contents and reprints of, 278–79n14; price of, 268; romanized script for, 267, 280n27
domestic transit duty (*lijin, likin*), 54–55
Do Van Ninh, 131
Dupuis, J., 51–52
Dutch merchants: commodities focused on, 86; iron goods purchased by, 23; marine-products trade of, 434–35; opium smoking spread by, 85; tin trade of, 28, 29–30; zinc and tin purchased from, 135. *See also* Batavia; Netherlands; Verenigde Oostindische Compagnie (VOC)

Earl, George Windsor, 33, 225–26
early colonial period: approaches to, 8–9; areas discussed, 201. *See also* books and printing trade; gem trade; junk cargoes; textile trade
East India Company (British, EIC), 85, 229
East India Company (Dutch). *See* Verenigde Oostindische Compagnie (VOC)
edible birds' nests (*yen-wo*) trade: area

discussed, 405; blood nests in, 414–15, 430nn28–29; Chinese monopoly in, 408–9; cleaning of, 413–14; collection of, 420–21; earliest documentation of, 409–11; early history and folklore of, 416–18; healing and therapeutic effects of, 411–16; illicit collecting of, 423, 426; plight and prospects for, 426–27; price of, 407, 414–16, 415–16; *semah* ritual and, 425–27; social relations of production and, 421–22, 424–26; summary of, 11–12, 427–28; value of, 407–8, 427–28
edible sea cucumbers. *See* trepang (*bêche-de-mer*, edible sea cucumbers)
EIC (British East India Company), 85, 229
Elsevier, Christiaan, 237, 245–46
Elvin, Mark, 3
Eredia, Manoel Godinho de, 27
ethnicity and ethnic identity: alliances and struggles among (Burma), 459–60, 474; as approach to trade analysis, 172–74; assimilation vs. affirmation of, 305; of captains in tortoiseshell trade, 185–86. *See also* language issues; *specific groups*
Europe: attitudes in, toward indigenous peoples, 69, 72; Chinese rare books extant in, 272–74, 282nn42–44; migration patterns of, 66; textile trade of, 283–84, 286, 299n35; timber imports of, 495; tin imports and production of, 30, 31; tropical products demanded in, 95. *See also* colonial powers; France; Great Britain; Netherlands; Spain
Evers, Hans-Dieter, 142
exclusionary laws, against Chinese immigration, 79–80

Faure, David, 3
feicui. See jade and jadeite
Field, Stephen, 80

fish farming (Tonle Sap Great Lake and River): area of, 303, 360–61; boats and trade in, 436, 442; capital difficulties and seasonal fluctuation in, 365–66; Chinese roles in export operations, 361, 364–65, 367–68, 370–72, 374; crisis of intensive, unregulated fishing, 373–74; emergence and growth of market-oriented, 362–67; expansion of, 41, 361, 440–41; regulations established for, 361, 375; revenue farming replaced with direct taxation, 372; revenue farming system and speculation in, 367–72; statistics on, 364, 366, 367, 373; summary of, 10–11, 374–75; Vietnamese role in, 361–66, 368, 370–72, 374–75

Fitzgerald, C. P., 57

Fogden, Michael, 413

Forbes, Andrew, 55

France: anti-opium movement in, 99–100; opium monopoly of, 97; Tonkin occupied by, 54–55; tortoiseshell trade of, 180–81

Fujian Province: book trade of, 259, 268–72; coin circulation in, 131, 143n4; copper trade of, 44; Japanese control of, 321; junk cargoes and, 227, 229; map of, 87; merchants' association of, 45; migration from, 66; Ryukyu trade and, 5, 7, 114, 120; swiftlets of, 410–11; Taiwanese investment in, 10, 314–17, 325–26; Taiwanese migrants in, 306, 310, 312, 320–21, 330n17; Taiwan's trade with, 318, 322; urbanization of, 325–26. See also Minnan; Minnanese dialect

Fuzhou: book trade of, 271; dialect of, 310; location of, 87, 108; missionaries and Bible distribution in, 396; political changes in, 317; Ryukyu trade and, 108, 123, 125–26; Taiwanese occupa-

tions and investment in, 306–7, 312, 314–18

Gan Tin Wee ("Banhap"), 95–97

Gathorne-Hardy, John (earl of Cranbrook and Lord Medway), 419–21

gemstones: descriptions and classification of, 8, 205; list of, 208–9. See also baoshi (rubies, sapphires, tourmaline); jade and jadeite

gem trade: approach to, 203–4; area discussed, 201; China as driving force in, 204, 214–16; feicui introduced, 207, 210–11; feicui more popular than baoshi, 212–14; in Ming period, 204–5, 208; in Qing period, 205–6, 208–9, 211; summary of, 8, 12, 214–16. See also gemstones; jade trade

gender roles, 27, 414, 431n46

Gittinger, M., 297n11

global Chinese network, 305, 328

global commodity-chain approach: concept of, 12–13, 482–83; timber trade in, 492–95, 501–2; transnational alliance capitalism concept and, 493, 501–2

global patterns: commodity trade, 53–54, 338, 383, 438; migration, 79–80; political economy and capitalism in, 447

gold-mining, 25–26, 90

gold-to-silver ratio, 125, 144n22

gold trade, 25, 133–35. See also coin business

Gomez, Edmund Terence, 3

governments: opium monopolies of, 97–100; promotion of conflict timber trade and, 486–90; rice production concerns of, 337–38

governments, interventions of: copper mining linked to increased, 46; increased, after uprising, 40–41; in rice

324–25; Taiwan ruled by (1895–1945), 305; timber imports of, 495; tortoise-shell sales in, 180; tributary voyages of, 129n11. *See also* Japanese migrants; Ryukyu Kingdom; Taiwan

Japanese migrants: destinations of, 307, 308–9, 311; passports and registration of, 309, 319–20; Taiwanese migrants compared with, 325

Java (Jawa): Cochinchinese coins in, 137; cotton imports of, 283–84, 286–87; cotton production organization in, 291–95; cotton trade, summarized, 295–96; cotton trade development in, 284–89; cotton yarn of, 290–91; Dutch control of Northeast, 290–91; Dutch intervention in cotton trade of, 289–91; edible birds' nests collection in, 408; foodstuffs supplied by, 93; governance divisions of, 298n22; iron imports of, 23; maps of, 87, 201; marine-products trade of, 434–35; opium farming and trade of, 84–86, 92, 97–98; Ryukyu trade relations with, 108, 108, 110–12, 116–18, 127–28; tin imports of, 27; tributary missions to China by, 119–22. *See also* Batavia; junk cargoes

Jennings, John, 327

Jiménez, José Antonio Cervera, 277–78n9

Ji Yun, 213

junk cargoes: area discussed, 201; books largely absent from, 259; Canton to Southeast Asia, listed, 136–37; celebration and fairs at arrival of, 225–26, 234–36; Chinese reforms of maritime trade (post-1727), 231–33; commodities in 1750–1759, 246, 248–54; customs, fees, and taxes on, 227–29, 227, 232–33; decline of, 246–47; Dutch attempts to control, 223–24, 235–37; Dutch debates about using own vessels

vs. junks, 228–31; economic importance of, 234–35; limits of quantitative data on, 226–28; limits of written accounts of, 221–22; number at Batavia (1750–1759), 237, 238–44, 244–45; pilfering and extortion complaints concerning, 233; prosperity embodied by, 161; salt trade of, 363–65; Siamese depiction of, 163, 169–70n48; sinking of Tek Sing, 247, 255; size of, 244–45; summary of, 7–9; time and spatial contexts of, 222–26; trepang and tortoiseshell on, 185–86, 188–89. *See also* luxury goods trade

Junk Ceylong. *See* Phuket

junk traders: coin circulation of, 138; crew and passengers of, 244–46, 255; details on nachodas, 237, 244; fish farming linked to, 11; marabouts hunted by, 362; newcomers as, 245; routes of, 222, 224–26; rutters and guidebooks of, 222, 276n4; Singapore central to, 94

Kachin Defense Army (KDA), 485

Kachin Independence Army (KIA), 465–66, 485

Kachin Independence Organization (KIO), 482, 485, 487, 491, 497–500

Kachin State (Burma): areas opened to logging, 484; cease-fire logging concessions in, 504n20; cease fires signed in, 480–82; Chinese role in timber trade of, 485–86, 490–92; environmental damage in, 499–501; HIV/AIDS rates in, 506n67; jade mines and trade of, 464–68, 474, 477n23; local livelihoods and political power in, 498–502; map of, 456; military economies linked to timber trade in, 484–85; national and local promotion of timber trade of, 486–90; opium pro-

Malay Archipelago (*continued*)
in, 354; rice imports of, 339–40; rice millers' ties with peasantry of, 338, 352–54; rice milling in, 338, 340–41; Taiwanese occupations and investment in, 313; timber resources of, 247; tin mining of, 27–33, 31–32. *See also* British Malaya; Burma; Kedah State; Malaysia; rice trade; Singapore; Thailand; *specific locales*

Malaysia (post-1963): edible birds' nests exports of, 407; map of, *303*; marine-products trade of, 436, 444–45; rice imports of, 336; rice production in, 338. *See also* Sarawak State; Singapore

Malenee Gumperayarnnont, 170n51

Manchukuo and Manchuria (under Japanese control): Japanese spoken in, 312; leased territory of, 328–29n3; Taiwanese occupations and investment in, 311, 317; Taiwanese trade with, 322–24, *323*, 326

Manila: bookselling activities in, 265, 269, 281n32; Chinese settlement in, 259–60; marine-products trade of, 443–44; Ryukyu trade relations with, 124–25

Marco Polo Bridge Incident (1937), 327

marine-products trade: approach to, 432–33; area discussed, 405, *439*; of coasts of Southeast Asian mainland, 440–41, 443; contemporary connections in, 437–45; Dutch attempts to control, 178, 181, 183–84; historical connections in, 433–37; in Indonesia, 179–86; seaweeds (agar-agar) in, 179, 185, 190; Singapore as example of, 444–47; Sinification of, 184, 191, 409; specialists in, 195–96n47; summary of, 12, 447–48. *See also* fish farming; tortoiseshell trade; trepang (*bêche-de-mer*, edible sea cucumbers)

Markovits, Claude, 39
Marx, Karl, 3, 64, 400
Massey, Douglas S., 460
Matsuo, Hiroshi, 283
Maung, Mya, 484
Mayor, Tomás, 266–68, 279n17, 280n29
Meagher, Arnold, 66
Medhurst, Walter, 388, 389, 396
medicinal traditions. *See* edible birds' nests (*yen-wo*) trade
Melaka. *See* Malacca
Menegon, Eugenio, 281n30
merchant associations (*huiguan*): copper traders, 45; cotton/silk traders, 49–50; factors in building, 48; origins of, 51–52; Taiping Rebellion's effects on, 53; temples of, 45, 49–51
merchant diasporas. *See* diasporas
metals technology: in Borneo, 22–24; development and spread of, 21–22; in tin mining, 39. *See also* mining and metalworking trade; *specific metals*
migration: analytical approach to, 1–2, 5, 172; contract labor and global patterns in, 79–80; culture of, 306–12, 460; exclusionary laws against, 79–80; historical overview of, 86–88; in macroregion model, 37–38; use of term, 306. *See also* Chinese migrants, generally; diasporas; Japanese migrants; Taiwanese migrants
Milne, William, 385–86, 389, 397
Milne, William Charles, 389, 393
Ming xin baojian (Cobo's translation of Confucian book), 262–63, 276–77n5
mining and metalworking trade: area discussed, 19; Chinese expansion in eighteenth century, 24–25; circulation patterns of, 39–41; coin business linked to, 7; goldfields in, 25–26; ironworking in, 22–24; merchant organizations and networks linked to, 45;

spread of, debated, 21–22; summary of, 4, 33–34; Taiwanese investment in, 315–16. *See also* coin business; jade and jadeite; metals technology; tin mining; *specific metals*

minjian (popular realm) perspective: concept of, 460, 476n12, 503–4n13; Yunnanese migrants and jade trade in, 457–63, 466–75, 475n3, 477n21

Minnan (Fujian), Chinese settlement in, 259, 277n7

Minnanese dialect: Mindong compared with, 268; missionaries' learning of, 261–62, 267–68; radio broadcasts in, 310; romanized script for, 280n27; song collections in, 270–71, 270–71; texts in, 265, 268, 270, 273, 276–77n5

missionaries (Catholic Dominicans and Jesuits): attempts to censor Chinese books, 269; attitudes toward Chinese in Philippines, 275–76; motivations of, 9, 260, 262, 275–76; movable-type printing preferred, 265–66; Protestant attitudes toward, 388, 392, 397; translations and printed works of, 260–68, 261, 264

missionaries (Protestants): arrests of, 395; Catholic book printing compared with, 275; Catholic missionaries as competition of, 388, 392, 397; children of, 389, 402n27; Chinese as, 386–88, 395; disunity of, 389–90; hopes for Taiping Rebellion, 390–95; training of, 399–400. *See also* Bible distribution

Moluccas ("Spice Islands"), spice trade of, 174, 176, 178, 223, 299n35

Mongols, 204, 215

Morrison, Robert, 385–86, 389

Morse, H. B., 133

Mossel, Jacob, 230–31

Mouhot, Henri, 365

Moura, Jean, 362, 364–66, 378n63

Mukden Incident (18 September Incident, 1931), 317, 324, 327

Murao Susumu, 170n48

Murray, Dian, 87

Muslim merchants: gold trade of, 25; rebellion of, 53; tin trade of, 27–28; tortoiseshell trade of, 177, 191; tribute trade of, 125; of Yunnan, 475–76n3, 479n39. *See also* Arab merchants

Myanmar. *See* Burma

Nanhai, ancient trade of, xii

Nanyang. *See* Southeast Asia

Nat Chumsai, M. R. W., 170n50

Nationality Law (China, 1909–1957), 310

Navarrete, Domingo, 263

NDA-K (New Democratic Army–Kachin), 485, 490, 492, 496–97, 504n20

Neale, F. A., 154, 167n25

Netherlands: anti-opium movement in, 98; cotton yarn and textile production of, 284; cotton yarn demand in, 290; opium monopoly of, 97–98. *See also* Batavia; Dutch merchants; Verenigde Oostindische Compagnie

networks of human societies: centrality of, 1–2; continued salience of, 447–48; role of capital in, 9–10; scholarship on trading and commodities in, 433–34; trade and culture-based, 317–18

New Democratic Army–Kachin (NDA-K), 485, 490, 492, 496–97, 504n20

Niah Caves (Sarawak): birds' nest collection process at, 420–24; description of, 418–21; history and folklore of, 417–18; Iban of Rumah Chang and, 419, 422–26, 428; plight and prospect of, 426–27; semah ritual at, 425–27; social relations of production at, 421–22, 424–26

Nieva, Diego de, 262

Nieva, Domingo de, 266, 268, 279n17
Ningpo (Ningbo): junk cargoes destined
for, 246, 251–52; junk cargoes from,
230, 239–41, 243; redemption fees on
junk cargoes in, 227, 227
Nidhi, Eoseewong, 170n49
Ni Tui, 207, 211–12, 214
Norodom (king of Cambodia), 367–71

O'Connor, Stanley, 22–23
Okinawa. *See* Ryukyu Kingdom (now
Okinawa)
Ong, Aihwa, 2
opium: British attitudes toward, 97,
99–100, 393; Chinese laborers' use of,
89–90, 337; farming of, 86, 90–92,
95–97; forms of, 84–85, 101n3; as
prime commodity, 100–101; rice production linked to, 337–38; as work and
recreational drug, 84, 102n16
opium trade: area discussed, 19; British
Singapore's role in, 92–95; centrality
of, 100–101; deforestation linked to,
499; economic role of, 101, 337; European complicity in, 393; government
monopolies of, 97–100; historical
overview of, 84–90; increased scrutiny
of, 96–97; Japanese policy on, 327;
major centers of, 87; summary of, 5
opium wars: Bible distribution suspended in, 395–96; British occupation
after second, 72–73; China's political
prestige degraded in, 7, 149–50
Owen, David E., 85

paddy kunca, 352–54
Pakistan, rice exports of, 336
Palembang: Chinese settlement in, 116;
Ryukyu trade relations with, 108, 108,
110–12, 117; textile imports of, 288–89,
293, 300n48
Pan-Southeast Asia: map of, 19; mining

frontier of, 21–34; opium trade of,
84–101
Panthay (Hui) Rebellion (1856–1873), 51,
53–55
Pasisir trade, 236, 287, 289–90
Passiak, junk cargoes for, 136–37
Passport Act (Japan, 1878), 319
Patani, Ryukyu trade relations with, 108,
108, 110–12
Pearson, Michael, 173–74
Peking Convention (1866), 74
Peleggi, Maurizio, 160
Pelras, Christian, 13
Penang: crises (political and natural)
affecting rice trade in, 346–47, 347;
investors from, 322; labor migration
and, 69, 77; marine-products trade
of, 436; missionaries and Bible distribution in, 275, 385–87; opium trade
of, 90–94, 96, 98, 100; rice milling in,
338, 340–44, 342–45; rice production
in, 349–50; rice trade of, 337–40; tin
trade of, 32, 32
pepper trade: area discussed, 105; Ryukyu relations and, 113–16, 119, 122–25;
summary of, 7
Petillot, Loÿs, 378n51
Phan Huy Chu, 221, 224–25
Philippines: Anglo-English school for
Chinese in, 282n45; attitudes toward
Chinese in, 274–76; books of missionaries in Spanish period, 260–68,
261, 264; book trade of, 265, 268–72,
281n32; Chinese settlement in, 259–
60; first publications in, 263; Hispani-
cization in, 267; map of, 201; marine-
products trade of, 436–37, 443–44;
missionaries' acquisition of Chinese
books, 271–74; opium banned by U.S.,
99; rice imports of, 336; Ryukyu trade
relations with, 124–25; Spanish Catholic missionaries in, 9, 401–2n23; Tai-

shipping: Canton to Netherlands, 224; Chinese trade via foreign vs. Chinese, xii; competition in, 99; junks vs. Western square-riggers, 221; measuring junks and, 231–32; post-1875 new technologies of, 54; repairs in others' ports, 114, 120; Ryukyu tributary ship, 113. *See also* junk cargoes; junk traders

Siam. *See* Thailand

Siamese ruling class: attitudes toward Chinese luxury goods, 150, 156–57, 159, 165n5; luxury goods imported, listed, 153–54, 155–56; political and social context of, 149–50, 162, 164; Sinicization of, 159–64, 162–63; tributary relations with China and, 151–53. *See also* Thailand

silk cloths and trade: cotton trade linked to, 49; Palembang imports of, 288, 299n25; as rewards in tribute system, 154, 158, 167n24, 167n27

silver: coins of, 139, 246; mining frontier of, 24–25; in Ryukyu trade, 124–25. *See also* coin business

silver-to-gold ratio, 125, 144n22

Simmel, Georg, 432

Singapore: as area trading center, 92–93; Bible Society of, 398; coin circulation in, 139; as contract labor recruitment center, 68, 79, 93–94; contract labor regulations and depot in, 75–79; financial role in timber trade, 494; fishing boats in port of, 436; fish product imports of, 368; location of, 303; marine-products imports of, 444–47; missionaries and Bible distribution in, 385–87, 396; opium trade of, 90–96, 100; rice trade of, 339; Taiwanese occupations and investment in, 313

Sinification (Sinicization): of evangelization, 387–88; of luxury goods trade

and Siamese ruling class, 159–64, 162–63; of marine-products trade, 184, 191, 409

Sino-Japanese War (1937–1945), 311, 324–25

Sino-Southeast Asian Studies, 13

Skinner, G. William, 3, 37–38, 433–34

slaves and slavery: British abolition of, 393; coins used in purchase of, 139, 147n57; trade in, 197n62; vocabulary about, 63–64, 66–67, 72

Smith, Kent, 46

smuggling: cotton goods, 289; cross-cutting relations in, 189; of people, 245, 320; tortoiseshell, 178, 181–83, 188, 197n71. *See also* pirates and piracy

social obligations: actors' participation in, 173; labor in context of, 64–65. *See also* cultural ties in economic relations; networks of human societies

South China: anti-Japanese sentiment in, 324; contract labor recruitment from, 72–73; copper circulation of, 41–48; Japanese migrants in, 307, 309; Japanese occupation of, 324–25; maps of, 19, 40, 105, 201, 303, 307, 405; Taiwanese investment in, generally, 313; Taiwanese merchants' role in, 316–17; Taiwanese migrants in, 306–7, 308–9, 309–10; Taiwanese trade and cultural networks with, 317–18. *See also specific locales*

South China Sea: networks connected via, 434; Ryukyu trade network in, 107–28, 108; trade routes in, 222, 224–26

Southeast Asia: anti-Japanese sentiment in, 324; Bible distribution in, 380–400; Chinese diaspora and culture in, 259–60; contemporary Chinese business interests in, 437–45; contract migrant labor of, 62–80; Dutch

tortoiseshell trade: approach to, 172–74; area discussed, 105; collecting a cargo in, 182–83; color and markings in, 180; context of, 174–78; cross-cutting relations in, 189–91; geographic sources of tortoiseshell, 179, 183–86; prices and profits in, 182, 184, 188, 196n59, 197n60; smuggling in, 178, 181–83, 188, 197n71; summary of, 7–8, 187–91; transcommunal interdependence in, 174

trade embargos, 49–50

transcommunal interdependence, concept of, 174

transnational alliance capitalism, concept of, 493, 501–2

transport industry, specialization of, 51–52. See also caravan and overland trade; junk cargoes; shipping

Treaty of 1869, 350

Treaty of 1906, 99

Treaty of Beijing (1860), 73

Treaty of Commerce and Navigation (1896), 307, 309, 319

Treaty of Nanjing (1842), 380

Treaty of Shimonoseki (1895), 318–19, 326

Treaty of Tordesillas (1494), 124

trepang (bêche-de-mer, edible sea cucumbers): collection ports of, 189–90, 198n78; growth of trade in, 8, 177–78, 184–85; market limits on, 191; monopoly of, 409; tortoiseshell trade linked to, 179, 185–87

tribute systems: China's policy changes in, 126–27; core-periphery model of, 125–26; goods accepted in, 114–16, 123–24, 127–28; Java's and Malacca's tributary missions described, 118–22; personnel of tributary missions (and rewards), 118–19, 122, 157, 158, 159; protocol of, 128–29n8; royal golden

missive sent in, 161, 169n47; Ryukyu and China relations in, 108; Ryukyu king's tribute and private trade, 122–24; Ryukyu ship depicted, 113; sham tally in, 121–22; Siamese tribute to China and luxury goods trade, 151–54, 156–57, 160, 164–65n1. See also luxury goods trade; Ryukyu Kingdom

tropical timber. See conflict timber trade

Turnbull, Mary, 33

turtles, hawksbill: current status of, 196n48; diving for, 187; environment of, 180; geographic sources of, 179, 183–86. See also tortoiseshell trade

Tu Shuliang, 213

United Bible Societies, 398–99

United Nations Office on Drug Control (UNODC), 499

United States: anti-opium policy of, 99–100; assistance for Dutch (1800) by ships of, 224; Chinese immigration to, 79–80; investments of, 95; Philippines controlled by, 437; rice exports of, 336; timber imports of, 495, 505n6; tin imports of, 30

urbanization, 46, 325–26

Valentijn, François, 180

Van Dyke, Paul, 135, 138

Vera, Juan de, 265–66, 279n18

Vera, Pedro de, 266

Verenigde Oostindische Compagnie (VOC): Batavia headquarters of, 224; coin casting of, 135, 146n43; coins purchased by, 143n12; competition for, 223–24; cotton trade of, 294–96; customs, fees, and taxes collected by, 229; data on shipping of, 226; debates about using own vessels vs. junks, 228–31; edible birds' nests trade of, 408; irony in records of, 197n65; junk

trade's differences from, 246; military expansion in Malacca, 176; money of account for, 197n64; opium commercialized under, 85; spice trade of, 176, 178, 181, 223, 299n35; tin trade of, 28; tortoiseshell trade and, 180–85, 187–91, 197–98n76, 198n77; trade control sought by, 177–78, 223–24, 235–37, 289–91; zinc purchases of, 132. See also Batavia; Dutch merchants; Netherlands

Vienne, Marie-Sybillede, 305

Vietnam (Annam): anti–Chinese brotherhood actions in, 91; coin casting of, 130–31; copper imports of, 42–43; edible birds' nests exports of, 407; fishing entrepreneurs of, 361–66, 368, 370–72, 374–75, 376n22; map of, 105; marine-products trade of, 440; mining frontier of, 24–25; opium farming in, 91, 97; rice exports of, 336; Ryukyu trade relations with, 108, 108, 110–12; Taiwanese occupations and investment in, 313; tributary missions to China of, 126; zinc imports of, 43–44. See also Cochinchina; Tonkin

VOC. See Verenigde Oostindische Compagnie

Vosmaer, J. N., 180

wage slavery, use of term, 64. See also labor as commodity

Wajorese traders, 183–84, 186, 188–89, 198n84

Walker, Andrew, 463

Wallerstein, Immanuel, 173

Wang Dayuan, 23

Wang Gungwu, xi–xiii, 1, 305

Warren, James F., 236

Weber, Max, 3, 432

Weld, Fredrick, 96

Wen Eang Cheong, 133

White, James, 71–72

Whittall, J., 74

Wilberforce, William, 382–83

Williams, William, 69

women, 71–72, 79–80. See also gender roles

Wong, Roy Bin, 3, 433–34

Wong Lin Ken, 31, 33

Wu Daxun, 212

Wu Lingjun, 327

Wyatt, David K., 159–60

Xiamen. See Amoy (Xiamen)

Xianluo. See Thailand

Xiao family, 316

Xu Jiong, 206

Xu Xiake, 210–11

Yang, Mayfair, 476n12

Yang Duanliu, 325

Yanghang (ocean guilds), 224, 232–33, 244–45, 247

Yoshikawa Toshiharu, 165n4

Yule, Henry, 49–51

Yunnan Province: Burmese gems in, 204–7, 210, 212; circulation patterns in, 39–41, 55–57; copper circulation of, 41–48; cotton (and silk) circulation of, 48–55; currency in, 472, 478n35; demographics of, 38, 46–48; economic orientation toward Southeast Asia, 478n37; first large-scale family-run firms (shanghao) in, 51; Han communication records on, 455–58, 472, 475n1; jade trade of migrants from, 457–63, 466–75, 475n3, 477n21; maps of, 19, 47; migratory flexibility and overland practices of, 472–73; mining frontier of, 24; post-1870s changes in trade of, 53–55; timber imports and processing of, 480, 482, 484–97, 501–2; zinc production of, 133. See also Canton

Wen-Chin **Chang** is an associate research fellow at the Center
for Asia-Pacific Area Studies, RCHSS, Academia Sinica, Taiwan.

Eric **Tagliacozzo** is an associate professor of history at Cornell
University. He is director of the Comparative Muslim Societies
Program and the Cornell Modern Indonesia Project, and is editor
of the journal INDONESIA.

Library of Congress Cataloging-in-Publication Data
Tagliacozzo, Eric.
Chinese circulations : capital, commodities, and networks in
Southeast Asia / Eric Tagliacozzo and Wen-Chin Chang, eds. ;
foreword by Wang Gungwu.
p. cm.
Includes bibliographical references and index.
ISBN 978-0-8223-4881-8 (cloth : alk. paper)
ISBN 978-0-8223-4903-7 (pbk. : alk. paper)
1. China—Commerce—Southeast Asia. 2. Southeast Asia—
Commerce—China. I. Chang, Wen-Chin. II. Title.
HF3838.A783T34 2011
382′.0951059—dc22 2010041586